THE CASE
AGAINST
THE GENERAL

****

THE CASE
AGAINST
THE GENERAL

****

Manuel Noriega and the Politics
of American Justice

STEVE ALBERT

Charles Scribner's Sons
New York

Maxwell Macmillan Canada
Toronto

Maxwell Macmillan International
New York Oxford Singapore Sydney

Charles Scribner's Sons
Macmillan Publishing Company
866 Third Avenue
New York, NY 10022

Maxwell Macmillan Canada, Inc.
1200 Eglinton Avenue East
Suite 200
Don Mills, Ontario M3C 3N1

Library of Congress Cataloging-in-Publication Data
Albert, Steve, 1950–
   The case against the general : Manuel Noriega and the politics of American justice / Steve Albert
      p.   cm.
   ISBN 0-684-19375-2
   1. Noriega, Manuel Antonio, 1934– —Trials, litigation, etc.   2. Trials (Narcotic laws)—Florida—Miami.   3. Drug traffic—United States.   4. Drug traffic—Panama.
KF224.N64A43   1993
363.4'5'0973—dc20   93-22819
                                                                              CIP

ISBN 0-684-19375-2

Macmillan books are available at special discounts for bulk purchases for sales promotions, premiums, fund-raising, or educational use. For details, contact:

Special Sales Director
Macmillan Publishing Company
866 Third Avenue
New York, NY 10022

10   9   8   7   6   5   4   3   2   1

Printed in the United States of America

CONTENTS

To my parents
Marilyn and Robert Albert

PART I
★★★★★★

Tracking the General

CHAPTER 1
★★★★★★★

A Trail of Evidence

This is the story of the American trial of Gen. Manuel Antonio Noriega, the leader of the country of Panama from 1983 until December 1989.

On December 20, 1989, George Bush, the President of the United States, ordered a military invasion of Panama. One of the president's stated goals was the capture and return of Noriega to stand trial in the United States. American prosecutors had accused Noriega of trafficking in illegal drugs and money laundering.

Not since the times of Ancient Rome had one nation launched an invasion of another with the goal of bringing its ruler to trial.

"My view is that he should have been prosecuted a long time ago. I guess the only thing you can say now for General Noriega is that he has been relying on the friendship of people in high positions in the U.S. Government and that he had a right to expect he would continue to get immunity from prosecution for criminal conduct, but I think it is long overdue."

New York City District Attorney Robert Morgenthau was seated in a United States Senate hearing room. It was Monday, February 8, 1988. Senator John Kerry, the Massachusetts Democrat, was chairing the Senate Foreign Relations Committee's Subcommittee on Terrorism, Narcotics, and International Operations. Besides Kerry, two other members of the Foreign Relations Committee listened closely to Morgenthau.

The Thursday before, two federal grand juries—one in Miami, the other in Tampa—had delivered indictments naming Noriega as a cornerstone in a broad drug trafficking and money laundering conspiracy. The immediacy of the indictments gave the hearing a more important air than the usual congressional dog-and-pony show.

"Certainly people in law enforcement have known for a long time that General Noriega was corrupt, and I think that kind of tolerance of corruption in foreign countries undermines our own respect for the law and respect for the law among people in law enforcement, and could lead to corruption in our own police departments," Morgenthau said.

★　　　　★　　　　★

Norman Bailey had been a Reagan administration special assistant for national security affairs from 1981 to 1983, more than five years before the delivery of the Miami and Tampa indictments. He had served as a senior staff member of the National Security Council, the president's advisers on foreign affairs. On Tuesday, March 29, 1988, he testified before the House of Representatives Select Committee on Narcotics Abuse and Control. Congressman Charles Rangel, the New York Democrat, was chairman of the committee.

"Available to me as an official of the NSC and available to any authorized official of the U.S. government is a plethora of human intelligence, electronic intercepts, and satellite and overflight photography that, taken together, constitute not a smoking gun but rather a twenty-one-cannon barrage of evidence," Bailey told the committee concerning Noriega's drug involvement.

Top American officials watched, he said, as Noriega and his military wrested control of the Panamanian government from its civilian leaders. As Panama was militarized, it was also dragged into a mire of drug trafficking–related corruption, Bailey said.

"It saddens me to think that for reasons deemed good and sufficient, Democratic and Republican administrations, liberal and conservative administrations, career officials and political appointees have all conspired for years to protect and abet a group of despicable international outlaws."

In his brief tenure at the NSC, Bailey said, he discovered a trail of evidence of "startling length and breadth." That evidence linked high officials of Noriega's Panamanian Defense Forces to drug trafficking and money laundering. The PDF was "extensively and directly engaged in or engaged in aiding and abetting" drug trafficking, including the loading and unloading of ships and planes, Bailey said.

The evidence showed that high Panamanian officials, including Noriega, had hosted Colombian drug barons in Panama and had facilitated the movement of ships and planes and the use of Panama as a transshipment point in the drug trade.

The evidence showed, Bailey said, that PDF officials had helped run guns to the Nicaraguan Sandinista rebels prior to the overthrow of the Nicaraguan dictator Anastasio Somoza in 1979. The PDF had later run guns to the followers of Somoza—called the Contras—who were trying to win the country back from the Sandinistas. And the PDF had run guns to guerrillas fighting in El Salvador and leftist and rightist guerrilla movements in Colombia.

Bailey said he had turned over his findings to President Ronald Reagan's national security adviser, Vice Admiral John Poindexter, and to officials in the Defense Department and the State Department, including Elliott Abrams, the undersecretary for Latin American affairs.

In the early 1980s narcotics problems seemed to have a "very low priority" at the White House, Bailey said. He called the situation in Panama "a story of how clear and incontrovertible evidence was, at best, ignored and, at worst, hidden and denied by many different agencies and departments of the government of the United States in such a way as to provide cover and protection for these activities." However, Bailey said, how Noriega escaped closer scrutiny by U.S. officials was explainable.

"Foreign policy is a very complex matter and is a matter of setting off or balancing a number of different considerations of various kinds. The government goes through that exercise all the time with reference to people who are by no means admirable."

From the ratification of the Panama Canal Treaty during the administration of President Jimmy Carter to concerns over the security of American military bases in Panama and the supply of weapons to the Nicaraguan Contras during the Reagan administration, American officials "felt they were getting more than they were giving up," Bailey told the congressmen.

"The whole history of our relationship with the Republic of Panama is a severe indictment of the United States' ability to handle its relationship with any foreign country," said Retired Army General Paul Gorman, the former commander of the U.S. Southern Command based in the Canal Zone, who had gone to the Joint Chiefs of Staff in 1983 and tried to explain the danger of the emerging cocaine cartels and what he believed was Noriega's acquiescence. Like Morgenthau, he was testifying before the Subcommittee on Terrorism, Narcotics and International Operations.

"I was trying to draw the attention of the Department of Defense to the large strategic issues, the more enduring strategic issues. In those years nobody wanted to talk about anything but El Salvador."

Gorman recollected visits by Noriega to Washington, D.C., in the early 1980s. The visits were not sponsored by the State Department or "the White House specifically," he said. Noriega's hosts were the Central Intelligence Agency and the National Security Council.

Gorman said, "Let us start by saying that if one wants to organize an armed resistance or an armed undertaking for any purposes, the easy place to get the money and the easy places to get the guns are in the drug world.

"Money is what fueled the Salvadoran guerrillas—not Marxist ideology, but money. Without money there would have been less violence. The most ready source of money, big money, easy money, fast money, sure money, cash money is the narcotics racket."

"It was November 1984 when I got a call from a buddy agent of mine, an immigration agent in Miami I had worked with on some smuggling cases."

Danny Moritz was thirty-four years old in November 1984. He had been with the U.S. Drug Enforcement Administration for about two years. Before that he had spent five years as a federal immigration agent, and before that five years as an Internal Revenue Service agent.

"He said he had stumbled across a Panamanian by the name of Edgar

Espinosa. Espinosa told him about an organization he was working for out of Panama that he believed was involved in large-scale drug-trafficking activities and money laundering.

"'Dan, this guy, he's telling me about this major Panamanian. You want me to hook you guys up? See if this guy has got any information?'"

He made the arrangements.

"I met the guy, talked to him, spent a few hours debriefing him. He told me about this guy, Floyd Carlton Caceres. He was a major guy out of Panama, moving large amounts of cocaine and money back and forth. Espinosa said this Floyd had very close connections with the Panamanian government, specifically with Manuel Noriega. He said that a guy named César Rodríguez was involved. Besides Noriega, most of the names, off the top of my head, I never heard of."

Moritz told Espinosa he would do some checking and try to verify his statement.

"Some of the stuff was right on. Some of it was well documented in our intelligence files. We had the names Floyd Carlton and César Rodríguez. I called Espinosa in and said, 'You want to go to work for the government?'"

Espinosa had been like a man Friday to Floyd Carlton. He looked after his Miami house, paid the bills, picked him up at the airport. Carlton would go back and forth to Panama. He was in Miami one week a month.

Espinosa said that when Carlton was in Miami he hung out at DIACSA, Inc., a dealership for new and used Cessna airplanes and parts. DIACSA is owned by Alfredo Caballero.

"At the initial briefing, Espinosa told me about DIACSA and Alfredo Caballero, that when Carlton went to the United States with his entourage they would meet at DIACSA at Miami International Airport. It was a central meeting place for this trafficking organization.

"They'd go to Caballero's conference room on the second floor. There they would make their calls, coordinate their loads."

Moritz sat down with his supervisor.

"We decided to try and infiltrate the organization. Now, there are only two basic ways to infiltrate a South or Central American trafficking organization, particularly those involving Colombians, and this one was supposed to be tied directly to Pablo Escobar, the head of the Medellín cartel. That's where Carlton got his cocaine.

"The ways to get hooked in were either to provide transportation or provide money-laundering capabilities. The bad guys need those two specialties.

"Transportation was out because that's what Carlton did. He had a transportation organization. The only other choice was to provide a money-laundering service."

The plan was to have Espinosa talk to Caballero, who, it appeared, was helping Carlton move the money. Espinosa's instructions were to let Caballero know that he had met someone who had a good connection with banks in Miami and could convert large amounts of cash into checks and wire transfers.

Moritz went undercover. He became Danny Martelli. He drove a mauve Jaguar SJX and wore a gold Rolex watch, a gold bracelet, a neck chain, and Carrera sunglasses. He met Caballero in January 1985.

"It was clear to me from the beginning that DIACSA was the place to be. Every time I went in there it was a beehive of activity, with lots of pilots. Caballero had the exclusive Cessna dealership for South and Central America, both aircraft and parts. He was buying and selling aircraft for the bad guys."

Moritz said he could launder cash risk-free for a price: 3 percent for wire transfers and 5 percent for cashier's checks. No amount less than $100,000.

Caballero decided to test the gringo with $200,000 in cash. He wanted a certified check.

"No problem. We had a money-laundering operation in place, Operation Pisces. We cleaned the money at a DEA facility.

"Once I passed the first test, slowly but surely they started calling me. I spent an hour or two over there every day, hanging out, developing the under-cover role."

Floyd Carlton was in Panama when he got word of the new laundry man. Pretty soon Pablo Escobar had heard of Danny Martelli.

"Carlton gave instructions for me to be at his place of business in early March. He wanted to meet me. It was his way, the organization head's way, of giving the final stamp of approval on this new business associate."

Carlton had been flying cocaine for Escobar since late 1981. He had kept at it until the assassination of Rodrigo Lara Bonilla, the crusading antidrug justice minister of Colombia, on April 30, 1984. Escobar and the other heads of the Medellín cartel had had Bonilla murdered. During most of this time Carlton had utilized the country of Panama as a transshipment point in his cocaine smuggling.

"This is where Noriega came in, but we did not know this until the arrest of Carlton. It was Carlton who specifically outlined Noriega's involvement."

Moritz knew that he had to make the best case he could on his target, Carlton. The only way to get higher—to the Colombians, to anyone higher, to Noriega—was to make such a good case against Carlton that he would have no choice but to cooperate with the DEA. That was the plan.

But by late 1984 and now, in 1985, the structure of Carlton's organization had changed from when he had been using Panama. Carlton's connections with Noriega had all but stopped, and his organization was now using the country of Costa Rica, paying off officials there for the right to take off and land the dope planes. The cartel had been run out of Panama by Noriega's demands for more money per load. Carlton would later say that Noriega wanted $100,000, then $150,000, then $200,000 per load.

"The man's a thief," Escobar had bawled to Carlton. "He's stealing from us."

Escobar told Carlton not to use Noriega anymore. Carlton shifted his refueling and off-loading operation to Costa Rica and then Mexico.

Drug-trafficking organizations are compartmentalized and are set up like Fortune 500 corporations. There's an organization involved in growing and processing the coca leaves. There are brokers who take the orders and coordinate the loads, and there are transportation experts.

"For example, there may be a guy in Medellín who takes orders from the guys in Florida. One guy needs one hundred kilos, another needs one hundred kilos, and another needs two hundred kilos. The broker comes up with an order for five or six hundred kilos of coke," Danny Moritz said.

"He calls the contact with the transportation groups, similar to trucking companies. He'll deal with three, four, or five different transportation groups. He may call Carlton and say, 'We have a load of five hundred kilos that we need to get to Miami by next Saturday. Can you handle it?'

"Floyd says, 'Yeah, we can put it together. Where do you want our plane?'

"So on Saturday at ten P.M. Carlton's pilot shows up at Escobar's ranch. That's the way it starts."

Moritz explained that Carlton had a number of pilots, off- loaders, and refueling sites. He negotiated with the broker and got paid anywhere from $3,000 to $3,500 a kilo, including transportation of the cocaine from Colombia to the contact in Miami.

"Out of that $3,000 he has to pay his expenses."

The transportation leg of the operation worked this way: All of the aircraft were kept in Miami. The pilots would take off and fly to northern Costa Rica, land, and refuel. One of the pilots would stay on the ground in Costa Rica to sleep. The other would fly the leg from Costa Rica to Colombia. He would pick up the cocaine, refuel, and fly back to Costa Rica, where he would leave the plane. The pilot on the ground would then fly the leg from Costa Rica back to the United States, or to Mexico if there was a group to ferry the dope across the border.

Carlton's pilot expenses would run from $150,000 to $250,000 per load depending on what leg the pilot flew. The off-loaders would receive about $50,000 per load, sometimes more. In Costa Rica one of the chiefs of the air national guard was getting $50,000 per load to provide government security and refueling. The head of the Nicaraguan Contras in northern Costa Rica was also in on the take for a while. Add to these the cost of couriers, and that would be the cost of running a transportation organization.

"It was like moving flour," Moritz said.

Because Carlton wanted to stay one step ahead of law enforcement and avoid suspicion, he would change planes often. That's where DIACSA came in. Carlton had met Caballero during a legitimate business deal and then started to buy more and more planes from him. Soon Caballero was not only handling the titles of Carlton's planes but hiding the movement of currency through his business.

When Moritz showed up, Caballero made the decision to get out of the money-laundering business.

"I'd go over, and he'd have a suitcase or a box full of money—$300,000, say. We would have to wire-transfer $200,000 to this company, and another $100,000 had to go to an account in Panama. I would take 3 percent for the service. That's how I went undercover," Moritz said.

Because Moritz was spending so much time at DIACSA, he soon was able to identify the tail numbers of the aircraft Carlton's organization was using. Since he was notified in advance that his money-laundering services would be needed on a specific day, he could identify cocaine loads and their size by the amount of cash to be laundered. This was the intelligence DEA needed.

In late April 1985, Carlton was suddenly removed from the picture. Then a load of 537 kilos being flown north by Carlton's organization got lost somewhere in Costa Rica. The load left Colombia but never arrived in Costa Rica. No one was ever sure what happened to the cocaine. There was some speculation that the Contras in northern Costa Rica stole it and then traded the drugs for arms.

"The long and the short of it was that 537 kilos disappeared, and there were some very mad Colombians," said Moritz.

"Carlton was in charge, so he was responsible. The cartel said to move the cocaine; they didn't tell him how to do it. This was a lot of money's worth of product."

Carlton was called to Medellín to explain what had happened. He couldn't, and he was about to be shot when Pablo Escobar interceded. Escobar told Carlton he could live for one day and could use the day to do what he pleased. Carlton left Medellín and went into hiding.

In Miami, Carlton's organization was taken over by Carlton's two top pilots. From them Moritz learned more and more about the operation. Moritz had reached the point where all he needed to put together an airtight case was the capture of a large load of cocaine.

By late September 1985 that shipment had made its way up from Colombia, through Mexico, and was about to be flown from Texas into Miami. Carlton entered the tail number of the plane in the DEA's intelligence computers. On September 22 agents began tracking the plane from Brownsville, Texas. The plane's pilot, Tony Azpruia, quickly recognized that he was being followed. He flew until he ran out of gas and was forced to land on an unfinished stretch of I-75 at the edge of the Everglades near Fort Lauderdale.

Azpruia escaped into the swamp even though one of Moritz's DEA supervisors, Ken Kennedy, had picked up the chase on the ground and arrived as the plane's propellers were still turning.

The Carlton group had lost another load—again, more than five hundred kilos of Colombian cocaine.

"The guys at DIACSA were frantic," said Moritz. "After that they were nervous and they wanted out."

Carlton's pilots trusted Moritz so thoroughly that they offered to turn the organization over to him. They wanted to retire alive.

"We were getting close to the end. We couldn't let these guys disappear."

Moritz went to the number two man in the Miami U.S. attorney's office, Richard Gregorie, who had followed Moritz's undercover work. Moritz boasted to Gregorie that he could deliver Noriega.

"The pilots had decided their last load would be in January 1986. Dick Gregorie and I decided to take them down on the last load," Moritz said.

In December 1985 an indictment naming Carlton and his operatives was prepared.

On January 23, 1986, a plane full of cocaine was seized near the border in Mexico. A sweep of arrests followed, and Carlton's operatives were taken to the interview room of Miami's DEA.

"They had been dealing with me for a year," Moritz said. "I was sitting behind the desk at the DEA when they started bringing these guys in one by one. You could see it on their faces as they walked in and saw me sitting there. They knew they were in a world of trouble."

One by one, members of the Carlton organization "flipped," agreeing to cooperate with the government. Every detail of the organization was fleshed out. Eventually, a stronger superseding indictment replaced the original.

"But we knew we needed Carlton to get to Escobar and the major Colombians, and to get Noriega."

Carlton was set up and lured out of Panama, where he claimed he had enjoyed Noriega's protection since fleeing Medellín. Carlton traveled to San José, Costa Rica, to meet Caballero, who had promised to provide him with details about the arrests in the United States and to give him copies of the indictment and court documents.

But now Caballero was working for the DEA. As Caballero and Carlton sat down in Carlton's room in the Cariari Hotel, room service arrived. In a borrowed waiter's uniform, Moritz and backup agents placed Carlton under arrest.

"I was telling Gregorie the whole time, 'If we get Carlton, we have Noriega,'" Moritz remembers. "Every time I saw Gregorie, he said, 'Hey, Dan, where's the big man?' And he said, 'You'll never get him.'

"I told him, 'I'll deliver Carlton and Noriega on a silver platter, and then I don't want you wimp U.S. attorneys to make any excuses why you can't do the case.'

"When we got Carlton, Gregorie said, 'You'll never get him extradited.'"

Carlton sat in a Costa Rican prison for six months while Moritz filed extradition papers. In January 1987, Moritz was told that Carlton was his.

Moritz and Ken Kennedy flew to San José. Within hours Carlton was seated aboard a DEA Cheyenne turbo prop. When the plane was airborne, Moritz placed Carlton under arrest and read him his rights.

Carlton was ragged. He had spent six months in a Central American prison. Noriega had not helped him. The cartel had not helped, though it had offered the prison warden $1 million to allow him to escape. Carlton was going to the United States to face a twenty-count indictment. If convicted on only the first count, he would spend the next fifteen years in prison.

"I leaned over and said, 'Hey, Floyd, Noriega is not coming to your assistance. The Colombians are still after you. We are your only friends. You have nowhere to turn.'"

Carlton had had six months to think about the moment. He knew that to save himself he would have to give up others who were more important.

He said, "What do I have to do? What do you want?"

Moritz stared into Carlton's face. "*El General*," he said.

And Carlton smiled.

While Carlton was hiding out in Panama, he had contacted the DEA's in-country agent, Thomas Telles, and had offered to trade information about Noriega for an exemption from prosecution. He could give the DEA documents that would prove Noriega's complicity in money laundering, drug trafficking, and arms smuggling, he said. He had Noriega's phone number in his notebook, and Escobar's and Daniel Ortega's. Ortega was the leader of the Sandinista junta in Nicaragua.

Telles had known of Moritz's undercover operation. He passed on Carlton's offer.

But now, back in Miami, Carlton knew Moritz would deal.

"We want the whole story from day one," Moritz told Carlton.

Moritz, Richard Gregorie, and a Spanish interpreter sat with Carlton for three days, eight or nine hours a day. It was February 1987.

Since the summer before, there had been allegations in the American press that Noriega, the de facto leader of Panama, was involved in drug trafficking. That didn't mean much to Richard Gregorie, a career federal prosecutor. To go to court there had to be evidence and corroboration.

In late January, Moritz had debriefed Tony Azpruia, who explained how he had been the pilot for the president of Panama. He said he had information on Noriega. As Noriega's personal pilot, he had flown money for him and also ether, a chemical used in the production of cocaine, to a clandestine lab in the Darien province of Panama, near the border of Colombia.

"We already had the beginnings of the downfall of Noriega," Moritz said. "Gregorie kept saying we needed more corroboration."

In three days' time Carlton became the case's major witness, and he would be the central figure in the structuring of the Miami Noriega indictment. The first thirteen overt acts listed in what would become the Miami indictment came from Carlton's testimony. Tony Azpruia's testimony would corroborate Carlton's.

"Our position was that we didn't care if this guy was a general," Moritz said. "He was a drug trafficker.

"There was concern about the indictment. This was a head of state. They wanted corroboration. There were a lot of people along the way who weren't convinced. As soon as he was indicted, the DEA was thrown out of Panama. People tried to protect themselves.

"My supervisor came to me and said there were people at headquarters who were concerned about our direction. They thought maybe we should consider shutting down. I said, 'You tell them to send me a memorandum, and then I'll shut it down.'

"We had to make certain that everything we got was corroborated. We took a lengthy briefing report. We had Carlton's history in drug trafficking—how he had met Noriega, the officials in Costa Rica, the Sandinistas, the Contras. Everything.

"I sent a lengthy teletype to Washington in early March, and then there was trouble. Shortly after, in April, I received notice that I was being transferred."

The U.S. House of Representatives Committee on Foreign Affairs delivered a staff study on U.S. narcotics control programs overseas on February 22, 1985. The study had surveyed the period from August 1984 to January 1985, and made these observations.

*"Corruption continues to be one of the biggest obstacles to effective anti-narcotics action in Panama. As one knowledgeable U.S. source put it, 'The Panamanian Defense Force is the axle around which the wheel of corruption turns.' This corruption is endemic and institutionalized; in fact, under previous governments members of the PDF were encouraged to take second 'jobs,' including drug trafficking, to supplement their income. Allegations persist that high-ranking military officials are involved in protection or actual trafficking themselves.

*"Probably the most significant antinarcotics enforcement action in 1984 in Panama was the discovery of the construction of a major cocaine processing plant near the Panama-Colombia border. The lab was apparently financed by Colombians with the complicity of a senior PDF officer, Colonel [Julian] Melo. Although both Colonel Melo and a number of Colombians were arrested in the PDF raid, none were prosecuted due to 'lack of evidence.' Colonel Melo was last believed to be in Miami, and the Colombians were deported to Colombia where they were released.

*"Panama has historically been a transshipment point for precursor chemicals moving south. In 1984, the government of Panama made a major seizure of 180 metric tons of ether, which may have had an impact on Colombian cocaine production. However, the study mission was unable to establish whether all of the ether seized has actually been destroyed.

*"There was also a major shipment of cocaine seized in Miami which was

carried on a Panamanian plane owned by Inair. Some observers believe there is a connection between this seizure, the cocaine lab that was raided, and the ether seizure.

*"The PDF (formerly known as the National Guard) is the sole entity responsible for narcotics enforcement. Within the PDF a forty-man unit (DENI) investigates narcotics cases. Panamanian customs officials refer all currency entering the country to the PDF.

*"With more than one hundred banks, the U.S. dollar as the national currency, and strict bank secrecy laws, Panama is an ideal haven for laundering narcotics money. Unlimited amounts of money may be brought into and out of the country with no reporting requirements, and money laundering is not a crime.

*"Given the importance of the banking community to the country's economy and as the employer of eight thousand people, Panama is extremely reluctant to alter its bank secrecy laws. Although the banking community has adopted a 'code of ethics' on banking procedures, it is voluntary and has no legal force.

*"Panama has no conspiracy law and no extradition treaty with the United States applicable to narcotics traffickers. Wiretaps, which could be used to prosecute narcotics traffickers, are illegal."

★★★★★★★

CHAPTER 2

Panama: A Short History, up to the Summer of 1987

Panama is a country roughly the size of Virginia. It lies on the S-shaped Isthmus of Panama, which joins North and South America. It has a population of 2.4 million people, about the size of Brooklyn, New York.

Until the arrival of the Spanish in the sixteenth century, the isthmus was occupied by several Indian groups. Panama was the center of Spain's New World commercial system until about 1740. In 1821, Panama proclaimed its independence from Spain and then joined the Colombian union immediately to the south.

Just before the discovery of gold in California in 1848, the building of the Panama Railroad was negotiated. The United States entered a convention that guaranteed Panama would remain neutral and that transit across the isthmus would be restricted.

Although the Spanish had once thought of building a canal across Panama, the French were the first to try. The work commenced in 1880, but by 1898 the privately owned construction company was bankrupt and work stopped.

The United States Congress in June 1902 authorized President Theodore Roosevelt to pay $40 million for the assets of the French company and complete the construction of the canal. In 1903 the president of Colombia agreed to transfer a strip of land for the canal to the United States, but the treaty was rejected by the Colombian senate.

Panama proclaimed its independence from Colombia on November 3, 1903. The presence of U.S. naval forces off the Pacific and Caribbean coasts of Panama deterred a Colombian effort to stop the secession. A treaty between Panama and the United States giving the Americans occupation and control of the Panama Canal Zone in perpetuity was signed on November 18, 1903.

The canal treaty was negotiated by the American secretary of state and a French citizen acting on behalf of the new republic. The treaty granted to the United States the ten-mile-wide, ocean-to-ocean Canal Zone. The treaty allowed the United States to govern the canal as "if it were the sovereign." The Panama Canal was opened in August 1914.

In the years that followed, Panamanians became irritated by the presence of the Americans. Even though Theodore Roosevelt had promised that the United States would not run the Canal Zone as a foreign colony bisecting Panama, the Panamanian people felt their sovereignty had been imposed upon and grew embittered. In an effort to improve relations between the two countries, several subsequent treaties were negotiated.

The Panama Canal Treaty of 1977 terminated all prior canal treaties between Panama and the United States. It abolished the Canal Zone and gave Panama sovereignty over the canal and the surrounding land. It also gave the United States the right to continue to manage and operate the canal.

A Neutrality Treaty was also signed in 1977 guaranteeing the permanent neutrality of the canal. The treaty said that after its expiration on December 31, 1999, only Panama would operate the canal, and no other country would be allowed to maintain military bases inside Panama. But the treaty reserved the right of the United States to use military force to keep the canal open.

The Republic of Panama adopted its first constitution in 1904. By 1919 provisions were added to allow for the popular election of a president and vice president. Through most of its modern history, however, Panama has had a tumultuous political life with many internal upheavals. Presidents were elected, defeated, exiled, and assassinated. And sometimes Panamanian restlessness broke into open rioting.

In May 1968, Arias Madrid was elected president of Panama. Eleven days later he was removed from office by the country's military, called the National Guard. The Guard took control of the government and formed a ruling junta. The leader of the coup was Col. Omar Torrijos. In 1972 he was given full executive powers for a period of six years. Panama's National Assembly named a new president in 1978, but Torrijos retained control of the National Guard and political power until his death in an airplane crash in July 1981.

Gen. Manuel Antonio Noriega became the commander of the National Guard in August 1983. At that time he reorganized and enlarged the Guard and renamed it the Panamanian Defense Forces. Noriega extended the influence of the PDF into nearly every realm of public life in Panama.

In May 1984, Nicolás Ardito Barletta, Noriega's chosen candidate, became Panama's first elected president in sixteen years. Barletta's election came by a small margin, however, and many suspected the military had influenced the vote.

In 1985 when Barletta, following popular sentiments, announced that he would investigate the murder of Hugo Spadafora, a leading critic of Noriega's regime, he was removed from office. He was succeeded in September 1985 by Vice President Eric Arturo Delvalle.

In the 1970s and 1980s, Panama's stance in regional politics was shaped by the presence of American managers and troops in the Canal Zone, its desire to remain neutral and at arm's length from Central American conflicts, and its desire to assert its sovereignty and demonstrate nationalistic pride.

By 1983, after Manuel Noriega had effectively asserted control over the government, Panamanian officials raised objections to U.S. support for the Nicaraguan Contras. (In 1978 and 1979, Omar Torrijos provided sanctuary for Sandinista guerrillas engaged in the anti-Somoza revolution in Nicaragua. When the Sandinistas prevailed in 1979, he immediately recognized the new government.) The Panamanians also protested the use of military bases in Panama for the deployment of U.S. advisers to El Salvador. That, they said, was an infringement on Panama's neutrality. The Panamanians asked the U.S. to limit its military flights to defense of the canal and also refrain from naval maneuvers off Panama's coast.

During 1984, Panama hosted meetings of the Contadora Group, which included Colombia, Venezuela, Mexico, and Panama. The group sought to promote peace in the region and, by freezing arms sales, the size of armies and the number of foreign military advisers.

While Panama officially positioned itself apart from the United States, Noriega maintained close ties to the Central Intelligence Agency and U.S. defense intelligence operations. He served as a back channel go-between for the United States and Fidel Castro. He secretly met and sometimes assisted top officials of the Reagan National Security Council, which was mounting its own unlawful effort to assist the Nicaraguan Contras.

But Noriega was not without his detractors. In February 1986 the U.S. ambassador to Panama criticized Noriega for his heavy-handed approach to human rights. And about the same time, the evidence that Norman Bailey had uncovered at the NSC in the early 1980s began to receive wider distribution. In April, Elliott Abrams, the U.S. undersecretary of state for Latin American affairs, criticized the Panamanian leader for his involvement with drug traffickers before a Senate subcommittee. In June the charges were restated in a lengthy *New York Times* article.

By the fall of 1986, members of Congress were growing increasingly concerned about Panama and Noriega. Conservatives, who were still smarting from what they considered too-generous concessions made in the Panama Canal Treaty of 1977, disliked Noriega for his dealings with Fidel Castro and Nicaraguan president Daniel Ortega. Liberals were displeased with the growing evidence of human rights abuses in Panama. And moderates abhorred Noriega's abuse of the democratic process during the May 1984 election.

In June 1987 a former officer of the PDF, Col. Roberto Díaz Herrera, alleged publicly that Noriega was responsible for the planting of a bomb aboard Omar Torrijos's plane in 1981. The former colonel, who once had vied for leadership of the PDF with Noriega, also charged that Noriega had been behind electoral fraud in the May 1984 election, had ordered the murder of the Panamanian dissident Hugo Spadafora, and was involved in corruption and drug smuggling.

Herrera's accusations—together with years of recession that had left Panama with a national debt approaching $4 billion—triggered months of demonstrations and strikes against Noriega's rule. More than one hundred civic groups joined together in the summer of 1987 to form what came to be known as the Civic Crusade. The crusade organized general strikes and street protests against Noriega's regime.

In the United States, conservative North Carolina Senator Jesse Helms attached an amendment to an intelligence bill; it required the CIA to disclose what it knew about Noriega's involvement with drug trafficking, arms dealing, money laundering, human right abuses, and his relationship with Cuba and the Sandinistas. The effort elicited a single typewritten page from the intelligence agency.

But popular protests and finally economic sanctions imposed against Panama by the United States were unsuccessful in moving Noriega from power.

When Noriega's own hand-picked president, Eric Delvalle, tried to fire him, Noriega instead removed Delvalle from the presidency.

In June, after growing protests had forced Noriega to suspend both freedom of the press and the right to assembly to maintain his authority, U.S. Secretary of State George Shultz urged Noriega to step aside. The U.S. Senate, in turn, on June 26, chastised Noriega and called on him to demonstrate a modicum of respect for human rights. The Panamanian military, on June 30, responded with an orchestrated gang attack on the United States Embassy in Panama City. The next day the United States temporarily suspended both military and economic aid to Panama.

Still, Noriega continued to pique the Reagan administration and his critics in Congress when he welcomed Nicaraguan president Daniel Ortega on an official visit to Panama in July.

On August 12, Noriega went on the offensive. He accused the United States of inciting the growing unrest in Panama. The United States was stirring up opposition to his rule, Noriega claimed, as an excuse to roll back the 1979 Panama Canal treaties that would return control of the canal to Panama in the year 2000.

CHAPTER 3

★★★★★★★

To Battle a Hydra

From the perspective of the twelfth-floor office of Miami U.S. Attorney Leon Kellner, it sometimes seemed as though all of society was falling apart. Right after he took over the top prosecutor's job in south Florida in the summer of 1985, he was up to his neck in crime and cocaine. He could look down from the window of his corner office on the cesspool that was the Miami River, which had become sort of a symbolic thoroughfare for drug dealers and murder.

In the summer that Kellner became U.S. attorney, seven off-duty City of Miami policemen staged their own private raid on a ship loaded with four hundred pounds of cocaine. The ship was moored just a few blocks from Kellner's office. Three drug smugglers, thinking they were about to be busted, jumped into the Miami River and drowned. The seven and eleven other policemen were eventually convicted or pled guilty to federal corruption or narcotics charges. The rogues became known as the Miami River Cops.

As Kellner looked down on the hundreds of rusty steel-hulled ships that regularly made their way from ports in Haiti or the Dominican Republic or Panama, he could only guess which ones contained stacked kilos of plastic-wrapped cocaine. From his window he could also look three miles west, over the low-slung rooftops of Miami's Little Havana neighborhood, to the very edge of the great, flat Everglades. Just inches above the muck of that slow-moving forty-mile-wide stream stretched the runways of Miami International Airport.

Early on, the drug police had run stings on baggage handlers in cahoots with drug runners out of Colombia. But by the time Kellner had taken over as U.S. attorney, the feds were arresting entire planes. Customs Service and DEA agents would tow the planes to the end of the runway and spend hours, sometimes days, searching nose cones, landing gear compartments, and false ceilings. Cocaine showed up everywhere: in cut-flower shipments, prefab concrete fence posts, even hollowed-out yams.

What didn't come in by way of the Miami River or Miami International Airport came in on cigarette boats feeding off fat drug-laden mother ships lying off the coast or in squadrons of small planes flying low under radar and landing on small airstrips or sections of uncompleted highway. The dope headed north, and in a week or two—converted into stacks and stacks of cash—flowed right back through Miami and offshore to banks in the Bahamas or Panama.

The drug trade translated into a crime wave. It had not always been that way. In 1970 the Miami U.S. attorney's office had had just seven prosecutors working in the criminal division. South Florida was a place to visit and play golf in the winter. President Richard Nixon's two daughters could water-ski on Biscayne Bay without a flotilla of Secret Service agents floating alongside.

That began to change by the late 1970s. The growing drug trade lacked sophistication, which led to violence. In south Florida, hundreds of competing smugglers—small-time operators—set up shop. Free enterprise in the drug trade created a murderous frenzy as dope smugglers and dealers competed for territory.

By 1979 and 1980 a war broke out among south Florida's so-called cocaine cowboys. It became literally a "shoot first and ask questions later" environment. The murder rate in Miami and surrounding Dade County soared from 349 in 1979 to 569 in 1980 and 621 in 1981. Law enforcement estimated that 40 percent of Miami's murders were drug-related. About 25 percent of the victims were killed with automatic weapons. Murder reached such epidemic proportions that by 1985 the Dade County medical examiner had to park two refrigerated trailers outside his front door to store the backlog of bodies.

The situation was exacerbated by the large flow of immigrants into south Florida. In 1980, Cuban president Fidel Castro lifted emigration barriers in Cuba and allowed 125,000 refugees to make their way to south Florida. This was known as the Mariel boat lift, for the Cuban port from which it originated, and thousands of those who arrived in Miami were hardened criminals turned loose from Castro's prisons.

Crime became so pervasive that Miami's top business leaders banded together shortly after the election of President Ronald Reagan to ask the White House for special assistance. The citizenry feared for its safety. Every president since Nixon had recognized the growing drug problem, but none had figured out how to solve it.

It was clear by the 1980s that stemming the drug trade would have little to do with continuing programs of small-time street arrests. In the 1970s and early 1980s, as the number of street arrests rose, the quantity of illegal drugs coming into the United States did not decline but rose. So-called bang-and-bust arrests—banging on doors and busting small-time peddlers—were not working. By the summer of 1987 auditors from the Justice Department had determined that Florida's southern district was the busiest federal crime fighting unit in America. The numbers spoke for themselves. The 120 assistant U.S. attorneys in Kellner's office had handled 328 felony jury trials in 1986, twice the number tried in the Central District of California, which included Los Angeles. In 1987 federal prosecutors in south Florida filed 1,365 felony cases, more than the number filed in Los Angeles and 100 more than the number of felonies filed in Manhattan and the southern district of New York.

In 1987 government agents seized thirty tons of cocaine in and around Miami. That amounted to 62 percent of all the coke seized in the entire United States. Seizures in excess of one thousand pounds were common. One captured shipment alone weighed four tons.

But it seemed that no matter how hard Kellner's prosecutors worked to stem the drug trade, no matter how hard the DEA and Customs agents worked to make cases for the prosecutors, the situation only got worse.

Kellner knew that one way to gauge the effectiveness of the drug traffickers or, conversely, the drug war was to measure the cost of cocaine. If law enforcement was putting a crimp in the supply, the cost of a Colombian kilo would rise, following the economics of supply and demand. But between 1982 and 1988—between the first day Kellner had come to work in Miami, as the chief assistant U.S. attorney, and the end of his third year as U.S. attorney—the cost of a kilo of cocaine had not risen. It had dropped in price by 400 percent, from $50,000 to $10,000. There was no getting around the fact that south Florida and Miami lay squarely in the path of the biggest illegal cocaine transshipment route ever established.

All of this had come about even though the administration of President Ronald Reagan had made the drug and crime problems of south Florida a top priority.

On January 28, 1982, Reagan announced the formation of a special cabinet-level task force to fight the drug scourge in south Florida. To hammer home just how important and what a top priority this effort would be, he charged Vice President George Bush with leading the newly created task force. The vice president of the United States would head the drug war.

"The nearly two million people of south Florida are unfairly burdened financially in addition to being denied their constitutional right to live in peace without fear and intimidation," the president said. It was intolerable for Miami to continue as "the nation's major terminal for the smuggling of illegal drugs," he said.

Within weeks federal crime-fighting offices in Miami were filled with reinforcements. The Customs Service added 130 agents, the DEA 60 agents, and the FBI 43 agents. The Internal Revenue Service pledged an attack on money laundering. The Bureau of Alcohol, Tobacco and Firearms added 45 agents to sniff out illegal caches of automatic weapons.

Still, in southern Florida, drugs made a mockery of the drug war. In the tony Miami suburb of North Bay Village, in the midst of upscale shops and the condos of well-to-do retirees, three cops were convicted of providing protection for dope dealers.

Five blocks from Kellner's office, the City of Miami police department was a honeycomb of drug corruption. Fifteen officers had been kicked off the force for stealing and distributing hundreds of kilos of cocaine. Some cops, like the Miami River seven, had even murdered dope pushers to take over their caches. The government's efforts seemed outmatched by the billions of dollars in illegal profits at the disposal of the drug cartels.

Sometimes the drug fight made Kellner literally sick. It was unrelenting. It was always there.

"The drugs were not being used in south Florida to any greater or lesser extent than anyplace else," he said. "But it was the entry point. What I wanted to do from the time I became U.S. attorney was not go after the boat captains. That would not solve the problem. The only way to solve the problem was to go after the heads of the drug families, the cartels, and the public officials helping them. It had to be an international fight. That was the only way."

Early in the Reagan administration, Justice Department officials decided that the leadership of drug organizations had to be identified and the trafficking networks dismantled. Law enforcement's challenge was to find its way from the low-level boat captains and street dealers to the drug barons and the hearts of their organizations. Most agreed that the federal conspiracy law known as the Racketeer Influenced and Corrupt Organizations statute—called RICO—was the way. RICO had been enacted by Congress in 1970 and was the culmination of decades of effort to fight organized crime, specifically the Mafia. The effort had begun in the 1920s and '30s with Prohibition. Liquor bootlegging, like the latter-day cocaine trade, required large organizations of smugglers, manufacturers, and distributors.

Crime organizations—which after the repeal of Prohibition turned to gambling, extortion, and labor racketeering, often across state lines—necessitated the involvement of federal law enforcement.

Federal efforts to fight organized crime began with the Anti-Racketeering Act passed by Congress in 1934. That law prohibited extortion in connection with interstate or foreign commerce. In 1950, Senator Estes Kefauver of Tennessee led a congressional investigation that concluded a nationwide crime syndicate existed. That conclusion was reinforced in 1957 when sixty-three organized crimes bosses from around the country met in New York State.

In 1963, after the inner workings of the Mafia were laid bare in televised congressional hearings that featured testimony by Mafia members such as Joseph Valachi, President Lyndon Johnson appointed a commission headed by Attorney General Nicholas Katzenbach to study organized crime further. In a 1967 report the Katzenbach Commission reported that the Mafia was essentially made up of "twenty-four groups operating as criminal cartels in large cities across the nation."

The Commission proposed a broad enhancement of federal law enforcement powers to attack the mob. In addition to beefed-up law enforcement resources, the recommendations included a law authorizing federal and state wiretapping, a law permitting witnesses to be immunized and compelled to testify, and the creation of a program to protect witnesses who cooperated with the government.

The Katzenbach Commission's recommendations, along with two congressional bills aimed at amending antitrust laws to stop the infiltration of organized crime into legitimate businesses, became the foundation of the Organized Crime Control Act of 1970, which created RICO.

In the 1970s, RICO—through the efforts of special Justice Department units called Organized Crime Strike Forces—targeted Mafia operations. Case by case, federal prosecutors began to dent the mob's work. At the same time, however, a debate began over whether Congress—which had designed RICO to counter the Mafia—intended the law to be used against other criminal activities. The answer came in two landmark U.S. Supreme Court cases, in 1981 and 1983. In *United States v. Turkette* and *Russello v. United States*, the Supreme Court adopted an expansive reading of Congress's intent. Prosecutors could use RICO to launch a broad attack against all organized crime and its illicit wealth. Specifically in *Turkette*, the Court found that groups of people, "associated in fact" whether as gang members or business acquaintances, could be held commonly responsible for a criminal act. In other words, every member of a criminal conspiracy from the top to the bottom could be held responsible for the criminal acts of every other member of the conspiracy.

The Court established that RICO targets could be any person engaged in organized crime, from the leader of a huge corporation to a lowly street thug. If associates shared as a goal the commission of a crime or profit from a crime, they could be labeled a criminal "enterprise" and subject to RICO prosecution.

The list of "RICO predicates" or racketeering activities that triggered enforcement of the expansive law was extensive. Among the acts that could bind conspirators together were murder, kidnapping, robbery, gambling, and bribery (all state crimes), and drug trafficking, obstruction of justice, and mail, wire, and securities fraud (all federal crimes). RICO said that the commission of any two racketeering acts with a common goal established a "pattern of racketeering activity." For prosecutors to bring RICO charges they needed to show the existence of a criminal enterprise with the intent to commit a pattern of racketeering activity.

RICO contained an additional provision that made it a crime to conspire to violate the law, a conspiracy being an agreement between two or more persons to do anything unlawful. Conviction on conspiracy, RICO said, did not require proof that the criminal objective was accomplished or attempted but only agreed upon. A conspirator did not have to agree that he personally would commit a crime but only that someone should.

To break up a drug-trafficking organization using RICO, prosecutors would have to show that conspirators had agreed, either expressly or through their actions, that they intended to smuggle drugs. Even though only a handful of people might actually load and transport a drug shipment or smuggle drug proceeds out of the country, the conspiratorial agreement could be proven by showing that the conspirators had discussed or agreed to the plot.

Moreover, RICO said that a conspiracy could be established by circumstantial evidence showing that the conspirators had banded together to perform various roles that would accomplish the illegal ends. That meant the leader of a drug operation, the person who came up with the idea and the financing to produce cocaine for export, for example, never had to meet or speak with the person who transported the cocaine. It made no difference that the pilot of the plane flying drug profits out of the country never met the accountant who tallied up the sales profits. All could be found guilty of conspiracy to import cocaine and money laundering.

Like the Mafia, the drug cartels were hydras. The Medellín cartel, for instance, was actually made up of some two hundred individual trafficking groups that had banded together to coordinate the production, transportation, and distribution of cocaine. Unlike the great Middle Eastern oil cartel that was most effective in the 1970s, the Medellín cartel—while its members frequently gathered socially—had no regular meetings specifically to coordinate drug trafficking or set the price of cocaine.

The members of the Medellín and the Cali cartels, both named for cities in Colombia, did not set the price of a kilo of cocaine, as the oil cartel might have set the price of a barrel of oil. Nor did the cocaine cartels set production quotas. Rather, each trafficking group operated autonomously and voluntarily to facilitate the safe transportation and delivery of their product to the big markets and to deal with threats from outsiders.

The drug cartels had come together almost by happenstance in the early 1980s. The Colombian cartel kingpins had started as small-time dealers and crooks in the mid and late 1970s. Pablo Escobar, for example, who would emerge as perhaps the preeminent member of the Medellín cartel, in 1976, at the age of twenty-seven, was known to the Colombian equivalent of the FBI as a petty criminal. He was a short, plump, unremarkable-looking man who had gotten his start in the criminal world by stealing cars.

Escobar rose quickly, however. When he was arrested for the first time on a drug charge, it was for the largest cocaine seizure ever up to then in the quiet Andean university city of Medellín.

Jorge Ochoa, born in 1949 and two months older than Escobar, was also destined to become a cocaine smuggling kingpin. Ochoa's introduction to the drug business came through his uncle, who had a made a life as a small-time smuggler in the developing cocaine trade. By 1977, at the age of twenty-eight, Ochoa had traveled to Miami to coordinate the receiving end of his uncle's business.

If one event was to mark the rise to prominence of the Colombian cartels, and particularly the Medellín and Cali cartels, that event came in late 1981. Up until then traffickers in the cities of Medellín, Cali, and Bogotá had never truly coordinated their actions. But in November 1981, Jorge Ochoa's youngest sister, Marta, a university student, was kidnapped by a Colombian leftist guerrilla group known as the M-19. One of three major guerrilla groups in Colombia, the M-19 had tracked the rise of the drug business. To help fund the purchase of weapons, M-19 turned to extortion. Drug traffickers, whose wealth was growing, were a target.

The kidnapping of Marta Ochoa particularly incensed drug traffickers throughout Colombia. In December 1981, 223 of Colombia's top traffickers met for a "general assembly" led by Escobar and Ochoa. The traffickers agreed to work together to protect their families and businesses. The gathering issued an eleven-point communiqué that promised death to anyone who "targeted people like us, whose hard-earned money has brought progress and employment to this country." Each of the traffickers pledged men and money to carry out the enforcement of the communiqué.

Shortly afterward, ten M-19 guerrillas were kidnapped and tortured. Three months later, in February 1982, Marta Ochoa was released. The episode cemented the bond among the traffickers. They found mutual benefit in cooperation.

In 1982 the Ochoa family joined with Pablo Escobar and a third trafficker, José Gonzalo Rodríguez Gacha, a Bogotá trafficker, to create Medellín & Company, a complete cocaine production and trafficking enterprise. The organization coordinated the efforts of coca growers, paste manufacturers, chemical suppliers, cocaine producers, transporters, distributors, and money launderers.

One of the Medellín cartel's first efforts was the creation of three modern cocaine processing laboratories on a remote jungle river island in southern Colombia. The laboratories, named Tranquilandia, or Quiet Village, numbers one, two, and three, were completed in 1983. They could produce twenty tons of cocaine each month. The facilities, including recreation rooms and medical clinics, were constructed and then staffed by hundreds of workers. By the mid-1980s the Medellín cartel's transportation and distribution networks were vast. In the United States alone, the Drug Enforcement Administration estimated, the cartel employed as many as six thousand people in Los Angeles and five thousand in Miami.

Less than a decade after the Medellín cartel had gotten its start, the American business magazine *Forbes* ranked the Ochoas as the fourteenth richest family in the world. Pablo Escobar and Jorge Ochoa were named among the world's billionaires.

CHAPTER 4

Floyd Carlton's Excellent Memory

Danny Moritz was amazed by Floyd Carlton's recollections. Usually an informant's memory is fragmented. But it seemed as though Carlton had anticipated the day he would be debriefed by a DEA agent: He had dates, times, and places on the tip of his tongue. Even after subsequent debriefings, Carlton's information remained the same. The facts were the same; the people were the same; the payoffs were the same.

"It was as if he had a photographic memory. And subsequently it was all corroborated," said Moritz. "You didn't have to say, 'Let's go over it again.'"

Assistant U.S. Attorney Richard Gregorie and Moritz spent three days with Carlton in a debriefing room hidden away in the basement of the Miami federal courthouse.

Carlton knew about the murder of Hugo Spadafora, one of Noriega's leading critics. He said he believed Noriega was responsible and that he had arranged for the bomb to be put on Omar Torrijos's plane. He told of Noriega's work with the Medellín cartel; he had worked directly with Pablo Escobar. And Carlton had been close to Noriega; both of them were raised in Chiriquí, Panama's westernmost province, and had met when Carlton was still a teenager.

"All our witnesses told us from firsthand experience that Carlton had been close to Noriega and Escobar. Carlton was in the room when Escobar and the whole crew were discussing the assassination of Lara Rodrigo Bonilla. We knew Carlton was of personal consequence. Escobar stayed in Carlton's beach house after the assassination of Bonilla. Noriega had been paid $5 million to shelter the cartel from the Colombian government," said Moritz.

Carlton talked about his involvement with the Sandinistas. He said that he and a colleague, César Rodríguez, had flown guns at Noriega's direction to the Sandinistas. Carlton speculated that Noriega was also involved with the Contras. He said that the Colombians were involved in the utilization of Nicaragua as a transit country for their cocaine.

Moritz sent his initial debriefing to DEA 6, the agency's reporting element. The report received a short circulation in Miami and at headquarters in Washington. The response was less than lukewarm. Some thought Carlton was shooting off his mouth, that he had a vendetta against Noriega. Noriega had been a friend to the DEA. He had taken down some traffickers in Panama, had joined in crop eradication efforts, and had put his agents behind a major DEA money-laundering sting. Since 1980 the government of Panama had granted every request by the United States to board Panamanian-registered vessels on the high seas. Panamanian authorities had been very cooperative in expelling directly to the United States those U.S. fugitives caught in Panama.

Moritz was told to prepare a general intelligence file. There was no slam dunk here—no powder on the table, as they liked to say in the agency. Carlton was handing up a dry conspiracy. That meant the trail was cold. It would take a dozen witnesses to corroborate Carlton's story in a fashion that could win a conviction. At headquarters, there were two schools of thought. One said the agency didn't go around busting its friends. Noriega, after all, was the only game in town when it came to Panama. He cooperated. He intercepted ether, acetone, and cocaine shipments. He sprayed marijuana fields with paraquat, unlike the leaders in other Central and South American countries. On the other side, some said the general was a drug trafficker, probably knocking off his competition. For that, he should be indicted.

Then in April 1987, Moritz was transferred out of Miami. Richard Gregorie was furious. Moritz had busted his back on the case, and there was more to do before packing it in. By now Gregorie had made it his personal mission to go after the leaders of the Medellín cartel. He had cut his teeth as a prosecutor in the Organized Crime Strike Force, a Justice Department group that made a living out of making tough cases against the Mafia and organized crime figures, and he had been one of the first prosecutors in the United States to deliver an indictment against the cartel. Any case that had to do with Pablo Escobar, Jorge Ochoa, or José Gonzalo Rodríguez Gacha—the cartel's leaders—was a case for Gregorie.

He called Ken Kennedy, assistant special agent in charge of the Miami DEA, and asked him to put another agent on the case.

"Gregorie saw Noriega as an extension of the cartel," said Kennedy. "It wasn't Noriega so much, it was Panama he wanted to pursue at this point. He knew pilots were flying cartel dope from Panama to the United States. He knew the Medellín cartel's principal flow of narcotics proceeds was coming back to Panama. A lot of us figured there was government sanction there. We knew the importation of cash into Panama was not illegal, but conspiracy to launder narco dollars in the United States was."

Kennedy sent another agent, Steven Grilli, to see Carlton.

Grilli flinched at his nickname, "Professor" (he had been a history Ph.D. candidate). He loved paper trails. He was as big as a defensive end, so he had had to pick his undercover assignments carefully. Then he turned to conspiracy work. It was the perfect thing for a scholar with a head for adventure.

"Kennedy said to see if I could make a case with this guy," Grilli remembered.

Grilli went to see Carlton. He was impressed.

"Carlton had a mind like iron. He could instantly recall dates, people, involvement, and chains of events. It was super dramatic for me when I talked to him."

Grilli, Carlton, and a DEA agent who spoke Spanish sat in a bunker below the Miami federal courthouse, which had been dubbed "the submarine."

At first Carlton spoke only in Spanish, but in two or three weeks he began to pick up English. On breaks he consumed magazines in Spanish and English. Sometimes he read two books a day.

Grilli saw Carlton as the kind of guy who could fade into a group. He wasn't a gold chain guy; he was sheepish. Grilli couldn't figure how Carlton had fallen into working for the cartel. He went over Carlton's story inch by inch.

For two and a half weeks beginning in mid-July, Grilli sat with Carlton and filled up five legal pads with notes.

"If you are going to investigate a conspiracy, the guy has to be briefed completely," said Grilli. "You have to get into the specifics, especially concerning people. You really don't know in the beginning how they fit. You want every little piece of evidence that might lead you to another piece of evidence that can corroborate what the guy is telling you. So you have to spend a lot of time."

Grilli's debriefing matched Moritz's: It was right on the money.

"He could remember within two or three days the dates that he actually traveled. This was in 1987, and he was talking about flights in 1982 to Colombia to meet Escobar," Grilli said of Carlton.

Using telephone patches through Panama so that the calls could not be traced, Grilli and Carlton began contacting Carlton's friends and asking them to smuggle out of Panama any papers or documents that would corroborate Carlton's story.

While the debriefing was still going on, Grilli began to receive Carlton's own documentation: his personal telephone book.

"When you opened the phone book, there were numbers for Pablo Escobar, for Escobar's contact in Managua, for La Playita, Noriega's beach house," Grilli said. "The numbers were all there: Ricardo Bilonick's, the guy who eventually transported Carlton's loads from Panama to the United States. David Rodrigo Ortiz's in Medellín, the guy who taught Carlton how to fly the Cheyennes." And there were airplane tickets and hotel receipts indicating where Carlton had stayed in Medellín. These more than corroborated his story. It was amazing.

Carlton said that he had been the middle man between Noriega and the cartel. He said that he had set up drug flights between Colombia and Panama and that he had paid protection money on behalf of the cartel to Noriega through an intermediary. He also said the Medellín cartel had once paid

Noriega at least $4 million for the right to use Panama as a refuge from Colombian authorities.

Noriega had probably never touched a drug shipment. He had just made it easy for the traffickers to do their business.

Within a month Grilli went back to Kennedy. "I think we can make a case," he said.

CHAPTER 5
★★★★★★

Getting to a Grand Jury

By the end of the summer in 1987, Steve Grilli and Richard Gregorie had heard enough of Floyd Carlton's story to know they could take it to a grand jury.

Noriega was now almost constantly in the news. Accusations of his involvement in drug trafficking were swirling. One of Noriega's former military officers, Roberto Díaz Herrera, had publicly accused Noriega of helping the Medellín cartel run drugs. These accusations had appeared in the *New York Times*. On Capitol Hill in Washington, senators and congressmen were openly critical of Noriega. Massachusetts Senator John Kerry was even preparing to hold hearings into Noriega's dealings with U.S. intelligence agencies.

But Gregorie knew there was a difference between a congressional hearing and going to court to try a criminal case. The first could rest on innuendo; the second meant gathering evidence. And a conviction meant evidence beyond a reasonable doubt. "I felt it was important to treat this as a criminal case, not a political football," he said. "In a Senate hearing they ask leading questions. They try to tilt the questions toward whatever political point they want to make. Sometimes the senators are fighting with one another."

It had been two years since Danny Moritz started following Noriega's trail. Gregorie knew he had to get his witnesses to a grand jury before a committee of senators began mucking with the record.

"I could just see a defense lawyer standing in front of Floyd Carlton saying, 'Didn't you tell the Senate thus and so?' 'Well that was the answer I gave, but that's not what I meant.'"

Gregorie summoned the grand jury in early October 1987. It was made up of twenty-three citizens, and the foreperson was a middle school principal.

A grand jury is a group of ordinary citizens who are called to court to determine whether government lawyers and law enforcement agents have collected sufficient evidence to prove that an alleged wrongdoer has committed a crime. The jurors see evidence and listen to testimony in secret. The secrecy allows witnesses called by the government to speak freely before them without inhibition or fear of retaliation. It also protects the identity of the person being investigated. Should the evidence prove insufficient and the jurors decide against issuing an indictment, the accused is usually not publicly identified.

29

But a grand jury does not decide whether the accused is guilty or innocent. Getting the indictment is one thing; taking the case to trial and proving the charges beyond a reasonable doubt is another.

"Our grand jury sat one day a week, on Thursday," Grilli remembered. "Six hours a day with a lunch break."

Besides Carlton, Gregorie and Grilli had Tony Azpruia, the former Panamanian pilot. Through the summer they had lined up about a half-dozen witnesses. Each had been debriefed. They went over the stories line by line.

Carlton was the first to be called in. He sat before the grand jury for more than two days. Next came Azpruia. Then a Colombian drug trafficker named Ramón Navarro. There was a cartel pilot named Boris Olarte, followed by a major in the Colombian National Police. The testimony outlined a conspiracy in which Noriega, the de facto leader of Panama, had used his position to foster drug trafficking.

Noriega had protected cocaine shipments from Panama to the United States, sold chemicals vital to the manufacture of cocaine to the drug cartel, allowed the cartel to set up a cocaine manufacturing lab in his country, protected money shipments from the United States to Panama, provided safe haven to the leaders of the Colombia-based cartel after they had ordered the assassination of the Colombian minister of justice, and accepted at least $4.6 million in bribes from the cartel to look the other way while it made itself at home in Panama.

The witnesses outlined a clear sequence of events. First, there had been four cartel drug flights through Panama using Carlton or his transportation organization. Second, there had been a Noriega-sanctioned drug voyage of a pleasure yacht called the *Krill* from Panama to Colombia. Third, there had been the Noriega-sanctioned deliveries of ether and acetone, chemicals used in the production of cocaine, to cartel laboratories, one located in Panama. Finally, there had been the laundering of money earned in the drug trade. The events spanned nearly five years from the fall of 1981 until March 1986.

The conspiracy, or "the enterprise," as prosecutors like to call such criminal organizations, included, at the bottom, drug smuggling pilots and, at the top, the world's richest and most powerful cocaine trafficker, the head of the Medellín cartel, Pablo Escobar. In the middle, but most prominently, was Noriega. He had aided the traffickers by protecting their scheme.

"The enterprise itself was like the Parthenon," said Grilli. "The Medellín cartel was like the roof, and the pillars were the various episodes of the case. Carlton's flights were pillars that spanned a number of years."

More simply, it was like a puzzle. You had to see each event in the context of others to understand exactly how the enterprise worked. "In law they call it the doctrine of verbal completeness," Grilli explained. "In other words, if you have one side of a conversation, you can't understand it unless you have both sides. In this case, if you don't follow the events in Colombia, you can't really follow the events in Panama."

The shipment of ether and acetone through Panama in and of itself was not startling or suspicious or illegal, for instance. But when you understood that the shipments ended up in the jungle and that the cartel was running a drug lab there, the picture became clearer. And when the cocaine being produced in the jungle was shipped back through Panama and on to the United States, the picture was complete.

"Why did members of the cartel show up in Panama after the killing of the defense minister, Rodrigo Lara Bonilla, in Colombia?" Grilli asked rhetorically. "The reason is that there was this outrageous manhunt in Colombia. There was a declared war on the traffickers. They went to their friend Manuel Noriega. Without the part that they had killed the defense minister, there can be no understanding of what Noriega was doing."

Nobody had taped any of these events. There was no documentary evidence. Before the grand jury, Gregorie and Grilli would have to build their case piece by piece.

"We had to put Floyd Carlton in historical context and then go back and find every piece of corroborating evidence concerning Carlton. We had to make Carlton trustworthy in the eyes of the grand jury."

The problem with a conspiracy is that evidence erodes over time. If a crime is committed tomorrow, three weeks later there will be an erosion of the evidentiary base—just like the ink runs on a piece of paper left in the rain. Gregorie and Grilli were trying to go back. They were reaching back to 1981, into a country run by a military dictator who was an intelligence-trained officer. It was very, very difficult. With the four flights of Carlton, the *Krill* affair, the ether and acetone, and the money laundering, it looked like four different cases.

To fit the events—what the prosecutors called overt acts—together to make a RICO case, Gregorie and Grilli needed to link the acts through a continuing criminal enterprise. They thought they had found that association in the Panamanian Defense Force. PDF officers had been linked to each of the events in one way or another, either facilitating trafficking or actually participating. Since Noriega and all of his cronies were associated with the PDF, the force seemed the likely enterprise.

Carlton and Azpruia had put together the drug flights. Ramón Navarro had tipped Grilli to the *Krill* voyage. There were airport witnesses who told about the ether and acetone shipments and the money laundering. Throughout, members of the PDF had participated. Their goal had been to enrich one another and the Medellín cartel.

Nearly all the characters that DEA agent Danny Moritz had first heard about two years before had a place in the story.

Five weeks into the grand jury investigation, Grilli stopped by Gregorie's office. "Dick, when are we going to have enough? Where are we going with this thing? Are we going to indict?"

Gregorie looked at Grilli. There was never enough. There could always be more. "Steve, what do you think grand juries are for?" he asked.

Grilli went back and started digging for more.

★   ★   ★

In Washington, Senator John Kerry, who chaired the Foreign Relations Committee's Subcommittee on Terrorism and Narcotics, had his own staff working on following up Noriega leads. Kerry had gotten word of the Miami investigation through a letter from Tony Azpruia, who had been sitting in the Metropolitan Correctional Center, the federal lockup in Miami, for months. He was ready to trade what he knew to anyone for freedom.

Even before Azpruia went before the Miami grand jury, he had written to Kerry claiming he had the goods on Noriega. Not all of what Azpruia had recounted to Moritz and Grilli panned out, and he had flunked a lie detector test on his direct dealings with Noriega. But Kerry didn't know that.

Late in the fall, Jack Blum, Kerry's special counsel, started asking Kellner's office to make some of its grand jury witnesses available to the Senate subcommittee.

"The investigation could have continued longer, but we didn't want our grand jury testimony made public," said Grilli. "We were getting calls from the Senate. Our witnesses were under wraps. It was like a shell game—who was going to get these guys first."

"I didn't want to see this case become a political football," said Leon Kellner, the U.S. Attorney and Gregorie's boss. "I did not want it to become a matter of Latin American policy, arms trafficking. This was a dope case. This guy had been dealing dope for years, and the United States looked the other way."

CHAPTER 6

★★★★★★★

Prosecution Politics

Miami U.S. Attorney Leon Kellner was tired of seeing politics run through his career.

In early 1986, eight months before the Iran-Contra scandal had first come to light, one of Kellner's young assistants, Jeffrey Feldman, uncovered what he believed to be the trail of an arms supply network that led to the Nicaraguan Contras. At the time the whole idea seemed preposterous.

Feldman believed that the arms and the money to pay for them flowed through Miami, went to Costa Rica, and then on to the Contras. He believed that an American rancher in Costa Rica named John Hull was involved and that an American colonel by the name of North was involved.

Feldman sent a memo to Kellner: "We have sufficient evidence to begin a grand jury investigation . . . (that) would ultimately reveal criminal activities including gunrunning and Neutrality Act violations." It was against the law for U.S. citizens or the government to run guns to the Contras.

Kellner wrote on Feldman's memo: "I concur that we have sufficient evidence to ask for a grand jury."

Feldman traveled to Costa Rica in search of the rancher John Hull. But Feldman first ran into the Central Intelligence Agency's Costa Rican station chief, Joseph Fernández, who was curious about what Feldman wanted with Hull.

Feldman never found Hull, and Fernández made sure that Feldman was safely packed back to Miami.

It may never be known what exactly happened next, but some believe that Fernández contacted his superiors at the CIA and told them about Feldman. And some believe CIA Director William Casey then contacted Lt. Col. Oliver North at the National Security Council, who told NSC Director John Poindexter about Feldman's visit.

Poindexter, like U.S. Attorney General Edwin Meese, was a member of the president's inner circle. Meese was, of course, Leon Kellner's boss.

What is certain is that Kellner changed his mind about going forward with a grand jury investigation into the gunrunning Feldman suspected. Upon Feldman's return to Miami, Kellner wrote in a memo: "A grand jury at this point would represent a fishing expedition."

Feldman later recollected that he was told the investigation was dropped because "politics are involved."

Kellner, who was later called—along with Feldman and two other assistant U.S. attorneys from Miami—to testify before a congressional panel looking into the Iran-Contra affair, said he was never told by the attorney general or anyone else to drop the Feldman investigation.

A Senate subcommittee investigator disagreed. He said he was convinced that Kellner "was part and parcel" of the Reagan administration's effort to cover up its Contra resupply network. Kellner responded: "Pure and simple, the evidence was not there."

Whatever had happened, Kellner did not plan to become the object of political wrangling a second time. If there was evidence of Noriega's drug involvement, then an indictment would go forward.

"I did not want the indictment to be perceived as political because it would violate everything I believed in. I wanted to do it before anybody made a big show with our witnesses. That was important to me. I wanted it to look like the grand jury investigation it was, rather than a circus." Which meant that Kellner did not like what he saw in Washington.

"Kerry was doing this to show that the administration was soft on drugs. He wanted to make our indictment look as if it was a response. It was all too political. I thought it was inappropriate for him to do this when I had a law enforcement investigation going on. Congress mucking around in a law enforcement case is a mistake. Look what happened with Iran-Contra. I was not going to let them destroy my indictment."

In early December 1987, Kellner called Associate Attorney General Stephen Trott, the top official in the Criminal Division of the Reagan Justice Department

"We have the case," Kellner told Trott. And he laid out the scenario.

Trott had known about the development of the indictment since even before the grand jury had begun meeting in October. In late September, Steve Grilli and Ken Kennedy had met with David Westrate, the DEA's deputy administrator in charge of operations, and briefed him on the investigation. Westrate had passed the information on to Jack Lawn, the agency's administrator. Lawn had told Trott, who was then kept abreast of all developments.

Trott now asked Kellner to prepare a Prosecution Memo outlining the facts and the charges. Prosecution Memos weren't prepared in every case, just in major cases utilizing RICO. The prosecutors were asked to lay out the evidence and the laws that would apply to the evidence. The memo was to discuss the downside of indicting and was to be a complete analysis of the case.

Trott had gone to the Criminal Division at Main Justice in 1983. Under Attorney Generals William French Smith and then Edwin Meese, he had seen the department's Office of International Affairs expand.

"It was called 'The Justice Department Goes International,'" said Trott. "We blew out all over the world: drug cases, terrorist cases. The notion was to make sure we weren't sitting ducks for people operating beyond our immediate reach, beyond our borders. Transnational criminals, multinational criminals, stateless criminals, traffickers, money launderers, gunrunners, white-collar criminals, the whole show." The department had stepped up its drug prosecutions. One objective was to go after the top of the drug families. "If you follow the drugs, you'll get only the lower-level people. If you follow the money, you get to the top."

Trott had been called to testify before Congress about Panama, to certify that Panama was engaged in fighting drugs. Certification was a prerequisite for American aid.

"We weren't fools," said Trott. "We knew what was going on. At one point it was pretty clear that Noriega was playing us off against everybody else and that he was putting on a show down there. He essentially had his own drug operation. If you didn't play ball with him, then he would turn you in to the DEA. He was throwing crumbs our way.

"We had reason to believe that he was playing both sides of the street, but we were not about to turn down the people he was throwing to us. We decided to play both sides of the street also: take what he gave us but go after him quietly on our own terms."

CHAPTER 7

The DEA's "Deep Appreciation" for the General

A letter dated May 8, 1986, from John C. Lawn, administrator of the U.S. Drug Enforcement Administration, to Gen. Manuel Antonio Noriega, commander in chief of the Panama Defense Forces:

> Dear General Noriega:
> I would like to take this opportunity to reiterate my deep appreciation for the vigorous anti-drug-trafficking policy that you have adopted, which is reflected in the numerous expulsions from Panama of accused traffickers, the large seizures of cocaine and precursor chemicals that have occurred in Panama, and the eradication of marijuana cultivations in Panamanian territory.

Jack Lawn testified before the Senate Foreign Relations Committee's Subcommittee on Terrorism, Narcotics and International Operations on Wednesday, July 12, 1988. He said as follows:

> The DEA has had a long and generally positive working relationship with the government of Panama. Our joint efforts concern crop eradication, narcotics investigations, money laundering, and drug interdiction.
> Since 1980, the government of Panama has granted every request by United States authorities to board Panamanian-registered vessels on the high seas. Panamanian authorities have also been very cooperative in expelling directly to the United States those United States fugitives caught in Panama.

DEA managers overseas are sometimes aware of allegations against the individuals with whom they work, people like Noriega, said Lawn. But, he added, "often the allegations cannot be proved or disproved. Often the allegations are malicious."

Between 1970 and 1985, the DEA had received on average three complaints each year alleging that Noriega was involved in corruption. The complaints were among more than four hundred thousand pieces of new information received in each of those years, Lawn said.

The DEA was not aware that National Security Adviser John Poindexter had visited Noriega in 1985, but the agency was aware that the State Department and the NSC were concerned about Noriega's alleged involvement in corruption.

The DEA did not receive information from the CIA or other intelligence sources regarding Noriega. The CIA was often reluctant to share information for fear it would be released in legal proceedings. That may have been one reason the DEA did not know the truth about Noriega. The DEA would not have known if the CIA, the NSC, or any other agency were actively supporting a foreign leader, Lawn said. The first "corroborative information" about drug-trafficking involvement by Noriega came through Floyd Carlton, Lawn said. He said that his 1986 letter to Noriega and others was "case specific," not "character references."

"For a long time now I, at least, and many others in the government, have been asking the Justice Department what was the state of evidence against General Noriega."

Elliott Abrams was the assistant secretary of state for Inter-American Affairs. He was testifying before the Select Committee on Narcotics Abuse and Control of the House of Representatives. It was Wednesday, March 29, 1988.

"The state of rumors was terrific. The belief that he was engaged in assisting drug trafficking was very high. But that's not evidence. Evidence is something that's solid and something that ultimately you hope you can go to a grand jury with."

Abrams said that when he went to the State Department in 1985, it was generally understood "without any particular evidence" that Noriega and the Panamanian Defense Forces, under his direction, were engaged in corrupt activities, including drug trafficking.

"I think you need to distinguish between evidence that produces a foreign policy result and the kind of legal evidence you can take to a grand jury. The fact that evidence does not rise to the level of being something you could take to a grand jury, it certainly has been sufficient to move on foreign policy grounds."

According to Abrams, Poindexter visited Noriega in Panama in late 1985 to tell him to quit his criminal activities.

"The main purpose of the trip was to tell Noriega that we could not tolerate what we believed to be the growing increasing pattern of PDF corruption, and it had to change."

The State Department's intelligence and drug enforcement information units believed that Noriega was involved in drug trafficking before he became the subject of criminal investigations in Miami and Tampa, Abrams testified. But the evidence, he said, had not yet risen to the level at which a grand jury could indict.

"As soon as it rose to that level, the Justice Department, two separate U.S. attorneys, moved."

"Not a sparrow falls in Panama without General Noriega getting a feather from that sparrow."

Francis McNeil was the former United States ambassador to Costa Rica. He was the senior deputy assistant secretary of state for intelligence and research, the number two man in the State Department's intelligence operation from 1984 to early 1987.

On Monday, April 4, 1988, he testified before the Senate Foreign Relations Committee's Subcommittee on Terrorism, Narcotics and International Communications.

As early as 1984, McNeil said, it was "fairly commonly believed" that Noriega was involved in drug dealing. The growth of the Panamanian connection to the drug cartels began in 1983 when Noriega became commander in chief of the Panamanian military. A State Department analyst at the United States Embassy in Panama City had reported that Panama was "slowly going to Hades in a hand basket, with Noriega taking over more and more control, the corruption becoming more and more evident . . ." McNeil said.

The conclusion at the State Department then, and again in 1985, was that Noriega "had to know what was going on, and he had to be involved," McNeil testified.

Why was the corruption in Panama ignored during the early years of the Reagan administration? McNeil's response: "Your State Department, your Central Intelligence Agency, White House staffs, military, tend to react to national priorities as they perceive them."

McNeil testified that following a 1986 *New York Times* article about Noriega's involvement in corruption, an intelligence and policy review was conducted by the Panama Regional Interagency Group, which included State Department, CIA, and Department of Defense officials. Some members of the group believed Noriega should be dealt with. Others argued that Noriega's help to the Nicaraguan Contras warranted alternatives. In the end, McNeil said, Elliott Abrams decided that Noriega might be an important ally in assuring a Contra victory. McNeil said the CIA and the State Department intelligence operation reached the same conclusion.

After the policy review, McNeil said, a conscious decision was made within the administration to delay dealing with Noriega. "At the time, the statement was made that Panama—that Noriega should be put on the shelf until Nicaragua was taken care of. . . . The decision to do anything about Noriega was postponed . . . for the cause of the Contras."

While the State Department sometimes took Noriega to task, CIA Director William Casey and officials at the Defense Department openly viewed Noriega as a "valuable support for our policy in Central America, and particularly in Nicaragua," said McNeil.

Noriega received mixed signals. In 1984, a year after Noriega had assumed power in Panama, Nicolas Ardito Barletta, Noriega's candidate for the Panamanian presidency, won in a flawed election. Yet the United States recognized Barletta's election and sent Secretary of State George Shultz to his inauguration. The United States hoped that Barletta, a capable civil servant, would bridge the gap to democratic civilian rule in Panama.

While the State Department hoped that the necessity of transition to real civilian rule would get through to Noriega, McNeil said, "the body language that Noriega saw from the CIA, military intelligence, and some in the [Department of Defense] suggested otherwise, that if he could consolidate his hold, his friends in Washington would take care of things."

In 1985, after the murder of Panamanian opposition leader Hugo Spadafora, there was a failure of will in the administration. Barletta clashed with Noriega and was deposed, but the State Department did not go to Barletta's defense. "Perhaps some kind of shortsighted 'he's a bastard, but he's our bastard' argument carried the day," said McNeil, "linked to [security of] the canal and Noriega's putative support for the Contras."

McNeil said that when Noriega was called to Washington in November 1985 to receive a dressing down for his behavior from members of the intelligence community, wires got crossed and no one scolded Noriega. CIA Director William Casey, McNeil said, reported that Noriega left "reassured."

"It is obvious that the meeting with Casey and the message from him confirmed Noriega's belief that the people who counted in the [U.S. government] were backing his grab for power and that he had no reason to listen to mere ambassadors and State Department babble," McNeil said. "If he could keep us happy on Nicaragua, he could do as he pleased."

The mixed messages continued.

In December 1985, NSC chief John Poindexter went to Panama and "upbraided Noriega about narcotics," according to McNeil. But within weeks NSC senior staff member Lt. Col. Oliver North sought Noriega's clandestine help in arranging Contra sabotage missions inside Nicaragua.

"Noriega's cozy relationship with American intelligence agencies may have protected him from close scrutiny. What is certain is that the value attributed to the relationship with Panamanian intelligence led our intelligence agencies to depend on the Panamanian service for handouts, treating them as an allied service," said McNeil. "This was a true intelligence failure, the accountability for which rests with the intelligence folk who had become Noriega's clients." In the end, Noriega provided the United States with little help in assisting the Contras, McNeil said. Noriega's value to the Contra cause was "vastly oversold. The administration made the same mistake that it made with respect to the Contra program: It indulged in wishful thinking, in the illusion of omnipotence."

CHAPTER 8

★★★★★★★

At Main Justice, the CIA, and the NSC

José Blandon was Noriega's chief political adviser and Panama's New York counsel. For much of the fall of 1987 he had worked to try and ease the growing tension between Noriega and his critics in the United States.

In October, Noriega asked Blandon to find some way out of the growing discord. The Civic Crusade in Panama had led workers in strikes against the government. Roberto Díaz Herrera had openly challenged Noriega's rule. And relations with the United States were in a shambles. The American secretary of state and much of the U.S. Congress had called upon Noriega to give up his power. Noriega thought that perhaps it was time to lead a transition to a civilian government and politicize the Panamanian Defense Forces. Blandon came up with a plan. It called on Noriega to leave power no later than April 1988, and it also provided for the retirement of all Panamanian Defense Forces officers who had completed twenty-five years of service. Essentially, Panama would get out of the grip of the PDF.

Secretly, Blandon also asked Assistant Secretary of State Elliott Abrams to guarantee Noriega's safe departure from Panama and to assure that Noriega would not be prosecuted in the United States.

It seemed as though the plan would work. Noriega took it under consideration.

But in mid-November, Daniel Murphy, a retired U.S. Navy admiral, ex-CIA man, and former chief of staff to Vice President George Bush, arrived in Panama. Murphy was ostensibly on a private trip looking for business opportunities. He was accompanied by one of South Korea's leading businessmen. Murphy asked for and got a private one-on-one meeting with Noriega.

Noriega was clearly under the impression that the United States, especially Congress, wanted him out of power. But in their meeting, Murphy proposed a four-point plan that would allow Noriega to stay on as the leader of Panama until after the elections scheduled for May 1989. That was a year longer than the timetable under the Blandon plan. Noriega would remain while Panama's authoritarian government was remodeled along democratic lines.

Noriega later described Murphy as an American envoy. He told Blandon

40

that Murphy had represented himself as the private emissary of Secretary of State George Shultz and new NSC chief Lt. Gen. Colin Powell. Murphy later confirmed that, in fact, he had been briefed by the State Department and the National Security Council before going to Panama, but he denied that he represented himself as an official U.S. emissary. Nonetheless, Noriega was heartened by the visit and believed that he had gained new support in Washington. He said Murphy had told him that "anything could happen" after the 1988 U.S. presidential election.

Following his meeting with Murphy, Noriega began to lose interest in the Blandon plan. By December 21, Noriega had called Blandon in New York to tell him to stop working on a compromise. Blandon wired a message back to Noriega saying that if he sought only to protect himself, "history will forget you." Three weeks later, on January 14, 1988, Noriega fired Blandon.

Within days, Blandon, who was now convinced that Noriega's presence hurt Panama, honored a request to appear before the Miami grand jury. When he arrived in Miami, he was met by Kellner, Gregorie, and Grilli, who took him to a DEA safe house. The next day, on January 21, 1988, Blandon became the last witness to appear before the grand jury. In five hours of testimony he provided what Gregorie and Grilli later termed the "Castro nexus."

Blandon revealed how Noriega, as the head of Panama's military intelligence service for thirteen years, had placed a number of close aides in key positions to control immigration, the airports, harbors, passports, and visas. He had obtained payoffs and hidden profits of millions of dollars for himself and civilian associates. Simultaneously, Blandon said, Noriega had put together a network of civilian business associates who became his personal links to the drug trade and to other illegal commercial ventures.

By the time Noriega had assumed control in Panama, Blandon said, his connections with the Colombian drug traffickers were firmly cemented. In 1984, top Panamanian officers were paid a $5 million bribe from the Medellín drug cartel in exchange for allowing a cocaine manufacturing plant to operate inside Panama near the Colombian border. Later, when the lab was raided by the PDF and the U.S. DEA, leaders of the cartel became angry with Noriega. Noriega met directly with Cuban president Fidel Castro to discuss the raid and to negotiate a settlement, Blandon testified. "We were wrong to take the money," Blandon said Noriega told him. Noriega said: "We have to make everything good."

Present at the Havana meeting, Blandon told the grand jury, were representatives of the cartel. Castro mediated the two sides' differences. The revelation amounted to direct evidence that Noriega had taken a bribe from drug traffickers.

Gregorie called Blandon's testimony "the icing on the cake."

With Blandon's testimony, Gregorie and Kellner were ready to ask the grand jury to indict not only Noriega but also several of his cohorts in the Panamanian Defense Forces, among them Noriega's chief of staff, Col.

Narcos Justines; chief of the air force, Col. Lorenzo Purcell; director of the
National Department of Investigation, Nivaldo Madrinan; and Noriega's personal aide, Maj. Luis del Cid, all of whom, according to Blandon, had also
been involved with drug traffickers. The prosecutors were prepared to name
the entire Panamanian Defense Forces as a "racketeering enterprise."

Leon Kellner's conference room was stacked with pizza boxes. In the corner, the Super Bowl was on television, but the volume was turned low.
Kellner, Gregorie, Mark Schnapp, the head of the office's Criminal Division,
Steve Grilli, and Ken Kennedy were literally pasting together the Noriega
prosecution memo and indictment. Kellner had promised to deliver the
memo and indictment to Stephen Trott the next day.

"We'd argue about who to put in, and then we would go back to my office
and start cutting and pasting and changing," Kellner recalls. "We'd do it
again, go back and yell again, 'No, it's not good enough.' We'd take this guy
out, and we'd change it again." The debate went on right through the Super
Bowl. "Do we have the evidence. Should we put it in or not? We'd go over
the evidence again. We'd attack it. Defend it."

Kellner, Gregorie, and Schnapp would be on the plane for Washington at
six the next morning, and Kellner was nervous. If anyone dared suggest he
was going slow on this prosecution, he would go ballistic.

Gregorie figured he had already taken care of the "go slowers." He had
called Brian Ross, an NBC investigative reporter, and told him to be on the
steps of the Justice Department the next morning and to bring a camera. The
Miami U.S. attorney's office was going to deliver the indictment of Manuel
Noriega.

Gregorie expected the worst. He hadn't been through the wringer as
Kellner had in the Iran-Contra affair, but he had gotten a dose of official
Washington in 1984 when he indicted Medellín cartel chiefs Pablo Escobar
and Jorge Ochoa. Later in the year, Ochoa was arrested in Spain along with
the head of the Colombian Cali cartel, Gilberto Rodríguez Orejuela. Gregorie
went to Spain to arrange the extraditions, but no one in the United States
Embassy would give him the time of day.

There was a drug war on, but two of the top cocaine kingpins in the world
couldn't move the foreign service. Before Gregorie could get anyone's attention, Ochoa and Rodriguez were deported to Colombia—Ochoa on a warrant
for importing show bulls without proper papers. It was a joke. Almost the
same thing happened again two years later. Ochoa was arrested in Honduras,
but the State Department let him slip away.

"I honestly believe that when our government decides, as a matter of priority, that there is something it wants, it can get it. If you have a man with
the kind of notoriety that Jorge Ochoa has, why would you stand by and allow
him to be shipped back to Colombia?" Gregorie said.

Gregorie had the same feeling when he began developing the Noriega
indictment. He had gone to the Internal Security Division of Main Justice,
which handles intelligence agencies. He asked for clearance to see the top-

secret files on Noriega. If he was going to indict Noriega, he wanted to make sure there weren't some compromising secrets that would end up embarrassing everyone.

Internal Security sent Gregorie to a bus bench two blocks from the Justice Department. A few minutes later, an unmarked bus stopped, and the driver called Gregorie by name. In a half hour Gregorie was at CIA headquarters in Langley, Virginia.

At Langley he sat in a bare room, and soon a folder marked "Top Secret" was delivered to him—the CIA's secrets on Noriega. He was told he could take notes, but the notes could not leave the room. In the folder were a couple of old newspaper articles.

Gregorie was convinced that if politics wound its way into the indictment process, somebody would try to kill the legal action. He had gone with Steve Grilli and Ken Kennedy to DEA headquarters in the fall when they were preparing special charts for the grand jury. The experience was unnerving. It wasn't hard to tell that there were some people in the government who thought indicting Noriega or any other national leader was bad form.

But only the attorney general and the president could block a U.S. attorney's indictment from going forward. Such action occurred only when the case itself was flawed or if the indictment could damage national security.

At about eleven o'clock in the morning on Monday, February 1, 1988, Kellner and Gregorie arrived at Main Justice. They walked past the NBC camera and went to see William Weld, the assistant attorney general in charge of the Criminal Division.

In a conference crowded with representatives of the Justice Department's organized crime and narcotics sections, and agents from the FBI and the DEA on hand, Weld went through Kellner's indictment point by point. He read each count aloud and asked for a presentation of the evidence. Then he turned to those gathered and asked for questions.

On the opposite side of the table from Kellner sat Robert Merkle, the U.S. attorney from Tampa. Merkle's office had launched its own probe of Noriega but had concentrated on marijuana smuggling. Nevertheless, when Merkle heard about Kellner's investigation, he found witnesses, too.

Merkle had come to Washington with his own prosecution memo and draft indictment. The Tampa case was closely tied to the testimony of convicted marijuana smuggler Steven Kalish. The allegations were that Noriega had protected the delivery of two hundred thousand pounds of marijuana to the United States in June 1983 and then had approved a scheme to launder the proceeds. It was a much more modest set of charges than the nearly six-year span of events alleged in the Miami draft.

Some thought the two sets of charges should have been rolled into one, but neither Kellner nor Merkle would hear of such a thing. Kellner had his reputation to restore, and Merkle, who had personally taken Medellín cartel kingpin Carlos Lehder to trial in November 1987, was preparing to run for U.S. senator in the June Republican primary. Neither would give an inch.

As the meeting wore on, it was clear that the draft indictment favored most was Kellner's. To begin with, there were more overt acts. If the two indictments weren't going to be merged, then the best chance of a conviction—assuming it went that far—was to use the shotgun approach. The more acts a jury was given to convict on, the more likely Noriega would end up doing time.

The questioning was direct but not that tough.

When the meeting adjourned, Weld took Kellner and Gregorie around to see Trott. Trott looked over the indictment. There were no surprises. The only concern, he said, was what evidence Noriega himself might have.

After that, Weld took Kellner to see Attorney General Edwin Meese, who already knew about the indictment. Every report about Noriega that came to Main Justice from Miami made it sooner than later into Meese's office.

With Meese was Arnold Burns, the head of the Justice Department's Civil Division. Meese shook Kellner's hand and asked how he was. "Do you think you have a case?" Meese asked. Kellner said, "Yes. I've got the case." Meese looked at the indictment. "All right," he said.

The entire meeting lasted not much more than five minutes.

Weld said he was taking the indictment from the Justice Department to the White House. There it would get an airing before the policymakers.

"Can I come?" Kellner asked.

"Sure, why not? You did this, you might as well come," Weld responded.

When Weld and Kellner arrived at the White House Situation Room, it was nearly four o'clock. Kellner was surprised at the informality, an almost jovial atmosphere. There were admirals and generals and gray suits from the State Department and the CIA. There were two rings of chairs around the wood-paneled room—one around the long conference table, the other around the walls.

Kellner started to sit at the far end of the room on the outside ring.

"No, no, no," said John Negroponte, the assistant national security adviser. "You come up to the table. You're the one who caused this."

Deputy Secretary of State John Whitehead sat at the table, Assistant Secretary of State for Inter-American Affairs Elliott Abrams sat to one side of Kellner, and Negroponte and his deputy, Nicholas Rostow, sat at the other end of the room.

Even though Kellner sensed that the group was prepared to let the indictment go forward, he grew tense as the discussion began. It was clear, given the events in Panama over the past year and the ongoing congressional investigations, that Noriega had to go. The question was, Was an indictment the way to get the job done? Could it get the job done?

Rostow, the NSC's legal adviser, turned to Kellner. "What business was it of a U.S. attorney to be making foreign policy?"

"The man's a crook," Kellner responded. "We indict crooks."

There were scattered questions around the room. "Tell us about the indictment," one person said. "Give us a copy of the indictment," another said.

Kellner explained the grand jury process. He said an indictment, until announced, was secret.

A military officer at the near end of the table cocked his head toward Kellner. "What are we supposed to do when we meet him from now on?" he asked. The question could as easily have been a statement: You won't get him.

Kellner paused. "Make sure to read him his Miranda rights," he said.

There was not a sound in the room.

"I was surprised there were not more reservations," said Kellner, remembering the meeting. "Maybe there were, but no one talked to me about them."

In a day's time the only truly grim look Kellner received was in his meeting early in the morning with Jack Lawn, the administrator of the DEA. Lawn sat with Kellner, Gregorie, Grilli, Kennedy, and DEA Operations Chief David Westrate. He had never said, Don't do this, but he didn't look pleased.

When the Miami prosecutors and agents walked out of Lawn's office, Westrate followed.

"David," Lawn said as the Miami contingent departed, "come in here. We need to talk."

At the end of the day, Weld huddled with Kellner. There was one objection, he said. The indictment named the Panamanian Defense Forces as part of the criminal enterprise. Kellner and Gregorie were not only naming the leader of Panama but its entire military as well. Was that necessary? Weld asked. And couldn't the indictment run into technical legal problems for "overreaching."

The indictment as written would not work to isolate Noriega at all. Instead it would act to unify him with his troops. The prospect of dislodging the entire Panamanian military was remote. If there was to be any prospect for reform in Panama, there had to be someone left in charge.

That evening Kellner sat with Gregorie and Paul Coffee, the Justice Department's expert on racketeering indictments, and rewrote the indictment. The indictment was rephrased to say the conspirators "included Panamanian military and civilian associates of Manuel Antonio Noriega and international drug traffickers."

Kellner and Gregorie were surprised that the whole process had gone remarkably smoothly. There had been tougher fights over lesser indictments, and no effort was made to dissuade Kellner from going forward.

The next morning there was a second meeting at the White House Situation Room. This time Kellner was asked to wait outside.

Inside, the security group discussed Presidential Directive 27, a procedure for approving indictments where the interests of one or more federal agencies is involved. Could the indictment of Noriega endanger American intelligence agents or soldiers abroad? Could it bring harm to the national security?

Weld and Elliott Abrams said they saw no reason the indictment should not go forward. There were no other comments.

"Well, we'll go ahead," Negroponte said.

★   ★   ★

"I think it is fair to say as an agent and an investigator [that] we look at information in the context of prosecution and corroboration. Others would have
to answer the question about foreign policy and the level and degree to which
information received is believed and causes people to make political decisions
and/or foreign policy decisions."

David Westrate was the assistant administrator in charge of operations for
the Drug Enforcement Administration. He was testifying before the Senate
Foreign Relations Committee's Subcommittee on Narcotics. It was Tuesday,
July 12, 1988.

"As an investigator, we have to have somebody who will raise [his] hand and
testify in a court of law in order to bring a case. And that has to be corroborated.
And in most cases, more than one witness has to do that about the same event
or there has to be corroboration through other kinds of documentation. That is
often very difficult to get, and typically what we see in these allegations is
third-party or hearsay information which we cannot pursue very well."

"It is said that you can get a grand jury to indict a ham sandwich, and the
reason you do not [ask] is because you do not want to be embarrassed if you
cannot get it convicted," said Richard Holwill, deputy assistant secretary of
state for inter-American affairs since October 1983, before the Kerry
Committee on Monday, July 11, 1988.

"I would argue that the evidence should be quite strong if you are going to
proceed in a manner to indict a foreign head of government or someone else
who is in that circumstance. Knowing that you cannot possibly bring him to
trial, you should not risk the other benefits of the relationship, which
includes rather extraordinary cooperation, in pursuit of only a specious
indictment. Some prosecutors think that, as a consequence of international
relations, they will never actually have to bring their cases to trial."

Holwill conceded that there had been a "tension" between the priorities of
the drug war and the priorities of foreign policy for two years prior to the
delivery of the indictment. "I do not think that we would ever put the drug
war totally on the shelf, but we cannot at the same time abandon decency
and democracy."

Stephen Trott was the top attorney in the Reagan Justice Department's
Criminal Division. He was among the first outside of Miami to know that an
indictment of Noriega was in the works.

"The whole thing fell into one of our major objectives at DOJ—to extend
the rule of law and the ability of the United States to enforce federal criminal
laws around the world. If you don't have a program that reaches worldwide in
every respect, then you are behind the eight ball on drug trafficking, money
laundering, gunrunning, terrorism. Somebody like Noriega fit the profile. We
didn't care who it was. We had a case. We were going to go out and make it."

Trott and Jack Lawn of the Drug Enforcement Administration learned of the investigation at about the same time. Trott immediately told Attorney General Edwin Meese: "I met with the attorney general every morning at eight o'clock. It wasn't a great shock or surprise to him. We were all over the world after everybody." By October 1987, the National Security Council and other intelligence groups were told what was going on.

"We went over to the White House and sat in the secret rooms and brought in the State Department, the CIA, military intelligence, and the National Security Agency. Colin Powell, the national security adviser, was there a couple of times," said Trott. "I said that we now had reason to believe that Noriega was a drug trafficker. At the Justice Department we don't deal with rumors, we need evidence. When I went to the White House, I told them the pieces of a case against Noriega were now lying around, and we were working in a grand jury context to put them together. I told them we had probable cause to believe this guy was an active drug trafficker. It was not just speculation. It was not inference. It was not triple hearsay. We had witnesses, direct and circumstantial evidence."

Long before Kellner was invited into the White House Situation Room, Kellner and Lawn had brought a series of progress reports to the intelligence agencies. Kellner remembers: "I said, 'Where is this going? I can't tell you. But it is moving toward an indictment. So everybody ought to know that right now for many obvious reasons.' I said, 'I don't care if he's Noriega or the king of England or whoever, if he's breaking the law, we're moving. Everybody is equal under the law.' I looked around and said, 'You're in the military. You're in the State Department. You're in the White House. You're the CIA. If there are national security concerns that we are unaware of, that indicate we ought to do something other than what we are doing, then somebody tell me. We stopped at every juncture and examined the ramifications of everything that we were doing. We wanted every iron in this fire.' I said, 'If you have righteous concerns that ought to be considered, say so. Unless there is a higher interest here to which I am not privy, this is where we are going.'"

There were discussions of worst-case scenarios, possibilities. "We talked about whether we could get him. What we would do to get him. There wasn't any sense in indicting somebody we would never get, especially the head of a foreign government. This was discussed in a thousand different what-if's and extrapolations. We had to make sure that when we pulled the trigger, we had a good bullet.

"One of the concerns was discovery," Kellner continued. "We knew that if there was anything around that could be embarrassing to the government, Noriega would go after it. He'd go after the CIA, the Defense Department, the DEA. He'd go after everything and start demanding documents. We said we had reason to believe that a lot of this stuff was classified and that intelligence agencies may develop heartburn at the probability of having to turn it over and make it public. We told the agencies to get back there and find out everything there was to find out, assess it in the worst possible light, and if it ended up going public and they wanted to put that on the scale of whether we went forward or not, to let us know.

"We clued everybody in, but they pretty much knew it already. These were pretty savvy people we were dealing with. They pretty much knew."

Stephen Trott of the Justice Department told the intelligence agencies to assume that "everything is coming out. There are no secrets. You can't keep secrets. If you can't justify what you did, you'd better let us know. . . . Today's dictator is tomorrow's fugitive. Noriega might be a big guy now, but we might catch him running for his life to Monte Carlo later."

Did President Reagan know about the indictment? According to Trott: "I left that up to the National Security Council. I assume that it was cleared at the appropriate levels. Whether they thought it had to be cleared by the president, I don't know. [Attorney General Edwin] Meese sure knew about it. We kept Meese advised the whole way. He was very encouraging. He was fully on top of the program. . . . This case was played straight, aces to deuces straight, at Justice and at the other agencies. Nobody ever came in and tried to side-swipe this. Finally, we made a judgment call. We said, Now we have a case we can go with. We have reasonable cause. We are pretty certain that we can win. The decision all around the table was go. So we went.

"If you take a shot at the king, you don't miss. You don't wound him. You take him out."

While Kellner and Gregorie put their finishing touches on the indictment, the State Department and the CIA secretly completed studies of what could be expected from Noriega, ranging from a break in diplomatic relations to an accelerated effort to take control of the Panama Canal. There could be military action against the canal or the United States Embassy in Panama City. Noriega could turn to Cuba or the Sandinistas in Nicaragua, or he could fall victim to a coup by military dissidents.

The State Department had determined that immediately following the announcement of the indictments, department officials in Panama City would publicly state that the indictments were directed only at Noriega, not the Panamanian government, the Panamanian Defense Forces, or the Panamanian people.

U.S. Ambassador to Panama Arthur Davis and Lt. Gen. Frederick Woerner, Jr., commander of the U.S. Southern Command in the Canal Zone, were ordered to stay clear of Noriega. Then the message would be clear: "No more business as usual."

On Thursday, February 4, 1988, at 3:45 in the afternoon, the Noriega grand jurors left their meeting room in the new wing of the Miami federal courthouse and walked across the enclosed courtyard to the old section of the courthouse. One court security officer led them and another followed.

They filed into Federal Magistrate Peter Palermo's courtroom and there handed over their thirty-page indictment.

There were twelve counts of racketeering.

The indictment alleged that Noriega, as the de facto head of Panama, had used his official position to foster drug trafficking.

Twenty-one pages of the document outlined a sixteen-member racketeering conspiracy led by Noriega. The conspiracy had protected and engaged in cocaine processing and smuggling and money laundering.

The indictment alleged that the enterprise had engaged in criminal activities from the fall of 1981 until March 21, 1986.

Specifically, the indictment alleged that Noriega protected cocaine shipments from Panama to the United States; that he sold ether and acetone seized in the drug war back to the cartel; that he allowed the cartel to set up a cocaine processing lab in Panama; that he protected drug money shipments from south Florida to Panama; that he gave safe haven to the leaders of the Medellín cartel after the assassination of the Colombian justice minister in 1984; that he negotiated a dispute with the cartel that was mediated by Cuban president Fidel Castro, and that he accepted $4.6 million in bribes from the Medellín cartel.

Noriega was named in eleven of the twelve counts. If convicted on every count, he could be sentenced to as many as 165 years in prison.

Also named in the indictment were Pablo Escobar, the leader of the Medellín cartel and considered the richest and most powerful cocaine smuggler in the world; Gustavo Gaviria, Escobar's cousin and also a leader of the cartel; Lt. Col. Luis del Cid of the Panamanian Defense Forces and Noriega's personal aide; Amet Paredes, the son of the former military commander of the National Guard of Panama; Ricardo Bilonick, a former Panamanian diplomat and part owner of Inair, a Panamanian cargo airline; Brian Davidow, a Miami college student and real estate broker; pilots Eduardo Pardo, Daniel Miranda, David Rodrigo Ortiz, and Roberto Steiner; and William Saldarriaga, Francisco Chavez Gil, Herman Velez, Jaime Gómez, and Luis Fernando Escobar Ochoa, alleged traffickers.

Only one of the sixteen, David Ortiz, was in the custody of law enforcement. Ortiz, once a pilot for Escobar, had been arrested with a cocaine shipment on the island of Guadeloupe in the Caribbean in 1987. He now sat in a French prison.

The following morning, Friday, February 5, at eleven o'clock, Kellner in Miami and U.S. Attorney Robert Merkle in Tampa held simultaneous news conferences. The Tampa grand jury had come back with its indictment of Noriega on marijuana smuggling charges at the same time the Miami indictment was delivered. To make sure neither Kellner nor Merkle stole the other's thunder, both had agreed to make their indictments public at the same time.

But the indictments were little-kept secrets. Most major newspapers around the United States had run stories about the expected announcements that morning. More than one hundred newspaper and television reporters had crowded into a conference room in Miami to hear what Kellner had to say.

"In plain language, what [Noriega] did was use his position to sell the country of Panama to the traffickers," Kellner said. The cartel was to blame for "the avalanche of narcotics that enters this country. They are destroying our children with narcotics, and that has to stop." Kellner said his prosecutors and the agents working the case had encountered "no hindrance" in the course of their investigation. Without elaborating, he said, "I recognized the implications of indicting a person who controls a country, and General Noriega controls Panama." Seated next to the lectern were Richard Gregorie and Mark Schnapp. Between them were two empty chairs, one for DEA agent Steve Grilli and the other for DEA supervisor Ken Kennedy, both of whom had been ordered not to attend. "Headquarters told us that [it] would put the lives of our agents in Panama in jeopardy," Kennedy said.

In Washington, at the Justice Department and at DEA headquarters, there were no announcements. There was no comment from the White House or from the State Department.

The indictments, in their detailed chronicling of Noriega's alleged wrongdoing and in their timing, raised several questions. If all of the allegations were true, if the alleged events had occurred between 1981 and 1986 at a time when the Reagan administration was paying close attention to Central America, why had the president or his administration not pushed for action against Noriega sooner?

Why, if Noriega was an outlaw, had the DEA and the CIA and even top officials in the National Security Council continued to deal with him?

Had the Reagan administration covered up or conveniently overlooked Noriega's wrongdoing?

Since the administration already had tried unsuccessfully to use aid and economic embargoes against Noriega—expressly, according to U.S. Secretary of State George Shultz, to try to push Noriega from power—were the indictments simply another tool in the Reagan administration's campaign against Noriega?

Had Noriega's failure to fully support the Contras left him irrevocably on the outs with those who had once supported him?

Because there was no extradition treaty between the United States and Panama, there was little hope, even if Noriega did fall from power in Panama, that he would be turned over to U.S. prosecutors. It was revealing that the indictments had not been sealed. Prosecutors often offer sealed indictments as leverage against public figures, who then turn themselves in or begin negotiations to reach a settlement.

In Panama, Noriega's reaction was quick, though only verbal. The indictments, he said, were "strictly a political act" and "totally false, no more than another step in the plan to menace and terrorize nationalist leaders and Latin

American patriots who dare to confront the United States." A statement from the Panamanian foreign ministry said: "The government of Panama energetically and indignantly rejects . . . the obsessive campaign of lies and calumnies against" Noriega and "the attempts by the North American administration . . . to isolate Panama and destabilize its government."

Noriega charged that the indictments were the result of his refusal, beginning in 1986, to back U.S. policy in Central America. To his supporters he explained that U.S. National Security Adviser John Poindexter had asked him to help in the fight against the Sandinistas by allowing Contras to be trained in Panama. Poindexter had hinted that with Noriega's help an invasion could be launched from Panama against Nicaragua. When Noriega refused to assure the NSC chief that he would help, Poindexter, Noriega said, told him to "expect the consequences."

On Saturday, February 6, two Miami criminal defense lawyers, Raymond Takiff and Frank Rubino, flew to Panama City. A third, Neal Sonnett, remained behind and prepared to go to Washington to represent Noriega before a Senate subcommittee. In Panama, Rubino and Takiff sat down with Noriega and reviewed the indictment. Noriega insisted that he was not guilty.

After the meeting, Frank Rubino issued a statement: The people of Panama were "shocked and outraged that the United States government would resort to the use of wholly untrue criminal indictments to achieve their political goals." Rubino said that the United States in desperation had opted to make foreign policy through indictment. "Indictment diplomacy," Rubino called it.

The indictments, fulfilling U.S. Attorney Leon Kellner's worst fears, had become political almost immediately upon being made public.

The Monday after the indictments were announced, José Blandon, the former Panamanian diplomat who had testified in Miami, went to Washington, D.C., to appear before John Kerry's Senate subcommittee. Blandon said that Noriega had taken an active role in the smuggling of arms to leftist guerrillas in Colombia and El Salvador. He had also worked for American intelligence, including the CIA. While Noriega was working with the Medellín cartel and Castro, Blandon said, he was also working with Oliver North of the White House's National Security Council.

Democratic Congressman Charles Rangel, chairman of the House of Representatives' Select Committee on Narcotics Abuse and Control, had words for Undersecretary of State Elliott Abrams: "I don't care what you people in the State Department use to reach your political objectives in dealing with foreign countries, but it bothers me that you are saying that, as relates to Noriega, the best evidence that we have was the decision reached by the U.S. attorney in the Southern District and the decision made by the twenty-three faceless people that indicted him."

When the president and the State Department failed to get foreign policy right, they let the task slip into the courts, Rangel charged.

Three months after the delivery of the indictments, presidential spokesman Marlin Fitzwater would concede that the indictments had gone forward without the president's direct approval.

"It did not go to the president," he told reporters. "We had been following the legal process but had also been careful not to be involved in any way that would taint the legal process. Certainly NSC officials and others were aware of the indictments coming down and the legal process that had been in the works for many months."

"It's just another example of the hands-off president," observed Senate Majority Leader Robert Byrd, a Democrat. "His people don't see the necessity of checking with him."

In Panama, Noriega's predecessor, Gen. Rubén Dario Paredes, whose son had been named in the Miami indictment, observed to a reporter for the *Miami Herald*: "Noriega is a prisoner of power. He has shared power with many politicians and military officers who now think they would lose everything if he goes."

"Panama is not in the hands of its leaders. It is in the hands of drug traffickers and those who obey them. There is a multinational force being created, one headed by drug traffickers, that has power over Central America," José Blandon told Senator John Kerry's foreign relations subcommittee in the week following the delivery of the indictments. The traffickers had penetrated most of Central America's military forces, including Noriega's, Blandon said. Noriega had deceived the DEA by feigning cooperation with U.S. narcotics agents while letting Colombian drug runners enjoy a nearly free rein over Panama. Blandon said Panamanian officials charged with overseeing drug enforcement cooperated with drug traffickers. Noriega had sold a cache of smuggled weapons to the Colombian M-19 guerrilla group in 1980. The band sometimes acted as an enforcer for the traffickers.

The Sunday after the indictments became public, Noriega was interviewed on the American television program "60 Minutes." He claimed that DEA Administrator Jack Lawn had sent him personal letters of praise for his drug enforcement assistance. It seemed as though either the allegations in the indictment were not true or the United States' top drug enforcement organization had been duped or, worse, had purposely ignored Noriega's drug involvement.

DEA spokesman Bob Feldkamp tried to put the best light on the situation: "All we're saying as an agency is that when we asked Noriega to do something for us in the narcotics area over the last several years, he always did it."

The indictments momentarily helped the Reagan administration look tough on international drug traffickers, but the euphoria was short-lived. That the administration had in effect let foreign policy fall into the hands of the judiciary could be a ticket to uncontrolled revelations. Now Central

American policy had moved into the domestic arena. In 1988, an election year, that was likely to only further politicize the situation.

On Wednesday, February 17, Assistant Secretary of State for Inter-American Affairs Elliott Abrams met with Panama's nominal president, Eric Arturo Delvalle. Abrams hinted to Delvalle that the indictments against Noriega might be dropped if Noriega and his top associates withdrew from power and went into exile. A country like Spain would likely take Noriega if he decided to leave, Abrams told Delvalle.

Word of the discussion appeared in the *New York Times* in late February. A State Department spokesman said that Abrams had discussed the dropping of the indictments only in response to a hypothetical question by Delvalle. "We all see the drug problem as tremendously important to the United States. . . . We have every intention of carrying through the indictments," the spokesman said.

But Abrams had first spoken to Associate Attorney General William Weld, who headed the Justice Department's Criminal Division and would later be elected governor of Massachusetts. Weld had explained that the indictments could be dropped by the president. Weld made it clear, however, that the Justice Department would strenuously oppose such a move. Dropping the indictments would not look good for the American justice system, Weld explained. It would leave the impression that the charges had been filed simply for bravado's sake. Once the press caught up with the story, the Justice Department moved to distance itself from the notion that the indictments could easily be dropped. A Justice Department spokesman, in a press briefing, explained that only the president or the attorney general could petition for the withdrawal of an indictment or decide not to prosecute the case. Such a decision, should it come, would most likely be founded on concerns over the exposure of national security materials in an open court of law.

"There is nothing in the indictments that we can see that would be sensitive information that couldn't be submitted in camera to the judge and privy to both the prosecutor and the defense attorneys," Justice Department spokesman John Russell told the *New York Times*.

Charles Redman, another Justice Department spokesman, said the indictments were "obviously based on strong evidence, and we're not going to dismiss the indictments unless the president orders it."

On Thursday, February 25, Panamanian president Eric Delvalle announced that he was "firing" Noriega as commander of the Defense Forces. The next day, at Noriega's order, the Panamanian National Assembly stripped Delvalle of the presidency. Delvalle immediately went into hiding. The indictments had not humbled Noriega.

Through back channels, U.S. State Department representatives searched for a way that would give Noriega an easy out. On Friday, March 11, Spain offered to give Noriega asylum if the United States agreed not to seek his extradition. Four days later, on March 15, as sentiment in the U.S. Congress was building against dropping the indictments, Justice Department and State Department officials went to the White House to discuss whether Noriega's extradition should not be demanded if he fled Panama.

President Reagan said to tell reporters, "All I can tell you is, we do want Noriega out of there and a return to civilian democratic government."

A few days later, six weeks after the indictments had been delivered, U.S. Undersecretary of State John Whitehead certified that the United States did not recognize Noriega's leadership of Panama. Within hours the United States froze Panamanian assets in the United States. Because the official Panamanian currency is the U.S. dollar, the action cut Noriega's government off from money that it could use to pay military and government workers in Panama.

Noriega, in turn, issued a decree claiming that the United States' efforts to force him out were little more than an attempt to interfere in Panama's domestic affairs and to find a way out of its obligations under the 1979 Panama Canal treaty.

"There exists a real situation of a non-declared war," Noriega's March 20 decree said.

On Thursday, March 31, Secretary of State George Shultz went to a meeting of the National Security Planning Group at the White House Situation Room with a bold proposal. A few days before, on March 25, members of Panama's Civic Crusade, mostly middle-class Panamanians, had taken to the streets to protest Noriega's rule. Several Americans had been detained by Noriega's troops.

Shultz argued that it was time to get tough with Noriega. The United States should enhance its military presence in Panama. Noriega should either be dislodged from power through a CIA-fostered military coup or kidnapped and brought to the United States to face justice. Limited military action against Noriega should not be ruled out, Shultz argued. This did not sit well with Defense Secretary Frank Carlucci, however. In essence, the Defense Department was being asked to bail the State Department out of a failed diplomatic situation. Floating these ideas in public—they were soon reported in the *Washington Post* and the *Los Angeles Times*—could easily have been another attempt to scare Noriega out of Panama.

White House spokesman Marlin Fitzwater told reporters: "There have been any number of offensive plans raised, but to this point, they have been rejected." Fitzwater said the administration was now "willing to take a look at all the hard options." The implication was that at any moment, if Noriega were to continue to remain recalcitrant, the United States could get tough. "It's always been a principle that we will protect American citizens as best we can," Fitzwater said. "And while we have said that we don't plan to go in militarily, it's also important to note that there are limits [to U. S. patience]."

Behind the public posturing, both sides continued to search for an out. Noriega's three Miami attorneys, Raymond Takiff, Frank Rubino, and Neal Sonnett, spent much of the spring traveling between Washington, D.C., and

Panama. Sonnett and Rubino had opened up channels of discussion between Noriega and the State Department. The easiest way out for both sides was never to walk into court.

By the end of April, after a week of intense negotiation, a deal was struck that would call on Noriega to yield power in Panama by the end of the summer. The indictments would remain in place, but Noriega would not be extradited to the United States. He could remain in Panama as long as he opened a dialogue with his opposition. An interim government would be appointed, and elections would be scheduled for May 1989. In the meantime, the United States would continue to recognize Eric Delvalle as the president of Panama.

But on Saturday, April 30, 1988, the day after the deal was struck, the Reagan administration—under severe criticism from the Panamanian opposition—began backing away from the agreement. Panamanians, not the United States, should be negotiating with Noriega, the opposition leaders said. The White House had no right to say Noriega could remain in Panama free from prosecution. That afternoon Noriega appeared before a gathering of union leaders in Panama City, wielding a machete and waving it above his head. He would not bow to the United States, he promised. But even as Noriega was denouncing the United States, negotiations between Noriega's attorneys and Michael Kozak, the State Department's point man in the effort, continued.

By the second week of May another deal was in the works. With the realization that economic and diplomatic sanctions would not move Noriega, real discussions about dropping the indictments began.

On Thursday, May 12, State Department officials began floating the idea of dismissing the indictments in return for Noriega's resignation. The deal would bring a semblance of democracy to Panama, which was the State Department's chief aim. After resigning, Noriega would ask the Panamanian legislature to limit the terms of future military chiefs to five years. Such a law would prevent Noriega himself from ever legally regaining power. As word of the proposed deal spread, Reagan administration officials defended it, saying that the ouster of Noriega was more important than the indictments. "What this amounts to is a plea bargain," said White House spokesman Marlin Fitzwater.

White House Chief of Staff Howard Baker, Jr., told reporters that dropping the charges "would be the most fruitful and productive plea bargain that we have seen in a long time. If you got a deal like that, it'd be the best plea bargain I ever heard of." To make the deal, Noriega said, the United States must pay Panama $20 million. That would help restart Panama's sanction-wracked economy, he said.

Arriving at what amounted to a plea bargain had been no small accomplishment for the Reagan administration. The final decision was taken at the end of a long discussion in the private quarters of the White House. On hand were President Ronald Reagan, Vice President George Bush, Secretary of State George Shultz, Assistant Secretary of State Elliott Abrams, National

Security Adviser Colin Powell, White House Chief of Staff Howard Baker, Defense Secretary Frank Carlucci, Attorney General Edwin Meese, CIA Director William Webster, and Deputy Assistant Secretary of State Michael Kozak. Afterward, the president made it clear what he thought of the deal. "If we can use it to get him out of power, that's the best use of it," he said. The indictments were a tool, after all.

CHAPTER 9
★★★★★★★

The Vice President Decides

George Bush and his handlers had spent much of the Reagan presidency adeptly steering the vice president clear of controversy. The Iran-Contra scandal had swirled through the Reagan presidency and around Bush but had never seemed to touch him.

Bush continuously and steadfastly maintained that he had not been aware of the Iran-Contra deal. On December 3, 1986, eight days after the arms sales to Iran and the diversion of profits to support the Contras was made public, Bush said that he had been aware of the president's decision to sell arms to Iran and approved of it. He said that it had been an attempt "to begin a dialogue with Iran."

But Bush said he had heard nothing of the diversion of funds to the Contras, even though administration records show that he was present at several meetings in 1984, 1985, and 1986 at which secret aid to the Contras was discussed. "We were not in the loop," Bush told a reporter for the *Washington Post* in August 1987.

As the presidential primary season heated up in the late spring of 1988, Bush's opponents worked to draw him into the Noriega crisis. The clatter had begun with Democratic Senator John Kerry's hearings on Panama. The subtext of the hearings, which had begun in February, shortly after the indictments were delivered, and would stretch into July, was that the Reagan administration had grossly misunderstood Noriega and failed to take action against his drug trafficking.

Bush had been the director of the CIA in the mid-1970s, and he had headed President Reagan's south Florida drug task force and drug war effort since 1982. He had met with Noriega, but as with Iran-Contra, the vice president said that he had not been aware Noriega was involved in drug trafficking.

Bush's position changed, however, during the first weekend of May 1988 when the *New York Times* reported that Bush had been briefed about Noriega's drug-trafficking involvement more than two years before, in December 1985, by the U.S. ambassador to Panama, Everett Briggs, who now confirmed that the conversation had occurred. The disclosure left Bush campaign aides with little choice but to concede that the discussion probably did take place.

On Monday, May 9, Bush clarified his previous denials of having known about Noriega's trafficking activities. It was not that he hadn't heard about Noriega's involvement with the drug trade before the February indictments, he said, but rather that it was not until the delivery of the indictments that be had become aware of actual "evidence" linking Noriega to drug trafficking.

In Miami the press reports of a pending deal between the administration and Noriega infuriated U.S. Attorney Leon Kellner. He was seeing the work of his office and his reputation sullied by politics once again. He decided he would not sit idly by while his indictment was turned into kindling. He called Attorney General Edwin Meese.

"Why am I not being informed?" Kellner asked Meese. Meese apologized. He said he knew what was going on but had not called.

"This makes it like a political indictment," Kellner told Meese. "It makes it look as if I was indicting this guy so that Washington could use it as a lever."

Meese was without an explanation. He could only apologize.

There had to be a way to turn the tide against scuttling the indictment. Kellner called a Bush fund-raiser in Florida named Alex Courtelis who had played a key role in delivering Florida to the Republicans in the 1980 and 1984 elections. Kellner asked him to arrange an appointment with the vice president. On Thursday, May 12, Kellner flew to Washington.

Kellner first went to the Justice Department and saw the attorney general. Meese assured Kellner that Main Justice had not wavered in its commitment to seeing Noriega prosecuted. Kellner was not convinced. He next went to see DEA Administrator Jack Lawn, who assured Kellner that quashing the indictment would only cheapen the DEA's work and damage agents' morale. Lawn would stand behind the indictment. Just before lunch Kellner arrived at the White House. The vice president was expecting him. They had met several times before on Bush's visit to south Florida as head of the president's drug task force. Bush showed Kellner into his private office in the basement of the White House and closed the door.

Dropping the indictment would be a terrible mistake, Kellner told the vice president. The indictment would be nothing but political fodder if the administration continued to negotiate with Noriega. It was a disgrace and it looked bad. The indictment was being "politicized," Kellner said. Playing loose with a dictator would end up being political suicide for Bush's presidential campaign, he told the vice president.

Finally, Kellner said, "Mr. Vice President, do you want to know the real reason why this indictment should go forward, the unvarnished truth?"

Bush nodded.

"Because if it doesn't, the voters are going to think that you're a goddamned crook and that the administration and you are being blackmailed."

Recent newspaper articles had suggested that the administration was trying to cut a deal with Noriega because Noriega could prove that Bush had known about Noriega's drug involvement all along. It all came out on Bush's face. He grew red.

"That's bullshit. That's a lie," Bush told Kellner, his voice rising. Bush stood up and turned away. He turned back. "You do what you have to do," the vice president said.

Kellner reflected later: "It never bothered me that the vice president said he hadn't known about Noriega's drug trafficking. What does it mean to know? Almost from the day I became an assistant U.S. attorney I knew Noriega was involved in drugs. Did I *know* it? No. Did I *believe* it? Yes. I was convinced from Bush's reaction that he did not know."

Later, Kellner received a telephone call from Democratic Congressman Charles Rangel, whose House Committee on Narcotics was looking into the allegations of Noriega's drug trafficking.

"Are you going to dismiss this indictment?" he asked.

Kellner said, "No."

"Is the attorney general?" Rangel asked.

Kellner said, "I don't know."

"I'm not totally naive," Kellner said later. "The Reagan administration would have bought the deal in thirty seconds. Had Noriega agreed to give up everything and go to France and sit on the beach for the rest of his life, the deal would have been cut."

On Friday, May 13, before he got on a plane to return to Miami, Kellner spoke with reporters at the Justice Department. He confirmed only that he had spoken to Attorney General Meese, who had assured him, Kellner said, that he would tell the president that dropping the indictment "would send the wrong message to the people of this country."

Whatever effect Kellner's visit to Washington had on the attorney general and the vice president, it did not carry over to the president. Five days after Kellner's visit, President Reagan at a White House press briefing was unwilling to say what he would do about Noriega or the indictments. "I will not comment on the negotiations that are going on in Panama, and at the appropriate time I expect to have a full statement and make it to the American people," the president said.

The same day, Tuesday, May 17, on Capitol Hill, the Senate voted 86 to 10 to approve a "sense of congress" resolution expressing opposition to any deal to drop the indictments or negotiations that could lead to such a deal.

The next day, at the Coast Guard Academy commencement in Connecticut, the president called the problem of illegal drugs "a national emergency." He said there would be a new resolve in the drug war and called for a "special executive-legislative task force to advance America's unified response to the problem of illegal drug use."

So much for Vice President Bush's six-year-old south Florida drug task force.

But the same day, across the country at the Los Angeles Police Academy, Vice President Bush took a stand during a campaign speech. He followed Kellner's advice. Lagging far behind Michael Dukakis in the polls, Bush moved to distance himself from the Reagan administration. He did not mention Noriega by name but said, "Drug dealers are domestic terrorists, killing kids and cops, and they should be treated as such. I won't bargain with drug dealers either, whether they're on U.S. or foreign soil."

But no matter what the vice president said, four days later, on Sunday, May 22, the rest of the Reagan administration went another way. In television appearances, both National Security Adviser Colin Powell and Secretary of State George Shultz confirmed that Noriega had been offered a deal under which the indictments would be dropped in return for his stepping down. The deal was the best chance to restore democracy in Panama, they argued.

"So you ask yourself, which situation are we better off in? To have Noriega more or less in charge in Panama and us with an indictment that we can't do much about . . . or having Noriega give up power in Panama and leaving Panama, but also having paid the penalty?" Shultz asked. "It is a difficult judgment," he said. But obviously the decision had been made.

Two days after the administration had decided justice could still be served if Noriega never walked into an American court, evidence that would have supplemented the indictment in Miami seemed to have disappeared.

A confidential informant had gone to DEA agents Steve Grilli and Ken Kennedy in Miami and told them of bank records that would link Noriega to the cartel. The records were in Panama, but they could be secretly shipped to Miami. Grilli and Kennedy made the arrangements. A contact in Panama City brought the bank computer printouts and the log books of two Panamanian pilots to the United States Embassy. They were left to be sealed and shipped aboard a diplomatic flight to the United States. But when the evidence arrived in Miami, the computer printouts were missing. Prosecutor Richard Gregorie was reminded of his visit to CIA headquarters in Virginia. His first thought was to impanel a grand jury to find out what had happened to the evidence. He would start by subpoenaing DEA and CIA agents in Panama stationed at the embassy. But going that route would have meant disclosing the evidence so far accumulated against Noriega.

Three days after Secretary of State Shultz and National Security Adviser Colin Powell appeared on television announcing a negotiated deal with Noriega, the deal was off.

On May 25, Shultz had delayed his flight to Finland where the president was to meet with Mikhail Gorbachev. Shultz was intent upon resolving the ongoing Panama crisis and had urged Noriega to do the deal. The secretary of state had imposed a deadline. Three months had dragged by since the indictments were made public; Congress was mad, and the administration had grown weary. Do the deal by the twenty-fifth, Shultz had told Noriega, or there will be no deal.

The deadline had passed and Noriega had not responded. Shultz left for Finland.

La Republica, a Panamanian government–backed newspaper, said the next day that the talks had collapsed when the United States failed to assure that Manuel Solis Palma, Noriega's hand-picked president, would be allowed to stay in office.

That day Noriega mocked the United States, saying American officials liked to "invent big dangers in small countries. When they do not find monsters, they have to invent them." Again, Noriega claimed that his problems with the United States had started when he refused American requests "at the height of the Iran-Contra to participate in aggression against Nicaragua."

Noriega had left George Bush the high ground. Bush had warned about dealing with dictators and drug traffickers. The day after Noriega's comments, Bush spoke to reporters. "We want to bring [Noriega] to justice. We want to get him out, and we want to restore democracy to Panama."

Once the Reagan administration dropped its efforts to negotiate with Noriega, Panama and Noriega quickly fell out of the news in the United States. From the end of May until the U.S. election in November, the foreign policy issue that had captured the attention of the administration for more than a year disappeared from all political radar.

Efforts to revive the issue failed. In August, three months before the election, two Democratic congressmen asked the General Accounting Office, an arm of Congress, to look into what effect, if any, drug trafficking by foreign officials might have on U.S. foreign policy. The request blatantly aimed to focus attention on Noriega and Panama and what, if anything, George Bush knew about Noriega's drug involvement.

But the Reagan administration—and the Bush campaign—ignored the request. The State and Defense departments and the CIA quickly rejected GAO records requests. A lawyer for the National Security Council, in turning back the GAO's request, said the investigation "raises important statutory and constitutional issues" involving access to sensitive law-enforcement and intelligence data."

Later, as the presidential campaign was coming to a close, the Reagan administration blamed the failure of Panama policy on the Democrats, even though the Democrats had had no substantive control over foreign policy in eight years.

A month before the election, Elliott Abrams told the *New York Times,* "The Carter Administration did absolutely nothing to help the development of democratic government in Panama. The Carter Administration did the easy thing about Panama, which was to hand over a piece of paper that said, 'This is the Panama Canal Treaty, and it gives Panama title to the canal.' We were left with this guy Noriega, to whom we're supposed to give the Panama Canal.

It's an impossible situation." The next president, Abrams noted, under the conditions of the 1977 treaty, would have to name a Panamanian as the canal's administrator. That appointment would be due on January 1, 1990. Noriega would then be handed control of the Panama Canal. "Obviously," said Abrams, "the president and the Senate are going to be in trouble with that nomination if Noriega is in charge and appoints a Noriega crony."

On January 20, 1989, Manuel Noriega celebrated the end of the Reagan administration with a Panama City street festival. Waving in the breeze above Noriega's party were signs proclaiming "Reagan is leaving and Noriega is staying."

Panama and Noriega had of course been all but out of the news since the previous spring. When it came to Noriega, picking up where the Reagan administration had left off was not a high priority for the new administration of George Bush. By late February the U.S. commander of American forces in Latin America, Gen. Frederick Woerner, Jr., complained that the Bush administration's Panama policy seemed beset by a "vacuum." But the new president had secretly approved a covert plan aimed at making sure that Noriega or his candidate did not win the Panamanian presidency in the general election scheduled for May.

A bold plan designed to remove Noriega from power through a CIA-supported coup had been developed in the waning months of the Reagan administration but had been turned back by the Senate Intelligence Committee. There was a fear that Noriega might accidentally be assassinated in a coup attempt. That would be a violation of U.S. law. The new Bush administration–sanctioned plan called for a more democratic approach to Panama's problems. It proposed to pump about $3 million into the election campaigns of the anti-Noriega candidates, though the money was hardly needed. The Sunday, May 7, election in Panama turned into a runaway for the Noriega opposition. The opposition presidential ticket, led by Guillermo Endara, won the popular vote by a three-to-one margin, according to the account of Catholic Church observers.

But despite the presence of international observers—including former U.S. presidents Jimmy Carter and Gerald Ford—an incensed Noriega wasted little time voiding the election. He ordered Endara and his two vice presidential running mates severely beaten. Noriega brought the new Bush presidency its first foreign policy crisis.

"The will of the people should not be thwarted by this man and a handful of these . . . thugs," Bush said. "I would love to see them get him out."

Since April 1988 sporadic and sometimes violent confrontations had taken place between Canal Zone Americans and the Panamanian military. Tensions increased following the May election. Bush ordered American dependents in Panama onto U.S. bases and dispatched a brigade of combat-ready troops—nearly two thousand soldiers—to join the eleven thousand servicemen already stationed in Panama. Administration officials termed the deployment purely defensive.

"I am worried about the lives of American citizens, and I will do what is necessary to protect them," the president said on Thursday, May 11. "We will not be intimidated by the bullying tactics, brutal though they may be, of the dictator Noriega." Asked at a White House press briefing if the United States would back a coup against Noriega, Bush said, "I've asserted what my interest is at this point. It is democracy in Panama; it is protection of the life of Americans." Three days later, however, the president was more forceful, barely stopping short of calling for a coup. He said the Panamanian people and the Panamanian Defense Forces—who followed Noriega's command— "ought to do everything they can to get Mr. Noriega out of there."

The president had adopted a not-so-subtle message of divide and conquer. That message was reinforced by the U.S. ambassador to Panama, Arthur Davis, who a few days later said, "I do not want my words of condemnation of Noriega . . . to denote condemnation of the entire Panama Defense Forces.... I know there are honorable professional officers and soldiers in the PDF who deplore the cowardly use of violence against his own unarmed population."

The U.S. Senate added its own note of displeasure on June 1 when it passed a resolution saying that it would refuse to confirm the appointment of a Noriega-named Panamanian as administrator of the Panama Canal, an appointment that was to become effective the following January. Further, the Senate called on the president to certify that Panama's government be "democratically elected" before a Panamanian administrator was confirmed.

Still, the effect on Noriega's rule was negligible. In Central and South America sentiment was building against Noriega. On July 20, the thirty-one-member Organization of American States, trying to find a multinational diplomatic solution to the Panamanian crisis, called on Noriega to establish a transitional government by September 1. That government would be followed by a new presidential election. The September deadline corresponded to the date specified by the Panamanian constitution for the installation of a new president if the May 7 election had not been invalidated.

"There must be a transfer of power through democratic means by September 1," U.S. Deputy Secretary of State Lawrence Eagleburger said following the OAS resolution. "For that to happen, General Noriega must go."

But when the deadline came, Noriega still had not responded. Eagleburger again took the point for the administration, reciting the litany of charges in the Miami indictment. He added that the United States had determined that Noriega's fortune was worth between $200 million and $300 million and that three days after Noriega had been indicted in 1988, he had ordered the transfer of nearly $15 million from a bank in London to a bank in Luxembourg.

In early September, one of Noriega's Miami attorneys, Frank Rubino, called Michael Kozak, undersecretary of state in charge of Central American affairs. Kozak had led the Reagan administration's failed negotiations with Noriega in May 1988.

"Nobody was getting anywhere," and Panama was being hurt by the economic sanctions, Rubino would later say of his reason for calling Kozak. "I was authorized to open a line of communication to see what we could do about this problem." That included dismissing the indictments, Rubino said.

But on October 3, 1989, before a dialogue could develop, several little-known Panamanian Defense Force officers secretly informed American officials that they were about to move against Noriega. When they did, the results were disappointing and bloody. Though Noriega was held at gunpoint for several hours, the coup was soon put down, and ten officers who had led the venture were killed.

A call for assistance to Americans in the Canal Zone had gone unheeded. U.S. military on the ground in Panama had waited for direction from the White House, but the administration in Washington failed to act either quickly or decisively.

For days afterward there was wild finger pointing in Washington. At first the administration said a change in top American military personnel in Panama in the days shortly before the coup had created a short-term gap in responsiveness. Later, White House officials blamed the failure of the coup on the plotters themselves, saying they had failed to communicate what sort of help they wanted and when. And the plotters also had failed to promise that Noriega would be handed over for extradition to the United States.

The bottom line escaped no one, however. For all of its tough talk, the administration and the president simply had failed to make a commitment to plan for the removal of Noriega.

The failed coup did give a boost to the settlement negotiations that Noriega's attorney Frank Rubino had called for in early September. On October 12, Rubino flew to Washington to meet with Michael Kozak. Present at the 2 P.M. meeting were State Department legal adviser Michael Matheson and Robert Mueller III, the number two man in the new Bush Justice Department, now headed by Attorney General Richard Thornburgh. Before Rubino could utter a word, he was told that Secretary of State James Baker and Attorney General Thornburgh were in their respective offices awaiting a report on the meeting. The attorney general and secretary of state, Kozak and Mueller told Rubino, would take news of the meeting directly to the president. Rubino swallowed hard.

The essence of Rubino's message that afternoon was, "How can we make each other happy?"

Mueller and Matheson made it clear that the Bush administration would not go as far as the Reagan administration's offer to dismiss the Miami indictment. If Noriega left Panama, however, perhaps things could be worked out. A condition of any agreement, Kozak explained, was that Noriega resign as commander of the Panamanian Defense Forces.

Rubino, who had represented Noriega for nearly two years now, since the indictments had been delivered in February 1988, told the U.S. representatives, "The general is not going to leave Panama and risk extradition."

Mueller and Matheson said the Bush administration would settle for Noriega's stepping down. The deal, then, was that "they would not move to extradite him" to face trial in the United States, said Rubino. Mueller clearly and unequivically said the U.S. would not dismiss the indictments. But Kozak tempered Mueller's position by saying, "The president of the United States is morally opposed to dismissing the indictments." Rubino took Kozak's comment as an opening to negotiation, all dependent upon Noriega stepping aside. The important thing was that Noriega leave. Rubino said it was doubtful that his client would go to Spain or any other country where he might risk extradition. A simple resignation would suffice, Kozak and Mueller said. They suggested November 3, Panamanian Independence Day. Kozak and Mueller said the United States would play no part in determining Noriega's successor in the PDF. That was an internal Panamanian matter, they said. As far as the voided May election, it could be ratified or a new election could be held, the Americans suggested.

Rubino took the news of the U.S. position to Panama. He went immediately to see Noriega at his home. "The Americans want a specific proposal from you to step aside," Rubino said. "They are hot to make a deal." Rubino informed his client that he was convinced "the indictment was negotiable" and that the U.S. government "is willing to talk."

The State Department had said that it would not dismiss the indictments in May 1988 and then reversed itself. The same thing was happening all over again, Rubino told Noriega.

The administration, in the meantime, had learned its lesson well: Talking with Noriega had a way of not resolving any problem. The failed coup had been a deep source of embarrassment and criticism. Whatever was to happen, Bush and his advisers vowed not to be caught napping the next time an opening to remove Noriega presented itself. Shortly after the October coup's failure, senior administration officials began considering lifting a 1976 executive order that prohibited the CIA from participating in the assassination of foreign leaders, and in mid-November the president approved a covert action that would allow the spending of up to $3 million to recruit Panamanian military officers and exiles to plan and carry out Noriega's overthrow. Essential to the authorization—called a presidential finding—was a new legal interpretation of the 1976 executive order.

The president had asked the Justice Department to explore the available legal loopholes, and the department had responded by saying that American law would not be violated if a foreign leader's death occurred accidentally during an American-supported coup. If the leader's death was not the goal of the coup, and the death was thus an indirect, not direct, result of the coup, then U.S. law would not be violated.

Not surprisingly, Rubino's discussions with Mueller and Matheson had no discernible effect on Noriega. Again, he failed to take the opportunity to leave Panama or to make a counterproposal. Instead he chose to stand pat. Later Rubino would observe: "One of Noriega's greatest strengths was his inaction. That's how he weathered so many crises, by doing nothing. This was an occasion when he did nothing."

On Tuesday, November 14, the Organization of American States' Human
Rights Commission issued a report calling Noriega's government "devoid of
constitutional legitimacy." Noriega's response was to order his military officers to begin to subtly challenge American military personnel and their
dependents traveling outside the Canal Zone. The point was simply to show
the Americans who was boss. Noriega believed he would be free to do as he
wished as long as he stopped short of moving against the canal itself.

On Monday, December 11, a Panamanian judge acting at Noriega's
request ordered the arrest of Gen. Maxwell Thurman, commander of U.S.
forces in Latin America, as well as the arrest of Thurman's second in command, Maj. Gen. Marc Cisneros. No charges were specified, but the warrants,
Noriega believed, would confine the Americans to their bases, much as the
U.S. indictments had confined Noriega to Panama. Here was Noriega giving
the Americans a taste of their own medicine.

PART II
★★★★★★★

The Way to Trial

CHAPTER 10

★★★★★★★

Invasion Justice

For two years the U.S. government carried on a running war of words with Noriega. Calling the Panamanian general a thug and a narcotrafficker—as President Bush had at photo opportunities—was one thing, but the president wasn't going to have to walk into court and prove the allegations of the 1988 indictment. Someone else would. If Noriega was brought to an American court, he would have to be tried on more than rhetoric. The moment Noriega walked into court, rules of procedure would kick in. How Noriega fared would depend on the skill of his attorneys and their ability and imagination in interpreting the law and fending off the prosecutors. The law and the court's rules would go a long way toward leveling the playing field.

It was easy to convict a so-called banana republic dictator in the press; it would be something else to convict him in a court of law. In other words, it would be one thing to capture and arrest Noriega, should that somehow prove possible, but it would be another thing entirely to convict him.

In early December 1989, Attorney General Thornburgh met with the president. What kind of case do we have? Bush asked. If we get Noriega, can we convict him?

Thornburgh wasted little time calling in his top lieutenants. Weld and Trott, the assistant attorney generals who had overseen the delivery of the indictments in 1988, were gone. Weld had returned to Boston and was campaigning to become governor of Massachusetts. Trott was named a federal judge in 1988, shortly after the indictment had been delivered.

If Noriega were captured and tried, the direct responsibility for seeing that the case was handled properly would likely fall to Robert Mueller. Mueller was the attorney general's most trusted aide. He would be Thornburgh's direct line to the prosecutors in Miami and Tampa.

Mueller was a career Justice Department lawyer, unlike the attorney general, who was a political appointee. Mueller knew firsthand the logistics of handling a U.S. attorney's office and directing online prosecutors. He had only recently served a stint as head of the U.S. attorney's office in Boston.

The attorney general also called in Mark Richard, the deputy assistant attorney general in charge of the department's Criminal Division, who also oversaw the Office of International Affairs and its narcotic and dangerous drug section. Richard was used to dealing firsthand with line prosecutors handling conspiracy and narcotics cases. Also on board was William Bryson, the deputy solicitor general and an appellate specialist who would be asked to make the prosecution's case airtight to appeal, given a conviction.

Thornburgh got to the point. He wanted the most thorough preparation ever given to a Justice Department prosecution. This would be the most important drug prosecution ever undertaken by the U.S. government. Not only was the prestige of the department at stake but also, more important, if the president decided to go after Noriega, he would be banking the integrity of the United States and its justice system on a conviction. Reading between the lines: The case was more than law and justice, it was also foreign policy and politics. Let there be no doubt, Thornburgh told each of the three, nothing was to happen in the Noriega case that had not received the utmost scrutiny.

As one top aide to the attorney general put it, referring to the location of the attorney general's office at Main Justice, "This was a fifth-floor case from start to finish."

Of course there was one small problem. No one at Main Justice, in Miami or in Tampa, had ever really given truly serious thought to prosecuting Noriega. He was, after all, the de facto leader of a foreign country. The United States government had never prosecuted the sitting leader of a sovereign nation. If anything, especially in 1987 and through at least May 1988, State Department officials had tried to find a way to let Noriega off the hook and not bring him to justice. Since the indictment, and off and on through October 1989, the State Department had worked hard trying to find a way to simply get Noriega out of power and out of Panama. No one had ever entertained the notion that the general would be tried in an American courtroom.

For almost two years the Miami case, which was clearly the more substantive of the two indictments, had sat virtually dormant. Since the indictment, the case had passed through the hands of three different Miami assistants. There had not been much for them to do other than baby-sit the file.

Noriega's defense attorneys had filed motions challenging the government's jurisdiction in the case in 1988, but since Miami U.S. Attorney Leon Kellner had left in June 1988 and his chief prosecutor, Richard Gregorie, had departed the following January, little attention was paid in Miami to *United States v. Noriega*. The same was true in Tampa where U.S. Attorney Robert Merkle had quit to run for the U.S. Senate in mid-1988. (He lost.)

Jorge Ochoa, Pablo Escobar, and Manuel Noriega were just names on the U.S. marshal's list of fugitives. The cartel leaders had succeeded in making second careers out of avoiding capture and extradition to the United States.

For months, until October 1989, the Noriega files had sat undisturbed in two file cabinets outside of U.S. Attorney Kellner's old office. In August, Myles Malman, the new deputy assistant to the new U.S. attorney, Dexter Lehtinen, returned to the office from two years in private practice. Malman dusted off the Noriega files and decided to assign himself the case. There were other big cases in the office, including indictments of the Medellín cartel's top leaders, but Malman thought the Noriega case was the most interesting. And after all, it wasn't impossible that sooner or later Noriega would himself unravel his hold on Panama. Then he might find himself at the mercy of American law enforcement officials. Malman called it his "old street bones." It was just a feeling that Noriega might one day leave Panama or get snatched.

That feeling got a little stronger after October 3 and the failed coup. If the United States had fully committed to the coup, Noriega could have been in Miami for Halloween. In the next couple of weeks Malman reread Gregorie's prosecution memo and the grand jury minutes, and he looked over the grand jury testimony of the Panamanian pilot Floyd Carlton and the cartel drug trafficker Boris Olarte. Malman even went to see Carlton, who was serving out his nine-year drug-smuggling conviction in the Witness Protection Program. Carlton would make a good witness, Malman thought after spending two hours with him. Olarte, who told the grand jury that he had personally talked drug dealing with Noriega, also made a good presentation, Malman thought.

The call from Mark Richard came in early December. Richard asked U.S. Attorney Lehtinen to come to Washington to talk about the Miami Noriega case, its strengths and weaknesses. The question was, if Noriega did come into U.S. custody, why should the Southern District have first crack at prosecuting him rather than Tampa?

Next, Lehtinen called in Malman for an evaluation of the case. The case was not strong, Malman told Lehtinen, but there was more to consider. If Noriega was brought back to the United States, witnesses would begin pouring out of the woodwork. Anyone who had ever been accused or had ever gone to jail for dealing drugs through Panama and knew anything about Noriega would be knocking on the government's door with information in an effort to cut a deal, Malman predicted. No one could guarantee a conviction, but if he had to bet, Malman told Lehtinen, he'd say they had 90 percent of a sure chance of conviction.

Malman and Marcella Cohen, Lehtinen's chief assistant, and James McAdams, the chief of the Miami Criminal Division, sat down and organized their Washington presentation. They divided the indictment into sections— the drug flights, protection of the Darien lab, the voyage of the *Krill*, and so forth—and each analyzed the strength of the work in hand. Point by point they compared the Miami case to the Tampa case. Malman put together a briefing sheet and charts to take to Washington.

Within a week of the attorney general's meeting with the president, the prosecutors from Miami and Tampa were at Main Justice. It was Friday, December 15, the same day Noriega stood before his National Assembly in Panama City and had himself proclaimed "Maximum Leader." Also on that day, Gustavo Gaviria, one of the leaders of the Medellín cartel, was shot dead by Colombian police.

Besides Lehtinen and his three assistants, Tampa U.S. Attorney Robert Merkle and his assistant Greg Kehoe, and about two dozen lawyers and agents from Main Justice, the DEA, Customs Service, and FBI sat in a large conference room down the hall from Mark Richard's office. Richard's question was simple: Could a prosecution of Noriega be successful? And who should go first, Miami or Tampa?

Malman stood and outlined the Miami case, which made the most sense, he said. Noriega was subject to more prison time in Miami. There were more charges, and they involved cocaine. In Tampa there were only two counts involving marijuana. There were more witnesses in Miami; the Tampa case was based almost exclusively on the word of one witness. If Tampa missed, it would be a loss. Certainly not all of the charges in Miami would miss their mark, and Noriega could still be put away.

In the Miami case, prosecutors knew they could rely heavily on the testimony of convicted drug pilot Floyd Carlton. His testimony would closely link Noriega to the Medellín cartel, though not quite. Carlton would say he had flown cocaine from Colombia to Panama under the protection of Noriega and that he personally had gone to the cartel on Noriega's behalf to arrange protection fees of more than $200,000 per flight.

The Tampa case involved the importation of marijuana. It was less sexy, and it was an older case, meaning it could be harder to dig up corroborating witnesses. And the load charged had never actually made it to the United States. Even though the case seemed relatively cut and dried by drug case standards, the Tampa prosecutors seemed unsure of their chances. A conviction was fifty-fifty, they said.

And what about Noriega's ties to U.S. intelligence or law enforcement, Richard asked, looking at the agency representatives seated around the room. If Noriega indeed had connections to the underside of the DEA or CIA, now was the time to say so. Top DEA officials had praised Noriega for his efforts, but that kind of praise was easy to come by and was more diplomatic than real, the DEA's representative told Richard.

It was true that no one, at least in Justice, had conducted a hands-on review of Noriega-related national security material at the CIA. Even though Justice Department policy called for such reviews before the delivery of sensitive indictments, Richard Gregorie, the Noriega prosecutor who visited the CIA in 1988, had walked away after seeing only old newspaper clippings. Gregorie complained about the CIA: "We don't know what's in the intelligence files, and they aren't telling us."

Even though the talk that afternoon was about gearing up for trial, the Miami prosecutors, looking back, never suspected that they would soon be hustling to bring their case to court. There was nothing overt in Richard's manner. No hints. Around the room there was no special sense of urgency. McAdams remembered later, "We'd been around long enough to know these things don't happen in a vacuum, but I can say that nobody was thinking . . . that an invasion was going to occur. It was just clear to us that the message was to be prepared."

In two hours the meeting was over. The general impression was that Miami would go first, but Richard said he would let the prosecutors know for certain in a day or two. As they were leaving, McAdams turned to Lehtinen and suggested that he take the few hours before their return flight to Miami to begin getting his top secret security clearance. Someone would have to begin checking classified documents. Be prepared.

From the first moment Mueller and Richard began looking over what their prosecutors had presented, they knew they were readying themselves to walk into a virtual mine field of legal problems. Noriega's lawyers would be sure to keep their nearly two-year-old promise to demand access to classified material. Specifically, the defense would ask for secret documents from the CIA and the DEA, documents that would show Noriega's involvement as an undercover U.S. informant beginning in the early 1970s. A way would have to be found to guide the prosecution around defense requests that could result in the case's being dropped because intelligence agencies were unwilling to reveal secrets and discuss their dealings with Noriega. Just in the past two years, Main Justice had abandoned an Iran-Contra–related case rather than give up intelligence materials.

Moreover, the Noriega case was a historical or dry conspiracy case, meaning it was devoid of physical evidence linking Noriega to drug trafficking. The case was based on the testimony of witnesses like Carlton who would say they had known Noriega to be involved in drug trafficking. No U.S. agent—such as a police officer running a street corner sting—had actually watched Noriega move drugs or heard him plot with others about doing so.

And because the conspiracy was alleged to have begun in 1981 and ended in 1986, witnesses were going to be asked to recall events that would strain the memory of even the most credible of them. Most of the government's informants were in jail and would be trading their testimony for less time or better prison conditions. The defense would certainly make much of such dealings.

On December 16, the day after Mueller and Richard had met with the Miami and Tampa prosecutors, Panamanian soldiers in Panama City shot and killed a U.S. Marine lieutenant at a PDF roadblock. An American Navy officer and his wife who had seen the attack were detained and roughed up. The Panamanians claimed the Marine and three others had taken potshots at Noriega's military headquarters, wounding three people. The American embassy denied the charge. Two days later, on Monday, December 18, a U.S. Army officer wounded a Panamanian police corporal. The American claimed the policeman was drawing his weapon.

Noriega's earlier pronouncement of a "state of war" was hyperbole, but in two days the situation was escalating. Bullets had flown, and the events were garnering a fair amount of press in the United States.

On Monday evening, Miami criminal defense lawyer Raymond Takiff, who had been hired by Noriega the week before the indictments were handed up in 1988, gave Noriega a call at home. There was a very real possibility the Americans could mount some sort of military action, Takiff warned Noriega. The United States had rolled trucks into Panama City intersections during the October failed coup. They could be more assertive the next time, Takiff told Noriega.

Takiff knew Noriega was not afraid to go toe to toe with U.S. forces stationed in the Canal Zone. Noriega expected machinations and bluster from the Americans, but he, not President Bush, ran Panama. Takiff suggested he fly down to Panama City. Together they could review Noriega's options if events grew more heated. Noriega agreed, and Takiff said he would leave Miami on Wednesday morning.

The next day, Tuesday, December 19, Attorney General Dick Thornburgh arrived at the White House after lunch. Thornburgh told the president that his department's review of the Noriega cases was complete. The Miami case was solid. Further, department lawyers had reviewed international treaties and law as well as American statutes and had concluded that the United States would not be barred from seizing suspected criminals in foreign countries even without the permission of those countries. A department memorandum had been drafted that declared the U.S. military had a legal right to arrest accused drug traffickers and other fugitives in foreign countries.

In addition, Thornburgh reported that Justice and State Department lawyers had reviewed the United Nations charter, the charter of the Organization of American States, and the Panama Canal treaties. Their conclusion: An American president was not bound by international law unless it was codified in American domestic law. Article 51 of the United Nations charter could be interpreted to allow for a nation's exercise of the right to self-defense on foreign soil. "Clearly a legal authority under both U.S. law and international law" had been established for the U.S. government to send its agents into Panama in order to bring Noriega to justice, Thornburgh told the president.

Noriega's de facto declaration of war against the United States, the killing of the Marine lieutenant, and the subsequent beating of another American military man was enough. The United States had the "right" to take the steps necessary to remove Noriega, the attorney general concluded.

At 7:20 A.M. on Wednesday, December 20, President Bush told the American people in a live television address from the Oval Office that overnight he had dispatched twenty-four thousand American troops to Panama. For nearly two years, the president said, the United States and other countries had tried to deal with Noriega, but every effort had been rejected by "the dictator of Panama . . . an indicted drug trafficker."

The goals of the invasion were simple, the president said: "to safeguard the lives of Americans, to defend democracy in Panama, to combat drug trafficking, and to protect the integrity of the Panama Canal treaty."

Later in the morning the president sent a memorandum to Secretary of Defense Richard Cheney. The president authorized American military units to apprehend Noriega and others in Panama under indictment in the United States for drug-related offenses. He directed that those apprehended be detained and arrested if necessary and turned over to U.S. law enforcement officials as quickly as possible.

From one end of Panama to the other, American troops wasted little time taking control of the country and displacing Noriega's Panamanian Defense Forces. Before daylight on the early morning of December 20, U.S. infantry and airborne soldiers had secured the Panama Canal, had surrounded Panama's major military barracks, and had all but leveled Noriega's military headquarters in Panama City. The fight was a mismatch from the outset. At best the PDF had five thousand armed soldiers.

Specially-trained Navy commandos disabled high-powered boats and Lear jets docked and hangared around Panama City. Any means that Noriega might have employed for escape were crippled. For the first time ever, two U.S. Air Force stealth fighter planes made combat appearances, dropping concussion bombs around outlying PDF barracks. U.S. helicopter gunships all but filled the sky above Panama City, even though Panama had no real air force or navy to offer resistance.

Without a doubt, Operation Just Cause, as the president and his top military men had labeled the invasion, was a rout—in all ways but one: The invasion's foremost objective, to capture the dictator Noriega and to bring him to justice, remained unmet. Though Panama was suddenly brimming with American military, Noriega eluded capture.

On Wednesday morning in Miami, television and radio gushed with news of the invasion. Miami's Hispanic community, including thousands of Panamanian exiles, was beside itself with glee. A Latin American dictator had gotten his comeuppance; if only it had been Castro.

At Ray Takiff's Coconut Grove law office, the phone did not stop ringing. Reporters were clamoring to find out what had happened to Takiff's most important client. What had become of Noriega? Where is the general, Ray? Now what? That afternoon, the office was full of reporters, and Takiff was full of bluster.

"General Noriega is not the type of man to run away," Takiff told those assembled. "He's probably going to die in Panama." The prototypical Miami "white powder" defense lawyer, Takiff was loud, bombastic, filled with panache, and a master of the hard sell. He wore gold rings, gold bracelets, and a diamond-studded Rolex watch. He drove a red Cadillac. Big and bearded, his motto had always seemed to be *Don't back down*.

"I'm talking about fighting to his death," Takiff asserted. "He will not come back to stand trial." The general's indictment had been nothing short of "indictment diplomacy," Takiff scoffed, repeating Frank Rubino's memorable phrase. And Takiff reasserted Noriega's promise that someday he would embarrass the American government and embarrass George Bush. "Oliver North did all the shredding," Takiff said. "Mr. Noriega shreds nothing. What Oliver North shredded, Noriega still has." Takiff claimed that Noriega had prepared a statement to be released upon his death. That statement had been given to his lawyers. Murder Noriega, and George Bush would have to live with the truth of his own actions revealed, Takiff promised.

Beside Takiff stood Frank Rubino. Rubino, forty-four, a former Secret Service agent, had been a defense lawyer for nearly fifteen years. His approach was slightly more low key than Takiff's. But he, too, derided the American action. The indictment was a blatant, politically motivated attempt to remove Noriega from power. It was retribution for the general's inflexibility on the Panama Canal treaties and his lack of support for the Reagan administration's Contra policy in Nicaragua, he said.

"The general is alive, well, and somewhere in Panama, and he is on top of the situation as far as leading his forces," said Rubino. "He's a fighter," Rubino asserted.

The next day, Thursday, December 21, the American victory was all but complete. There were only a few pockets of resistance remaining in Panama; most of the PDF's top leaders had surrendered rather than risk death. Still, Noriega had not been captured.

(That morning Frank Rubino was a guest on the "Morning Zoo," a Miami rock-and-roll radio wake-up show. Panamanian politics; the interior of Noriega's elegant Panama City home; the outrageous invasion—Rubino had something to say about it all.)

Within hours of the touchdown of U.S. troops, large portions of the Panamanian countryside were secured. Most important to the Bush administration, Noriega's homes and offices, where the Maximum Leader had been most expected to make a stand, were overrun.

Because press freedom had been restricted by American officials, initial reports from Panama were all but orchestrated by the administration. Reporters went where the U.S. Army took them and reported on what the Army showed them.

With Noriega on the lam, the next best thing, to some members of the media pool, was to see where the dictator had been. The pictures out of Noriega's headquarters were not pretty. The Noriega *comandancia* seemed nothing less than a den of iniquity, though there was speculation the scene was doctored by American troops.

There were vats of blood and animal entrails, and what seemed to be a witch's diary. It was, no doubt, the scene of pagan animal sacrifices and rites. Also found: a pair of women's high heels, phallic objects, and pornography; a framed picture of Adolf Hitler; a collection of German-made Luger pistols and Uzi automatic weapons. Near two decorated Christmas trees was a stash of $120,000 in cash and what appeared to be 110 pounds of cocaine. The field leader of the invasion, Gen. Maxwell Thurman, told reporters the conclusion was easily drawn: Noriega was "clearly not only a narco trafficker but . . . he condoned or used the stuff himself."

Noriega was "a man who has graduated from a narco trafficker indicted in the United States to a narco terrorist," Thurman told reporters. In Washington on December 22, Rear Adm. Edward D. "Ted" Shaefer, head of intelligence for the Joint Chiefs of Staff, told reporters that Noriega was nothing more than "a corrupt, debauched thug."

That the capture of Noriega was one of the Bush administration's chief objectives in the invasion of Panama was demonstrated in the lack of breadth to the invasion. Panama City and the areas around Noriega's headquarters were the clear focus of the American thrust. In Chiriquí, the westernmost province of Panama and one of the country's most prosperous, PDF troops had gone all but ignored—even though the province was commanded by Lt. Col. Luis del Cid, a onetime secretary and aide to Noriega, who also was named in the Miami indictment. Although U.S. Army and Justice Department officials claimed that American forces met stiff resistance in Chiriquí, only a few Americans had entered the province, and there was virtually no fighting. In fact, soon after the invasion, del Cid telephoned the U.S. Southern Command headquarters in Panama City and quietly offered to arrange a peaceful surrender of his troops. Del Cid also promised to abdicate his military command to the newly installed government of Guillermo Endara. After a day or two of telephone negotiation, del Cid agreed to a full surrender and disarmament of his troops. In exchange, U.S. commanders assured del Cid that he could surrender to an officer of equal rank and that his rank and the rank of the officers serving under him would be respected.

The day before Christmas, without one shot being fired between PDF and American troops, del Cid's soldiers put down their arms. Del Cid then met an American lieutenant colonel in the province capital of David and gave himself up. Del Cid believed he would be taken to Panama City and kept under the authority of the newly formed Endara government. But when del Cid arrived in Panama City in the custody of the U.S. Army, he was immediately handed over to DEA agents who placed him under arrest and put him on an agency plane to Miami. On Christmas night, with deep black bags under his eyes, del Cid sat in an isolation cell at the federal Metropolitan Correctional Center in Miami. He had arrived with $7,000 in his pocket. A public defender was assigned to his case.

Outside of the United States, much of the world seemed to share Takiff's and Rubino's outrage. Especially in Latin American, the talk was of a return to gunboat diplomacy. It didn't make sense: an entire army sent to capture one man. At the United Nations, France, China, and the Soviet Union denounced the invasion. In Moscow, a Soviet military leader quipped sarcastically that it was "surprising that a huge country like Panama had carried out aggression against such a tiny country as the United States." Both the United Nations and the Organization of American States took up debates aimed at condemning the U.S. action.

But disappointment was greatest among the American military itself. There were twenty-three U.S. soldiers dead and another three hundred wounded, yet there was no caged dictator to show off.

The American invasion was overwhelming. Even a military man like the general could never have imagined it. Now Noriega knew his main task was to stay alive and to find a way out of Panama. For the first few days after the invasion, accompanied by a few military aides, Noriega remained in hiding, initially moving into a small apartment but then into a house.

He learned that his wife and daughters had found asylum in the Cuban embassy, but the diplomatic path to escape had been quickly cut off when the Americans surrounded both the Cuban and Nicaraguan diplomatic compounds. With the news of del Cid's surrender, Noriega's hopes of fleeing into the countryside and rallying an insurgency effort were dashed.

By Sunday, December 24, the game was up. A Noriega intermediary telephoned the Vatican embassy and requested that Noriega be granted asylum. Within an hour an embassy car was dispatched to fetch the general from the parking lot of a nearby Panama City Dairy Queen and to return him to the white-walled Vatican compound on Balboa Avenue.

This surrender of sorts was good news for the White House. That Sunday morning the president went to the Pentagon for a briefing on the Panama situation. The administration was already working to fend off criticism that its failure to capture Noriega was fueling looting and civil disorder in the Panamanian capital. At least with Noriega's whereabouts now known, the president could breathe a sigh of political relief. "I am pleased that the general is now under the control of diplomatic authorities," the president said in a statement. "His reign of terror is over."

Bedraggled and exhausted, Noriega spent the next ten days in the papal embassy while Vatican, American, and Panamanian officials searched for both a diplomatic and a legal solution to his asylum. Under diplomatic tradition, Noriega would be safe from arrest as long as he remained inside the embassy, but clearly the deposed Maximum Leader had no command over his fate. U.S. officials refused to allow him to flee to Cuba or Nicaragua. Countries that might have considered granting him asylum in the past, such as Spain, now felt obliged to honor their extradition treaties with the United States. Day by day Noriega's options dwindled.

On Christmas Day the embassy was surrounded by U.S. armored personnel carriers and dozens of soldiers. U.S. helicopters circled overhead. "It is U.S. policy that we would like to have Mr. Noriega," said Secretary of Defense Dick Cheney, who had been dispatched to Panama by the president.

In Corpus Christi, Texas, on Wednesday, December 27, President Bush told reporters that the United States was doing all that it could to gain custody of Noriega and to return him to Miami for trial. Though Noriega was wanted on criminal charges in his own country, the president said, the new Panamanian government was leaning toward turning him over to the United States. (Indeed, the new Endara government probably would not have known what to do with Noriega; Panama City's only maximum-security jail had caught fire and burned to the ground during the invasion.) "We made it clear to the Vatican our preference to bring the man to trial and subsequently to justice," said Bush. "We're trying to solve a difficult problem here." And, the president said, if Noriega was brought to the United States for trial, he himself had no fear that Noriega would disclose CIA or other American intelligence information that would embarrass the United States. "You may get into some release of certain confidential documents that he may try to blind-side the whole justice process, but the system works, so I wouldn't worry about that," the president said.

In fact, the system had already begun working in Miami the day before. On Tuesday, December 26, former Panamanian Defense Forces Lt. Col. Luis del Cid was arraigned on charges of racketeering, drug trafficking, and conspiracy to transport cocaine. If convicted, del Cid would spend seventy years in an American prison. Del Cid, forty-six, walked into the courtroom clearly stunned by the events that had befallen him. In less than a week's time the swagger had left the legs of this career military man.

He turned to look at Miami U.S. Attorney Dexter Lehtinen, who had risen to tell the court the government's intention regarding the defendant. The Panamanian shook back a convulsive sob. It was as though he had looked at the face of the devil himself. Lehtinen had minced few words with reporters before entering the courtroom:

"Luis del Cid and others were importing cocaine into our country and destroying our children," the prosecutor told the reporters and cameras. "We're confident we have the evidence to convict them."

Bold words for a prosecutor who had not yet impaneled a jury. Prospective jurors sitting in front of their television sets in Miami that evening heard a still untried and still innocent man labeled a destroyer of children.

It was as though the government were saying: We are unafraid of tainting the jury pool. Give us publicity, and we can still give this man a fair trial. After all, the president had called Noriega and his band "thugs." The rules of criminal procedure were not going to be easy to obey.

Lehtinen was itching for a fight. He had been ever since he took over the Miami prosecutor's job after Leon Kellner resigned in April 1988. If he could lead troops in Vietnam, which he had, the Miami U.S. attorney's office wasn't going to be a problem, Lehtinen told the attorney general.

He decorated his office with Vietnam battle flags. A Revolutionary War flag over his desk read DON'T TREAD ON ME. When the plane carrying del Cid to the United States landed at an Air Force base south of Miami in the middle of the night, Lehtinen was there.

Del Cid's lawyer, Miami Federal Public Defender Kenneth Swartz, was outraged that Lehtinen had gone to reporters with inflammatory accusations about his client. When Swartz protested to Miami U.S. District Judge William M. Hoeveler, the judge agreed. Federal rules of procedure prohibited lawyers from personally attacking opposing parties. Criminal defendants must get a fair trial, not a trial in the media.

Lehtinen was chastised, but he insisted that the commander in chief himself had pronounced the indictment against del Cid and Noriega "winnable." His remarks, Lehtinen said, were intended to show that del Cid and Noriega were such a threat to the United States that American soldiers had fought and died to try to bring them to justice.

Still, Lehtinen was not finished putting del Cid on the defensive. He argued that even though del Cid had come to America with only $7,000 in his pocket, hardly enough to marshal a legal defense, it was del Cid, not the taxpayers, who should pay the cost of his defense. On that point the judge agreed. "If he can afford it, he cannot have a public defender," Hoeveler told Swartz. The judge gave del Cid thirty days to prove he was destitute or to get his own lawyer. But for now, del Cid wasn't talking. When asked if he had money to pay a lawyer, the former Panamanian military officer—who reports said had somehow lived in a $300,000 home on a $1,000-a-month salary—invoked the Fifth Amendment. The talk at Main Justice was that del Cid and Noriega, too, had undoubtedly stashed away more than enough money to pay for their own lawyers. On Wednesday, December 27, the Justice and State departments teamed together to ask Switzerland, France, Luxembourg, and Great Britain to freeze accounts in their countries belonging to Noriega and his family. By some estimates, Noriega's wealth could be as much as $300 million.

By the time Frank Rubino had been hired by Noriega in 1988 he had tried more than 130 cases. Picking juries and going to trial were what Rubino did best. His clients were major drug dealers and organized crime bosses. But it had not always been that way for Rubino, who was forty-three when Noriega hired him.

Rubino was born in Philadelphia and raised on the seashore in New Jersey. He went to college at Seton Hall University and moved to south Florida after graduation. There he worked first as a street cop and then joined the Secret Service and helped protect President Nixon on his visits to his resort home on Key Biscayne. But Rubino wanted more and entered night law school, finally graduating from the University of Miami in 1975.

Rubino was adamant about how he and the general's three other lawyers should meet the incessant drumbeat of derogatory government statements about Noriega: Fight fire with fire.

"If the president and the government have a right to tell their side of the story, does the poor general just have to sit back and have no one speak on his behalf?" Rubino asked. "The president of the United States stood and said [Noriega] is a criminal, he is a drug dealer, not an alleged one." Rubino shook his head. No, that was wrong to say. Now "it is etched in stone that he is evil."

It was unfair, said Rubino. Pure and simple, the indictment was political, and if the government aimed to inflame the public, it was only fair that the defense, in turn, be able to heap hyperbole and ridicule on the U.S. government.

But for one of the general's lawyers that was not so. Neal Sonnett, long one of Miami's most respected criminal defense lawyers, had joined the general's defense team a month and a half after the delivery of the indictment, in March 1988. Sonnett was the only one of Noriega's three lawyers who actually had a law firm of more than a half-dozen lawyers and a staff of paralegals behind him. Only he could lay out a defense position and then marshal the horses to do the necessary legal research to pull the load.

With flaming red hair and beard as well as a commanding base voice and a piercing stare, Sonnett would appear to have assumed the role of team wild man. But Sonnett's approach was scholarly, quiet, and matter-of-fact tough. The one thing he could not countenance was showboating. President of the National Association of Criminal Defense Lawyers, Sonnett had more than once found himself sitting across the table from senior Justice Department lawyers negotiating mutually acceptable interpretations of fine points of criminal procedure and law. No case was won in the press. Being able to deal with the no-holds-barred Reagan and Bush Justice Departments was hard enough without getting into the bad habit of exchanging snipes. So Rubino's and Takiff's posturing bothered Sonnett. Takiff, particularly, with his over-charged ego, was the polar opposite of Sonnett. Since the invasion, the posturing had shifted into overdrive in anticipation of Noriega's capture.

On one return trip from Panama, Takiff and Rubino were met at the the airport by a reporter. Takiff blustered that they had just met with Noriega and had returned with "political dynamite." Rubino was speechless. They had nothing. But Takiff carried on. Sonnett advised Takiff to quit grandstanding. But Takiff could not help himself.

On Wednesday afternoon, December 27, Sonnett went to Judge Hoeveler and asked to withdraw. Almost from the minute he had joined the defense team, Sonnett told Hoeveler, a series of conflicts had developed between counsel. "Those conflicts involved, among other matters, serious differences of opinion regarding the proper scope of representation and the appropriate-ness of certain statements, not directly related to the pending case, which have been made to the media by co-counsel." Sonnett said he had thought about quitting almost a year before but was persuaded to stay on. Now, he said, the media focus on the case was overwhelming and the hype was becoming unmanagable. Sonnett explained that he had "always insisted on drawing a clear line of demarcation between functioning as a lawyer in a spe-cific legal matter and assuming a broader role as a client's general representa-tive or public relations spokesperson." His desire was to provide a client with a "zealous" defense. After all, this was "the very foundation of our democratic system of justice." But it was a matter of professional judgment, Sonnett said, that he could not function well as part of the team now defending General Noriega.

Takiff was his usual incredulous self. "We've had no problems whatsoever, just general differences of opinion," he said when he heard about Sonnett's decision to quit the case. "It's just too hot in the kitchen," he added.

With Noriega as close as ever to being dropped into the hands of U.S. law enforcement, new concerns about the strength of the case began to emerge at Main Justice. So far, DEA and Justice Department investigators and lawyers sent to Panama with the invasion force had failed to uncover any new evidence or documents that could link Noriega to drug trafficking.

In the days immediately after the invasion, special Army document collection units located and carted off more than fifty file cabinets' worth of materials: intelligence memorandums, including reports on U.S. military activities, Panamanian military records, maps, letters, Noriega's personal financial records, including American Express Gold Card and VISA receipts, a wide assortment of materials that might conceivably be evidence against the general. The U.S. investigators had hoped to find tape recordings and specific financial records and intelligence reports that would make their case, but nothing had turned up.

In fact, the 110 pounds of stacked and packaged white powder that Army brass had crowed about recovering from one of Noriega's offices—the cocaine that would irrevocably prove the general's debauchery and collusion with the cartel—on closer inspection had turned out to be tamale fixings.

The boxes and boxes of documents that military leaders had been so careful to preserve in the course of the invasion were proving to be no paper trail. What the U.S. forces had captured instead was a Pandora's box of legal questions grounded squarely in the Constitution. What role did the military have in seizing potential evidence? What right did it have to seize it? What were American soldiers looking for when they went into Noriega's offices? And in what form were the seized records found? How could the United States prove that the documents it had captured had not then been doctored?

The defense—if Noriega did go to trial—would surely argue that any documents seized in Panama had almost undoubtedly been seized illegally. Only evidence found "in plain view" could properly have been seized. After all, the Fourth Amendment clearly barred "unreasonable" searches, and the government would be hard-pressed to prove that its evidence was obtained legally and had not been tampered with in the utter chaos of invasion.

"I highly doubt they will be admissible in court," Rubino said of the boxes of documents the government claimed to have captured. "Rules of evidence don't provide for armed troops to kick your doors down and seize evidence for use in a criminal case."

Rubino also made a direct appeal to the American sense of fair play. How was Noriega going to receive a fair trial given the unprecedented publicity surrounding the case? he wondered. When the president of the United States says your client has been "poisoning the children of the United States of America and the world," one might reasonably argue that such a statement is an obstacle to a fair trial, Rubino said. "I'm going to have to find people on the dark side of the moon," said Rubino of the prospect of choosing a jury.

On Monday, January 1, 1990, Daniel Miranda, another alleged conspirator named with Noriega in the 1988 indictment, arrived in the United States. Miranda, an airline pilot, had been apprehended the day before at a Panama City apartment house. U.S. soldiers and DEA agents broke in on him at six in the morning. The indictment alleged that in May 1983, Miranda, along with another pilot, Eduardo Pardo, had transported $800,000 in drug proceeds from Fort Lauderdale to Panama.

Miranda, thirty-six, became the fourth Noriega co-defendant to be rounded up, joining Lt. Col. del Cid and Brian Davidow, a Miami real estate agent, and the Colombian William Saldarriaga, an alleged drug trafficker who had been arrested in October. For his role in the alleged scheme, Miranda faced five years in prison and a $10,000 fine. Again, Miami U.S. Attorney Lehtinen had gone to Homestead Air Force Base south of Miami to meet Miranda as he got off the military plane that brought him from Panama.

The next day, Miranda, short and dark-haired, was arraigned. Also on January 2, del Cid went to court for a bond hearing. Del Cid had hired Miami criminal defense lawyer Samuel Burstyn. Miranda, in the morning hours after arriving in the United States, had contacted an old family friend, Miami criminal defense lawyer Michael O'Kane, who accompanied him to court

O'Kane and Burstyn wasted little time getting to the point when their clients were brought before the federal magistrate. Miranda, on O'Kane's instructions, stood silent. O'Kane said Miranda "was standing mute" because the United States simply did not have the legal authority to arrest a foreign citizen in a foreign country. Clearly, said O'Kane, the United States had decided it was "willing to break the law to achieve its ends." The very notion, said O'Kane, was disturbing.

Burstyn, standing next to del Cid before Judge Hoeveler, on the question of bond said, "This is a vigilante kind of posse use of the armed forces. The U.S. military can't be an international police that goes around arresting people all over the world. As much as American citizens might like to see justice done to criminals, the United States is not an international police force. The United States just can't go out and invade other countries and arrest whoever it wants."

Both O'Kane and Burstyn argued that the United States had violated the Geneva Convention and U.S. law in arresting and transporting their clients. Their clients had been seized and returned to the United States illegally by U.S. military and law enforcement agents, the two lawyers said. They further argued that the mere mention of Noriega's name would almost guarantee prejudice toward Miranda and del Cid. "If you had Mother Teresa sitting at the table next to Noriega, she'd have trouble getting past the jury," O'Kane told the judge.

The lawyers for Davidow and Saldarriaga went to court the next day, Wednesday, January 3. Davidow, who had been accused in the indictment of conspiracy to distribute cocaine, was represented by Miami criminal defense lawyer Richard Sharpstein. Saldarriaga had hired Miami criminal defense lawyer Steven Kreisberg. Both asked Judge Hoeveler to grant their clients separate trials, but for different reasons.

Kreisberg argued that Saldarriaga, forty-five, had been named in only one of the specific criminal acts listed in the indictment—meeting with Noriega and others in March 1986 to plan the shipment of about three hundred kilograms of cocaine aboard a luxury yacht. Saldarriaga, Kreisberg argued, had not been included in the broad first count of the indictment that outlined the conspiracy to conduct a racketeering enterprise. It would be unfair to take Saldarriaga to trial and subject him to the "spillover" of evidence that would come in against the other co-defendants allegedly involved in the broader conspiracy.

A jury would be "bombarded with days, if not weeks, of testimony and reams of documentary exhibits," all "inflammatory," Kreisberg told the judge.

Sharpstein had his own reason for seeking a separate trial for Davidow: The publicity surrounding the events in Panama had been so widely spread and so volatile that Davidow, who had given himself up to authorities shortly after the indictment had been delivered in 1988 and who had gone about his business trying to sell real estate in suburban Miami, would suddenly find himself sucked into the vortex of bad press that any person accused with Noriega would suffer. Davidow had never even met Noriega, argued Sharpstein.

But Lehtinen and Malman argued that the charges against the two were not so complicated that a jury could not distinguish who was being accused of doing what. Moreover, the federal rules of criminal procedure said that there was no need to separate co-defendants for trial if evidence would be duplicated at two trials. The rules clearly said that a defendant's right to a fair trial must be balanced against the interests of judicial economy. There were only so many judges and so much money to go around, the government said.

As far as either Saldarriaga or Davidow was concerned, Judge Hoeveler said it was just too early to say that either one would suffer as a result of the publicity surrounding the case or its chief defendant, General Noriega.

"At present we have four defendants. However, if the situation in Panama should resolve itself in another week and if we have five defendants—and one of them is General Noriega—then the whole situation changes," the judge said.

That night the situation changed.

★   ★   ★

For ten days Noriega lived in the guest wing of the three-story Vatican embassy. With a single bed, a nightstand, a broken television, and a crucifix on the wall, Noriega went almost sleepless listening to the incessant din of the rock music played over U.S. Army loudspeakers.

Soon the soldiers cut off the electricity to the embassy and with it the air conditioning. Then they began blasting excerpts from speeches by George Bush.

All the while, in the background, Noriega could hear the chanting of angry Panamanians who stood behind the military blockades. He was not safe in the country whose "internal security" he had once guaranteed.

On Wednesday afternoon the papal ambassador went to Noriega. The Vatican had decided that the general was a refugee from criminal, not political, charges. Noriega's asylum would end the next day at noon, and then the general would be on his own. The choices were spare: He could face the new Panamanian government, which certainly would have very little control over the unhappy and revenge-minded demonstrators now in the streets, or he could take his chances with the Americans.

Through Vatican officials Noriega asked for assurance from the Americans that if he were to surrender, he would not face capital punishment in the United States. No, he would not, the reply came back. In that case, Noriega asked to be granted a few wishes: the use of a telephone to speak briefly with his family and his mistress; a promise that the surrender be kept a secret until he walked out of the embassy; a surrender in full military uniform to an officer of equal rank. The Americans agreed.

At 8:50 P.M. on Wednesday, January 3, 1990, dressed in his general's uniform, dark brown pants and a tan shirt with military emblems, Noriega walked to the iron gate of the Vatican compound.

"I will pray for you every day," Reverend Xavier Villanueva told Noriega as he walked him to the black iron gates.

"*Gracias*," Noriega said quietly.

Villanueva handed Noriega a keepsake Bible, and Noriega handed the priest a letter addressed to the Pope. "I express my gratitude for having taken me in . . . and for the bright light that you gave me," Noriega wrote. Then the general stepped through the gate and presented himself to the American invading soldiers. The United States' two-year campaign to remove Noriega from power was over.

Noriega was immediately searched for weapons and then briskly escorted across the street to an athletic field where an Army Blackhawk helicopter sat ready for the five-minute flight to Howard Air Force Base in the Canal Zone. Less than forty minutes later, Noriega was walked up the rear ramp of an American C-130 cargo plane flanked by DEA agents and U.S. military personnel. He was given a medical examination by two Army doctors and pronounced fit for flight, and he was then told to change into a rumpled green flight suit for the five-hour and fifteen-minute flight to Miami. A chain was placed around the general's waist and handcuffs attached.

At 9:30 P.M. the American plane left Panamanian soil carrying the former Maximum Leader to the United States to stand trial. Flying alongside the cargo transport were two U.S. fighter planes.

The U.S. law enforcement agents had had plenty of time to think about Noriega's capture and what should happen next. Shortly after the American plane cleared Panamanian airspace, the DEA agent sitting next to Noriega turned and formally placed him under arrest. Now there would be no question of the agents' territorial authority to make the arrest.

Noriega was read his rights in Spanish. He had the constitutional right to a lawyer and to remain silent. Then the formal charges were read, first in English and then in Spanish.

Flying across the Gulf of Mexico, Noriega clutched three Catholic rosaries and the Bible he had been given at the papal embassy. All the while a DEA agent read aloud from the scriptures in Spanish.

While Noriega was airborne, President Bush talked to the American people in a television address. The invasion had been a success, the president said. The final goal, to capture Noriega, had been achieved.

"The United States is committed to providing General Noriega a fair trial," the president said, reading from a statement that had been carefully reviewed by White House lawyers in an effort to make sure potential jurors would not be prejudiced. "Nevertheless, his apprehension and return to the United States should send a clear signal that the United States is serious in its determination that those charged with promoting the distribution of drugs cannot escape this scrutiny of justice."

With dozens of anti-Noriega protesters standing at the gates of Homestead Air Force Base, the plane carrying Noriega touched down at 2:45 on the morning of Thursday, January 4, 1990.

"Good-bye, Pineapple Face," the protesters yelled in the distance, mockingly referring to Noriega's acne-scarred face.

Within minutes of his having landed at Homestead, Noriega was besieged by a phalanx of U.S. marshals who hustled him to a Lear jet sitting across the tarmac. In another fifteen minutes the plane touched down on a far runway at Miami International Airport. The flight had cut short the forty-minute drive from Homestead to the Miami federal courthouse. Noriega was placed in the backseat of a sedan. With three other sedans loaded with heavily armed marshals, a police special tactics van, and two Miami city police cruisers, the caravan sped through nighttime Miami to the federal courthouse. At 3:30 A.M. the caravan rounded the corner at Miami Avenue and disappeared down the underground drive leading into the building. Noriega was hunched over in the backseat, with a flak jacket draped over his shoulders and flanked by deputy marshals. Noriega was taken from the sedan and led through a maze of underground hallways and tunnels to a maximum-security cell that sat squarely under the oldest section of the courthouse. The ten-by-twelve-foot cell, with a bed, a television, and a toilet, was so secret, marshals' service personnel refused to acknowledge that it existed. The windowless lockup, enclosed by interior walls on four sides, was approachable only through heavily guarded passageways and was so hidden that it had been dubbed "the submarine."

That same night another co-defendent named in the indictment, pilot Eduardo Pardo, was arrested in Panama and loaded on a military plane bound for Miami. Like Daniel Miranda, he, too, was accused of having flown drug profits to Panama from the United States.

Later that morning, across the street from the courthouse in the jury pool parking lot, two dozen television satellite dish trucks had set up shop. Half of the lot's spaces were crisscrossed with television cables, and along the curb, folding patio chairs were filled with cameramen, reporters, and producers drinking coffee in the sun. It was a picture-perfect Miami day.

Around the corner, at the entrance to the court's ten-story courtroom tower, Panamanian exiles, anti-Castro Cuban Americans, hangers-on, and the curious had already filled the sidewalks. "*Justicia!*" (justice) and "*Asesino*" (murderer), some yelled. Soon the chant began in Spanish: "Down with Noriega, up with Bush."

T-shirt vendors were there, too. NORIEGA: ENEMY NO. 1 OF DEMOCRACY read one, OPERATION JUST CAUSE another. MIAMI: SEE IT LIKE A NATIVE, with a likeness of Noriega looking out from behind bars, was another.

Reporters with cellular telephones gathered in knots close to the court's front entrance. The word from the marshal's office was that there would be forty seats set aside for the press in Courtroom 9 that afternoon for Noriega's arraignment. By 10 A.M., two hundred reporters, some from as far away as Japan, Germany, and all around South America, had placed their names on the seating lottery list.

Overnight every federal marshal in south Florida had been put on alert. Plainclothes marshals with walkie-talkies and binoculars peered from the balconies reaching up the side of the courtroom tower. Miami police officers with automatic weapons and dressed in full battle gear stood at the corners of nearby intersections.

By mid-morning Ray Takiff, Frank Rubino, and Steve Kollin, another lawyer who had replaced Neal Sonnett, had arrived at the courthouse and were taken to see their client. The three had not met since before the invasion. The general was happy to see some familiar faces.

But Takiff had news for Noriega: The stress of the case, he told Noriega, had thrown his heart into arrhythmia, and his cardiologist had told him to quit the defense.

Decades of heavy smoking and a rich diet had finally caught up with the feisty Takiff. In little more than a year's time, Takiff had suffered two massive heart attacks and undergone two bypass surgeries. My "stress is elevated and [my] health [has been] placed in serious jeopardy," Takiff explained to the general. If I keep this up, Takiff continued, if I stay on this case, it "might well lead to disastrous consequences." Suddenly the team was down to two, Rubino and Kollin.

Courtroom 9 was packed. Reporters filled the first three rows of the gallery and spilled over into the empty jury box; also present were a half-dozen television sketch artists. No photographers are allowed in federal trial courts. Twenty members of the public, most of whom had stood in line since early morning, sat in the remaining twenty seats along the back of the courtroom. Beyond the double doors, in the foyer, milled another 150 reporters, who were cut off from the courtroom by a line of deputy marshals; they would rely on the reporters inside to report on Noriega's arraignment. In each corner of the courtroom stood two plainclothes marshals. Four stood at the foyer door, and eight more lined the railing between the gallery and the prosecution and defense tables.

Facing the bench on the right sat U.S. Attorney Lehtinen, his chief assistant, Myles Malman, and four other young assistants. Behind them sat six other lawyers, four from Main Justice and two from the State Department. On the left, at the defense table, stood defense lawyers Rubino and Kollin.

At 4:20 P.M., twenty minutes behind schedule, Judge William Hoeveler strode up the stairs from his chambers and took the bench. Six feet, four inches tall, Bill Hoeveler looked out commandingly at his courtroom. If ever there was a quintessential federal judge, Hoeveler was it. It had become a courthouse cliché to call the tall, lean sixty-seven-year-old jurist "Lincolnesque." His manner was soft, his speech measured. Had Hollywood set out to find an actor to play the part of a judge like Hoeveler, it would have gone straight to Jimmy Stewart.

After fourteen years on the bench, the Harvard Law School–trained Carter appointee was known by the Miami defense bar to be as tough on criminal defendants as the Nixon and Ford appointees who had preceded him and the Reagan appointees who followed. In the three years before Noriega's arrest, Hoeveler had been appealed in twenty-eight criminal cases. In every one, the Atlanta-based Eleventh U.S. Circuit Court of Appeals had affirmed him.

Still, despite the judge's law and order record, Frank Rubino, who would soon stand on behalf of the general, said of Hoeveler, "He's tough, but he's fair. There's no judge we would rather have on this case."

Hoeveler was now just five months from being eligible to take senior status, which would allow him to reduce his caseload. But he refused to cut back. In every year that he had been on the bench, Hoeveler had presided over one hundred–plus criminal cases. That was slightly more than the average for the sixteen federal judges sitting in the Southern District of Florida. At one time or another just about every criminal law issue had come before Hoeveler. Though he was known to take his time in ruling, his affirmation record told the story.

And Hoeveler was not new to the case. He had already presided over the early jurisdiction skirmishes. In February 1988, on the day the Miami indictment was handed up, the case had been randomly assigned to Hoeveler off what the judges called "the wheel," a computerized assignment system.

"Well, here we go again," Hoeveler told his wife when he walked in the door that evening. It seemed he had been drawing one tough case after another.

"What?" asked Mary, who everyone called "Griff" after her maiden name Mary Griffen Smith. (The two had been married since the early 1950s, when Hoeveler had come to Miami to join the law firm in which Griff's father was a partner.)

"I drew Noriega," he said.

"That could be a biggie," Griff said.

"No," Hoeveler replied, after a moment. "It'll never go to trial. They'll never get him."

That had been two years before. Now, the white-haired judge took his place behind the bench.

"Sorry for the delay," he began, looking out over the courtroom.

"We'll now call the case *United States versus Noriega,* number 88-79." Hoeveler asked counsel to state their names for the record.

"Where is the defendant?" the judge asked, looking to the defense table and seeing that Noriega was not present.

"Your Honor," Rubino said, "at this time General Noriega would waive his right to appear." A defendant, if he chooses, and with the judge's permission, does not have to be present to answer the charges leveled against him. With a judge's permission the defendant can sit out his own arraignment.

"This is not a case I want to go by waivers," said Hoeveler after a pause. He directed the marshals to bring Noriega into court.

All heads turned toward the courtroom's side entrance. Thirteen hours after he had arrived in Miami, Noriega, flanked by marshals, walked into court. The former general wore a freshly starched beige short-sleeved shirt with four silver stars on the epaulets, dark brown pants, and black boots. His black hair was lightly oiled back. He looked bewildered and small and oddly passive. Noriega turned slightly toward Kollin and then to Rubino. He clasped his hands behind his back and faced the judge, who said, "Please state your name."

"Manuel Antonio Noriega."

"Are you in good health today?" the judge asked.

"Sí," Noriega answered in Spanish. A court interpreter standing to the side translated the questions and answers.

"Have you used any drugs or medication in the last twelve hours?" Hoeveler asked.

"Absolutely not," Noriega answered.

The judge asked the general if he understood his rights as a defendant in a

U.S. criminal prosecution. Through the interpreter Noriega said he did.

Then Rubino stood to address the court. General Noriega would not enter a plea to the charges leveled against him, Rubino told Hoeveler.

"General Noriega most respectfully refuses to submit to the jurisdiction of the court," Rubino said. "General Noriega's appearance here today is made under protest."

Noriega would "stand mute before the court," Rubino continued. As a head of state he was immune from prosecution, Rubino said. "General Noriega is a political prisoner in the United States," Rubino explained. The U.S. invasion of Panama was illegal, and the twelve-count indictment was politically motivated. The general was in court "under coercion and intimidation," and he had been coerced into surrendering. "He was told at the noon hour today that the only person who would enjoy diplomatic immunity was the papal nuncio himself," said Rubino. "In order to avoid any unnecessary bloodshed and to prevent loss of life in the compound, General Noriega felt compelled to acquiesce."

"Very well," said the judge when Rubino had finished. Hoeveler then looked to the U.S. attorney. "Mr. Lehtinen, what say you?"

The question of Noriega's immunity was long settled, Lehtinen began. He noted that Hoeveler himself had rejected defense claims of immunity a year before. Noriega was now legally in custody, the prosecutor said. "It is the position of the government that all our actions were proper under domestic and international law," Lehtinen said.

When Lehtinen had finished, the judge looked thoughtfully at Noriega. Did he understand what was being said, and was it his wish not to speak or enter a plea? the judge asked.

"My attorney has explained everything," Noriega answered.

Then Hoeveler said: "If the defendant refuses to plead, it is the duty of the court to enter a plea. I shall enter a plea of not guilty."

Lehtinen stood again and said the government was prepared to go to trial. He estimated a trial would last about two months. Rubino stood. He could not be ready for trial in less than nine months, he said. The defense lawyer estimated a trial would take six months.

Rubino said Noriega would waive his right to a bond hearing. Lehtinen requested that the former general remain jailed until trial.

Noriega's first appearance in an American court was over in twenty minutes. He was led away to be photographed. Just a few weeks shy of age fifty-four, he was U.S. prisoner 41586.

Late that afternoon, Attorney General Richard Thornburgh released a prepared statement in Washington: The capture of Noriega and the killing in December of Medellín cartel boss José Gonzalo Rodríguez Gacha by Colombian police had delivered a "one-two punch against the international drug traffickers. We're satisfied that there's no bar whatsoever to going forward with the charges, using the evidence that we have, to sustain the charges contained in the indictment." Thornburgh's statement was an indirect response to Noriega's challenge that the court could not have authority over him. "We're not worried about anything that may be raised by way of defense."

Rubino and Kollin met with Noriega again after the arraignment. It was their third meeting of the day. They sat in the anteroom to Noriega's underground holding cell, the same room in which prosecutors Richard Gregorie and Mark Schnapp and DEA agent Steven Grilli had interviewed Floyd Carlton more than two years before.

Noriega was animated, and he grew more vigorous as the day went on. He asked if the lawyers had heard from his wife or three daughters. Were they safe?

"He was not in any rush to leave us," Kollin said late that afternoon. "He probably would have spoken to us for hours, but we were very tired."

At 6 P.M., as the sun began to fade, the television floodlights lit up along the sidewalk across the street from the courthouse. Simultaneously, nine television reporters delivered live updates.

In Washington an anonymous senior Justice Department official suggested to a *New York Times* reporter that the administration would be willing to consider a plea bargain with Noriega if he would provide information about Colombian drug dealers. There was still one way to avoid a courtroom showdown. Noriega could flip. It was an idea for the defense to think about. But no one in the Bush administration—having just completed the first invasion since Roman times aimed at returning home the leader of another country— would dare such a suggestion on the record.

On the morning of Friday, January 5, Attorney General Thornburgh went to see the president and brief him on the legal strategy to be followed in the prosecution. The Justice Department was not going to offer Noriega a plea bargain, Thornburgh told the president, but should Noriega want to talk, the prosecutors had been instructed to listen. All indications were that the prosecution would be strong. Even now, investigators in Panama were seeking new witnesses and continuing their search for a paper trail. The idea was to proceed full throttle toward a prosecution but not cut off the possibility of a plea.

And, Thornburgh told the president, now more than ever efforts must be made to avoid giving the defense the slightest reason to move for a mistrial. Even the president must avoid trying Noriega through public statements.

At a midday news conference, President Bush reflected the Attorney General's counsel. "The time for rhetoric is over," the president said, reading from a prepared statement. "Our government is not seeking a deal with Noriega. Our policy remains that we have brought him to this country for prosecution. Well, this morning I met with the attorney general, Dick Thornburgh, to discuss the legal process related to the prosecution of General Noriega. We are committed to a fair trial and to providing all the protections guaranteed by the United States Constitution and law. The attorney general assures me that our case is strong, our resolve is firm, and our legal representations are sound. Our government is not seeking a deal with Noriega. Our policy remains that we have brought him to this country for prosecution. I will be ever mindful of this legal process in the days ahead and will not comment on any aspect of this prosecution or any matters that could even inadvertently affect the outcome of this case. And I'm going to ask others in this administration to do the same."

What about a plea bargain? a reporter asked.

"There is no such plan," said the president. Noriega "has a right to do what he wants, and then let the legal process determine how that should work out."

"Then you're not ruling it out?" a reporter followed.

"Well, I'm not ruling it in," the president said. "I'm just saying he's got his rights, and we ought not to stand up here and try to define narrowly what they are."

And what about Republican Party National Chairman Lee Atwater's pronouncement that the invasion of Panama and the capture of Noriega was nothing less than a "political jackpot" for the president.

Bush replied testily, "I did it to protect American lives. A president's called on to take certain actions. We're not going to try to furbish a political image. That's ridiculous."

Two days later, on Sunday morning, Rubino appeared as a guest on the ABC-TV program "This Week with David Brinkley."

"The government chose to bring General Noriega to trial, and they shall have their trial," Rubino said. Plea bargains were for the guilty, the defense lawyer said. The innocent don't plea bargain.

And as for evidence of guilt or innocence, Rubino was not giving anything away. "One thing I have never done in sixteen years of practicing law is to guess what may happen."

CHAPTER 11
★★★★★★★

After the Capture:
The First Days

One-on-one, Dexter Lehtinen, the Miami U.S. attorney, could be very likable. He was a south Florida boy, raised in Homestead, a horse town fifteen miles south of Miami, wedged between Biscayne Bay and the southern tip of the Everglades. He would invite the assistants in the U.S. attorney's office over to his suburban Miami home for dessert. Illeana, his wife and now the first Cuban-born woman in the U.S. Congress, would even serve coffee and cake.

But as southern Florida's top federal prosecutor, Lehtinen was piss and vinegar. As the U.S. attorney on the front line of the drug war, he wanted to be the first one over the top, always carrying the battle flag. His predecessors had been very different. Leon Kellner was a Harvard man. So was Stanley Marcus, who had come before Kellner. Kellner was now back in Washington, in private practice, and Marcus had ascended to the federal bench.

As in Vietnam, where Lehtinen had been an Army lieutenant and a platoon leader and where he had lost the fleshy part of his face to an enemy rocket, Lehtinen was a take-charge guy.

Lehtinen had never been afraid to mix it up with anyone. Only a couple of months on the job in 1988, he had boldly made a play for the public spotlight by issuing a "report to the community" in which he had decried the shortage of federal prosecutors in southern Florida.

Main Justice, starting with the attorney general, was furious. Nonetheless, the trick had worked. The report brought south Florida to the attention of Washington, and money and bodies were parachuted in almost immediately.

But Lehtinen also had managed to anger his own assistants. The problem with Lehtinen, many of the assistants thought, was that he didn't make it fun to be one of his good guys. On modest government salaries, a fourth or fifth of what an average criminal defense lawyer could take home in a year, Lehtinen's troops were required to book sixty-five hours of overtime every month. And then the praise was thin.

Morale in the office was not made better by the Bush administration's failure, in more than a year's time, to advance Lehtinen's name to the Senate for confirmation. Even though other U.S. attorneys had served longer without Senate confirmation, some Miami defense lawyers began to charge that Lehtinen's work as U.S. attorney was invalid. They had even gone to court claiming that he should be nominated or quit signing indictments. Lehtinen did not make things any better for himself by souring relations with the press. The press was trying to get a handle on exactly how the biggest drug case ever would be tried and what would happen next. Though President Bush and top-ranking administration officials had had plenty to say about "narco thugs" and drug trafficking before the invasion, they quickly grew silent.

Following del Cid's arraignment on December 26, Lehtinen talked loudly about the defendants being poisoners of children. But a January 4 press conference scheduled by Lehtinen was canceled. Instead, a prepared statement was read to reporters following Noriega's arraignment: all questions regarding the case, the release said, should be directed to Attorney General Thornburgh's office.

On Wednesday, January 10, Samuel Burstyn, del Cid's lawyer, decided to call the administration's hand on Lehtinen. He filed a motion challenging the acting U.S. attorney's right to prosecute the case without Senate confirmation. "Mr. Lehtinen is not a duly qualified attorney for the government," Burstyn charged.

With Noriega's arrival in Miami, the president's appointment people had pushed ahead an FBI background check on Lehtinen in an effort to get him confirmed as soon as possible. Unfortunately, the check turned up unsubstantiated allegations that only confirmed what everyone suspected: Lehtinen had a tendency to fly off the handle. Still, Lehtinen was popular in Miami, and his new wife, Illeana Ross-Lehtinen, was a congresswoman whose campaign manager had been Jeb Bush, the president's son.

While attempts like Burstyn's to challenge the legal standing of an unconfirmed U.S. attorney had failed in the past and would certainly fail now, clearly Main Justice could see it was time to gather a tight rein on the prosecution. Key decisions in the case could not be entrusted to Miami, the attorney general and his aides decided. Thornburgh directed Robert Mueller and Mark Richard to take personal control over the makeup of the prosecution team. If Lehtinen wanted a say, fine, but the ultimate decision was the attorney general's. The case wouldn't be "scripted," said one Main Justice insider, but there would be "very close involvement" by Washington.

Specifically, Mueller and Richard decided that Main Justice would take close control over three basic areas likely to become the focus of the case. The first was the issue of jurisdiction: whether or not the head of state of a foreign country could be captured by U.S. law enforcement officials and summarily extradited to the United States for trial. The department's Office of International Affairs under Richard would prepare briefs and motions on this issue.

The second was Fourth Amendment questions of search and seizure:

whether possible new evidence captured during the invasion could be used in the case or in the drafting of a superseding indictment to replace the 1988 indictment.

The third area was classified information and whether government documents would be revealed should the defense, as expected, try to learn if Noriega had taken directions from U.S. government agencies such as the Central Intelligence Agency. These questions would go to the department's internal security section, also under Richard's direction.

Decisions on tactical trial preparation—how the government would go about making its factual presentation of the case—would be left to Miami with the help of Charles Saphos, the head of the department's narcotic and dangerous drug section in the Criminal Division. Saphos' office was routinely involved in the development of major drug cases.

There was no question that putting the right prosecutor in front of a jury could mean the winning edge when it came to trial. The phrase at Main Justice was "comfort level." No one questioned Lehtinen's smarts, but he was a loose cannon. Myles Malman, Lehtinen's hand-picked asistant, was an unknown. Noriega's would be the most important drug prosecution ever undertaken by the government. "Seldom are U.S. attorneys replaced in cases," said one Justice Department official, "but here you had one of the most publicized alleged criminals of the century. The 82nd Airborne fell out of the sky to catch this guy. That's pretty extraordinary." Thornburgh called Lehtinen. "The ultimate responsibility is yours," he told Lehtinen. But there was no way one man could run one of the biggest U.S. prosecutor's offices in the country and first-chair the Noriega case, he continued. You can be the U.S. attorney, or you can be the Noriega prosecutor. The decision is yours.

Across the country in California, Michael P. "Pat" Sullivan had just arrived at his parents' home outside Long Beach. Sullivan, tall, lanky, and silver-haired at age forty-two, had been in San Diego talking to an assistant U.S. attorney who was an expert on Bolivian drug smuggling. Sullivan was one of the Justice Department's two top litigators in Miami—he held the prestigious title of senior litigation counsel—and he was preparing for the upcoming trial of Arce Gómez, a former Bolivian army colonel who had already been extradited.

Sullivan had been a federal prosecutor for eighteen years, joining the U.S. attorney's office in Miami in April 1971, fresh out of the University of Florida's law school. He had served as the chief of the office's Criminal Division for two years beginning in 1978 and then had put in two years with the Miami Organized Crime Strike Force, the federal mob fighters. Soft-spoken and low-key, Sullivan was known as one of the hardest working prosecutors in the office. His record for winning complex criminal cases was as high as they come, only a case or two below 100 percent. The January before, after Richard Gregorie had left the U.S. attorney's office, Mark Schnapp, then head of the Criminal Division, had asked Sullivan whether he would be interested in taking on Noriega. Sullivan wasn't, but Schnapp explained that the prosecutors in the Narcotics Conspiracy Division on the tenth floor had done nothing but bicker over who would get Noriega since Gregorie had left.

Sullivan took the case, but the assignment was only to look after the file. He gave the file a cursory preliminary examination. After reading the indictment, the grand jury minutes, and the transcripts of the testimony of Gregorie's top witnesses, Floyd Carlton and Boris Olarte, his assessment of the case was harsh: It was a loser, he thought. It was a loser from day one. Evidence was lacking in both quality and quantity. The witnesses' testimony just didn't add up in some places and what corroboration there was was also thin.

At the end of every government prosecution, defense lawyers, as a standard practice, make a motion to dismiss the government's case for lack of evidence. Such motions were laid out in Rule 29 of the Rules of Criminal Procedure. Sullivan thought the Noriega case probably had enough to get by a Rule 29 on some of the twelve counts but not all. Would a jury convict based on what Gregorie and Steve Grilli had put together? As it stood, this case would fail, Sullivan thought. In August 1989, Sullivan gladly gave up the Noriega case to Myles Malman, who had returned to the Miami U.S. attorney's office from private practice as Lehtinen's deputy in July.

In 1987, Malman had won convictions of two defendants in a drug money case that involved members of the Cali, Colombia, cocaine cartel in what was then the longest federal criminal trial in south Florida history. The Noriega case was more complex and clearly very important. It immediately caught Malman's eye. Six months later the case was making history, and in California, Sullivan looked on at his colleagues back home in Miami who were in the middle of it.

By Wednesday, January 11, the attorney general's mandate had sunk in, and Lehtinen made his choice. Sitting first chair, representing the U.S. government at Noriega's arraignment and then at the bond hearing, was being part of history. It called for the presence of the U.S. attorney. But the case was bound to take at least eighteen months of pretrial preparation and then would likely drag on before a jury for several months more, Lehtinen knew. Lehtinen had an office of 160 prosecutors to run. Putting a full-time prosecution team in place was clearly important. It was what the attorney general and probably the president expected.

Mueller, Thornburgh's assistant, told Lehtinen that Main Justice was prepared to handle the substantive legal issues involving the invasion, international treaties, extradition, and fundamental constitutional issues of search and seizure and jurisdiction. After some back-and-forth discussion, including a personal visit to Miami by Mueller, Lehtinen and Mueller agreed that William Bryson, forty-four, the deputy U.S. solicitor general, should join the prosecution team. Bryson, who had helped keep classified information from being disclosed in the Iran-Contra trial of Lt. Col. Oliver North, would work from Washington and go to Miami as necessary.

Bryson was chief of the appellate section of the Justice Department's criminal section and special counsel to the organized crime and racketeering section.

Main Justice suggested another candidate for the prosecution team, Michael Olmsted. Olmsted had had extensive experience dealing with classified documents during the Iran-Contra proceedings. He worked on Mueller's staff, and while he was clearly qualified to join the Miami prosecutors, the scuttlebutt around the Miami office was that Olmsted was a Main Justice plant whose job it was to spy for Mueller and the attorney general.

Mueller made it clear that Lehtinen, with final approval from the attorney general, of course, could have his say about the trial team itself. The choices for Lehtinen were obvious. Malman already had charge of the Noriega file and had spent hours reviewing it in preparation for the presentation to Mark Richard almost a month before. At forty-three, he had big trial experience, plus he really wanted the case and was a friend. He was in.

With the president himself and the rest of the world watching, Lehtinen didn't need Mueller or the attorney general, for that matter, telling him that the team had to have a "long-ball hitter," as Main Justice had put it. The other choices also seemed to be obvious. Norman Moscowitz, a Harvard-trained lawyer, was the other senior litigation counsel working in Miami with Pat Sullivan. Senior litigation counsel were the department's most experienced, brightest trial lawyers. There were only fifty in the whole country. Sullivan had the deepest trial experience; he would be offered the first chair, Lehtinen decided. Moscowitz would also be put on the team but would be held in reserve for ancillary issues.

Moscowitz had recently assisted in a still-secret grand jury investigation of possible corruption among state judges. A cooperating witness in the case was none other than Raymond Takiff, Noriega's lawyer until just after the invasion. Should indictments ever be returned in that investigation, Moscowitz might have to be called on to handle questions involving the legality of Noriega's lawyer serving as an informant for the government in a separate investigation.

James McAdams, who headed the Miami office's Criminal Division and had also been in on the December 15 meeting with Richard, already was on board, lined up to handle the classified information and secret document side of the case. Lehtinen was confident that this lineup would get the case moving.

With Lehtinen's choices in hand, Richard checked with assistant U.S. attorneys across the country who had spent time in Miami. Main Justice rarely got involved in local work, but if ever there was an exception, this was it. Main Justice had to know exactly who it was putting on the front line. One by one, each of Lehtinen's nominees checked out.

With the attorney general's go ahead, Lehtinen found Sullivan at his parents' home. "I would like you to lead the Noriega prosecution," Lehtinen told

Sullivan. The case was big, and it was important. Sullivan was his and the department's number one choice for the first chair, Lehtinen said.

"My reaction was, 'What did I do to deserve this?'" Sullivan said later. "I knew what was in the file. I knew that it was not a very strong case. In all truth, I was loath to try the case."

But Sullivan said okay. He was on the next flight out of Los Angeles to Miami.

On Saturday, January 13, Lehtinen called a press conference. Because he had refused to comment for the past ten days, the media assumed he would lead the prosecution. He wouldn't. "I don't want to be the individual that spends months in court full-time and eighteen months preparing the case," Lehtinen told the dozens of reporters. "I could not devote the time to the Noriega case that would be needed for its proper presentation to the court," he continued. Sullivan, Malman, and Bryson would play pivotal roles in the prosecution. McAdams and Moscowitz and other assistants would round out the team as needed.

"I will continue to work closely with the team in coordinating the prosecution of this case," Lehtinen said. "The ultimate responsibility is mine. The attorney general phoned me personally and said that. I never said any different."

Yet Main Justice, Lehtinen, and his staff knew little about the defendants and their alleged crimes. Sullivan's take on the case was correct. Washington and Miami fell into a near mad scramble to fortify the case. They had simply not been prepared for the capture of Noriega or any of his codefendants. On January 2, Malman, with Lehtinen at his side, argued at a bond hearing for del Cid that the Panamanian lieutenant colonel had been both Noriega's personal secretary and the head of Panamanian Defense Forces' military intelligence unit called G-2. Malman also asserted that del Cid surrendered to U.S. troops only after he had been hopelessly surrounded and outgunned. The portrait of del Cid was sinister, its effect electric. The media reported the accusations unquestioningly.

But less than two weeks later Samuel Burstyn brought his client back to court and told the judge he simply couldn't understand what Malman was talking about. Burstyn said his client insisted he had never run G-2, and he produced a statement from Noriega himself that said, "At no time was Lt. Col. Luis del Cid head of intelligence or the G-2 branch of the Panamanian Defense Forces. At no time was Lt. Col. Luis del Cid my personal secretary." As far as del Cid's surrender at the barrel of a gun, Burstyn said the U.S. Army could verify that del Cid had telephoned the American command long distance from the City of David offering to lay down his arms and give up.

The government's embarrassment could not be hidden.

"When I said del Cid was the head of intelligence, I misspoke," Malman admitted to the judge. But del Cid was the friend of the man who had held the intelligence post, Malman said, trying to minimize the mistake.

In fact, said Malman, offering the court a photograph of del Cid, Noriega, and Fidel Castro, del Cid had once carried out a highly sensitive mission for Noriega. In 1984 he had accompanied Noriega to Havana where Noriega asked Castro to help arrange a reconciliation between himself and the Medellín cartel. Obviously, Malman asserted, del Cid was Noriega's right-hand man.

Del Cid, Burstyn responded, was only a part of a long-arranged diplomatic mission to Cuba. The photograph, which like Noriega's mug shot soon appeared on the front page of the *Miami Herald*, was clearly the government's attempt to "inflame" Dade County's anti-Castro Cubans and the potential jury pool, Burstyn charged. He asserted that del Cid would demand his right to a speedy trial, which was to begin within seventy days of his arraignment.

"We don't claim that he worked with the CIA," Burstyn told the judge. "We don't need any classified documents. They [the government] have no idea who this lieutenant colonel is. They feel because he was seen at times with General Noriega . . . [that] he's like Attila the Hun."

The government's rejoinder came the next day, but not in court. Burstyn had called to the witness stand two sisters who now lived in Miami but who had once lived in Nicaragua; they had fled that country with del Cid's assistance. They spoke of del Cid's help and praised his character. The next day federal Immigration and Naturalization agents knocked at their door and demanded to see their immigration documents.

"Obviously this immigration inquiry was not a routine or ordinary investigation," Burstyn later complained to Judge Hoeveler. "The timing reflects vividly that this is a retaliatory measure aimed at intimidating these and other defense witnesses."

At this point the administration and its prosecutors needed more time to make its case. The hope and expectation in the Miami U.S. attorney's office and at Main Justice was that the invasion would turn up the evidence which would directly link Noriega and his codefendants to drug trafficking. Special teams of Justice Department lawyers and Defense Department document specialists had been dispatched to Panama immediately. Within a few days of the invasion, more than a dozen agents and attorneys from the FBI, Immigration Service, Customs, the DEA, and the international office of the Justice Department's Criminal Division were in Panama sifting through documents. Almost all were fluent in Spanish, and they had the assistance of military computer operators. Fifty tons of documents were captured. The materials filled seven rooms of a U.S. military warehouse, covering six thousand linear feet of shelf space. In Miami and Washington the prosecutors worked to identify high-priority subject categories that would assist their case. Each document was compared against the priority categories, identified, and indexed if relevant.

Among the items American agents had gathered during the invasion were

Noriega's personal papers, PDF personnel files and intelligence files, government and personal financial records of Noriega and the codefendants. The new Panamanian government also began handing over bank and telephone records almost immediately. "Realize there were two cases," explained Thomas Cash, the DEA special agent in charge of the Miami division, "the case before the invasion, when we had little, and the case after the invasion when we gained access to Panama." Yet few new leads were uncovered. There was no obvious paper trail to corroborate the grand jury testimony of Carlton, Olarte, or Blandon. Even the capture of Noriega's personal papers and documents had not strengthened the case.

What the seizure of the documents had done, however, was open up new questions about the role of the U.S. military in seizing potential evidence, a job usually designated for law enforcement. Even though the Justice Department had sent lawyers and agents to Panama with the invasion force to make sure records were not tainted or compromised, the invasion was still not a police action aimed at gathering and preserving evidence but a military action.

Rubino would argue that any documents seized in Panama were evidence illegally seized. Their use would violate the Fourth Amendment protection against illegal searches and seizures. (Courts had generally refused to admit improperly obtained evidence even though at that moment the U.S. Supreme Court had before it a case which argued that constitutional guarantees did not apply outside the boundaries of the United States.) Rubino asserted that if the Army gathered any so-called evidence which was not in plain view, then it had gathered that evidence illegally. He noted that the Americans had not bothered to obtain search warrants either from U.S. or Panamanian courts. Doors were broken down and offices and houses ransacked. "I highly doubt they will be admissible in court. Rules of evidence don't provide for armed troops to kick your doors down and seize evidence for use in a criminal case," he said.

Perhaps of greater concern was the reality that some evidence may have been destroyed or stolen. Panamanian citizens had been hard upon the heels of U.S. soldiers going into Noriega's offices and homes. Some carried off Noriega's personal belongings. Within days of the invasion, relatives of U.S. soldiers living in California were offering for sale Noriega memorabilia, including stationery, business cards, telephone logs, and letters. Who could tell what may have been hidden away, lost, or destroyed?

And at the specially established U.S. document-processing center at Fort Amador in Panama City, Army intelligence officials said they became concerned the day following the invasion when CIA personnel told members of the Army's 407th Military Intelligence Brigade to vacate the building. Some suspected the CIA agents cleared the building so that they could rummage through files before anyone else knew what was there or what was missing.

The defense did not have to be reminded of Prosecutor Richard Gregorie's experience. As he testified before the U.S. Senate in 1988, documents pertaining to the Noriega investigation had been boxed up at the United States Embassy in Panama City and sent to Miami, but when the box was opened at the other end, the documents were missing. As the defense also argued, captured documents could cut both ways. Just as they might show the involvement of Noriega and the codefendants in drug trafficking, they might also show Noriega's efforts to stop drug running and to cooperate with American law enforcement agents.

With reports that no effort had been made to protect Noriega's offices and home from looters and because no assurance could be given that the United States had acted to prevent the stealing or destruction of documents, Daniel Miranda's attorney, Michael O'Kane, bluntly accused the government of ineptness. "The government has shown that it cannot act responsibly to preserve these documents," he charged in a motion asking the judge to step in. O'Kane proposed that the National Archives should oversee the document collection and storage process.

Steve Kollin, one of Noriega's lawyers, told the judge he did not know if documents had been destroyed, but he wanted to make sure that none were. He said some documents in the government's possession certainly would show that Noriega had acted to slow drug trafficking. In particular, Kollin said, there were papers at the Departmento Nacional de Investigaciones, the Panamanian equivalent of the FBI, that would show how Noriega had assisted the United States. Those records should be turned over to the defense, he said.

Even though Judge Hoeveler had placed legal questions of preserving evidence in the hands of Miami federal magistrate William Turnoff, who from early January 1990 monitored the government's efforts to catalog and identify evidence and documents to be handed over to the court and defense, by early February the lawyers grew suspicious that the government was not doing its best.

Kollin charged that U.S. military personnel had stolen documents and other evidence. "We are now aware that items are being misplaced and mishandled purposefully," he told Magistrate Turnoff. "In other words, they are being stolen by members of the U.S. military occupation forces in Panama. We are concerned that things that are critical to the defense, including intelligence documents, will not be there when we go to take our own inventory." Turnoff was sympathetic to the prosecutor's assertions that they were working as hard, as fast, and as honestly as they could ("Due to the recent events in Panama, evidence is still being gathered and analyzed," one government motion said), but he ordered the government to catalog the items belonging to Noriega that had been seized in the invasion. Nothing, he said, was to be destroyed or turned over to the Panamanian government until Noriega's lawyers and the lawyers of the codefendants had the opportunity to determine its relevance to the defense. Still, the government's slowness in processing evidence grated on defense counsel.

"My guy's been sitting in jail since October 1, and now they're procrastinating," said Steven Kreisberg, the defense lawyer for William Saldarriaga, a codefendant who had been arrested in Miami even before the invasion. "It's hard for us to prepare for trial without getting the discovery. This is just a further example of their unpreparedness to go to trial."

That unpreparedness was perhaps more profound than the defense imagined. The Malman gaffe about del Cid and the G-2 reflected the prosecution's basic ignorance about what Sullivan called "the big picture in Panama. We [didn't] know all the identities of all these other parties who were important in the case," he complained. "We just know so little." It wasn't Malman's fault, Sullivan knew. DEA was on the scene in Panama. The agents had supplied the information on del Cid, and they were wrong. "You tend to lose confidence in your sources of information," Sullivan said.

Sullivan and Malman knew they were drowning in still disorganized facts. Twice a day, once in the morning and once in the evening, Sullivan and Malman would sit down and talk about the case. On Fridays and on the weekend they would be joined by James McAdams, who for all practical purposes had taken up residence in a hotel across the street from Main Justice in Washington. McAdams was now spending four days a week coordinating the secret document search in Washington, returning to Miami on the last flight each Thursday evening.

Two books about Noriega's rule of Panama had appeared within a week of the invasion, one by *Wall Street Journal* reporter Frederick Kempe and the other by National Public Radio editor John Dinges. Both had been months in preparation, and the prosecution pored over them, dog-earring and tagging the pages. Sullivan and Malman also launched into David McCullough's history of the construction of the Panama Canal, *The Path Between the Seas*, even though the book stopped fifty years short of Noriega's ascension to power.

Sullivan called all of the prosecutors and agents in Miami together. There were a thousand leads to follow, he told them: witnesses sitting in jail, informant files, the files in Panama. The prosecution would be divided into teams. A young, up and coming assistant U.S. attorney in the office, Guy Lewis, twenty-nine, had been added to the trial team. Sullivan, Malman, and Lewis would divide up the major witnesses and codefendants. Each would be responsible for developing a part of the case and coordinating with the DEA and FBI agents who were investigating leads. McAdams, working in Washington, would continue to head the document search, teaming up with Michael Olmsted, who was already on the assistant attorney general's staff at Main Justice.

With the initial flurry of Noriega's first court appearance past, Sullivan met with DEA SAC Tom Cash and agents Ken Kennedy and Thomas Raffanello. The investigation needed serious teeth, Sullivan told them. The case was too shallow. Cash, a DEA veteran, wasted little time. He ordered Kennedy and Raffanello to take charge of a special team set up just to assist the Noriega prosecutors. It was dubbed Group Nine. While traditional DEA investigative units were made up of a dozen agents, Group Nine had twenty.

Raffanello was given day-to-day charge of the Miami investigators. He set up a separate office for Group Nine, ordered that every request from the prosecutors be recorded and followed up in writing, that every witness lead be pursued. Within days, a new six-man special documents team was sent to Panama. Within a few months, more than five hundred interviews of potential witnesses had been conducted from California to France to South Korea. Later, Raffanello would only half joke: "Every chicken in Panama was counted."

Together, the investigators and prosecutors began fashioning a prosecution profile. The profile included the names of witnesses, defendants, and subject areas that might be contained in the volumes of documents being studied in Panama and Washington. Agents would need names and dates to help in the investigation.

"We're looking for all kinds of leads," Sullivan told Raffanello's investigators, "for those documents that have some relevance to the case. We're looking for documents that could be the smoking gun either for or against us." What we need today may change tomorrow, Sullivan told them.

"It was a massive, massive undertaking," Sullivan recollected. "The major problem in the case was management of information—keeping everyone updated so you could make decisions about what was relevant, incriminatory or exculpatory information. We were looking for anything that contradicted the testimony of our witnesses, anything that would corroborate our witnesses."

On Wednesday, March 14, less than two months after the invasion and only a month since the first legal challenges to admissibility of evidence gathered in Panama were filed, the U.S. Supreme Court ruled that the Constitution's protection against unreasonable search and seizures did not apply to foreigners outside the United States. The decision, which overturned a 1988 Federal Appeals Court case, *United States v. Verdugo-Urquidez*, came in the marijuana smuggling case of René Martin Verdugo-Urquidez, a Mexican who was also convicted of a role in the kidnap and torture-murder in Mexico of U.S. drug agent Enrique Camarena. Evidence of Verdugo-Urquidez's drug smuggling was uncovered in a warrantless search of his Mexican home. The 5-to-4 decision was seen by many as little less than a slightly disguised boost to the Bush administration's effort in Panama. One defense attempt to undermine the government case was short-lived.

Chief Justice William Rehnquist, in writing for the Court's majority, said the Fourth Amendment, when adopted in 1791, was not "intended to restrain the actions of the federal government against aliens outside of the U.S. territory."

The opinion did not refer directly to Panama but certainly came close, especially in noting two of the very reasons the president had given for launching the invasion. "The United States frequently employs armed forces

outside this country—over two hundred times in our history—for the protection of American citizens or national security," Rehnquist wrote.
"Application of the Fourth Amendment to those circumstances could significantly disrupt the ability of the political branches to respond to foreign situations involving national interest."

But Justice William Brennan, Jr., in a dissent, said it was unfair for the
United States to trample on the rights of foreigners. "When we tell the world
that we expect all people, wherever they may be, to abide by our laws, we cannot in the same breath tell the world that our law enforcement officers need
not do the same. By respecting the rights of foreign nationals, we encourage
other nations to respect the rights of our citizens. If we seek respect for law
and order, we must observe these principles ourselves. Lawlessness breeds
lawlessness."

Attorney General Thornburgh said the decision would "clarify and assist"
U.S. law enforcement in overseas drug cases. He added, "Drug traffickers and
terrorists will take no cheer from the Court's opinion."

And because there was no distinction, the Court said, between foreign
searches and arrests, attacks on the court jurisdiction filed by both Rubino
and Burstyn had all but evaporated.

Del Cid's defense lawyer, Samuel Burstyn, called the Court's ruling "the
death knell for any jurisdiction attack" in the Noriega case. "The last remaining challenge to the power of the court to proceed with this case has just
gone out the window," he said.

But there was still the issue of classified information. Soon Sullivan came
to Judge Hoeveler and asked that a tight rein be placed on defense disclosures
and requests for government files. Specifically, Sullivan asked Hoeveler to
promulgate rules under a federal law called the Classified Information
Procedures Act, or CIPA, that would prohibit defense lawyers from disclosing
matters involving classified information.

Strict procedures for releasing sensitive documents that might show
Noriega's involvement with the CIA and the DEA or other government agencies was necessary, said Sullivan. Many government records classified "Top
Secret" would likely be sought and "could reasonably be expected to cause
serious damage to the national security of the United States" if released, he
said. Without specific guidelines in place, Sullivan told Hoeveler, the government would have to come to the judge every time a bit of classified information was disclosed. More important, Sullivan argued, "the unauthorized
disclosure and uncontrolled dissemination of such information would cause
exceptionally grave damage to the national security."

CIPA was a 1980 law that not only mandated the safe handling of secret
information in court but also required that requests for sensitive information
and arguments about their relevance in a case be made in closed hearings.
Under CIPA, the government would be required to conduct a thorough
search of its records in an effort to uncover information useful to the defense.
The judge would determine whether the records sought, if found to exist,

were in fact necessary or relevant. By Wednesday, February 8, both the government and the defense had taken preliminary measure of what their CIPA cases were likely to be.

McAdams, working in Washington, had determined that there were tens of thousands of classified government documents to be reviewed. Not only had his investigators been searching for documents that fit the prosecution profile of information needed to boost the government's case, but they had also been seeking information that the government would be required by law to reveal to the defense lawyers. Under what had come to be called the Brady rule or due process doctrine, the prosecution was required to disclose to the defense evidence "favorable to the accused." A 1963 U.S. Supreme Court ruling in *Brady v. Maryland* had mandated that prosecutors who failed to turn over such exculpatory evidence, even if not specifically requested by the defense, could be found to have violated a defendant's right to due process. In turn, the defense was obliged to help the prosecution understand exactly what it needed. But in telling prosecutors what it wanted, the defense, to varying degrees, also could be put in the position of exposing its case. Even though federal rules of criminal procedure required neither the government nor the defense to reveal the outlines of its case in advance, to some extent CIPA was bound to help each side predict its opponent's course of action.

By early February, Rubino, who with the departure of Ray Takiff and Neal Sonnett was clearly in command of the defense, signed on two other attorneys. One was Jon May, thirty-four, an intense former federal prosecutor who with his wife had a small appellate practice in downtown Miami. May was not a criminal trial lawyer by any stretch of the imagination. He had built a solid reputation in the appellate section of the U.S. attorney's office before striking out on his own, and his practice now centered on helping trial lawyers build and submit appeals on their clients' convictions. Like most appellate lawyers, May had a bookish, scholarly appreciation of the law and an understanding of how missed opportunities at trial could help reverse a conviction.

In late January, Rubino, with the media widely second-guessing his ability to handle a case as complex as Noriega's, also added David Lewis, a New York criminal defense lawyer with experience in handling classified information cases. Lewis, who had defended CIA renegade Edwin Wilson, the so-called "Pizza Connection" heroin trafficker and IRA gunrunner, was a rotund, bearded man cut from the classic New York defense lawyer mold.

At a February 8 hearing, McAdams spoke first about the government's search for relevant secret documents. He said he and Michael Olmsted, who joined him at the prosecution table, were making their best effort to discover what files the government had pertaining to Noriega and his codefendants. Justice Department lawyers had even been dispatched to the CIA headquarters in Langley, Virgina, McAdams said, but by his best guess so far they had reviewed less than one-third of what was there.

McAdams said the time had come for the defense to make its requests—as specific as possible—for the documents they believed the government had.

Such requests would, in turn, under CIPA, give the government thirty days to determine whether it had the items sought. Then a special hearing could be set at which the defense, the prosecution, and the judge would determine the relevance of the documents to the case. The first CIPA hearing could take place in July, and perhaps by September all of the parties involved would be ready for trial, McAdams estimated.

Defense counsel David Lewis immediately contradicted McAdams's prognostication. "It would be almost impossible," Lewis told the judge, "to guess what schedule this process will follow. There's a tremendous amount of exculpatory material that the United States has. You're in what we call in my practice a megatrial," Lewis told Hoeveler. The defense did not intend to start by seeking specific documents, Lewis said. Instead, "My intention is to file a CIPA notice in the broadest way." The search for evidence, Lewis said, would include, among other things, requests for intercepts of Noriega's conversations by the National Security Agency. Those intercepts, Lewis said, would include "a series of wiretaps" of conversations recorded by the NSA, conversations between Noriega and ambassador-level officials that would show Noriega's direct participation in joint drug-enforcement actions between the United States and Panama. That evidence, Lewis said, would go "straight to the heart of the defense." NSA interceptions had never been turned over for trial use, Lewis told Hoeveler, but then again, this was no ordinary case.

Lewis said he expected a fight from the government, and that would take time. In the Oliver North case, the document-request process had ground on for nine months. This case was likely to be no different, he said. Noriega had received foreign intelligence over the years, and that would need to be reviewed—intelligence not only from the United States but also from Israel and Libya and many other countries. "This case will not be before a jury for a minimum of one year to eighteen months," he said. "This trial is not going to be an ordinary trial. This is a megatrial. I know in my heart the government's estimate is not realistic." Most important, said Lewis, some way must be found to construct a Chinese wall between the prosecution and the defense so that the prosecution could not prepare its case by studying the documents that the defense requested.

Rubino stood next to Lewis. "Your Honor," he said, "the pretrial motion stage will take ninety to one hundred and twenty days. We have extensive memorandums of law to litigate. It will take David Lewis nine months to a year to get the documents he will need," Rubino continued. "After that it will take us six months to go out and conduct interviews. We are requesting eighteen to twenty-four months to go to trial. Right now we will execute a waiver of speedy trial."

Behind Noriega's lawyers sat lawyers for five of Noriega's codefendants. Samuel Burstyn spoke for the group when he rose behind Rubino and said, "Your Honor, what we've seen here today is the tip of the iceberg as to what a trial of General Noriega will mean." If Noriega's codefendants were to get a fair and speedy trial as they were entitled to, Burstyn said, their cases were going to have to be tried separately, their cases severed from Noriega's.

Richard Sharpstein, the lawyer for Brian Davidow, the only American among the codefendants, stood beside Burstyn. His client had no need for classified documents or government secrets, he said. To drag along a codefendant who had never even met General Noriega but had somehow been implicated in this conspiracy was patently unfair, Sharpstein said. Davidow, Sharpstein told the judge, could be found guilty for simply sitting in the same courtroom with a man who had been vilified by the president of the United States. It was guilt by association.

"There may be several defendants sitting here," said Sharpstein, "who are not interested in CIPA issues. CIPA will enormously elongate this case. We have been announcing that we are ready for trial. Maybe at this point, Judge, the roads should part." Sharpstein wore cowboy boots, and his hair was stylishly combed back.

There was one other thing, he said. "Usually you have the spillover effect," he said, referring to the detrimental impact a well-known defendant can have on other, lesser-known codefendants. "In this case, it's the atomic bomb effect." Sharpstein looked at Noriega, who sat motionless, his head resting on his palm, listening to a translation of the proceedings through a translator's headset. "Everyone within a thousand miles gets killed," Sharpstein said. The gallery behind the defendants was packed with reporters. Sharpstein had just delivered the quotable line of the day.

Sullivan rose for the government. To separately try codefendants brought together in the same indictment and alleged to have participated in the same conspiracy would be time-consuming and wasteful, he said. In essence, separate trials would mean trying the same facts and presenting the same evidence and witnesses twice, asking two juries to do the job of one, asking the judge and the prosecutors to do twice what could be done once.

"The government contends that they"—Sullivan turned and pointed to the defense table where the five codefendants, including General Noriega, sat squeezed together with their lawyers—"were indicted together so they should stand trial together. They carried out instructions from the top, and they should stand trial together. The government does not believe they should be severed."

As the judge was about to speak, Rubino rose. Because the preparation of the general's case would take as long as two years, Rubino said, his client would provide an affidavit or testimony, if necessary, attesting to the codefendants' lack of criminal involvement. Noriega would do this, Rubino said, if severance were granted.

Rubino's offer was a tactical move. If a separate and earlier trial for the codefendants took place, Rubino knew that Noriega might gain an advantage at his own trial. A trial of one or more of the codefendants would expose the weaknesses and strengths of the government's evidence and witnesses before Noriega's turn came. The allegations against Noriega bisected the charges against each of the other codefendants at one point or another. The grand jury witnesses who had implicated the codefendants had also accused Noriega. A separate trial of del Cid, in particular, would certainly mean that Noriega's lawyers would get a look at Floyd Carlton, the government's key witness against both del Cid and Noriega.

Carlton had accused del Cid of delivering $200,000 in drug proceeds to Noriega. Watching Carlton on the witness stand under direct and cross-examination could open up new avenues of defense for Rubino. It was in Noriega's interest to help the codefendants win severance.

But the odds were with the government, however. There were too many defendants and not enough judges and courtrooms. If there was a way to try the defendants in one indictment all together, Hoeveler had an obligation to do so.

Hoeveler was not impressed by the statements that placed the start of the trial two years off. Ten lawyers in one courtroom equaled a great deal of posturing. In short order, evidence would begin to manifest itself, and all sides would gain a more realistic notion of when a trial could begin. The judge warned, "I will say this: Motions will be made, and I will rule. It's important that this case not flounder. I do propose to go forward. If expansion is needed, expansion will be granted . . . but in no event will this trial start later than January 1991," he ended.

That morning as Noriega had entered the courtroom accompanied by two deputy U.S. marshals, he had paused to shake hands with Luis del Cid, already seated at the defense table. It was the first meeting between the two since their capture. Noriega still wore his general's uniform, crisply pressed. He had regained some of the color in his face, color that had seemed all but drained at his arraignment. His hair was coal black without a hint of gray. His demeanor and bearing had returned.

Del Cid, by contrast, was slouched and apparently still bewildered by all that was transpiring around him. He parted his hair on the right. It was casually pushed back from his rounded face. As he sat at the defense table, his paunchy middle-aged stomach seemed to hang forlorn. Yet when Noriega entered and offered his hand, del Cid immediately rose to his feet, still a lieutenant colonel to the general; there was the snap to attention. For a moment they were again commander and officer taking up a common defense.

Already, though, Del Cid's lawyer, Samuel Burstyn, had approached the prosecutors about cutting a possible plea bargain that would allow del Cid to plead guilty to one of the five counts against him in exchange for the government's dropping the other charges. Burstyn had defended scores of alleged drug traffickers, and he knew that whatever the government's evidence, del Cid was in trouble. The indictment accused del Cid of drug smuggling, racketeering, and conspiracy, saying that he was a go-between and bagman for

Noriega. Conviction on all counts with the maximum sentence meant del Cid faced seventy years in prison. If the forty-seven-year-old-former soldier was ever going to spend any time with his wife and children again, the chances were good that he was going to have to turn on Noriega. If he was not severed from Noriega and Noriega was convicted, then del Cid was bound to take a very hard fall. A good defense lawyer, Burstyn believed, never ruled out a plea, given the right offer.

The key to keeping del Cid out of prison for the rest of his life, Burstyn figured, was making sure the government knew there was serious interest in a deal. The next step was keeping the pressure on. Malman's gaffe over del Cid's leadership of the G-2 was a godsend. In court, Burstyn could hold the government's feet to the fire. They don't know what they've got or what he's done, Burstyn told the judge, the press, and anyone else who would listen. From the start, Burstyn led the charge, filing a pleading, questioning the court's jurisdiction, the legality of the invasion, and the U.S. Army's right to search and seizure in Panama. He hoped that in the end it would all add up.

For the government, the formula for dealing with del Cid and the other codefendants was clear. Whatever happened and no matter how it happened, the case had to equal a Noriega conviction. Anything less was not enough.

Sullivan, Lehtinen, and Malman had known for almost a year how weak the indictment was. But Malman and Lehtinen had promised Main Justice a 90 percent chance of conviction before the invasion because they had counted on turning, or flipping, codefendants. They would not approach any codefendant or Noriega himself with an offer, but neither would they turn away anyone who wanted to talk. The prosecutors knew the best way to fortify the case—apart from the efforts already under way to document wrongdoing—was to cut deals with codefendants.

Burstyn made his first move within days of Noriega's capture. His client could help the government's case against Noriega, he told Lehtinen. Del Cid might not have been the head of G-2, but he could make a government deal worth its while. Del Cid would plead to one count and testify against Noriega. When Lehtinen came back with a tough counter—guilty plea to two of the counts with a total exposure of forty years—Burstyn decided to wait.

For Sullivan and the prosecutors, del Cid was not the only game in town. In Panama, the U.S. military had detained 5,200 Panamanians for questioning following the invasion. By mid-January most of those had been released, but at least 130 Noriega loyalists still remained in custody, most high PDF officers or civilian officials. There was always hope that one might lead investigators to an undiscovered bonanza of new information and evidence.

In Miami, Sullivan, Malman, and Lewis divvied up the indictment's main witnesses and set about learning all they could from them. First, that meant one- to two-hour telephone calls to the prisons or Witness Protection Program sites around the country where they had been sent.

Floyd Carlton, whose name was repeatedly cited in the indictment, was among the first interviewed by Sullivan. Carlton's grand jury testimony had helped him get his own drug-trafficking sentence reduced. His demeanor was even-keeled and matter-of-fact. He was believable, Sullivan decided.

In 1986, Carlton told a Senate committee that if drug smuggling happened in Panama, then Noriega knew about it. "He would deal with God and the devil at the same time," Carlton said of Noriega. "Nothing can be done in Panama without Noriega's approval—that is, if you want to be successful."

Malman contacted former Noriega loyalist and adviser José Blandon, the man Noriega had acrimoniously dismissed as Panama's New York consul general in early 1988. Blandon was also sure of himself but a little too pat, Malman thought. When his grand jury testimony was compared to Carlton's, dates and events didn't match. One of the two had been wrong.

Defense lawyer Frank Rubino said of Blandon: "He said one thing in Panama and changed his tune here in America. It seems whoever feeds him is the person he cheers on."

Malman's prediction that witnesses would "come out of the woodwork" once Noriega was in custody proved true. Suddenly every two-bit dope trafficker stuck in the Metropolitan Correctional Center outside of Miami, south Florida's federal lockup, had a Noriega story to tell and to trade time for. But no offer was more surprising than one that came in mid-January from Carlos Lehder, the cofounder of the Medellín cartel who had been convicted of cocaine smuggling in Jacksonville, Florida, in 1988 and sentenced to life in prison without parole plus 135 years. Lehder, through his lawyer, invited prosecutor Guy Lewis and DEA agent Henry Cuervo to visit him at the federal prison in Marion, Illinois.

There were some, however, who simply could not help the government as much as they might have liked. Richard Sharpstein, codefendant Brian Davidow's lawyer, said his client, after being given all the talk about plea bargaining, found himself at a disadvantage. Davidow had never met or spoken to Noriega, Sharpstein said, so he had nothing to bargain with. Michael O'Kane, codefendant Daniel Miranda's lawyer, said his client also was at a disadvantage given the flurry of plea bargain talk. "My client has nothing to say about Noriega," O'Kane told reporters. "He doesn't know him and never met him."

O'Kane still insisted that was true on Thursday, February 15, when Eduardo Pardo, the pilot Miranda had flown with from Fort Lauderdale to Panama, went to court and became the first codefendant in the case to enter a plea of guilty. Trembling and near tears, Pardo, forty-four, admitted that he had worked for Floyd Carlton, Noriega's chief accuser, and that the plane he and Miranda had flown to Panama from Fort Lauderdale contained "secret compartments" filled with drug proceeds. Pardo's guilty plea corroborated parts of Carlton's grand jury testimony. That corroboration would be the prosecution's first step in making Carlton a more credible witness at trial. In a few short minutes, Pardo had reduced his jail time exposure from seventy years to ten. And ironically, given the federal guidelines for jail time—if the defense was correct about pretrial work taking as long as two years—Pardo could be out of jail in time to sit in the courtroom and watch the Noriega trial as an observer.

After watching Pardo enter his guilty plea in court, Frank Rubino said, "If Mr. Pardo tells the truth, he can't hurt us."

Even with the Pardo plea and the progress in reaching a plea agreement with del Cid, Pat Sullivan still sensed that there simply was not enough evidence to get a Noriega conviction. It was already a full-time job keeping pace with the rush of defense motions and court hearings, and directing the debriefing of witnesses. Now Sullivan thought maybe the right strategy would be to combine the Miami and Tampa allegations into one big superseding indictment that would cover all of the bases.

The three-count Tampa indictment accused Noriega of assisting a U.S.-based marijuana smuggling operation in return for about $1 million in payments. Sullivan set about learning all he could about the Tampa case, hoping there was a thread that would tie the two together, perhaps enough to repackage the charges with those in Miami to make a juggernaut case which the defense would have trouble surmounting, if not in whole then at least in part.

Sullivan found that the main Tampa witness, Steven Kalish, had been intimately involved in the facts of both cases. Kalish had grown up in Houston and spent his aborted high school career selling marijuana to classmates. After dropping out of school, he had gone on to make hundreds of millions of dollars smuggling dope. At the height of his drug career he admitted to overseeing a two-hundred-person smuggling organization. The business was so lucrative, he later testified, that "currency filled entire rooms. . . . We used money-counting machines, but we could not keep up with the volume."

By the early 1980s, Kalish started shipping cash in batches of $2 million to $3 million from Tampa to Panama, where it could be laundered through dummy bank accounts. The huge influx of money garnered the attention of Noriega, the PDF *comandante* since the death of Gen. Omar Torrijos in 1981. According to the Tampa prosecutors, in the early 1980s, Noriega and Kalish met and conspired, along with Enrique "Kiki" Pretelt, a Panama City jeweler, to smuggle marijuana into the United States. Kalish, the indictment said, paid bribes to Noriega to get the proceeds laundered in Panama. The Tampa indictment, based almost exclusively on Kalish's testimony, also alleged that Noriega and Pretelt had banded together with Kalish to smuggle 1.4 million pounds of marijuana into the United States.

Sullivan also discovered that Kalish claimed to have direct knowledge of Noriega's involvement with the Medellín cartel and events related in the Miami indictment. Kalish's drug dealings had brought him a web of Central American underworld friends. When the cartel's newly established cocaine-processing lab in Darien, Panama, was raided by the PDF in May 1984, the cartel dispatched an envoy to Kalish. Could Kalish help the cartel get in touch with Noriega and find out why a $5 million payoff had not bought protection for the lab as intended?

Kalish was surprised by the visit but also recognized it as an opportunity to ingratiate himself with the cartel and perhaps open new avenues of business. Kalish introduced the cartel's messenger to César Rodríguez, Noriega's old pal. In short order Rodríguez learned that the cartel's $5 million payoff had gone to PDF Col. Julian Melo, who was Noriega's top military aide.

According to Kalish, Noriega was informed of the double-cross, and though he was traveling in Europe, had Melo discharged from the PDF. He also had the drug lab workers who had been captured in the Darien raid released and sent home to Colombia without being charged. Kalish claimed that the cartel's envoy later told him that Noriega had ordered the repayment of the $5 million as well as the return of a helicopter seized in the raid. Kalish said the cartel then paid him $500,000 for helping to straighten out the mess.

Events surrounding the Darien lab were the basis for two of the twelve counts against Noriega in the Miami indictment. To Sullivan, who ended up spending much of the first six months of 1990 tracing Kalish's involvement with Noriega, that was all the more reason to combine the Tampa and Miami indictments. He began pushing for a reindictment, but the effort turned into a hard sell. It turned out that time was working against him. Though Lehtinen, Malman, the Tampa prosecutors, and finally Main Justice agreed that a superseding indictment could become a substantial step in ensuring a Noriega conviction, the statute of limitations had almost run out.

Under the statute of limitations covering conspiracy, the government's charges had to be delivered within five years of the alleged wrongdoing. The 1988 indictments included activities stretching back to 1983, but if Noriega and others were reindicted in 1990, then the activities charged would have had to occur since 1985. A new indictment would have to exclude the events surrounding the Darien lab. Only the conspiracy to ship drugs aboard the yacht *Krill*, as alleged in the indictment, would fit into a new indictment's time frame. In the end, a superseding indictment wouldn't work, Sullivan decided. That was too bad, he thought, because as he looked further and further into Noriega's actions during the 1980s, Sullivan found that he was also guilty of something else the defense was bound to seize upon—cooperation. Sullivan said, "While we indicted Noriega for supplying ether to Colombia, actually what was going on was that the PDF was seizing hundreds of thousands of gallons of ether that was being transshipped through Panama on the way to Colombia and destroying it."

There was a real puzzle here, Sullivan thought. Hadn't Gregorie and Schnapp recognized that Noriega cooperated with the DEA in interdicting chemical shipments through Panama? The indictment accused Noriega of allowing ether to move through Panama to Colombia, but both U.S. and PDF records showed that Noriega had directed the seizure and destruction of hundreds and hundreds of gallons of drug-processing chemicals destined for the cartel.

As Sullivan went through files being uncovered in Panama and

Washington, he grew worried. "It just cuts the wrong way," he thought, "when you are trying to say that Noriega was allowing ether to be trans-shipped." Some fine distinctions were going to have to be made. A winning prosecution was not going to be easy. There was no way this case could go to trial for at least a year, Sullivan told himself by the middle of April. No way.

CHAPTER 12

★★★★★★

A Prisoner of War

On February 8, one month and four days after he was arraigned, Noriega was back in Judge William Hoeveler's courtroom.

Once again he sat impassively, staring straight ahead. Occasionally the former dictator adjusted the headphones that a translator had given him shortly after he entered through the side door. Surrounded by deputy marshals, the deposed general refused to look around or acknowledge that the visitors' gallery was packed with reporters all craning to get a glimpse of him.

Again, Noriega was dressed in his general's uniform—smartly pressed green army slacks and beige short-sleeved shirt with four gold stars on each shoulder. After a month of near isolation in the courthouse holding cell downstairs, the general looked remarkably rested. The glaze of strain and bewilderment that had been so apparent the day of his arraignment on January 4 had slipped away. Now Noriega seemed engaged with the work of his attorneys. But still he looked impassively at the courtroom deputies who flanked the bench. It was as though he refused to acknowledge that he was at the mercy of the court.

At 9:35, Judge Hoeveler strode up the stairs from his chambers and took the bench. Seated, Hoeveler looked at the prosecution table and then to the defense. He formally opened the hearing. "All right. I am going to call the case of *United States versus Noriega* and others," he said. "It is 88-79. Would counsel announce their appearances."

Pat Sullivan stood and introduced himself. He then turned to introduce Myles Malman and James McAdams. He also introduced the attorney general's representative, William Bryson, who had arrived from Washington early that morning.

Seven days earlier, on January 27, Noriega's lead attorney, Frank Rubino, had set the prosecution on its heels by coming to court and declaring the deposed general a prisoner of war. The move came after the government, to avoid possible appeal, asked Hoeveler to take up the issue of bond for Noriega. Rubino and Steven Kollin had conceded that the court would never set their client free to await trial. Still, a bond hearing might, at best, Rubino thought, end with the disclosure of a government document or two that the defense knew nothing about. Any such revelations might give the defense a look at what the government planned to use against their man at trial.

Since federal rules of evidence allow prosecutors to effectively—if not quite ethically—keep secret incriminating evidence until just before the commencement of trial, good defense lawyers are continually looking for government lawyers to tip their hand. The alternative was lonely: to prepare the best defense one could and hustle when the government finally put its cards on the table.

Rubino decided the moment was right for high drama. After Hoeveler had called the case and after Lehtinen's assistant, Myles Malman, had briefly but strongly argued that Noriega would surely escape to an unfriendly country if freed on bond, Rubino stepped to the lectern squarely before the judge. In a strong, measured cadence he said: "His name is Manuel Antonio Noriega. His rank is four-star general. His serial number is 0001."

A murmur filled the courtroom. Not quite sure he had heard Rubino right, the judge asked, "How's that again, Mr. Rubino?"

Rubino repeated Noriega's name, rank, and serial number and then continued: "The government of the United States must immediately repatriate General Manuel Noriega to a third country or to his homeland."

A handful of reporters jumped from their seats and sped to the telephones in the elevator lobby beyond the double courtroom doors.

"General Noriega, commander in chief of the Panamanian Defense Forces of the Republic of Panama, hereby claims the status of prisoner of war," Rubino continued. General Noriega wanted to claim all of the rights, privileges, and immunities granted to prisoners of war under the Geneva Convention.

The television and newspaper sketch artists seated in the empty jury box directly across from the prosecution table looked back and forth from the prosecutors to Rubino. Reporters behind the defense and prosecution tables cupped their ears to make sure they were hearing him right.

Hoeveler shifted once, then twice, looking on sternly. Clearly this was a surprising turn of events. The defense had failed to file a motion laying out its intentions. The judge, as well as the prosecution, was caught off guard. More reporters jumped from their seats and hurried for the telephones. Rubino, knowing full well he was turning the court on its ear, straightened his tie, turned, and sat down.

As the near palpable shock finished its swirl through the courtroom, Hoeveler looked first toward Noriega, still sitting and staring ahead at the translator, and then at the prosecution. "Well," the judge said after a moment, "the matter before me today, Mr. Rubino, is the question of your client's bond."

Hoeveler paused. He seemed to be dismayed, perhaps even angry, that he had not been informed of the defense move in advance. "Your client is before me," he said. "The case is before me. Mr. Rubino, you may respond to the government's motion to deny your client bond."

Again Rubino stood. "Your Honor, most respectfully on behalf of my client, we refuse to cooperate with this court," he said.

At that, annoyance edged into Hoeveler's voice. "Well then, I am afraid I have no choice but to keep Mr. Noriega in the custody of the marshal."

The judge looked at Noriega. He paused and took a slow, deep breath. "Bond is denied," he ruled.

Within days the Bush administration and the prosecution came back with a surprise of their own.

"The United States has determined as a matter of policy that Noriega . . . should be given the protections accorded prisoners of war under the Geneva Convention," government prosecutors said in a memorandum to Judge Hoeveler filed on February 2.

The government, in short, would not object to Noriega's claiming status as a POW. The government "as a matter of policy" would not object to the defense's invocation of the Geneva Convention of 1949, which offered standards of treatment to be accorded prisoners of war. Treating Noriega as a prisoner of war, the government said, would have little effect on the general's day-to-day life in prison. Noriega could see a Red Cross representative and have a U.S. Army officer visit him to make sure his everyday needs were being taken care of, just like every other POW.

Under the convention, prisoners of war were entitled to adequate food, clothing, housing, and medical care. The seriously ill were to be repatriated. If prisoners faced trial, the convention established the right to counsel.

But Rubino and the defense, in asserting that Noriega was a prisoner of war and should be repatriated to Panama or a third country, were also prepared to argue that provisions of the Geneva Convention should allow Noriega to be tried by an international tribunal such as the World Court headquartered in Switzerland. The invasion, Rubino argued, had violated the sovereignty of the Republic of Panama. Noriega should not be tried before a U.S. judge.

The government, of course, had not missed Rubino's main point—that Noriega should go free. The prosecution's February 2 memorandum said the defense was in the wrong if it planned to demand that the court under the Geneva Convention be required to send Noriega to a neutral third country. Nothing in the Geneva Convention provided support for the contention that an American court lacked jurisdiction to try Noriega on drug-trafficking charges, the government's memorandum said; in fact, the Geneva Convention specifically allowed prisoners of war to be prosecuted in the civilian courts of a detaining country.

The question of the removal of Noriega from the jurisdiction of the court was before Judge Hoeveler. Now, on February 8, Hoeveler turned to Rubino.

"The first matter we are going to take up, Mr. Rubino," he said, "will be your motion attacking the jurisdiction of the court."

Hoeveler looked out at the courtroom over the top of his glasses.

"Motions have been made. I am ready to hear argument on them. I am ready to rule on them, if I should, and I think on this POW point I should. This case is too important to let drift."

Rubino adjusted his brown double-breasted suit jacket, cleared his throat, and moved to the lectern before the judge.

In the week since Rubino had last stood before Hoeveler and offered only his client's name, rank, and serial number, it had become increasingly clear that the defense strategy was to focus attention away from the narcotics charges against the general onto the deeper political questions. Rubino had promised from the day of Noriega's arraignment that the defense would seek classified documents detailing Noriega's long association with U.S. intelligence agencies. That would put the government on the defensive. So, at least for a while, would the POW issue.

"At no time have we ever stated that the issue before the court is one of the dismissal of the indictment," Rubino began when standing before the judge. "I want to make that point as clear as I can. We are not asking you to dismiss the indictment. The motion simply asks this court to relinquish jurisdiction."

Rubino looked to his notes jotted in longhand on a yellow legal pad. He continued: "The government says that there were four reasons for the invasion of Panama. The first was to protect American lives that had been endangered by escalated harassment and violence on the part of Noriega's regime. Well, the government failed to mention that the harassment and aggression was first committed by the United States Army. Members of the United States Army left the military bases in Panama to which they were assigned. They went out into the countryside."

Rubino spoke smoothly and extemporaneously as he looked up from his notes.

"They blockaded bridges and roads in a halfhearted effort to support a military coup against General Noriega. This was just another step in the historical effort by the United States to assist in violent overthrows of foreign governments, governments that they do not approve of."

Rubino was referring to the October 3 coup attempt by junior Panamanian military officers. The officers had seized the Maximum Leader's military headquarters in Panama City and had held it during five hours of heavy fighting. After Noriega loyalists finally crushed the takeover attempt, Noriega had gone on Panamanian television to denounce the Bush administration for supporting the effort. Even though there had been no blatant evidence of covert American support for the coup attempt, it was true that American military police in Panama City had blockaded roads near the Panama Canal administration building during the fighting.

Drawing a parallel, Rubino recollected the murder of American Army Maj. Arthur Nicholson by a Soviet soldier at a Berlin border crossing in March 1985. That incident, he said, was clearly on point. "The United States government, based on Nicholson's killing, did not invade the Soviet Union."

Still looking toward the prosecutors, Rubino chided the government's invocation of the United Nations charter and the charter of the Organization of American States to justify the American invasion. Clearly Rubino's approach was to appeal to the court's sense of fair play, reminding the judge how unfair the invasion had been.

Looking to Hoeveler, Rubino continued: "They fail to tell Your Honor that by a clear three-fourths majority, the United Nations condemned the U.S. action. They fail to tell the court, the U.S. also was condemned by the OAS."

On these points Rubino was only partly correct. The thirty-two-member Organization of American States had not actually condemned the U.S. invasion. The organization said it "regretted" the invasion. What is more, the U.N. vote had been quickly followed by signals from all but a few nations that they would willingly—despite the vote—adapt to the U.S. move against Noriega.

Pointing to Sullivan and Bryson, both taking notes, Rubino continued: "They rely on the Panama Canal Treaty, and they say that the treaty gives the U.S. government the right to invade the sovereign Republic of Panama." Wrong, said Rubino. What the 1903 treaty said was that the United States was entitled to use armed force in Panama only if armed force was being used against the canal, said Rubino. "The thing that interests me the most is that the Panama Canal, under General Manuel Antonio Noriega, was never shut down for one single minute. The canal was never shut down until the United States government invaded Panama to protect the canal. Then the United States shut it down for three days and denied the rest of the world the use of the canal. How the U.S. government can be heard to say they were protecting it so others could use it when they, in fact, shut it down defies logic."

Rubino walked to the defense table. He leaned over and picked up a copy of the government's motion.

"The United States says that 'the operation, the invasion, had the objective of assisting the lawful and democratically elected government of Panama to return to power.' The United States, in its self-appointed role as world policeman, has decided to take sides in a purely Panamanian matter," said Rubino, his voice rising. "The U.S. government has absolutely no right to intervene in the internal politics of Panama."

Rubino was glossing over Noriega's annulment of the May 7 Panamanian election results. By the accounts of nearly all international observers, the vote had easily been won by Panamanian opposition candidate Guillermo Endara. Noriega's installation of his own candidate, Francisco Rodríguez, as Panama's new civilian president drew vehement criticism from South American and North American diplomats alike. Following the sham election, many countries withdrew their ambassadors from Panama. Even with the election stolen, Noriega ordered vigilante groups known as Dignity Battalions to find and beat Endara and his two vice presidential running mates. Rubino also did not mention that after the failed October coup attempt, the dictator ordered the roundup and imprisonment or execution of dozens of his own military officers. In essence, Rubino was boldly asserting that the internal politics of Panama or any other country—whether good or bad—were no business of the United States.

"I ask by what authority does the United States swear in a new government in a foreign country other than under the theory of government by invasion?" asked Rubino.

Rubino arrived at the heart of his argument. Did the United States and this court have jurisdiction over the deposed general? Was Noriega accused of a crime for which he could be prosecuted by the American justice system? The defense's answer was no. Noriega, under international rules governing prisoners of war, absolutely could not be tried for a crime that was committed prior to armed conflict between nations. To do so would be a violation of the Geneva Convention and international law, he said.

Noriega's case should be moved beyond the reach of American law and an American court. Rubino knew full well that U.S. appeals courts, even the U.S. Supreme Court, had ruled in three fundamental cases dating back more than one hundred years that once a defendant was before an American court— almost irrespective of how he or she had gotten there, by force or not—that court had jurisdiction.

From the moment Noriega had been arrested by U.S. troops, legal scholars in the United States and around the world had publicly agreed that there was little legal justification under international law for what the United States had done. But American law said that the manner in which Noriega had been brought to the United States was valid and legal; international law would not affect the U.S. government's efforts to prosecute the general.

Besides, the official U.S. position was that Noriega had not been seized but rather had surrendered voluntarily. Had he personally been taken by force? No. He walked out of the Vatican embassy and gave up.

Still, a senior lawyer at the World Court said shortly after the general's surrender, "Go back in history about two thousand years ago. It was like the Romans leading back defeated leaders and taking them to the circus to be displayed."

Standing before Hoeveler, Rubino next pointed to the 1904 extradition treaty between Panama and the United States, a treaty still in force. The agreement cited thirteen crimes for which the two countries agreed extradition was possible, crimes such as murder, arson, robbery, forgery, counterfeiting, embezzlement, fraud, perjury, rape and piracy. Nowhere in the treaty was drug trafficking and conspiracy to deal drugs mentioned, Rubino said. "You are presented today, Your Honor, with a case of first impression of monumental implications," he continued. "If we move away from the international law of long-standing agreements with other nations, that law will be just totally reduced. The question posed to the court is more than a legal question. It is one of international policy considerations. You are being asked to set the tenor and the tone for how the world will interpret the Geneva Convention or how the rest of the free world will look at what rights prisoners have under that convention."

Rubino paused again, looked to the prosecution and then to the judge. "We have got to go into the real matter before this court, which is one of international policy, which is one of how does the United States—"

But Hoeveler sensed where Rubino was going. "Wait a minute," the judge interrupted.

Hoeveler was not about to be moved away from federal statutes and into the realm of international politics and policy. There are no federal laws regulating international invasions. "I think you are in the wrong forum when we start talking about international policy," Hoeveler said. "This is a court of law. I've got to decide the law. I don't make international policy."

But Rubino disagreed. "In all due respect," he said, "you are going to make international policy by this decision."

"Whether I like it or not?" asked the judge, pressing Rubino.

"Yes, sir," said Rubino. "Because what you are going to do is, Your Honor, you are going to decide whether we are going to strictly construe the Geneva Convention or whether we are going to, so to speak, just push it aside a little bit so we can sneak General Noriega through and try him in this court."

Raising his arms palms out toward the judge, Rubino ended matter-of-factly and with respect: "I don't envy your position, but I know you will do a good job of it."

Rubino turned toward Noriega and then back to Hoeveler. That was it. Rubino could only hope he had altered Hoeveler's ideas on how international and American law intersected. At least for the moment, Rubino could be satisfied that the defense had given the prosecution more than a routine drug case.

Under the best circumstances, a drug case is difficult to defend. Statistics show that nearly 95 percent of the defendants charged with drug-related crimes in the federal Southern District of Florida ended up entering pleas or being convicted. And Noriega was infamous to boot. But even before Rubino stood before Hoeveler, criminal defense experts had agreed that the defense of Noriega was not without hope. If the DEA wanted information at the highest levels of the most secret cocaine cartel in the world, how would they get it? They would use someone like Manuel Noriega, observed Miami federal public defender Kenneth Swartz. "It's a mountain for the defense to climb, but truth is stranger than fiction, and Manuel Noriega may have the last laugh," Schwartz said.

With Rubino seated, it was now the government's turn. Bryson, the deputy solicitor general, walked to the lectern.

"Mr. Bryson," the judge said.

With his gray suit hanging on his loose frame, Bryson stood before Judge Hoeveler and said he would be brief. "I think the basic point to be made is that, yes, we have agreed to treat General Noriega as a prisoner of war," Bryson began. "We have agreed to make the Geneva Convention provisions fully applicable to Mr. Noriega."

Bryson looked at his notes and then looked up at the judge. He held the government's twenty-four-page memorandum in his hand. The Geneva Convention clearly authorized the prosecution of crimes of the sort charged in the government's indictment, he said. If Rubino wanted to argue the Geneva Convention, Bryson was prepared. The convention clearly had contemplated that there could be prisoners of war tried for acts committed prior to their capture, for conduct that occurred prior to a prisoner's coming into the custody of a detaining power. "The crimes that are being tried here are acts that are made criminal by virtually all civilized nations," said Bryson. His practiced, closely reasoned manner bespoke his frequent appearances before the U.S. Supreme Court.

The defense, Bryson said, had read the Geneva Convention in a conveniently narrow fashion. The defense was wrong, he said. The convention and other treaties, many decades old, did not have to specifically name drug trafficking or other crimes as criminal acts for those acts to be outlawed. All nations could agree that some acts were illegal. Certainly, the recent rise of international cocaine trafficking was a perfect example.

Bryson, along with senior Justice Department lawyers in Washington, had prepared the government's arguments and memorandum. They had spent hours carefully crafting their arguments. And when Bryson spoke, he spoke for legal principles considered at the highest level of the U.S. government.

Miami prosecutors Sullivan and Malman looked on as the attorney general's man set out to refute the arguments of international law raised by the defense. The case, Bryson said, should proceed on the narrower issue of criminal liability for narcotics trafficking. Noriega's was a drug case. Noriega was a drug trafficker, pure and simple. Does international law harbor drug traffickers? Of course not.

If treaties between Panama and the United States didn't spell out the illegality of cocaine trafficking, then there were other international agreements that did, said Bryson. Both Panama and the United States had signed the Single Convention on Narcotics Drugs. That 1961 United Nations convention clearly condemned the international trafficking of illegal drugs and called on all nations to assist one another in prosecuting drug-running conspiracies that crossed international boundaries.

"I think, Mr. Bryson," Hoeveler said, interrupting, "that if I heard Mr. Rubino correctly, he is saying that he is not asking me to dismiss this case, but he thinks I ought to, under the Geneva Convention, transfer this case to some other country, maybe even to Panama."

Bryson nodded in agreement. "He argues, Your Honor, [that] he's not seeking dismissal. He says he calls it relinquishment of jurisdiction. I am hard-pressed to understand the distinction. If the court relinquishes jurisdiction over Mr. Noriega, it will have, in effect, dismissed the indictment. There isn't any proceedings pending anywhere."

Hoeveler agreed. "I think that's probably right," the judge said.

The government's response was very simple, continued Bryson. The Geneva Convention and other treaties did not bar the jurisdiction of American courts. On that point, the Justice Department had been sure before the invasion. The 1886 Illinois case of Frederick Ker, who had been brought before a Chicago court on larceny charges, was upheld by the U.S. Supreme Court. In that case, Ker had fled Illinois authorities and escaped to Peru. When state agents caught Ker in South America, they kidnapped him and brought him back to Chicago. The Supreme Court ruled that Ker's seizure, kidnapping, and subsequent conviction were legal.

International law might not be specific in recognizing the authority of civilian courts in prosecuting domestic cases, but U.S. courts, even the U.S. Supreme Court, held that American courts had the authority to try almost any cases that came before them. Noriega's case was before the court by virtue of the deposed general's presence, Bryson said.

"Is it possible for a person in General Noriega's position to occupy two statuses," asked Hoeveler, "one as a prisoner for charged crimes and the other as, if you will, a prisoner of war? Does one really cross the other at some point, or can they go down parallel streets?"

"That's exactly the point," responded Bryson, following Hoeveler's lead. "He is a defendant before this court. This court has jurisdiction over him. The court can enter orders with respect to him, but he is also a prisoner of war. The Geneva Convention says that with respect to his status as a prisoner of war, he is to be treated in the same way a military person in our armed forces would be treated. In fact, if a military officer in the United States Army had committed these crimes, he would be sitting right here in this court because the district court has parallel jurisdiction with the military courts."

That in a nutshell was the U.S. government's position. Noriega, accused of a serious crime, was being given exactly the same treatment he would be given if he had been an American military officer. That, the government said, is exactly what the Geneva Convention entitled him to. Noriega was not being singled out. He was not being treated differently. He was being treated like any other prisoner of war accused of a crime, like any other man accused of a crime in America.

And with that, Bryson stopped.

The U.S. government had Noriega, Bryson had argued. It was not—barring an order of the court and the Supreme Court—about to let him go. No one, not even the general's lawyers, should expect the United States to release Noriega on a narrow reading of a law or treaty. He would not go free on a technicality. American law allowed for the prosecution of Noriega, and that's what the United States would do.

"Mr. Rubino, a brief response," Hoeveler offered.

"Please," said Rubino, returning to the lectern. He looked again at the judge and spoke without notes. Again he would appeal to the court's sense of fair play.

"Panama would not attempt to bring an American citizen to Panama to stand trial for crimes which the Panamanians alleged were committed on American soil," said Rubino.

He pointed toward Sullivan and Bryson. "The government at no time has ever said that General Manuel Antonio Noriega came to the United States and committed a crime."

The U.S. government was not charging Noriega for a crime the government alleged he committed in the United States. The United States was charging Noriega with a crime that, if he had committed it at all, he had committed in Panama. The whole notion was ridiculous, said Rubino. The United States was not the world's policeman.

Rubino raised his arms. "This is not a motion to dismiss the indictment. The government seems to think it is, and the court seems to think it is, too. I am asking you, Your Honor, most respectfully, to follow the Geneva Convention and say, 'I don't have jurisdiction of this POW.'"

Rubino paused. Hoeveler held up his hand as if to stop him.

"Well, what happens then?" the judge asked. If the defense was suggesting that Noriega not be tried in the United States, then where?

"Then what happens?" said Rubino, echoing Hoeveler. "Then what happens is that you have no jurisdiction. The court divests itself of jurisdiction. The indictment still stands.

"He can either be repatriated back to Panama, and then the U.S. government can see if they can get him fair and square down there and bring him back here again." Meaning, Rubino did not have to say, that the Bush administration could have another go at capturing Noriega without the help of twenty-four thousand American troops.

"My initial request and suggestion," continued Rubino, "was to send the general to a third country."

Whispers cut through the bank of reporters sitting behind Rubino. Anyone who had sat through a half day of federal magistrate court in Miami knew there was little chance that Noriega or anyone charged with drug trafficking and conspiracy in Miami would walk out of the federal courthouse without first telling his or her story to a jury.

Rubino now seemed to be angling for the very deal that Noriega had rejected nearly two years before. The Reagan administration had tried in almost every way to convince Noriega to agree to leave Panama, even offering the dictator deals to avoid prosecution in the United States. With Noriega in custody, the defense seemed to be getting that old-time religion. It was a valiant but certainly doomed attempt at conversion.

"Needless to say," continued Rubino, "if we have any choice in the country we would like the United States to send General Noriega to, it is going to be one that doesn't have an extradition treaty with the United States.

"This is the ultimate result we seek. It is a legal one under all international principles."

The judge thanked both lawyers and then called for a short recess. He walked out a side door to his chambers.

For the next twenty minutes Noriega sat quietly. He looked once toward the prosecution but never around at reporters, kept two rows at bay by deputy marshals.

Two months before, Noriega, once a master of psychological warfare, had stood on a Panama City balcony waving a machete over his head in defiance of the American government. He had thwarted two presidents before Bush. Each had coddled him and then regretted it. When the deposed general walked out of the Vatican embassy carrying a Bible and a toothbrush, one U.S. official on the scene said the fallen dictator "really looked like a whipped and beaten little man." Even so, the man whom George Bush had ordered captured dead or alive was still very much alive. He was not finished. As time would surely tell, his defense team was only warming up.

When Hoeveler took the bench again, he wasted little time rendering his decision:

"Now, I am going to rule on the question of the Geneva Convention," he said. "I will begin with the ending. However you describe your motion," the judge said, looking at Rubino, "whether it is a motion to dismiss or whether it is a motion to divest myself of jurisdiction, whether it has some other name that I haven't yet determined, the motion will be denied. I have an indicted case here. The charges are, as stated in the indictment, against several defendants."

The judge was measured in his speech. He looked toward Noriega as he referred to the Geneva Convention. That convention, Hoeveler said, allowed for the detention of prisoners of war against whom criminal proceedings were pending. The government was right in maintaining that where the offenses were the same as those that could be charged against a military person in the detaining country, those offenses could be prosecuted against one who has the status of prisoner of war.

"The court does have jurisdiction. You have presented me with the question of whether or not I have the right to proceed, and I answer that question by saying yes, and we will," the judge said.

So it was decided that Noriega, a prisoner of war, as both defense and prosecution agreed, could be tried for drug trafficking. He was back to legal square one.

A rush of reporters to the telephones began even before the judge was finished. Hoeveler paused, then repeated himself with finality: "We'll proceed with the matter."

CHAPTER 13
★★★★★★★

Shocking to the Conscience

Jon May and Frank Rubino went back to Judge Hoeveler on March 22, again asking that the case be dismissed. The grounds for dismissal, they asserted, were that General Noriega had been brought before the court in a manner that was "shocking to the conscience and in violation of the law and norms of humanity."

May outlined the defense argument in a thirty-page motion, attaching forty more pages of exhibits. The motion alleged that the invasion of Panama violated the due process clause of the Fifth Amendment of the Constitution. Due process, as set forth in the Fifth Amendment, demands that the law not be unreasonable, arbitrary, or capricious and that it be enforced in a manner that bears some reasonable relation to the object being sought.

The short of it, asserted May, was that the launching of a twenty-four-thousand-man invasion to capture one person was "illegal and immoral," clearly an absurd overreaction and a breach of due process. Even if Noriega's capture wasn't a violation of due process, May argued, the judge should dismiss the indictment simply to prevent the court from becoming a party to the government's misconduct.

Drawing on reports by two human rights groups, Physicians for Human Rights, a Boston-based organization formed in 1986 to assess the medical consequences of armed conflict, and the ad hoc Independent Commission of Inquiry on the United States Invasion of Panama, headed by former U.S. Attorney Gen. Ramsey Clark, May's portrayal of the invasion was not pretty.

In the middle of the night on December 20, American troops had dropped into Panama. They brought the "most sophisticated and powerful weaponry in the world": tanks, bazookas, mortar artillery, M-60 machine guns, M-113 armored personnel carriers, AC-130 Spectre gun ships, and even Stealth F-117 fighter bombers, dropping two-thousand-pound bombs. They faced a Panamanian military with eight thousand men and no air force.

In a few hours at least 300 and perhaps as many as 4,000 civilians—certainly not 202, as the U.S. government claimed—had been caught in the fighting and killed, May asserted. Another 3,000 had been wounded, 18,000 had had their homes destroyed, and more than 50,000 were left homeless.

"The United States has tried to give the impression that this was a quick and clean surgical military operation," said May. It wasn't, he said. "Witnesses will testify that in the streets and in the hospitals bodies were lying everywhere. Many people were killed or injured from shrapnel and exploding bullets. United States troops used flamethrowers to burn piles of dead bodies. Tanks flattened automobiles, homes, and bodies. Whole shanties were blown apart by mortar fire with residents still inside. Soldiers collected bodies in plastic bags and transported them away from the scene of destruction," said May, drawing on the inquiry commission report.

Quoting from the Physicians for Human Rights report, May continued: "A U.S. helicopter circled a fifteen-story slum apartment building, firing rockets at one or more armed persons who were shooting from the thirteenth floor early in the afternoon on December 22. Rocket fire from the helicopter hit several surrounding civilian dwellings and two schools. In one home, a grandmother preparing dinner was killed, and her brother, brother-in-law, and daughter suffered shrapnel wounds. The family's home was entirely destroyed, and the husband remains anguished. 'Her legs were destroyed, her insides came out,' he told the physician team." May said that during the course of the invasion, cluster bombs were dropped on civilians. When the cluster bombs exploded, they released flechettes, tiny darts that pierce human skin and inflict internal injuries.

All of this happened, May contended, while the international media were kept at bay by U.S. forces. When a Spanish photographer standing in front of a Marriott hotel in Panama City failed to quit taking pictures after an American soldier had yelled "Stop" to a group of journalists, the photographer was shot between the eyes, May charged. When confronted, the Army claimed that the journalist had been killed in cross fire. The independent commission identified five mass grave sites in Panama City, May told the court. All of this to capture one man? the defense asked. "We believe that the conduct engaged in by the United States military far exceeds anything ever considered by our courts," he told the judge. "While the courts have upheld the right of agents to participate in some criminal activity in order to infiltrate criminal enterprises, the courts have recognized that there are limits to permissible conduct."

May quoted a 1973 ruling by then Supreme Court justice, now chief justice, William Rehnquist: "We may someday be presented with a situation in which the conduct of law enforcement agents is so outrageous that due process would absolutely bar the government from invoking judicial processes to obtain a conviction. That someday is now."

The standard by which the U.S. government should be judged, May said, had been laid out in a 1974 federal circuit court case called *United States v. Toscanino.* The Toscanino case had carved out an exception to the so-called Ker-Frisbie doctrine established by the Supreme Court. The reference was to the 1886 case of Frederick Ker in which the Supreme Court held that an overseas seizure by law enforcement was legal, and the 1952 case of *Frisbie v. Collins* in which the Supreme Court rejected the argument that a violation of federal law could divest a court of jurisdiction over a criminal defendant. Toscanino's story was a Kafkaesque miscarriage of justice. Francisco Toscanino was an Italian citizen living in Montevideo, Uruguay. In the 1970s he was wanted in New York State on charges of drug trafficking. One day Uruguayan policemen, acting as paid agents of the United States, lured Toscanino and his pregnant wife to a deserted area in Montevideo. There he was knocked unconscious with the butt of a gun, bound, blindfolded, and thrown into the back of a car as his wife looked on. He was kidnapped at gun point and taken to Brazil where, Toscanino claimed, he was tortured and interrogated for seventeen days by Brazilian police, who also were agents of the U.S. government. Toscanino was denied sleep and food for days. He was forced to walk up and down a hallway for seven or more hours each day, and if he fell he was kicked and beaten, he claimed. To induce him to respond to questioning, his fingers were pinched with metal pliers, alcohol was flushed into his eyes and nose, and electrodes were attached to his ear lobes, toes, and genitals. All of this happened, Toscanino claimed, with the knowledge of the U.S. attorney in New York—who even, he alleged, received reports on Toscanino's interrogation.

Toscanino was returned to the United States and later convicted, but when a federal appellate court heard of Toscanino's treatment and learned that the trial court declined to hold a hearing on whether Toscanino's rights to due process were violated, the court reversed his conviction. The appellate court ruled that if Toscanino had proven at a hearing that his right to due process had been violated, the district court would have had to divest itself of jurisdiction over him.

Since the days of the Ker and Frisbie rulings, which established the general rule that a court's jurisdiction over an accused is not impaired by the manner in which the government acquired control over him, May asserted, the Supreme Court had expanded due process to bar the government from extreme misconduct—what Justice Felix Frankfurter in a 1952 ruling called "conduct that shocks the conscience." May noted that the Ker and Frisbie decisions came at times when questions of due process applied only to the fairness of procedures at trial.

The appellate court in the Toscanino case said that the agents who returned Toscanino to the United States violated not only a U.S. kidnapping law but also two international treaties. The government's conduct was so egregious that it warranted dismissal of the charges, the court ruled.

Because the Toscanino case had gone before the federal Second Circuit Appellate Court in New York State and had never reached the U.S. Supreme Court, it was not the law of the land but instead was case law in the federal Second Circuit. That meant Toscanino had not set a precedent which needed to be followed in the federal Eleventh Circuit that encompassed Florida and the court Noriega found himself in.

But May, in his argument to Judge Hoeveler, noted that there were cases in the Eleventh Circuit that "left open the possibility of dismissal in that hypothetical situation where the conduct of the agents shocks the conscience." The Eleventh Circuit had said that there could be exceptions to the Ker-Frisbie doctrine of extreme cases.

So, argued May, "Ker-Frisbie does not speak to that unique case where the action of government agents is not merely illegal but in violation of the norms of civilized conduct."

May said the government had conceded as much in a response to a motion by Noriega codefendant Luis del Cid filed a month earlier. Del Cid's defense lawyer, Samuel Burstyn, had argued that Hoeveler should not accept jurisdiction over a case in which it found that "the United States government deliberately and unreasonably exploited illegal conduct in an outrageous fashion so as to effectuate an extraterritorial arrest." Ker and Frisbie did not apply where the United States had trampled international treaties.

Burstyn put it this way: "The actions of the United States government are particularly egregious where the United States government never even sought to procure [the defendant's] presence through any less violent and invasionary means. One of the principal elements that the Toscanino court relied upon in finding a due process claim was the extent of the violence in that case. The instant case presents an outrageously greater case of violence and destruction. Hundreds of persons were killed. Billions of dollars in property were destroyed. The incredible magnitude of this violence, which was engaged in for the purpose of effectuating the defendant's arrest, is shocking and should shock the conscience of this court."

And Burstyn added: "The policy ramifications of what occurred in this case are chilling. If this court finds [the defendant's] arrest lawful, then the judiciary of the United States will send a message to the world that any nation that does not comport itself consistent with the laws of the United States is subject to invasion and the military and governmental agents of said foreign nation subject to arrest and involuntary transmission to the United States for trial."

In the government's response to Burstyn's motion, May noted, the prosecutors conceded that the Eleventh Circuit hinted there could be some version of the Toscanino exception which "might be embraced in a particularly egregious case of brutality or torture." Given the death and destruction inflicted on Panama as a result of the invasion, May told Hoeveler, "plainly the facts of this case are so egregious, so at odds with the norms of civilized conduct, that dismissal of the charges is warranted."

May said that the invasion violated the obligations of the United States under the charter of the United Nations and the charter of the Organization of American States, which obligated members to respect the territorial integrity and political independence of other nations. "The waging of war for the express purpose of effectuating the arrest of a single individual is unprecedented in the history of mankind. Our concern for human rights . . .

cannot be conveniently turned on and off as our foreign policy dictates. The true meaning of what we say is not lost on the world, nor is it lost on international terrorists who will use our acts to justify acts directed at United States citizens. As we seek to give our laws extraterritorial effect, we must also extend our notions of due process, or we will surely suffer the consequences of our own hypocrisy. If the exercise of a court's supervisory powers is ever called for, it is in a case such as the one herein, where the United States government did not merely abduct an individual from a foreign country but killed hundreds and possibly thousands of innocent people in the process. The killing of men, women, and children occurred here as a direct result of state policy, policy intended to effectuate the arrest of a single individual. If the killings committed by our government had occurred at any time but during a war, they would be called murder. Indeed, had they not been committed by the victors of this conflict, they would have been termed an atrocity.

"Nothing General Noriega is accused of could ever justify such a deliberate taking of human life. If ever there were a case of the ends not justifying means, if ever there were a case where our courts must act to deter such conduct from occurring again, such a case is this."

After receiving the defense's motion on Thursday afternoon, March 22, the judge scheduled a hearing to take up the request on the morning of April 2, a week and a half later. A hearing would give the defense the opportunity to present to the court the issues of fact and law behind its motion. The government, too, would have a right to be heard. Though less formal than a trial, a hearing would also give the defense its best shot at presenting evidence which would prove to the judge that the invasion had been an uneven-handed and outrageous way for the Bush administration to deal with Noriega. In all likelihood the judge would allow the defense to put on witnesses and present evidence. Rubino and May knew this was their final shot at getting the case dismissed, at least on the issue of jurisdiction.

May sent subpoenas to Ramsey Clark, the most prominent member of the ad hoc Independent Commission, two medical school professors belonging to Physicians for Human Rights, and the chairman of the Joint Chiefs of Staff, Colin Powell. Clark and the doctors had all been to Panama shortly after the invasion and reported firsthand the death and destruction reflected in the defense motion. Powell was asked to produce documentation pertaining to civilian deaths and injuries and pre-invasion forecasts of casualties. The subpoena to Powell was direct; it asked, in part, for "plans and details for the disposal of dead bodies and any and all reports written after the invasion detailing how these dead bodies were disposed of."

But by Thursday afternoon, March 29, it was clear the two doctors and Powell would not appear the following Monday. After a ninety-minute telephone conference, the judge agreed with lawyers for the physicians and quashed the subpoenas, saying the doctors simply had not been given enough notice. The same was true for Powell, although the judge also said the information the defense had requested of Powell might be classified. Prosecutor Myles Malman argued that the Powell subpoena was an "intrusion" and "the materials sought are potentially classified materials."

At the Monday hearing in Hoeveler's ninth-floor courtroom, the defense's oral argument followed closely the prepared motion before Judge Hoeveler. "This is a unique situation," began Rubino, standing before the judge. "This is the first time the United States has invaded a country and leveled it to arrest one man."

Rubino played a fifteen-minute video collage of news footage from the American television networks ABC, CBS, CNN, and NBC and also from Panama's Channel 13. The footage included rocket attacks and graphic portrayals of death. Through it all, General Noriega, who had not said a word in court since his arraignment nearly three months before, sat with his hand to his mouth, studying the images.

"All of the death and destruction the court has seen," said Rubino when the monitor went blank, "is for the arrest of one man."

Noriega looked ahead at the judge.

"I object," said Pat Sullivan. "This is not what we are here for, for editorial comments."

"Is this evidence?" the judge asked Rubino, taking up Sullivan's point. Rubino had not offered the video as evidence, and now he was adding his own commentary, not arguing the issue.

"It certainly is hearsay evidence," Rubino replied.

"Even given everything alleged here, there is still no relief that can be offered," Sullivan said.

"The question of your basic premise does need to be explored, Mr. Rubino," the judge said. "The premise, 'to catch one man,' seems to be begging an awful lot of questions."

"We are asking this court to say this conduct"—Rubino motioned toward the video monitor—"is shocking to the conscience. This man seeks justice from you, not from the executive branch," Rubino said, turning fully toward the judge. "Just because the executive branch does something doesn't mean that can be shoved down the throat of the judiciary. In fairness, don't slam the—"

"The doors of justice will not be slammed in your client's face," Judge Hoeveler said, finishing Rubino's sentence.

"If this conduct is not shocking," Rubino continued, "I don't know what is, except nuclear weapons and leveling the earth. Would I have to bring my client here with no arms and no legs? The intent was there."

Rubino called Ramsey Clark to the witness stand. Dressed in khaki trousers and a corduroy jacket, Clark looked more like a high school history teacher than a former attorney general.

Clark sat in the witness box to the judge's right. He said he had gone to Panama to see the fruits of the American invasion for himself. He was horrified by the death and destruction that had befallen Panama City. He visited the Garden of Peace Cemetery and stopped to talk with children who played among the headstones. "One youngster took us back to where there had been a huge cut in the ground," Clark said. "It was six paces wide and forty paces long, about eighteen by one hundred and twenty feet. The children said the Americans had come with trucks and dumped green bags. We were told that some bags contained more than one body. You have to think about it to understand what that means. It would seem that many bodies were disposed of so that they would not be counted. It's clear an accurate count will take some time. I felt I knew there were hundreds, maybe thousands of deaths."

"What we're talking about is a holocaust," said Jon May after Clark stepped down from the witness stand. "Nothing General Noriega is accused of justifies such a wanton taking of human life. Every place where Noriega could be, they bombed. It's the death of these individuals that demonstrates how horrendous our government's conduct was."

May said the government's argument that there was a political doctrine at work here—that only the executive branch itself, not the judiciary, could judge its own actions—was designed to undermine the court's authority.

"I have alleged war crimes," May said, his voice rising. "They don't think they have to respond. They think the court should just ignore this. Warfare brutalizes everyone. At some point the methods we use make us worse than the people whom we accuse. The government always has to take the morally superior position. Regardless of how this court rules on Toscanino, it is important to recognize that what happened was wrong and immoral. And the government has a long road to travel to justify what it did."

It seemed, Judge Hoeveler observed, that May was trying to make a "political" rather than legal argument.

"The children, the people who died in Panama had a right to live," May implored.

Hoeveler turned to the prosecution for a response. William Bryson stood. As usual, he was brief: "We think the court can rule as a matter of law," he said. The invasion deaths were not on trial, Bryson continued. "That's a political question. . . . Our argument is that the [defense] motion can be decided as a matter of law."

"Mr. May makes a moving argument," Hoeveler responded. "Wouldn't this be placing the imprimatur of the court on the killing of people?"

"You don't punish society by letting a presumptive criminal go to make another point," Bryson said matter-of-factly. What U.S. troops did was irrelevant to the issue of Noriega's due process, said Bryson. The defense intended to "embroil this court in questions of foreign policy and military strategy unsuited to resolution in a judicial forum." Simply, "Noriega's allegation of 'war crimes' and other atrocities are irrelevant" to the charges filed against him in federal court, Bryson said. The U.S. government had a right to take action in Panama, according to Bryson. The federal courts had never dismissed a case on the ground of "outrageous" conduct. The U.S. action was far broader than bringing just one man to justice, he concluded.

The judge turned to May for a response.

"Your Honor," May started, "how many people does it take to make the government's conduct outrageous? The administration has whipped up a patriotic fervor. The press has accepted what happened uncritically. And what really happened was murder. The primary reason for the Bush administration's action was frustration," May said. "This makes us much worse than any drug dealer."

"All right," said Hoeveler when May finished. The judge said he would take the defense's motion under consideration. "For now, we are done."

The government's written response to Noriega's motion had been filed shortly before the April 2 hearing. The Miami prosecutors had sent a copy of the defense's motion and its forty pages of supporting documents to Main Justice the same day it was filed, on March 22. Within hours, Assistant Attorney General William Barr had called in Bryson and Deputy Assistant Attorney General John McGinnis to draft a reply. Though the memorandum would be signed by the Miami prosecutors, the legal heavy lifting had actually taken place in Washington. Barr, who in two years' time would become attorney general following the resignation of Richard Thornburgh, composed the response himself.

Bryson's arguments in court summarized Barr's memorandum. Noriega's claim that the U.S. invasion was shocking to the conscience and violated the norms of international conduct were wrong, the government response said. Noriega's due process rights under the Fifth Amendment had not been violated, the government asserted.

Barr's response called the report of Ramsey Clark's Independent Commission of Inquiry on the U.S. Invasion of Panama "extraordinarily biased and inaccurate in many respects." Whatever the defense's allegations, whatever conclusions one might draw from the invasion, the law, Barr wrote, would not support a dismissal of the indictment.

Taking up the defense motion point by point, the response called the Toscanino ruling simply no longer good law. Supreme Court and Eleventh Circuit decisions had left Toscanino without teeth. Rulings in those courts established that the correct response to outrageous or brutal conduct toward a defendant was not the dismissal of criminal charges against the defendant himself but civil or criminal action against the offenders.

In other words, if Noriega or del Cid or any other defendant felt he had been wronged by the government, he was free to sue. But an error by the government would not relieve a defendant from facing prosecution for the allegations lodged against him. To let a defendant go because the government had misbehaved, the courts had ruled, was "too extreme and too costly to society to employ as a sanction for improper government conduct in obtaining custody of the defendant."

Barr asserted that the defense motion was simply out of line. "First," he said, "decisions concerning the deployment of military force overseas are committed to the political branches of government, not the courts." The Constitution, continued Barr, provided no standard by which the courts could judge whether military action was contrary to civilized conduct. "Under our system," said Barr, "it is for Congress and the executive branch, not the judicial branch, to determine United States military policy and to accept the political consequences of that determination."

Noriega's claim that the U.N. and O.A.S. charters or other international treaties prohibited the United States from seizing him and bringing him to trial were wrong. Treaty provisions, Barr further argued, do not create private rights that can be invoked by individuals in U.S. courts. Rather, treaties set forth principles by which nations agree to abide. The right to protest a treaty violation belongs to the state, not the individual. Since the legitimate government of Panama, led by Guillermo Endara, had not objected to the United States' invasion of Panama or the arrest of Noriega, then there was no basis for Noriega to claim as an individual that his arrest had violated the U.N. or O.A.S. charter.

With the briefs in and arguments made, Judge Hoeveler considered his decision for several weeks. His ruling came in an omnibus order on June 8. In ruling on the defense's assertion that Noriega's arrest had been illegal and the prosecution's response to that assertion, Hoeveler began with Jon May's Fifth Amendment due process argument. He said there was no question, according to the law, that the manner in which a defendant was brought before the court normally had no effect on the ability of the government to try that person. The Ker-Frisbie doctrine said that a court is not deprived of jurisdiction if the defendant's presence was procured in an unlawful way. But, as Noriega's lawyers pointed out, Hoeveler noted, there was the Toscanino exception in cases where the government was deliberate and unreasonable in its invasion of an accused's constitutional rights.

The type of government conduct necessary to trigger the Toscanino exception and warrant what Hoeveler called "the drastic remedy of dismissal" was behavior that was "shocking to the conscience"—that is, conduct such as torture and brutality. Toscanino, the judge agreed with the defense, did establish that there is a difference between conduct which is merely illegal and conduct so egregious it shocks the conscience.

But Hoeveler said the invasion of Panama had not violated any of Noriega's personal rights, a requirement for dismissal under the due process clause of the Fifth Amendment. "The defendant does not claim," Hoeveler said, "that he was personally mistreated in any manner incident to his arrest, at least not in any manner nearly approaching the egregious physical abuse stated in Toscanino."

Noriega's due process claim, the judge said, was instead based on the rights of third parties, Panamanian citizens who had been harmed in the course of the invasion. The due process clause, said the judge, was activated only when the rights of the defendant were violated. "Nothing in Toscanino or in the other decisions cited by Noriega undermines that principle or in any way suggests that the due process rights of third parties may be vicariously asserted," Hoeveler said. "Here, Noriega is not merely invoking the due process rights of third parties but further urges that the indictment against him be dismissed as a result of alleged violations of those rights. . . . The only party interested in having the indictment against Noriega dismissed is Noriega." Though Toscanino would require a court to divest itself of jurisdiction in some cases, it would not do so in this case, the judge said.

As for Noriega's claim that his capture and arrest violated international law, Hoeveler agreed with the government that individuals lack standing to assert violations of international treaties when there has been no protest from the offended government; nowhere in the U.N. or O.A.S. charters or in other international conventions cited by the defense are individual rights addressed.

To require Noriega to present the protest of the Panamanian government before he personally could claim a violation of his rights might be viewed as a form of "legal bootstrapping," Hoeveler admitted. There was some force to the argument that Noriega as the de facto head of Panama was the government of Panama and "to permit removal of him and his associates from power and reject his complaint because a new and friendly government is installed" did seem to turn on the doctrine of sovereignty standing on its head.

But, said Hoeveler, "the United States had consistently refused to recognize the Noriega regime as Panama's legitimate government, a fact which considerably undermines Noriega's position." And further, Noriega had nullified the results of the Panamanian presidential election shortly before the invasion. Thus, "the suggestion that his removal from power somehow robs the true government of the opportunity to object" is weak, the judge said.

Hoeveler next turned to the defense assertion that even absent a constitutional or treaty violation, the court should refuse to hear the case, dismissing it so as to prevent the court from becoming a party to government misconduct in invading Panama and bringing Noriega to trial. Hoeveler said the invocation of what he called "supervisory power to dismiss an indictment" was a harsh remedy that should be reserved for the flagrant or repeated abuses of government conduct. Supervisory authority, he said, was a vehicle for correcting problems that were neither constitutional nor related to statutory law but problems that a court nonetheless found "repugnant to fairness and justice."

Noriega's claim that his arrest came as the result of "deliberate and indiscriminate atrocities" during the invasion and thus merited the court's move to distance itself from that government action was not convincing, said Hoeveler. He said Supreme Court Justice Louis Brandeis was right in 1928 when he said, "Crime is contagious. If the government becomes a lawbreaker, it breeds contempt for the law, it invites every man to become a law unto himself; it invites anarchy."

But in Panama, said Hoeveler, the U.S. soldiers and agents had not "deliberately killed and tortured individuals for the sole purpose of discovering a fugitive's whereabouts in order to secure his arrest." Rather, said Hoeveler, "a military war in which innocent lives were unfortunately lost in pursuit of foreign policy objectives" was waged. "Although the motives behind the military action are open to speculation, the stated goals of the invasion were to protect American lives, support democracy, preserve the Panama Canal Treaties, and bring Noriega to the United States to stand trial for narcotics offenses."

Because the president had ordered Noriega arrested in the course of carrying out military operations in Panama, "the capture of Noriega was incident to the broader conduct of foreign policy," the judge said. The government's rationale for invading Panama was not beyond challenge and need not be blindly accepted, but the defense had offered no evidence to the contrary, Hoeveler said.

In fact, the judge added, if anything, the exhibits that the defense attached to its motion for dismissal and the report of Ramsey Clark's Independent Commission supported the notion that the American invasion was an exercise in foreign policy. The defense had conceded that U.S. economic and military interests seemed truly to be behind the invasion. "The additional fact of Noriega's declaration of war against the United States shortly before the invasion only further undermines that premise," Hoeveler said. "That foreign policy objectives rather than just law enforcement goals are implicated radically changes the court's consideration of the government conduct complained of and, consequently, its willingness to exercise supervisory power," the judge said. Once foreign policy becomes a focus of a government action, then "the political question doctrine" would preclude the court from resolving issues more properly left to the political branches of government.

Since as early as *Marbury v. Madison*, the 1803 Supreme Court decision establishing judicial review, judges have been careful to limit their scope of inquiry, seldom venturing into areas reserved for the executive and legislative branches of government. True, the "exact contours of the political question doctrine are ambiguous and remain a source of some confusion," Hoeveler said, but clearly "broad challenges to an executive's conduct of foreign policy" are not to be answered in court but are best left to the executive and legislative branches that were constitutionally empowered to handle foreign policy questions. Questions of constitutional authority, such as whether or not the president had usurped Congress's exclusive authority to declare war, could be reviewed in court, said Hoeveler. But in this case Noriega was challenging the conduct of foreign policy. Noriega "asks this court to find that the deaths of innocent civilians and destruction of private property is 'shocking to the conscience and in violation of the laws and norms of humanity.' At bottom, then, Noriega's complaint is a challenge to the very morality of war itself. This is a political question in its most paradigmatic and pristine form. . . . Questions such as under what circumstances armed conflict is immoral [and] whether it is always so are not ones for the courts but must be resolved by the political branches entrusted by the Constitution with the awesome responsibility of committing this country to battle. In this case, the decision to send troops into Panama was made by the president in his capacity as commander in chief, and he is on this matter 'accountable only to his country in his political character, and his own conscience,'" Hoeveler said, quoting *Marbury v. Madison.* "The court has no authority to pass moral judgment upon that decision."

Hoeveler said that as a judge he had to recognize the constitutional separation of powers and functions. He added, "Any suggestion that rejection of defendant's position is somehow an approval of governmental conduct described as egregious is misplaced."

In 1973 a federal court declined to decide whether President Nixon had illegally escalated the war in Vietnam by ordering the bombing and mining of harbors in North Vietnam, and in 1984 another federal court declined to determine whether the deployment of cruise missiles in Great Britain would create a heightened risk of nuclear war.

Following upon these decisions, Hoeveler said, "If the courts are incapable of determining whether bombing constitutes an escalation of war or what the effect of missile deployment is on world peace, it would likewise seem beyond our province to determine whether or under what circumstances war is immoral. What would be the criteria for determining when armed conflict is 'shocking to the conscience'? Defendant's counsel makes much of the numbers of innocent civilians killed and the extent of property damage, but the court fails to see what that argument proves; the death of one woman or man is one too many."

Even with Hoeveler's February 8 ruling from the bench on Noriega's POW status, the defense still had questions about the court's right or jurisdiction to sit in judgment of the general. A motion to dismiss the indictment against Noriega had been pending with the court since October 1988, six months after the delivery of the indictment.

In April 1988, shortly after the indictment was delivered, Judge Hoeveler ruled that even though Noriega had not come before the court personally, he had a right to counsel and a right to challenge the validity of the indictment without surrendering himself. Neal Sonnett, Raymond Takiff, and Frank Rubino, Noriega's lawyers at the time, had filed a motion in late March 1988 asking the court that they be allowed to make a special appearance even though Noriega was not in custody and there was no prospect he would soon come into the custody of the court. They had told the judge that they sought to file a motion that would go "to the very heart of the prosecution." The motion, they said, would "attack the right of the government to bring an indictment against General Noriega and the jurisdiction of this court to hear the case against him."

A month later Hoeveler ruled that even though the government had argued that the courts in general had not allowed fugitive defendants to make special appearances and even though an exception in Noriega's case could open the "floodgates" to similar motions by thousands of defendants, he would exercise his own discretion and allow Noriega's lawyers to do so.

In his ruling, Hoeveler said the Noriega indictment was out of the ordinary.

"The present indictment is surrounded with special circumstances which militate in favor of allowing the defendant to attack its validity," the judge said. The case was one of a kind, a "case of first impression."

"The case is fraught with political overtones," he continued. "I do not propose to engage in any political inquiries beyond those properly raised by legal argument. However, the best way to avoid the appearance that this indictment has assumed the character of a political proceeding rather than a legal one is to determine its legal validity upon the arguments of counsel."

In granting the defense motion to take up the question of the court's jurisdiction, Hoeveler told the government that it should welcome, not shun, any procedure that would "negate the perception that this prosecution may be politically motivated." He said, "It should be observed that for all the notoriety surrounding this indictment and this defendant, he is under our legal system innocent until proven guilty."

And so, seven months after the Miami indictment had been handed up in February 1988, Sonnett, on behalf of the defense, filed a motion asking Judge Hoeveler to dismiss the indictment. That request preceded by more than fifteen months the arrest of General Noriega in Panama. (The judge deferred ruling on the motion until June 1990, six months after Noriega's arrest and arraignment.)

Sonnett's motion explained why the defense believed Noriega was beyond the court's jurisdiction. He conceded that American courts, including the Supreme Court, had generally upheld the exercise of jurisdiction over acts in other countries, acts that were intended to have an effect within U.S. borders. But that jurisdiction simply did not apply in the case of General Noriega, he said. The reason: Noriega was the leader of a sovereign nation, and he had never done anything overtly illegal in the United States.

Sonnett told Judge Hoeveler that one of the basic underpinnings of international law was that the jurisdiction of any one nation is dependent on whether it would be reasonable, given the interests of other nations, to exercise that jurisdiction. It was not for one nation to go about enforcing its own peculiar or specific laws at the expense of other countries who enjoyed their own sovereignty and laws. Would it be fair for the leader of Libya, for instance, to send police officers to Washington, D.C., to arrest members of Congress who had violated Libyan laws? No, of course not; that would be unreasonable, said Sonnett's argument.

There were fair and internationally accepted tests of a nation's extraterritorial jurisdiction, Sonnett told the judge. Those tests had been widely agreed to by most nations. Nations had agreed that a country has the jurisdiction to set down laws with respect to activities and persons within, or substantially within, its own territory and with regard to conduct outside its territory that has or is intended to have a substantial effect within the nation; a nation can enforce its laws on its own citizens even if those citizens are outside its national boundaries; and, finally, a nation can enforce its laws on people outside its borders and who are not nationals if those people threaten the security of the nation or other interests.

But enforcing one nation's laws in another nation is not without limitation, Sonnett told Judge Hoeveler. When a person's or nation's acts have no direct physical consequences or if the effect is at best ambiguous, then there is clearly a "reasonable" question of jurisdiction. If a nation exercised jurisdiction over an action that took place wholly in another country, what would stop nations from exercising jurisdiction whenever it became expedient? There could be virtually no limit to a nation's exercise of jurisdiction. It was just that point, Sonnett told the judge, that thirteen Caribbean countries, all members of the Caribbean Community and Common Market, embraced shortly after Noriega's 1988 indictment. The group wrote to President Reagan protesting the Justice Department's "derogation" of the laws of Caribbean nations and accusing the United States of violations of their sovereignty by investigating allegations of drug trafficking in the Caribbean and Panama.

The problem, Sonnett told Hoeveler, was this: "There is no 'bright line' rule of who is entitled to head of state immunity, and as one might expect, no decision has ever been rendered in a criminal case." Even though General Noriega was not the elected head of the state of Panama as defined by the Panamanian constitution, his position as the acknowledged de facto leader of Panama clearly qualified him for immunity.

There could be no doubt, Sonnett argued, that although many terms had been used to describe Noriega's rule in Panama—some pejorative, such as "military strong man" and "dictator"—"the point is crystal clear: It simply cannot be legitimately controverted that General Noriega is the effective de facto leader of the nation of Panama, regardless of the source of his power or the nature of his rule."

And there were two other reasons that robbed the judge and American courts of jurisdiction over Noriega, Sonnett argued. One was called act of state immunity and the other diplomatic immunity.

Act of state immunity, Sonnett reminded Hoeveler, was a judicially created concept that "requires courts to refrain from adjudicating claims that challenge the legality of official acts committed by foreign officials in their own territories." The doctrine had been laid out in an 1897 Supreme Court ruling that said: "Every sovereign state is bound to respect the independence of every other sovereign state, and the courts of one country will not sit in judgment on the acts of the government of another, done within its own territory."

The American government could not judge why Noriega did what he did as the leader of Panama, Sonnett argued. The motives of a foreign head of state are not for an American court to judge.

But Sonnett's most impassioned argument for dismissal was based on what he termed the "discriminatory and selective nature" of the prosecution. "We submit that the prosecution of General Noriega amounts to intentional and purposeful discrimination against him in that the government's selection of him for prosecution has been invidious, in bad faith, and based upon impermissible considerations, including political and foreign policy consider-ations," Sonnett told the judge. All recognized that under the American sys-tem of justice the government retains broad discretion as to whom to prosecute. But, he added, "the government's discretion is not unfettered and is subject to constitutional restraints."

If the prosecution of General Noriega or any other person was undertaken with an "evil eye" or "unequal hand," as Supreme Court Justice Stanley Matthews once described it, it was unacceptable, said Sonnett. And that, he argued, was exactly what was happening. "Without question, General Noriega is being prosecuted—yes, punished, based upon impermissible politi-cal and foreign policy considerations by the highest levels [of the U.S. govern-ment]," Sonnett told the judge. He said the Miami prosecutors, the assistant U.S. attorneys who had drafted the indictment, were not specifically to blame; rather, the wrong reached much higher. "Political and foreign policy tactics so infected this case as to require dismissal," he said.

Sonnett recounted the United States government's "changing attitude" toward Noriega beginning as early as mid-1984 when the Reagan administra-tion first sought modification of provisions of the Panama Canal Treaties. Even though American officials described Noriega as "extremely cooperative" as late as 1987, the tenor of relations had begun to change in 1986 as Senate committees began probing Noriega's rule in Panama. Efforts to persuade Noriega to leave Panama escalated into economic boycotts and the suspen-sion of all military and economic aid in 1987.

But it was only after the delivery of the indictments, Sonnett said, that it became apparent just how politically motivated the prosecution really was. In March and May 1988, State Department officials began private meetings with Noriega's lawyers aimed at persuading the general to leave Panama in exchange for guarantees that the United States would not prosecute him.

The political intentions behind the indictment, Sonnett told the judge, became transparent after the May negotiations faltered. Sonnett quoted a late May 1988 statement by Assistant Secretary of State Elliott Abrams that summarized the Reagan administration's thinking about the indictments: "The indictments drove Noriega crazy and gave us a terrific bargaining tool."

The government's response to Sonnett's motion was equally sure of itself. For Noriega to claim that he did not fall under the jurisdiction of the court because he was the leader of a sovereign nation was frivolous, the govern-ment said.

The response, written by Sonia Escobio O'Donnell, the chief appellate counsel to the Miami U.S. attorney, said the question at hand was twofold: Did Congress have the power to enact laws having extraterritorial effect, and had it enacted a law prohibiting the activities alleged in the Noriega indictment? The answer to both, the government said, was yes.

"Many of the overt acts enumerated in the indictment are alleged to have occurred within the territorial United States or to have been directly aimed at bringing narcotics into the United States," O'Donnell argued. She pointed to the indictment's allegation that Floyd Carlton had flown a shipment of 2,141 pounds of cocaine from Panama to Miami in June 1984 and that in March 1986 he had purchased a Lear jet in Miami that was to be used to fly drug proceeds from Florida to Panama.

The government also argued under a separate theory of jurisdiction that if the national interest is injured by a criminal offense, even by a person acting outside the U.S. borders, and that action threatens national security or threatens to interfere with the operation of the government, then that person can be held criminally liable. "Certainly the greatest threat to the United States comes from beyond the limits of its territory," O'Donnell argued. "Simply stated, it is entirely reasonable to subject the defendant to the jurisdiction of the United States when he is alleged to be an active coconspirator, offering protection to narcotics dealers whose aims are to inundate our shores with illicit drugs."

O'Donnell told Hoeveler that Noriega's claim that he was the de facto head of state was without merit. Head of state immunity, she said, cannot be asserted by individuals but must be requested by the sovereign state. The status of head of state, she said, is an attribute of state sovereignty, not an individual right.

O'Donnell also told the judge that Noriega was equally wrong to claim immunity from prosecution under the act of state doctrine. Like sovereign immunity, act of state immunity only protects individual officials acting on behalf of their sovereign governments. Official acts are those taken on behalf of the state and not those taken on behalf of the actor, the government said. The indictment alleged a series of private acts committed by Noriega and his coconspirators for their own personal financial gain. The indictment did not allege, said O'Donnell, that Noriega had "engaged in the enterprise and committed the drug transactions and money-laundering acts in furtherance of Panama's state policy or to serve an unspecified national interest."

In his June 8 omnibus order, Judge Hoeveler again agreed with the government on all major points. The ability of the United States to reach and prosecute acts committed by aliens outside of the U.S. borders was well established. All nations have recognized the principle that if a man outside of a country willfully puts in motion a force that causes a crime to be committed in that country, then that man is answerable where the evil is done. Appellate courts, Hoeveler said, have "on numerous occasions upheld jurisdiction over foreigners who conspired to import narcotics into the United States but never entered this country nor personally performed any acts within its territorial limits. All prosecutors needed was proof of an overt act committed within the United States by a coconspirator."

Hoeveler went further, noting that international law principles had expanded to permit jurisdiction upon a mere showing of intent to commit a crime. Proof of an actual criminal act or the effect of a crime within the United States was not even required for a court to claim jurisdiction, he said.

In assessing the reasonableness of extraterritorial jurisdiction, Hoeveler said, one factor that he or any other judge must consider is the activity in question and the importance of regulating that activity. In the case of drug trafficking, the issue was clear: It must be stopped. "Given the serious nature of the drug epidemic in this country, certainly the efforts of the United States to combat the problem by prosecuting conduct directed against itself cannot be subject to the protests of a foreign government profiting at its expense. In any case, the court is not made aware of any instance in which the Republic of Panama objected to the regulation of drug trafficking by the United States. Because Noriega's conduct in Panama is alleged to have resulted in a direct effect within the United States, the court concludes that extraterritorial jurisdiction is appropriate as a matter of international law."

Hoeveler said, in ruling, that if the court could claim jurisdiction over the actual trafficking in drugs, then it could also claim jurisdiction over those who had conspired to traffic in drugs. "The same must be said for an aiding and abetting charge," he continued. "If anything, the act of aiding and abetting is even more intimately connected to the underlying crime." The RICO charges in the indictment also reached Noriega, the judge ruled, even though neither side had asked, he said.

Criminals could not escape RICO by locating their operations abroad, Hoeveler said. "As long as the racketeering activities produce effects or are intended to produce effects in this country, RICO applies."

Hoeveler next turned to the defense's assertion that Noriega was immune from prosecution based on sovereign immunity. Simply, the judge said, for Noriega to assert head of state immunity, he would first have to be recognized as the head of a state, and that had never happened.

To decide that immunity from prosecution must be granted regardless of a leader's source of power "would allow illegitimate dictators the benefit of their unscrupulous and possibly brutal seizures of power," Hoeveler said. He also ruled that case law had established that in order for act of state immunity to apply, Noriega would have to establish that his activities were acts of state, that they were taken on behalf of Panama and not on behalf of himself. "The court fails to see how Noriega's alleged drug trafficking and protection of money launderers could conceivably constitute public action taken on behalf of the Panamanian state. . . . The defendant does little more than state that, as the de facto ruler of Panama, his actions constitute acts of state. This sweeping position completely ignores the public/private distinction and suggests that government leaders are, as such, incapable of engaging in private, unofficial conduct."

CHAPTER 14
★★★★★★

Follow the Money

By the first week of April 1990, it was becoming increasingly clear to Frank Rubino, Jon May, Steven Kollin, and David Lewis that the time had come for the defense to move beyond legal questions regarding the court's jurisdiction. The judge was not going to enter his omnibus order regarding the legality of the invasion, Noriega's arrest, or the general's POW status until June, but he already had made his position on the issues clear in open court. The case was going to go forward, and Hoeveler expected a trial to begin in March 1991, less than a year away.

After the arraignment and as the first big issues began to be resolved, representatives of the world press began gradually to fade away. The invasion was becoming more and more a memory.

Now there was real work to do.

On the prosecution side, there were three or four other assistant U.S. attorneys working with Sullivan, Malman, and Guy Lewis, as well as nearly two dozen DEA and FBI agents. The team in Washington had McAdams and five Justice Department lawyers; the investigators in Panama numbered close to thirty.

The defense team, by comparison, looked positively ragtag. If Rubino counted Jack Fernández, a lawyer investigator, Leon Tozo, another lawyer who worked in Rubino's office, a couple of investigators, a paralegal, and a few secretaries, the defense added up to, at best, less than a dozen bodies.

Noriega had been under indictment for twenty months before his surrender and had had the full force of the PDF and the Panamanian government to construct a defense. The general should have had a full defense in hand by the time of the invasion. His own G-2 had complete access to anything U.S. officials had put in writing and just about everything that might have been said within earshot of PDF listening devices. A virtual library of exculpatory material should have been assembled by now, especially if one were to believe his own words.

"The Beast is going to defend itself!" Noriega had written to Ray Takiff and Rubino in May 1988. "Bush is going to end up like a torn American flag blown to pieces by an Atlantic wind. He is going to disappear." He told

Takiff, "They are S.O.B.s! Send them all to hell for me! This is the message you have to deliver. I have the cassettes in my hands!"

That was the message Takiff and Rubino had delivered to the U.S. government and the world. Noriega possessed documents and tapes that would show the complicity of the American government in Noriega's work. Whatever drug trafficking and money laundering had occurred in Panama happened with the implicit if not explicit knowledge of U.S. officials, Takiff and Rubino repeated.

"I'll tell you one thing," Takiff told one reporter. "What Oliver North shredded, Noriega still has. I don't think Noriega will ever be tried because of what he will bring up in his defense. The world has not heard the last of either Ray Takiff or Tony Noriega."

But now Takiff was gone, Noriega was in jail, and Frank Rubino was going to have to eat his own words. The fact was that Noriega once arrested had nothing. And neither did his defense lawyers.

While Noriega had the foresight to stash his money in secret overseas bank accounts and buy property in foreign countries, he had failed to do the one thing that would ensure a successful defense against an American prosecution: to gather and hide the documents and tapes that he said would prove his link to the U.S. government.

With the TV lights dimmed and the jurisdiction pleadings filed, Rubino now faced the task of uncovering whatever there was that would prove the link Noriega had boasted about. The simple truth was that, for all of its ravings, the defense had no defense. A defense was going to have to be built the old-fashioned way, with hard work. And that was going to cost money.

Takiff once boasted that Noriega handed over $2.9 million to the defense team before the invasion. If that was true, Rubino didn't know where the money had gone. By Rubino's figures, Noriega had paid the defense—Takiff himself and Neal Sonnett—about $900,000 over the past two years. That was $2 million less than Takiff's total. "That was distributed among four or five lawyers in the case," Rubino later said. "If there is $2 million additional out there, I didn't get a dime of it, and I don't know anyone else who did." Rubino swore the same to Judge Hoeveler.

The $900,000 had paid for the initial pleadings, the negotiations with the State Department between February 1988 and October 1989, and visiting Noriega almost once a month for the past two years. To build the defense, hire investigators to go to Panama to find the documents that would back up Noriega's story, and to pay David Lewis, Jon May, and himself to pore over classified documents ferreted out in the United States was going to cost money, and the going rate was going to start at $250 an hour.

Rubino relied on Lewis's estimate: The job would be labor-intensive and take at least a year. Just to pay his own office overhead, Rubino figured he would need $20,000 a month. Lewis was flying back and forth to New York. May had a new baby at home. There would be the cost of sending investigators to Panama. Some estimates said the government expected to spend $25 million to build the prosecution. To do its case right, the defense was going to spend between $500,000 and $1 million on investigators. There would be travel to Panama; interpreters to translate and transcribe documents; three more lawyers and four or five law clerks, plus support staff. All told, a tight-fisted defense was going to cost at least $3 million to $4 million, Rubino figured. But $900,000 had been spent, and within a week or so of the invasion, Rubino found that whatever additional money Noriega had accumulated, legally or illegally, was out of reach.

Even before Noriega surrendered, U.S. officials had begun to identify assets owned or controlled by him that would be subject to forfeiture as the products of alleged criminal activity. Under federal law the government is permitted before a trial to freeze a defendant's assets by placing liens on bank accounts and real estate as long as it can show that the property is, or might be, profit from a criminal act. Such action protects assets from being dissipated by a defendant until a trial is completed. Hours after placing Noriega in custody, the U.S. and Panamanian governments, using international mutual legal assistance treaties and international requests for judicial assistance through letters rogatory, moved to have countries around the world freeze accounts that the Treasury, State and Justice departments had linked to Noriega. Under the treaties, even countries with bank secrecy laws agreed to comply with efforts to search out tainted drug money. Within days, twenty-seven bank accounts, mostly in Europe, containing $20 million, were placed out of the reach of Noriega, his family, or associates, even though only one of the accounts actually bore Noriega's name. Since a letter rogatory is a request by one court of another court in an independent jurisdiction to assist the administration of justice through methods of court under the latter's control, once the identified accounts were frozen in countries such as France, Switzerland, Austria, West Germany, and England, they fell out of not only Noriega's control but also the control of the U.S. government.

Much the same happened to Noriega's personal possessions. After the invasion, U.S. soldiers seized Noriega's homes, automobiles, and personal possessions, including $5.8 million in cash from his Panama City home. But even though Noriega was placed under arrest by U.S. agents, everything captured by American troops was quickly handed over to the new Panamanian government.

In essence, Noriega had been summarily dispossessed. Though he found himself under the control of the American judicial system where he would be called upon to defend himself against U.S. prosecutors, his means to pay his lawyers had almost vanished—all without a judicial finding of probable cause to show that his assets had been tainted by illegal narcotics activity.

Hoping against hope that the prosecution would be turned back either by the court or by public opinion, Rubino said nothing about the lack of funds for three months. But now Rubino had to find out exactly when the government intended to release some of the seized money.

In the second week of April, Rubino called Dexter Lehtinen. Under federal

law the government was obliged to hold a hearing before the judge if it
intended to continue to keep tight reins on the money. The government certainly would concede that not all of Noriega's wealth was subject to forfeiture
under U.S. law, Rubino told Lehtinen. After all, Noreiga had received a salary
as a general, was known to have sold information to the intelligence services
of various nations, and had his own business interests. His wife, too, had
come from a well-to-do family, had been a teacher, and had her own businesses. Clearly, Noriega had some untainted money.

But Lehtinen explained that the worldwide effort to freeze Noriega's
assets had not been undertaken by his office but by others in the Justice
Department. Noriega's Panamanian assets were now under the control of the
government of Panama, and the international accounts were under the control of the courts of those countries. There was nothing the Miami prosecutors could do. Lehtinen promised he would contact Main Justice and relay
Rubino's concern.

On Friday, April 27, Pat Sullivan called Rubino and May. Their request
that the U.S. government do something to ensure Noriega's defense had gone
to the "highest levels" in Washington, Sullivan told them. The answer had
now come back. There was "no way" the U.S. government could help. There
was no assurance that the money Noriega wanted would ever return to the
control of the American government, and the government was not going to
pay Noriega's defense.

"I don't even have money to pay for copies," Rubino told Sullivan. "I have
a mortgage to pay and a kid in college, and I have to fund this case out of my
own pocket?"

Since January, Rubino said, he had spent three hundred hours on the case.
With the government certain to begin turning over materials found in the
course of their investigation and the beginning of the classified information
discovery, hours and costs were going to skyrocket.

The answer was "No way," Sullivan repeated.

Rubino was infuriated. So was the rest of the defense team. David Lewis
put it directly: Without money, he was out.

That weekend Rubino and May hammered out three pleadings to present
to Judge Hoeveler on Monday. One was a motion to compel the government
to identify all the frozen assets that the government believed belonged to or
were controlled by Noriega; the second asked that the government return or
unfreeze those assets; and the third, calculated to have the greatest impact,
requested that the defense be given permission to withdraw as Noriega's
counsel.

The motion to withdraw got straight to the point. The government had
frozen Noriega's assets in an effort to deprive him of a defense, to deprive
him of a fair trial.

"The government has so tipped the scales in its favor that this court can
have no confidence that the defendant will be able to receive a fair trial,"

Rubino and May told Hoeveler in their motion. The government's unwilling-
ness to negotiate was confirmation enough that it intended to play hardball
with Noriega even at the cost of his constitutionally guaranteed rights. News
of the defense's intent to withdraw had leaked to the *Miami Review* and had
gone out on the national wire services before the motion was even filed. By
noon on Monday, Rubino's office was jammed with reporters.

Whatever advantage the government hoped to gain by not being sympathetic toward the defense's lack of funds was soon far overshadowed by
Rubino, May, and Kollin's plea for fundamental fairness. With the reporters
at hand, Rubino declared that the government would have Noriega's lawyers
go bankrupt trying to defend the general. "The U.S. government in its never-
ending persecution of General Noriega has frozen all his funds," Rubino said.
"We feel there is no way we can adequately represent him if we do not have
the resources we need."

After four months of full-time work, Rubino said he and the three other
defense lawyers had received less than $100,000. The burden of defending
Noriega had prevented them from taking on other clients; their practices
were withering. The defense had reasonably asked the government for only a
"small percentage" of Noriega's assets and had been turned down.

The Bush administration could have only one thing in mind, Rubino said.
"We have no doubt that the administration's refusal to negotiate over legal
fees is in part motivated by its belief that without experienced counsel and
adequate resources [Noriega] will decide to fold. They have taken every single
thing in his house, his cars, his bank accounts, his children's bank account,
his wife's bank accounts, essentially everything he owns, with the exception
of the clothes on his back." What could the government hope to gain by acting this way? Rubino asked.

"I'm sure they are hoping that the general will be given a court-appointed
lawyer, one that has a year or two of experience and has maybe tried two or
three cases, maybe with the aid of one part-time investigator. That's how
they want to try the case. Actually, it's like they want to shoot fish in a barrel," he said.

Rubino said the defense had gone forward without pay in an effort to
prove that General Noriega could get a fair trial. He said to let the government know any sooner that the defense was without money might have
caused the government to work harder to freeze assets. The only way Noriega
was able to maintain his sanity and determination, given all that had befallen
him, was through the confidence he placed in his lawyers. At risk, said
Rubino, was Noriega's right to due process of law and effective assistance of
counsel. Show that the assets seized were subject to forfeiture, Rubino said.
Return the assets that were unfairly seized or dismiss the indictment.

One defense pleading said that of the $20 million seized, $17 million had
been derived from legitimate sources. The U.S. government's own records,
Rubino said, would show that Noriega had been paid as much as $200,000 a

year by the U.S. government for his assistance to the CIA and the Defense
Intelligence Agency. U.S. government money paid to Noriega had gone into
an account at the Bank for Credit and Commerce International. That
account was directly under Noriega's control, Rubino said.

A claim by U.S. Undersecretary of State Lawrence Eagelburger in a speech
in August 1989 to the Organization of American States that Noriega had
wealth of as much as $300 million was wrong, Rubino said. After a worldwide
search, the Bush administration was now claiming that Noriega had assets of
$20 million but was still asserting that it was all tainted drug money. "Come
on, be fair," Rubino said.

Across town, Lehtinen, at the U.S. attorney's office, issued the government's response in a short written statement: "Mr. Noriega has been accorded all the protections of due process and right to counsel. Nothing the
government has done regarding illegally obtained assets has infringed on
these rights in any way."

Judge Hoeveler reviewed the defense's motions on Monday afternoon and
told reporters, "It's a real dilemma; there will be some due process implications from this." The judge said he would hear from both sides in person on
Friday afternoon.

Before Monday was out, the prosecution team sat down to draft a formal
response to the defense motion to withdraw. How could the defense say it
was ill-prepared to go forward or in need of additional resources when it had
been on the case for more than two years? In January, Rubino had bragged to
a federal prosecutor in Orlando that he had received a "seven-figure" retainer
for the case.

Moreover, to imply that the government's request to freeze the bank
accounts denied Noriega the counsel of his choice was off base; the guarantee
afforded defendants under federal law was the right to "adequate representation." The Supreme Court had ruled "those who do not have the means to
hire their own lawyers have no cognizable complaint so long as they are adequately represented by attorneys appointed by the court. A defendant may
not insist on representation by an attorney he cannot afford."

What Noriega and his lawyers were really up to, the prosecutors said, was
"an attempt to require the government to pay defense counsel a higher fee.
Obviously, counsel are dissatisfied with the substantial amount of money
already received. . . . Counsels' desire for larger fees is no legal or ethical justification for withdrawal. This attempt to force the government to pay additional attorneys' fees should be rejected."

The following Friday, Hoeveler directed both the prosecutors and the
defense team to present their arguments in court. Hoeveler told both sides
that he had not been impressed with the events of the past four days. Noriega
was entitled to a fair trial and the perception that there would be a fair trial,
the judge lectured. "We have got to recognize that our justice system is on
display and that [Noriega] is entitled to be represented to every extent possible by those he wants to defend him," Hoeveler said. Noriega was entitled to

a defense, and he should be allowed to pay for it. That would depend on differentiating between monies that were "the product of drug dealing" and those "from other sources." Certainly Noriega "must have acquired some assets of his own in twenty years in the Panamanian army free of taint," the judge said.

"Your Honor," Rubino said, "I don't know if you consider money paid by the CIA to be taint-free." That's where a good portion of Noriega's money had come from, he said. Rubino said he had subpoenaed the Central Intelligence Agency, the Defense Intelligence Agency, the Department of Defense, the chairman of the Joint Chiefs of Staff, the National Security Council, the Secretary of State, the National Security Agency, and the DEA to provide records of money paid Noriega. Unless the U.S. government considered its own funds tainted, then clearly there would be money in the general's accounts "above reproach," Rubino told Judge Hoeveler.

The subpoenas told the real story, Sullivan protested. What the defense wanted, he said, following Rubino to the lectern, was to use the motion to draw out the government's involvement with Noriega and whatever evidence it had gathered.

Hoeveler interrupted. That might be so, he said, but Noriega's right to counsel could not be ignored, and until that issue was resolved, a lingering perception would remain that Noriega was being treated unfairly. Hoeveler said he would give the prosecutors one week to prove that all the assets seized were tainted. In addition, he said he wanted a detailed list of those assets and what efforts the government had made to differentiate between tainted and untainted funds.

In the next days, the prosecutors, with help from Main Justice and the State Department, went back to the same countries that earlier had heeded the request of the letters rogatory. Not only did the prosecution need a detailing of the accounts but it also needed to know if the accounts could be unfrozen to help pay Noriega's legal expenses. The results, however, were disappointing. The initial survey found few governments particularly sympathetic toward the former dictator. Once frozen, the accounts had become subject to forfeiture under the drug laws of the host countries. To unfreeze those monies and turn them over to the United States would be the same as giving away small fortunes.

Matters became more complicated when the new Panamanian government said that not only would it refuse to make available assets seized or frozen in Panama, including the value of Noriega's personal possessions, but it would also challenge the release of assets to Noriega anywhere in the world. The Endara government said that whatever Noriega had stashed or hidden in Panama or elsewhere was either stolen or misappropriated and thus did not belong to him. The Panamanian government had already frozen more than two hundred local bank accounts that it believed were connected to Noriega and the Medellín cartel. In the days after the invasion, the Endara government had formed a task force to try to retrieve money allegedly stolen by

Noriega. The new government said it would seek the recovery of money it believed was lost during twenty-one years of government corruption. In the United States only one relatively small bank account had been seized.

Intelligence agencies in Washington had begun scrambling to answer the defense subpoenas that asked for "any and all records pertaining to all funds paid directly or indirectly to General Manuel Antonio Noriega from January 1, 1970, until the present." Such records would serve two purposes for the defense: First, U.S. pay stubs would immediately demonstrate that Noriega had had a legitimate source of income apart from his salary as a Panamanian soldier. Second, pay records would also demonstrate that Noriega had been on the front line of the drug war *for* the United States; the records would implicitly if not explicitly link Noriega to the efforts of American law enforcement and would serve as a cornerstone to a defense that would show that, whatever he might be accused of, Noriega was working in concert with the United States. Thus, as a U.S. agent, like countless other U.S. agents, it would be highly plausible that Noriega had acted in an undercover role, working closely with drug traffickers in an effort to ultimately snare the wrongdoers.

One week was not going to change what the government already knew. The prosecution was going to have to admit that it had no idea whether the frozen accounts were tainted.

To further complicate matters, the agency record search in Washington had turned up U.S. payments to Noriega. Though there were no records of payments by the DEA, there were payment vouchers from the CIA and the Defense Department. By making intelligence-gathering-related payments available to Noriega's lawyers, it was likely the prosecution would pave the way for even more defense requests and disclosures. The last thing Main Justice wanted was to engender a gray mail or so-called Oliver North defense, where defense requests for government information become so sensitive that national security secrets are jeopardized, and rather than capitulate, the government gives up its case.

There was only one way for the prosecution to avoid embarrassment: pay for Noriega's defense. On Friday, May 18, Lehtinen called Rubino and May with a three-part deal. First, the government would pay defense costs retroactive to the beginning of January if the defense would agree to drop its subpoenas. Second, the government would tell Judge Hoeveler what it had paid Noriega, but not the defense, at least for now. Third, if the frozen accounts were subsequently unfrozen and returned, Noriega would reimburse the government for the money it had paid the defense. If Noriega was convicted, his assets would be forfeited. This course would bury the question of whether the prosecution had acted legally in seizing Noriega's assets without giving him the opportunity to contest the actions.

On Monday, May 21, in a private meeting with Judge Hoeveler and the defense, Lehtinen laid out the deal, explaining that under a federal law called the Criminal Justice Act it was permissible for the government to help an indigent defendant pay his legal fees. Because the government had frozen all of Noriega's accounts without proper authority, he was technically bankrupt and entitled to a public defender, Lehtinen said. Noriega agreed to sign an affidavit attesting to the fact that he was penniless, and he promised to repay the government if some assets were recovered, Lehtinen said.

The judge turned to Rubino.

So far, Rubino told Hoeveler, the defense had incurred $1 million in expenses. To match the government's effort, the defense would need money to pay for investigators, translators, computer specialists, paralegals, and, of course, lawyers. For the type of complex case at hand, Rubino said he and attorney Steven Kollin proposed to be paid $350 per hour. Jon May and David Lewis should receive $300 per hour. And other attorneys, such as Leon Tozo, who was fluent in Spanish and would assist in the debriefing of Noriega, should receive $250 per hour. In the end, Rubino told the judge, the defense was likely to cost in excess of $3 million. "Essentially he has no assets that are not under seizure," Rubino told the judge. "He has no way to pay."

Hoeveler was familiar with the Criminal Justice Act, which allowed for a fee of $60 per hour for an attorney's work in court and $40 for out-of-court work. There seemed to be quite a disparity between what the act allowed and what the defense was requesting, Hoeveler observed.

That was true, Lehtinen said, but the act allowed for higher fees in cases that were "exceedingly complex."

"I can safely say I've never had this situation before," the judge said. But given the circumstances, he continued, he would tentatively agree to the deal, provided it received final approval from the chief judge of the Eleventh Circuit Court in Atlanta, Gerald Tjoflat.

Three days later, on Thursday, May 24, Hoeveler called the prosecutors and the defense back to court.

Hoeveler's demeanor was stern, and he was clearly not pleased. He began by explaining that he had spoken to the chief judge. Judge Tjoflat had been adamant, Hoeveler said. No fee higher than $75 could be paid to the defense, and under the Criminal Justice Act, no compensation totaling more than $10,000 would be paid.

"We're back to square one," Hoeveler said. "Frankly, I would rather General Noriega pay his own legal bills than U.S. taxpayers. . . . The government is going to have to make some decisions on what they want to produce and not produce." Noriega, the judge said, was "no different from so many other defendants who appear before this court." But "the government has taken all of his money, and we have to determine what portion of that money he is entitled to."

Rubino asked to speak, and he wasted little time returning to the attack. The prospect was that the court would appoint new lawyers at low hourly rates to take over the case, Rubino said. By unjustly freezing Noriega's assets, the government would force him to rely on a public defender. "If the court were suddenly to give him court-appointed attorneys at the usual rate, it would take the new team six months just to get up to speed in this complex case," Rubino said, his voice rising. "Our American system of justice will be on trial for the whole world to see. I think the eyes of the world are on our justice system. If this court would rule at a rate of $40, $60, or $75 an hour to try this case, I think in all sincerity it would make a mockery of due process."

Hoeveler ordered both sides to begin preparing for a full hearing on the status of the general's assets and whether the government acted properly. The prosecution, Hoeveler said, would have to demonstrate that the Justice Department had the legal right to freeze the $20 million. Now the government would be required to give evidence showing that Noriega's money was illegally obtained.

Lehtinen rose. Noriega had not submitted a list of assets that he suspected were frozen, he protested.

The government is required by law to notify a defendant of the assets it seizes, Rubino replied. Noriega did not submit a list of assets because the government had never filed notices of seizure or requested a warrant to "arrest" his property as required. "There is indigency, and there is forced indigency," Rubino added. "No man after twenty-five years has acquired nothing in his life. The janitor in my building has acquired something in his humble life. To say that everything Noriega has acquired is related to the charges is ludicrous."

In a week's time the government—with the attitude of the judge clearly seeming to harden toward its position—submitted a written response to the defense's early May motions seeking disclosure of the frozen assets.

The government, Sullivan and Malman argued, did not have to identify the assets seized from Noriega because it had never formally sought the forfeiture of those assets. In fact, they argued, none of Noriega's assets had actually been seized, they were only held in foreign countries. The letters rogatory were requests for assistance, not formal forfeiture proceedings, they argued. If Noriega wanted to challenge the freezing or seizure of assets, he would best do so in the courts of the countries involved, they said.

When Hoeveler received the government's response, he was nearly beside himself with anger. The prosecution's logic was twisted. Rubino was right: It certainly appeared as though the government was willing to deny Noriega not only his assets but also his right to counsel. The time had come to make the government understand in no uncertain terms that the court would not tolerate the perpetration of an injustice upon Noriega or any defendant.

"The precise issue before this court is whether the government may deprive a criminal defendant of his only assets available for attorneys' fees without any showing that the assets are connected to illegal activity and without affording the defendant an opportunity to contest the seizure," Hoeveler said. "Unless the constitutional rights to due process and counsel of choice are to be stripped of all meaningful content, the court must necessarily answer in the negative."

Hoeveler said it was the fundamental provision of the Fifth Amendment that a person not be deprived of life, liberty, or property without due process of law. "Consistent with that fundamental guarantee, due process traditionally requires that a defendant not be deprived of his property without adequate notice and opportunity for a hearing."

At stake in this instance, said Hoeveler, was Noriega's Sixth Amendment right to his counsel of choice. But that right was not absolute, Hoeveler conceded; it was dependent on his ability to pay. An indigent defendant is entitled to counsel but not necessarily the most expensive counsel, he said.

One of the most disturbing elements of the dilemma Noriega now found himself in, Hoeveler said, was that the government had not just deprived him of his assets pending the outcome of a trial, as was usual in asset seizures in drug cases, but that it was prepared to deprive him of counsel before trial. Noriega had been given no meaningful opportunity to be heard, and the government had shown no probable cause. The letters rogatory had even short-circuited judicial review, Hoeveler said.

"What the government believes as to the nature of [Noriega's] assets is nothing more than an accusation at this point," the judge said. "The government has not articulated any interest in justifying its actions in this case."

Hoeveler continued: "No one doubts that an indigent defendant has no constitutional right to counsel of his choice. At most the indigent defendant is entitled to some legal representation in the form of a court-appointed counsel. But by the same token, a defendant cannot be forced into indigence without due process and then be told that he has no right to representation he cannot afford. Noriega is not asking for expensive counsel beyond his financial means; rather, he simply desires to pay his attorneys with assets the government may not be able to prove are the product of criminal activity. Elementary concepts of fairness suggest that no one, government or otherwise, should take and hold another's property which it has no legal right to hold.

"Certainly the government has an interest in combating the drug epidemic which plagues this country," Hoeveler continued, "but its effort must never be at the expense of an accused's constitutional rights."

Neither the Congress nor the people intend the Bill of Rights to be a fatality in the war on drugs, Hoeveler said.

The prosecution's claim that the government could not be strictly held to the formal forfeiture laws because they had never been invoked was lame, Hoeveler said. "The government is always bound by the minimum constitutional requirements imposed under the Fifth Amendment."

Hoeveler, who had let the administration and President Bush have their due when it came to the jurisdictional questions surrounding the invasion, said that power of the executive branch was not limitless. "The power of the Executive to deal with foreign governments is unquestionably great," the judge said, "but it does not extend so far as to impinge on a criminal defendant's right to due process."

And as far as the prosecution's claim that it had no power to persuade foreign governments to unfreeze Noriega's assets, Hoeveler said he didn't buy such an argument. "That the government was able to persuade foreign authorities to freeze the assets in the first place belies its suggestion that it has no influence over the accounts in question," he said.

Not to make the government justify its seizure of Noriega's assets would be a violation of Noriega's Fifth Amendment right not to be deprived of property without due process and his Sixth Amendment right to be represented by counsel. "The danger that an innocent person may be convicted because of unfair deprivation of assets that would have been used to retain his counsel of choice is simply too great to permit a freeze to go unchallenged," Hoeveler said.

The judge then ordered that in one week's time, on June 20, the government would have to show that its actions were justified and that Noriega's assets were tainted. Otherwise, Noriega himself would be allowed to testify as to exactly where he had earned his money, who had paid him, when, and for what reason. In a week's time, Noriega, in his own words, would be able to reveal his relationship with the U.S. government in open court.

Jon May read the judge's order and called it a "stunning, stinging defeat." At last the government had been reprimanded for its behavior, May thought.

The bite of Hoeveler's words were not lost on the prosecutors in Miami or on the top brass at Main Justice, either. Hoeveler was about to get very harsh, Sullivan and Malman knew.

The letters rogatory had become an albatross. The accounts were frozen, and despite what the judge thought, the countries that had frozen them had agendas of their own that might not include paying Noriega's legal bills. The judge was known to be extremely patient and fair, but only to a point.

Letting Noriega take the stand was out of the question; proving that the frozen funds were drug-tainted would be impossible, the prosecutors knew. But the judge had to be appeased.

Two days before the June 20 hearing, Sullivan called Rubino with a proposal: The government would agree to use its best efforts, formal requests, to influence foreign governments to unfreeze the accounts and to give Noriega sufficient funds for his defense. In particular, the administration would do what it could to unfreeze three accounts with assets totaling between $4.5 million and $6 million. In addition, Sullivan promised that the government would reveal the names of the accounts, the signatory parties, and the amounts on deposit of the accounts it would seek to unfreeze. In return, Sullivan proposed, the defense would quit its effort to litigate Noriega's right to counsel, and both sides would stipulate to the agreement and forgo the calling of witnesses on June 20.

The agreement was the picture of expedience from every angle. The defense would give up the noble constitutional question of whether the government had acted properly in seeking to freeze or seize Noriega's assets, but it would pocket the cash it said it needed.

The government would not have to justify what it had done.

Both sides put a righteous spin on the agreement.

"This approach should settle this collateral issue so that both sides can focus on the underlying criminal case," Lehtinen said. "This avoids distracting litigation and premature presentation of evidence that would only sidetrack us from the real issues."

Rubino said: "We feel we now will have the ability to go forward and give General Noriega the defense he deserves. This gets the ball and chain off our leg. We appreciate that the government saw fit to do the right thing."

The judge, too, was impressed. He said the agreement was the "fair and right thing to do."

But before either side could walk out of court, a lawyer with the Washington, D.C., law firm of Williams & Connally stood and asked to speak on behalf of the government of Panama.

Attorney Gregory Craig said that he objected to the release of any frozen monies to Noriega. His clients' interests, he said, "were broader than the interests of this court." The Panamanian government would file a $5.3 billion suit against Noriega, accusing him of racketeering, murder, theft, and fraud against the Panamanian people.

Wherever the government of Panama had to go, whatever court it had to appear before, Craig vowed, Noriega would not have the Panamanian people's money.

As the summer stretched on, it turned out that Noriega would not have his money, either. Even with the June 20 agreement, Main Justice warned there was no guarantee that funds would automatically be released. Formal requests for the releases went out to the governments of Britain, Germany, Luxembourg, Switzerland, and the Cayman Islands.

In particular, the Justice Department targeted three accounts where it felt most confident of getting the $5 million to $6 million it had promised the defense: at the Union Bank of Zurich in Switzerland; the Deutsch-Suedamerikanische Bank AG in Hamburg, Germany; and the Credit Lyonnais in Marseille, France.

By the end of July there was frustration enough to go around. While the prosecution proceeded to contact witnesses and search through captured documents in Panama and secret files in Washington, the defense was all but dead in the water.

David Lewis stepped out of the case, and though he continued to be listed as a defense consultant, there was barely money to pay for long-distance phone calls between Miami and Lewis's New York offices. Steven Kollin, who had been in the defense almost from the start, was close to leaving the team. There was no money to hire investigators to sift through the voluminous documents being held in Panama. Rubino had already decided that if push came to shove, only he and May would stay on. Rubino would be the stand-up-in-court man and May would handle the substantive legal research. It would be no way to run a defense, but it would be cheap.

On Wednesday, July 25, Rubino finally sat down with Lehtinen, Sullivan, and Malman. After three hours he sent a formal letter to the judge.

The government had made its appeals to the banks, and the defense had followed with subpoenas for records to the American branch offices of the three banks, Rubino told Hoeveler. The German bank had not responded. The French bank's New York office said it did not have access to records of accounts in Marseille, and the Swiss bank said it could not make disclosures without authorization of the account holder, and Noriega was not an account signatory.

Rubino said the defense could not proceed. "We're still broke," he told the judge.

Hoeveler, for his part, was all but powerless to make the international banking community stand up and pay attention to his orders. The banks had asked the court to quash the defense subpoenas. They argued that the defense subpoenas violated principles of international comity by forcing them to violate their own country's bank secrecy laws. The defense, the banks said, should have the decency to respect the laws of sovereign nations.

For its part, the Panamanian government made every effort to stay ahead of Noriega's lawyers, sending representatives to banks where Noriega was believed to have deposited money and requesting that funds not be turned over to the United States or the general's lawyers.

Under Hoeveler's direction, a federal magistrate denied the banks' motions to quash the defense subpoenas. Hoeveler said that his efforts to allow Noriega's case to go forward without questions of constitutional violations outweighed the interests of other countries' bank secrecy laws, especially when those laws served the privacy needs of individuals and not national interests.

Some headway was gained in August when the Zurich bank agreed to share account information with the U.S. government, which could then share the information with Noriega's lawyers. And in September the Hamburg bank agreed to open its records; it said the account was now empty but had once contained $11.8 million. But still, no money was forthcoming.

By the middle of October, Rubino still had no money.

"We are at square zero," Rubino told Hoeveler on October 19 at a case status conference.

Months had passed since Hoeveler set Noriega's trial to start on January 28, which was more than a year after Noriega had made his first appearance in court.

"January 28 is unrealistic," Rubino told Hoeveler. "If I got all the money in the world, I couldn't investigate the case before then—and I can't find a dozen investigators to work for free."

Hoeveler was growing more and more frustrated. This mess was the prosecution's making. While the defense sat idle, the prosecution was using the delays to build its case. In the meantime, Noriega's codefendants continued to insist that they were being denied a speedy trial. Hoeveler could not be absolutely sure Rubino had not stashed some of Noriega's money away and was simply holding out for more.

"We've got to press on with this," Hoeveler finally told Rubino. The case was bogging down. The choice was either to remove the defense team and appoint court-paid counsel or reappoint Rubino as a federally paid attorney.

Not much of a choice, Rubino thought.

On Wednesday, October 24, the Panamanian government made good on its threat to stymie Noriega's defense and try to make the former dictator uncomfortable for the rest of his life, if that were any more possible given the circumstances Noriega already found himself in. In a civil suit filed in the Miami federal court, the Republic of Panama claimed that Noriega had looted the national treasury, killed political opponents, and operated the PDF as a criminal enterprise engaging in assassination and torture. In his twenty-eight years as a soldier, officer, and leader of the PDF, Noriega had diverted government revenue and had illegally sold visas and passports, among other things.

The list of crimes recited in the complaint also included drug trafficking, money laundering, racketeering, embezzlement, and abuse of authority. The complaint read like the indictment Richard Gregorie and Mark Schnapp would have delivered against Noriega in 1988 if they hadn't met opposition from Reagan administration officials in the State Department and the National Security Council.

Besides the sale of visas and passports, the complaint listed other ways that Noriega had allegedly enriched himself at the expense of Panama. Specifically, the suit claimed that Noriega had once sold eight government military aircraft and then pocketed the money. It claimed that Noriega once appointed his daughter Lorena an executive secretary in a division of the attorney general's office at an annual salary of $40,715, but the young woman never showed up for work.

The suit sought the recovery of between $300 million and $500 million in assets that Noriega and his associates had spirited out of Panama. In addition, the thirty-two-page complaint asked for punitive damages of $5 billion.

The one basic flaw of the complaint was that Noriega had never been a U.S. citizen and had not lived in the United States during the time he was alleged to have defrauded the Panamanian people. Jurisdictionally, the claim seemed to be misplaced.

Rubino, seeing the complaint, called it a publicity stunt and a nuisance. Its intent, he said, was to see that Noriega was strangled by litigation in the United States and wherever his assets might be and that he wouldn't be able to defend himself. Panama's Washington, D.C., lawyer, Gregory Craig, all but confirmed that notion and perhaps revealed the true intent of the Bush administration when it came to the asset question: He said that much of the information in the complaint had been supplied by the prosecutors.

CHAPTER 15

★★★★★★★

Transitions

Daniel Miranda could help corroborate parts of Floyd Carlton's story. He could verify Carlton's absences from Panama. He had worked for Carlton and could verify Carlton's legitimate businesses. He could verify certain comings and goings. He could identify some of Carlton's planes. He could help the government make Carlton look more credible. But that's all Miranda could do. He knew nothing about the alleged cocaine-smuggling enterprise outlined in the 1988 indictment. He knew nothing of Noriega's alleged involvement. He had never met or dealt with members of the Medellín cartel. It was true that Miranda had copiloted a Lear jet from Fort Lauderdale to Panama and that that plane carried a duffel bag which pilot Eduardo Pardo had told Miranda contained $65,000 in cash. But that was in 1983.

Maybe now Miranda would be suspicious of a duffel bag with $65,000 in cash, but no one had ever heard of the Medellín drug cartel in 1983, and it was not generally suspected that Manuel Noriega was involved in drug running. Panama was a peaceful place. When Pope John Paul went to Panama in 1982, he spoke of divorce and birth control. When he went to Nicaragua on the same trip, he talked about human rights, the desecration of churches, and the problems the Vatican was having with the Sandinistas. There was no talk of international drug conspiracies.

Given that airliners going to the Third World frequently took large amounts of cash to pay for fuel, $65,000 was not an unheard-of amount. Miranda was never told that the bag actually contained $800,000. He was never told that the money was narcotics proceeds. In the scheme of the 1988 Miami indictment, Miranda, the copilot on one briefly described flight, was insignificant.

Even his attorney, Michael O'Kane, believed Miranda was so insignificant to the case that if his defense was vigorous and presented enough problems to the prosecution, eventually it would be to the government's advantage to cut a deal with him and make sure he didn't go to trial. But the government would have to make Miranda a good deal. Eduardo Pardo proved there was no advantage to pleading guilty. In January, Pardo had pled guilty to the indictment without a plea agreement. On Thursday, May 17, with tears running down his face, Pardo was sentenced. He declined to speak on his own behalf, but his attorney, William Meadows, told the judge that his client knew "he did something wrong. He regretted it immediately. He was deeply remorseful for it, and he said he has not done anything similar before or since." Judge Hoeveler sentenced Pardo to thirty months in jail, including the five months already served. The judge said he would consider motions for a reduction of that time if Pardo cooperated with investigators.

The sentencing was good news for O'Kane. Miranda—because he was in exactly the same position as Pardo, maybe better since he was only the copilot—would not serve more than thirty months. And because the case was what was referred to as a pre-guidelines case, that is, an offense that took place before stiff federally mandated prison sentences went into effect in 1987, O'Kane figured that Miranda would do even better. With good behavior, he would probably serve two-thirds of thirty months, the last six months in a halfway house. That was with no plea. For Miranda to plea and to testify for the government—or, more important, to get out of the way and not complicate a Noriega trial—O'Kane decided that the prosecution would have to offer a deal of no more than fourteen months real time, plus residence status in the United States after jail, and the return of Miranda's pilot's license.

If pleading guilty or a guilty verdict at trial meant thirty months, O'Kane could wait. The key would be making sure that Miranda became the fly in the ointment. O'Kane had already upset the prosecutors with his "public disclosure" of a Panama City telephone book map, a map that pinpointed the location of the National Security Agency listening post. Breach of national security, the government had charged.

Then O'Kane rejected as unnecessary the suggestion that he, like other defense counsel, obtain classified information clearances. O'Kane reckoned that doing so would only play into the government's hands. Now anything he disclosed in court would be something he had learned not from a secret document but from his own investigation and interviews. It would only aggravate the government to know it wasn't the only source of information, O'Kane thought.

The government's final remedy for keeping classified information out of the court record was dismissal of an indictment. Not agreeing to keep secrets secret—even if O'Kane didn't know for a fact that the information he had was classified—was a way to hold a gun to the prosecution's head. If the government wanted to keep a lid on Noriega's involvement with the U.S. government, O'Kane wasn't going to help.

Samuel Burstyn, Lt. Col. Luis del Cid's lawyer, also didn't want anything to do with Manuel Noriega. Burstyn had called the initial January hearings for Noriega, del Cid, and the other codefendants "circuses."

Everything about the case looked like trouble to Burstyn. Things hadn't gotten any better as time went on. There was the photograph of Noriega, del Cid, and Castro meeting in Havana in 1984. The photo had been introduced in court and then reproduced on the front page of the *Miami Herald*. There had been all the talk about Noriega and del Cid being the poisoners of children. No one seemed to remember that Luis del Cid had surrendered his troops to the Americans without a shot being fired.

But now the best place for del Cid was as far away from Noriega as he could get, Burstyn decided. If del Cid were to go to trial, it would be better for him if the trial was separate from Noriega's. Perhaps an even better alternative, Burstyn thought, was not to go to trial at all, to cut a deal and be rid of the Noriega burden. On Wednesday, January 10, a little more than two weeks after del Cid's surrender and initial appearance before Judge Hoeveler, Burstyn filed a motion seeking a separate trial.

The severance motion was not unlike those already filed by attorneys for Brian Davidow, the Miami real estate salesman, and William Saldarriaga, a Colombian, both charged in the indictment as well. Burstyn's motion asserted that del Cid was in reality a relatively minor figure in the indictment. Though he had been charged with four of the same counts Noriega had been charged with, the quantity of evidence admissible against him was going to be small. By contrast, the government's case against Noriega was likely to depend heavily on testimony of those who were allegedly involved with Noriega and the Medellín cartel in the transshipment of drugs. Noriega's defense was likely to admit some criminal offenses on the grounds that U.S. law enforcement and intelligence agencies had condoned them. Such a defense could be used to implicate or graymail the government or, alternatively, to claim that Noriega had been entrapped.

Such a defense would be antagonistic to del Cid, who, Burstyn decided, would claim that the charges against him were based on "hearsay evidence" at best. There was an "enormous disparity" between the alleged roles of del Cid and of Noriega as outlined in the indictment, Burstyn told the judge.

There was another good reason to seek separate trials in Burstyn's mind: the spillover of negative pretrial publicity. Any literate person in south Florida who knew who General Noriega was probably had a negative opinion about him. It would be "manifestly unfair" to require del Cid to be tried in the same courtroom as Noriega, Burstyn argued.

On this point, other defense lawyers had already agreed. Davidow's lawyer, Richard Sharpstein, had likened Noriega's presence to that of an "atomic bomb producing fallout which would kill anyone tried with him." Saldarriaga's attorney, Steven Kreisberg, had asked for severance because the media and U.S. officials had placed Noriega in the company of "Ivan the Terrible, Attila the Hun, and Jack the Ripper."

The Noriega "atomic bomb" went off again in June. On the eighth, in Tampa, Enrique "Kiki" Pretelt entered a two-count felony plea admitting he had conspired with Noriega in 1983 and 1984 to smuggle 1.4 million pounds of marijuana into the United States and to launder the profits.

Pretelt, a wealthy Panama City jeweler who also ran a string of duty-free shops and had been in business partnerships with Noriega, agreed to testify that he had conspired with Noriega, Steven Kalish, and César Rodríguez to make the dope shipments from Colombia through Panama to the United States. Kalish headed the operation, but Pretelt had agreed to take care of the false labeling of containers and Noriega was a "silent" partner, the Tampa indictment charged. The scheme was aborted in July 1984 when Kalish was arrested before it could get off the ground.

For his help in tying up the Tampa indictment, Pretelt, forty-seven, would get no more than ten years in prison, and the government would recommend that the Immigration and Naturalization Service not deport him to Panama where he was also wanted on charges. If convicted on the Tampa charges, Noriega would face thirty-five years in prison.

The ten-page plea agreement was a "great deal" for Pretelt, his lawyer said afterward.

Noriega attorney Jon May said, "The government is desperate to obtain whatever witnesses it can to shore up its case. All of these people are testifying because they are getting great deals, not because they are great citizens."

On June 13, Michael O'Kane filed a motion with Judge Hoeveler in which he accused the U.S. government of providing a false inventory of documents seized in Panama. Since January the prosecution had been under a discovery order approved by Judge Hoeveler that called on the government to preserve documents seized during the invasion. But O'Kane charged that an investigator he had sent to Panama discovered a "secret" inventory of captured materials that had never been identified to the court. "Elements" in the U.S. government may have removed documents potentially embarrassing to the United States from records seized in Panama, O'Kane surmised. The five-page inventory, which O'Kane's investigator had found wadded up in a box, included a list of Panamanian military intelligence files and records on political parties. There were thousands of pages of evidence unaccounted for, O'Kane alleged.

It was unclear if the Miami prosecutors knew of the list or of the secret documents, O'Kane said, or if they, too, were "the victim of a cover-up effectuated in Panama by unknown elements within the government of the United States."

The motion drew a clipped response from Gen. Maxwell Thurman, the American who was in charge of the Panamanian invasion forces and the U.S. Southern Command. He said there had been no tampering with records seized in Panama, now under the stewardship of the Command's 470th Intelligence Group.

The prosecution reacted differently: Lead prosecutor Pat Sullivan, at a hearing a week later on O'Kane's motion, conceded that not all of the documents seized had been turned over to the defense. For that matter, said Sullivan, not all of the documents had even been inspected. There was, he said, a "linear mile" of documents in storage, and it would "take months" before they were all sorted, perhaps up to the first day of Noriega's trial, scheduled to begin January 28, 1991.

O'Kane was a nuisance to Noriega's defense team as well. O'Kane's refusal to obtain a classified security clearance and his insistence that Noriega's lawyers not share any classified information with him irritated Frank Rubino.

But what really tipped the Noriega defense against O'Kane was his filing of a civil suit on behalf of two European photographers who said they had been wounded during the invasion. O'Kane did not sue the U.S. government but Noriega. The general, the suit said, had "let loose the dogs of war" by declaring a state of war with the United States. The suit asked for damages and an injunction to prevent Noriega from transferring funds out of south Florida.

Angered and frustrated, Rubino, on June 27, motioned Judge Hoeveler to sever Noriega's trial from Daniel Miranda's. "Mr. O'Kane's actions can best be described as a loose cannon rolling on the deck, with no one having any idea in which direction he may fire next," Rubino wrote in his motion. O'Kane, said Rubino, had "distinguished himself from all other lawyers in this case by his wild and reckless actions."

But O'Kane's assertion that there might be uncataloged or secret files energized Rubino and his colleagues. Following O'Kane's lead, the Noriega defense demanded a list of secret documents seized in Panama. Some of the documents were undoubtedly Noriega's personal property, Rubino asserted, and should be returned to Noriega. "Somehow they [think they] have the right to the documents through sheer power of war," complained Rubino to the judge. It was unfair and a violation of court rules for the prosecution alone to decide which documents should be turned over to the defense, Rubino complained.

On August 2, Judge Hoeveler agreed. He called the defense and prosecution together and instructed Sullivan to make a list of documents available. Though Sullivan complained that some of the documents could have "ramifications both inside and outside of Panama," the judge would not relent.

Prior to that decision, on July 18, Amet Paredes, the son of Gen. Rubén Darios Paredes, the former commander of the Panamanian Defense Forces and Noriega rival, became the seventh defendant to turn himself in. Amet Paredes, who was also the brother of Rubén Paredes, a would-be drug smuggler who had been murdered in 1986 along with César Rodríguez by the cartel in Medellín, gave himself up to the DEA at the United States Embassy in Panama City.

The indictment alleged that Amet and Rubén had smuggled cocaine with the help of Rodríguez. Amet Paredes had conspired with Noriega to smuggle 332 kilograms of cocaine aboard the yacht *Krill.* The drugs were supposed to have gone from Colombia to Panama to the United States, the indictment charged. Although Joel Rosenthal, Paredes's lawyer, had struck no formal deal with the prosecutors before his client gave himself up, it was understood that Paredes's cooperation would bring him much less than the ninety-five years in prison he faced if convicted by a jury.

The value of cutting a deal with the government became amply clear less than a month later in Tampa when Enrique Pretelt returned to court on August 16. Although his lawyer conceded that Pretelt had "liability all over the place," Pretelt's agreement to testify against Noriega made his future look much brighter. The U.S. attorneys in Tampa and Miami agreed to recommend that Pretelt's sentence be capped at ten years—twenty-five years off the maximum he faced—and although Pretelt had admitted earning more than $500,000 in drug trafficking, he forfeited only $108,000.

Judge Hoeveler answered the severance question on Tuesday, October 9. Noriega, Miranda, del Cid, Davidow, and Saldarriaga would have to stand trial together.

The preference for joint trials is dictated by factors of convenience and economy, Hoeveler said. If the same charges and facts were presented twice, then quite simply the taxpayer would pay twice for the time and efforts of a judge and prosecutor.

The ultimate issue in granting severance, Hoeveler said, was whether a jury would be able to compartmentalize and independently appraise the evidence admitted as to each defendant.

"There is no reason to believe that the jury will be unable to distinguish evidence of an attempted smuggling of cocaine aboard a boat from evidence of, for example, Noriega's alleged protection of a cocaine laboratory, provision of secure airstrips in Panama, protecting of cocaine shipments, assurance of the safe passage and laundering of narcotics proceeds in Panamanian banks, and receipt of payments from cartel members for [these] activities," Hoeveler said.

As for the assertion that inflammatory media publicity surrounding Noriega would result in guilt by association without severance, the judge said it was too early to speculate about whether a careful questioning of prospective jurors would not avoid such a problem. Besides, said Hoeveler, if it appeared as though it would be impossible to find an unbiased jury in south Florida, the remedy would not be severance but a change of venue, moving the trial and all of the defendants to another city.

A trial date was scheduled for January 28, 1991, less than four months away.

CHAPTER 16

"I Never Expected a Fair Fight": Fair Trial and Free Press

For the first month of his life in U.S. custody, Noriega was locked away in the basement of the old section of the Miami federal courthouse. His cell, the "submarine," had been the home of prisoners and federal witnesses who had appeared before the grand jury that prepared his indictment in late 1987 and early 1988.

Windowless and below street level, the submarine was connected to the new wing of the courthouse by a series of heavily guarded underground tunnels. When Noriega was scheduled to appear in Judge Hoeveler's ninth-floor courtroom, located in the court's new wing, he was taken in shackles through the tunnels to a private elevator. This elevator, which also provided judges secure access to their chambers, ran up the west side of the courtroom tower to a private foyer just outside the courtrooms and chambers. Going to court, Noriega was escorted by four deputy marshals. After he stepped off the elevator, the handcuffs were removed and he was allowed to walk into court without restraints.

But the submarine had not been designed as a long-term home for any prisoner. For one thing, it had no access to fresh air or to the recreation facilities required by federal prison officials and by the Red Cross, now that the general had been officially recognized as a prisoner or war. There had been talk of relocating Noriega to the federal penitentiary in Atlanta, but as Noriega's lawyers had pointed out in early January, that would have essentially cut Noriega off from his attorneys, who were only beginning to prepare his defense.

The only option was the Metropolitan Correctional Center, a federal medium-security prison twenty-four miles south of the courthouse. MCC is a modern forty-eight-acre campuslike facility on the edge of the Everglades in a scrub pine forest. On a quiet day prisoners taking exercise can hear the roar of tigers coming through the trees from the not-too-distant county zoo.

MCC was already the home of Luis del Cid and other Noriega codefendants rounded up during or after the invasion of Panama. Speculation was that Noriega would soon be joining the prisoner ranks, albeit apart from those he was accused of having conspired with.

By late January construction crews had converted a small one-story detached building, which once housed four inmates, into a special segregated lockup just for Noriega. The lockup was a sort of prison suite consisting of a seven-by-eleven-foot cell with a bed, desk, chair, toilet, and a ten-inch color television; an adjacent cell of the same size that could be used by Noriega to meet visitors; and a third multipurpose cell, fifteen feet by fifteen feet, that included a shower. Adjacent to all three rooms was a fourth room for guards.

Noriega's transfer to MCC occurred on January 28. At MCC he was able to settle into a routine of sorts. His only contacts with the outside world were visits from his attorneys, the guards who accompanied him on nightly walks around a small lake that had a concrete alligator, and a daily diet of soap operas.

The multipurpose room adjacent to his cell was outfitted with a broken-down Schwinn bicycle mounted on a wooden platform and thus converted into an exercise machine, a word processor, two document safes, a copying machine, a paper shredder, a folding table, and six plastic chairs.

Apart from watching television, Noriega spent much of his time writing letters. He tried to answer every letter he received, even letters from school-children who wrote wanting to know what life in prison was like. There was also work to do in preparing the defense. Some days Rubino, May, and Kollin visited two or three times. They would all sit in the conference room discussing the government's allegations or new motions to be filed with the court. Noriega dissected the indictment, trying to remember incidents and the names of people who might have helped the government bring its charges. The idea was to try to second-guess what witnesses had told the grand jury and to come up with the names of others who could undermine the government's case. It was also important, Rubino kept reminding Noriega, to recollect incidents and U.S. government contacts that would help to counter the government's conspiracy assertion. Lonely and isolated, Noriega missed his family and his wife and his mistress. Felicidad, Noriega's wife, and his three daughters were now in the Dominican Republic. At first they had taken refuge in the Cuban embassy in Panama City. Soon after the Panamanian government allowed them to quietly slip into exile.

Noriega's eldest daughter, Lorena, had married a well-to-do Dominican, and Felicidad took her daughters Sandra and Thays to join Lorena in Santo Domingo. The State Department and U.S. immigration officials had blocked all efforts by the family to come to Miami to visit Noriega. Vicki Amado, Noriega's longtime mistress, remained in Panama City with her mother, Norma, a confidante of Noriega's, and his mother, Mama Luisa.

By March, almost the only remaining connection to the outside world and the way life had been for Noriega was the telephone. Prison rules allowed free access to a phone as long as charges on long-distance calls were reversed. That meant Noriega could call just about anywhere and anyone he wanted. There was only one stipulation: As with all inmates, all his calls, unless to counsel, could be monitored. The rule made common and legal sense. Prison officials did not want inmates planning or directing illegal activities from within prison. Phone calls to attorneys, on the other hand, could not be monitored, ensuring protection of attorney-client communication, as guaranteed by the Sixth Amendment.

For most of MCC's inmates, telephone calls were made from a specially designated phone bank. But for Noriega, separated from the main cell block, all calls had to be placed by the guard on duty sitting outside of his cell. The guard would dial the number at Noriega's direction, note the number and time in a logbook, and then hand the receiver through the cell door.

The actual monitoring of calls was automatic through a central prison recording system. Like all prisoners at MCC, Noriega signed a waiver on his first day at the prison agreeing that his calls, except for those to his attorneys, could be reviewed. A sticker attached to the phone saying so served as a reminder.

The telephone became important to Noriega. Within a few days of entering the prison, he began making upwards of five calls each day, some days spending as much as eight hours in conversation. His calls went everywhere: Panama City, Spain, Hong Kong. For overseas calls he often telephoned Frank Rubino's office and had the secretary there connect him through the law office switchboard.

It was hard for Noriega to keep his hand out of Panamanian politics. Some former PDF and Panamanian officials were still in Panama City; some had taken up residence in the Cuban embassy there. Noriega was curious to know if those loyal to him saw any chance of manipulating the uneasiness of transition in Panama. Noriega had despised the Endara-led opposition. That the invasion now had made Guillermo Endara president of Panama was not easy for Noriega to accept. "It is important to keep the morale of our people high," Noriega told one former pro-Noriega legislator by telephone.

Marshaling resources for the defense effort was also important. Somewhere there must be bank accounts unaffected by the American and Panamanian governments. Norma Amado, well versed in Noriega's business dealings, might be instrumental in finding whatever money had gone unfrozen. But many of Noriega's conversations were bittersweet realizations of the course his life had suddenly taken.

"Yo, Dad, what have you got to say?" his daughter Sandra greeted him once in a call from the Dominican Republic.

"Here I am like Tres Patines," Noriega responded only half-jokingly, referring to a popular Cuban radio comedy character who continually found himself in court. "Hah," Sandra said with a laugh and then giggled.

The number of Noriega's phone calls quickly caught the attention of the prosecutors. Sullivan and Malman learned from DEA case agents and prison officials that Noriega's calls were mounting. Somewhere along the way Noriega might mention a name that would nail down a link to the cartel, they believed.

Malman signed the government's first subpoena to the custodian of records at MCC on February 8. It was the first of eight subpoenas seeking the telephone logs and tape recordings of telephone calls by Noriega. The tapes, according to the subpoenas, had potential evidentiary and investigatory value. The subpoenas noted that MCC's custodian of records would likely be asked to appear and testify in court.

A preliminary review of the logs showed that despite the volume of calls, Noriega regularly failed to notify his guards when he was making a privileged call to his attorney. The waiver he had signed said he understood his calls would be monitored unless he specified he was making a privileged call.

The lack of privileged calls struck Pat Sullivan as odd. Steve Grilli and Tom Raffanello, the DEA case agents, also thought the lack of attorney-client–designated calls was unusual. Sullivan wrote a March 6 memo to the prosecution team: "If attorney-client conversations are included on a tape, then the tapes must immediately be sealed and segregated from the others. If only portions of the tape contain attorney-client conversations, then only a sanitized copy or transcript will be made available to Noriega agents and prosecutors."

There would be a review of Noriega's calls first by a prison bureau employee at MCC and then by a Spanish-speaking DEA agent not assigned to the investigation. Each would listen to make sure no attorney-client calls were on any of the tapes that eventually got passed on to the investigators or prosecutors. A first batch of twenty-one tapes was produced by MCC in April and quickly reviewed. Soon another seventy-one tapes were ready for review.

The screen was working, but there was one unexpected hitch. After the first tapes were screened, Sullivan met with the agents and asked, "What are we obtaining from these tapes that has evidentiary value?"

The agents' answer was unexpected. "We don't know for sure what he's talking about," they said. Noriega's lengthy conversations made little if any sense. The former intelligence officer was speaking fragmented, coded sentences. It seemed as though some of the conversations, particularly with old confederates still in Panama, were aimed at directing opposition efforts toward the Endara government. Other calls seemed to revolve around the recovery of hidden bank accounts. But no one was sure. Toward the end of April, the DEA agent who had been assigned to review the tapes was sent back to his home office in Chicago. The tapes began piling up again.

Sullivan thought the idea had turned into a big fizzle. There were no leads. But Steve Grilli, who had been on the case since the beginning, working first with Assistant U.S. Attorney Richard Gregorie, thought José Blandon could help. Blandon was the former PDF senior intelligence officer and Panamanian counsel to New York who had once been close to Noriega. That was until he had testified against the general before the grand jury and also before a Senate subcommittee in 1988. If anyone could understand what Noriega was talking about, Grilli thought, Blandon could.

Blandon was now living in Houston and was likely to be a witness at Noriega's trial. He agreed in June to make a special trip to Miami to review the tapes. He started with a batch of twenty-two tapes.

On June 27, he briefed six DEA agents working the case. Yes, Blandon said, the conversations had to do with the movement of money, but it was unclear what was being moved where. Some of the conversations were with Noriega's friends and family members and also with former Panamanian military and civilian officials, he said. The agents asked Blandon to write a memo outlining what he had heard in the tapes. They would pass the memo on to Sullivan.

Blandon's longhand report covered six pages. He passed it on to Grilli, who without reading it passed it on to Sullivan. Sullivan sat down to read the memo in July and right away found a problem. One conversation, Blandon reported in his synopsis, involved a discussion between Noriega and one of his lawyers. Sullivan stopped reading, called Grilli immediately, and ordered the memo and the tapes sealed and placed in a safe.

What Blandon's memo went on to describe was a discussion about two potential witnesses: Alfredo Sánchez, a convicted drug smuggler who was once employed by the U.S. Defense Intelligence Agency, and Felipe Camargo, a former Panamanian intelligence officer. Sánchez was in the federal Witness Protection Program, and Camargo was being held in a Panamanian jail on charges of beating political opponents. The conversation, Blandon's memo said, was between Noriega and Rubino's chief investigator, Jim Hawkins.

"Think what you know about them and whatever they can know about you, whatever they could say," Hawkins told Noriega. Noriega replied that he could vaguely recollect Camargo, but he did not know Sánchez.

Blandon, unlike the agents who had preceded him in the review, had not been warned about steering clear of attorney-client conversations. The prosecution's sanitizing effort had failed. The tape review as an investigative tool was a bust. Sullivan at the end of July ordered the effort dropped. In five months' time the government had subpoenaed 162 tapes containing more than one thousand conversations. Agents had reviewed fifty-two of the tapes, Blandon another twenty-two. None of the tapes contained information that would be useful at trial.

Frank Rubino had known from the first day Noriega arrived at MCC that his client's phone calls were subject to monitoring. The only safe call, Rubino told Noriega, was a call to his lawyer.

Copies of the government's subpoenas requesting the tapes of MCC had never been delivered to Rubino. They hadn't been sent to the judge, either, even though such action was required under court rules. So Tuesday, November 6, turned out to be a day of surprise for Rubino. That morning Rubino took a call from two reporters for the Cable News Network—Marlene Fernandez and John Camp—who wanted to come by to discuss an important development in the case. The network wanted Rubino to listen to a tape recording on camera. Rubino agreed. Although the recording was scratchy and in places unintelligible, Rubino said the conversation—which involved Noriega's discussion of Alfredo Sánchez and Felipe Camargo—clearly concerned legal strategy and potential witnesses. The voices, Rubino verified, were those of Noriega and investigator Jim Hawkins. The tape was one of seven recordings the network had obtained of Noriega's telephone conversations while at MCC, the CNN reporters told Rubino.

Rubino was dumbfounded. The recording had been made by the federal government, and the conversation clearly seemed to fall under attorney-client privilege, yet a news network had a copy of it.

"It's the most grave violation of [my client's] constitutional rights I have ever seen," Rubino said as the CNN camera continued to roll. The government had sought to learn Noriega's defense strategy. The government seemed prepared to do anything to win a conviction. The next day Rubino called CNN reporter John Camp and explained that broadcasting the Noriega tape could jeopardize his right to a fair trial. The network had to provide the defense with a written assurance that it would not air the tape, Rubino said.

CNN could make no such promise, the reporters told Rubino. As it stood, the network would broadcast the report the next evening.

Late that afternoon Rubino with Jon May went to Judge Hoeveler and told him about the tapes. A fair trial would be impossible if the tapes were aired, Rubino argued. The defense requested that CNN be enjoined from broadcasting attorney-client conversations. Hoeveler set an emergency hearing for the next morning, Thursday, November 8, at 8:30.

When word of the hearing reached CNN, lawyers for the network, including CNN general counsel Steven Korn, met with members of the news staff. At 7 A.M., an hour and a half before the scheduled hearing, CNN broadcast its report. Noriega, the network said, had used his prison telephone to make plans for an insurrection in Panama and a possible return to power. The Bush administration had learned of these plans through its taping of Noriega's conversations, some of which were discussions between Noriega and his legal team. The government could be guilty of misconduct in the case, the broadcast said. Although portions of Noriega's conversations were included in the broadcast, only one was translated from Spanish, and the conversation between Noriega and Hawkins was inaudible.

When Rubino went to court that morning, he feared that CNN would play the privileged conversation or others in future broadcasts. Even though the report had raised the specter of government misconduct—which could lead to a dismissal of the indictment—there was still the question of attorney-client confidentiality and a fair trial, Rubino told Hoeveler. CNN must be barred from airing the prison tapes.

"It's becoming more and more difficult in this case to assure that both parties get a fair trial," the judge observed. Hoeveler was not at all pleased with the turn of events. He paused to consider what he was being asked to do. The defense wanted him to restrain the press from publishing information that it had gathered in the course of its work. Such requests were rare because the law had long been settled: News organizations were free to decide what information should be broadcast or published. It was not for the government or the courts to decide. When prior restraints had been imposed in the past, they were almost always overturned on appeal. Supreme Court Chief Justice Charles Evans Hughes said it best in a 1931 case: "Any prior restraint on expression comes to this court with a presumption against its constitutional validity."

Judge Hoeveler looked at Daniel Waggoner, the CNN lawyer who had flown to Miami for the hearing.

"I think the First Amendment may be the most important amendment we have," the judge said. "The question is, here we have privileged conversation between a lawyer and his client going to the question of the preparation of his case, something to which nobody else is entitled. I am not entitled to it. You are not entitled to it. Nor is anyone else except those lawyers and the client. Now, why should you be able to publish that?"

The attorney-client privilege had been violated not by CNN, Waggoner told Hoeveler, but by the government when it taped the conversations. Protecting Noriega's right to a fair trial was important, but the defense had not yet demonstrated that right was in jeopardy, the lawyer said.

There were other ways besides a prior restraint to make sure Noriega got a fair trial: The judge could quiz the prosecution concerning what it had learned about the defense through the tapes, and the jury could be questioned concerning what it had learned about Noriega through media accounts.

But Hoeveler said that he had to know what was on the tapes before he could know for certain if Noriega's rights had been breached. Allowing millions of Americans to listen to attorney-client conversations would be like "shooting [Noriega's] defense right in the head. I cannot conceive of the right of someone else to know what a lawyer and client are talking about," the judge said.

Two fundamental constitutional rights were at stake: "the sacrosanct First Amendment right of the press to be free from any prior restraint on speech and the fundamental right of an accused to a fair trial," Hoeveler continued, opting to risk prior restraint. CNN would be temporarily restrained from airing any privileged attorney-client conversations, the judge ruled. The easiest and quickest way to determine if Noriega's rights were jeopardized would be for the network to turn over its tapes and allow them to be reviewed. "I would be glad to desist from this procedure if CNN considers this further and elects to act in a way or in a manner which I think comports with the desire of all involved in this case to assure that the defendant is able to have a fair trial," the judge said.

But CNN's attorney said the judge should go to the government. "Their beef is with the government," Waggoner said of the defense. "The barn door is already opened, and the cows are out."

Hoeveler called Myles Malman forward. The government would be ordered to produce a list of all conversations Noriega had had with his attorneys using the prison telephone, the judge told him. Malman assured Hoeveler that the prosecutors had not listened to any of the tapes and had not seen transcripts of the tapes. The FBI was now looking into how CNN had obtained the tapes, he said. The hearing ended.

Hoeveler could see that if the case was dismissed it would likely happen on Sixth Amendment grounds. Noriega's right to counsel and his ability to consult a lawyer without interference could cause dismissal.

In Washington, Assistant Attorney General Robert Mueller said it was false that the government had improperly taped Noriega's telephone calls with his counsel. Mueller had received that assurance from Miami U.S. Attorney Dexter Lehtinen. Lehtinen had ordered senior litigation counsel Norman Moscowitz to debrief the prosecutors and agents. Moscowitz said their stories checked out. Noriega, Mueller said in essence, had been told how to make unmonitored calls to his attorney.

Mueller's statement caused consternation at CNN. The Justice Department seemed to be taking exception to CNN's assertion that attorney-client conversations had been recorded. (What Mueller said, in fact, was that no conversation had been *improperly* recorded.) Now it seemed as though the Justice Department was questioning the network's credibility. The tapes existed, and Rubino had identified the voice of a member of the defense team talking to Noriega. CNN viewers hadn't actually heard the conversation yet; it had been made inaudible by a voiceover in the first report, but it could easily be broadcast. And broadcast of the Noriega-Hawkins conversation would put the lie to the Justice Department's assertion, the CNN producers decided.

The judge had ordered that no privileged conversation could be broadcast, but Rubino, on camera, had identified this conversation as being between his investigator and Noriega. Rubino had in effect waived attorney-client privilege by publicly affirming the conversation, the network's lawyers had decided.

Judge Hoeveler again called the CNN attorneys and Noriega's lawyers back to court on Friday afternoon, November 9. The government had turned over the log of Noriega's calls, but the log entries gave little clue as to the contents of the conversations. The judge again asked CNN to turn over its tapes so that the court could finally decide if Noriega's rights were in jeopardy. "We have an important constitutional right of privacy and a privilege that's involved here, and unless we know what we're talking about, the court can't rule on it," Hoeveler said.

"The initial question presented by the case is whether the press can constitutionally be prohibited from publishing privileged attorney-client communications," he said. His order in part was based on protecting the privacy of conversations between defendants and lawyers.

"I cannot conceive that the law of prior restraint is so sacrosanct and so encompassing that there can be no situation which would justify enjoining publication of communications between attorney and client," Hoeveler said. CNN still refused to give up the tapes. The court had no business meddling in the network's editorial process, said Terry Bienstock, a Miami lawyer representing CNN. The damage had been done by the government, not the network, he said.

The Miami hearing ended at 4:45 P.M. At CNN's headquarters in Atlanta, the decision was made to air the Noriega conversation during the 6:30 newscast. Word of the impending broadcast quickly made its way to Hoeveler's ninth-floor chambers; he could look out his floor-to-ceiling office windows at the mobile news vans parked around the courthouse.

The network had put him in an impossible situation, Hoeveler believed. The judge called Rubino, May, and Bienstock back to his chamber at 5:30. He would extend the broadcasting ban for ten days. Hoeveler was pointed in his comments. "If they publish those tapes, they will be doing so in contempt and violation of [my] order," he said. That could mean jail time for network executives, and fines. Rubino grinned. "Six million payable to us would be nice," he said, thinking of the still- lingering question of how the general would pay for his defense. Jon May offered that if the network would hold its broadcast one more day, he would fly to Atlanta the next morning to present arguments to the circuit court.

The network would not wait, Bienstock said. "This case has been a series of nightmares for freedom of the press," he said. "CNN has been responsible from Day One. They could have published before your order," he told the judge. The government should be called to account for having improperly recorded Noriega, not the network. The court should not be involved in the editorial process of the network, Bienstock said.

"The tapes are what they are," Hoeveler said, his voice rising. "There is nothing editorial in them."

The Noriega-Hawkins conversation was broadcast at 6:30. The CNN report said Noriega's right to a fair trial had been compromised by the taping.

From what he had heard, Rubino said, CNN had received the tapes from a high official in the Panamanian government who had gotten them from someone at the State Department, who had gotten them from the prison. "If our information is correct, then this fact may be sufficient grounds for dismissal," said Rubino. Then he continued, "The government is an eighty-headed snake." How many other things had the government done and not been caught at, he wondered aloud.

The next afternoon, Saturday, November 10, Rubino and May went to Judge Hoeveler with a motion to hold CNN in contempt for violating the order not to broadcast the privileged conversation. Later in the afternoon the Eleventh Circuit, in an opinion that shocked the CNN lawyers, upheld Hoeveler's prior restraint and ordered CNN to produce the tapes to the court. The circuit court had taken strong exception to CNN's Friday evening broadcast, a broadcast the court felt had clearly violated Hoeveler's order. "CNN has shackled the district court by refusing that court's reasonable request for review of the audiotapes it has in its possession and which CNN desires to broadcast," a three-judge panel of the appellate court said.

"While appealing to our nation's judicial system for relief," the panel said, referring to CNN's own appeal, "CNN is at the same time defiant of that system's reasonable directions. No litigant can continue to violate a district court's order and attempt to have that district court's order reviewed at the same time. . . . The First Amendment interest of the press and the Republic will be best served by the immediate production of the tapes held by CNN so that the district court can conduct the difficult balancing of constitutional rights required under these circumstances, an obligation which the district court is required to discharge." For CNN there were now few alternatives: produce the tapes or continue the appeal right to the Supreme Court.

By Monday morning, November 12, as CNN lawyers in Atlanta began preparing their brief for the Supreme Court, Hoeveler again asked CNN to delay more broadcasts. "No one is going to get breathless waiting to hear a conversation between General Noriega and his girlfriend," the judge said. "I can't tell you what to do. I've tried once."

Noriega's lawyers said they would suspend their request for civil contempt charges—a fine they proposed to be $300,000 per broadcast—if CNN agreed not to make any more broadcasts until the Supreme Court ruled. The network agreed. May said the defense was satisfied. "Our concern is to keep General Noriega from being denied a fair trial. I'm not here to squeeze blood out of CNN," he said. "My interest here is stopping CNN from disseminating the conversations, pending review by the Supreme Court, and that's what we've done."

With the free speech issue dealt with, May and Rubino decided to ask that the drug-trafficking charges against Noriega be dismissed on the grounds that the government had violated the right of a defendant to meet privately with his lawyers. It wasn't just the prosecutors that the defense was worried about, May said. There were others. "There's a whole bunch of other people in the United States who may have these tapes, including the State Department and the CIA," he said.

Still unresolved were the questions of unfreezing Noriega's overseas assets to pay for his defense.

Rubino had taken to likening the government to a Medusa's head of slithering snakes, one biting at the next. "With the wink of an eye," Rubino said, one part of the U.S. government could be urging governments to unfreeze these accounts and another could be saying to freeze them again. "No matter how much dancing or argument they give us, we still don't have the money," Rubino told Hoeveler at a hearing on Tuesday, November 13. "I believe these gentlemen are acting in good faith," Rubino said, pointing to Sullivan and Malman. "My problem is a lot higher up."

Hoeveler had called the hearing specifically to hear what progress the prosecution had made in trying to release funds for the defense. Sullivan had asked the director of the Justice Department's Office of International Affairs to come and tell the judge exactly what was going on. "It's rather, Your Honor, like trying to 'unring' a bell," said Drew Arena, the office's director. "The answer we're getting back is that even though we have submitted requests, the foreign governments are unable to unfreeze." Once foreign governments had invoked their own drug laws, they became reluctant to reverse the process.

"Thus you have no idea when, if ever, we will be able to secure those assets?" Hoeveler asked.

"I believe that's a fair characterization," Arena replied.

General Noriega sat at the defense table next to Frank Rubino. It was his first appearance in court since the tape issue had arisen. As usual, he wore a freshly pressed uniform, dark brown trousers, and a tan short-sleeved shirt, but his face seemed unusually pale from the months of confinement. Noriega alternately stared ahead or into his lap. He would sit motionless for minutes at a time, his eyes closed.

The prosecution had been unable to carry out the judge's June order to unfreeze the $4 million to $6 million in Noriega's overseas accounts.

"After how many months?" Hoeveler asked. "We're nowhere. It is obvious that we may not be able to secure any money. . . . The need for this case to go to trial has never been made more clear than by events of the past three or four days," the judge said. "As long as this case lingers, we face the prospect of new issues causing more delays."

Hoeveler said he had received permission from the chief judge of the Eleventh Circuit to appoint two lawyers to defend Noriega. The two could be paid $75 an hour under the Criminal Justice Act, and of course Rubino and May would have the first chance to continue with the case. First, Noriega would have to declare himself a pauper to qualify for the government assistance.

But what hope would a defense team composed of two lawyers have against the government, Rubino wondered aloud. The prosecution had probably assembled a team of twenty-five to thirty lawyers and fifty investigators, Rubino told the judge. "Their budget is probably $25 million," said Rubino. "These are more than guesstimates. . . . There has never been a case of this magnitude," continued Rubino. "Now we are going to the United States Supreme Court. . . . Honest to God, no two lawyers or three lawyers can render effective assistance in a case of this magnitude. David and Goliath, that's how this battle is shaping up."

The battle before the Supreme Court began on Thursday, November 15, when CNN filed two briefs with the Court. One was an emergency application asking the Court to immediately lift the temporary restraining order imposed by Hoeveler, thus allowing it to go forward with further broadcasts.

The other was a formal appeal asking the Court to review the circuit court's ruling upholding Hoeveler's prior restraint as well as Hoeveler's order to turn the tapes over to the court.

"The First Amendment simply does not permit the district court to act as censor and review in advance of an upcoming telecast," the CNN petition to the Court said. "If Oliver North, John DeLorean, and the Watergate defendants can obtain fair trials in the face of massive nationwide publicity, so, too, can Noriega," CNN's lawyers argued. "Gagging CNN will neither cure nor avoid any breach by the prosecution. It will serve only to punish a news medium which has faithfully executed its constitutional role by reporting on criminal proceedings and allegations of unlawful government action. It is the government's interception of Noriega's prison conversations that has frustrated Noriega's claim to [attorney-client] privilege, not CNN's actions in telecasting information about possible government misconduct," the CNN brief said.

That afternoon in downtown Atlanta, two FBI agents spoke with security personnel at the Omni International Hotel. A box of tapes marked "Noriega" had been found in a vacant room at the hotel, which was contained in the complex of buildings that also included CNN's headquarters. The room had been registered to Marlene Fernandez, one of the CNN reporters working on the network's Noriega stories.

On the morning of Friday, November 16, Rubino, May, and David Lewis, who had flown in from New York for the hearing, went to the courthouse early. General Noriega had already been brought to the basement holding cell from MCC.

The four sat and talked about the day's prospects. Once again they would ask the judge to find a way for the defense to be paid. As the three lawyers looked on, Noriega signed an affidavit of indigence. If the prosecutors could not unfreeze the European accounts, then the judge should find a way for the government—perhaps through the administrative office of the federal courts—to pay Noriega's defense costs. Noriega's poverty had been government induced, after all. Rubino had also prepared a motion for dismissal of the indictment as a consequence of the government's actions. As far as Rubino was concerned, the prosecution was guilty of conspiring to deny General Noriega a fair trial and effective assistance of counsel. Not since Watergate had the government acted in such a way to derail justice.

Rubino's motion had three parts. First, it accused the prosecutors of trying to deny Noriega a fair trial by obtaining the details of the defense's strategy and evidence through telephone recordings and then disseminating the details to others. At first the prosecutors said no government agent had heard the tapes, then they said a DEA agent had.

"We still do not know whether our conversations at MCC were recorded or whether our conversations in our offices and homes were recorded," the defense motion said. "Given the fact that these acts were committed by law enforcement agencies, we doubt that we will ever find out the level of governmental intrusion into our professional and personal lives. Nor will we even know the extent that General Noriega's defense has been compromised. In all likelihood the United States now knows how we intend to discredit its witnesses and how we intend to prove that this is a political prosecution." The tapes had been given to the government of Panama by the State Department, and it was probable that the State Department had gotten the tapes from the Justice Department, the motion said. There could have been only one reason for the tapes to end up in the hands of CNN, Rubino said, and that was "to provide otherwise unavailable information to the prosecution team, its agents, and its witnesses, and to poison the minds of potential jurors. . . . There can be no clearer evidence that the United States will stop at nothing to ensure a conviction in this case."

Rubino's motion to the judge said there was more: Two months earlier, a government witness had approached the defense and offered not to testify in exchange for a bribe. "We now believe that this was a setup designed to entrap defense counsel into committing a crime," the motion said. Further, Rubino said that government agents had contacted his former clients and offered them "inducements" if they would provide information of criminal conduct by Rubino. Where would it all stop? Rubino asked.

And as for the question of assets, nothing had changed, the motion continued. Absolutely nothing had come of the June 20 agreement. "The government entered into this agreement in order not to have to justify to this court its seizure of assets which General Noriega sought to use for his defense," the motion said. "It is our belief that the State Department has actively worked to undermine the agreement entered into by the United States and has suggested to the foreign governments that they independently freeze the accounts. It is clear that the United States has engaged in a coordinated effort to sabotage General Noriega's chances of receiving a fair trial," Rubino asserted. "This effort has worked at different levels and has involved different agencies."

In court, Rubino handed a copy of the dismissal motion to the prosecutors. The judge had been given a copy beforehand. Sullivan asked that the prosecution be given two weeks to respond; he said Rubino's disclosure of contact by government witnesses smacked of "trial tactics." Otherwise, why hadn't he come forward sooner? Sullivan asked. As for the financing of the defense, Sullivan said the government was doing all that it could.

Rubino stood again. "The defense has worked tirelessly for eleven months without one penny of compensation," he said. "In all due respect to this court, and most respectfully to General Noriega, we can no longer go on. To go on would be financially impossible. Each one of us is a sole practitioner and not a member of a large firm. For us to continue would be economic suicide."

Then Rubino paused. He looked at the prosecutors and then at the judge. Noriega sat on Rubino's left, erect in full military uniform. The general's eyes were fixed on the judge, and his lips were drawn tight.

"Your Honor," Rubino continued, "this may be an unusual request, but it's a very sincere one. At this time General Noriega himself would most respectfully wish to address Your Honor in open court."

Hoeveler looked out over the court. He looked at Noriega. The request was indeed unusual, but until this moment—after what would soon be a year of legal wrangling—the general had said nothing on his own behalf. At first it was unusual having a de facto leader of a country sitting in court, but everyone, including the judge, had come to accept Noriega's presence. The prosecution did not object.

"He may," Hoeveler said, motioning for Noriega to step forward.

The general rose from his chair and walked to the lectern. He seemed slightly bowed, but an air of confidence seemed to fill him as he stood before the judge. He carried three pages of notes, and when he spoke his first public words for more than ten months, his voice was strong and polished and matter-of-fact.

"When I was brought to the United States, I mistakenly believed that I would be able to receive a fair trial," Noriega began in Spanish. "In order for this to come true, I also believed that I would be able to use my money to hire the lawyers of my choice. It is painfully obvious that the United States government does not wish me to be able to defend myself, and has done everything possible to deprive me of a fair trial and due process. They have taken my money, deprived me of my lawyers, videotaped me in my cell, wiretaped my telephone calls with my lawyers, and even given them to the Endara government and to the press. The government of the United States has ignored my status as a prisoner of war and violated the Geneva Convention. Worst of all," Noriega continued, "they have not acted in a humanitarian manner. Despite repeated requests by the International Red Cross, they have violated my human rights by denying my wife and children visas so that they may come to the United States to visit me. To deprive a woman and children of the basic human right to visit their husband and father is shameful and a violation of international law."

Noriega seemed to grow more erect and taller as he spoke.

"I am a military man, and I understand a good fight. I never expected a fair fight from the government of the United States. I never expected an equal fight from the government of the United States. But I also never expected to face a virtual army of prosecutors and investigators on such an uneven field of battle. The United States government wishes me to engage in combat in the courtroom with them, but my army is to consist of only three unpaid soldiers whose loyalty is unquestionable but are only allowed to be armed with handguns and no support staff while the prosecutor's office has nuclear weapons. This they call a fair fight.

"Obviously, it is to the benefit of the government that I cannot defend myself, for they fear what I know. The battle I face ahead is very similar to when the United States invaded my country. That was one-sided and unfair, and so is this battle."

Noriega paused for a moment and looked away from his notes. The interpreter who was translating his statement to the court paused also and shifted.

"The one shining light through this legal nightmare has been Your Honor, Judge Hoeveler," Noriega continued. You have been as honest and fair as anyone could hope for. You have done your very best to protect me and my rights from the overreaching and oppressive conduct of the government. You have ordered the government to release my funds to pay my lawyers. It is not your fault that the government went behind your back to deprive me of my chosen attorneys. I realize this case has implications to the highest levels of the United States government, including the White House, and I also realize that many forces are at work beyond Your Honor's control. I know you have done your best for me, and I thank you. I thank my lawyers for their diligence, hard work, and unending loyalty to me and this case. They have worked for ten months with no remuneration whatsoever, and for this I will always be in their debt. I cannot and do not expect them to go on to the point of bankruptcy.

"It pains me to know that I am being deprived of their services when the solution to the problem is so simple. When I was the leader of the Republic of Panama, the United States would ask many different things of me. They would ask me to arrest people, to allow the search of Panamanian flag vessels, to send people to the United States for trial, and to freeze bank accounts. I know that when the United States seriously requests something from a foreign government, they get it. The purported efforts of the United States government to unfreeze certain of my funds to pay my lawyers and finance my defense were a sham. If the United States government sincerely wanted those accounts unfrozen, they would have been unfrozen. I am now at the mercy of a totally unfair and unjust system that chooses my prosecutors and now chooses my defense lawyers."

A controlled anger had begun to fill Noriega's voice.

"This is not justice. Why are we pretending to make it look like justice?"

Noriega stopped and looked at the judge. The courtroom was completely silent. The general turned and walked back to his seat.

It was Judge Hoeveler's turn to speak, but he let the silence go on. It was clear to Hoeveler how Noriega had come to be the leader of a country. His style had been confident and commanding.

"Yes, sir," Hoeveler finally said. If the defense was to quit, other competent counsel would assuredly take its place, Hoeveler said, speaking directly to Noriega. "I want the defendant to understand he is not being cast adrift by the court, the judicial system. So I say this for his benefit, that this case will not lag. He is entitled to a trial. He is entitled to a fair trial."

The next day, Saturday, November 17, at the Supreme Court's request, both the government's and Noriega's lawyers filed briefs addressing CNN's appeal of Hoeveler's prior restraint. Rarely did the Supreme Court ask for briefs to be filed on a Saturday. It was conjectured that the Court planned to rule at its regular sitting the following Wednesday.

In a twenty-page brief, U.S. Solicitor General Kenneth Starr sided in part with Noriega's lawyers, arguing that Hoeveler had been justified in temporarily blocking CNN from broadcasting Noriega's conversations. Starr conceded that a prior restraint was justified in only the most extraordinary of circumstances, but under the "peculiar circumstances" of the Noriega case—where the judge had no idea what was on the tapes—a temporary restraint should be tolerated until "the court can make the factual findings necessary to determine whether an injunction is justified."

Starr, however, did not go as far as Jon May, who again argued that the case "presents fundamental questions concerning the balance between the First Amendment right of freedom of the press and the Sixth Amendment right of the accused to a fair trial and the effective assistance of counsel. The fundamental question presented this Court is whether any defendant can receive effective assistance of counsel and a fair trial if each day he and his lawyers face the possibility of their most trusted confidences being revealed to four hundred million viewers of Cable News Network," May said. "The answer to that question must be no."

The next day, Sunday, November 18, the Supreme Court, in a 7-2 vote, declined to accept CNN's petition to lift the original restraining order issued by Hoeveler, which meant the Court had ruled against CNN's request that Hoeveler be required to lift his ban on the broadcast of the tapes.

The decision stunned many First Amendment lawyers, and it stunned Noriega's defense team. It was the first time the High Court had ever affirmed that a news organization could be prevented in advance from publishing or broadcasting information of any sort. Even though the Court had ruled only on Hoeveler's temporary ban—the network would be free to return to the Supreme Court if Hoeveler permanently banned broadcast of the tapes—the decision still amounted to an affirmation of a prior restraint. CNN would now have to turn the tapes over to the judge for review.

Justices Thurgood Marshall and Sandra Day O'Connor dissented from the majority, saying the Court's action had "extraordinary consequence" for freedom of the press.

Marshall wrote in his dissent: "Our precedents make unmistakably clear that any prior restraint of expression comes to this Court bearing a heavy presumption against its constitutional validity and that the proponent of this drastic remedy carries a heavy burden of showing justification of its imposition. I do not see how the prior restraint imposed in this case can be reconciled with these teachings."

"The refusal of the Supreme Court, over the dissent of Justices Marshall and O'Connor, to hear at this time CNN's challenge to the prior restraint imposed upon it is a loss of a battle in a continuing war against censorship," CNN president Thomas Johnson said.

In fact, CNN had virtually invited a prior restraint by first announcing that it had the tapes. But the existence of the tapes had excited CNN more than what was on them. "This is a case of the messenger shooting itself," Jon May summarized. "To whatever extent the media may complain, this is a significant adverse decision. CNN has only itself to blame."

On Monday morning, November 19, Noriega's lawyers wasted little time subpoenaing CNN's records on how many times the tapes had been aired. The defense would ask for a contempt hearing and seek a fine of $300,000 for each broadcast of the tapes. Such a fine could reach as high as $12 million, May estimated. That would pay for Noriega's defense.

The next day, CNN handed the tapes over to Hoeveler, who, to make sure he was not exposed to any potentially privileged communications, immediately gave them to a magistrate for review. But CNN said the review would show that it had not broadcast any tapes that would jeopardize a fair trial. "We are confident that after Judge Hoeveler considers the content, he will hold that continuing prior restraint is not appropriate," the network said in a statement. "If he does not, his holding will be subject to further appellate review, and we would vigorously pursue our rights." By late Tuesday afternoon, transcripts of the CNN tapes were ready for Hoeveler and the defense lawyers' review.

The subject on Monday, November 26, was assets. It had been a week and a half since Noriega had stood and addressed the court. Hoeveler had ended that hearing by saying that he had no intention of letting the case flounder or letting Noriega go defenseless. Several top lawyers had contacted him about representing Noriega should the defense finally withdraw. All said they would do it for the legal cap of $75 an hour; a few said they would do it for free. Hoeveler was convinced that Noriega would get good representation and a fair trial, but even so, the best solution was to keep Rubino and as much of his team as possible on the case.

Judge Hoeveler was detached. He was uncharacteristically cold. He said he intended to hold off just a little longer on deciding to appoint new defense lawyers.

"I am deeply concerned about the image that this case seems to be acquiring, that the defendant is not going to get a fair trial," he said. "I've heard this joked about, spoken about in public. I'm sensitive to what is occurring, and it's because of this series of events with which we have been involved. I'm bound and determined that this defendant is going to get a fair trial, so I want to dispose of these collateral issues."

"We have a case that is being watched by so many, and it is incumbent on this court to do all the law requires and permits to make sure that he does indeed get a fair trial." Hoeveler asked Sullivan what progress the government had made in unfreezing the foreign bank accounts. When Sullivan answered that there had been none, Hoeveler said he would hold an evidentiary hearing at which the government would be required to prove that Noriega's money had been acquired illegally. And if the government couldn't, then he would enter such a finding and order the money turned over. With the finding and order, Hoeveler said, perhaps the Justice Department could convince the foreign governments to unfreeze the accounts.

The controversy over the content of the CNN tapes came to a whimpering end on Wednesday, November 28. The judge and the defense had had eight days to study the tapes and seventy-two pages of transcripts prepared by the magistrate.

The tapes contained conversations of Noriega talking to his wife, his three daughters, his mistress, his mistress's mother, Rubino's legal secretary, and the defense team investigator. There was family small talk as well as talk about government policies in Panama. There were cryptic references to former allies, the weather, and food. There was even talk about Frankenstein. Most of the time Noriega simply listened and responded "Yes." Rubino called it all "boring stuff." Only one of the seven tapes contained attorney-client conversation, the one that CNN had broadcast. "Had CNN showed us the tapes two weeks ago, we could have avoided all this," Rubino said.

Rubino agreed with Hoeveler that there was nothing on the tapes that would jeopardize Noriega's defense. He agreed that the ban should be lifted. "A ban now is like shutting the barn after the horse escapes," he said. But the defense would pursue its motion to dismiss the case on the grounds of government misconduct. And, he added, CNN should still be held in contempt for broadcasting the tapes after Hoeveler's ban.

Hoeveler said he would make sure of one thing: to order the Bureau of Prisons not to give any government agency further access to any prison tapes without his approval.

From the first revelation, the tapes had been nothing short of an unmitigated disaster for the government. There had been no intention on Sullivan's part to eavesdrop on the defense team. The prosecution had only hoped to pick up a few leads that would help nail down some of the allegations in the indictment.

The subpoenas should have been disclosed to the defense and the judge; that they hadn't been made the prosecution look bad and only spurred on those who contended that the whole mess was one more example of the Bush administration's vendetta against Noriega.

Sullivan could not deny that much of what had happened smacked of government misconduct, even if all could be explained away as unintentional. It was a disgusting situation for a career prosecutor to find himself in.

On a very practical level, once all the defense's dismissal motions were turned back, which Sullivan felt sure they would be, the leak of the tapes gave rise to another concern. How much could the prosecutors trust some of the chief witnesses who had helped secure the 1988 indictment? The tapes had supposedly come to the CNN reporter from a source in Panama. But how had that person gotten the tapes? It was clear that José Blandon, future star witness for the government, had leaked them. When Blandon was brought to

Miami DEA headquarters to review the tapes, he also carried his own pocket tape recorder. As he sat in a small office listening to the tapes—with agent Steven Grilli sitting only a few feet away—he secretly made his own copy of the tapes. Blandon leaked the tapes to friends in Panama, and, in turn, to CNN. Blandon had been a solid choice to review the tapes. He could certainly recognize obscure names and references in Noriega's conversations. But, as Sullivan learned the hard way, there was also a matter of trust. If Blandon could not be trusted to review the tapes in confidence, then how could his testimony be trusted? Sullivan had already begun to suspect it couldn't. He had spoken to Blandon both on the phone and in person. There was something about his story that didn't add up: His testimony didn't fit the facts.

The Darien lab had been raided by the PDF in May 1984. All of the lab workers had been rounded up and then released within five days and flown back to Colombia. In his testimony to the grand jury, Blandon asserted that Noriega had been paid a bribe by the cartel to protect the lab, and after the raid, the cartel wanted revenge for the double cross. Blandon told the grand jury that at the Havana meeting a nervous Noriega, who feared the cartel might assassinate him, had negotiated a truce with the drug leaders through Fidel Castro. The cartel would call off its hit squad if the Darien lab workers were set free, Blandon testified.

The only problem with Blandon's testimony, Sullivan found, was that it wasn't true. The lab workers had been released a full six weeks before the Havana meeting, and Blandon had to know that. In fact, as far as Sullivan could tell, the Miami prosecutors, Gregorie and Kellner, had known it as well. Yet a major allegation in the indictment was the quid pro quo set at the Havana meeting.

That was not to say Noriega had not been bribed by the cartel—Sullivan continued to believe he had—but putting Blandon on the witness stand to say so at the trial was highly questionable. And with the CNN tape fiasco, there was now no way that Sullivan would let Blandon come under cross-examination by the defense, not if he had been exposed to privileged material. The prosecutors would have to find an alternative way to prove the charge of bribery for the lab's protection.

There was shortly, however, one bit of good news on the witness front. On Tuesday, December 14, the government and Luis del Cid finally came to an agreement. After nine months of back-and-forth negotiation, del Cid agreed to plead guilty and testify against Noriega. In return, the government would drop three counts against del Cid, leaving him to plead to just one count of conspiracy under the Racketeering Influenced Corrupt Organizations Act. The count carried a prison term of up to twenty years and a $50,000 fine.

The del Cid plea was a boost for Sullivan. Del Cid was now the second codefendant to agree to cooperate. It had been a long dry spell since Eduardo Pardo had pled guilty in February.

★   ★   ★

On Friday, January 11, 1991, more than a year after General Noriega's first appearance in court, Sullivan himself became the first witness to give testimony in *United States v. Noriega*. It was an unusual turn of events.

The question of whether the government had deliberately monitored Noriega's prison conversations with his attorneys had festered since the beginning of November. Rubino and May called upon Judge Hoeveler to hold an evidentiary hearing at which Sullivan, Malman, and the DEA agents who had dealt with the prison tapes, as well as José Blandon who had reviewed them, could be called as witnesses. The objective was to find out exactly what the prosecution had learned from the tapes and when they had learned it. "To sweep this under the rug would be a denial of due process for the general," Rubino said. At the very least the government had violated federal rules of evidence by failing to disclose the existence of the tapes. If it was worse, the case should be dismissed because of the prosecution's prejudice, Rubino asserted.

"The United States maintains that no privileged calls were ever taped because Noriega was fully advised that all of his telephone calls would be monitored unless he followed a specific procedure for privileged calls to his lawyers," the government said in a pleading opposing the dismissal motion. "Noriega never invoked that procedure; therefore, all of his calls were properly monitored. During the entire period of his incarceration, Noriega has never requested the opportunity to make an unmonitored attorney call."

But for Hoeveler, the appearance of justice, as well as its true guarantee, had become more important than ever. The case had spawned one ugly episode after another, the judge complained to his clerks privately. The tapes were just the latest. The defense, Hoeveler decided, was entitled to hear directly from the prosecutors what they had intended. Letting the defense have its day in open court would serve to help cleanse the case publicly. So Rubino called Sullivan to the stand. The prosecutor was sworn and took his seat not more than fifteen feet away from Noriega, who sat listening through headphones.

Sullivan was tight-lipped, uncomfortable, and uncooperative. To one question after another he was vague and almost oblique in his answers. As the questioning slowly progressed, Rubino finally complained to the judge: "Your Honor, Mr. Sullivan is probably the most adverse witness I have ever faced in seventeen years of practicing law."

Sullivan conceded that he had subpoenaed the tapes without telling the judge or the defense.

"Was it to keep us in the dark?" Rubino asked.

"My intent was not to disclose to the defense attorneys that we were listening to conversations," Sullivan replied.

On cross-examination by government senior litigation counsel Norman Moscowitz, Sullivan told of how he had been surprised that the Blandon memo contained references to an attorney-client conversation. "I didn't think there would be any," Sullivan explained. "When I came to the part about Noriega speaking to his lawyers, I stopped."

Sullivan was followed to the witness stand by assistant lead prosecutor Myles Malman and then by DEA agents Tom Raffanello and Steven Grilli.

The DEA agents testified they were more than confident that Noriega knew his calls were being monitored. At times Noriega and his lawyers had even mentioned in small talk that they had to be careful because of the monitoring, the agents said.

Grilli conceded that while Blandon was working to decode the tapes in the DEA's Miami headquarters, there were times when he was only intermittently supervised. Blandon could have secretly duplicated the tapes. But Blandon would not tell his story—not now, perhaps never. The government had cranked up a criminal investigation into the tapes diversion, and Blandon was the chief suspect. Anything he might say in court could be used against him. "My advice to him is that since there is an impending investigation, he should not testify without immunity," Blandon's Dallas attorney, Stan McMurry, said. Otherwise he would invoke the Fifth Amendment and decline to answer, his attorney said.

So the defense was going to have to take the prosecution's word for it, Moscowitz finally told Judge Hoeveler. The prosecutors had received excerpts from Noriega's attorney-client conversations, but they had not gleaned any sensitive information that would compromise the defense, Moscowitz said.

Hoeveler ruled on the dismissal motion two weeks later, on Monday, January 28, and few were surprised.

"I am concerned about the way these things have developed," the judge said. "While there were some irregularities," he said, referring to the manner in which the tapes were obtained, "I'm going to follow the law, which says that dismissal is too great a sanction. I don't think the defendant has been hurt to the extent that he has been denied a fair trial." Hoeveler said he would consider suppressing or restricting evidence that had been "tainted" by the tapes if the defense could prove that was the case. "I am concerned about the way access to the tapes was obtained," he said. In fact, the government had violated federal rules of criminal procedure governing the discovery and handling of evidence. "Nonetheless, it is clear that these violations have not resulted in any prejudice to Noriega. The conversations consisted mostly of incomprehensible dialogue, discussions of Panamanian politics, and occasional trivia which contained nothing of value to the prosecution." Neither Noriega's Sixth Amendment right to counsel nor his Fourth Amendment right to privacy had been irreconcilably harmed, the judge said.

If the matter of paying the defense could be finally settled, Noriega's trial would begin on June 24, 1991, the judge said, slightly less than six months away.

The dilemma of financing the defense was finally settled in the last days of January 1991. But as usual things came with an odd turn and twist.

On January 18 the government grudgingly admitted that Noriega had been on the U.S. payroll, but its payout to him over thirty-one years had been meager. All told it added up to $320,000 in cash and gifts. In papers filed with the court, Sullivan said that the Army and the CIA had made payouts to Noriega. The details were sketchy. The Army had paid a total of $162,168, almost half of which had been in the form of gifts and incentives. In 1955, Noriega had received a check for $10.70. In 1982 he received a sound and projection system worth $50,000 and $6,176 in cash.

The CIA had paid Noriega monthly stipends of $1,949. His top earning years were 1979 ($24,000) and 1985 ($25,000). In 1977 and 1978 he had received nothing.

The government said in its filing that it would not explain what Noriega did in exchange for the payments, but it called the payouts "stipend, subsidy, or salary" and said Noriega had signed receipts for most of the payments. Notably, no payments to Noriega had come from the DEA, according to the government pleadings.

The pleadings were clearly designed to rebut the defense notion that Noriega had received millions. Rubino and May scoffed at the figures. "The prosecutors knew less than I thought," said May. "I can only say that the evidence that will come out at trial will establish a much higher figure than the government has revealed."

The best news for the defense came in the final two days of January when the government of Austria agreed to release $1.6 million from an account frozen in Vienna. Judge Hoeveler gained approval at last from the federal Administrative Office of the Courts and the Eleventh Circuit's chief judge to appoint two of Noriega's attorneys to continue to work on the case at the government's expense. In a matter of hours, Rubino and May agreed with the judge that the $1.6 million from Austria would be used to pay the defense's costs through the end of December 1990. As for the future, the entire defense team would withdraw from the case effective immediately, and Rubino and May alone would accept the case on court appointment at the flat rate of $75 per hour. Steven Kollin and David Lewis had slowly been pulling themselves out of the case anyway. The defense would continue with just two lawyers. "All right," Hoeveler told Rubino. "Then I will consider for all practical purposes you are in and Mr. May is in. And I must say, regretfully, as far as our other counsel are concerned, they are out. So be it."

CHAPTER 17

★★★★★★★

The Voyage of the *Krill*

Ramón Navarro was a thin Colombian with curly salt-and-pepper hair and an olive complexion. Some called him "Loco." Many called him "El Turco."

He drove a red 1989 BMW, which he had stolen, carried a gun, had a wife and a twenty-two-year-old Colombian girlfriend. He listed his occupation as importer-exporter. He said he had a yearly income of $24,000 but lived in a $350,000 house. In 1986 he slipped out of Colombia just as the National Police were about to arrest him for being part of a scheme to smuggle cocaine to the United States aboard a fifty-foot pleasure yacht named the *Krill*. Shortly after he found his way to the United States where he hid out in Miami. In 1987 he was caught trying to buy two handguns, a federal offense for an illegal alien.

At the Metropolitan Correctional Center south of Miami, the same federal lockup that would eventually house Noriega, Navarro met José Louis Acosta, a marijuana smuggler doing sixty years and trying to work off part of his sentence by soliciting prisoners to cooperate with federal prosecutors. Navarro learned that a Miami federal prosecutor named Richard Gregorie was trying to put together a case against Panamanian strongman Manuel Noriega. For immunity from prosecution for his past crimes and a pass on the gun charges, Navarro agreed to tell Gregorie and a federal grand jury about a scheme to ship guns to Colombia from Panama, to trade the guns for cocaine, and then ship the cocaine to the United States. Involved in the business with the Medellín cartel were a business associate of Manuel Noriega, the two sons of General Manuel Rubén Paredes, and an American real estate broker, Navarro claimed.

The *Krill*, Navarro told the Miami prosecutors, had been sold to William Saldarriaga, an in-law of the Ochoa cartel family, and Navarro, allegedly with Noriega's permission. At a meeting on March 10, 1986, Navarro told the grand jury, Noriega learned the specifics of the deal, the amount of cocaine that the Panamanians and Colombians planned to smuggle, the destination, the deferred payment for transportation, and how the cocaine would be acquired. Not only did Noriega approve the sale of the *Krill* and the smuggling scheme, Navarro said, he also assisted in having the *Krill* removed from Panamanian registry and provided Rubén Paredes, Jr., the son of the onetime head of the Panamanian National Guard and one of the smugglers, a second passport. He also autographed a photograph to be placed aboard the *Krill* to ensure its safe passage. Navarro claimed he was not the only witness to Noriega's involvement in the smuggling scheme. At the planning meeting held in a restaurant owned by César Rodríguez atop the Bank of Boston building in Panama City were Noriega, the Paredes brothers, Brian Davidow, the American real estate salesman, and several others.

Following the March 10, 1986, meeting, Rubén Paredes, Jr., and César Rodriguez, Noriega's longtime business associate, were found murdered in Medellín. And a little more than two weeks later, on March 26, the *Krill* and 322 kilograms of cocaine were seized by the Colombian National Police at San Andrés Island, Colombia.

Before the 1988 grand jury, Navarro followed Carlton to offer testimony. DEA agent Steven Grilli had also rounded up Orlando Villarreal and his son Toti. They followed Navarro.

Navarro's assertion became the foundation for counts nine and ten of the Miami indictment. Count nine accused Noriega, Amet Paredes, Davidow, Saldarriaga, and two other Colombians of conspiring to import and distribute 322 kilograms of cocaine into the United States. Count ten accused the group of actual distribution of the cocaine.

Now, in March 1991, five years had passed since the *Krill* venture had been planned. Four years had passed since Navarro told his story to the Miami grand jury. The failed voyage of the *Krill* remained one of the most tantalizing tales associated with the Noriega case, but some of the luster associated with Navarro's story had begun to fade.

Sullivan considered the trafficker a pathetic character, too brash and loud. From the first moment they met, Sullivan searched for a way to avoid using Navarro to help prove the allegations at trial. Malman felt the same way. Nothing about Navarro's garish dress, manner, or speech rang true, Malman thought. Navarro looked like a drug dealer right out of a bad television movie. Since Navarro had given his story to Gregorie, in fact, the DEA had become convinced that Navarro was continuing to deal drugs. Getting a conviction wouldn't take much work, but there was a real dilemma within the Miami DEA about making a case. To do so would all but pull the rug out from under the Noriega indictment. The agency had paid Navarro a $50,000 informant's fee to work on two drug stings in 1988 and 1989, but he was never called to testify because prosecutors knew almost any good defense lawyer would be sure to use Navarro's own criminal record to discredit him, and even the DEA suspected Navarro had used his informant's fee to buy drugs.

Whether to risk using Navarro at trial became a more pressing question by the second week of January 1991. The effort to find a way to pay for Noriega's defense had now dragged on for a year. Meanwhile, Noriega's remaining codefendants—the ones who had not entered plea agreements with the government, Brian Davidow and William Saldarriaga—waited patiently for a trial date. Their speedy trial rights demanded that they be given a chance to go to court soon. Following a mid-January hearing, Judge Hoeveler agreed that the two should not have to wait any longer. The judge granted severance and set a trial date for Monday, February 25.

Now, with the trial of Davidow and Saldarriaga less than two weeks off, Pat Sullivan was faced with calling as his star witness one bad actor. Sullivan tried to measure just how useful Navarro would be. He had told the grand jury that he'd met person to person with Noriega about the *Krill*. But then there were no other witnesses who would say that had happened. Even worse, there was at least one witness, Amet Paredes, who would say specifically that Noriega never met face-to-face with the other conspirators.

Paredes was named in five counts of the Miami indictment, including counts that he participated in two racketeering conspiracies, manufactured cocaine for sale, conspired to import cocaine, and distributed cocaine. Each count was connected directly to the *Krill*. If convicted on every offense, Paredes faced up to ninety-five years in prison and a $1 million fine. Shortly after the delivery of the 1988 indictment, Paredes's father, the former general, called the DEA in Miami. He spoke to supervisor Ken Kennedy and Steve Grilli. Paredes wanted bond for his son. Amet would give himself up, General Paredes said, but he must be allowed to bond out and be given permission to return to his family in Panama.

But U.S. Attorney Leon Kellner was skeptical. Kellner said that if Amet turned himself in, he could not guarantee he would be allowed to return to Panama. For the next year and a half, Grilli and Kennedy kept tabs on young Paredes. Amet was often seen in Panama, but with Noriega in power there was little hope he would ever be returned to the United States.

Life changed radically for Amet Paredes with the U.S. invasion of Panama. Although his movements had been restricted by Noriega after the indictment, he had also enjoyed protection from prosecution. With the invasion, for the first time, he felt truly at risk of being arrested and taken to Miami to face the indictment. He gave formal statements five times that he was not involved in the *Krill* venture, but still he was wanted.

With the invasion Paredes went into hiding. For the fifteen days that Panama remained in a state of war and under siege, a period during which the country's civil laws were suspended and American troops and DEA agents were legally free to remove Paredes to the United States—just as they had with Luis del Cid—Paredes could not be found.

But by January 1990, with Noriega in custody, it was clear to the Paredeses that it was only a matter of time before the Panamanian government itself would deal with Amet. In February the family hired a Miami lawyer to begin searching for a way to make a deal with the Miami prosecutors. "We were confident that Amet would get his things together, finish his business arrangements, say good-bye to his kids and his family," Steve Grilli said later. "We felt it was guaranteed that he was going to come up here and face the music."

Sullivan wasn't sure exactly what Paredes would offer, but he knew he could be an important witness. And there was Amet's father, the general. It was possible the elder Paredes could help stitch together a broader case against Noriega. And maybe the senior Paredes could exert some influence on the now former members of the PDF to come forward with information. There were several former officers who had firsthand knowledge about the work of the PDF under Noriega. If they could be identified and located, they might be used to double-check new evidence and information being gathered in Panama.

Three months after the invasion, General Paredes, through Miami attorney Joel Rosenthal, contacted Grilli. Amet was ready to deal. General Paredes flew to Miami and with Rosenthal met with Grilli and U.S. Attorney Dexter Lehtinen's chief assistant, Marcella Cohen. The best thing for Amet to do was give himself up, Grilli said.

Cohen was adamant that neither the U.S. attorney's office nor the DEA would negotiate a surrender. Amet was a fugitive. Sooner or later he'd be caught, and then things would not go as well as if he returned voluntarily.

On July 17, seven months after the invasion, Amet walked into the United States Embassy in Panama City and surrendered. The next day he was arraigned in Miami.

But Paredes did not make any promises about aiding the Noriega prosecution. In five statements in Panama, he continually maintained he knew nothing about the *Krill* or Noriega's involvement. When he arrived in Miami, it was the same story.

Grilli kept on Paredes sixteen hours a day. Amet was not yet thirty. Grilli could see he was smart enough to know that sitting in jail the rest of his life was not the answer.

The 1986 murder of his brother Rubén and César Rodríguez in Medellín had never been solved. Some speculated that the two had shortchanged the cartel, skimming off for themselves some of the *Krill* cocaine. Cartel chief Pablo Escobar may have paid hitmen to be rid of the pair. Others thought maybe Noriega himself had decided to cut out the middlemen in the *Krill* deal. No investigation in Colombia or Panama had ever gotten to the bottom of the killings.

Grilli kept after Amet. The prosecutors knew about the March 1986 meeting in Panama City, Grilli told him. Navarro had testified that Amet and his brother were there. Grilli kept after Amet for six months. Finally, on February 14, 1991, with the Davidow and Saldarriaga trial near and with no hope for a deal once the trial began, Amet "remembered" that Noriega had spoken to the conspirators on a speakerphone. He would say so in court.

Paredes's attorney and Sullivan reached a deal. For his testimony the government would agree to drop four of the five counts against Amet. Forgotten would be the counts that had charged him with being part of the overall racketeering conspiracy as well as with the manufacture and distribution of cocaine. Overnight Amet's jail exposure would drop from ninety-five years to no more than ten.

For the government, Paredes's flip was a godsend. The Davidow and Saldarriaga trial would be the first test of the Miami indictment. The press, Noriega's defense team, the Justice Department, and all of official Washington would be monitoring the trial to see just how strong the Noriega prosecution really was. Now with Paredes, Sullivan could use the repulsive Navarro more sparingly. Maybe Navarro wouldn't even have to be called. Amet's testimony alone would show that a conspiracy existed and that Davidow, Saldarriaga, and Noriega were involved. Paredes wouldn't put Noriega at the March meeting, as Navarro had alleged, but he would put Noriega on the phone with the other coconspirators.

At Paredes's plea hearing on Thursday, February 14, one week before the codefendants' trial was to begin, Sullivan told the story of the *Krill*. "The *Krill* was loaded with arms supplied by the Panamanian Defense Forces to be taken to Colombia and traded for approximately four hundred kilos of cocaine," he began. Secret compartments were built into the vessel. The *Krill* sailed for Colombia, but the boat was seized. When Rubén Paredes, Jr., and César Rodríguez went to Medellín to meet with the cartel, they ended up murdered, Sullivan told the judge.

Paredes's attorney, Joel Rosenthal, then told the judge that Amet's testimony would be the next step in "putting a major family tragedy behind him." Rosenthal went further than Sullivan: "Amet Paredes will say Noriega ordered the killings, and he will place Davidow and Saldarriaga at a meeting in Panama City where the *Krill*'s voyage was planned."

Both Richard Sharpstein, who was defending Davidow, and Steven Kreisberg, who was defending Saldarriaga, had relished the opportunity of taking apart Ramón Navarro on cross-examination. But Amet Paredes would corroborate Navarro's story. Sharpstein and Kreisberg would have to pit Navarro's and Paredes's testimony against each other. Here were two admitted drug smugglers trying to ingratiate themselves with the government at the expense of Davidow and Saldarriaga, two defendants who had claimed all along that they were innocent.

At a pretrial hearing on Wednesday, February 20, Sharpstein opened his attack on Navarro, asking Judge Hoeveler to allow the defense to reveal at trial that Navarro had been granted immunity and had been paid $170,000 by the government for his cooperation. Sharpstein also told Hoeveler that the jury should know of Navarro's criminal background and the deals he had been given by the government.

Steve Kreisberg had other concerns. Following Sharpstein to the lectern, Kreisberg asked Hoeveler to bar at trial the admission of a 1990 letter of confession sent by Saldarriaga to the prosecutors. In the letter Saldarriaga asked what he could gain if he were to plead guilty and cooperate. But the letter was not an admission of guilt, Kreisberg argued, it was an inquiry. It should not be allowed in court because of rules that ban evidence developed during plea bargain negotiations. There was no reason for the jury to be told that Saldarriaga had simply asked about a plea agreement. Kreisberg also asked Hoeveler to bar testimony relating jailhouse conversations Saldarriaga had with other inmates at MCC—Sullivan and Malman had gathered more than a half-dozen inmates who said Saldarriaga had confessed to them in jail. The judge said he would take the requests under consideration.

On Monday, February 25, Brian Davidow, twenty-nine, and William Saldarriaga, forty-four, went to court for the beginning of jury selection. Saldarriaga faced forty years in jail and a $500,000 fine if convicted on two conspiracy counts. Davidow faced fifty-five years on two conspiracy counts.

The two accused looked as different as the two worlds they had come from. Davidow had turned himself in within hours of delivery of the 1988 indictment and was quickly released on bond. In the three years since, he had earned a bachelor's degree from Florida International University and had become deeply religious. He wore a yarmulke, a sign of Orthodox Judaism.

Saldarriaga, a short, solid, and weathered Colombian, looked the part of a boat dealer–turned-smuggler or smuggler who sold boats as a cover. He had been sitting in jail for almost a year and a half. He was the first codefendant arrested in the Noriega case, having been picked up by a Metro-Dade police officer during a routine traffic stop.

Neither spoke to the other or said much to their lawyers as they sat through jury selection. Surprisingly, the selection process lasted only a day and a half. Though Sharpstein and Kreisberg had spent the best part of a year voicing concern about seating a jury that could separate their clients from Noriega, in the end the task seemed not that difficult. Few of the seventy potential jurors voiced a distaste for Noriega.

By midday on Tuesday, February 26, the prosecutors and defense lawyers agreed on a jury: ten men and two women. Only three of the twelve said they had ever heard of Davidow and Saldarriaga or the charges against them. All but three said they had heard of Noriega.

On Monday, February 25, with the jury out of the courtroom, Sullivan informed the judge that the government had decided to drop its racketeering conspiracy count against Brian Davidow, the young American. Instead, Davidow, like Saldarriaga, would face only two of the indictment's overt act charges, counts nine and ten. Instead of facing sixty years in jail, Davidow would face forty.

The move was tactical for the prosecution. Instead of having to present extensive evidence about the conspiracy itself and Noriega's alleged role in the enterprise, the prosecutors now could focus simply on the *Krill* episode. By dropping the first count, Sullivan knew, Noriega's lawyers would not now be able to sit through the codefendants' trial and learn the government's evidence against their client.

On Wednesday, February 27, Judge Hoeveler listened to six inmates tell how Saldarriaga had regaled them with tales of his life as a drug trafficker. Brought one by one, handcuffed, into the courtroom, each said Saldarriaga had talked about his legal troubles almost incessantly. Kreisberg argued that he feared the inmates had been planted by the government to solicit incriminating statements from Saldarriaga. But the judge disagreed. The inmates would be permitted to testify; they were not government agents. Saldarriaga's letter to the prosecutors, however, would not be presented to the jury.

While the jury continued to wait in the jury room for opening arguments, Kreisberg met with Hoeveler and Sullivan in the judge's chambers. He requested a delay while he discussed a plea agreement with the government. But with Paredes's testimony already in place, Saldarriaga didn't have much to offer. There would be no deal.

At 1:30 that afternoon, the jury was brought into the courtroom. Judge Hoeveler invited the government to present its opening argument. Pat Sullivan walked to the lectern.

"It's a fairly simple charge," Sullivan began, "that from November 1985 to March 1986, Brian Davidow and William Saldarriaga, and the other codefendants who are named, including Manuel Antonio Noriega, conspired together to distribute cocaine—in excess of 322 kilograms of cocaine—that was located in Colombia, place it aboard the vessel *Krill*, and sail it to Miami, intending that the cocaine be unlawfully imported into the United States aboard the *Krill*." The defendants faced two charges, Sullivan explained: one for distribution of cocaine, the second for importation. One codefendant, Amet Paredes, Sullivan continued, had pled guilty and had agreed to testify for the government. But others also would testify. Of those others, some had received "use immunity"—an agreement that the government would not prosecute them for what they said in court. "Those witnesses were conspirators who have not been prosecuted, and their testimony will not be used against them," said Sullivan. "There are a fair number of people who have that arrangement." Not once did Sullivan mention Ramón Navarro as an expected witness.

Sullivan turned to the story of the *Krill*.

Saldarriaga and Davidow had been present at several meetings where drug dealing was discussed. Davidow, Sullivan said, pointing toward him, had agreed to help distribute the cocaine once it arrived in Miami. "At one point, César Rodríguez called on the telephone General Manuel Noriega," Sullivan said. Noriega would protect the voyage of the *Krill*. Noriega spoke to the group, said Sullivan, on a speakerphone. Among those who would testify for the government, Sullivan said, was a *Krill* crew member and another sailor who had put into the same ports as the *Krill* on its voyage from Panama to Colombia. "There will be no real issue in this case that the *Krill* was packed to the gunwales with cocaine. The issue will be the participation of these two defendants in placing the cocaine on the *Krill*."

Richard Sharpstein followed Sullivan to the lectern to deliver the first of two opening statements for the defense. The *Krill*'s voyage to Colombia, Sharpstein explained, was a venture conceived by César Rodríguez, Rubén Paredes, and Ramón Navarro. Shortly after the *Krill* was confiscated by the Colombian police, Rodríguez and Paredes were murdered. That, said

Sharpstein, was an "unsolved mystery" that "ties directly into this case." Ramón Navarro, said Sharpstein, was the person who planned and directed the venture. He would be a witness in this trial. It was Navarro, said Sharpstein, who had traded his story about the *Krill* for immunity. It was Navarro's story that had become the foundation of the *Krill* portion of the 1988 Miami indictment. "Ramón Navarro is an individual of the most incredible, incredulous, scurrilous background," said Sharpstein. Navarro had been a drug trafficker since 1976 and had brought thousands of pounds of cocaine and marijuana into the United States.

"And this man now comes into this courtroom under the guise of the United States government, under a grant of immunity," Sharpstein said. "He has never been prosecuted, will never be prosecuted, has never spent one day in jail for his acts, and never will." In a month's time, said Sharpstein, Navarro's liability for the *Krill* episode would expire with the statute of limitations.

Sharpstein stepped toward the jury box. "You're going to hear about a lot of people who were given deals, sweet deals, that they would never be given because they can point their finger in the direction of General Noriega. You must understand the politics, the American politics, the Panamanian politics behind it to understand how all of this came to be."

Amet Paredes, Sharpstein said, had told at least five different stories about the *Krill* and Noriega's involvement since he had first been interviewed by Panamanian officials in 1988. Navarro, by Sharpstein's count, had given seventeen different versions of the *Krill* story since he first came in contact with Colombian and American law enforcement.

When the *Krill* sailed for Colombia in 1986, Sharpstein said, it carried guns supplied by Rodríguez and Panama City gun dealer Orlando Villarreal, Sr. Ramón Navarro was the gun smugglers' contact in Colombia. How could Noriega be involved in the *Krill*? How could Noriega be involved in 1986 with Rodríguez at all? Two years before the voyage of the *Krill*, in 1984, Rodríguez was thrown in jail—by Noriega—for running guns and drugs through Panama. The two had not spoken to each other since, he said. The government's contention that Noriega would somehow find himself in 1986 in one room with both the son of General Paredes, a political enemy, and a man he had imprisoned was quite unlikely.

At least one thing was for sure, said Sharpstein: Amet Paredes had for three years denied any involvement in the *Krill* affair and had never said anything about Brian Davidow. "The only testimony you'll hear at trial comes from individuals, all of whom have a reason to lie and are using my client to perpetuate those lies for their own benefit," Sharpstein said.

Steven Kreisberg, sitting at the other end of the defense table next to William Saldarriaga, rose and stepped before the jury. He would deliver the second opening statement for the defense.

"I think the question here is not what will the evidence be but what will the credible evidence be?" he began, looking from one end of the jury box to the other. "Your job is sifting through the chaff to get to the wheat, if there is any wheat, and I think what you're going to see in the next couple of days is that there's a whole truckload of chaff that is going to be dumped in this courtroom. A lot of what you'll hear has nothing to do with Mr. Saldarriaga," said Kreisberg. "A lot of what you'll hear will not be in dispute. We don't intend to dispute that Mr. Saldarriaga had the misfortune of knowing Ramón Navarro."

Navarro, it was true, had contacted Saldarriaga in 1986. In the course of his jewelry and small-appliance business, Saldarriaga made frequent trips to Panama, and he agreed to scout out a boat for Navarro on one of those trips, said Kreisberg. In fact, Navarro had convinced Saldarriaga that the *Krill* was a good investment. With Saldarriaga's financial help, Navarro told his fellow Colombian, the *Krill* could be bought and quickly resold at a huge profit. The two agreed to become investors together, Kreisberg said.

"Now, Ramón said nothing to Saldarriaga about any drugs being put on the boat, nothing to him about the fact that when Ramón and the boat were in Panama, Ramón apparently had these secret compartments built. He told him nothing about guns. Why should he tell? Ramón Navarro, as you will see, is the kind of person who, if there was money to be made, would want to make it all for himself. The question"—Kreisberg pointed to his client—"is whether William had anything to do with that cocaine. The credible evidence will show that he did not, but, rather, that his investment was perfectly legal; that he had nothing to do with the guns on the boat, with the compartments, with the cocaine, with Noriega, with any of this."

Kreisberg next made a peremptory strike at the government's jailhouse witnesses. "The people the government is going to bring in and ask you to believe will come in here and say, 'Well, Mr. Saldarriaga must be guilty because he confessed to me.' The evidence will show that these people are not here for nothing. They're not here as good citizens. They're trying to get out of jail."

Don't be fooled by the government's desperation, Kreisberg told the jurors. "They spent millions of dollars and American lives to bring Mr. Noriega to court. The government would stop at nothing to find William Saldarriaga, Brian Davidow, and Manuel Noriega guilty," Kreisberg said.

The first witness would be called the next morning.

At a little past 11:30 that night. Ramón Navarro was in his red 1989 BMW, driving east on Southwest 184th Street, just twelve miles south of the Miami federal courthouse. He had just been to visit his girlfriend and was on his way home to his wife. He had just a couple of blocks to go.

Heading toward Biscayne Bay on the straight two-lane road—bordered on each side by sprawling ranch-style homes with broad lawns—the BMW was going seventy-five miles an hour when it crossed the center line and plowed through seventy-five feet of wooden-slat fence, shearing off a heavy Florida Power & Light electrical transformer before coming to a crumpled rest. There was no explosion or fire, but the noise roused neighbors, who ran to the accident. One said he saw a red Camaro speeding away. Another said a man in a black Chevrolet Blazer stopped long enough to take Navarro's pulse. Navarro was cushioned by the BMW's airbag, but slats from the wooden fence pierced the car's windshield and scissored Navarro's neck.

The government's star witness was dead, all but decapitated. There were no skid or braking marks at the scene. A loaded pistol was found under the front seat of Navarro's car. The passenger door was open. At 11:36 P.M., a coroner called to the scene pronounced Navarro, age forty-one, dead.

Later, Miami attorney Steve Glass, who advised Navarro on his dealings with the government, said he knew of no threats against his client. He added, "When the government's chief witness becomes a cadaver on the eve of trial, yes, that's suspicious."

On Thursday morning, February 28, before the jury was brought into the courtroom to begin the second day of trial, Pat Sullivan informed Judge Hoeveler that Navarro had died the night before. "He is not going to testify— not in this plane of existence," Sullivan told the judge. Sullivan asked that the defense be ordered to return copies of Navarro's 1987 grand jury testimony. Sharpstein and Kreisberg had shaped Navarro's credibility as the key to the defense cases.

Sharpstein rose and requested a mistrial. "In light of my opening argument and their opening regarding Mr. Navarro, the jury has heard an awful lot about him," Sharpstein told Judge Hoeveler. "His credibility was lacking, and the truth would come out if he was here. His absence only inures to our detriment."

Sharpstein's law partner, his wife, Janice Burton Sharpstein, stood and explained that there were at least three reasons to grant a mistrial: first, the jury had already heard the opening statements; second, and related, the defense's strategy had been revealed; and third, a natural prejudice was bound to arise from the death of a witness.

Kreisberg followed her and moved for a mistrial as well.

The defense was in a dilemma of its own making, Sullivan responded, standing at the prosecution table. Sharpstein and Kreisberg could have chosen to reserve or postpone their openings so as to respond more fully to the government's case. That was something not uncommonly done by defense lawyers. Instead, both had chosen to argue their cases and to attack Navarro up front. Sullivan looked at Sharpstein: "He knows very well that oftentimes witnesses don't say what you think they'll say, and if you commit yourself in opening statement, you may be embarrassed later on. He also knows witnesses sometimes don't appear or appear and take the Fifth. Things don't happen the way you always fully expect them to happen."

Hoeveler reflected for a moment and then denied the motions for a mistrial. "I can't believe that a jury would hold it against either side for not being able to fulfill a promise in connection with a witness who has died in an automobile accident," the judge said. "I can't see that anybody is really injured.

Perhaps the most injured is the government. They no longer have one of their principal witnesses." If it was found that Navarro had been shot or his car tampered with, the issue would be revisited.

The next morning, as the trial was set to begin its third day, one juror reported to the judge that she had heard of the accident on the television news. Even though Hoeveler had asked each juror to be careful not to read the newspapers or listen to television or radio reports, it happened. The juror was called to a sidebar with the judge and the attorneys.

What did you think when you heard it? Sharpstein asked the juror.

"That somebody wiped him out," she replied.

"This is a thought that will probably stick with you, isn't it?" Sharpstein asked.

"Well, probably," she replied.

A mob of reporters surrounded Pat Sullivan as he walked out of the courthouse that evening. "We're going straight ahead [with the trial]," he told them. "Damn the torpedoes."

In Washington, Assistant U.S. Attorney Robert Mueller released a statement saying that government officials "obviously have an interest in [Navarro's death] and will look into the circumstances." The Justice Department, he said, would review the findings of the local police, and if it was found that Navarro's death came as a result of an effort to keep him from testifying or was a murder-for-hire, the FBI and the DEA would take over the investigation.

Late in the morning on Friday, March 1, the government called its first witness to the stand. Sullivan and Myles Malman had decided to build the case against each of the two defendants separately, calling first one or two witnesses against Saldarriaga, and then one or two witnesses against Davidow. The plan was to alternate back and forth, slowly drawing the two together and toward Noriega.

Gabriel Taboada, a Colombian cocaine and marijuana smuggler who was serving a twenty-year sentence at MCC, testified that he had met Saldarriaga and Navarro and had seen the *Krill* on an island in Colombia in 1986. Taboada said that he was invited aboard the *Krill* and there saw a large portrait of General Noriega in a white dress uniform. "I was impressed that the picture of a general was on a boat where cocaine was going to be transported," Toboada told the jury. He said Saldarriaga and Navarro told him the boat "was under the protection from Panama of General Noriega."

A second witness, a seaman named Manuel Sánchez, said he had been hired to work on the *Krill* after Navarro and Saldarriaga bought the vessel from the Paredes family. Before the *Krill* left Panama, Sánchez said, a carpenter built secret compartments on board. Later, Sánchez said, he watched the *Krill* being loaded with cocaine. By Friday afternoon, Sullivan and Malman were satisfied with the way the government's case was proceeding. Navarro's death was, so far, a minor setback.

On Monday morning, Sharpstein renewed his motion for a mistrial. Suspicion that Navarro's death had been the result of foul play was everywhere, he told Judge Hoeveler. "Wherever I went—to the barber, the video store, everywhere—everyone had the same cynical and suspicious conclusion: that there was something sinister, not just a mere accident." Sharpstein argued that if the public was suspicious, then the jury would be suspicious. That could result in prejudice against the defendants.

Hoeveler insisted that worry over public suspicion was not enough to spark a mistrial. "That's a TV-type reaction," the judge said. "When you say to [a jury] there is no foul play involved, they accept it."

At the Metro-Dade Police Department, leads were thin. The Navarro crash had been turned over to CENTAC, a special drug-homicide unit. But the only thing investigators had found was a pending IRS investigation against Navarro for failure to pay $200,000 in taxes and a tip that Navarro had recently fenced stolen jewelry.

For Frank Rubino and Jon May, who were now busy preparing Noriega's defense, Navarro's death meant little. The dead man's testimony would have centered only on the *Krill*, they knew. By Rubino's count, the government still had at least six strong witnesses against Noriega on the *Krill* count alone.

In court on Tuesday morning, March 5, the prosecution began its effort to link Davidow to the *Krill* and to Noriega. Sullivan called to the witness stand Sandra Ferro, the former personal secretary to César Rodríguez. Ferro said she kept detailed phone logs and that Davidow had called and visited Rodríguez several times in 1984 and 1985. Ferro said she took phone messages from Davidow and even helped him rent an apartment in the Panamanian capital. On December 17, 1985, Ferro said, Marcella Tessone, Noriega's secretary, called looking for Davidow. Ferro also said that in 1985 she witnessed meetings of Rodríguez, the Paredes brothers, and Navarro. And though Noriega was never present at any of the meetings, Ferro said that Tessone had called frequently with messages for Rodríguez to call Noriega.

But under cross-examination, Ferro's testimony did not seem to hold up. She conceded that the calls from Noriega's office to Rodríguez stopped in 1984. She also said that the messages from Noriega's office to Davidow requested that he call Tessone, not Noriega. Ferro admitted that Davidow bought dresses from her as gifts for Tessone. On cross-examination, Ferro denied that she had been granted a promise of immunity for her testimony and had been paid $6,500 in expenses. But before she took the stand, Pat Sullivan said both were the case.

With Navarro dead, the government's star witness became Amet Paredes. Now there was no one to contradict his version of the *Krill* scheme and the meeting that he said involved Noriega. Paredes went on the witness stand on Wednesday, March 6. Paredes's testimony, Sullivan hoped, would inextricably entwine Davidow, Saldarriaga, and Noriega in the *Krill* conspiracy. Paredes would bring Noriega's name squarely before the jury, and if the jurors had any compunction about doing the right thing for their country and the war against drugs, they would believe him.

Amet Paredes took the stand looking like a young businessman, in a coat and tie. He looked serious and spoke with assurance.

The March 1986 *Krill* meetings, he said, were held at César Rodríguez's offices and home. In attendance were Rodríguez, himself, and his brother, Rubén, as well as Davidow, Saldarriaga, and Navarro. As fate would have it, the only persons who attended the meetings and were still alive to tell about it were now seated in Judge Hoeveler's courtroom: Paredes, the accuser, and the two defendants, Davidow and Saldarriaga. General Noriega's involvement with the *Krill* was very real, Paredes testified, but Noriega never participated in the March 1986 meetings in person, only by speakerphone.

Under Sullivan's questioning on direct examination, Paredes outlined the *Krill* deal: eight hundred to one thousand M-16 rifles would be supplied by Noriega and the Panamanian Defense Forces; 350 to 400 kilograms of cocaine would be supplied by Saldarriaga; the guns would be traded for the cocaine in Colombia; Davidow would distribute the cocaine in Miami. "The general said, 'I'm going to send a guy over there . . . and make sure the guns are delivered,'" Paredes told the jury. The guns were delivered and loaded on the *Krill* a few days later, Paredes said.

At another meeting, Paredes said, Rodríguez told Noriega, "General, everything is ready. Everyone is here and ready to go. We just need to do some paperwork." That paperwork, Paredes told the jury, involved $12,000 in back taxes owed on the *Krill*. Without a tax clearance the *Krill* would not be able to pass through the Panama Canal. "Noriega said, 'Okay, let me work on it,'" Paredes told the jury. Within a few days the *Krill* was given permission to begin its voyage. No taxes were ever paid, Paredes testified.

As for the profits from the *Krill* venture, Paredes said the shares were determined in advance, with Noriega receiving his cut from Rodríguez. Davidow, Paredes said, made his money on each kilo sold in the United States.

Paredes conceded that his father, General Paredes, and Noriega had once been political enemies, but Amet and Rubén, Jr., asked their father to tone down his criticism of Noriega because the family business was suffering. The reversal in the family's business fortunes following the senior Paredes's exit from military service drove the Paredes boys to drug trafficking, Amet told the jury.

On cross-examination, Richard Sharpstein asked Paredes about the six different versions of the *Krill* meetings that he had given to investigators between 1988 and 1991. Each time it seemed Paredes lied to the prosecutors and to the DEA, Sharpstein noted. The last time Paredes lied about the *Krill*,

Sharpstein pointed out, was just before he pleaded guilty. "Why?" Sharpstein demanded of Paredes.

"I was afraid," Paredes responded. "You get convicted in the States, you get deported from the States."

Paredes said that if he was forced to go back to Panama, he could become the victim of retribution by former members of the PDF or National Guard.

Are you telling a story right now? Sharpstein asked.

"It's not a story," Paredes replied adamantly. "It's the truth. I don't make stories. I made mistakes."

"Did they read *The Boy Who Cried Wolf* in Panama?" asked Sharpstein before turning away from Paredes.

The next day, Thursday, March 7, the government took its next step to link Davidow and Saldarriaga to the *Krill*. The prosecution called Elizabeth Verbel, the common-law wife of Ramón Navarro.

Before Verbel could take the stand, Sharpstein and Kreisberg renewed their motions for a mistrial. If Verbel testified, there would have to be an explanation of why her husband was not going to be a witness. The jury would learn of Navarro's bizarre death.

Hoeveler again rejected the dismissal motions. "If this is a bona fide accident, it shouldn't be prejudicial," he told the two defense lawyers.

The judge called for the jury to be brought into the courtroom.

"He died as the result of an automobile accident," the judge told the jurors. "The death is in no way attributed to anyone in this lawsuit and should not be considered by you in any way."

Verbel took the stand, her blond hair tied in a tight bun. She was dressed head to toe in black mourning clothes.

Under direct examination by Assistant U.S. Attorney Guy Lewis, Verbel said that she and her husband never discussed his business. She believed her husband was a boat dealer. She said she knew little about his dealings, but she was sure he conducted business with Davidow and Saldarriaga.

Sharpstein on cross-examination asked Verbel if she had ever seen Davidow after 1984. Her reply was almost inaudible. "Never," she said.

The next day, Friday, March 8, Myles Malman took over for the prosecution. He called Orlando "Toti" Villarreal, Jr., to the stand. Toti was married to Amet Paredes's sister and with his father ran one of the biggest gun shops in Panama. With Villarreal's testimony, Malman intended to link guns to the *Krill*. First, he asked about Villareal's family connection to Noriega and a tangential scheme to sell Panamanian visas.

Villarreal said that he used his father's "drinking partner" acquaintance with Noriega as well as his own in-law relationship to the Paredes family to help beef up the family's government contracts business with Panama's National Guard. In 1983, Villarreal said, he got the idea to sell passports to Cuban and Chinese immigrants who wanted to flee to the United States via Panama. Noriega, Villarreal said, was the man to see because he not only ran

Panama's G-2 intelligence service but also headed the country's immigration and passport offices. "I went to his office and I sat in front of him," Villarreal told the jury. "I asked him to help me secure visas."

Noriega promised to "try to help," Villarreal said.

The meeting came at the start of a four-to-six-month period when he sold visas for $800 each, Villarreal said. In time Noriega and the G-2 saw that the scheme was profitable and began slapping a surcharge on the visas he obtained.

Villarreal said Noriega also helped him and his father get the necessary permits and import licenses to open Panama's largest gun shop. The shop had a huge supply of rifles and shotguns that the Villarreals stored in a National Guard warehouse. It was true that some of those arms ended up in the hands of Colombia's M-19 guerrillas, he said.

Richard Sharpstein protested that Malman was using the broad brush of insinuation; Villarreal's allegations had nothing to do with Davidow or Saldarriaga. Sharpstein asked for a mistrial. Again Hoeveler denied Sharpstein's request.

Malman turned to Villarreal's knowledge of Davidow's activities.

Villarreal said that he and Davidow discussed drug dealing in Miami on several occasions. Meeting at the real estate office of Davidow's stepfather, Villarreal said Davidow showed a keen interest in drug trafficking and through 1985 asked many times how he could contact drug dealers in Colombia.

On cross-examination, Sharpstein referred back to Villarreal's 1987 testimony to the grand jury. Not once, Sharpstein noted, had Villarreal then spoken of meetings with Davidow.

On Monday, March 11, before the trial resumed, Steven Kreisberg requested that his client be allowed to address the court. Sniffling and clearly ill, William Saldarriaga said he had spent a miserable weekend at MCC. The previous Thursday he had been placed in solitary confinement following a disagreement with another inmate. The inmate charged that Saldarriaga threatened him. The words led to a scuffle. With outdoor temperatures in the forties, unusually cold for Miami at any time of the year, Saldarriaga said, he was stripped to his undershorts and given only a sheet to keep warm. At the same time the prison's air conditioning continued to run at full blast.

Kreisberg said that guards had taken all of Saldarriaga's belongings, including his Bible and toothbrush. The treatment, Kreisberg charged, was clearly aimed at convincing Saldarriaga to roll over and plead guilty.

"That's outrageous, if indeed that is the fact," the judge said after listening intently to Saldarriaga. Hoeveler ordered Malman to contact the prison immediately and make sure Saldarriaga was not being ill-treated.

For the rest of Monday and much of Tuesday, Saldarriaga's ill treatment grew worse; only now, however, it was at the hands of the prosecutors. Two witnesses, Héctor López and Jesús Héctor Velez, both convicted drug dealers and both intent on reducing their jail time, spent the balance of the two days linking Saldarriaga to the Medellín cartel. López testified first, saying that he had dealt cocaine with both Saldarriaga and his wife, Marta. The two, López said, were known to have close ties to the Ochoas of the Medellín cartel. López identified cocaine packages found aboard the *Krill*. The packages' yellow wrappings were a sign they had come directly from the Ochoas, he said.

Velez testified next. Under questioning by prosecutor Guy Lewis, he told of dealing cocaine with Saldarriaga. Velez said that both he and Saldarriaga's wife were cousins of the Ochoas; he had known Marta since they were both children. Velez testified that he had met Saldarriaga again at MCC, where Saldarriaga told Velez that the drugs aboard the *Krill* had come from Medellín and the Ochoas. "The pure truth is that the merchandise belonged to your cousins," Velez said Saldarriaga told him.

Velez, under cross-examination by Kreisberg, admitted that he had traded his cooperation with the government for less jail time. The prosecutors, he conceded, reduced his sentence for drug trafficking and money laundering from sixty years to less than three.

"Then things worked out pretty well for you, didn't they?" Kreisberg asked.

"Very well," Velez answered.

With Velez, the parade of jailhouse witnesses against Saldarriaga began in earnest. A smuggler of guns and cocaine named Francisco Rodríguez Milanes testified that Saldarriaga repeated again and again the story of the *Krill*. Saldarriaga wanted to tell the prosecutors but was afraid because be feared his family in Colombia would be harmed, Rodríguez Milanes said.

Noriega ordered the trade of rifles for drugs, Rodríguez Milanes said Saldarriaga told him. César Rodríguez was "in charge" of relaying the weapons to the Colombian drug lords. "General Noriega provided them in order to make an exchange of cocaine in Colombia," Saldarriaga had said. When the *Krill* arrived in Colombia, there were only 320 kilos aboard—80 kilos short of the agreed-upon amount, Saldarriaga told him. Saldarriaga telephoned the news to "a person connected with Noriega." Later, César Rodríguez and Rubén Paredes were murdered in Medellín. Saldarriaga believed Noriega had something to do with the murders, Rodríguez Milanes testified.

The following Wednesday, March 13, Tirso Dominguez, an inmate who had testified during the pretrial hearing regarding Saldarriaga's jailhouse confessions, returned to court. Dominguez testified that Saldarriaga told him about the murders of Rodríguez and Paredes. When the *Krill* had shown up eighty kilos short, Saldarriaga said he called someone in Panama to relay the news of the shortage and avoid taking the blame. "He believed Noriega had these people killed for a shortage of drugs on board the *Krill*," Dominguez told the jury.

Following Dominguez, Hewitt Gaynor McGill, a boat captain, testified that Davidow and Navarro ordered him to captain a drug boat in 1984. Sullivan's final evidence before the prosecution rested was the introduction of telephone records showing dozens of calls from Davidow's Miami real estate office to Colombia and Panama. The numbers called, Sullivan pointed out, matched the phone numbers of Davidow's contacts in the drug world.

The burden of proof in a criminal prosecution is always on the government. The question for the jury is: Has the government proven guilt beyond a reasonable doubt? In many cases the defense strategy is to present no defense at all. That forces the prosecution's case to overcome the reasonable doubt in a jury's mind. Where no defense case is presented, jurors are always instructed that the lack of a defense is not to be considered in reaching a verdict.

When a defense is presented, the strategy is almost always to demonstrate where gaps exist in the evidence and the testimony of the government's case and to demonstrate that the prosecution's witnesses were not credible. During cross-examinations, Sharpstein and Kreisberg had hammered away at the criminal records of many of the government's witnesses. "The problem of conflicting witnesses would have been one of their big problems had Navarro testified," Kreisberg later said. Navarro and Paredes together had spelled trouble for the government.

"Navarro's grand jury testimony said Noriega was sitting at the table. It described what he was wearing. Subsequently you get Amet Paredes who says Noriega wasn't there. Now, if you sit down and discuss drugs and arms with Noriega, you are going to remember that. You don't make a mistake if he was there in person or on the speakerphone. That's not a detail people could be confused about. Somebody is lying, or they are both lying."

On Thursday, March 14, Sharpstein called the defense's first witness, Orlando Villarreal, Sr. He had come to Miami to testify on behalf of the prosecution, but he had not been called. He had spent the three weeks since the beginning of the trial lounging about in a Miami hotel, all expenses paid by the U.S. government. Villarreal denied the testimony of both his son, Toti, and Paredes. He said he had nothing to do with planning or supplying the *Krill*'s guns-for-cocaine voyage. He further denied that he had ever attended the *Krill* planning meetings, nor had he supplied M-16 rifles or the permits for the rifles, as Paredes had alleged. He did not know the *Krill* was used in the conspiracy. He did not know that Davidow and Saldarriaga were part of the conspiracy. "I was never in any meeting having to do with anyone to discuss weapons, guns, or drug deals to do with the *Krill*," Villarreal told the jury. He had never gotten along with Noriega. He stored weapons in the National Guard's warehouse only because Noriega's police required him to do so. Noriega, Villarreal told the jurors, was an "extremely evil person"; he was not a person he would have done business with.

Villarreal said Brian Davidow always seemed more interested in selling real estate to the Panamanians than having anything to do with drug dealing.

The message for the jury, Sharpstein hoped, was that Paredes and Toti were unreliable witnesses.

Villarreal insisted he was not lying and had never lied in court. Unlike Paredes, he told the jury, his account of the *Krill* had not changed once over the years. Villarreal said his testimony now was exactly the testimony he had given the grand jury, the same facts he had been relating to prosecutors and DEA agents since 1987. And unlike Paredes, Sharpstein pointed out, Villarreal had not been given immunity to testify in court.

On cross-examination, Sullivan found himself in the uncomfortable position of trying to discredit a witness that the government had relied upon in bringing its indictment and had invited to trial. Villarreal soon conceded that he had sold guns to people connected to Noriega, and he admitted that he had jumped bond in 1986, two years prior to testifying before the Miami grand jury.

As a character witness, Sharpstein next called Asher Kimchi, Brian Davidow's stepfather. Kimchi simply insisted that Brian had never been involved in drug dealing.

On cross-examination, Myles Malman began to ask about a January 1, 1985, incident in which Davidow reported his own kidnapping. Sharpstein objected. With the jury out of the courtroom, Malman explained that Davidow's brother had called police to report that Brian was kidnapped. Police monitored the brother's phone. When Davidow called back, he said his kidnappers were demanding that they be paid. "Bring $21,000 or a kilo," Davidow had told his brother.

"A kilo of what?" his brother replied.

Recounting the incident would prove that Davidow was not as innocent as he claimed. Davidow's own words placed him in the company of drug dealers. But the judge ruled the incident irrelevant to the case at hand.

For Saldarriaga, the defense was thin. Kreisberg maintained that Saldarriaga was a businessman who had been sucked into the *Krill* story by Navarro. "They had William coming and going," Kreisberg said later of the government's case. "They had him in too many places. If the jury believed their witnesses, they had him."

The defense was brief. The heart of its counter to the government's case came in the cross-examination of the prosecution's witnesses. The government relied upon the testimony of seven convicted drug dealers, four jail inmates, and the son of a onetime Panamanian presidential candidate who had pleaded guilty to the indictment and told six different stories about the *Krill*.

There had been very little hard evidence linking Davidow and Saldarriaga with the alleged smuggling scheme. The Villarreals could not agree on what had happened, and Paredes and Navarro would not have agreed. But Navarro was never heard from.

The following Monday, March 18, Hoeveler's courtroom was packed for closing arguments. Reporters played up the case, labeling it a "window" on the

Noriega trial. The government's case against Noriega would be based on many of the same kind of witnesses, and an acquittal of either Davidow or Saldarriaga would raise doubts about the strength of the Noriega prosecution. A loss would reflect poorly not only on the prosecutors but on the Bush administration as well.

Myles Malman would first deliver the government's closing, and then the defense would close. Finally, Pat Sullivan would offer the government's rebuttal.

Malman sat tensely at the prosecution table. He had delivered many closing arguments before, but it was his nature not to relax until the jury walked out of the courtroom for the last time.

The jury was seated. Hoeveler called Malman forward.

Brian Davidow and William Saldarriaga schemed with Manuel Noriega to swap rifles for cocaine as part of "criminal partnership," Malman began. "This whole enterprise had the protection of Manuel Noriega. This was about arms for cocaine." Malman paused. "The last thing in the world they expected was an honest Colombian cop. Conspiracies are secret," he said. That's why there was no hard evidence.

The government's witnesses weren't "choirboys," he admitted. "They aren't little angels. But they all came in here and were able to look you in the eye. If they cooperate, yes, they can help themselves. If they lie, they get slammed."

The government's case, Kreisberg and Sharpstein responded, was based on the tales of liars and convicted drug dealers whose motives for testifying were early release from prison. The case was flimsy.

Kreisberg stood before the jury dangling a large key. "The government is using the power of the key," he said. "This case represents a corrupt side of the system. The witnesses are almost encouraged by the kind of deals the government gives to lie." Kreisberg held out the key. "To dangle this in front of people without hope . . . does not foster truth. That fosters perjury."

The "N factor" had not only dirtied the witnesses, it had dirtied the prosecutors as well, Sharpstein said, following Kreisberg. "If it wasn't for the Noriega factor," he told the jury, "they wouldn't be handing out the deals they are. They wouldn't be spinning this web of deception and deceit."

Sullivan stood. The fact of the matter, he said, was that Davidow and Saldarriaga had worked with Noriega, whether they had a choice or not. "We were proving that Noriega controlled them, that he could make them do his will, that they were subservient to him." Noriega, said Sullivan, was "the iron fist in the velvet glove."

For five years, Sullivan told the jurors, the government worked on this case. Five long years, he said. The witnesses did not all agree on exact dates, but their stories fit together like the pieces of a mosaic. Every painting has a flaw, said Sullivan, but the picture remained of how the defendants and their coconspirators agreed to and commissioned a crime. After five years, it was time for the case to end. "It's time for the voyage of the *Krill* to end now," Sullivan said.

On Tuesday morning, March 19, Judge Hoeveler read the jury its instructions and outlined how it was to weigh the evidence presented. "You don't wear black robes and your term of office is shorter than mine, but in every sense of the word you are judges in this case," Hoeveler said.

He explained that the indictment itself was not evidence of guilt, that the defendants were presumed by the law to be innocent. "The law does not require a defendant to prove his innocence or to produce any evidence at all, and no inference whatever may be drawn from the election of the defendants not to testify," Hoeveler told the jury. "The government has the burden of proving a defendant guilty beyond a reasonable doubt, and if it fails to do so, then you must acquit the defendant."

The government's burden of proof was heavy, the judge said, but it was not necessary that the defendant's guilt be proved beyond all possible doubt. "It is only required that the government's proof exclude any reasonable doubt concerning the defendant's guilt."

A defendant could be proved guilty by either direct or circumstantial evidence, Hoeveler explained. Direct evidence is the testimony of a person who asserts actual knowledge of a fact, like an eyewitness. "Circumstantial evidence is proof of a chain of facts and circumstances establishing the guilt or innocence of a defendant," he said. The law made no distinction between the weight given to either direct or circumstantial evidence. "It requires only that the jury, after weighing all of the evidence in the case, must be convinced of the guilt of each defendant beyond a reasonable doubt before any defendant can be convicted."

All of the evidence was to be considered, said Hoeveler, looking at the jury. But that did not mean all of the evidence had to be accepted. "You are the sole judges of the credibility or believability of each witness and the weight to be given to his or her testimony." It was not the number of witnesses presented but their credibility that should be weighed, Hoeveler said. However, the testimony of witnesses who had been offered favorable treatment or who had struck a bargain with the government should be considered with caution.

In his final words to the jury, Hoeveler said, "The word verdict is a derivative of the Latin. It means to speak the truth. Let your verdict speak the truth."

At 11:15 in the morning of Tuesday, March 19, the jury walked out of the courtroom to consider the verdict.

Word came four hours later that the jurors had finished their work. Brian Davidow and William Saldarriaga were guilty on both counts, conspiracy to import cocaine and distributing cocaine.

William Saldarriaga covered his face with his hands. A deputy marshal led him out of the courtroom before Steve Kreisberg could say a word.

Brian Davidow shuddered when he heard the verdict. Richard Sharpstein reached over and put his arm around him. Davidow's wife, sitting in the gallery directly behind him, burst into tears.

Saldarriaga and Davidow would be sentenced on May 14, Hoeveler said. Each faced forty years in prison.

Pat Sullivan told reporters that the trial was not a preview of the Noriega trial. The charges proven, he said, were only a small part of the larger indictment.

CHAPTER 18
★★★★★★★

The Government's Secrets

Frank Rubino on the defense of Noriega: "Jon and I sit here together, and then you've got the government with its trial team and its classified information team. And they have a litigation team. They have an appellate team. They even brought in a team to handle CNN issues. They have six, seven different teams comprised of two, four, or five lawyers in each team. It's not like Jon and I get to deal only with our counterparts who are Pat and Myles. No. We still have to deal with all the other teams the government has put together. Jon and I must have lost two months' worth of work on CNN alone. But Pat and Myles just move on with trial prep."

The way Rubino and May saw it: "The indictment is a pure and simple garden-variety drug case," according to Rubino. "That's what the indictment is. But that isn't what the defense is. That isn't what the case is."

The defense would have two objectives: First, meet the prosecution's case, the drug case, and defend against it with straight rebuttal. Second, the defense would prepare an entirely separate and distinct defense that would put the indictment in context. For example: "The indictment specifically states that General Noriega accepted a bribe from the cartel to protect the Darien lab. Then, after the PDF raid, he went to Fidel Castro to mediate this alleged dispute with the cartel. We want to [present] General Noriega's relationship with Fidel Castro in toto. If the jury doesn't know that he met with Castro fifteen other times—ten before and five after—they won't get the context. I believe it won't make sense. You know, we use the term 'the truth, the whole truth and nothing but the truth,'" said Rubino. "We should be entitled to show not just the truth of that particular meeting but the whole truth. And show how that meeting fits in a pattern of meetings, a context of meetings. And then show that the truth was caused by the United States, that General Noriega was probably our main liaison man between Washington and Havana."

Another example, Rubino said, was the *Krill*. Davidow and Saldarriaga were guilty. But that does not mean General Noriega was guilty. Should a jury believe that because the general's picture was hanging in the *Krill*, he was giving it protection?

"César Rodríguez was [once] General Noriega's pilot. The general gave

Rodríguez an autographed photo, as I am sure he gave thousands of auto-graphed photos. As I am sure George Bush has given thousands of auto-graphed photos. You've got to get where the photo came from. How is he going to protect this vessel on the high seas? Because his picture was hanging up in it? I don't deny that Saldarriaga and Davidow filled a boat full of dope and tried to bring it. That doesn't mean Noriega had any knowledge of it, let alone participation."

And, according to Rubino, "the prosecution says Noriega was turning Panama into a drug haven, but at the same time he [was] cooperating with not only the DEA but the CIA and the National Security Agency as well. Much of what Noriega was doing for the United States was classified, secret. But the government chooses from hundreds of incidents, isolates those acts, and then claims that is the whole picture."

"There is a whole story to be told," Rubino repeated. "To fit it all in con-text, you can't just say, like the government wants to, that General Noriega did this. You've got to show General Noriega's cooperation with the govern-ment, to refute the claim that he turned Panama into a drug haven."

May would handle the preparation of the defense's political case. Rubino would prepare to counter the prosecution's case, preparing for the govern-ment's witnesses and the cross-examinations. In theory, though seldom in practice, if the defense did a good job on cross-examination, it could win an acquittal without ever calling a witness. When the government rested, the defense could seek what was known as a Rule 29 motion for acquittal. Rule 29 of the *Federal Rules of Criminal Procedure* states that if the government's evidence was insufficient to sustain a conviction, the judge could automati-cally acquit the defendant. The defense would never put on a case, and the jury would never deliberate.

The key to that sort of success was for the defense to know the govern-ment's case as well as or better than the prosecution itself. It meant knowing the whole record for every witness or potential witness, each witness's back-ground and the deals the government had cut. That was Rubino's job. In sev-enteen years of practice, Rubino had tried more than 100 cases. He was well suited to the courtroom work ahead.

May's training was almost perfect for the "political" task that lay ahead. His practice had focused on research, on ferreting out little-known prece-dents in the preparation of appeal briefs. May had gone to Emory University as an undergraduate journalism major and probably would have become an investigative reporter if the *Wall Street Journal*'s Atlanta bureau chief hadn't told him to go to law school first. He liked piecing puzzles together.

But for May there was something extra that made the Noriega case espe-cially interesting. It was more than just another drug case; one could see that Noriega really had had an involvement with the U.S. government. The more he learned about Panama and Central America, the more May believed that the United States was wrong—wrong about Noriega, wrong about Panama and Central America. "If we win this case, it will be because the jurors will think that this whole thing was manufactured by a very powerful country for political reasons," May said. "That, or the jury will have decided that General Noriega is pretty much a minor player compared to all of the other people the U.S. government is going to give great deals to."

Despite all of the defense's initial posturing, there were no secrets and no tapes or classified documents that Noriega had kept. Just as Assistant U.S. Attorney Richard Gregorie had come up empty-handed at CIA headquarters in Langley, Virginia—there were only old newspaper clippings in the agency's Noriega file—so Noriega's attorneys had not found or been given any information that helped their client's case.

The defense strategy now was simply to find some kind of smoking gun, some sort of exculpatory evidence. Somewhere in discovery, if the requests for discovery material were broad enough, there might be a germ of information that could make all the difference.

When the first defense funds became available in February, May, along with three investigators, began poring over some of the documents the U.S. government had captured in Panama. Those documents along with newspaper and media accounts and General Noriega's personal recollections would be shaped by May into a narrative for Judge Hoeveler. That narrative would describe what exactly the defense planned to offer at trial. Such a presentation was required under a federal law known as the Classified Information Procedures Act, or CIPA, enacted by Congress in 1980 in response to growing concern among government and defense intelligence agencies, the State Department, and the Department of Justice over the disclosure of national security information in the prosecution of espionage and criminal leak cases. A Senate subcommittee in 1978 had learned from CIA Director Stansfield Turner and top Justice Department officials that the prosecution of defendants for disclosure of national security information often required disclosure at trial of the very information that the government was seeking to protect. In fact, the more sensitive the information that government lawyers sought to protect, the more difficult the protection was becoming. The problem was "graymail," or the threat by a defendant to disclose classified information in the course of a trial or pretrial discovery.

Rather than going forward with some prosecutions and risking the disclosure of the material through the media or newspaper articles—a disclosure just as real as if the information had been handed to a foreign agent—the government found itself forced to let the misconduct go unpunished. Justice Department officials said the prickly question they faced was "To what extent must we harm the national security in order to protect the national security?" CIPA, an omnibus pretrial proceeding to be used in cases where national security secrets were likely to arise in the course of a criminal prosecution, required a defendant to put the prosecution and the court on notice of all motions, defenses, and arguments he intended to make that would require the discovery and disclosure of intelligence information or the use of intelligence community witnesses. That would allow the judge to rule in advance of the trial on the admissibility of the intelligence information and on the scope of a witness's testimony as well as the general relevancy of the motion or defense prior to the discovery of secret information to the defendant. Under court procedures prior to CIPA's adoption, the relevance and admissibility of evidence was normally decided as such questions arose at trial. Pretrial hearings on CIPA matters instead allowed the government to propose unclassified alternatives to the disclosure of secret information and, if unsuccessful in substituting unclassified alternatives for relevant classified information, to assess the risks posed to national security by a trial before the classified information was publicly revealed and national security compromised.

May's narrative, submitted to Judge Hoeveler under seal on March 18, 1991, and running to 107 pages, was the defense's first notice that it intended to disclose classified information at trial. Such a notice under CIPA was named a Section 5 submission after section five of the law. The submission recounted Noriega's long history of involvement with the U.S. government and ignored the drug charges.

"The Panama Canal was the United States' most important strategic asset in the Western Hemisphere," the brief began. "And General Noriega was the one person relied upon most to maintain the security of the canal. Noriega was repeatedly called on to defuse situations which threatened American interests in Central America and elsewhere," the brief said. May promised that the defense would detail Noriega's relationship with the United States, Israel, Cuba, Costa Rica, and Nicaragua. It would discuss Noriega's assistance to the United States in arming the Sandinistas and later in arming and training the Nicaraguan Contras. The submission would also reveal the CIA's knowledge that pilots flying weapons to the Contras also transported drugs to the United States. The CIA, May asserted, failed to stop those pilots despite warnings from Noriega. In the submission's first section, May outlined what he called "acts by the Central Intelligence Agency in destabilizing and changing foreign governments. What occurred in Panama is nothing new," May said. "The United States has been changing foreign governments to suit its needs for years. The United States tried many ways to get General Noriega out of power with no luck. They then came upon a new twist, 'indictment.'"

The submission's second section outlined Noriega's relationship to the United States. "In order for the jury to properly understand the defense, they must know the lengthy and ongoing relationship between General Noriega and the United States. They must be appraised of the many secret missions Noriega conducted as well as the contacts he made on behalf of the United States with numerous world leaders."

Noriega's relationship with the United States had begun in 1958 while he was a young military cadet. In early 1959, Fidel Castro overthrew Cuban dictator Fulgencio Batista. Shortly, communism had a base only ninety miles from Florida. One of the CIA's most important tasks became keeping a close watch on revolutionary seedbeds such as military academies where the region's future military leaders were trained. Noriega went on the CIA's payroll.

In 1962, as a second lieutenant in the Panamanian National Guard, Noriega came under the command of Maj. Omar Torrijos. Torrijos took Noriega under his wing and made him chief of the transit police. In addition, Torrijos, also on the CIA's payroll, gave Noriega command over a modest intelligence-gathering operation commissioned by the CIA. Noriega's cooperation led to intelligence and counterintelligence training under American officers both in Panama and at Fort Bragg in the United States. Following a Torrijos-led coup overthrowing Panamanian president Arnulfo Arias in October 1968, Noriega was quickly promoted to command positions with the Panamanian military. In 1970, Torrijos named Noriega head of the country's military intelligence, G-2. As the head of G-2, Noriega became an "official institutional link that included access to large sums of CIA contingency funds."

"The money was virtually unaccountable in the CIA's budget and was invisible from outside the CIA," May asserted. "It was officially justified as support for 'institutional cooperation,' but in fact it was a slush fund turned over to the head of the 'cooperating' intelligence agency to do with as he desired." Noriega was expected to use the money to pay agents working for G-2 and the CIA. Over the years, the CIA secretly gave Noriega $11 million. "Noriega became the CIA's man in Panama, an alternative to the man considered a dangerous leftist by American intelligence, Omar Torrijos." In time, Noriega became as indispensable to the Americans as he was to Torrijos, the submission contended. By 1976, Noriega was the liaison to the CIA, FBI, Customs, DEA, and several military intelligence agencies.

During the Carter administration, CIA Director Stansfield Turner cut off payments to the then colonel, but Noriega thrived anyway. He continued to provide sensitive data on Latin American military and guerrilla movements to American intelligence. When the Sandinistas took over Nicaragua in 1979, Noriega provided intelligence on them to the United States.

In 1980, Noriega took charge of protecting the deposed Shah of Iran, a favor to the administration of President Jimmy Carter. During this period Noriega also assisted American law enforcement. In 1984 he agreed to assist in the establishment of an undercover money-laundering operation for the DEA.

Noriega's assistance to the DEA led agency administrator Jack Lawn to commend Noriega in a letter sent on May 8, 1986. The letter stated the DEA's "deep appreciation for the vigorous anti-drug-trafficking policy that you have adopted, which is reflected in the numerous expulsions from Panama of accused traffickers." The DEA, Lawn later told a congressional committee, had been granted every narcotics request ever made to the Panamanian government. In 1987, Lawn again commended Noriega for his assistance in bringing about the indictment of twenty-nine defendants for laundering $433 million in drug money for the Medellín cartel. Less than eight weeks before Noriega was indicted, DEA Administrator Lawn told a former aide to Vice President Bush that there was insufficient evidence against Noriega. "The U.S. relationship with Noriega continued to be a close one up until the moment he was indicted by the United States," May wrote.

The third part of May's Section 5 submission was called "The United States Involvement in the Illegal Supply of Weapons to the Contras and the United States' Solicitation of General Noriega to Have Panama Invade Nicaragua."

May's assertion here was strong. "The jury must hear how the United States was involved in the attempted violent overthrow of the Nicaraguan government. They must further be appraised of how agents of the United States used drug money to finance this endeavor. This section goes to the very heart of the indictment against General Noriega. The United States was clearly involved in a 'guns for drugs' policy, whatever it took to win in Nicaragua." After the Sandinistas seized power in Nicaragua in 1979, Noriega provided intelligence about military equipment that the Sandinistas were getting from abroad. Later, Noriega passed hundreds of thousands of dollars from the CIA, at Director William Casey's order, to the maverick Contra leader Eden Pastora, until Pastora fell out of favor with the United States, the submission said. The Medellín cartel itself sent $10 million in aid to the Contras. At least one pilot who said he flew guns from the United States to the Contras testified that he received payments from cartel middlemen and flew drugs back to the United States.

In late 1984, Noriega went to Washington, D.C., and on a cruise down the Potomac he privately visited with Marine Lt. Col. Oliver North, who was then attached to the National Security Council. North told Noriega he was concerned about allegations that the Contras were connected to drug trafficking. He asked Noriega to do whatever he could for the Contras, although he made no specific requests. North told Noriega to call him at the White House if he ever needed to talk. Later, Reagan National Security Adviser John Poindexter specifically asked Noriega to commit Panamanian troops to assist the Contras in an invasion of Nicaragua from the south. When Noriega balked, Poindexter "responded by threatening Noriega specifically and Panama in general." More requests for Panama's assistance to the Contras would come to Noriega from Oliver North, often through emissaries who claimed President Reagan's and Vice President Bush's support. In September 1986, Noriega met North in London where North requested that Panamanian commandos join with the Contras to assist in acts of sabotage within Nicaragua. Noriega made no commitment. Later in Panama, Dewey Clarridge, the CIA's Latin American operations chief, called on Noriega at home. During this period, the Boland Amendment prohibited official U.S. government assistance to the Contras.

The logic of having drug money pay for the pressing needs of the Contras appealed to a number of people who became involved in the covert war. Indeed, senior U.S. policymakers were not immune to the idea that drug money was a perfect solution to the Contras' funding problems. "As DEA officials testified last July before the House Judiciary Subcommittee on Crime, Lt. Col. Oliver North suggested to the DEA in June 1985 that $1.5 million in drug money, carried aboard a plane piloted by DEA informant Barry Seal and generated in a sting of the Medellín cartel and Sandinista officials, be provided to the Contras. . . . The testimony of convicted drug dealers establishes that the cocaine and marijuana were flown directly into the U.S. bases in south Florida," the submission continued. "Because they were flying guns down to the Contras, such flights had the protection of U.S. government agencies. Intriguingly, the head of the South Florida Drug Task Force interdiction project during these years was none other than Vice President George Bush."

The submission's final part, called "U.S. Efforts to Control the Government of Panama," focused on Noriega's relationship with George Bush and his relationship with the CIA, military intelligence, and the National Security Agency.

In June 1971, the United States and Panama began negotiations over the future of the Panama Canal. Because the canal issue seemed low on the Nixon administration's list of goals, Torrijos decided to raise global awareness of Panama and the canal. He made entreaties to leftist Latin American governments such as Cuba as well as the United States' European allies. Torrijos even managed to embarrass the United States at a meeting of the United Nations Security Council in 1973.

All the while, Noriega was often called upon to provide the CIA with detailed briefings on Panama's relationship with other countries.

In 1976, when negotiations over the canal treaty became deadlocked— Panama reacting in part to a campaign speech by Ronald Reagan in which he said, "When it comes to the canal, we bought it, we paid for it, it's ours, and we shall tell Torrijos and company that we are going to keep it"—the CIA plotted with the Torrijos government to set off explosives in the Canal Zone. The idea was to make Americans living in the Canal Zone see how tenuous their lives were in the absence of a treaty.

In December 1976, Noriega traveled to Washington and met with then CIA Director George Bush. At that meeting the two discussed unrest in the Canal Zone. Bush later sent a letter to Noriega thanking him for his assistance.

Noriega had contact with Bush again shortly after Bush was elected vice president in 1980. During the Reagan presidency, Bush held a variety of high-profile antidrug positions, and Noriega came in contact with Bush's chief antinarcotics staffer, former Admiral Daniel Murphy. While Panama had come under criticism from the media in the mid-1980s for being a center of drug money laundering, Noriega assisted U.S. law enforcement in catching drug traffickers and breaking up cartel money-laundering operations.

In December 1983, Vice President Bush visited Panama briefly and spoke specifically about the dangers of Cuban influence in Nicaragua and Central America. He alluded to U.S. concern about money laundering in Panama but

told Noriega and Panama's President Ricardo de la Espriella, essentially a fig-
urehead president serving at Noriega's behest, that he had not heard of specific drug-involvement allegations against Panamanian officials. Bush's
comments followed a pre-meeting briefing at which State Department, DEA,
and Pentagon officials told Bush that drug allegations against Noriega were
unproven.

The defense submission also recounted the details of the Reagan administration's covert efforts in the early and mid-1980s to fund and deliver military
supplies to the Nicaraguan Contras.

Noriega's help with the U.S.–Contra effort, May said, came largely
through providing training and assistance to the Contras. And while Noriega
refused to provide direct assistance in an invasion of Nicaragua, he helped
coordinate the training of Contras in Panama. Further, May asserted, Noriega
also helped the United States gain intelligence on new Soviet President
Mikhail Gorbachev and even helped the CIA provide Exocet missiles to
Argentina during its war with Britain over the Falkland Islands.

Noriega had helped the U.S. antidrug effort, and he had aided the United
States with covert operations around the world. But that had not been
enough, May concluded. "General Noriega was finally threatened that if he
did not [cooperate with the United States], certain things would occur to
him. One of those things that ultimately did occur was, in fact, that he was
indicted, his country invaded—that threat came true."

A little more than a week after May submitted the Section 5 on March 27, he
and Rubino followed up with a so-called Brady motion, a request for evidence
or records from the prosecution that could be helpful to the defense. Though
the motion was not necessary, since under federal rules of procedure the government is supposed to come forward on its own with such materials, the
defense lawyers were not leaving anything to chance. Better to make it clear
up front, they believed.

"It is our contention that the charges against General Noriega were manufactured as a result of General Noriega's refusal to commit Panamanian soldiers to an invasion of Nicaragua through Costa Rica," the motion began. "It
is our contention that evidence of General Noriega's cooperation with the
United States in maintaining peace and stability in Central America and in
fighting the scourge of narcotics trafficking demonstrates the falsity of the
allegations contained in the indictment."

The Brady motion requests were as broad as the Section 5 submission. The
defense wanted any information pertaining to all U.S. operations directed
against foreign governments since 1945; information on operations in which
U.S. officials had made false statements to Congress or disseminated false evidence in support of U.S. foreign policy; congressional reports containing classified information on intelligence activities; information pertaining to U.S. agent
or asset involvement in the Far Eastern opium trade, particularly in Burma and
Thailand in the 1950s and 1960s; similar information on U.S. agency or asset

involvement in the Central and South American marijuana and cocaine trades, and particularly efforts to finance the Contras through drug trafficking; information on violations of U.S. law regarding aid to the Contras; information on U.S. military and paramilitary activities intended to overthrow regimes in twenty countries around the world, including China, the Soviet Union, Vietnam, Iran, Syria, Guatemala, Costa Rica, and Panama; attempts to assassinate world leaders, including Castro and Panama's Torrijos and Noriega; and information on many top secret U.S.-run covert operations.

The defense also demanded the release of materials that would show Torrijos's and Noriega's relationship to U.S. agencies, officials, and operations; proposals by U.S. agents to overthrow or destabilize the Panamanian government, including plans to assassinate Torrijos and Noriega; materials pertaining to the training of Panamanians by U.S. government military and intelligence agencies; information showing Noriega's assistance to U.S. intelligence and law enforcement; details of Panamanian, Israeli, and Saudi assistance to the Contras; and finally, information formulated to ruin Noriega after he had refused to assist the United States in opening a southern front against the Sandinistas.

When James McAdams and Michael Olmsted, the assistant U.S. attorneys heading the government's classified information team, began reading through the defense's Section 5 submission and Brady motion, they were flabbergasted.

Since shortly after Noriega's arraignment, they had reviewed more than one hundred thousand documents, searching federal law enforcement, intelligence, and military files for references to Noriega and cataloging the thousands of documents captured in Panama. The orders from the top of Main Justice were that there should be no surprises arising out of secret government files. McAdams and Olmsted, who some at Main Justice had started calling the Starsky and Hutch of the Noriega case, were convinced they had covered the field. But the defense's Section 5 and Brady requests spanned four decades and involved operations around the world. Neither McAdams nor Olmsted could understand, for instance, what relevance an event in Burma in the early 1950s could possibly have to the specific drug charges facing Noriega.

Key to Noriega's emerging defense was a special pleading filed under seal in late September 1990, six months before the Section 5. That pleading was called a 12.3 Notice of Defense Based upon Public Authority. The notice was named after Rule 12.3 of the *Federal Rules of Criminal Procedure*, which required a defense to notify the judge and the prosecutors if it intended to claim that the defendant was acting as an agent of law enforcement or a federal intelligence agency at the time an alleged crime occurred. The notice required the identification of the government agencies involved and any members of those agencies that knew a crime was being committed. Noriega's 12.3 had singled out the DEA and the CIA as agencies that knew what Noriega was up to, including three former DEA directors and seven former CIA directors. McAdams and Olmsted would be charged with filing the government's response to the classified information proceedings and ultimately would lead the challenge against Noriega's CIPA defense at the special hearings on the Section 5 submission.

From the prosecutors' perspective it looked as though Noriega and his lawyers intended to admit that the acts charged against him in the indictment *had* occurred. But Noriega was going to say that his role came at the insistence and with the authority of the DEA and the CIA and were part of his long-standing relationship with those agencies and their leaders. Still, much of what the defense was demanding was manifestly unrelated to the charges or the times specified in the indictment.

On April 12 McAdams and Olmsted filed a response to Noriega's requests. The response followed reasoning developed at Main Justice. Even if Noriega had been the U.S. secretary of state himself, the reasoning went, if he participated in drug activities, he would be indicted and tried. Under Rule 12.3, McAdams and Olmsted pointed out, Noriega had to identify specifically the person who had authorized him to commit crimes, even if only by a "wink and a nod. The government is at a loss to understand, assuming Noriega truly believes he had a grant of public authority, why the defendant is having so much difficulty with the simple tasks of identifying his witnesses and describing the circumstances of the alleged grants of authority," McAdams and Olmsted noted.

As for the Section 5 submission, the prosecutors said it, too, was so broad as to be almost useless in trying to help define what Noriega really wanted. "While it may constitute a mini-treatise on United States foreign relations following World War II, [it] does not even attempt to identify the classified information that the defendant reasonably anticipates will be disclosed at trial. It never addresses any act set out in the indictment, nor does it begin to address any defense relating to the indictment."

The Section 5 notice is central to a CIPA defense, and it can't be vague, McAdams and Olmsted argued to the judge. Not only did Noriega's Section 5 fail to state specifically what confidential information the defense expected to disclose at trial, it also, and more fundamentally, the prosecutors said, made reference to so many irrelevant events that it was impossible to know what the defense thought was important. "Unless there is some minimal threshold requirement of relevance attendant to a Section 5 notice, the [special hearings, called] Section 6 proceedings and the trial which follow will be an unfocused and unmanageable free-for-all," the prosecutors said.

As for Noriega's Brady requests, McAdams and Olmsted said it appeared the defense planned to argue that "any act, real or imagined, by the United States government that now appears to be immoral or illegal or even mildly embarrassing shows that the current act of bringing this indictment is also misguided, illegal, or wrong. This entire argument is ludicrous."

Clearly, the prosecutors said, what the defense sought was to revisit the

Vice President George Bush met with General Manuel Antonio Noriega in Panama City in 1983. Bush then headed the Reagan administration's war on drugs and Noriega, according to the Miami indictment delivered five years later, was a co-conspirator with the Medellín drug cartel of Colombia. At Noriega's trial, the defense tried unsuccessfully to have this photograph admitted as evidence. (AP/Wide World Photos)

Manuel Noriega (*left*) met with Fidel Castro (*center*) in Cuba in July 1984. The Miami prosecutors alleged that Noriega asked Castro to mediate a dispute with the Medellín cartel during this meeting. At the extreme right is Noriega's military assistant Luis del Cid. (Courtesy of Miami U.S. Attorney's Office)

Lt. Col. Julian Melo (in uniform, standing next to Noriega) was alleged to have been Noriega's point of contact with the Medellín drug cartel. Soon after the May 1984 raid on the cartel's cocaine lab in Panama's Darien province, Noriega expelled Melo from the Panamanian Defense Forces. (Courtesy of Miami U.S. Attorney's Office)

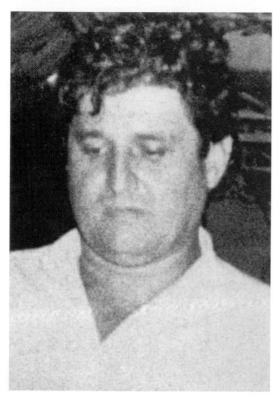

Jorge Ochoa, the Medellín cartel boss, allegedly hosted Noriega in Colombia. Later–following the murder of Colombian Justice Minister Rodrigo Lara Bonilla–Ochoa evacuated the cartel to Panama and paid Noriega $4 million for protection. This photo was introduced at trial by U.S. prosecutors.
(Courtesy of Miami U.S. Attorney's Office)

Pablo Escobar, one of the chiefs of the Medellín cartel, allegedly met with Noriega in Colombia to arrange a cocaine transportation route through Panama. This photo, from the early 1980s, was introduced as evidence at trial.
(Courtesy of Miami U.S. Attorney's Office)

Assistant U.S. Attorney Richard Gregorie directed the Miami grand jury investigation in late 1987 and early 1988 that led to the indictment of Noriega. (Courtesy of *Miami Daily Business Review*)

Leon Kellner, the Miami U.S. Attorney, met with reporters when the Noriega indictment was released on February 4, 1988. Three months later Kellner met privately with Vice President George Bush and pled that the Reagan administration not cut a deal with Noriega. (Courtesy of *Miami Daily Business Review*. Photo by Michael Germana.)

U.S. Attorney Dexter Lehtinen inherited the Noriega case from Leon Kellner only a few months after the indictment. The case lay idle for more than a year until October 1989, when Attorney General Richard Thornburgh directed that it be revived. Three months later Panama was invaded. (Courtesy of *Miami Daily Business Review*. Photo by Barbara Ellen Koch.)

Gathered in the central courtroom of the U.S. district court in Miami, the Noriega prosecution team (*from left*): Assistant U.S Attorneys Guy Lewis, Michael "Pat" Sullivan, and Myles Malman. Sullivan boasted one of the best prosecution win records in the Justice Department. Malman was also a veteran prosecutor and assistant to Miami U.S. Attorney Dexter Lehtinen. Lewis was only a few years out of law school. (Courtesy of U.S. Attorney's Office)

U.S. district judge William Hoeveler was appointed to the bench by President Jimmy Carter. The Harvard Law School graduate was one of the least reversed federal district judges. He presided over the case from the outset and completed the trial despite open heart surgery.

(Courtesy of *Miami Daily Business Review*)

Jon May joined the defense team in early 1990 to handle substantive law matters. The former Assistant U.S. Attorney and appellate specialist later took over the preparation of Noriega's secret documents case. Later he delivered the defense's opening statement at trial.

(Courtesy of *Miami Daily Business Review*)

Frank Rubino, a former Secret Service agent, had defended more than 100 cocaine smugglers and others before Noriega hired him in 1988. Rubino entered secret negotiations with the Justice Department prior to the December 1989 U.S. invasion of Panama. Later Rubino was Noriega's chief defense counsel at trial. (Courtesy of *Miami Daily Business Review*. Photo by Barbara Ellen Koch.)

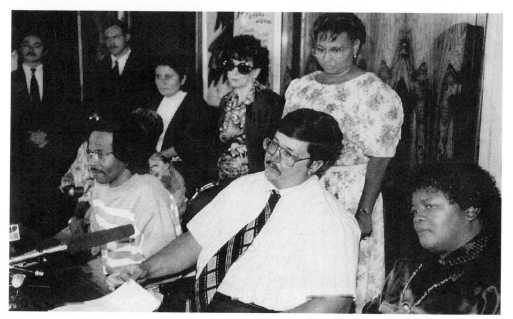

Members of the Noriega jury include (*standing from left*) Nova Rodriguez, Jean Hallisey, Ethel Bussey Johnson, and (*seated from left*) jury foreman Lester Spencer, James Hogan, and Thelma Sturdivant. During four days of deliberation Hogan and another juror expressed doubts about Noriega's guilt. (AP/Wide World Photos)

The Noriega prosecution team met with reporters on April 9, 1992, following Noriega's conviction by a Miami federal jury. It was their first meeting with the press. From left: Assistant U.S. Attorney Myles Malman, the second chair of the prosecution; Justice Department attorney Michael Olmsted, who worked on preparation of classified documents; then Acting U.S. Attorney James McAdams, who headed the secret document preparation; Assistant U.S. Attorney Michael "Pat" Sullivan, the lead prosecutor; and Assistant U.S. Attorney Guy Lewis, the third chair of the prosecution.

(Courtesy of *Miami Daily Business Review*. Photo by Barbara Ellen Koch.)

Lead defense counsel Frank Rubino met with Noriega almost daily following the dictator's incarceration as they prepared for trial. From his capture in January 1990, Noriega
maintained that he was a prisoner of war, and Rubino searched for a way to introduce
the United States' involvement in Central America into the trial. Throughout the trial
Noriega wore his general's uniform. (William Gentile, *Newsweek*)

Iran-Contra investigations. While such a recounting might "have some value for public titillation," it had no relevance to this case, said McAdams and Olmsted.

"The defendant argues only that United States support for the Contras encouraged certain elements of the government to value Noriega's help more than they valued the possibility of bringing an indictment, and when Noriega proved he would not support United States policy, the government no longer valued his help and permitted an indictment to be issued. This 'spin' on the events preceding the indictment is irrelevant even if true. The fact is that for years the intelligence community received inconclusive and circumstantial evidence that Noriega was involved in drug trafficking, but they were unaware of hard evidence. Eventually, new witnesses became available, and slowly but surely prosecutors assembled facts before the grand jury."

As for somewhat more specific requests for information that drugs were used to finance the Contras, McAdams and Olmsted noted that "if such material existed, it would be discoverable," but so far it had not been found. And if the Contras did fund their weapons purchases with drug proceeds, it still would not be relevant to the case at hand unless that drug trafficking was committed by Noriega with the authorization of a U.S. agency. Not every drug crime ever committed could be linked or relevant to the Noriega case, the prosecutors said.

"In general," McAdams and Olmsted wrote, "the government acknowledges that Noriega was a paid asset of the Army and held a paid relationship with the CIA. He provided information to the government in return for that payment. . . . In addition, he supported U.S. government programs in Panama, some of which were important intelligence operations and some of which were routine military or diplomatic exercises. Unless Noriega's participation undermines the charges in the indictment or relates to drug trafficking generally, the government objects to the demand for documents referring to that participation. . . . It appears generally that Noriega's estimation of his role in U.S. intelligence gathering is somewhat overblown."

Specifically, Noriega's assertion that his indictment and the invasion were the direct result of his failure to carry out a National Security Council request to open a southern front against the Sandinistas was "a complete fabrication."

The prosecutors said that the government saw its case against Noriega as "first and last a drug case. . . . The government seeks to confine this case to the indictment and to the facts normally admissible in such a case. The trial should concern those issues admissible in proving or rebutting the charges set out in the indictment," the prosecutors said. "The history of foreign relations in the United States is not on trial in this case; neither is the record of foreign relations by Noriega. Noriega, due to his position in history, is attempting to recast that history to his benefit. As an accomplished intelligence officer, he extracts facts which are neutral to him and attempts to reset them in a contrived context which casts him in a positive but decidedly historically revisionist light."

★   ★   ★

Now Judge Hoeveler would decide what information was relevant and admissible at trial. May was optimistic that Hoeveler would allow the broader context to come out. "I think he really wants the whole truth to come out. He doesn't want graymail. He doesn't want to just throw it out because it's sensationalism. But if we can show him that we believe what we have, how it really fits in context, how it is really relevant to the total picture, he'll let us have it. I believe he will. I hope he will." The judge scheduled the first hearing over the classified information question for Tuesday, April 30.

That day, Frank Rubino addressed the court first. He repeated that he and Jon May would need thousands of documents to show that Noriega had helped U.S. authorities battle drug trafficking in Panama. Some of those documents were in the United States and were classified top secret, others included files that Rubino said he had helped assemble in Panama between the 1988 indictment and the 1989 invasion. "Not only are these the general's files but also my files," Rubino said. "I didn't know we were going to have an invasion, or I would have brought them back. We are not asking for secret documents in Washington, we are asking for access to our documents."

Noriega had left forty-seven file cabinets filled with his own materials relevant to the defense in Panama. Some of those files contained notes of Noriega's meeting with George Bush and with the commanders of U.S. forces in Central America and U.S. ambassadors to Panama. Some contained documents "acquired by Noriega" outlining U.S. efforts to assassinate Torrijos and Noriega. The files, Rubino said, had been assembled with the help of Capt. Luis Quiel, former chief of the narcotics section of the Panamanian Defense Forces. The papers would show how Noriega acted to destroy a cartel drug lab and how Panama confiscated $18 million in drug money and turned it over to the United States, Rubino told the judge.

Pat Sullivan, in turn, addressed the judge. He said the government had turned over seven thousand pages of documents to the defense so far. The documents would prove irrelevant because the case was simply about drug trafficking. Noriega's work for law enforcement did not give him an excuse for breaking the law, Sullivan argued.

At a hearing on Thursday, May 5, Judge Hoeveler, although not yet ready to rule, gave Rubino and May an idea of his feeling. "What you are seeking," the judge said, "is a couple of truckloads of materials, about 98 percent of which would not be admissible in any way."

Rubino took the judge's hint. "Let us scale it down," Rubino interupted. "I am not going to try to stand here and feed you some garbage. Certain things in here are really vague and ambiguous. We are more than willing to go back to the drawing board on request for production and try to nail it down in a far more pointed way and not 'give me everything about training in Panama.' You are right."

A week later, on Monday, May 13, Hoeveler gave the defense a good part of what it wanted. The judge ruled that Noriega should have access to some documents, including those showing his cooperation with U.S. drug probes. But Hoeveler also said he needed more proof about other files requested by Noriega, including some relating to Cuba and others that allegedly would show weapons purchases for the Panamanian military. The judge observed: "The defense will, it appears, argue that evidence of Noriega's efforts to combat narcotics trafficking is admissible on the question of intent and tends to support his innocence of the activities charged in the indictment."

Jon May called the judge's ruling a victory.

"Judge Hoeveler hasn't ruled on the admissibility of evidence, but to the extent that he thinks the information is relevant to our client's intent, he at least is giving us access to the information. We'll argue admissibility later on," May said. "I assume it is going to be an uphill battle when it comes to admitting evidence," May later said privately. "The judge is going to approach these issues with a fair degree of skepticism. It is going to take us to convince him both as to the legitimacy of our defense and the need for the documents."

But the broad shotgun approach of discovery in the three defense submissions had seemed to work, May admitted. "We are making progress on a lot of different fronts. We are starting to see how we can do things and accomplish things."

Yet May conceded that no matter how much the judge finally allowed the defense to discover, it could already be too late.

"I have a great deal of respect for the prosecutors in this case, and I would never think that they would willfully suppress anything," he said, but "I certainly would not be surprised if critical evidence had been removed months ago by different agencies of the United States government that had access to it," he added. "It is likely that there are things that may not be there that were there at one time. I have no way of proving it. There are some things in life you just can't do anything about, you just have to deal with it the best way that you can."

But if records had disappeared or could not be found or had never been made, there was little Noriega could do to convince a judge or a jury that what he said was so. "The U.S. government, any government, operates on the doctrine of plausible deniablity," May said. "So long as they can deny it, no one ever knows if it really is true."

By Friday, July 19, McAdams and Olmsted had assembled more than two hundred top secret government documents that were responsive to the defense requests.

In the almost two months since the filing of the defense's requests, both the prosecutors and the defense had been holed up in the basement of the old federal courthouse locked away in the top secret document vault called SCIF, the Sensitive Compartmented Information Facility, reviewing each document.

Document by document, in some cases paragraph by paragraph, May and

Rubino, at the special CIPA hearing, would tell the judge why each document was important to Noriega's defense and should be allowed at trial. The prosecutors, in turn, would be given an opportunity to object to each document's admissibility.

Judge Hoeveler would have the final say concerning the use, relevance, and admissibility of the classified information at trial. The judge would be the final arbiter of what the jury would hear.

In early June, Hoeveler once again had to delay the trial. Then he hoped for a July 22 start date. But though the government had made nearly all of the discoverable material available to Rubino and May, the two lawyers had found it impossible to read through it fast enough to prepare, even though they were working twelve to sixteen hours a day, seven days a week. Rubino and May had managed to keep their sense of humor, but their bodies were worn out. "We just need more time," Rubino told Hoeveler. "Your Honor, I've had to go to the doctor. I get stomach cramps, diarrhea."

Hoeveler was sympathetic, but this would be the last delay. Ready or not, the trial would begin in early September, he told the lawyers.

The classified document hearing closely followed the defense's Section 5 and Brady motion. Event by event, assertion by assertion, the classified documents, each given a five- or six-digit identification number, came before the court. Documents 01141 to 01143 explained the defense's cocaine-Contra "pipeline theory." Jon May gave reasons for the importance of the three documents to Noriega's defense, and James McAdams argued why they should not be used at trial. Documents 01163-01164 contained nothing of relevance except for one paragraph concerning the *Krill*, McAdams asserted. The whole of the documents were important, the defense argued.

Documents 01299-01327, which had been pulled from DEA files in Washington, clearly showed Noriega's and Panama's assistance in the area of narcotics law enforcement. But the time frame, McAdams argued, had nothing to do with the acts and the time period alleged in the indictment. May responded that the fact Noriega had assisted was fundamental. It placed Noriega's actions in the context of the time and demonstrated his relationship with the DEA, May said.

Back and forth, through Friday, July 19, for four hours on Saturday, and all day Tuesday, Wednesday, and Thursday, the Section 6 hearing continued. Outside Hoeveler's ninth-floor courtroom, behind three deputy marshals, television and newspaper reporters sat. Little about what was going on inside would ever be reported. Each day security personnel swept the courtroom for listening devices. The electronic sweep left a residue of tension. This is like a marathon, Jon May thought to himself.

On the right side of the courtroom, facing the judge, sat the prosecutors: James McAdams, who would do most of the talking for the government, Michael Olmsted, Pat Sullivan, Myles Malman, and Guy Lewis, and DEA agent Steve Grilli. Behind them sat lawyers from the State Department, the

CIA, and other intelligence and defense agencies. To the defense it looked like a cast of thousands.

On the left side of the court sat Rubino and May, with lawyer-investigator Leon Tozo, who sat next to Noriega. In front of Noriega sat the court translator. Noriega mostly sat quietly, stone-faced, but occasionally he would turn to Tozo and explain the broader context of a document under discussion. Tozo would then whisper to May or Rubino.

The government objected to some of the documents entirely. On others, the government made suggestions for substitutions or redactions. Hoeveler pushed the lawyers through the case, sometimes word by word. "I have nothing to do with whether these documents are made public or not," Hoeveler said of his role in the process. "I have nothing to do with whether they're classified. What I have to determine is relevancy."

Each time May stood to explain why a document was important, the government learned something more about the overall defense strategy—or lack thereof. The Section 5 submission and the Brady motion had been broad and sometimes vague by design.

Rubino and May in fact had asked Judge Hoeveler to exclude the prosecutors from the hearing. The request not only went counter to CIPA but made little sense, the judge said. If the government was going to be called upon to make substitutions or redactions in admissible classified documents, clearly the government's lawyers had to be present to receive the judge's instructions.

But there was also the chance that in the review process the government might decide a document was too secret to be revealed. Refusing to hand it over could give the judge an opportunity to dismiss the case.

Even before the Section 6 hearing began, one thing had become almost certain about Noriega's defense. There was almost nothing to support a 12.3 public authority defense. In the weeks prior to the hearing, Rubino and May searched frantically for anything that directly connected Noriega to the DEA and the CIA. The best they had been able to do was uncover a couple of letters of commendation written by DEA Director Jack Lawn to Noriega, thanking him for his role in one narcotics bust or another. DEA officials called the almost generic ones "atta boy" letters, which were letters often sent to cooperating law enforcement agents following successful operations.

Without a strong 12.3 case, the context of Noriega's actions became strangely disconnected. There were no solid connections. If Noriega dealt drugs or participated in the indictment's alleged conspiracy as a confidential informant for the U.S. government, then his handlers had ensured plausible deniability. To anyone looking at the events now, it appeared more and more as though the general had been out there on his own.

Though the defense had traced Noriega's role in U.S. foreign policy back nearly a quarter of a century, the law that would determine how Hoeveler, as the judge, looked at all of that was quite settled. The indictment and the issues raised in the indictment provided the basic framework for determining what could be used as evidence at trial.

The case at hand had to do with a drug conspiracy alleged to have existed between the fall of 1981 and March 1986, a conspiracy that had as one of its members Manuel Noriega. The relevant facts were laid out in the indictment: Noriega had allegedly used his official position to transform Panama into a base of operations for international drug traffickers in exchange for payment. He was alleged to have permitted the use of airstrips in Panama to transport cocaine shipments from Colombia to the United States; arranged for the transportation and sale of ether and acetone, the chemicals necessary to produce cocaine, to the Medellín cartel; provided a hiding place for the cartel's top leaders when Colombia sought to crack down on them; and allowed cocaine proceeds to be deposited in Panamanian banks. He also had allegedly traveled to Cuba and met with Cuban president Fidel Castro, who mediated a dispute between the cartel and Noriega arising from Noriega's seizure of cocaine from a laboratory he had been paid to protect.

These were the events that governed the case. The law said that the evidence admitted at trial would go to show either Noriega's guilt as to these alleged facts or his innocence. For Hoeveler, evidence that indicated Noriega's innocence or mitigated his criminality had to fall within the time frame of the acts alleged in the indictment.

But Hoeveler also knew that there could be a subtext to events that the government might willingly be overlooking. That a piece of evidence was classified was not reason enough for that evidence to be ignored at trial. There could well be exculpatory evidence that one government agency or another had deemed secret just to avoid its exposure in a trial like this.

In adopting CIPA, Congress made it clear that a defendant was entitled to use classified information in his defense. The right to a fair trial and due process was paramount. A judge was not to balance the national security interests of the government against the right of the defendant to obtain information and put on a defense. Where information was central to the question of guilt or innocence and a defendant's constitutional guarantees were at stake, Congress had said that there should be no alternative but public disclosure. If dismissal was the only alternative to protecting the rights of the individual, then, Congress said, so be it.

Hoeveler would weigh the materials discussed during the Section 6 hearing by the same rules of evidence used in any other criminal case. All evidence was judged by two criteria: relevance and admissibility. Relevant evidence was evidence that tended to make the existence of any fact or action of consequence in the case at trial more probable or less probable. Admissible evidence was evidence so specifically pertinent to the case that the judge was bound to receive it. Evidence found relevant during pretrial might not be found admissible during the course of trial, and not all admissible evidence was relevant. The arguments Hoeveler had heard during the

Section 6 hearing were almost wholly directed toward relevance. Both the defense and the prosecution realized that admissibility would be determined during trial as the case unfolded witness by witness.

It was not enough, Judge Hoeveler ruled, that evidence be "minimally relevant" or bear some abstract relationship to the case. Rather, it was up to Noriega to show that the information in question was both relevant and helpful to the defense. Some of the classified information that the defense had requested was not, Hoeveler said.

Not admissible, according to the judge, was material relating to wiretapping, money laundering, narcotics interdiction, gun smuggling, Contra aid and supply, Contra training, Contra intelligence gathering, sabotage, the Panama Canal, spying on foreign governments and listening posts, and the operations of the CIA, the DEA, the NSA, military intelligence, and the State Department in Panama from 1981 to 1989. "Requiring production of all material relating to all of the above operations would place the government under the extraordinary burden of delivering a warehouse of documents which have no conceivable connection to this case," the judge said.

Further, classified materials detailing payments made directly or indirectly to Noriega, the government of Panama, or any entity that Noriega had access to and that offered support for any of the named U.S. government agencies was also not admissible. That would include monies for expenses, salaries, gifts, bribes, reimbursements, operational projects, and joint activities paid directly or indirectly by any agency of the U.S. government to Noriega or Panama or any Panamanian entity that Noriega had access to.

In requesting records of U.S. payments to Noriega, Rubino and May had hoped to get sufficient evidence to counter the government's claim that Noriega must have dealt in drugs to have grown so rich on a soldier's salary of $50,000 a year. Only two weeks before, the government itself revealed that it had obtained bank records and VISA, MasterCard, and American Express receipts that showed the Noriegas spent up to tens of thousands of dollars every month. The government dubbed this their "unexplained wealth" or "net worth" theory.

Though the government admitted that Noriega had been paid by the CIA and the U.S. Army, the payouts had been less than $400,000 in total, according to the prosecutors. Not so, the defense countered. In an affidavit filed in late July, Noriega said that the money paid him by the U.S. government had in fact totaled about $10 million since 1970. That money was to be used as he saw fit, he said, the only proviso being that the operations he was contracted to oversee were carried out.

But to allow the defense to use the money argument would confuse issues and divert the jury's attention away from the indictment, said Judge Hoeveler. If the government had documents that showed Noriega had pocketed operational funds, then those documents should be produced, Hoeveler said, but "the court will not require the government to dig up every receipt for every operation involving Noriega." If Noriega wanted to show that he was paid large amounts of money by the United States, then he could present evidence of such payments.

The judge ruled that the U.S. records of arms flights going from Panama to Costa Rica, Nicaragua, Honduras, El Salvador, and Guatemala between 1981 and 1986, and drug flights from those countries to the United States during the same period were not necessarily relevant. He recognized the "validity of Noriega's pipeline defense," Hoeveler said, but the discovery request was too broad. Only "pipeline" materials that related to Panama, not all of Central and South America, and to the charges covered in the indictment were relevant. If there was no connection to Panama, then the allegations had no consequence for the indictment. Hoeveler said he would rule on the admissibility of such evidence at trial.

As for the relevance of Noriega's meetings with U.S. officials in Washington and his meeting with George Bush in Panama, meetings that the defense contended were related to the Contra pipeline, Hoeveler said he found no reason to connect the meeting to the Contra operations, and the defense would not be allowed to discuss the meetings at trial. Material pertaining to plans by the U.S. government to open a southern front in Nicaragua and expand hostilities there, as well as materials relative to U.S. government assassination plans or attempts against Noriega and intelligence information furnished by Noriega to the U.S. government with respect to Cuba or Nicaragua during 1981 through 1989, was also not relevant, the judge said.

But Hoeveler said he would not deny the whole of the defense's requests in regard to Noriega's relationship with Cuba and its president, Fidel Castro. The government would charge that Noriega and Castro met in Havana in July 1984 to settle a dispute that had developed between Noriega and members of the Medellín cartel over the seizure of a cocaine lab in Panama. The seizure, the government said, was in retaliation for the cartel's failure to make adequate payment to Noriega. But, Hoeveler noted, the defense would say that the meeting had to do with foreign policy matters, and that was not unusual. The defense would seek to show that Noriega regularly acted as an intermediary between the United States and Cuba and that his meetings with Castro came at the behest or with the approval of the United States. Within certain limits, the judge agreed, Noriega should be able to introduce evidence of an ongoing relationship with Castro. "Evidence that Noriega had several contacts with Castro unrelated to narcotics would make this version of events more credible and tend to support his assertion that the meeting identified in the indictment was similarly unrelated to narcotics," Hoeveler wrote. "Noriega is entitled to have the jury consider the July 1984 meeting within the broader context of his relationship to Castro." Still, the substance of any intelligence provided to the United States as a result of the visit was irrelevant, Hoeveler ruled.

Also not relevant was material that would show Noriega aided the United

States in causing minor explosions at the Panama Canal in order to expedite the Panama Canal Treaty negotiations. The court "fails to see the relevance of this material," the judge wrote in his order.

But some U.S. agency materials were relevant, the judge said. He ordered that the DEA discover all materials that showed Noriega or his government's assistance to the United States in the extradition of drug fugitives, including those sent to the United States through Panama. Similarly, any material revealing any joint operations between the DEA and Panama in the seizure of drugs, money, aircraft, and boats, drug labs, and precursor chemicals should also be provided to the defense, the judge ordered. Such material, Hoeveler said, clearly would demonstrate Noriega's assistance in drug interdiction and narcotics-related law enforcement.

Because the indictment broadly charged that Noriega had allowed Panama to be used as a safe haven for drug traffickers, evidence that Noriega had permitted the DEA to conduct operations in Panama would tend to negate such an allegation by showing the extent to which Noriega had made Panama inhospitable to drug traffickers.

Internal U.S. agency documents had concluded that there was no reliable evidence connecting Noriega to drug trafficking. Those, along with other documents that showed Noriega had assisted the United States and particularly the DEA in various law enforcement efforts related to narcotics, such as ship boardings and joint sting operations, were important to a so-called lack-of-intent defense. Also relevant was information that would show money paid to government witnesses against Noriega and to those who had provided information to the CIA.

"Information which shows that persons identified as Noriega's associates in criminal activity were employed by the CIA would, at the very least, tend to support Noriega's defense that the activities with which he is charged were part of an operation run by the United States," Hoeveler said. Such material could be used to prove his innocence. As to whether or not the defense was entitled to know the nature of any of those persons' covert involvement, that would depend on the activities and if they bore any connection to the defense, the judge said.

Judge Hoeveler issued his forty-one-page CIPA ruling on August 7. Though the defense requested that the order be made public, since the judge had had to make several direct references to the content of classified documents, he ordered the ruling sealed.

CHAPTER 19

★★★★★★★

Cutting Deals

The closer the case moved to trial, the more it seemed the prosecution was put on the defensive. The day after the judge's CIPA order was handed down, the *Washington Post* and *Newsday* reported that the Customs Service had inadvertently allowed an accused cocaine smuggler who had been one of the government's chief witnesses before the Noriega grand jury to return freely to Colombia.

Boris Olarte testified that he had delivered $4.25 million of the $4.6 million in payoff money that had been given to Noriega from the Medellín cartel. The spring 1984 payment, Olarte said, was to ensure the protection of cartel operations in Panama. The indictment said there had been no other witnesses to the payoff. The alleged bribe was a key part of the government's case.

Olarte had pled guilty to smuggling charges in 1987 and had since been cooperating with the DEA. For his cooperation in the Noriega case and two other drug cases, he had been placed on probation and released from prison. He also had pocketed nearly $70,000 in government money for his undercover work. Over anxious Customs agents could not wait for Olarte to testify and "deported" him to Colombia so that he could work undercover.

One *Washington Post* headline said WITNESS SENT TO COLOMBIA MAY MISS NORIEGA TRIAL. A Customs spokesman said, "The disclosure of this information not only endangers lives but could cause the collapse of any productive long-term investigation." The truth was that Olarte had to be retrieved.

Rubino called Olarte's disappearance a curious and fortuitous turn of events for the prosecution. "His testimony is contradicted by two other government witnesses about how the alleged payoff occurred," Rubino said. The implication was that Olarte had been disposed of, though not quite as permanently as Ramón Navarro.

But things were not all bad news for the prosecutors on the witness front. Brian Davidow had agreed to cooperate with the government. At Davidow's scheduled sentencing on May 23, Sullivan told of Davidow's expected testimony against Noriega and his cooperation in a separate case. Rather than sentence Davidow to as much as forty years now, Sullivan asked that the judge delay sentencing until his help in the Noriega case could be measured.

William Saldarriaga, Davidow's *Krill* codefendant, declined to cooperate, however, and when he came before Hoeveler on May 24, he was handed a twenty-year prison term. This was ten years more than the sentence given defendants who had come before and offered to cooperate. Eduardo Pardo, the pilot who had carried drug profits to the cartel and who had pled guilty in early 1990 after Noriega's arraignment, was released from prison on June 13. He had been sentenced to thirty months but was released early for good behavior. The quickest way out of prison was to help the government.

The sixth Noriega codefendant to sign a plea agreement came forward on Tuesday, August 6. David Rodrigo Ortiz, thirty-five, a former Colombian air force pilot, was accused of flying drugs to Panama and teaching Floyd Carlton how to fly a smuggling plane for Pablo Escobar.

In jail in France, where he was serving a fourteen-year sentence on an unrelated drug charge, Ortiz listened carefully to Assistant U.S. Attorney Myles Malman when Malman went to the French prison to solicit Ortiz's help. For his testimony, Malman told him, Ortiz would be taken out of the French prison and brought to the United States, where the racketeering charges against him would be dropped. The maximum jail time Ortiz would face in the United States would drop from thirty-five years to ten, and his French sentence would also be satisfied. Standing before Judge Hoeveler on August 6, Ortiz admitted that he had piloted cocaine at the direction of Pablo Escobar and that he had taught Carlton how to fly a Piper Cheyenne aircraft in November 1982.

Ortiz said that soon after meeting with Carlton in December 1982, he learned that Carlton had met with Noriega and negotiated another drug flight through Panama for which Noriega had demanded $150,000 in advance protection money. The money was paid, and later that month, Ortiz and Carlton flew nearly nine hundred pounds of cocaine from Escobar's Hacienda Napoles ranch in Colombia to an airstrip in Panama.

On Friday, August 16, the prosecution received one of its biggest breaks since Floyd Carlton's grand jury testimony in 1988. In Panama, after weeks of negotiations with the DEA and the Miami prosecutors, Ricardo Bilonick, onetime top Panamanian diplomat, businessman, and Noriega confidant, agreed to turn himself in. With only two weeks to go before the start of the trial, Pat Sullivan and Myles Malman were still trying to nail down the case. The prosecution strategy had not changed from the beginning: to amass as many witnesses as could be found who would either directly or indirectly link Noriega to the acts charged in the indictment. As the old law enforcement adage went, you have to squeeze the ones you have to get the ones you want. That meant using the testimony of convicted drug dealers to work up the ladder to the organization or conspiracy's leaders.

Apart from Carlton, most of the witnesses who had come forward or had been flipped so far could offer only indirect knowledge of Noriega's involvement. Bilonick was different. He had been Noriega's business partner and had direct access to Noriega. If Noriega was on the take, if he had sanctioned drug dealing, then Bilonick had been in a position to know about it.

"He will provide extremely important testimony at the trial," Malman told Judge Hoeveler shortly after Bilonick's surrender. "Bilonick would act as a conduit of cocaine flights from Colombia to the Republic of Panama flown by Floyd Carlton and others. Bilonick would receive instructions from heads of the cartel. Bilonick has deep historic ties to the Medellín cartel," Malman said.

Noriega had received about $10 million in payoffs from the cartel to protect between fifteen and twenty tons of cocaine bound for the United States between 1982 and 1984, Bilonick told the prosecutors. He said he knew this was true because he had been the chief intermediary between the cartel and Noriega, supervising drug shipments through Panama.

Bilonick was part owner of a Panamanian cargo airline called Inair. He said that he had arranged for nineteen cocaine flights through Panama, that he had taken his instructions from Pablo Escobar, and that Noriega had been paid $500,000 for each flight. What Floyd Carlton had been doing with Cessnas, Bilonick had been doing with commercial cargo planes.

The indictment said that one of Bilonick's Inair planes was seized at Miami International Airport in 1984 with more than a ton of cocaine aboard, but Bilonick told the prosecutors that the amount of cocaine which had gone undetected had been much, much more. As many as ten to fifteen additional multi-hundred-kilo loads of cocaine had gone to south Florida from Panama between 1982 and 1984, he told the prosecutors.

Bilonick said that he began dealing with the cartel in 1981 when the daughter of cartel leader Jorge Ochoa was kidnapped by a Colombian M-19 guerrilla group. It was Bilonick who had arranged for Noriega to broker the negotiations between the traffickers and the guerrillas at Noriega's Panamanian beach house. The traffickers ultimately paid a ransom of $1.2 million, and Noriega received an arbitrator's fee of $125,000.

With Bilonick, the number of codefendants who agreed to testify against Noriega had grown to six. The first to come forward had been the just-released Panamanian pilot Eduardo Pardo, forty-five, who had flown a Lear jet loaded with $800,000 in drug proceeds from Fort Lauderdale to Panama in 1983. Though Sullivan called Pardo a "minor player" in the case against Noriega, Pardo would be able to corroborate the testimony of star witness Floyd Carlton.

Next was Luis del Cid, forty-eight, the former lieutenant colonel in the Panamanian Defense Forces and a Noriega military aide, who was accused of being a bagman and a liaison between Noriega and the cartel. The indictment said that he had carried up to $150,000 at a time from the cartel's pilots to Noriega. He had attended the meeting of Noriega and Castro to mediate the dispute between Noriega and the cartel. Named in three counts of the indictment and facing fifty years in prison, for his testimony del Cid was allowed to plead guilty to one conspiracy count carrying a maximum sentence of twenty years and a $50,000 fine.

Roberto Striedinger, forty-three, the chief pilot for cartel leader Pablo Escobar, was accused of conspiracy to import and distribute cocaine and distributing four hundred kilos of cocaine by flying a load from Escobar's Colombian ranch to Panama. His testimony was expected to corroborate Floyd Carlton's. Striedinger would testify that he had been present during a visit by Noriega to the cartel offices of the Ochoa family. Though Striedinger, misidentified in the indictment as Roberto Steiner, faced thirty years in jail, his deal with the government called for no more than ten years.

In the three months leading up to the September 3 trial date, Sullivan and Malman had gathered enough new evidence against Noriega to bolster the charges. Though Sullivan had ruled out a superseding indictment, he now promised that the government's case against Noriega would also demonstrate that Noriega had aided Bolivian drug smugglers, handed out phony passports to the top echelon of the Medellín cartel, helped smuggle expensive sports cars to the cartel in Colombia, protected more cocaine shipments than the indictment alleged, and accepted bribes to return to the cartel a drug-laden ship seized by the U.S. Coast Guard off the Panamanian coast.

Flipping codefendants had not been the extent of Sullivan's, Malman's, and Guy Lewis's work, however. The prosecutors, along with DEA agents Tom Raffanello, Ken Kennedy, Steve Grilli, Lenny Athas, Henry Cuervo, and others, had also coaxed several others to come forward. Besides Floyd Carlton, the prosecutors had lined up drug trafficker Gabriel Taboada, Panamanian businessman Enrique "Kiki" Pretelt, American marijuana smuggler Steven Kalish, and banker Amjad Awan.

Taboada, a drug trafficker and luxury car dealer, said he was present when Noriega visited the Medellín office of the Ochoa family. During that meeting, which Roberto Striedinger also said he attended, Taboada claimed Noriega accepted a bag filled with $500,000 in cash.

Kiki Pretelt, a former close friend and business partner of Noriega's, had been indicted with him in Tampa in 1988 and was accused of conspiracy to import 1.4 million pounds of marijuana into the United States. Pretelt had accompanied Noriega on his 1984 visit to Castro. He would testify that Noriega intended to lay the blame for the events leading to the indictment on one of his officers, Lt. Col. Julian Melo, saying that Melo had been the one who dealt with the cartel, not him.

Steven Kalish—who had been indicted separately in Tampa—would testify that he had given a $300,000 gift to Noriega for permission to launder his drug proceeds in Panama. He also would say that he had helped win the release of cartel operatives arrested in Panama.

Noriega's "personal banker," Amjad Awan, would say that he directed the flow of $23 million from Noriega's Panama bank account to accounts around Europe. Awan, a convicted money launderer, had worked for BCCI, the Bank of Credit and Commerce International. He would say that Noriega's secretary and Panamanian soldiers had delivered cash to him.

With just a week to go before the start of the trial, Sullivan acknowledged that a good portion of the government's case probably would be made by those who had traded their testimony for time off prison sentences, cash, or both. In a letter to Rubino that the defense had requested, Sullivan said that the prosecutors had paid more than $1.5 million to six men likely to testify during the trial. The highest amount, $510,921, had gone to Panamanian drug pilot Tony Azpruia. Azpruia, the pilot whose capture eventually led to the capture of Floyd Carlton, had been one of the government's key witnesses before the grand jury in 1988. Even though he had been convicted of drug trafficking, the government paid him for information. The one problem for Sullivan, however, was Azpruia's continued failure to pass an FBI lie detector test.

Boris Olarte, who was now in Colombia as a Customs Service undercover agent even though the DEA and the prosecution were counting on his testimony, had been paid $199,000 for information on Noriega. But unless the Customs Service could convince Olarte to return, it was unlikely he would make a significant contribution to the prosecution's case.

Ramón Navarro, who was now dead, had been paid $170,000 for his help, the government said. And José Blandon, whom Sullivan had scratched from the witness list because of his purloining of the Noriega prison tapes, had been paid $169,000.

One witness whom Sullivan expected to testify, Max Mermelstein, had been paid at least $250,000 for information. Mermelstein would testify about the makeup and structure of the Medellín cartel. Even though he had been linked to four murders and had admitted to importing more than fifty-six tons of cocaine into the United States, part of Mermelstein's agreement to testify was a reduction in his prison time from life without parole plus ninety years to two years and twenty-one days.

But perhaps the most problematic deal of all was the government's agreement with Carlos Lehder, a cofounder of the Medellín cartel. DEA agents began talking to Lehder in the late spring of 1990. Shortly after Noriega had been captured, Lehder, who was serving a sentence of life without parole plus 135 years, contacted the government about testifying. That Lehder would become a witness for the United States was truly odd.

For years Lehder had been the U.S. government's chief enemy in its war on drugs. Federal prosecutors had once called him the Henry Ford of the cocaine trade because he had perfected the cartel's drug delivery system into the United States, personally directing the delivery of 80 percent of the cocaine in the early 1980s, using sophisticated air drop and speed boat routes to move it through the Caribbean and eventually into south Florida. Lehder had proclaimed cocaine a "revolutionary weapon against North American imperialism."

Tampa U.S. Attorney Robert Merkle, who had tried and convicted Lehder in Jacksonville in 1988 and who had also headed the Tampa investigation and indictment of Noriega, was appalled by the Noriega prosecutor's decision to use Lehder as a witness. Merkle called Lehder "a liar from beginning to end."

But Lehder could make the ultimate link between the cartel and Noriega. Sullivan and Main Justice knew it.

The government's deals were no surprise to the defense. Making deals was not out of the ordinary for prosecutors handling drug cases. Flipping defendants to get to the higher-ups was standard fare. Without written documents or videotapes to present as evidence, the prosecution's case, the defense knew, would be built on drug dealers, money launderers, and other felons. And spending $1.5 million on witnesses was only a small part of the government's total bill, considering the cost of the invasion itself.

"We knew that when this case ultimately went to trial it would be the government putting on a Cecil B. DeMille production," Jon May said.

Remaining to be dealt with were attorney Michael O'Kane and his client, Daniel Miranda, Noriega's codefendant. Miranda was as far removed as one could get from the heart of the alleged conspiracy; he was accused of copiloting the drug cash–laden plane that Eduardo Pardo had flown from Fort Lauderdale to Panama in 1983. Miranda had never met Manuel Noriega. There was little he could tell about the alleged conspiracy. Miranda said he hadn't even known the plane he was copiloting carried drug cash.

For a year and a half O'Kane had done nothing but get in both the government's and the defense's face. He had refused to seek a separate trial for his client. He had challenged the defense fee deal and then refused to participate in the classified information search. All this was part of O'Kane's strategy. There was no way, O'Kane believed, that Pat Sullivan would muddy a trial of this magnitude by allowing an absurdly insignificant second defendant in the courtroom. The government had already cut deals with felons who had committed crimes infinitely more serious than Miranda's.

O'Kane told Sullivan that Miranda would cooperate with prosecutors if he got what he wanted: time served (fourteen months), the restoration of his federal pilot's license and his air-transport pilot's license, U.S. residency, and a work permit. Then he would be on the road to American citizenship. O'Kane did not waver in the deal he wanted for Miranda. He had made the same proposal early in 1990 and had been rejected.

But on September 4, with jury selection scheduled to begin, Sullivan agreed to O'Kane's terms. Dressed in a business suit, white shirt, and tie, and with a slight smile on his face, Daniel Miranda became the seventh Noriega codefendant to strike a deal with the government. He walked out of the Miami federal courthouse essentially a free man.

But there was one deal that could not be made. Shortly after the conviction of Brian Davidow and William Saldariagga in March, Sullivan privately suggested to Jon May that now was the time for Noriega to consider a plea. Even though the president himself had said shortly after Noriega's capture that the government would not plea bargain with the former dictator,

Sullivan knew better. For the right terms, the government always would negotiate a deal. The upside to a plea was usually guaranteed jail time and the assurance that an alleged criminal—through the quirks of the jury system—would not walk away free.

May and Rubino had their own ideas about plea bargains. For one, they would not allow their client to turn "snitch" against someone else. Noriega, conceivably, could finger Pablo Escobar, Jorge Ochoa, and other top drug lords. But "snitching" was something Rubino would never allow a client to do. "If that's what they want to do, fine," Rubino would say. "But first they have to find another lawyer." That was not a problem, however, with Noriega. From the start, he had insisted he was innocent. He had nothing to trade for a plea. A plea would have to be for time served, May and Rubino and Noriega decided.

But Sullivan didn't press the matter and months went by. Finally, in August, with just two weeks to go before the trial's start, Sullivan tried again. "What about a plea?" he asked Rubino. Rubino said he was willing to talk if the government was serious. Sullivan set up a meeting in U.S. Attorney Dexter Lehinen's office. Rubino and May came.

"Time served," Rubino answered when Lehtinen and Sullivan asked what Noriega would take to plea out and avoid a trial. "He will plead to one, just one, of the lesser counts," Rubino said. Rubino suggessted Count 10, which accused Noriega of assisting in the transfer of drug money from the U.S. to Panama. The maximum sentence was five years.

Sullivan and Lehtinen looked at one another. "You have to be kidding?" Sullivan responded. No, he said. Noriega would—at a minimum—have to plead guilty to Count One, the RICO conspiracy charge, which carried twenty years, and at least one of the other major counts, such as the Darien or Tranquilandia drug lab counts, which carried fifteen years. With a plea, the judge might see fit to let Noriega out of jail in ten or fifteen years.

Sullivan was all business. Main Justice would accept nothing less.

Rubino did not have to think it over. "Sorry," he said. "My client is innocent. He insists he's innocent. We will see you at trial."

CHAPTER 20
★★★★★★★

Finding a Jury

When Warren Burger, then the chief justice of the U.S. Supreme Court, visited the Central Courtroom of the old federal courthouse in Miami, he told James Lawrence King, federal district chief judge, that he thought it was the most magnificent federal courtroom in America. Indeed, there were few courtrooms that could have lent a more historic feel to what clearly would be a unique American trial.

The Central Courtroom sat off an open-air courtyard in the oldest section of the Miami federal court building. For fifty years the white limestone and coral rock building in the center of downtown Miami, just two blocks from Biscayne Bay, had served as both a post office and a courthouse. In the 1970s the post office was moved and the eleven-story court tower was added next door.

The Central Courtroom was a throwback to a bygone era. The checkerboard linoleum gallery with three rows of wood pewlike benches that could seat two hundred ended at a varnished oak bar beyond which deep red carpeting stretched past the prosecution and defense tables to the hand-carved witness box and judge's bench. Above was a coffered ceiling with gleaming gold Spanish-style chandeliers. Five large windows ran along each side of the courtroom, set at what would have been the second story of any other courtroom. Red velvet draperies were pulled back from the windows. Above and behind the spectators' gallery were oil paintings of the district's former chief judges. Behind the judge's bench was an oil mural, twenty-six feet by eleven feet, portraying south Florida's historical, commercial, and industrial history. When it was unveiled in 1941, the artist said it was his "conception of law and justice guiding Florida's progress from the savagery of the Seminoles to the modern skyscraper and airliner."

The mural included a schoolgirl, chemist, architect, fisherman, musician, bathing beauties, construction workers, mother and child, dockworkers, and laborers, forming a kind of pyramid at the top of which presided a black-robed judge.

The mural's black-robed judge looked out over the bench at which Judge Hoeveler would sit, past the witness stand to the jury box. Between the low oak balustrade and the oak wainscoting that circled the room were twelve wooden-backed, red-leather-cushioned chairs fixed to brass swivels.

233

All of the case's pretrial hearings—the POW and jurisdiction hearings, the hearings on Noriega's assets, the codefendants' trial, the classified information hearing, the plea hearings—had taken place in Judge Hoeveler's ninth-floor courtroom in the new courtroom tower on the other side of the courthouse. But on Thursday, September 5, jury selection in *United States v. Noriega* got under way at 10:30 A.M. in the Central Courtroom when the first dozen of about 170 potential jurors filed into the jury box.

The process of finding twelve jurors and six alternate jurors to hear the Noriega case had actually begun slightly more than four months before, on April 30. After weeks of negotiation between the prosecution and defense, Judge Hoeveler sent out a twenty-seven-page questionnaire to 1,204 residents of Miami and Dade County. The eighty-four questions were designed to bring together a pool of between two hundred and three hundred people who could fairly consider the case.

The questionnaire covered everything from the potential jurors' race, age, and education to the types of newspapers and magazines they read and the television programs they watched. One question asked whether the recipient had ever been employed by the M-19 or the Contras. One asked if the recipient, a close friend, or any member of the recipient's family had ever sought employment or been employed by the FBI, the CIA, the DEA, the National Security Agency, the Department of Justice, or the Defense Intelligence Agency. Another question asked if the recipient had formed an opinion about Noriega or the case, or the government's handling of the case. The questionnaire asked the potential jurors if they had ever heard or read about George Bush, Manuel Noriega, Ronald Reagan, Fidel Castro, or Oliver North, among others.

The winnowing process began as soon as the questionnaires started returning to Hoeveler's office. Sullivan, Malman, Rubino, and May took turns reviewing the potential jurors' answers. Some—like the one who asserted that Noriega should have been hanged in Panama—were easy to remove from consideration. About 60 percent of the returned questionnaires contained negative comments about Noriega, Rubino estimated.

More than 400 questionnaires came back undelivered; 136 recipients did not respond; 70 of those who responded were excused because they could not speak or understand English or had medical excuses; 7 were excused because they were government employees; 65 were excused for health or family reasons. In the end, slightly more than 170 were left.

The process beginning on this bright and muggy September morning was called *voir dire*, a phrase borrowed from the French that means "to speak the truth." It was an opportunity for the attorneys and the judge to examine the interests and competency of the potential jurors and to select those who would finally sit on the jury.

Voir dire, in fact, amounts to jury selection more by exclusion than inclusion. It affords attorneys the opportunity to exclude those who they believe are less likely to be sympathetic to their client and their argument. Jurors can be excluded from a jury in two ways: for cause, which usually means the potential juror exhibited a bias or has a relation to one of the two sides or, in the judge's determination, simply is not suitable; and by a peremptory challenge on the part of either side, which does not have a particular basis. Because both the prosecution and the defense must be able to accept the jury selected, it is almost a given that neither side will be truly happy with the results.

In federal court the defense is usually given ten peremptory challenges and the prosecution six, but given the media attention that preceded the start of the trial, Judge Hoeveler decided to double the number of peremptory strikes allowed: twenty for the defense and twelve for the prosecution.

The pool of potential jurors for the Noriega case was a true reflection of the county's multiethnic makeup—about one-third were Hispanic and about one-fourth were black. There were almost an equal number of women and men.

Judge Hoeveler told Sullivan, Malman, Rubino, and May that he was confident a jury could be selected in only a day or two. He knew the process would take longer, as did the lawyers, but he was nonetheless intent on making the case move quickly now that the first day of trial had finally arrived.

"Serving on a jury is one of the great privileges of citizenship in the United States," Hoeveler began, looking at the potential jurors. "Not often is the obligation incident to a case of this type."

The judge was convinced that not only could Noriega get a fair trial, but he could get one in Miami. Much had been made of south Florida's Hispanic population, more than 40 percent of those who lived in and around Miami. (Privately, Hoeveler worried that the Castro element might prove to be a problem in this case.)

Still, Hoeveler thought a fair jury could be had. "If anything, the time that this case has taken," the judge said, privately thinking back over the twenty months the case had taken to get to trial since Noriega's capture, "has got to inure to his benefit. The excesses of his regime grow dimmer as time progresses. Justice," Hoeveler said before the trial began, "is the achievement of truth."

The jury would not be sequestered until they began final deliberations, Hoeveler told the potential jurors. They would be able to go home at night and lead almost normal lives, except that they would not be able to read or listen to any news reports about the case. The trial would usually begin at about nine o'clock each morning and run until about four in the afternoon, four days a week, with Fridays off. But the trial, Hoeveler warned, could last from two to six months.

"You are here to determine whether or not the government can prove its allegations beyond a reasonable doubt," the judge said after he had read from the indictment. "There will be nothing in this case, as far as I am concerned, that has anything to do with politics. This case is going to be tried strictly within the confines of the indictment."

The potential jurors sat and listened. A young black man sat in the second row. He wore green shorts and a gold necklace with a charm in the shape of a machine gun. On his belt he carried a beeper. Another potential juror, a woman with blond hair pulled back into a knot, sat in the front row, taking notes.

Judge Hoeveler explained that the case would have to do with cocaine and drug money. "Even people you think are bad may be telling the truth," the judge told them. "Nobody is all good or all bad." There were several codefendants, the judge said, but none of them would stand trial with Noriega. The absence of the codefendants was not to be a concern, he explained. There would be some defendants and others who had pled guilty to crimes, but, still, their testimony could be truthful. Hoeveler said that he did not know if the defendant, General Noriega, would testify or not, but the jury should know that there was no requirement that he do so. How Noriega had arrived at this trial, Hoeveler continued, indirectly referring to the invasion, would not be the jury's concern.

Hoeveler told the prospective jurors that he "firmly believed" a jury could be impaneled. "Is there anybody here who knows the defendant, Mr. Noriega?" the judge finally asked.

Around the courtroom there was quiet.

Then Lesbia Reyna, an almost plain Hispanic woman, silently stood.

"Yes, ma'am," Judge Hoeveler said, inviting her to speak.

Reyna looked directly at Noriega, who sat stoically looking back. "I know him as a violation of human rights," she said in unpolished but pointed English. Then Reyna said that she did not know the defendant personally.

Jury selection, Hoeveler immediately thought, might be more difficult than he had anticipated.

Frank Rubino felt that his worst fears would be realized. Finding a fair jury in politically charged Miami was going to be very, very difficult.

As the judge and then Sullivan and then Rubino surveyed the potential jurors, several explained they had been born in Cuba and doubted they could be fair toward Noriega, particularly if Fidel Castro was to play a role in the case.

Later, several raised their hands when Hoeveler asked if there were any who could not judge Noriega solely on the evidence.

"Deep down inside, I know I'm prejudiced against the defendant," said one potential juror. "I lead a straight-track life." Others signaled that they did not think they could ignore the invasion.

The judge was edging toward frustration. "Do you folks understand, and I'm sure you do, that we are in a court of law?" he asked.

Finally, Hoeveler turned to Sullivan and Rubino. They could begin their questioning of each individual potential juror.

Juror number four's son had been arrested when he was seventeen. The police had treated the boy as an adult. It wasn't fair, the potential juror said. A woman who worked in a hospital explained that she had never read a word about Noriega in the newspapers. In almost two years, Noriega's dilemma had escaped her attention. One man, who held a small bottle of pills in his cupped hands, said that he had read much about the case and watched almost everything that had appeared on television. He had a strong opinion about Noriega. Could that opinion be changed, the judge asked. "Maybe," the man responded.

Another woman said her brother-in-law had worked for the CIA more than twenty-seven years before. He had gone to Cuba in the ill-fated Bay of Pigs invasion.

One man was the father of two soldiers who had participated in the 1989 invasion of Panama. Another man said that as a college senior he had infiltrated a high school as a police undercover drug buyer. One woman said that she was the ex-wife of the cartoonist who drew Spy vs. Spy in *Mad* magazine. Another was married to the chief executive of Southern Air Transport, a Miami-based air cargo company that had once been owned by the CIA.

On Friday morning, September 6, Rubino questioned twenty-two of the potential jurors. By the end of the morning five had been excused.

Sitting on the other side of Rubino from Noriega was Rebecca Lynn, a psychologist and jury profile expert. In late August, Hoeveler had approved hiring Lynn at $100 per hour. Using a jury selection expert was not uncommon, especially in complex criminal cases. Across the courtroom, the government's own jury expert sat behind Sullivan and Malman.

The defense's ideal juror would be intelligent and well read. The person would understand that the United States has made mistakes in the name of foreign policy. A cynic. A person who would not find it hard to believe that the U.S. government might engage in conspiracies. What to do with the Hispanics in the jury pool? One thought was to avoid seating them as much as possible because of the strong dislike for Castro. But Latin American immigrants might more fully understand the implications of United States foreign policy in Latin America.

As Rubino and Sullivan worked their way through the pool, Noriega wrote on a yellow legal pad. Often he would turn toward Rubino and Leon Tozo, and engage in animated three-way conversation. In his high school yearbook Noriega had listed psychiatry as an interest; in the military he had become a specialist in psychological operations.

In the first row behind Noriega sat his family—his wife, Felicidad, and his three daughters. Felicidad was a former schoolteacher from a well-to-do family. She had used her husband's position to expand her own business opportunities in Panama. Her black shoulder-length hair was drawn in a bun, and she was attentive to her husband's moves. She took notes as the *voir dire* continued.

Shortly after the invasion, Mrs. Noriega and two of her daughters had been placed under house arrest at the Cuban embassy in Panama City. In March 1990 the family was allowed to settle in the Dominican Republic, where the third Noriega daughter now lived. Since her husband's arrest and extradition to the United States, Felicidad had sought permission to come to the United States to visit him. The State Department had repeatedly denied her requests for a visa and visas for the three daughters. Finally, on August 12, with the trial's start less than three weeks away, visas good for just one U.S. entry were granted. Two days later the family arrived.

In the next week and a half, Felicidad and daughters Lorena, Thays, and Sandra, who had two infant children, went to the Miami federal courthouse where Noriega was once again jailed in the basement "submarine" cell. They visited five times before the end of August.

"It's difficult to hear somebody say bad things about someone who is not a bad man," Sandra told reporters. "Of course we got mad at people who were saying things that are not true. He's still our father. We have always seen him as our partner, our father, our friend."

On Friday, September 13, after six days of jury selection, the prosecutors and the defense had agreed on twelve jurors and six alternates.

Of the jurors, nine were women and three were men. Eight were black, two were Hispanic, and two were non-Latin whites. Demographically, they hardly matched the ethnic mix of Dade County, which was 45 percent Hispanic, 35 percent white, and 25 percent black.

One was a postal worker, one a laid-off fireman at a nuclear power plant, and three were retired. There was a first grade teacher, a woman who owned a silk flower business, a woman whose cousin was an official in Costa Rica's intelligence service, a veteran's hospital nurse, a woman auto mechanic, an insurance field representative, and a twenty-four-year-old graduate business student.

Of the six alternates, four were black and two Hispanic, three men and three women.

The number of middle-aged black women on the jury—six—surprised some. Given the damage illicit drugs had done to the black community, wouldn't they be extra tough on a drug defendant?

In the end, there were eighty-five finalists for the twelve jury seats and six alternate seats. The chosen eighteen would receive $40 a day for their services, free parking, and twenty-five cents a mile for the commute.

"You are now embarked on a very important project, and that is the trial of this case," Hoeveler told the jurors after they had been sworn in. "You must consider this case only from the standpoint of the evidence that is presented in this court."

CHAPTER 21
★★★★★★★

Unfinished Business:
The Government Snitch

Judge Hoeveler scheduled opening arguments for Monday, September 16.

But even before the final juror had been selected, there was unfinished business to attend to.

Three months before, on June 9, U.S. Attorney Dexter Lehtinen made a startling announcement. Ray Takiff, the defense lawyer who had represented Noriega in the days leading up to the 1988 indictment and for almost two years after, had worked—not in this case but in another—as an undercover agent for the U.S. government. On June 8, more than one hundred state and federal agents had raided the homes and offices of five current and former state judges in Miami. The agents came away with stacks of marked $100 bills. The bills had been passed out by Takiff.

Since August 1989, three months before the invasion of Panama, Takiff had been assisting in joint state and federal investigations. The assignment had been easy. Takiff, under investigation for tax evasion and money laundering, was to offer cash in exchange for favorable treatment of defendants coming before the judges in Miami's state courts. A federal grand jury had amassed enough evidence, Lehtinen said, including tape recordings made from a wire worn by Takiff to meetings with the judges.

Lehtinen explained that public disclosure of Takiff's cooperation had not been made sooner for fear it would compromise the undercover phase of the investigation. Lehtinen said that even though the operation was conducted in secret and Noriega's former lawyer was a key player, Noriega's case had not been affected.

"The government has taken all reasonable precautions to avoid interference with, or infringement upon, Noriega's defense and his right to counsel," Lehtinen said. The government had never asked for or obtained any privileged communication from Takiff relating to Noriega's defense, he said.

A filing by Lehtinen made the same day in federal court explained that Takiff had begun cooperating with the government on August 4, 1989, more than four months before the invasion of Panama. On November 20 he had signed a plea agreement in which he promised to drop his representation of clients in federal court. Lehtinen said that Takiff informed the government that he had terminated his representation of Noriega on December 28, 1989, four days after the start of the invasion.

When Takiff filed his withdrawal from the Noriega case, he claimed that his health was so poor he didn't know how much longer he might live. But as it now turned out, at age fifty-four and with three heart attacks and two major bypass surgeries behind him, Takiff had turned not to rest and recuperation but to carrying briefcases full of cash to judges while wearing an FBI wire on his chest. The indictments that were about to follow would make for the biggest judicial corruption case in Florida history and the second biggest in U.S. history.

Though Takiff said in a newspaper interview that he had not cooperated with the government for any personal gain, the government described it as a "plea agreement." Takiff did exactly as he had advised his clients on many occasions: saved his skin by working for the government.

For five years federal agents had been investigating Takiff on money-laundering and tax evasion charges. There were suspicions in the Miami U.S. attorney's office about Takiff's dealings with his drug-trafficking and money-laundering clients. It seemed that defense lawyers in Miami had some trouble drawing a distinct line when it came to getting involved with their clients' business dealings. Jack Fernández, who had worked with Takiff for years, was a perfect example. Fernández, an attorney, was now working for Rubino as an investigator on the Noriega case, but his client dealings had led to an indictment on federal money reporting violations. Fernández had taken a sabbatical from the Noriega case in early 1990 to serve his prison time.

By the summer of 1989, Takiff could clearly see the feds circling. The draft of a thirty-two-count money-laundering indictment had been prepared. At the same time, Assistant U.S. Attorney Norman Moscowitz, who would later defend in court the government's taping of Noriega at MCC, was with other assistants in Lehtinen's office looking into rumors that there was corruption in the state criminal courthouse in Miami.

Lehtinen would later maintain that the Takiff tax investigation, the judicial probe, and the Noriega case all coincidentally merged. Takiff claimed that he was the one who said he could reveal corruption at the courthouse. However, as it happened, in his November 1989 agreement with the government, Takiff traded his cooperation for the forgiveness of his $92,968 debt to the Internal Revenue Service, the discharge of the grand jury that had been looking into his tax problems, and the tearing up of the draft indictment. Takiff first spoke to federal agents on August 4, 1989. He made his first payoff to a judge on August 29.

Takiff's astounding success as a government undercover agent seemed a commentary on his standing in the Miami legal community. In less than a month's time he had parlayed a shady reputation into a payoff for the government. Takiff's sting was straightforward. He claimed that he represented a wealthy Central American drug trafficker who wanted to make sure his people stayed out of jail. In exchange for cash, Takiff asked the judges to lower bail, reveal the existence of arrest warrants, release confidential information, and suppress evidence.

The drug-trafficking clients whom Takiff represented, however, were FBI and state agents. By June 1991, Takiff had handed out $266,000 in government bribe money.

U.S. Attorney Lehtinen called the judicial probe "particularly important." He said, "This kind of corruption destroys public confidence in the criminal justice system."

In press interviews after Lehtinen's announcement, Takiff said he believed God had let him live so that he could do the right thing, to rewrite his legacy. Now, he said, his children could be proud of him. The same Ray Takiff had claimed after Noriega's indictment that he possessed material that would damn George Bush. That material had still not turned up.

Of his work for the government, Takiff said, "During the period of time in which I worked for the government, I did not compromise any client, particularly in the period of time I was lead counsel for Manuel Noriega." Takiff said that he had negotiated the dismissal of the indictment against Noriega, but Noriega had pulled out of the deal.

Frank Rubino was incensed by the revelation of Takiff's cooperation with the government. No matter what Takiff or Lehtinen claimed, it seemed as though Takiff's work for the government intersected with the Noriega case at too many points. U.S. and Panamanian confrontations had grown more alarming in October and November 1989. In November, Takiff had signed his plea agreement with the prosecutors.

Takiff said he resigned as Noriega's attorney on December 28, 1989. That was the same day Noriega surrendered to U.S. forces in Panama. Takiff had been in close, regular contact with Noriega until his surrender, even while Takiff was a government agent. He was a lawyer and an informant at the same time. And when Takiff did quit Noriega's defense, he did not bother to notify his co-counsel of two years of his resignation.

Would Noriega have taken the State Department's deal to leave Panama if Takiff had been more forceful? Why had Takiff not resigned as soon as be had become an informant? "I don't see how he could have been the general's lawyer if he was more interested in self-preservation and cottoning up to the government," Rubino told a reporter. There were ten thousand lawyers in Dade County. Why did the government choose to recruit Takiff as an informant? Even if he did go to the government with information, why had he been enlisted to spend the next year working as an undercover agent?

On July 7, Rubino had filed a motion to delay Noriega's trial until a hearing could be held on the Takiff matter. Rubino told Judge Hoeveler he believed Noriega's right to a fair trial had been compromised and threatened by Takiff's work as a government agent. Takiff had been intimately involved in the defense strategy for two years, Rubino said. During that time Takiff had met with Noriega and with assistants from the U.S. attorney's office. Clearly, Rubino said, Takiff had a conflict of interest, and Noriega had been denied effective assistance of counsel. If nothing else, Rubino said, Takiff had been under an obligation to tell Noriega that he was involved in another case that might affect his representation. "The guarantee of the Sixth Amendment right to effective assistance of counsel requires two related rights: the right to reasonably competent counsel and the right to counsel's undivided loyalty," Rubino told Hoeveler. Rubino requested an inquiry into the matter, a hearing where government agents and prosecutors and Takiff would be required to answer to the court under oath what information the government had received from Takiff while he was still representing Noriega.

Rubino expanded on his request for a hearing on Wednesday, September 4, when Judge Hoeveler listened to oral arguments.

Between August 1989 and January 4, 1990, when Noriega surrendered, Takiff had met "probably a dozen times" with Noriega, Rubino told the judge. Each meeting had to do with how to deal with Bush administration offers. Each could have led to a result other than the invasion, he said. On January 3, 1990, Takiff telephoned Noriega at the Vatican embassy and advised Noriega that it would "please the Justice Department" if he surrendered. Noriega did, and the next day as he was being transported to the United States to stand trial, Takiff announced his resignation for "health reasons. Had General Noriega not followed Mr. Takiff's advice, there is a real possibility that this indictment would have been dismissed and General Noriega would not be here today," Rubino said. "What we're saying is that Takiff served two masters."

Noriega had suffered no harm, Assistant U.S. Attorney Sonia O'Donnell said, responding to Rubino. No one on the Noriega prosecution team had learned anything about the Noriega case from Takiff, she said. Both Sullivan and Malman had filed affidavits saying Takiff had not revealed privileged information, O'Donnell told the judge.

Noriega's constitutional right to counsel did not apply outside of the United States. Noriega, O'Donnell asserted, had not submitted to the jurisdiction of the United States until his capture. While Takiff worked for the government and remained Noriega's counsel, Noriega had others who "zealously represented" him. Noriega's other lawyers could have advised him to follow another course of action.

During fourteen years on the bench, Hoeveler had never seen a case quite like this. At every turn there seemed to be some new, unexplored dimension. The case had been an exercise in constitutional principles almost from the start. It wouldn't make any sense for it not to be so now.

Hoeveler said he would take Rubino's request for a hearing under consideration. He later set a hearing for September 28. The trial would not have to be delayed. The issue could be considered separately, and if there had been government misconduct so egregious as to have hurt Noriega's right to a fair trial, the trial could be stopped and the charges dismissed. The defense, the judge decided, would have its day in court with Takiff.

PART III

The Trial

CHAPTER 22
★★★★★★★

The Small Man
in the General's Uniform

It was the first day of the trial itself.

Manuel Noriega wore dark dress trousers, a long-sleeved khaki shirt with a Panamanian Defense Forces insignia on each upper sleeve, a black tie, and four stars on each shoulder. He stood leaning into the defense table, facing toward the gallery. In the first row sat Felicidad and his youngest daughter, Thays. To Noriega's right stood Frank Rubino, wearing a dark Italian suit, white shirt and tie. Reading glasses hung at the edge of his nose. To the general's left sat Jack Fernández and next to him Jon May. Noriega and Rubino laughed.

Michael "Pat" Sullivan sat across the aisle at the prosecution table. He wore a gray suit, white shirt, and red tie. Next to him sat Myles Malman and then Guy Lewis. At the end of the table sat Steven Grilli of the DEA. James McAdams and Michael Olmsted, the prosecution team's two CIPA experts, sat in chairs directly behind the prosecution table.

In the first row of the gallery sat U.S. Attorney Dexter Lehtinen. He was flanked by Daniel Horgan, the U.S. marshal in south Florida, Thomas Cash, the Miami SAC of the DEA, and attorneys from the State Department, the DEA, and the CIA.

It was 9:30 in the morning. The gallery had packed quickly, beginning at 9:15. All had passed through two sets of metal detectors on their way to the Central Courtroom. The press had to show specially prepared IDs. Members of the public had to sign a roster. A contingent of deputy federal marshals equipped with radio earphones tracked the movements of the media and public as they filed into the courtroom fifteen minutes before the judge was scheduled to take the bench.

The middle front row of the gallery was crammed with television courtroom artists. (On the courthouse steps outside were two dozen still and video camera people.) Behind the artists and to the sides were assigned seats for fifty different news organizations that had committed to complete coverage. Another 140 reporters filled the remaining seats. One bench at the back of the courtroom was filled with fewer than a dozen members of the public. The few who had gotten in had waited in line for three hours.

A dozen deputy marshals took up positions around the courtroom, two in each corner, two behind Noriega facing the gallery, and two next to the jury box.

In the well before the judge's bench sat the court reporter and to his side the judge's courtroom assistant. At the table to the judge's left sat a classified information specialist from the Justice Department who would monitor the trial and advise the judge when a witness or evidence moved perilously close to divulging secret information. Next to her sat the judge's two law clerks.

The jurors were brought into the courtroom at just after 9:30. Two alternates sat at the end of each row of seven chairs in the jury box. In front of the jury box sat the other four alternates. Each juror had been handed a notebook and a pen as the group made its way into the box.

The crowd of reporters seemed to startle some of the jurors. Uneasy smiles came across their faces. Clearly, they had become the focus of the case.

At 9:42, Judge Hoeveler strode into the courtroom and took the bench. Behind him a printed plaque read: FROM JUSTICE AS A FOUNTAIN ALL RIGHTS FLOW. A momentary sigh of relief seemed to have eased across his face as he turned toward the jurors. Getting this case to trial had not been easy. It would be the first and perhaps only trial of a foreign head of state ever to take place in an American courtroom.

Hoeveler spoke to the jurors. The judge and the jury have separate functions, he explained. The judge was present to instruct the jury on the law applicable to the case, to make sure that a fair trial happened. "Whatever you have been or are," Hoeveler continued, "you are now judges. I have no question you can do the job. Jurors of all walks of life can rise to the occasion. Your term of office will not be as long as mine," he added with smile. "Close but not quite."

Hoeveler explained that the burden of proof rested on the government. First, the government would make its opening statement, not an argument but a statement about its case. The defense, the judge explained, had elected to defer its opening statement until the government had completed its case. So, following the government's opening, the prosecution would proceed with its witnesses. After the government concluded its case, the defense would follow, presenting, if it felt necessary, its own evidence and witnesses. After all the evidence had been presented, Hoeveler told the jurors, then each side would deliver its closing arguments, its statements about what its witnesses and evidence had proven.

"You are to determine the facts and the believability of the evidence," Hoeveler told the jurors. "We all have a tendency to reach conclusions as soon as we have facts. Resist reaching conclusions. Resist that temptation until the very end." The jury would be free to take notes, the judge said, but after the verdict was reached, the notes would be destroyed. In the meantime, Hoeveler told the jurors, do not discuss this case with anyone, not even among yourselves.

It was 10:09. Judge Hoeveler looked at Pat Sullivan. "All right, Mr. Sullivan, you may proceed."

Sullivan knew that what he would say in the next hour could very well determine how the jurors would view the government's case over the next two or three months. He knew his opening should not be just a recitation of facts but should paint a picture, draw an image of where the case would go. If his opening statement worked, the jury would listen to the entire case, perhaps even look forward to hearing the government's witnesses.

Sullivan buttoned his coat as he walked to the lectern. He faced the jurors and put his notes down. Pat Sullivan never had great flair; he was matter-of-fact, unflappable for the most part. His style was soft-spoken but authoritative. He looked at the jury for a moment.

"Good morning, jurors. Thank you for being here with us on this singular day. You are here to decide the case of United States versus General Manuel Antonio Noriega. The defendant is here in the courtroom. He is a small man in his general's uniform. He is the last military strongman from Panama. He looks small here in this cavernous courtroom, but he was a giant in Panama."

Noriega did not look up. He sat at near attention, but his head was bowed. He wore a black headset and listened to the courtroom interpreter.

Sullivan said he would explain what the evidence was going to be in the government's case. The opening statement was not evidence, it was what the evidence was about, he told the jurors. His summary, he said, would help the jurors put in context the testimony of each witness. Many times one witness's testimony wouldn't hold a great deal of significance, but in the context of a second or third witness it would, he said.

Because some of the events were as much as ten years old, the pieces of evidence, Sullivan warned, might not fit perfectly. Memory, he said, was like that. But all of the pieces would fit together to form a picture, like a giant jigsaw puzzle. Using the indictment, Sullivan said, the jury could measure and evaluate the evidence and testimony and determine whether the charges in the indictment had been proved.

Sullivan then took the jury through the ten counts of the eleven-count indictment, the ten counts that named Noriega. He pointed to a large black-and-white chart sitting on an easel that listed racketeering conspiracy, racketeering, trafficking conspiracy, distribution, conspiracy to manufacture. The racketeering counts, counts one and two, he said, were the center of the indictment. All of the major allegations against Noriega were contained in those two counts. Noriega, said Sullivan, was involved with a group of individuals—what the law called an enterprise—who used Noriega's official position to facilitate the manufacture and transportation of cocaine headed to the United States and to launder the proceeds. That enterprise was "an association of narcotics traffickers from Colombia and Panama who had the authorization and permission, encouragement and permission" of Noriega. Noriega, Sullivan said, was "at the top of a criminal enterprise to manufacture and import cocaine into the United States."

Sullivan pointed out the names: Gustavo Gaviria and Pablo Escobar of the Medellín cartel; Floyd Carlton, a witness in the case; Luis del Cid, who would tell the jury about his personal participation in the events. Next, Sullivan continued, came Roberto Steiner, whose real name was Roberto Striedinger, Francisco Chavez Gil, and David Rodrigo Ortiz. They had pled guilty and would also testify. Anticipating Rubino's cross-examination, Sullivan added, "They are cooperating in the hopes that their sentence after their plea of guilty will be lighter than if they did not cooperate."

Amet Paredes and Brian Davidow would also testify. And then Ricardo Bilonick, Eduardo Pardo, and Daniel Miranda, who also pled guilty.

Five witnesses would testify about Noriega's relationship with the Medellín cartel, Sullivan said. Striedinger and Gabriel Taboada, the Colombian trafficker, would testify about how they were present when Noriega visited the cartel's office in the summer of 1983. Max Mermelstein, a man who had pled guilty to trafficking in 1986, and Carlos Lehder, the convicted cartel member, would explain the inner workings of the cartel, its membership, and how Noriega worked with the cartel leaders. Floyd Carlton would also testify about the cartel and how the cartel had recruited him as a pilot because they knew he was close to Noriega. Carlton would tell of four flights he had made to Panama from Colombia for the cartel.

"On each and every occasion, Floyd Carlton consulted with Noriega that he was going to make a flight," Sullivan explained. "Noriega always told him, 'Do nothing without my permission. If you try anything that I don't know about, I will know about it, and you will suffer for it. You can only act with my permission.'"

Carlton was never present when Noriega had direct contact with the cartel, said Sullivan, but cartel money passed from Carlton to Noriega's military aide, Luis del Cid, to Noriega, Carlton would testify.

"Money was delivered by Floyd Carlton to Manuel Noriega. On all occasions Manuel Noriega wouldn't receive money in hand from Floyd Carlton. He would use an intermediary," said Sullivan. A cartel paymaster named Eric Guerra would corroborate that Carlton was paid for his cocaine flights and to bribe Noriega.

Carlton never used Noriega's name in front of the cartel leaders. "He would always just say, 'My man, my person in Panama has to be taken care of.'" But the cartel's leader, Carlton would say, always specified that they were dealing with Noriega.

Carlos Lehder, who sat in on the counsel meetings of the chiefs of the cartel, would testify that he had never met Noriega. But he would say that Noriega was just like "hundreds of crooked cops throughout Colombia, Panama, even Florida." Manuel Noriega was just another crooked cop, Sullivan said. Like crooked lawyers and corrupt politicians, they all worked for the cartel.

Noriega had come to the cartel's attention in the late 1970s because he was in charge of Panama's military intelligence and had broad law enforcement powers. The cartel knew that the only way to move their product to market was to either eliminate Noriega or buy him. "Their decision was to buy him," Sullivan told the jury.

The relationship was "hit or miss" until about 1982 when the cartel's business began to expand. Then, in an effort to open even more smuggling routes, the cartel sent emissaries to Panama to visit Noriega. The cartel's representatives met face-to-face with Noriega and gained his permission to fly small planes loaded with cocaine into the two airports in Panama City. For Noriega's protection the cartel would pay him $1,000 per kilo, Sullivan said. That meant Noriega would make $400,000 on an average load. The amount of money that flowed from the cartel into Noriega's bank accounts will "stagger you," Sullivan promised the jury.

The kidnapping of Marta Ochoa, as Lehder, del Cid, and Bilonick would tell the jury, Sullivan said, was a fundamental turning point in Noriega's relationship with the cartel. Noriega's successful mediation of the dispute impressed the cartel and cemented their relationship.

Through it all, Noriega continued to enforce the law in Panama, said Sullivan. He arrested drug traffickers, but always "the problem would be worked out. Payments would be made to release Colombians who got arrested. Payments would be made to release planes or boats that got seized." But one incident almost ruined Noriega's relationship with the cartel, Sullivan explained. In March 1984, the Colombian army raided and destroyed the cartel's Tranquilandia lab in the Colombian jungle. Within two months, Sullivan said, the cartel cut a deal with one of Noriega's lieutenants and set up a new cocaine manufacturing site in Panama's Darien province. In mid-May 1984, a PDF unit, thinking the lab was a guerrilla camp, raided it and arrested many of the cartel's workers. The resulting dispute between Noriega and the cartel, Sullivan told the jury, had to be mediated by Fidel Castro. In the end, all of the cartel's workers were released and its property as well as $4 million in protection money was returned.

Witnesses to all of these events would come into the courtroom, said Sullivan.

"You will hear their testimony. You will get to know them. You will put together their testimony, just like those jigsaw pieces, that will form one big picture. And at the end of all the evidence, jurors, you will use that to base your verdict on, and you will, I believe, decide that the government has borne its burden of proving beyond a reasonable doubt the criminal charges against Manuel Noriega."

Sullivan paused for a moment and then thanked the jury. His opening statement had taken nearly ninety minutes. Not once did he mention Noriega's relationship with the U.S. government or any of its agencies, such as the DEA. Sullivan's history had been selective, but then he had promised only to address the indictment, which he had.

Not before Sullivan's opening did the government assert that Noriega met face-to-face with the cartel. Now the government was saying that Noriega met personally with cartel members, not once but twice. The government previously contended only that bagmen and intermediaries had conducted the cartel and Noriega's business.

Through Sullivan's opening, Noriega sat impassively, his chin on his hand, as he listened to the Spanish translation.

Frank Rubino made notes as he followed Sullivan's presentation. The road map to the government's case had been spread before the jury and the defense.

It would now have been Rubino's turn to present the defense's opening. The decision to defer was a bit of a calculated risk. While the defense sat silent, except for cross-examining witnesses, the government case would have a chance to coalesce in the jury's minds. There was also the chance that the jury might not understand Rubino's objections through the course of the government's case. But Rubino had decided that if the government's case was really going to take as long as three months, then his opening would simply have been lost in time. When he did deliver Noriega's opening, Rubino believed, it would be fresh in the minds of the jurors, as they then went on to consider the defense case.

Rubino had spent the months before trial preparing for the government's witnesses and cross-examination; Jon May had worked to assemble the defense case. But Hoeveler's CIPA ruling had narrowed their options. May could continue each day to dig through the documents the government had turned over and try to undercover new investigative leads, but if the defense were forced to go on now, it would have to settle for a very conventional drug case rebuttal. It would be the Davidow and Saldarriaga defense all over again.

CHAPTER 23

A Man of His Confidence

The next morning, Tuesday, September 17, Pat Sullivan called his first witness.

Sullivan wanted first to show the jury just how large the Medellín cartel's operation was and how ruthless its leaders could be. In short order, the witness stand would become a parade ground for Spanish-speaking, dope-dealing Colombians, but to start, Sullivan intended to show another face of the cartel.

Max Mermelstein fit the bill, and he was no stranger to a federal court witness stand. Mermelstein was a forty-seven-year-old Brooklyn-born Jewish engineer who went into the cocaine-trafficking business through the back door; he had begun smuggling in-laws out of Colombia.

In 1978, living in Miami, Mermelstein made the acquaintance of Rafael "Rafa" Cardona. Cardona had come to the United States with Mermelstein's help, and once in Miami he began to coordinate cocaine shipments with the Ochoa family, whom he knew from his native Medellín.

Mermelstein's friendship with Cardona led, in time, to his own full-fledged involvement in the "transportation arm" of the cartel. Beginning in the early 1980s and continuing through 1985, Mermelstein, by his own estimate, smuggled nearly fifty-six tons of cocaine into the United States. That was, he believed, 25 percent of the total amount of cocaine brought to the United States by the cartel.

For Mermelstein, drug trafficking was a business. He hired pilots and couriers, managed inventory and distribution, and, as necessary, helped the cartel's leaders make sure that business ran smoothly. In 1985 that meant arranging the murder of a Louisiana drug-trafficker-turned-informant named Barry Seal. Mermelstein stalked Seal personally, but in the end gave the job to other cartel assassins. In June 1985, before Mermelstein was able to supervise Seal's murder (which the cartel successfully carried out in February 1986), federal agents caught up with Mermelstein and put him in jail on trafficking charges.

Faced with an eleven-count federal indictment for cocaine importation, conspiracy, and possession, which would have landed him in jail for life plus ninety years if convicted, Mermelstein flipped. Over the next six years, in addition to writing a book about his exploits with the cartel, Mermelstein served as one of the government's top witnesses against cartel members. From 1985 to the middle of 1991 the federal government paid Mermelstein almost $256,000 for information on the drug business. In addition, Mermelstein and seventeen members of his family were enrolled in the federal Witness Protection Program, receiving more than $414,000 in living expenses.

Under Sullivan's questioning, Mermelstein guided the jury through a tale of the cartel's business dealings and leading personalities. Mermelstein's odyssey led to Panama in March 1983, when the cartel dispatched him to buy landing rights for its drug flights. In Panama, Mermelstein said, he met with people who he believed were top Panamanian officials. But those meetings never involved Noriega, he conceded. The closest Mermelstein ever got to Noriega was on a visit to the cartel's office in Medellín. There, Mermelstein said, he saw Noriega's name in a ledger book that contained cocaine transactions.

"What were the names you recognized in the ledger?" Sullivan asked Mermelstein as the direct examination wound its way around to Noriega after nearly four hours.

"My name, of course," Mermelstein said. "Going through it, there was one page that had Noriega's name at the top."

Sullivan had taken Mermelstein down a long road. Still, it had begun with the cartel and ended with Noriega.

Through almost the full four hours Noriega sat stoically, looking straight ahead. Only at the final mention of his name did he seem to perk up, but then only for a second. His expression in that instant was one of puzzlement.

The examination created a picture of the cartel and its dealings. Noriega's presence seemed removed except by inference. It would be for Rubino to explain to the jury that certainly Noriega could not be responsible for every official in Panama who had ever taken a bribe. And that Noriega's name had once been written in a ledger in Colombia did not make him a drug dealer.

The route of cross-examination for Rubino was clear and simple: hammer away at Mermelstein's character and credibility, and his obvious motivation to trade his testimony for staying out of jail. If the prosecution intended to put on a typical drug case, then the defense would be the tried-and-true drug case defense.

Rubino started by reviewing the government's eleven-count indictment against Mermelstein. As Mermelstein sat in jail, facing the rest of his life there, Rubino suggested, the idea of cutting a deal with the government began to look better and better.

"Now you sat in jail for a period of time, and eventually you began to negotiate with the government, correct?" Rubino asked.

"That is correct, sir."

"And you negotiated a deal with the government wherein they would allow you certain considerations. Am I correct?"

"What do you mean by considerations?"

"Well, right now today you are out, and you are not in prison, correct?"

"That's correct, sir."

"So, therefore, you are not subject to the continuing criminal enterprise where you may have spent the rest of your natural life and died in prison?"

"That's correct, sir."

"I would call that a consideration. Would you?"

"The charges were dropped, yes, sir."

"In fact, you negotiated with them and you traded things with them for your cooperation and your testimony, did you not?"

"It was a contract. A contract is give and take on both parts."

"And you gave them your cooperation and your testimony, and they gave you your freedom? And it was bartered and bargained for between you, your lawyer, and the government, correct?"

"That is correct, sir."

"You ultimately served two years, twenty-one days?"

"That is correct, sir."

Rubino's questioning seemed to be making points with the jury. Smirks spread across the faces of several jurors. Mermelstein was an easy target for Rubino, and he expanded his questioning.

"Now, let me ask you this: Did you also receive immunity so that you would not face any criminal liability for the murder you were involved in?"

Sullivan objected. Until this moment the jury had not heard about murder. Sullivan asked to speak to Judge Hoeveler at sidebar. Mermelstein had not been "involved" in murder, Sullivan told the judge. Rather, he had been involved in solicitation for murder. There was a difference.

Rubino said the government's own discovery material indicated that Mermelstein had been involved in two murders and had knowledge of two others. He had even testified as to his involvement in the Scal murder.

"He went out and hunted the man down like a dog," protested Rubino. "His testimony before the grand jury and other testimony indicate all the things he did in tracking this man down. . . . Just because you don't pull the trigger, because someone else does, that doesn't make it 'uninvolved in a murder.'" Rubino added that Mermelstein had been present in December 1978 when his friend Rafael Cardona had murdered a man.

Hoeveler allowed Rubino to continue his cross-examination.

"There was also another murder that you were present when it occurred here in Miami. Am I correct?" Rubino asked.

"That is correct, sir," Mermelstein replied.

"And have you received immunity for your involvement in that incident?"

"It was covered by my use immunity."

"Okay. Now, you have been involved in smuggling aliens. Have you not, sir?"

"Yes, sir."

And marijuana and cocaine, Rubino added.

"Yes, sir."

"And you have also been involved in converting firearms from semiautomatic to automatic? Basically, what that really means is you made machine guns, correct?"

"Correct."

"You made these to kill people, correct?"

"That was their ultimate intention. Yes, sir."

Rubino continued, "Now, the first contract murder was a contract put out by your *compadre*, Rafael Cardona, correct?"

"Which contract are we talking about now, sir?"

"It does get confusing with all these murders, doesn't it?" Rubino let his comment soak in for the jury.

He then asked about a late December 1978 murder committed by Cardona, who was accompanied by another man.

"Who was that gentleman?"

"Chino Arles."

"Now, you then left your home with Mr. Chino Arles and Rafael Cardona in the van, correct?"

"That's correct."

"And you were driving the van, right?"

"That's correct."

"And Mr. Cardona and Mr. Chino Arles were having an argument. Am I right?"

"Yes, sir."

"And the reason you were driving the van was so that the two of them could settle their differences, correct?"

"No, sir."

"Okay. Why were you driving the van?"

"Cardona had come over and said that they had just come from a party and they were both a little bit on the tipsy side, and he didn't want to have any words about being stopped by the police or anything. So he asked me if I would drive him home."

"Mr. Cardona, then, I assume, was concerned that he did not want to violate the law by driving under the influence of alcohol. Is that correct?"

"No, sir. He just didn't want any involvement with the police unless he absolutely had to."

"And the reason he didn't want any involvement with the police is because as you drove down the road in that van, Mr. Cardona pulled out a gun and in cold blood murdered Mr. Arles while you were driving the van. Is that not true?"

"That is true, sir."

"And then you pulled the van off to the side of the road, wherein the murder weapon was disposed of in a canal. Am I correct?"

"Yes, sir. It was one of the many stops."

"You stopped along the way to dispose of some of the bullets, too. Did you not?"

"Yes, sir."

"All the while, you are driving with a dead body and blood all over the van, correct?

"Correct."

In all, Rubino said, continuing, the government had agreed to drop drug, firearms, and tax-evasion charges and had granted Mermelstein immunity from prosecution in five separate killings.

"To be very candid about it, you're quite proud of the life you lived and the criminal activity you were involved in?" Rubino asked.

"I did it," Mermelstein replied. "I'm not proud of it, but I did it."

Mermelstein conceded that he never paid $2.5 million in back taxes on his illegal drug profits. He said he did pay taxes on the $255,000 in reward money the U.S. government paid him for his help in bringing about $50 million in drug-related seizures.

"It is about time. I am glad to hear that," Rubino said. "It wasn't enough that you only spent two years, twenty-one days in jail for all the things you have described. . . . The government has supported you since the day you got out of jail, haven't they?"

"Yes, sir."

"And they have supported you by putting a roof over your head, correct?"

"Indirectly. Yes, sir. I pay my rent. They pay me."

"And they pay your electric bill, don't they?"

"That's correct."

"And they pay your phone bill, don't they?"

"Yes, sir."

"And they buy all your groceries, don't they?"

"Yes, sir."

"And they pay your dry cleaning?"

"Yes, sir."

"And all the other expenses that one has in life?"

"Also correct."

"And not only do they pay these for you, they pay these for a large number of family members of yours, do they not?"

"Also correct."

Rubino next turned to Mermelstein's assertion that Noriega's name had appeared in a cartel ledger. That ledger was not in the possession of the government, Rubino quizzed Mermelstein. In fact, as far as anyone knew, it might not exist at all.

"There is some other book that you say exists, but it is missing. The one you saw in Colombia, right? The missing book?"

"It is not missing."

"Well, have you got it here in court to show to us today?"

"No, sir."

"And the two that are in court, the ones we can touch and feel, they don't have his name, do they?"

"No, sir."

"You know, when we get right to it, when all is said and done, the truth of the matter is you have never in your entire life met General Noriega, have you?" Rubino asked.

"No, sir," Mermelstein replied.

"And you have never in your entire life seen him commit any crime whatsoever, have you?"

"Correct."

"I have nothing further," said Rubino, and he turned and walked back to the defense table.

Through Mermelstein, Sullivan had succeeded in placing the cartel in Panama handing out bribes for the use of runways and public facilities, and Rubino had failed to counter the assertion. The prosecution's next move was to place Noriega more convincingly close to the cartel's work. Putting the cartel's money in Noriega's hands was a sure way to make that link.

When former PDF Lt. Col. Luis del Cid walked into the courtroom, he stared straight ahead, his gaze fixed on the witness stand. He had to pass within ten feet of Noriega, but del Cid refused to even glance at him, just as the prosecutors had instructed.

Short and squat, del Cid had spent twenty-two months in prison. He wore an open-collared khaki shirt, khaki trousers, and prison-issue blue tennis shoes. Grim-faced, he was about to turn on his former commanding officer of almost thirty years.

Myles Malman had prepared del Cid as a witness and now would lead him through his direct examination. Malman, forty-four, rose from the prosecution's second chair, buttoned his blue suit, and walked to the lectern. Malman's black hair was combed back, and he had a slightly graying mustache. Although some said he could do in twenty questions what any other prosecutor could do in ten, his presentations seldom lagged.

"How old are you, Mr. del Cid?" Malman asked.

Del Cid's response through the court's interpreter was forty-seven years old.

"Thank you. When you were eighteen, did there come a time when you entered the armed forces of Panama, also known as the Guardian National or National Guard?" Malman could see del Cid's nervousness. He moved to lead del Cid as much as possible.

"That's correct."

"Thank you. And what rank was Manuel Noriega then?"

And so Malman's questioning proceeded. In short, clipped bits, slowed only by the translation from English to Spanish and Spanish back to English, del Cid's twenty-nine-year history in the Panamanian military was sketched out, and his relationship to Noriega revealed. Del Cid had shadowed Noriega up through the ranks of the Panamanian military.

By understanding how the Panamanian military had evolved and the extent and manner of the power that Noriega had exercised over the military and eventually Panama, Malman believed, the jury would come to see that the only way the cartel could have operated in Panama was as a result of either Noriega's acquiesence or his consent. Del Cid described himself as Noriega's "errand boy."

What had del Cid done in the military? Malman asked.

"Followed orders," was del Cid's reply. "I was a man of his confidence. I had been working with him for many years."

Noriega had controlled and compartmentalized power and information in Panama. In the end, only he knew all that happened in Panama. As Noriega amassed power he consolidated the functions of the national intelligence, immigration, customs, and passport offices. From the early 1970s on, Noriega made sure that he knew the details of life in Panama.

"Nothing came in through the airports of Panama that General Noriega did not know about," del Cid told Malman and the jury.

Noriega's gradual takeover of what Malman termed "the essential building blocks" of Panamanian society led to a time when Noriega and his cronies, most of whom, like del Cid, Noriega had met early in Chiriquí, were able to secretly allow Panama to become a drug transshipment point.

"Specifically, what charges did you plead guilty to, sir?" Malman asked del Cid.

"To the charges of delivering money to Noriega from Mr. Floyd Carlton," the witness replied.

"When you say delivering money to Noriega from Mr. Floyd Carlton, what type of money?"

"Drug money," del Cid said.

Del Cid said that Noriega had begun receiving drug payoffs from Carlton in late 1982. Noriega, he said, would send him to the airport to meet Carlton, and then he would return with shoe-box-sized packages filled with money.

Later, said del Cid, Noriega sent him to the airport to meet the general's secretary. Once she arrived on a flight into Panama City with eight suitcases. The suitcases were taken to Noriega's office and placed in a safe.

"I imagine it must have been money," del Cid said.

As del Cid spoke, Noriega stared at his former lieutenant and rarely looked away.

The passing of the envelopes from Carlton to Noriega was one of the key acts in the indictment, that Noriega took payoffs.

Did del Cid tell Noriega that he once had met Jorge Ochoa? Malman asked.

Yes, del Cid replied, and Noriega knew who he was. Del Cid explained that Noriega's ties to the cartel became apparent in 1981 when Noriega coordinated the negotiations to release the kidnapped Marta Ochoa, sister of the cartel boss. Ricardo Bilonick, the former Panamanian ambassador-at-large and Noriega business partner, was summoned to moderate the negotiations between the cartel and the Colombian guerrilla group M-19. Del Cid was an observer.

"How frequently, if at all, did you report these negotiations to then Colonel Noriega?"

"Every day."

"And did you discuss this fact, that is, that the Ochoas were part of the Medellín drug distribution cartel with then Colonel Noriega?"

"Correct."

After three days of negotiations, the Ochoas and M-19 came to terms. The Ochoas paid a ransom of $1.2 million, del Cid said.

The success of the negotiations brought the cartel and Noriega closer. A deal allowing the cartel to transship cocaine through Panama followed.

Malman moved on to the raid of the Darien lab in May 1984. Del Cid said he learned that a cartel lab had been raided from Capt. Luis Quiel, the head of Noriega's antinarcotics unit. Quiel said the military had suspected a guerrilla encampment, but when they arrived they found a full-blown cocaine manufacturing lab. Two representatives of the cartel arrived in Panama City following the raid. They were demanding $6 million.

"Why?"

"Because they had paid for protection of the Darien lab, and it had been nabbed." The protection money, Quiel told del Cid, had been paid to one of Noriega's top military aides, Lt. Col. Julian Melo. Quiel, del Cid said, "told me to again try to get ahold of the commander to inform him inasmuch as it was a sensitive matter. A delicate matter," said del Cid.

"Why?"

"Because it involved a high-ranking officer of the armed Defense Forces."

Noriega, who then was on a state visit to Europe, was notified and flew from London to New York, New York to the Bahamas, and from the Bahamas to Havana, del Cid said. In Havana, Quiel met privately with Noriega and Fidel Castro, del Cid said. Noriega viewed a videotape of the laboratory raid brought to Havana by Quiel.

When Noriega returned to Panama, Melo was booted out of the military and "sent home," del Cid said, but he was never prosecuted.

Del Cid, following Malman's lead, said there had been other incidents of concern for Noriega.

Four years before, in June 1980, César Rodríguez, Noriega's sometimes pilot, had crashed a Panama air force plane in El Salvador. The plane had been loaded with weapons for the Salvadorian rebels. Del Cid and Quiel were sent to a hospital in Chiriquí where Rodríguez had been taken with a broken pelvis. Their job was to cover up the link between the Panama air force plane and the arms shipments to El Salvador.

Del Cid and Quiel told Rodríguez and Floyd Carlton, who had saved Rodríguez from capture, that they were to give false information to the Panamanian attorney general's office regarding the crash. They were to distance Noriega from the incident. Noriega, who del Cid described as very "concerned" about the Rodríguez mishap, later ordered Rodríguez and Carlton to quit flying arms to El Salvador.

"Did the attorney general of Panama take, if you know, false statements from Floyd Carlton Caceres and César Rodríguez covering up their involvement in this guns flight to El Salvador?"

"Correct."

"And at whose orders was that cover-up instituted?"

"Colonel Noriega's."

Through del Cid's answers, Malman was setting up the further piecing together of the prosecution jigsaw puzzle. Del Cid's recollections would lay the foundation for the eventual development of the Noriega–Floyd Carlton–César Rodríguez drug-trafficking axis.

The cover-up continued in March 1986, a month after the Miami indictment was delivered, del Cid said. Then he received orders from Noriega to report to the attorney general of Panama to give a statement about his involvement in the incidents named in the indictment.

Del Cid went, and in his statement he said that he had never received monies from Floyd Carlton. That was not the truth.

Who ordered you to lie? Malman asked del Cid.

"The general," del Cid answered.

Malman's direct examination of del Cid took two and a half days. Now the prosecution had placed cartel drug money in Noriega's hands, had linked him to the $6 million cartel bribe, and asserted that he had ordered del Cid and others to perjure themselves.

In the course of the examination, Malman introduced into evidence a photograph taken in Havana showing Noriega, Fidel Castro, and del Cid at the time of the 1984 meeting. Although the photograph had been offered as a means of identifying Castro, clearly the prosecutors had calculated its effect on the jury. Here was Noriega in the company of the Central American dictator whom Americans most loved to hate.

Before Rubino could begin his cross-examination, Malman had just two more questions. Malman was surprised by del Cid's rigid responses. In preparation, del Cid had been loose and even witty. Now, clearly, del Cid was terrified by Noriega's presence. Malman wanted to employ del Cid's fear.

"Mr. del Cid, do you see the person that you have referred to as Manuel Antonio Noriega in this courtroom today?"

"Correct."

"Would you please point him out."

Del Cid began to raise his arm, and for the first time since he had become a witness against his commander, dared to look toward Noriega. Before del Cid's arm was fully extended, Noriega snapped from his chair to attention. Reflexively del Cid, too, bolted to attention. As the two military men stared at each other, the courtroom fell into silence.

Malman gathered his notes. "Thank you," he told del Cid.

Del Cid's testimony had shown him to be exactly as he had described himself: an errand boy. His all-but-cursory knowledge of Noriega's dealings with the cartel raised questions about why he had pled guilty to racketeering conspiracy. The answer, his attorney Samuel Burstyn said, was that cooperating was easier than fighting the government. Del Cid would have been convicted, Burstyn said. At least this way he would be out of jail sooner.

On the courthouse steps the day before del Cid was to return to court for Rubino's cross-examination, Burstyn told reporters he had heard that Rubino had visited Cuba twice during the past summer and that talks were under way to take the videotaped testimony of Castro, who would be asked about the 1984 meeting in Havana that included Noriega and del Cid. Castro would testify, Burstyn said, that the meeting had nothing to do with the cartel. Castro would say that Noriega had been on a state visit and that such visits were not unusual. In fact, Noriega had served as a go-between with the United States in advance of the 1983 invasion of Grenada.

Noriega was furious. Del Cid had lied, he told Rubino. His recollections on almost every key point had not been correct. The $6 million bribe had been solicited by and paid to Julian Melo, Noriega insisted. There was no mystery about who had ordered the raid on the Darien lab. He had done it himself and immediately notified the U.S. Drug Enforcement Administration.

When Rubino met del Cid for the cross-examination on Tuesday, September 24, he began circling him with his own rope. He started by asking del Cid about his testimony that he had lied to the attorney general of Panama regarding his knowledge of the incidents contained in the 1988 Miami indictment.

"It was your testimony yesterday that when you were asked questions under oath in Panama, you lied?"

"Correct," del Cid responded.

Rubino turned to the oath del Cid had taken now in the Noriega case.

"You realize today you are still under that oath?"

"Correct."

"Yesterday when you were under oath, did you lie?"

"No."

Rubino showed Noriega's passport to del Cid and asked him to look closely at the Customs stamps that pegged Noriega's travels.

"You testified yesterday that General Noriega was in Paris when the lab was raided?"

"Correct."

But Noriega's passport clearly indicated that Noriega had not gone to Paris or anywhere outside of Panama until about a month after the raid on the Darien lab. Del Cid at first looked perplexed, then he seemed embarrassed.

"General Noriega, in fact, gave the order to raid the Darien lab, did he not?" Rubino asked.

Del Cid paused and looked toward the prosecutor's table. All Malman and Sullivan could do was stare back at del Cid.

"Correct," del Cid finally answered.

Rubino pushed del Cid: "When you testified yesterday that Captain Quiel came to you and you were looking to find General Noriega to tell him about the lab, and that you finally reached him in Europe, in Paris, that was a mistake?"

"I made a mistake."

"You have no doubt in your mind that the Darien lab raid occurred on or about May 23, 1984, do you?"

"Correct. I believe I made a mistake."

Pressed further, del Cid said that he had contacted Noriega in Europe, not when he had learned about the Darien raid but when the cartel's agents came looking for Julian Melo and the cartel's $6 million in protection money.

"So you in fact reached him to tell him about the Melo scandal?"

"Correct. I handed the telephone over to Captain Quiel."

"And Captain Quiel didn't tell him about the raid on the lab because he already knew about it for a month, correct?"

That was right, del Cid conceded. He looked from Rubino toward the jury.

The telephone call had been to inform Noriega that the cartel's representatives had come to Panama seeking Melo, who was publicly accused of taking payoffs from the cartel. Del Cid said that when Noriega learned of the allegations against Melo, he ordered him placed under arrest.

And so, Rubino pressed del Cid further, why had Noriega made the emergency trip to Cuba to see Castro which del Cid had testified about?

The visit, del Cid responded, had been planned for months. It had been on Noriega's itinerary all along. Cuba was not a diversion after the raid but a planned leg of the trip that had also included Israel, France, and the United States.

Rubino then turned to del Cid's testimony about having picked up drug money for delivery to Noriega. He asked del Cid if Noriega had ever said, "Go meet Floyd and get some drug money from him for me."

"Did he order you— Did he use the words 'drug money'?" Rubino asked del Cid.

"No," del Cid answered. "I used them because Floyd was into drugs."

"Did Floyd, when he gave you the envelope, tell you it was drug money?"

"He didn't tell me, but I knew it was drug money because Floyd was into drugs. That's what he was into."

Neither Noriega nor del Cid had ever said a thing about drug money, correct? Rubino pressed del Cid.

"Everyone in Panama knew that these people were into drugs," responded del Cid.

"So your basis of knowledge is hearsay, rumor, and gossip, correct?"

"Well, that is no gossip," said del Cid defiantly.

In fact, del Cid had never looked inside the envelopes, just as he had never looked inside the suitcases that Noriega's secretary had brought from the airport.

Did you know what was in the envelopes? Rubino asked del Cid.

"He didn't tell me, but it was drug money," del Cid responded. "I felt it, and I knew."

"You possess X-ray vision?" Rubino asked rhetorically.

"They didn't tell me, but when I picked it up, the envelope, I felt it and I knew it was money," del Cid said.

"You assumed it was money," Rubino countered. "And you assumed that the source of the money was drugs."

Under Rubino's questioning, del Cid conceded that he hoped his testimony would lead to a reduced sentence for the one count he had pled guilty to. It was for the jury to decide whether his distortions and backtracking under cross-examination had damaged the government's direct. It seemed they had. But Rubino did not make all of the inroads on cross-examination that he had hoped for.

Malman and Sullivan successfully blocked Rubino's attempts to broaden the scope of questioning. He tried to expand on del Cid's testimony that Noriega had visited Israel. Rubino wanted to explore Panama's involvement with Israel and Israel's involvement in the U.S. arms pipeline to the Nicaraguan Contras. The judge, at sidebar, warned Rubino off. It's "irrelevant," the judge said.

Judge Hoeveler also blocked Rubino from introducing a photograph taken at a December 1983 Panama City meeting. The photograph showed Noriega and George Bush, then the vice president, sitting at opposite ends of a sofa.

"You are getting into a prejudicial area," the judge told Rubino at sidebar. "I am going to keep the politics and certainly current politics out of this."

The next day, Wednesday, September 25, Assistant U.S. Attorney Guy Lewis, the third chair on the government's prosecution team, called to the witness stand Panamanian businessman Eric Guerra. On direct examination, Guerra said that he had once laundered as much as $20 million a week in drug profits for the Medellín cartel.

Guerra said that military officers commanded by Noriega routinely protected cash shipments that came into Panama City from south Florida aboard commercial flights. Guerra said he often drove his car onto the runway at Panama City's main airport to pick up the money. Sometimes, when he transported the cash to banks, he would receive armored car escort protection from the G-2.

"During this time period that you were working receiving money, did you ever have any problems from the Customs people out there at the airport?" Lewis asked Guerra.

"Never," the witness responded.

"Did you ever have any problems with the immigration people out at the airport?"

"Never."

"How about any of the people involved with narcotics [enforcement]?"

"Not that, either."

Guerra said that his money-exchange business handled $500,000 to

$800,000 each day for the cartel and that once a week he would receive $10 million to $15 million shipments, usually from Fort Lauderdale.

"The cash from Colombia and Miami would come in suitcases, all tied with rubber bands," he said. "If it was $20 bills, each bundle would be $20,000. If hundreds, it would be $100,000."

Guerra said that on several occasions the money arrived in a private jet, the jet that Noriega used as his personal plane.

And on three to five occasions in 1982 and 1983, Guerra said, he was told to deliver between $300,000 and $400,000 to Floyd Carlton, and Carlton told him the money would then be delivered to "a big chief."

Rubino's cross-examination was not long. Guerra first conceded that money exchanging or, in his work for the cartel, money laundering was not a crime in Panama during the early 1980s. As for the military escorts that made sure he got to a bank safely, they were provided to other businessmen as well.

The "chief" of the Panamanian military during the period Guerra had testified about, 1982 and 1983, was not Noriega, he also explained, but Rubén Dario Paredes, Sr.

CHAPTER 24
★★★★★★

The Cartel's Drug Runner

It was just two months short of seven years since DEA agent Danny Moritz had first heard of Floyd Carlton. The confidential informant who had told Moritz about Carlton in November 1984 had described him as a "major Panamanian." The description, when applied to the world of illegal drugs, had been right on target. Carlton conceded a close relationship with the top leaders of the Medellín cartel. He had been one of the cartel's top smugglers for five years, beginning in the early 1980s. Carlton could put the cartel's cocaine in south Florida.

Certainly, without Carlton, the government never would have brought its Miami indictment against Noriega.

Now, on Thursday, September 26, for the first time, Carlton—who had been debriefed nearly a half-dozen times and along the way had testified before a grand jury and a Senate subcommittee—would tell his story from a witness stand.

Carlton's appearance as the government's star witness would be, as Judge Hoeveler described it, "where the rubber hits the road."

Shortly after the jury was brought into the courtroom for the morning, Hoeveler asked the government to call its next witness. Pat Sullivan knew how important Carlton was to the prosecution. He rose and said, "The government calls Floyd Carlton."

Carlton was led into the courtroom by four deputy U.S. marshals, a marshal on each side, one in the front, and one in the back. He entered from the far right side of the courtroom and crossed in front of the defense table and before Judge Hoeveler on his way to the witness stand.

If one were to imagine what the world's largest cocaine cartel's top transportation captain looked like, one would never imagine Floyd Carlton. Less than six feet tall, Carlton was light complexioned and sported a stylish Ivy League haircut. He wore a blue blazer, white shirt, rep tie, and khaki trousers. He was forty-two but could easily have passed for a university graduate student.

As he sat down, Carlton looked back across the courtroom and nodded to Noriega.

With Carlton's testimony, Sullivan intended to lay out almost every facet of the broad historical conspiracy as outlined in the indictment. Essentially, the RICO charge—the establishment of an enterprise for the purpose of manufacturing and smuggling cocaine and the actual acts of smuggling— could be proven through Carlton's relationship with the cartel and Noriega.

The chronology of historical events as outlined in the indictment could be organized into four episodes: first, Carlton's cocaine flights between November 1982 and January 1984, flights for Pablo Escobar and the cartel sanctioned by Noriega; second, the cartel operations in Panama between March 1982 and July 1984, including a period when the cartel's leaders took refuge in Panama from Colombian authorities and operated a cocaine lab in Panama's Darien province; third, the Inair cargo affair between May 1984 and June 1984 when cartel leader Jorge Ochoa worked through Panamanian Ricardo Bilonick and Noriega to smuggle cocaine to Miami; and fourth, the *Krill* affair in February and March 1986. Of the four episodes, Carlton could offer direct testimony on the first two.

Sullivan's job was to lead Carlton through the two episodes, allowing him to offer his personal recollections of the cartel's operations and the cartel's interaction with Noriega. Later, other witnesses would corroborate Carlton's story and round it out.

Sullivan began by asking Carlton to relate for the jury his arrest in Costa Rica and his extradition to the United States. Then Carlton continued by explaining that after his agreement to cooperate with federal prosecutors, he, along with his wife and three children, had been placed in the federal Witness Protection Program. Since then he had not lived under his own name.

Sullivan asked Carlton to jump back to his early years in Panama's Chiriquí province. There, around 1966 or 1967, Carlton had first met Noriega, when Noriega was a lieutenant in the Panamanian National Guard and Carlton was a clerk in a government office. Even though Noriega was more than ten years Carlton's senior, the two became friends.

By the late 1970s, Carlton had moved to Panama City and, using his commercial pilot's license, went to work for Ricardo Bilonick. In 1977, Carlton decided to set up his own business and with an old friend from Chiriquí, César Rodríguez, began selling airplane parts at the Paitilla airport. Soon the two began operating an airplane charter service.

Carlton's first encounter with smugglers had come in mid-1977 when some Colombians came to his office and asked him to transport cocaine paste from Chile to Colombia. The flight never occurred, but in time the Colombians came back looking for Carlton's services.

In 1979, Carlton and Rodríguez went to work for the Panamanian government, clandestinely flying weapons from Panama to leftist guerrillas in El Salvador. The flights, which numbered about seventeen, were sanctioned by Panama's top general, Omar Torrijos. They required absolute discretion, Carlton explained, because Torrijos and his aide, Colonel Noriega, wanted to avoid an international controversy.

The officially sanctioned arms flights gave Carlton and Rodríguez free access to Panama's airports. Customs, Immigration, and military security had been instructed to look the other way. That, said Carlton, led to his first encounter with the Medellín cartel.

In September 1982, Carlton testified, he was invited to Medellín where he met Pablo Escobar and Gustavo Gaviria. The two cartel leaders asked him to fly cocaine.

"These people had noticed a certain ease with which we moved about," Carlton testified. "The first thing they did is they asked me about General Noriega. They asked me how the then Colonel Noriega was doing. I told them that he should be all right. Why were they asking me about him?"

Then they asked Carlton why he thought he had been invited to Medellín. Carlton said that the cartel's representative had told him he was going to be asked to transport money from different cities in the United States to Panama.

Sullivan asked, "What was the response to that?"

"I remember that Mr. Gaviria jumped up and he said, 'No, it has nothing to do with money. It is cocaine. Transporting cocaine from here to the city of Panama,' and I said, 'I have nothing to do with that. That is not my business. I am not into that.'"

To that Pablo Escobar said, "You go and talk to Colonel Noriega. Go and talk to Colonel Noriega."

Carlton replied, "Why do you think that Colonel Noriega has something to do with this?"

And to that Escobar retorted, "Isn't he your godfather?"

"No, sir," Carlton told Escobar.

Escobar explained that a vessel transporting cocaine for the cartel had been seized in Panama, and the cartel had paid a ransom of $800,000 for the boat. The money, Escobar told Carlton, had been paid to Noriega.

Carlton told Escobar that he would go back to Panama and talk over the cartel's proposal.

"I told them that I was going to talk it over, that there were certain people whom I had to ask."

"Did you use Noriega's name?" Sullivan asked.

"No," replied Carlton.

"Why didn't you?"

"I had no authorization from him. I had not discussed drugs with him. I had no authority to use the gentleman's name down there in that business." Carlton said he had never spoken to Noriega about drug trafficking.

But two or three weeks later, Carlton saw Noriega, and he told him about his visit to Medellín. When Carlton told Noriega that the cartel had proposed that he smuggle drugs, Noriega became angry. "He told me that I should be grateful because on the grounds of the friendship that existed, he would not send me to jail." Carlton said he asked Noriega to forgive him and to forget he ever brought the scheme to his attention.

But a couple of weeks later, on a visit to Noriega's beach house, Noriega pulled Carlton aside.

"We went over to a bedroom. He asked me what had happened about that business that I had brought up to him, and I was surprised. I told him that, no, I had forgotten about that; that I hadn't touched that subject again, and he told me to go ahead and talk to these people again, and to find out how this business was to be."

"Did either you or him—that is, Colonel Noriega—ever use the word 'cocaine' in that discussion?" Sullivan asked.

"I don't believe so," said Carlton.

"Did you mention or did he mention who these people were who were proposing this deal?"

"I never mentioned it to him, and he never asked me."

In mid-October 1982, Carlton said, he had another discussion with the cartel's leaders. Then he asked them how much his partner, "whichever they wanted to call him," would be paid.

"What person were you referring to?" Sullivan asked.

Carlton looked across the courtroom to Noriega and pointed. "To that gentleman there," he replied.

"Had Colonel Noriega asked you to do that?"

"Yes."

"What was Escobar's and Gaviria's response?"

"That it was going to be in the neighborhood of thirty, fifty thousand dollars, something like that."

"For making the flight or for what?"

"No—just for being my partner, for having authorized the flights to take place," replied Carlton.

Carlton then told Noriega how much he would receive for each smuggling flight that was unhindered by the Panamanian authorities. Noriega scoffed. The cartel must be crazy. Noriega said he would not allow cocaine flights through Panama for less than $100,000 for each flight.

Carlton then went back to Escobar and Gaviria and related Noriega's response. He never used Noriega's name, however.

To that Escobar and Gaviria laughed. "This guy is always going very high," Escobar told Carlton.

"Did they use his name?" Sullivan asked.

"Yes, sir," replied Carlton.

"Did you use Noriega's name?"

"No, sir," said Carlton.

"Why didn't you just use Noriega's name?"

"Because he told me that he did not wish to have his name involved in that type of problem and that if something happened, he did not know anything from nothing. That he had nothing to do with it. He did not wish to know the name of these persons, and he did not wish his name to be mentioned, either." Sullivan was convinced Carlton was telling the truth because Carlton, if he had concocted his story, easily could have said Noriega's name was used. Sullivan hoped the jury agreed.

Shortly after, on November 27, 1982, Carlton was called upon to make a flight for the cartel. In Medellín, a cartel ground crew loaded Carlton's plane with green duffel bags. Carlton took off, flew to Panama, and delivered the load. Only later did he learn that the bags had been filled with sand and stones.

Carlton returned to Medellín and met with Escobar. Escobar explained that the cartel had had bad experiences in Panama and on occasion had been double-crossed. Escobar asked Carlton if there would be a problem making a second flight. Carlton said he didn't think so, but first he wanted to contact "that person" in Panama.

"So what did you do?" Sullivan asked Carlton.

"I again called the colonel, and I informed him of these people's wish to again make a new flight. And he advised me that on this opportunity it wouldn't be one hundred thousand but one hundred and fifty thousand."

"Who said that?"

"Colonel Noriega."

Carlton then called Escobar in Medellín. When he explained that the second flight would cost $150,000 in protection money, Escobar responded, "Well, here we go again. There [are] always problems with Panama."

But Escobar agreed to the price.

Carlton oversaw another flight in December 1982 and a third in May 1983. Each time the price for protection was $150,000. Each time, Carlton said, he contacted Noriega's aide, Luis del Cid, and cash was passed to Noriega in advance.

Carlton's fourth and final flight for the cartel came in December 1983. Then, Carlton said, he went to Noriega, and the colonel asked how much Carlton was charging.

"I told him around $150,000, and he told me that I was giving away my work."

Noriega told Carlton, "These people think we are nothing but a tribe of Indians. One more flight," Noriega said. "Take advantage of the opportunity. Make money. Do you know how much they are selling a kilo for in Miami or the United States?"

Carlton said he didn't.

"You are a fool," Noriega told Carlton. A kilo of cocaine would sell for between $25,000 and $30,000 in the United States, Noriega told Carlton.

Because Noriega was now the commander of the Panamanian Defense Forces, working with the Colombian "mafia" would be bad for his image if a link was ever made, he told Carlton. The charge for the final flight, he said, would be $200,000 paid in advance.

Carlton's testimony had stretched over a day and a half. Throughout, the jury had paid close attention to the boyish-looking smuggler. His answers to each of Sullivan's questions had been measured and direct. Sullivan feared Carlton might have come across a bit meek and timid, but Carlton, unlike del Cid, had been unafraid of looking across the courtroom toward Noriega.

At the defense table, Noriega had sat impassively listening to Carlton, sometimes jotting notes on a yellow legal pad.

Sullivan was now ready to move to the cartel's operations in Panama between March 1982 and July 1984. Again, Carlton had direct knowledge of what had happened.

Carlton said that after the final cocaine flight in January 1984, he retired to a farm in Chiriquí. But shortly after, he received a phone call from Ricardo Bilonick, who said that Carlton's "father" was in Panama and wanted to see him. The "father" Bilonick was referring to, Carlton testified, was Pablo Escobar.

Carlton left Chiriquí and went to Panama City. There he found that the cartel had set up offices catercorner from the Nicaraguan embassy. When he went into the office, he found the *crème de la crème* of the Medellín cartel, Escobar, Gustavo Gaviria, and Jorge Ochoa, as well as members of the Cali cartel. All had fled Colombia following the assassination of the Colombian justice minister, Rodrigo Lara Bonilla.

Carlton asked Escobar why the cartel had come to Panama, given their harsh feelings toward Noriega and his steep protection charges. Escobar told Carlton not to be concerned, that everything was under control, that $4 million had been paid for the protection of the cartel.

"Did he say to whom $4 million had been paid?" Sullivan asked.

"Yes," replied Carlton. "To General Noriega."

Carlton said that in late May 1984 he helped Escobar move to Nicaragua where he would continue to hide out from Colombian authorities. Later, Carlton said, he learned that the cartel had begun using Ricardo Bilonick's Inair cargo company to transport cocaine to the United States. And even later he was invited by César Rodríguez to join in a cartel smuggling venture using the yacht *Krill*. But Carlton said he was then running his own smuggling operation using landing strips in Mexico and was not interested in becoming involved with the *Krill*.

In little more than two days, Carlton had directly established Noriega's relationship to the cartel, specifically through the four flights and the cartel's $4 million bribe to set up offices in Panama. He had also set the stage for more expansive testimony on the cartel's use of Inair and the *Krill* venture. Noriega had been the cornerstone of the cartel's Panama operations.

On Monday afternoon, September 30, Frank Rubino was given his opportunity to cross-examine Carlton.

As Rubino walked to the lectern, he looked toward the jury and smiled. Carlton's testimony had damaged his client, but the smuggler's story was not without holes, Rubino figured. He could retrace Sullivan's questioning and show the seeming gaps in Carlton's story. And he might be able to move past Carlton's direct testimony to show the fuller context of what had happened in Panama and Colombia in the early 1980s.

Rubino began by asking Carlton to think back once more about the four drug flights, the ones Noriega had allegedly been bribed to protect. Rubino asked Carlton to recollect again his first conversation with Noriega about the cartel's proposal to sponsor drug flights through Panama. Carlton testified that he had initially spoken to Noriega about working for the cartel as the two flew together from the Panama coast to Panama City. Carlton was piloting, and Noriega sat in the passenger seat.

"Was there anyone else on the plane besides you and General Noriega?" Rubino asked.

"Just he and I," Carlton replied.

"You had this conversation with him wherein you advised him of the possibility of drug flights, correct?"

"Yes."

"And there are absolutely no witnesses in this entire world, save you and General Noriega, to this conversation, correct?"

"Indeed, sir," said Carlton.

Carlton testified that Noriega had rebuffed him but later decided to go forward, to offer the cartel protection.

Again Noriega and Carlton had met alone.

"Your testimony is he takes you into a bedroom and talks to you there, right?"

"Indeed, sir."

"So, again, just like the airplane, there are absolutely no witnesses in this entire world to this alleged conversation, other than you and General Noriega?

"Indeed, sir."

Rubino then moved backward, to the meeting where Escobar and Gaviria had asked Carlton to approach Noriega.

"Is there anyone else present in the room besides yourself, Gaviria, and Escobar?"

"I don't think so, sir," replied Carlton.

"And at this time is when the discussion starts to begin about General Noriega?"

"Sir, I never brought up General Noriega's name with them. I never admitted to General Noriega's name with them."

"So again, or in this particular case, the only witnesses in the whole world to this conversation would be yourself, Mr. Escobar, and Mr. Gaviria?"

"Indeed, sir."

Gaviria was dead, Carlton acknowledged under Rubino's questioning. He had been killed by Colombian police in the month before the U.S. invasion of Panama. And Escobar was a prisoner under an agreement with the Colombian government that was worked out early in 1991.

Rubino turned next to the actual flights and Noriega's protection. Did Carlton tell Noriega when the drug flights would occur? Rubino asked.

"Do you tell him the date you intended to bring the cocaine into the country of Panama?"

"No, sir. I did not know it."

"And obviously you couldn't tell him the time of day, either, because you didn't know that, either?"

"Indeed, sir."

Rubino asked Carlton to explain how Noriega had acted to protect the flights. Carlton conceded that he had not told Noriega which planes would be used or when the flights would occur or what airports the planes would be flown into.

"You never told General Noriega when you were coming with the airplane full of what you believed would be dope, correct?"

"No, sir."

"And you never told him, obviously, what time of day, let alone what day?"

"Never, sir."

"And you never told him what airstrip you were coming to?"

"No, sir."

"And you never gave him any description of what type of aircraft—make, model, color, et cetera—you were flying, did you?"

"No, sir."

"How did General Noriega *allow* that flight to come in?"

Pat Sullivan stood and objected. The question called for Carlton to speculate about Noriega's actions.

Wisps of smiles came across the faces of several jurors.

There had been no overt protection, Carlton acknowledged, as Rubino pressed the questioning. No soldiers had met the planes. No Customs officials had faked inspections. The Defense Forces had not protected the runways, and the airport control towers had not given the flights special directions.

"To the best of your knowledge, what, if anything, did General Noriega do to aid, abet, assist, help in any way, shape, or form—help you get that load of drugs, or what you believed were drugs, into the country of Panama? . . . He did absolutely nothing, correct, to the best of your knowledge?"

"No, sir."

"In fact, to the best of your knowledge, he didn't have the faintest idea that you were coming, correct?"

"Indeed, sir."

"Your statement, then, is that he allowed you to make that flight, right?"

"Yes."

"How did he allow you to do it?"

"When I informed him about the intentions regarding the first flight, that I told him of that amount of $50,000 and he told me that he would not allow it for less than $100,000, I was morally authorized to make it."

Rubino looked at Carlton incredulously. "Morally, correct?" he asked.

"Unfortunately, sir, but that's the way it was."

Well, said Rubino, stepping toward Carlton, "isn't it true that you just stole an extra $100,000 from the cartel, put it in your pocket, and never gave anything to General Noriega because he didn't know about this?"

Carlton looked toward the jury and then back at Rubino. "No, sir," he said.

Rubino's voice rose. "You weren't just trading on his name as a high-level person?"

"I was afraid of those people. I wasn't about to— I was never capable of doing such a thing, sir."

"You are not capable of doing what sort of thing?" asked Rubino, picking up the attack.

"Stealing a thin dime from anyone, sir."

Rubino looked at the jury, then back at Carlton. "You will smuggle thousands of kilos of cocaine, but you won't steal a dime, right?" he said sarcastically.

Pat Sullivan stood and objected. "Argumentative," he said, appealing to the judge.

"Argumentative. Sustained," Hoeveler said.

Rubino reined himself in. "Is there a particular point in crime where you draw the line, certain things you will do and certain things you won't do?" Rubino pushed again.

"I object again, Your Honor," said Sullivan standing again.

"It is argumentative, counsel," Hoeveler said, looking at Rubino.

But the point did not seem lost on the jury. Several jurors looked toward Sullivan and the prosecution table.

Rubino circled and asked Carlton about how he had informed Noriega of the second of the four flights. Carlton testified that he and Noriega had spoken at Noriega's beach house during a party attended by two hundred people.

"Did you tell him about that at this party?"

"Indeed, sir."

"And is this done publicly, in front of others? Are there any witnesses, or is this another private conversation between you and him alone?"

Carlton was finding himself on the defensive. "Mr. Rubino, this was a cocaine deal. We weren't talking about cookies here, so we— I couldn't tell him about these things in front of everybody, the people there. From the very beginning, Mr. Rubino, I told you that he allowed me. We never did anything in Panama without him allowing it."

"So he allowed an event to occur that he didn't know was going to occur?"

Carlton hesitated. "He knew that something was going to happen sooner or later. He just didn't know when or where."

Rubino next turned to Carlton's plea agreement with the government. The agreement exempted Carlton from having to forfeit the property he had acquired in Panama using his drug-trafficking proceeds. It also paid him $211,000 in living expenses in the four years since he had been brought to the United States in 1987. The U.S. government had placed not only Carlton and his family in the Witness Protection Program but his baby-sitter as well.

"Yes," Carlton conceded.

Rubino looked at the four middle-aged women sitting in the first row of the jury box. "Good baby-sitters are hard to find, huh?" he said, turning back to Carlton.

"Yes, sir," Carlton replied.

The next day, Tuesday, October 1, Rubino resumed his cross-examination, turning to Carlton's testimony about running guns to Central American guerrilla groups. Carlton admitted that his pilots had flown arms to the Nicaraguan Contras between 1983 and 1984, and they were also flying cocaine to the United States for the Medellín cartel.

Rubino hoped the cross-examination would lay the groundwork for a defense that would show the U.S. government, in backing the Contras, had ties to drug traffickers, ties not unlike Noriega's.

Rubino began with Carlton's early flights to the leftist Salvadoran guerrillas.

"These weapons were being sent there to an opposition force of the government, correct?"

"Yes, sir."

"Now, this incident up until now is something that was not for public knowledge, something done in a very secretive and clandestine way, correct?"

"Yes, sir."

"Now, did you know that Lieutenant Colonel Noriega was notifying the United States of everything that was going on?"

Before Carlton could answer, Sullivan stood and objected. "It is obviously an argumentative question," he said.

Rubino backed off but reminded Carlton that he had testified on direct examination that the weapons destined for the Salvadoran guerrillas had come from Israel and Taiwan. "Now, this was an extremely, shall we say, 'touchy matter,' something that had to be handled very carefully and surreptitiously, correct?"

"Indeed, sir."

"Now, do you know, . . . during this period—when Taiwan and Israel are supplying weapons to the Salvadoran guerrillas—whether the United States was providing weapons to the Salvadoran government?"

"Objection," said Sullivan, standing.

Sullivan feared that Rubino was closing in on what the defense in pretrial pleadings had called the "arms for drugs pipeline." The theory was that cocaine was traded for weapons and that many insurgent groups in Central America were doing it, even the U.S.-backed Contras. Through Carlton and other prosecution witnesses, Rubino hoped to show that if Noriega was involved in gun and drug running, it was something that the United States likely knew about. The strategy was to move the case beyond drug trafficking to show the broader political context of Noriega's actions.

"Irrelevant," said Hoeveler, sustaining Sullivan's objection. "We really need not go into that area any further."

"Can we approach?" asked Rubino, calling for a sidebar.

"No, not on that point," Hoeveler replied.

Jon May stood next to Rubino. "Your Honor, can we approach the bench? We would like to make an argument as to this issue."

Hoeveler relented and called the attorneys forward. The judge stepped off to the side of the bench, out of earshot of the jury.

May explained that the weapons Panama was supplying to the Salvadoran guerrillas had originated in Israel, a U.S. ally. While Israel was supplying arms to the guerrillas, the United States was supplying the Salvadoran government. Torrijos and the Panamanian government wanted Carlton and Rodríguez to lie about their gun running so as to "keep a lid" on a potential embarrassing situation for Israel, the United States, and Panama.

Sullivan interrupted. The prosecution's direct examination was not intended to demonstrate the political cover-up but that Noriega could trust Carlton enough to ask him to lie to Panama's attorney general, he explained. Sullivan said the defense was trying to twist the evidence, and that was not right. "Evidence can be admissible for one purpose even though inadmissible for any number of other purposes," he told the judge.

Hoeveler said he agreed. When it came to the relevancy of the direct examination, "we have to look to his stated objective for that direct examination, and that was to show the relationship between Noriega and this witness and Rodríguez at the same time, not to get into the politics of the situation."

Rubino was about to continue May's argument when the judge interrupted: "Let me make my position clear right now. We are not going to turn this case into a political case. I have said that so many times, and I mean it."

"We have to start opening up the pipeline theory with this witness," Rubino said.

"When we get to the pipeline theory, I will rule on those aspects of it," Hoeveler responded, and dismissed the sidebar.

Rubino continued the questioning: "Now, General Noriega would instruct you to make arms flights to specific people, did he not?"

"Yes, sir," replied Carlton.

"Did you ever fly weapons at General Noriega's instructions for Colonel Oliver North?" Rubino moved to press the pipeline connection from another angle.

But Sullivan stood instantly. "Objection, Your Honor." It was likely outside of Carlton's direct knowledge whether Noriega was working with North.

"Sustained," Judge Hoeveler said.

Rubino was rushing the connection, leaping ahead. If he persisted, Sullivan would continue to object and Hoeveler would continue to sustain the objections. Rubino backed up and set out to move Carlton toward the connection more methodically.

Carlton testified that some of the flights that he and his pilots had made were for Noriega on behalf of the Contras. He conceded that some of the flights had been organized by Alfredo Cabellero, the Miami owner of DIACSA, the Cessna airplane dealership that DEA agent Danny Moritz had first focused on as the Noriega drug connection.

"Now, both guns and drugs were flown in and out of the United States by DIACSA, were they not?"

"Objection," said Sullivan.

"Sustained," said Hoeveler.

Rubino tried again: "Did you personally see any drugs at the office of DIACSA?"

"Objection."

"Sustained."

Rubino winced with frustration. "I should have the right to show—"

"Don't tell me what you have a right to show in front of the jury," warned Hoeveler, and he called the attorneys to sidebar.

At sidebar, Rubino explained where he was going: "I was narrowing it down to his drug dealings with DIACSA. Then I go to pilots under his control. Guns would be flown out of DIACSA or Nicaragua or Costa Rica, and they, in turn, would fly drugs back to the United States. Some of these flights, in fact, went through Panama. Then we'll get into the fact that DIACSA was a company funded by the United States government. We can carry it even further: Caballero and people in DIACSA were under the direct control of the Central Intelligence Agency, and the story will keep evolving."

On direct examination Carlton had said that after Rodríguez's crash in El Salvador, he never flew arms again. But, added Jon May, he did not say that the pilots he had trained and controlled had never flown arms again. They had, said May, and they flew drugs as well. That was the pipeline. "The same mechanism he used for flying arms was used for drug flights," May told Hoeveler.

The defense, Sullivan objected, was twisting the purpose of the direct examination to its own ends.

But, Rubino said, the jury was thinking that the last time Carlton flew arms was in El Salvador, and "that's not true." Connecting Carlton to the arms and drugs flights out of DIACSA would open the defense's theory of how the Contra arms pipeline was abused to move drugs as well, said Rubino. "The government is trying to show that the general allowed a haven for drug dealings in and out, and I can show, 'No, this was not true, but rather, it was to assist the United States government to assist the Contras.'"

Noriega knew about Carlton's arms flights, said Rubino, but he didn't know the other half of the story, Carlton's drug flights. That was a venture that Carlton had undertaken on his own and never told Noriega about.

"You can go show that he's not as nice a guy as he said he was," Hoeveler told Rubino. "But when you start connecting it up to the U.S. government and the CIA, you're on a venture of your own."

"In some respects I have to concede you are correct," said Rubino, "but the venture is the proof the general didn't do what he's charged in the indictment with."

"I don't know that yet," responded Hoeveler. "I'm going to have to be very circumspect about this phase of the case because it seems to me you're going

well beyond the direct. If he flew drugs back in connection with armed shipments—ask him."

"Say, first I establish DIACSA as doing guns and drugs," said Rubino.
"Once I establish that, I'd like to ask him about his knowledge of the U.S.
government funding DIACSA. May I ask him that?"

"No," said Hoeveler, concluding the sidebar.

Rubino resumed his cross-examination by asking Carlton about drug
flights. Carlton said that drug flights had been made in connection with
DIACSA. Then Rubino asked if arms had been flown in connection with
DIACSA. To that, Sullivan again objected.

"Just stay away from it," Hoeveler warned Rubino.

"Okay," said Rubino and then continued: "Now, was one of the people
involved in these drug flights a gentleman named Mario Calero?"

Rubino was not going to stay away from it. Calero had been a leader of the
Nicaraguan Contras.

"Objection. Irrelevant," said Sullivan.

Again Rubino asked for a sidebar. "We are not just blindly asking questions, hoping to get a good answer. I thought I could ask about the arms as
long as I didn't touch the CIA."

"The difficulty I am having is connecting your cross with the direct," said
Hoeveler.

Calero, said Rubino, could be an unindicted coconspirator.

"He happens to be one of the heads of the Contras," said Sullivan. "That's
where they are going."

"The plot thickens," said Hoeveler.

"Yes," said Sullivan.

Hoeveler said it was one thing to show that Carlton was no angel but
another to begin building collateral conspiracies, conspiracies that had nothing to do with the case at hand.

Rubino moved on to the May 1983 drug proceeds flight of Eduardo Pardo
and Daniel Miranda. The two had been hired by Carlton to transport drug
cash from the United States to Panama where it could be laundered through
cartel bank accounts. Again, Carlton confirmed, Noriega had not known
about the flight and had not provided protection. But still, Carlton insisted,
the general had been paid.

Rubino pushed further. Was the importation of large amounts of cash
into Panama a crime in the early 1980s? Was the deposit of large amounts of
cash into Panamanian banks a crime? No, Carlton conceded.

Rubino asked about Carlton's third drug flight for the cartel. Again,
Carlton confirmed, Noriega had no knowledge of the flight. Yet, Carlton
insisted, the general had been paid off.

"In fact, General Noriega provided, to sum it up, nothing to aid or assist
you so that that plane could land, did he?" asked Rubino.

"That's correct," replied Carlton.

"So essentially your testimony is—and you correct me if I'm wrong—that General Noriega was paid $150,000 in advance to do absolutely nothing?"

"That's correct, sir."

Finally, Rubino turned to a telephone conversation that Carlton had had with two Panamanian associates in early 1988. The conversation had been recorded by the G-2 intelligence unit of the Panamanian Defense Forces shortly before Carlton was to appear before Senator John Kerry's foreign relations subcommittee, which was the week after the delivery of the indictment.

A transcript showed Carlton saying that his Senate testimony would be his opportunity to "thank" Noriega.

The gist of the conversation, suggested Rubino, was that Carlton intended to get even with Noriega for failing to get him out of jail in Costa Rica and avoid extradition to the United States.

"That's not what I meant to say," said Carlton. "I wouldn't be so stupid to make accusations against the general while he was in power."

"Sir, is this not your chance, these last few days, to get even with General Noriega?" asked Rubino.

"No, sir," replied Carlton. "I swore before God, before this jury and this honorable judge, to tell the truth, and that's what I have done."

Rubino had one more question, but it was rhetorical and mocking: "Sir, before you would lie, would you spend the rest of your natural life in prison with no possibility of parole and then spend another one hundred and forty-five years?"

"Objection, Your Honor," said Sullivan, jumping to his feet.

"Sustained," said Hoeveler.

Rubino raised his arms from his sides and then slowly let them fall back. "I have no further questions," he said, turning to the judge and then back to the defense table.

The cross-examination had taken two days.

CHAPTER 25

Touchstone:
The Man in the White Suit

In his four days on the witness stand, the one thing that Floyd Carlton had not been able to do was put Noriega physically together with the cartel. An indirect relationship had been established with Carlton's testimony, that Carlton served as an intermediary between Pablo Escobar and the general. But Carlton was only an intermediary.

An effort to make the direct link came on Thursday, October 3, when the prosecution called cartel pilot Roberto Striedinger.

Just before and after Carlton, the prosecution had called cartel pilot David Ortiz to testify. Ortiz's testimony corroborated Carlton's friendship with Noriega and Carlton's work for the cartel. Carlton had told Ortiz that he worked for both. Ortiz also established that besides Carlton's, there were other cartel transshipment routes through Panama. That suggested that cartel payoffs had created a protection net that was perhaps wider than Carlton might have known.

Still, Ortiz's appearance had not offered a direct link between Noriega and the cartel either. That point had been driven home on cross-examination when Rubino asked: "The reason that you have not said anything about General Noriega is because you have no personal knowledge of General Noriega committing any crime whatsoever, do you?" To that Ortiz conceded, "I have never spoken with him, sir."

Roberto Striedinger, however, could offer more.

After his arrest the previous summer, Striedinger admitted that he had smuggled drugs for nearly seven years, amassing enough money to buy the Key Biscayne home of former president Richard Nixon. Now, as he walked into court, he was not the dapper businessman his neighbors had known but just another federal prisoner dressed in lockup khaki and a blue pullover sweater.

Guy Lewis, with wire-rimmed glasses and a Tennessee drawl, stepped forward to begin the direct examination. By chance, the Memphis State Law School grad, who had only been a federal prosecutor for a couple of years, had drawn the witnesses with "face time," those who said they had been in the same room with members of the cartel and Noriega. This was the link the prosecution wanted to make.

Striedinger testified that he had met Pablo Escobar and Gustavo Gaviria in early 1980. First he flew cocaine paste from Bolivia to Colombia for the cartel, and then he graduated to transporting cartel leaders and their families on business and vacation trips. On two occasions in 1982, Striedinger said, he flew to Panama City. Neither time was his plane or his passengers checked by Panamanian Customs or security officials. Then in May 1983, Striedinger said, he was summoned by Gaviria to the Medellín office of Jorge Ochoa. As he drove through the front gate and up the long driveway, armed bodyguards were everywhere, he said. He entered the house and stood in the foyer. In the living room was a group of sixteen- and seventeen-year-old girls. Striedinger was soon summoned upstairs to Ochoa's office.

There, he said, in animated conversation were Gaviria, Jorge Ochoa, Fabio Ochoa, a Colombian trafficker named Pablo Correa, a luxury car dealer and marijuana trafficker named Gabriel Taboada, and, dressed completely in white, Manuel Noriega.

"Now, prior to this time when you saw Noriega with these people, had you ever seen, face-to-face, Noriega before?" asked Lewis.

"No, sir," replied Striedinger.

"Well, did you know who it was?" asked Lewis.

"It is difficult to mistake him. Because of the photographs that came out in the newspapers."

As he spoke to Gaviria about preparing for a flight to Panama the next day, Striedinger said he overheard the group's conversation in the background. Fabio Ochoa was trying to convince Noriega to help import a Ferrari sports car into Colombia using Panamanian diplomatic channels.

What did Noriega say? asked Lewis.

"It would be the same as someone taking a photograph of him embracing Fabio and sending that photograph to the *New York Times*," said Striedinger. Then Noriega moved toward Fabio as if to hug him, and the group broke into laughter.

"They all were very euphoric," Striedinger said.

The next day, on Gaviria's instructions, Striedinger said, he flew six French women from Pablo Escobar's ranch in Colombia to a coastal airstrip outside Panama City where they went aboard a waiting yacht.

And a few days later, Striedinger said, he again flew to Panama from Medellín, this time with Floyd Carlton and this time carrying a cocaine shipment. When the two returned, they were met at a cartel airstrip by Gaviria and Noriega.

That was Striedinger's testimony.

Throughout, Noriega sat at the defense table between Frank Rubino and Jon May with his arms crossed. He showed no reaction to the charge that he had met personally with the cartel.

Rubino, however, bristled at each of Striedinger's anecdotes. Lewis, for no apparent reason and with no apparent connection, had elicited a link between Noriega and automobile smuggling; Noriega and sixteen- and seventeen-year-old girls; and Noriega and six French women. The prosecution was eliciting testimony about events not alleged in the indictment and perhaps not even crimes.

"This is a racketeering and drug conspiracy case," Rubino protested to Judge Hoeveler at a sidebar. What purpose did such testimony have if not to shock and prejudice the jury? Rubino asked. Hoeveler took Rubino's objections under advisement.

On cross-examination, Rubino first set out to discredit Striedinger's character and the prosecution's reliance on an admitted criminal's testimony. The pilot's plea agreement was a standard government giveaway, Rubino charged. It had allowed Striedinger to pay his attorney $500,000 to help negotiate the plea. The plea allowed Striedinger to keep a Mercedes-Benz, two trucks, an airplane, a yacht, and, of all things, a collection of assault rifles including AR-15s, Soviet AK-47s, Uzi pistols, and MAC10s.

Under Rubino's questioning, Striedinger conceded that the prosecutors had agreed to urge the governments of Belize, Bolivia, Germany, and Mexico not to press charges against him for admitted drug activities in those countries. The government also agreed to recommend to Judge Hoeveler that Striedinger serve no more than ten years of a maximum thirty-year sentence.

Questioned about his drug flights with Floyd Carlton, Striedinger admitted that his recollections differed from Carlton's. Striedinger testified that he was summoned to the cartel office in the summer of 1983 to discuss the Colombia-to-Panama drug flight with Carlton. Carlton testified that he had been in Europe on vacation during that summer. Carlton claimed the flight began at Escobar's ranch and involved 400 kilos of cocaine. Striedinger testified the flight had begun at a clandestine airstrip and carried only 150 kilos of cocaine.

In the end, Striedinger's testimony failed to match Carlton's, but the pilot had succeeded in putting the cartel and Noriega in the same room.

On Tuesday, October 8, the prosecution prepared to call its next witness, Gabriel Taboada, the Colombian luxury car dealer whom Striedinger saw meeting with Noriega and the cartel leaders in Jorge Ochoa's office. Word had spread among the press that Taboada was going to do severe damage to Noriega. Unlike Striedinger, he had not walked in on the middle of the Noriega-cartel meeting but had been present the whole time. Someone on the prosecution team dubbed Taboada the government's "smart bomb." Guy Lewis had prepped Taboada for trial and called him "100 percent." Taboada had taken four pretrial polygraph tests and passed each one.

But before the jury or Taboada was brought into the courtroom, Rubino and Jon May asked the judge for an opportunity to address the court. May handed Hoeveler a motion requesting the declaration of a mistrial.

"I bring this motion at this time because today the government will be presenting evidence that, if admitted, will further compound the error of Striedinger's testimony," said May. "It has been a longstanding principle of our jurisprudence that evidence of guilt by association has no business being introduced during the course of a criminal trial. Now, the United States government has found it necessary to present evidence concerning an incident having to do with a Ferrari, as well as an incident wherein minor children were present, and an incident where, supposedly, six French nationals were given as a present to General Noriega.

"None of these incidents are mentioned in the indictment. None of these incidents have any relevance, any probative value, as to any issue in this case. These incidents appeal to the passions, the prejudices, the emotions of these jurors, and make it much easier for this government to convince the jury that General Noriega must be guilty because he's an evil person." The jury, continued May, should judge Noriega on the credibility of witnesses and the quality of testimony, not on emotional appeals. "It is such an egregious violation of an individual's right to a fair trial."

The error, said May, would only be compounded if Taboada were allowed to come to court and give similar testimony. "We are moving for a mistrial based on the introduction of that evidence."

Sullivan took up the government's response. The prosecution's intent, he said, was not to prove guilt by association but to show a relevant association. "The government cannot prove guilt beyond a reasonable doubt if it merely shows association, but association amongst coconspirators and codefendants is an element of proof," he said. "If the government never put on any evidence in this trial that Noriega ever met with the heads of the cartel, I guarantee Mr. Rubino would be arguing to the jury that the government never even proved they ever met and spoke together."

That Noriega would mimic putting his arm around Fabio Ochoa and joke about sending their picture to the New York Times showed that Noriega knew he shouldn't be associating with drug dealers, said Sullivan. That Ochoa felt comfortable about asking Noriega to help obtain the Ferrari showed that they knew each other well enough to ask for favors. The French dancing women had arrived when Noriega was made commander in chief of the Defense Forces in August 1983. It showed that the cartel felt comfortable enough to offer Noriega a present.

"We are not attempting to inflame passions, if that's really possible," said Sullivan. "That kind of evidence shows the goodwill that existed between the cartel and their man in Panama, General Noriega. And it dates it as well."

But May countered, "Our argument is that these individuals are not telling the truth. . . . They want the vividness of that image to present to this jury. They are throwing mud to see what sticks," said May.

The judge was sympathetic to the government's response. He promised to consider the motion carefully. But the trial would continue.

Hoeveler called for the jury. When the jurors were settled, he asked the government to call its next witness.

Lewis called Taboada. Guided by Lewis's questioning, Taboada, thirty-five, told of how he had started out importing pickup trucks to Colombia from the United States and how his business had expanded to include Mercedeses, Porsches, and Ferraris. When the Colombian government restricted the import of luxury cars in 1982, Taboada turned to the diplomatic corps for assistance. Foreign ambassadors were free to import automobiles, and with the proper papers, Taboada could resell the cars to his wealthy clients, such as traffickers in Medellín, Cali, and Bogotá.

In 1983, Taboada said, Fabio Ochoa called on him to import a red Ferrari 308 into Colombia, a car just like the actor Tom Selleck drove in the television series "Magnum, P.I." Ochoa called Taboada to a meeting at his brother's office. Taboada said that when he walked in, Noriega was there. Ochoa told Taboada that Noriega was going to help arrange the importation of the car.

Like Striedinger, Taboada confirmed that Noriega and Ochoa joked about the difficulty of using Noriega or a Panamanian diplomat to bring the car into Colombia.

But after Striedinger left, Taboada said, a briefcase was brought into the room. Gaviria then turned to Noriega and said, "There's five hundred in here." Taboada said the briefcase contained stacks of one-hundred-dollar bills. Gaviria's reference, Taboada said he assumed, was to $500,000 in cash. When the meeting began to break up, Gaviria turned to Noriega and said, "Hey, Manuel, don't forget the briefcase."

Taboada's testimony ran counter to the defense's contention that Noriega was the victim of underlings who had traded on his name. In fact, if Taboada and Striedinger were to be believed, Noriega was very, very close to the cartel's trafficking network, although Taboada's testimony stopped short of placing the cartel's cash in Noriega's hands.

For the defense, however, Taboada and Striedinger were more of the same. The government kept coming close but could not make the connection. It was as though Noriega were some sort of "touchstone," explained Rubino. A prosecution witness would tell of a cartel crime, find a way to brush the incident up against Noriega, and then try to find another. More than anything, the government's case seemed to be aimed at Pablo Escobar, said Rubino. Escobar, so far, was behind each of the incidents related in the prosecution witnesses' testimony. Not one witness could say that Noriega was a member of the cartel or had actually done something criminal.

On cross-examination, neither Taboada nor Striedinger was able to offer independent evidence that Noriega had ever traveled to Medellín. There was stronger evidence to place Taboada and Striedinger in the exercise yard at Miami's federal lockup, Rubino suggested, a place where they could have concocted their story. "Here's this guy with a successful car business and all of a sudden he needs the general to bring this car in," Rubino said privately. "The entire cartel had gathered in this room for the sole purpose of getting this kid a Ferrari. And then this pilot walks in the room when the deal is going down. That is not the way dopers work."

And if Noriega was having face-to-face meetings with the cartel, as Taboada and Striedinger testified, why did he need Carlton as an intermediary? Why was Luis del Cid carrying packages of money to Noriega from Carlton if the cartel was handing briefcases full of money to Noriega personally? The prosecution's case didn't make sense, said Rubino.

CHAPTER 26

★★★★★★★

The Panama Witnesses

Pat Sullivan, Myles Malman, and Guy Lewis were undaunted by Rubino's attacks on cross-examination. Sullivan had told the jury that the case would come in pieces and that the pieces in the end, like a puzzle, would fit together.

Carlton and then Striedinger and Taboada had provided eyewitness accounts of Noriega's acquiescence and association with the cartel. By the end of Taboada's testimony, Carlton's four cocaine flights had been corroborated and a near-direct link between Noriega and the cartel made.

The prosecution's next step was to show how Noriega had allowed the cartel to operate almost worry-free in Panama. It was as though the case was moving north, from Colombia to Panama, and in time to the United States.

By Tuesday, October 8, more than a month into the trial, Sullivan was ready to introduce the cartel operations phase of the case. By Sullivan's calculations it would take more than a dozen witnesses to tell the story from beginning to end.

Retired Panamanian Col. Rogelio Alba, whose troops in 1984 accidentally came upon the Darien laboratory in the remote southeastern jungle of Panama, testified that at first he suspected a guerrilla encampment. Because he had only eleven men under his command, he radioed Noriega's *comandancia* in Panama City for reinforcements.

The next morning, before the reinforcements could arrive, Alba's troops cautiously moved into the abandoned camp and found barracks, a kitchen, and sophisticated processing equipment to turn coca paste into crystals or cocaine. Later, when two hundred men from Panama's elite Puma infantry company arrived from Panama City, Alba said their commander did not seem surprised to learn that what had been captured was a cocaine laboratory. Alba testified that he requested the lab be used as a training site for soldiers, but the Puma commander instead insisted the lab be destroyed.

At sidebar, Rubino and Jon May protested what they believed was an insinuation through the prosecution's questioning that Noriega might have orchestrated a "show" response to the lab's discovery. May told Hoeveler the government was trying to have it both ways. If Noriega didn't raid the lab, it was because he had been bought off. If he did, it was because he was trying to cover up.

Myles Malman, who had been questioning Alba, said the testimony showed that the raid had been a mistake, that Alba had accidentally discovered the lab and had put Noriega in the position of having to respond. "They had to put on the show," said Malman. For the time being, Hoeveler said, he would let Alba's testimony stand.

The former head of the nominal Panamanian Air Force, Col. Lorenzo Purcell, who had retired from the Panamanian armed forces in 1988 and now worked in a Fort Lauderdale pizzeria, next testified that he was present in the *comandancia* when Alba called for reinforcements. He said that when he heard the report, he knew the camp did not belong to guerrillas, that guerrillas did not haul around plywood to construct barracks.

Purcell testified that the camp was not destroyed but that Noriega had ordered it dismantled and brought to Panama City. "He told me to be very careful not to lose any of it," said Purcell of Noriega's order. The camp included "washing machines, stoves, electrical plants, generators, high-voltage light bulbs, and a great deal of plywood." In the days following the raid, about twenty-five Colombian nationals were captured in the jungle surrounding the lab, Purcell testified. They were placed in custody and transported to Panama City. Later, said Purcell, on Noriega's instructions they were flown to Bogotá.

A month later, in June 1984, Purcell said, he was with Noriega on a military hardware buying tour in Israel when late one night he was summoned to Noriega's room. There he learned that Noriega's chief of staff, Capt. Julian Melo, was being accused by some of those who had been arrested of taking a bribe to protect the Darien lab.

Purcell said Noriega called Melo to the meeting and scolded him in front of the general staff. Then he ordered Melo to return to Panama to face the charges. When he returned to Panama, Purcell said, he learned that several Colombians had gone to Noriega's general staff and charged that Melo had been paid "millions" to protect the lab and that he was supposed to have passed the bribe on to Noriega. "They handed money over to Melo in order to be able to conduct operations in this lab," and, in turn, "Melo was to hand over that money to the general," Purcell said.

"Did General Noriega respond to this?" Sullivan asked Purcell.

"Yes. He said that that was false." Purcell said Noriega then ordered Melo court-martialed.

"What happened to Melo, to your knowledge?" Sullivan asked.

"Well, the disciplinary board found him to be guilty, and they recommended that he be discharged from the armed forces and . . . be handed over to the civilian authorities." In the end, however, Purcell said, looking at the jury, the charges were dismissed.

Sullivan moved to focus on the Colombians' access to Noriega's staff.

"Would it be unusual for Colombians to come to a meeting of the general staff?" he asked.

"Yes," said Purcell, looking across the courtroom toward Noriega.

"Did you ever learn the names of those Colombians?" asked Sullivan.

"No."

Sullivan pressed Purcell on two additional points. First, Purcell confirmed that on Noriega's return from Europe, after he had sent Melo ahead to Panama, the Panamanian group stopped in Cuba. There, said Purcell, Noriega on one occasion met privately with Fidel Castro until three in the morning. Second, Purcell testified that César Rodríguez and another Noriega crony, Enrique Pretelt, who also was named in the Miami indictment, were given free access to the military portion of the Tocumen international airport in Panama City. The two, said Purcell, often arrived aboard international flights and passed through security and Customs without being checked.

Purcell's testimony seemed to suggest that Noriega had allowed drug traffickers to use Panama as a way station, and if the prosecution's assumption that the military response to the discovery of the Darien lab was nothing but a "show," then the arrest of Melo and his trial was also a show.

At one point during Purcell's testimony, Noriega jotted a note and pushed it across the table to Rubino.

When Sullivan finished, Rubino walked to the lectern. He asked Purcell about Noriega's relationship with César Rodríguez. Wasn't it true, he said, that the two had virtually quit talking by 1984?

Yes, said Purcell. "They got somewhat estranged."

And wasn't it true that the materials from the carefully dismantled drug lab were donated to Panama City's poor?

Yes, responded Purcell. "I think that the wood, everything that was wooden, was used at the civic action organization."

Wasn't it true, asked Rubino, that Noriega had "vehemently denied" any involvement in the cartel-Melo bribery scheme?

"That's correct, yes," answered Purcell.

And the disciplinary board that Noriega appointed to try Melo found him guilty, did they not? asked Rubino.

"That is correct," answered Purcell.

"And, further, that disciplinary board found no evidence that General Noriega had any knowledge of that incident, isn't that true?"

"Yes."

When court resumed on Tuesday, October 15, the prosecution was ready to resume its string of witnesses linking the cartel's operations to Panama.

Myles Malman called Noriega codefendant Eduardo Pardo to the stand. Pardo had pleaded guilty to flying $800,000 from Fort Lauderdale to Panama in 1983. He had both participated in and witnessed many of the cartel's operations. Pardo explained that he had been recruited to the cartel by Floyd Carlton. Carlton assigned Pardo to fly jets. That included transporting drug proceeds from the United States to Panama. On a visit to Medellín, Pardo said, he learned that a secret compartment had been installed in Pablo Escobar's jet. The compartment was to smuggle cash out of the United

States, Carlton explained. Later, in Panama, said Pardo, the cartel plane was seized by Noriega's G-2 when the secret compartments were discovered.

Frank Rubino objected to the relevance of Pardo's testimony. At sidebar he protested the government's continuing use of Noriega as a "touchstone" for every criminal action of the cartel.

But Malman explained that the seizure only further implicated Noriega. The real reason the G-2 seized the cartel plane was to "steal" it from the cartel, he said. "Your Honor, it is kind of like the Darien lab. Mr. Rubino makes an argument that the Darien lab was a perfectly proper, legal exercise of the Panamanian Defense Forces. They found this thing and they seized it, et cetera. We say that it was an accidental stumbling, and, therefore, it is relevant because the lab is, as other evidence will show as we go along, that Noriega was paid and that it was accidentally seized and the money was given back."

Hoeveler said he would allow the questioning to continue. The law said an innocent act could further an unlawful conspiracy, he reminded Rubino.

On cross-examination, Rubino aimed to let the jury know that Noriega could not have known about the schemes of every drug trafficker passing through Panama. Rubino started with the 1983 cash-smuggling flight.

"Now, on this particular flight, you never called General Noriega in advance to tell him you were arriving, did you?" Rubino asked Pardo.

"No, sir."

"You never requested his permission, did you?"

"No, sir."

"You never paid him any money to make this flight, did you?"

"No, sir."

"In fact, to the very best of your knowledge, General Noriega didn't have the faintest idea you made this flight, did he?"

"Correct," Pardo said.

Rubino pursued one final point. Carlton, in his testimony, had given a detailed description of Pardo's flight from Fort Lauderdale. When Pardo returned to Panama, Carlton said, he instructed Pardo to leave the duffel bag with $800,000 on the plane to be picked up later.

"Didn't Floyd Carlton tell you to leave the money locked up in the false compartment on the airplane and that he would go by the next day and pick it up?" asked Rubino.

"No, sir. That's not true," answered Pardo.

"Floyd Carlton didn't tell you that?" Rubino asked.

"No," Pardo insisted.

Later that afternoon, Pat Sullivan called the government's next witness, Enrique Pereira, an ex-bodyguard and associate of César Rodríguez. Pereira was a short black man, forty-five years old and street smart. Sullivan didn't consider Pereira a major witness, but his testimony would fit in to what Sullivan had dubbed the "Rodríguez strategy." The idea was to put Rodríguez—Noriega's now-dead business partner—as close to the cartel as possible. Many witnesses would agree Rodríguez was an intimate of Noriega's. If the jury also was convinced that Rodríguez was an intimate of the cartel's, then perhaps they would see a solid link between the cartel and Noriega. That's what Sullivan hoped.

Pereira began by saying that his job was "to watch over the money."

He testified that his boss, whom he called "the late César," flew $4.7 million in cash back to Panama from south Florida on three trips. After the first trip, Pereira said, Rodríguez ordered him to deliver a briefcase to Noriega's home.

"Take a briefcase to the old man's home," Rodríguez told Pereira. Pereira said he wanted to see what he was delivering, so Rodríguez opened the case.

"What did you see?" asked Sullivan.

"Money, lots of used money." The case was filled.

"Did César say how much money it was?" asked Sullivan.

"Yes. In that briefcase, yes, he did," answered Pereira.

"What did he tell you?"

"He said, 'Take this briefcase to the old man's house. Be careful because it's $250,000.' "

Pereira said he went to Noriega's home where he was met by Noriega's chief of security. "He said, 'Put it on the table. The old man is having dinner.' And so I put it on the table, and I took off."

Pereira said he did not know the source of the cash. He later delivered $1.7 million to Noriega's personal banker, Amjad Awan, who headed the Panama City office of the Bank of Credit and Commerce International, BCCI. In all, Pereira said, he delivered $300,000 to Noriega's home and office and $1.7 million to Awan.

The money was separate from the $600,000 delivered to Noriega by Carlton and the $500,000 Taboada said he saw the cartel give Noriega in Colombia.

Rubino made his cross-examination short. He picked up where he had left off with Eduardo Pardo.

"Sir, you're aware that César Rodríguez was involved in the shipment of arms to various places and countries, correct?" he asked.

"No, never," answered Pereira.

"Are you aware that César Rodríguez was involved in the shipment of arms to foreign countries?"

"Sir," Pereira answered, "I knew that because it was published in the press worldwide, so not only did I know that but the whole world knew that because he crashed in Central America in a small airplane."

"Do you know if the money that was being picked up on these three specific trips was money for arms shipments?"

"Sir, I did not know the source of the money."

"I have nothing further," said Rubino.

The government's next witness, Rodolfo Carcamo, had been an airport guard in 1984 when he said Fabio Ochoa's plane landed one day. On hand to pick

Ochoa up, said Carcamo, was a G-2 driver and car. The implication was that he had been sent by Noriega.

On cross-examination Carcamo conceded that at the time of Ochoa's visit Noriega was not the head of G-2.

"Did you ever see, during your entire military career, General Noriega in the company of Fabio Ochoa?" Rubino asked.

"No," responded Carcamo.

On Wednesday, October 16, before the prosecution could call its next witness, Judge Hoeveler called the prosecution team and defense attorneys together.

For nearly two weeks a serious problem had been brewing. On September 30, the federal Marshals Service in Phoenix had received for delivery a subpoena issued by the Noriega defense. Jon May had been spending hours each day buried in the courthouse basement researching the government's witnesses and cementing together the defense case. In the last week of September, May delivered thirty-eight subpoenas to the Marshals Service. The names included DEA agents, former ambassadors, and even Lt. Col. Oliver North. Once the potential witnesses were contacted, many would be interviewed. Then evidence would be gathered. Preparation of the defense case would take until Christmas, May and Rubino figured.

Because federal rules of procedure do not require either side to disclose the names of witnesses far in advance of their taking the witness stand, both Sullivan and Rubino had been very careful not to tip their hands. Disclosure of a witness list could give the opposition the advantage of extra time to prepare cross-examinations and even to modify the presentation of its case. But when a defense subpoena arrived in Phoenix, attached was a complete list of all the subpoenas to be delivered, all thirty-eight. The list was a shorthand outline of the defense case.

The Phoenix subpoena went to Lewis Tambs, a history professor at Arizona State University and a former U.S. ambassador to Costa Rica from 1985 to 1987. Tambs forwarded it to the State Department, whose attorneys would act as his counsel in arranging his appearance. Of course, the entire defense witness list was attached. The State Department, in turn, forwarded the list to the Justice Department. On October 3, Sullivan notified both Hoeveler and Rubino that a copy of "what appeared to be a witness list" had "inadvertently" come to the attention of the government.

The leak infuriated Rubino and May. The incident fit what seemed to be a pattern of government misconduct. First, Noriega's telephone calls were taped, leaked to CNN, and broadcast worldwide. Then Noriega defense lawyer Raymond Takiff was recruited as a confidential informant in a separate government case.

Only days before the subpoenas were delivered to the Marshals Service, on September 20, Judge Hoeveler had specifically ordered that the names of the subpoena recipients be kept secret.

Within an hour of receiving Sullivan's notification, May sent a letter to south Florida's U.S. Marshal Daniel Horgan. The disclosure, May charged, would do great harm to the defense. "There is no question in my mind that personnel within the United States Marshals Service came up with a very artful scheme to violate the confidentiality of our witness list," May wrote to Horgan. May then filed a motion with the judge's office requesting that the Marshals Service be disqualified from further service of defense subpoenas.

Now, on October 16, Judge Hoeveler had received the government's response to May's motion. He asked each side to explain what had happened.

May took up the defense's argument. He was still furious over what had happened.

"Apparently Ambassador Tambs decided that since he was not himself covered literally by the court order, that he was free to violate the spirit of the order. He telephoned the State Department, and he read off the entire list of our witnesses, or at least the list that had been submitted to the Marshals Service," May began.

"This is of major concern to the defense because we did everything that we thought we could and should do to protect the secrecy of our witnesses. Despite our best efforts, or at least what efforts we thought were our best efforts, the entire list of our witnesses falls into the hands of the Department of Justice, the one entity which we did not want to know the list of our witnesses." The court should take the task of delivering the defense subpoenas away from the Marshals Service, May told the judge.

James McAdams responded on behalf of the government. "We are not disputing that there was an administrative glitch here, in the sense that what happened was unintended." McAdams said the disclosure was not the fault of the Marshals Service. The marshal "had no way of knowing that the individual on the subpoena was either directly or indirectly related to a United States government agency."

Hoeveler was convinced that despite all of the government's missteps, none was intentional. Surely, if the government intended to subvert the process, it could have been done so more artfully, he thought.

Hoeveler looked at May. "There is not a great deal we can do about this, what has happened, except for me to assure you that I will assist you in any manner necessary to make sure that those subpoenas are complied with. . . . I can't find and do not find that this was an intentional act on the part of the Marshals Service."

From now on a private subpoena service would deliver the defense subpoenas, Hoeveler ordered. "What's done is done," he said, though May and Rubino were not convinced.

The prosecution's next witnesses, like Rodolfo Carcamo, had spent much of the early 1980s working at Panama City's major airports, where, the government said, they had front-row seats to the comings and goings of the cartel.

Panamanian Customs official María Morales said she saw up to $10 million in drug profits unloaded at Paitilla airport. The money came in boxes and suit-cases. She said money flights often arrived from the United States and that "there was an order from the commander's office that these planes were not to be touched. . . . Every week millions would come in," Morales said.

Morales said she finally asked Noriega himself about all of the money coming into the country. "He replied that this was a banking center, and that this was normal," she said. On one occasion she received a call from Lt. Col. Luis del Cid, Noriega's assistant, informing her to extend a "special courtesy" to a flight of César Rodríguez's. When the plane arrived, there was $10 million on board, Morales said.

Rubino objected. Rodríguez was dead, and Morales was not named as a coconspirator. The conversation was not within the scope of the conspiracy at trial, Rubino told the judge at sidebar. Rubino noted that Panama was the region's largest banking center and the possession of large amounts of money was not a crime.

If the prosecution could connect the money to narcotics, Hoeveler said, he would allow the questioning to continue. Sullivan promised that the connection would follow.

Guy Lewis resumed his questioning, and Rubino's objection was mooted when Morales said Rodríguez told her the money was from the drug trade.

On cross-examination, Morales conceded that large amounts of cash began flowing into Panama long before Noriega had taken charge of the country. Cash was coming to Panama as early as Omar Torrijos's rule and later during Rubén Dario Paredes's tenure as military chief, Morales confirmed.

"In fact, banking was the single largest industry in the entire country, was it not?" asked Rubino.

"Yes," Morales replied.

On Thursday, October 17, the prosecution called Anel Pérez, an air traffic controller. Pérez said that in 1983, on three separate occasions, he watched through binoculars as Noriega greeted cartel leader Jorge Ochoa after he had arrived at Panama's Tocumen airport. He said that at other times he saw boxes of money being unloaded from Noriega's small jet and taken away by intelligence officers and that he also saw drums of ether and acetone being loaded onto a cargo plane which then headed for an unspecified location on the border between Colombia and Panama. All this had come at a time, said Pérez, when there were increasing problems with undocumented flights coming into Panama from Colombia.

Guy Lewis led Perez through the questioning. Lewis picked up a two-by-three-foot blowup photograph of Jorge Ochoa and walked to the defense table. He stood with the photograph behind Rubino and next to Noriega, who was seated and staring straight ahead.

"Is this the man you saw with the defendant?" Lewis asked, referring to the photograph.

The courtroom grew silent, almost electric.

"Yes," Perez responded.

Noriega was furious at the tactic. Later, during a break, Rubino gave Lewis a message: "My client says you are despicable."

At sidebar, Rubino protested the government's inference that each and every undocumented flight was loaded with dope and that Noriega had issued some sort of order saying "every drug flight from Colombia can come to Panama."

The continuing press of inference was weighing on the defense. Rubino turned on Pérez personally.

"When did you volunteer to testify against General Noriega?" asked Rubino.

"When I found out that General Noriega was in this country and he was arrested. I looked for a way of helping," said Pérez. "I always wanted to come here and testify."

"And you always wanted to testify against General Noriega, didn't you?"

"Always. I tried to look for the means of getting here."

"Why don't you like General Noriega?" asked Rubino.

"I have never said that," answered Pérez, glancing toward the jury.

Pérez then conceded that he was fired from his air traffic controller's job in 1988 and had been bitter toward Noriega since then.

Rubino's questioning suggested that Pérez's observations were of little, if any, consequence. At sidebar he explained: "This man tells about these clandestine flights that are occurring. We don't deny these clandestine flights are occurring. Our posture is that he is simply nothing more than an air traffic controller. He's not involved in foreign policy. He has no idea." The boxes Pérez saw loaded and unloaded could as easily have carried guns as drugs or money, Rubino observed. In fact, he said, they carried arms for the Salvadoran guerrillas. "They are doing the drug case, and I am doing the arms case," Rubino told Hoeveler.

On cross-examination, Rubino further pressed Pérez about his testimony that he saw Noriega greet Jorge Ochoa. Had Pérez in his ten years as a controller seen Noriega greet any other dignitaries? Rubino asked.

Pérez said he remembered that once the president of Costa Rica had been forced to make an emergency landing at the airport, and he also remembered an official visit by U.S. president Jimmy Carter.

What Pérez didn't remember, Rubino pointed out, were visits by the presidents of Guatemala, San Salvador, Venezuela, Argentina, and Honduras, Daniel Ortega of Nicaragua, the vice president of the United States, George Bush, and Pope John Paul.

When Guy Lewis objected to the questioning, Rubino took the issue up at sidebar. "I just find it beyond coincidence that he's up in that tower and he only remembers Jorge Ochoa. He doesn't remember the Pope," Rubino observed.

★   ★   ★

Rubino was steadily punching holes in the testimony of the prosecution's witnesses, but the weight of circumstantial evidence was mounting. With Pérez, the trial had finished its fifth week of testimony, and yet the government was not halfway through its witnesses. There would be little Rubino could do to help the jury resist a guilty verdict simply on the volume of evidence.

By the next Monday, October 21, the defense lawyer's work had taken its toll. Rubino was at home with a 103-degree temperature. "The way he's been going, this was bound to happen," Hoeveler told the other attorneys. "We have got to really watch ourselves."

To complicate matters, one of the jurors, Arnold Andrews, had suffered a mild heart attack on Saturday and had been admitted to the hospital. Andrews's physician said that she did not know when he would be able to return.

Two days later, still weak, Rubino was back in court, but Andrews was still in bed recovering. He would need at least a week to recover. That's why juries had alternates, Hoeveler pointed out. "I hate very much to lose Mr. Andrews," Hoeveler said, but "we cannot afford to lose a week."

Next on the witness stand for the government was Colombian drug trafficker José Cabrera. Cabrera, who was now serving a thirty-year sentence for cocaine smuggling, said that cartel leader José Gonzalo Rodríguez Gacha told him in early 1984 that the cartel was going to murder Colombian Justice Minister Lara Bonilla. The cartel, Gacha told Cabrera, held Bonilla responsible for the raid and destruction of the Tranquilandia cocaine labs. The raid resulted in the seizure of ten tons of cocaine and momentarily hurt the cartel's supply of cocaine to the United States.

Cabrera said he tried to talk Gacha out of going forward with the assassination, but less than two weeks later, Bonilla was gunned down by a motorcyclist on a Bogotá street. The assassination immediately triggered a government crackdown on the cartel, Cabrera said, and the cartel's leaders fled to Panama.

In Panama, Cabrera said, the cartel had the protection of *El Tigre*, Noriega, to whom the cartel paid $5 million for protection. The charge to each cartel member protected was $100,000 per week, Gacha told Cabrera.

In Panama, the cartel's leaders, including Gacha, Jorge Ochoa, and Pablo Escobar, took up residence on a resort island. Shortly after the cartel's arrival, Cabrera said, Noriega visited. He walked into the cartel's hospitality suite and announced, *"Bienvenidos, muchachos. Ustedes no tienen nada que temer."* (You are welcome, friends. You don't have to worry about anything here.) Cabrera also testified that the cartel paid Noriega for money-laundering privileges and for landing privileges.

Later, Cabrera said, he left Panama and went to Spain. There he met Jorge Ochoa, who was mad at Noriega.

"Did you have any discussion with Jorge Ochoa as to what had happened in Panama, as to why he was so upset?" Sullivan asked Cabrera.

"Yes, sir. He felt betrayed by the Panamanian Defense Forces and the general." The Darien lab had been raided, Cabrera said.

Pat Sullivan next called Luis Ernesto Gilibert, the Colombian police colonel who had led the March 1984 raid on the Tranquilandia drug lab. Gilibert testified that he found at Tranquilandia barrels of ether and acetone, the cocaine-processing chemicals. The barrels may have been the same that previous government witnesses had seen loaded on planes at Panama City airports, the government suggested.

On cross-examination, Rubino asked Gilibert about the chemicals.

"No matter which route they took and no matter whether they came by airplane or by boat, if they had the proper documentation, the proper bill of lading showing they were coming through, say, the Canal Zone, would they then enter your country as legal cargo?" he asked.

"Precisely," Gilibert responded.

Rubino then asked about the operations of Pablo Escobar and Jorge Ochoa in Colombia in 1980, '81, '82, and '83. Was there, Rubino asked, a warrant for their arrests?

Gilibert said he could not recall.

"Well, can I assume if there was, you would have arrested them?" Rubino asked.

That was correct, responded Gilibert.

"Tell me this, sir: Was it General Noriega's responsibility to arrest Colombian drug traffickers for crimes they committed in Colombia?" Rubino asked.

Sullivan objected.

Rubino reworded the question. "Sir, at any time did the government of Colombia or any agency thereof, such as the police or the military, make any request, a law enforcement request, of General Noriega and him denying you that request?"

"As far as I know, no," answered Gilibert.

Rogelio Rodríguez, a Panamanian customs inspector, followed Gilibert to the witness stand. Rodríguez testified that Lt. Col. Julian Melo, Noriega's chief of staff, cleared the permits for the shipment of ether and acetone through Panama to Colombia. The chemical barrels were labeled FRESH PAINT, Rodríguez said. He testified that Melo told him not to worry about the permits for the chemicals because "the approval of the commander in chief had already been obtained."

On cross-examination, Rubino asked Rodríguez about the $16,500 that Panamanian businessman Jaime Castillo had paid him to help move ether shipments through Panama. The money was equal to five years of Rodríguez's salary. Rubino asked if the money was a payoff or a bribe because, in fact, Rodríguez was helping to commit a crime. The money was a "gift," Rodríguez insisted. He explained that at the time he helped Castillo, he had taken a leave of absence from his customs job.

"It wasn't a crime for me because, I repeat," said Rodríguez, "I was on vacation."

The government's case had taken shape. Noriega's Panama was a country awash in drug money, and a Colombian drug cartel operated as though it could buy just about anything it wanted in Panama. The prosecution's aim now was to draw the cartel closer and closer to Noriega. Three Panamanian businessmen—Ricardo Tribaldos, Jaime Castillo, and Enrique Pretelt—had testified to the relationship between the cartel and businessmen, between the cartel and military officers close to Noriega, and between the cartel and Noriega.

Ricardo Tribaldos had gone to junior college in Florida. When he returned home to Panama in the late 1970s, he went to work at his father's International Harvester dealership. Later, Tribaldos went into business with friends procuring equipment for the Panamanian military. This led to a friendship with Lt. Col. Julian Melo, who became an intermediary for Noriega, and Nicolás Ardito Barletta, a vice president of the World Bank, who was running for president of Panama in 1984. Melo asked Tribaldos to raise funds for Barletta. Melo said financial support could be found in Medellín, Colombia.

Frank Rubino objected and asked for a sidebar. "Now, the government wants to make the case political," Rubino protested to the judge. "I thought this was supposed to be a drug case." Malman explained that the government wanted to show Noriega's relationship to the cartel. "First, the candidate is chosen by Noriega and then, secondly, Noriega's candidate is supported by the cartel at the request of Noriega," Malman explained. "If we have a government of Panama in the person of Manuel Noriega later on allowing them to set up a lab, the cartel, allowing them to ship ether and acetone, allowing them safe haven, it is very relevant." Judge Hoeveler agreed. "Let's see where this takes us," Hoeveler said.

"Do you know with whom Colonel Melo was in contact in Medellín to get this economic or financial support for the presidential candidate?" Malman asked Tribaldos.

"Yes, sir. With Jorge Ochoa." Tribaldos said he flew to Medellín and met with Ochoa. The next day Ochoa pledged $200,000 to Barletta's campaign.

When Ochoa's money arrived in Panama, Melo took charge, Tribaldos said. Melo gave Tribaldos $15,000 and took part for himself. In the end, half of the $200,000 was given to Barletta for his campaign. Proof of the contribution was recorded in a photograph taken at a fund-raiser where Barletta was pictured with the money.

"What was the relationship between Colonel Melo and Manuel Antonio Noriega at that time?" Malman asked Tribaldos.

"Well, they were close friends," said Tribaldos.

A few months later, Tribaldos said, he and Melo were called to Colombia where they met with members of the Ochoa family. "They said they wanted protection for all their business in Panama. They said they wanted the protection of the National Guard of Panama, including General Noriega."

At first, the cartel offered to pay $1 million for protection, but Tribaldos said Melo told Fabio Ochoa, "General Noriega would not accept $1 million. General Noriega would accept at least $4 million." Ochoa at first balked. But if the money was for the protection of all the cartel's business in Panama, he said, including a new lab being built in the Darien jungle and the free movement of precursor chemicals through Panama, and if Melo could assure the cartel that the money would go directly to Noriega, then the $4 million amount would be provided.

Three or four days later, the cartel's money arrived in wooden crates. Melo divided up the money again, giving Tribaldos $400,000 and keeping $800,000 for himself. In the end there was $2.8 million left for Noriega. Tribaldos said he didn't know whether the bribe was ever delivered.

Even though Melo later told Tribaldos that the cartel was receiving Noriega's protection, proof was hard to come by. The 1984 raid on the Darien lab left Melo "scared," Tribaldos said. "The Colombians were very nervous and angry about what was happening. They asked Colonel Melo what was going on. They didn't understand. Colonel Melo said, 'Well, I did give the money to him. I don't know what's going on.' Melo told the Colombians that the raid was a mistake."

To make matters worse, Tribaldos said, shortly after the Darien raid, the Defense Forces began seizing the cartel's ether shipments headed for other labs. The Ochoas demanded a meeting.

"What was Colonel Melo's mood or attitude at that meeting?" asked Malman.

"He was very nervous, sir."

"Did he offer any explanation at all, or did he make any statement as to any reason that Manuel Antonio Noriega had had for seizing the ether?"

"Well, he didn't say much. He said, 'I don't understand what is going on with General Noriega. He must be crazy.'"

The explanation did not appease the cartel's representatives. Melo suggested, "Let's kill General Noriega."

The Colombians were dumbfounded by Melo's suggestion, Tribaldos said. "They said that they only wanted their problems solved" and said no.

Later, Tribaldos continued, after Noriega learned about the Darien raid and about Melo's call for Noriega's murder, Tribaldos and Melo and others, including the cartel's representatives in Panama, were rounded up and taken into custody by the G-2. He and others were questioned about the raid, the ether seizures, and the threat against Noriega. Then one of Noriega's officers ordered Tribaldos to sign a statement which he was not allowed to read. (At sidebar, Malman explained that the statement absolved Noriega of any involvement in the raid.)

One of Noriega's officers told the cartel there would be money returned.

★   ★   ★

Rubino was convinced the direct examination of Tribaldos opened opportunities for him to explore more than Noriega's relationship to the cartel.

On cross-examination, Rubino first established that Tribaldos's initial contacts with the cartel were on behalf of General Paredes, not Noriega. Pablo Escobar had made a gift of a $150,000 horse to Paredes at the time Paredes headed the Panamanian National Guard, Tribaldos said.

"Are you aware that Mr. Barletta was supported by the United States government, also?" Rubino asked. Barletta had a Ph.D. in economics from the University of Chicago, where U.S. Secretary of State George Shultz had taught. Malman objected.

At sidebar, Rubino explained that the reason Noriega and the Panamanian military switched its support from Paredes to Barletta was that the U.S. government had requested they do so. Barletta did not know the money belonged to the cartel, Rubino said, and neither did Noriega. Besides, Rubino said, there was also secret funding for Barletta from the CIA and the United States.

That might be true, Pat Sullivan pointed out, but if Tribaldos, the witness, did not know about the U.S. support for Barletta—which he didn't, Sullivan assured the judge—then the case had not come to "the bridge" which would take it into politics.

Hoeveler agreed. Rubino could push forward into the United States' involvement in Panamanian politics now only if Tribaldos was aware of such support. Otherwise, he must wait for the right witness and the right opening.

When Rubino returned to his cross-examination, Tribaldos agreed that Barletta was qualified to be president of Panama; his integrity and intelligence had never been questioned, Tribaldos agreed.

Rubino now turned back to rectifying the impression that Noriega was aware of Melo's contacts with the cartel.

"Now, do you know if Colonel Melo, in fact, had General Noriega's approval?" asked Rubino.

"No, sir. I didn't know," said Tribaldos.

"And right up to and including today, you honestly don't know, do you?"

"I don't know, sir."

Rubino reminded Tribaldos that his testimony on direct examination had been that in cutting a protection deal with Melo, the cartel had insisted that the $4 million bribe be delivered to Noriega. Tribaldos had said the cartel's representative told Melo, "You have to give it to General Noriega. As per our experience, if Noriega doesn't take that money or he's not in the play with it, we cannot do business in Panama."

"And, in fact, they didn't do business in Panama. Their lab got shut down and raided and arrested, didn't it?" Rubino asked.

"Yes," said Tribaldos.

"And they never got protection for a cocaine laboratory because it got busted, right?"

"I guess so," said Tribaldos.

"Tell this jury how much of that $2.8 million you know went to General Manuel Antonio Noriega."

"I don't know that, sir."

"In fact, you don't honestly know if one penny ever reached General Noriega, do you?"

"I don't know that, sir."

"Right after the time that Colonel Melo is taking all of this bribe money from the Ochoas is when the PDF, led by General Noriega, is seizing a lab and seizing ether shipments, correct?"

"Yes, sir."

"That didn't make a lot of sense to the cartel, did it?"

"I don't know that, sir," answered Tribaldos, looking at his hands.

Tribaldos was the sixth government witness to say that Noriega had received bribe money. But like the testimony of the others before him, Tribaldos's had seemed contradictory. None of the witnesses could confirm that Noriega had actually received money from the cartel.

Panamanian businessman Jaime Castillo followed Tribaldos to the witness stand on Tuesday, October 29. Castillo testified that in 1983 he established a phony company to help the Ochoa family smuggle ether and acetone through Panama's free trade zone to Colombia. He claimed that Julian Melo, the chief of staff to Noriega, had assured him his business would be profitable and unhindered because it had the general's backing.

"'Look,'" Castillo said Melo told him, "'You have all the protection because this deal belongs to El Viejo, the old man.'" El Viejo was Noriega, Castillo testified.

But after that, Castillo's testimony did not mesh with Tribaldos's. Even though the two had often met together with Melo to coordinate the cartel's smuggling, and even though they were both present at many of the same occasions, their testimony differed.

Castillo testified that Barletta was told directly that the $100,000 campaign contribution came from the cartel. Tribaldos testified that Barletta did not know. When the money was presented to Barletta, Castillo said, Melo prefaced the presentation by saying, "These are some gentlemen who represent certain families in Colombia, the Ochoa family and Mr. Escobar. They want to contribute to your political campaign because later on they are interested in making certain investments here in this country." Then, Castillo said, "Melo says, 'The commander already has knowledge of this.'"

After the Darien lab was raided, Castillo testified, he was present when Jorge Ochoa confronted Melo. Ochoa wanted to know why the cartel had not received the protection it had paid for. Melo was extremely nervous, Castillo said. Suddenly, the meeting was interrupted by a phone call.

Castillo remembered Melo saying, "Yes, my general. I am here meeting with all these people. And I am already telling them, at this point, that you are going to give me a solution to this problem. I am going to take care of everything here because I know that I have your support, my commander."

Melo made a show of receiving the call, Castillo said, but no one in the room besides Melo heard the other side of the conversation. "I have no personal knowledge that the person who was calling was the general," Castillo told the jury.

And when Castillo, Tribaldos, Melo, and the cartel's representative were detained after Noriega learned that Melo had suggested the cartel should consider murdering him, Castillo testified, Melo and Tribaldos tried to bribe their way out of trouble. They instructed Castillo to pass $65,000 to two of Noriega's top officers, Luis Quiel and Nivaldo Madrinan. But, Castillo said, instead of paying the bribe, he kept the money.

On cross-examination, Rubino first asked about the cartel's $100,000 campaign contribution to Barletta, emphasizing the contradiction between Castillo's and Tribaldos's testimony.

"Now, did Mr. Barletta accept the campaign contribution knowing it was coming from an illegitimate source, the Ochoas?" Rubino asked.

"Right," Castillo responded. "He told him that this was a contribution being made by the Ochoa family and Escobar from Colombia for his political campaign; that later on they would be talking about some investments that were going to be made in Panama."

"Now, did he make this statement quietly over in a corner, or was it said publicly?"

"It was in public."

"And Mr. Tribaldos and all the others in the room were present when the statement was made?"

"That is correct."

Rubino turned momentarily toward the jury and then moved on to Melo's alleged telephone conversation with Noriega, the one in front of an angry Jorge Ochoa. Melo's demeanor seemed aimed at making sure Ochoa was aware of who was on the other end of the line, Castillo said in response to Rubino's questioning. It was as though Melo was overemphasizing the conversation, Castillo testified.

"Is it a fair statement to say that Melo is in trouble with this group?" prompted Rubino.

"That's right," Castillo responded.

"And Melo is kind of trying to get himself out of the problem he is in, right?"

"I imagine so," said Castillo.

Rubino asked Castillo about a party hosted by members of the cartel which he said he attended in February 1984. The party, Castillo had testified on direct examination, was to celebrate the murder of Lara Bonilla, the Colombian justice minister.

Was Castillo absolutely sure the party had taken place in February? Rubino asked.

"Yes," Castillo responded.

Bonilla was murdered the following April 30.

CHAPTER 27

Doing Business with the General

Enrique "Kiki" Pretelt had just walked in the door after a weekend away at the beach when he got a call from his best friend, Manuel Noriega. It was Sunday, June 14, 1980, Father's Day in Panama. It had been a restful, enjoyable weekend for the Pretelt and Noriega families. They had gone away together to Rio Hato, a beach resort not a long flight from Panama City.

But now Noriega was frantic. News had just been received from El Salvador that a Panamanian Aerocommander had crash-landed outside of San Miguel in eastern El Salvador. The plane, whose real owners were Noriega and Pretelt, was loaded with rifles. The pilot, who somehow escaped, had already been identified in news reports as César Rodríguez, one of Noriega's and Pretelt's closest friends.

"You must find out what is going on," Noriega told Pretelt. Rodríguez must be found and instructed to disavow any relationship to the Panamanian military or himself, Noriega told Pretelt. "I really want this thing taken care of."

Pretelt found Rodríguez in a hospital in the Panamanian town of David. Floyd Carlton had rescued him and delivered him back to Panama. "Well, César," Pretelt told Rodríguez, "you know how the business is. You have to take all the responsibility in this accident."

Rodríguez agreed, but before Pretelt left, the injured arms smuggler explained that Noriega knew about the flight and that arms were being smuggled to the Salvadoran guerrillas. In fact, Rodríguez told Pretelt, Noriega was his partner.

The event helped bind Rodríguez, Pretelt, and Noriega together.

Over the next five years the three men's lives became inextricably intertwined. Rodríguez continued to smuggle arms and then drugs and later money. Pretelt, now an intimate of Noriega's, joined with Rodríguez to start an air taxi company. In August 1983, Noriega rose from the rank of colonel to general and became the commander in chief of the Panamanian military. All the while, there were business deals for the triumvirate.

On Thursday, October 31, 1991, more than a decade after Rodríguez's accident, Pretelt, wearing blue jeans and a black flight jacket, was sitting in the witness box looking across the courtroom at his old best friend.

Under direct examination by Pat Sullivan, Pretelt would draw Noriega even closer to the Medellín cartel. Noriega had not just allowed Panama to be used in the cartel's cocaine trade, Pretelt would say, he also permitted cartel marijuana smugglers and money launderers free use of Panama.

Pretelt knew something about marijuana smuggling. He had already pled guilty to the 1988 Tampa indictment that named him and Noriega as chief coconspirators. But before Sullivan asked, "Mr. Pretelt, what is the crime that you pled guilty to in Tampa?", he requested a sidebar.

Sullivan outlined to Judge Hoeveler and Frank Rubino what Pretelt was about to say. "General Noriega and Mr. Pretelt were charged together in the indictment in the Middle District of Florida, and it charges basically a conspiracy by this person 'Frank Brown,' who is an American . . . using Frank Brown as an alias. His real name is Steve Kalish, and he comes to Panama in September '83 and makes the acquaintance of this witness and César Rodríguez and, first, just to check out Panama, he brings huge amounts of money to deposit into the banks of Panama. He makes the acquaintance of the general. There will be testimony he makes a payment to the general to gain his goodwill. That's in September. He builds up a friendship and a relationship with those people, Pretelt and the general. Then in December, Frank Brown, also known as Steve Kalish, or the other way around, begins his plan to import a half million pounds of marijuana out of Colombia through Panama to the United States. He broaches that to Pretelt, Rodríguez, and the general; they come aboard. Further payments are made. Brown–Kalish gets involved, as does Mr. Pretelt, in the event that we have heard about from the last several witnesses: the house arrest there at César Rodríguez's house with the G-2, the plot by Melo to kill the general, and all those events that then flow from that. Brown and Pretelt get very intertwined in that and have numerous conversations, discussions with the coconspirators and the general, all about that, and that's because they are already involved and intertwined with the general in the marijuana conspiracy."

The testimony the jury was about to hear would fall under a federal rule of evidence, 404(b).

"Ladies and gentlemen," the judge said to the jury, "I want to give you an instruction relating to some testimony that is going to be offered by the government. You will hear evidence tending to show at some time other than the times stated in the indictment, although closely related to the times stated in the indictment, the defendant committed acts similar to the acts charged in the indictment in this case. Now, you may consider such evidence not to prove that the defendant did the acts charged in this case but only to prove the defendant's state of mind, that is, that the defendant acted with the necessary intent and not through accident or mistake. The crimes charged in this case require intent, criminal intent, before the defendant can be convicted. The government must prove beyond a reasonable doubt that the defendant willfully and knowingly intentionally committed the crimes that he's charged with in this case." The testimony was secondary to the case at hand, but it could bolster the notion that Noriega had "criminal intent."

★   ★   ★

In September 1983, Pretelt began, César Rodríguez was approached by "a gringo," Steve Kalish, who wanted "to try to establish some kind of a base in Panama," a base to smuggle marijuana and to launder drug profits. Kalish told Rodríguez and Pretelt that he wanted to launder between $50 million and $80 million over a six-month period. To conduct his business, the gringo, who called himself Frank Brown, would pay a gift to Rodríguez, Pretelt, and Noriega, their "silent partner."

In late September, Rodríguez and Pretelt took Brown to see Noriega. Brown brought a briefcase. "I didn't count it," Pretelt said, "but I saw it was filled with large bills. They were hundred-dollar bills." As they sat in Noriega's home office, Rodríguez and Pretelt told Noriega what Brown wanted to do. Brown seemed stunned, Pretelt observed.

"I told Brown our silent partner was General Noriega, and I think that he couldn't believe it."

Noriega asked Brown how much money he planned to bring to Panama. Brown could only say "large amounts." Pretelt observed, "I think he didn't want to commit in front of Noriega how much."

"Did Noriega respond?" Sullivan asked Pretelt.

"Noriega says that anything he will need in Panama, just let him know through César or through myself."

When Brown got up to leave, he left behind his briefcase. It contained a gift for Noriega, Pretelt said Brown told Noriega. Inside was $300,000.

Later, Pretelt and Noriega talked about Brown. They agreed they had "a big fish," Pretelt said. "A big man with big money. . . . The general told me that he thought that this gringo was going to be a good one," testified Pretelt.

"Did you say anything about what you thought about Frank Brown? What he was?" asked Sullivan.

"Yes," continued Pretelt. "I told him that I thought this was money from drugs because nobody could handle such amounts of money in cash."

"It is okay," Noriega responded, Pretelt said.

At first Brown agreed to pay a 5 percent charge on the cash he was allowed to launder in Panama. Later Rodríguez and Pretelt decided to make him a part of Servicios Turisticos, their joint venture with Noriega. Brown, said Pretelt, paid $400,000 in cash to work with the front company.

In December 1983, Rodríguez and Brown went to Pretelt with a proposal. Rodriguez and Pretelt's air taxi service, called VIP, should go into the marijuana-smuggling business. The marijuana would come from the cartel in Colombia and land in Panama, where VIP would "redo" the shipping papers. Then the shipments would proceed to the United States as though they had originated in Panama. The threesome waited until after Christmas season to take the idea to Noriega.

"We explained to Noriega that this was going to be a transshipment, that the marijuana was coming from the north part of Colombia to Colón and from Colón we'll be redoing new papers and that the cargo appearing in the manifest will be plantains from Colón to the United States, and that we don't see much risk on that. Noriega said that he thinks that this could work." The load of plantains would contain 400,000 pounds of marijuana. Brown agreed to pay $750,000 to his partners to let the scheme proceed.

But in mid-April 1984, Rodríguez informed Pretelt that they were being cut out of the deal. Noriega insisted he would work with Brown alone and use no intermediaries.

"César, I think that this is a message that Noriega is sending," Pretelt remembered telling Rodríguez. "He doesn't want us around.

"So that's how I withdrew from the conspiracy," said Pretelt, looking at the jury. From then, he said, the best he could do was remain Noriega's friend.

The following Monday, November 4, Pretelt took the witness stand again.

In July 1984, Pretelt told the jury, he went to New York to meet Noriega, who was returning from Europe. Together they flew on to Cuba. Noriega had just received word that Melo was being accused of taking a bribe to protect the Darien lab. "Noriega was very preoccupied about the situation in Panama," Pretelt testified.

In Havana, Noriega met privately with Castro. Afterward, Pretelt said, Noriega's mood changed. "He was more settled down, he was more relaxed, and he mentioned to me that now they will have to put all the blame regarding the raid on the lab on Melo. That Melo will be the scapegoat in this affair."

When Noriega arrived in Panama, there was more good news, said Pretelt. At the airport, after a press conference, Noriega met with Rodríguez, Brown, and Pretelt. In Noriega's absence, Brown and to a lesser degree Rodríguez and Pretelt had coordinated the return to Colombia of the lab workers, two helicopters seized at the Darien lab, and $1 million of the cartel's money. Jorge Ochoa was exceedingly pleased. Through Brown, Pretelt said, the cartel believed it had "formed a new connection with Panama." That connection would take care of all the cartel's money-laundering and drug-trafficking needs in Panama. Noriega pledged to Brown that he would be his friend and protect him. "That he will be his godfather," said Pretelt.

A year later, Pretelt continued, things were not so good. In late 1984, Brown was arrested in Tampa and charged with marijuana smuggling. The plantain-marijuana–smuggling scheme never materialized. And in May 1985, Noriega and Rodríguez had a falling out.

Noriega telephoned Pretelt at home and told him he had just received a letter from Rodríguez intimating that he might go public with what he knew about Noriega. "He mentioned about the trafficking of arms in Central America. He mentioned the money laundering, and he mentioned the drug trafficking. That Noriega was aware of all of that," said Pretelt, characterizing his conversation with Noriega. Noriega instructed Pretelt to speak to Rodríguez. Pretelt did.

Rodríguez said he was angry that Noriega was refusing to take his phone calls and that the Panamanian Defense Forces refused to pay $700,000 owed him on the sale of airplane equipment. Unless he was paid, Rodríguez told Pretelt, he would send a copy of his letter to the newspapers.

Pretelt looked at Noriega and then at the jury. Rodríguez received his money within twenty-four hours, he said.

Shortly thereafter, Pretelt said, Noriega sent him to buy Rodríguez out of their joint venture. Within weeks, Pretelt continued, Noriega cut him out of the venture as well.

For the prosecution, Pretelt's testimony was one of the "building blocks" that helped explain Noriega's relationship to the cartel. But Frank Rubino saw Pretelt's testimony as more insinuation. Brown's briefcase full of cash, in Rubino's view, could simply be seen as a "gratuity," part of doing business in Central America. At worst it might be considered a bribe. In any event, it did not rise to the level of a crime against the United States. In fact, said Rubino privately, it was not unusual for some people in the United States to trade on the name of a higher-up in government. It happened all the time in the Reagan-Bush administrations. Politics, patronage, and expediency were not exclusive to Noriega and Panama. It was no crime in the early 1980s for Frank Brown or anyone else to go to Panama and deposit large amounts of cash. Panama was known as a major banking center in South America. Pretelt conceded on cross-examination that large cash deposits were accepted in Panama long before Noriega became the country's leader.

"You and César now go to General Noriega and propose a drug deal to him with a man who is virtually a total stranger to General Noriega. Had you ever done a drug deal with General Noriega?" Rubino asked.

"No," Pretelt said.

As for Brown's scheme to disguise the 400,000-pound marijuana shipment in a load of plantains, Rubino asked, "No ship ever sailed, did it?"

"No," Pretelt said.

"And no marijuana ever came to Panama?"

"No."

"And no marijuana ever was transshipped to the United States, was it?"

"No."

And as for the cartel's payoffs to protect the Darien cocaine lab and the cartel's ether shipments, Pretelt conceded that Noriega had refused to take what Pretelt described as a $1 million offer to protect the chemicals, and Pretelt could not say if Noriega had ever received a part of the cartel's $5 million.

"Do you personally know if Melo ever paid Noriega?" asked Rubino.

"No, I never—This was Melo and Noriega's business. I got nothing to do with that."

"Do you know if Melo lied to the Colombians and said he had General Noriega's permission?"

"Not really. I have no knowledge of that."

"Do you have any personal knowledge, whatsoever—personal knowledge—that General Noriega was involved in that lab incident?"

"No," answered Pretelt.

Then Rubino asked Pretelt to look at the letter Rodríguez had written to Noriega. "Are you positive the letter mentions arms trafficking and drug trafficking?" Rubino asked.

Pretelt read the letter and then looked up. "No," he said.

"Doesn't this letter really expose you?" Rubino asked.

Pretelt fidgeted. No, he didn't think so, he said, looking past the jury to the prosecution table.

"Sir, you made a statement the other day. Do you remember this statement: 'It is better to be the minister's friend than the minister'?"

"Yes."

"In your case, it was better to be the general's friend than the general, correct?"

"Yes."

"Because you could trade upon his good name, correct?"

"Well, I won't put it that way."

On redirect, Sullivan asked Pretelt to recollect one of Noriega's three early meetings with Brown.

"Frank Brown, at this point, made the connections with the Colombians, the people from the cartel," Pretelt said. "And from now on, he was going to be the man in Panama for the people in the cartel. And he will be taking care of all the money through Panama and drugs going through Panama. This is what Brown explained to Noriega during this conversation."

"Did Brown say that he was going to be involved in a legal or an illegal business?" asked Sullivan.

"Well, we never mention the word legal or illegal, but it was understood that it was an illegal business," said Pretelt.

On Tuesday, November 5, thirty-eight-year-old Frank Brown, whose real name was Steven Kalish, took the witness stand. Kalish was born and raised in Houston, and by the time he was halfway through high school, he had determined he could make his fortune selling marijuana.

His business flourished. By the age of twenty-eight, Kalish had imported more than 500,000 pounds of marijuana into the United States and cleared a personal profit of $20 million. Though the law had been after him since 1980, Kalish was not arrested until July 1984. During his last year and a half of freedom, he came to know Manuel Noriega.

It all began in early 1983, Kalish explained during Pat Sullivan's direct examination. His marijuana business was so lucrative that he and his partners were grossing as much as $75 million a year. Unfortunately, the proceeds came in in small-denomination bills. Soon the Cayman Island bank where

Kalish laundered the money said it could no longer handle the bulk; it would accept nothing smaller than $50 bills. Kalish set out to find a new banker.

In September 1983 a friend took Kalish to Panama, where he met César Rodríguez. Kalish explained that he anticipated banking as much as $100 million in the near future. He had brought $2.5 million in cash to open an account.

Rodríguez lit up. For a 5 percent commission, Rodríguez explained, Kalish could enjoy the secrecy of Panama's banking system and the protection of the Panamanian government. To Kalish's surprise, "Rodríguez informed me that the leader of Panama was a man named General Noriega," said Kalish. "He was not the president but the head of the military, and they, in fact, retained all the power in Panama, and if I wanted anything done or we wanted to attempt to do anything, we had to have clearance from General Noriega. He informed me that General Noriega, himself, and Enrique Pretelt were partners."

That afternoon, Kalish continued, Rodríguez and Enrique Pretelt accompanied him to Noriega's house. Kalish told Noriega of his plans. "He seems very pleased over it" was Kalish's recollection of Noriega's reaction. "He seems happy to meet me, wishes me the best." Kalish told the jury that he had brought a briefcase with $300,000 in it. When he got up to leave, he left it behind. "As I was leaving, he hollered at me and noted that I had left my briefcase, and I signaled to him that the briefcase was, in fact, for him." And later on that evening he thanked Kalish for the gift.

Kalish said he was nearly beside himself. "I was quite impressed with what I had seen in Panama. It was obvious to me that there were no limits to what we could do in Panama; that with the right—having all the right connections, which it appeared to me that we had, Panama would provide us with just a number of important contributions to our operations, which it did." Kalish said his access to Noriega grew after he bought a one-quarter interest in Pretelt, Rodríguez, and Noriega's business for $400,000. Soon he and Noriega discussed using a Defense Forces Boeing 727 to transport drug proceeds from Washington to Panama, and by the end of 1983 they were discussing the shipment of 400,000 pounds of marijuana from Panama to New York; the load would be buried in containers of plantains. For Noriega's assistance in clearing the shipment's paperwork, Kalish said he paid Noriega, whom he called "Tony," $250,000.

As Kalish was finding Panama to be the perfect center for his business, he continued to develop his contacts with the Medellín cartel, his main supplier of marijuana. After the Darien lab was raided in April 1984, Kalish said, the cartel's representative, Guillermo Angel, came to him and explained that the cartel had set up the lab with the understanding that it was sanctioned by General Noriega. "They were very upset over the fact that they had lost millions of dollars, not including the bribe money that they paid to officials in Panama. He asked what my thoughts were on the subject. He explained that they had paid close to $5 million in bribes to secure a safe manufacturing

facility, and he explained that those monies had been paid to Colonel Melo
with the understanding that they would subsequently be paid to General
Noriega." Kalish said he told Angel that if Noriega had been paid, the lab
would not have been seized.

A smile crept across Frank Rubino's face. This was, after all, the government's own witness.

"I said that if—I stated that if General Noriega had actually been paid the
bribe monies for the lab, then I couldn't understand why they had been
seized, why the lab had been seized, and the Colombians deported," Kalish
continued. "He asked if I could check with my sources, General Noriega, and
anybody else, and get to the bottom of the situation." Then Angel told Kalish
that Julian Melo had suggested Noriega be murdered.

"I was shocked," said Kalish. "I was afraid they would kill the general."
That, Kalish said, would mean the "loss of my protection, loss of everything
I've vested in Panama. I'd been cultivating his favor for several months."

Together with Rodríguez and Pretelt, Kalish said, he arranged the return
of the cartel's bribe money, its workers, and some of its equipment. The cartel was so pleased and so impressed with his seeming clout with Noriega,
Kalish said, that its leaders asked him to be their main money launderer in
Panama.

Kalish went to Noriega and proposed that they work together to service
the cartel's banking needs. "I [told the general that it] was Jorge Ochoa and
others from Medellín, Colombia," Kalish told the jury.

"And what was your relationship going to be with that Ochoa organization?" Sullivan asked.

"I was going to be their connection in Panama to assist in the laundering
of their revenues from their cocaine sales in the United States."

"Did you tell that to Noriega?"

"Yes, sir, I did."

"What did he say to that?"

"He was satisfied with the arrangements."

But before the new business could begin, Kalish continued, he was arrested in Tampa and jailed. Kalish explained that he had pled guilty and traded
his testimony for a reduction in his sentence of life plus 285 years in prison.
His cooperation had led to Noriega's indictment in Tampa and a reduction in
his sentence to nine and one-half years. Kalish said he expected to be free by
June 1993.

Sullivan turned next to one of the few pieces of hard evidence that
the prosecution had gained since the invasion of Panama: a letter written
by Kalish to Noriega in September 1984 from a Texas cell block following
his arrest. It had been found in Felicidad Noriega's safe deposit box in
Paris.

The fourteen-page letter indicated that Noriega knew little or nothing
about the work of the cartel in Panama, and it indicated that Noriega knew

nothing of the $5 million bribe paid to Lt. Col. Julian Melo for the protection of the Darien lab.

Given the contradictory testimony he had just completed, Sullivan asked Kalish what the letter meant. Kalish said he had an ulterior motive for sending the letter:

"I wanted to assure the general that I was not cooperating with the United States authorities. I wanted to provide him with some sort of letter which would prove to him that I was not cooperating with the authorities or providing them with any sort of information." Though the letter was contrived and in part a lie, Kalish again said he continued to believe Noriega knew nothing about the $5 million bribe to protect the Darien lab.

 Referring to the letter, a copy of which Sullivan asked Kalish to read aloud, Kalish said, "I insisted that General Noriega had not been party to the manufacturing operation in the Darien province. This was my belief. This is what I was led to believe from my conversations. Colonel Melo was acting alone."

"What made you believe Colonel Melo was acting alone?" asked Sullivan.

"The fact that the lab had been seized. The fact that General Noriega had asked me if I knew the people associated with the lab. Also, my belief that it was a foolish operation to begin with."

"What do you mean by that?"

"It was unnecessary," said Kalish. "There were numerous other labs operating around the world. Why jeopardize Panama? Panama offered us a number of services. A safe haven for one. Our main banking facilities."

Frank Rubino's cross-examination had become nearly standard. Kalish was one more convicted drug smuggler who was trading his testimony for a reduced sentence. Worse yet, Kalish was going to offer testimony that clearly fell under Rule 404B of the Rules of Criminal Procedure. It was testimony pertaining to the facts of the Tampa—not Miami—indictment, testimony that could not be used to determine guilt in this case. Rather, it was being offered to provide context. Still, the way Rubino saw it, it was like having Lady Godiva ride into the courtroom and then telling the jury, "Disregard what you just saw."

Rubino knew what to expect. He had known Steven Kalish for almost ten years. Rubino had once represented Kalish's business cronies on drug charges. "Preppie doper," Rubino said privately. "He's well groomed, articulate, a tough witness even if he won't offer much about the allegations in this indictment."

Rubino asked about the millions in assets that Kalish acquired as a smuggler. On direct examination Kalish testified he had paid $500,000 to the IRS in unpaid taxes and that he had forfeited the proceeds from the sale of his $250,000 home in Tampa. But that left unspecified millions unaccounted for.

"The government allowed you to keep this drug money, didn't they?" asked Rubino.

"Yes, pursuant to my plea agreement in Tampa," Kalish responded. But he had made sacrifices, Kalish protested.

"You had to give up your forty-five-foot yacht, did you not?" Rubino asked.

"Yes, sir. That's correct."

"And you already told us about some gold. Gold watches? Sort of gold jewelry?" continued Rubino.

"Yes, sir," responded Kalish.

"I guess the hardest thing to give up was the red Ferrari, right?" continued Rubino.

"It was one of my more cherished possessions. That's correct."

"And you had to give up a Porsche, a Jeep Wagoneer, assorted artwork, and some home furnishings, correct?"

"That's correct."

Rubino turned, as he had before, to Panamanian law. It was not a crime in 1983, he reasserted, to enter Panama with large amounts of cash or to deposit that cash in Panamanian banks.

"That's correct," answered Kalish.

"Now, the country of Panama, at least at that time in 1983–84, was an independent sovereign nation," continued Rubino with a hint of sarcasm. "Was it not?"

"Yes, sir."

"It was in no way, shape, or form a colony or a protectorate of the United States, was it?"

"No, sir."

"And the United States government in no way wrote the laws of the country of Panama, did they?"

"No. They did not."

In all of Kalish's conversations with Noriega, had the word "smuggle" ever come up? Rubino continued.

"Did I use the word 'smuggling'? I don't know. Was there any question in my mind as to whether Noriega knew I was smuggling drugs? Absolutely not."

"Well," said Rubino, standing at the lectern and pointing his ballpoint pen first at Kalish and then toward Noriega, "we speak now of what was in the mind of the speaker. Let's talk about the mind of the hearer. Now, if you said that you intended on bringing $100 million to Panama from your ventures, for all he knew, you could have been anything from the owner of Exxon Oil to an Arab sheik to who knows what. Contrary to your most popular belief, other people besides drug smugglers make lots of money," said Rubino.

"Well, that's not my belief, Mr. Rubino," Kalish responded. "And Mr. Noriega certainly knew it wasn't from bingo proceeds or something of that nature."

In fact, none of the smuggling or money-laundering ventures that he testified about had ever occurred, Rubino pressed Kalish: not the money smuggling aboard the PDF's jet, not the 400,000-pound marijuana load to New York.

That was correct, responded Kalish.

And if they had, didn't it strain credibility that to go forward one would have to bribe the leader of a country?

Rubino asked about Kalish's testimony that an American Customs inspector had been bribed to allow the aborted 400,000-pound load into New York.

"Did you have to bribe the leader of the country to get a load of drugs into his country?" asked Rubino.

"No, you did not," answered Kalish.

"Do you know how high these bribes would have to reach in order to get a satisfactory result?" Rubino pressed.

"It depended on what particular operation you were involved in," said Kalish. "I mean—"

Rubino cut Kalish off, "Let me ask you this—"

"No," continued Kalish, anticipating Rubino's question. "It didn't go to the president of the United States."

"Exactly," said Rubino.

Essentially, said Rubino, Kalish was claiming that he had bribed Noriega to do "exactly nothing."

"I wouldn't say he was doing nothing," said Kalish.

On redirect, Sullivan allowed Kalish to expand where Rubino had cut him off. Noriega's assurances of protection—even if he never had to act on Kalish's behalf—were of value, were they not? asked Sullivan.

Yes, responded Kalish. Knowing that his assets were safe and that his bank accounts could not be examined by U.S. law enforcement was of tremendous reassurance, said Kalish.

Kalish said that in November 1983, when Noriega returned from a visit to Washington, D.C., he spoke to him on the tarmac at the Panama City airport.

"He said that the United States wants him to fight the communists in Nicaragua and open his banks to United States scrutiny," remembered Kalish. "He said he's going to fight the communists, but he'll never open the banks."

On recross-examination, Rubino pursued the opening. The government's own witness had opened up the area of Noriega's discussions with the U.S. government about fighting communists in Nicaragua.

"Do you know who asked General Noriega to fight the communists in Nicaragua?" Rubino asked.

"I know who was represented to have asked, and that was supposedly the president of the United States, Reagan," said Kalish.

Rubino moved to broaden Kalish's testimony.

"In fact, General Noriega did assist in fighting the communists in Nicaragua by supplying aid to the Contras, right?"

"Objection, objection," said Sullivan. The redirect was aimed at learning about Kalish's understanding of bank secrecy in Panama, not about the U.S. government's instructions to Noriega regarding the communists in Nicaragua. Rubino's question was not relevant, Sullivan protested after Hoeveler had called the attorneys to sidebar.

"But the other came along with it," Rubino said.

"They suggested that Noriega was standing up to the United States and saying he wasn't going to open up the banks," Jon May added, taking up Rubino's point. But in fact, May said, Noriega assisted the United States in its investigations into the banking system, and he assisted the Contras. In the end, May said, Noriega went along with the United States on both counts. Noriega's assistance was highly relevant, May argued.

The purpose of the recross, repeated Hoeveler, was the bank records. It was still not the moment to talk politics. "'A' for effort," said Hoeveler, turning to Rubino and May, "but I must sustain the objection."

On April 30, 1984, Jorge Ochoa and his brothers, Fabio and Juan David, their two sisters, and a business associate, Gustavo Gaviria, were leaving the bullring in Medellín. Within seconds the Ochoas' bodyguards emerged and with weapons barely hidden hustled the cartel's leaders to their waiting Mercedes.

Around the stadium's parking lot, car radios were blaring the news that in Bogotá, 175 miles away, Rodrigo Lara Bonilla, the Colombian justice minister, had just been machine-gunned to death.

The cartel's top leaders were sped to their business offices on the outskirts of Medellín. Jorge Ochoa ordered the leaders and top lieutenants of all of Colombia's top drug-trafficking families into immediate executive session. "It is better for us to see the bulls from outside the ring than to be inside the ring with the bulls," Ochoa told the gathering that evening.

The next day, as the Colombian National Police mobilized to hunt down Bonilla's killers and the men who had hired them, the cartel began a full-scale airlift to Panama. Every significant cocaine and marijuana trafficker in Colombia, as well as their wives and children and even their babysitters, were flown immediately to Panama. In less than a day the cartel had reestablished itself in Panama.

As the weeks passed and the Colombian police seized the homes and property of cartel members, on Balboa Avenue in Panama City, just two blocks from the United States Embassy, Ochoa and the cartel's top executives took their morning jog each day at about seven. In the heart of Panama, the cartel bodyguards were nowhere to be seen.

So testified César Cura, a rancher neighbor of the Ochoas who had become a cocaine trafficker and then fled with the cartel to Panama. Jorge Ochoa, Cura told the Miami jury on Tuesday, November 12, assured the cartel that "General Noriega had been paid [to protect] the safety of the Colombians." The price was $4.6 million, Ochoa said.

"It's the core doctrine or theory as to the safe haven and using Panama for the business of the Medellín cartel," Myles Malman told the court. "General

Noriega provided them a safe haven to be able to come to Panama to avoid and escape the wrath of the authorities in Colombia." Pointing to Cura, Malman said, "This witness was there."

Cura said he first learned that there was nothing to fear in Panama when Ochoa began sending him there to pick up boxes of the cartel's laundered cash. "Go on. Go on. Go pick up the boxes," Ochoa would tell Cura. "Everything is paid for. There won't be any problems." Cura said he was told the G-2 had been bought off. When he had any problems in Panama, Cura said, he would call César Rodríguez.

In early May 1984, Cura said, Noriega realized he had been bribed for perhaps more than he could handle. As the cartel took up residence in the Panama City Marriott and Holiday Inn hotels, coincidentally so, too, did dozens of top international diplomats, including former U.S. President Jimmy Carter. The Panamanian presidential elections were just a week away, and representatives from the United Nations and the Organization of American States were arriving to monitor the vote.

"El Tigre was very worried in reference to the amount of Colombians who were there in Panama," Cura said Gustavo Gaviria told him. Noriega, Gaviria told Cura, "was very worried because the United States government by that time had . . . its eyes upon him because all those narcotics traffickers were there in Panama."

Noriega was so worried, said Cura, that he called a special meeting of the leaders of the cartel and former Colombian president Alfonso López Michelsen. Perhaps Michelsen, Noriega thought, could negotiate a truce between the cartel and the Colombian government. A secret meeting was called at the Marriott Hotel, but any hope of a truce was dashed when word leaked to the press that negotiations were under way.

But Noriega's troubles with the cartel were only beginning, Cura said. Less than three weeks later, on May 21, the Darien lab was raided. The cartel's leaders were enraged. Though Noriega had left for France and Israel, the cartel leadership decided to have him assassinated.

"I overheard them when they made the decision to have him killed in Europe," Cura said. A contract was made with a Basque separatist group in Europe to murder Noriega, he continued. The assassin would be Ilyich Ramirez Sanchez, the Venezuela-born, Moscow-university-educated terrorist known also as Carlos the Jackal. The Jackal, it was said, had been responsible for the 1975 attack in Vienna on OPEC oil ministers. The attack had left three people dead and put Carlos on Interpol's most wanted list.

"They were furious with the general because they considered him to be two-faced because they were saying that the general was with the United States, that is, that he was with the authorities of the United States and at the same time he was with [the cartel]."

Ochoa, said Cura, held Noriega in contempt. He quoted Ochoa as saying, "Look at him. He goes and embraces President Reagan, and then he turns around and he is embracing Castro."

For Cura, the cartel's murder plans were disturbing. With Steve Kalish, César Rodríguez, and Noriega, Cura said, he had just assembled a huge marijuana shipment destined for the United States. Cura said he had personally invested $1.5 million in the load, and if Noriega were murdered, protection for the load through Panama would evaporate. Kalish was just as upset, said Cura. He had $2 million invested in the load.

Cura said he and Kalish went to Rodríguez, who, in turn, contacted Noriega's officers. The result was the meeting at which Noriega's top men guaranteed the cartel's representative that its bribe money, equipment, and workers would be returned.

Cura's testimony was dramatic but also problematic. Cura had contradicted two of the government's previous witnesses, Ricardo Tribaldos and Steven Kalish. Both had testified that Julian Melo, not the cartel, suggested Noriega's murder. Both insisted the cartel never took the idea seriously. And Cura also failed to mention the alleged role of Fidel Castro in mediating a settlement between the cartel and Noriega.

The fundamental problem with Cura's testimony, as Frank Rubino saw it, was that Cura was never actually present at any of the cartel leadership's discussions. Instead, he learned all that he knew from Jorge Ochoa and Gustavo Gaviria. That's where Rubino centered his attack on cross-examination.

"Now, Mr. Ochoa told you—Jorge Ochoa told you—that General Noriega had been paid. Is that not your statement?" asked Rubino.

"Yes, sir," replied Cura.

"Did Jorge Ochoa tell you that he personally paid General Noriega?"

"No, sir. I haven't said that. I haven't said that he personally paid General Noriega."

"Did Jorge Ochoa tell you who supposedly paid General Noriega?"

"He told me that they had paid the representative for Mr. Noriega who had been Colonel Melo."

"Do you know if Colonel Melo paid General Noriega?"

"No, sir. That would be very difficult for me to know, whether he paid him or not."

"All of the meetings that you've testified about involving General Noriega, you did not attend, did you?"

"You're right. I did not attend any of them."

"So essentially you're telling us what you claim somebody else told you, right?"

"Yes, sir."

"All of the meetings that you've testified about, essentially, you're repeating to us gossip, rumor, and hearsay, correct?"

The question, the prosecution protested, was argumentative.

Cura, Rubino responded, offered absolutely no personal knowledge whatsoever.

Rubino turned to Cura's seeming concern that Noriega not be assassinated.

"When I heard it, I immediately became very concerned," Cura testified.

"Were you concerned that a human being was going to be killed, or were you just concerned about it ruining your profits?" asked Rubino.

"That my profits would be ruined," answered Cura.

Rubino was successful in his cross-examination; he compromised a witness's credibility yet again. But it seemed more a tactical victory than a substantive one.

A Colombian housekeeper working in Miami passed along the tip in 1984: A Panamanian plane would be arriving at Miami International Airport with one thousand pounds of cocaine aboard.

Milo Grassman had spent more than twenty years with the Drug Enforcement Administration. Now he was working for the vice president's Joint Task Force, a special group formed of Customs and DEA agents. Grassman was assigned to the cargo group handling interdiction at the airport.

On June 15 two cargo liners arrived at Miami International from Panama. Grassman went first to the Inair cargo warehouse at the far end of the airport. The tip said the cocaine would be secreted in refrigerated equipment.

The Inair DC-8 had arrived at four o'clock in the afternoon. When Grassman and his partner Frank Easton got to Inair, it was already seven in the evening. The plane's load was in the warehouse; huge cargo pallets were covered with plastic and netting. The cargo manifest said perfume and automotive parts, but some of the boxes were marked SANYO FREEZERS.

To avoid burning the informant, Grassman decided to make his search look like a routine cargo inspection. He called in a Customs' dog handler. Dogs were used every day on a random basis at the airport. Within seconds the narcotics-sniffing dog went for the freezers. Inside were small, square, football-like plastic packages, most hand-marked with a Star of David. It was no surprise when the contents was discovered to be cocaine.

From Miami, Grassman's investigation worked backward to Panama.

The top narcotics investigator for the Panamanian Defense Forces, Lucinio Miranda, offered the PDF's full cooperation, and with its help a Colombian national living in Panama, Oscar Cardona Donato, was arrested. A month after the cocaine seizure at Miami International, Miranda himself flew with Cardona to Miami and handed him over to Grassman, claiming he acted alone.

In July, Grassman flew to Panama. The PDF had shut down Inair and pulled the company's flight charter. Grassman was still trying to determine if Inair's owners had anything to do with the load. Walking through the lobby of the Marriott Hotel, Grassman bumped into Inair's Miami warehouse manager. With him was Ricardo Bilonick, the owner of Inair, who was emphatic that the Miami seizure had closed down Inair and put sixty people out of work. He would do anything he could to clear up the problem and get Inair flying again.

"They were very interested in getting the whole situation resolved so that they could get on with their business," Grassman recollected.

Ricardo Bilonick was raised in Panama but was educated at the University of Scranton in Pennsylvania. He received his law degree from Tulane University in New Orleans. As a lawyer with one of Panama City's most important firms, he quickly distinguished himself and was called on by Gen. Omar Torrijos during the 1970s to serve as Panama's "ambassador at large" in Washington. During the Panama Canal Treaty negotiations in 1977, Bilonick was an important link between Panama and U.S. congressmen and senators. At home, Bilonick had become a force in Panama's small commercial aviation industry; he owned a majority interest in the country's top commuter airline.

All that had changed by the time Ricardo Bilonick was called to the witness stand on Thursday, November 14.

"Are you charged with using Inair airlines to fly in excess of one thousand pounds of cocaine to Miami International Airport from the Republic of Panama on or about June 15, 1984?" Myles Malman asked, standing before Bilonick.

Bilonick, forty-four, was dressed in a dark business suit and tie. He wore glasses and was chronically overweight.

"Yes, sir," he responded.

"Is there anyone here in this courtroom today with whom you did that?" Malman continued.

"Yes, sir. I did it with General Manuel Antonio Noriega, sitting right there at the table."

If what Bilonick said was true, the conspiracy alleged in the 1988 indictment and the testimony of all the government witnesses had just been brought full circle. The small, football-sized cocaine packages found in Inair's Miami warehouse bore the same Star of David marking that were found on similar packages seized at the cartel's Tranquilandia laboratory. That meant the ether and acetone that were shipped south through Panama's free trade zone to Tranquilandia and to the Darien lab were used to produce the very cocaine that was shipped north again through Panama and via Inair to the United States. If the government's witnesses were telling the truth, Noriega protected the cartel's raw materials and finished product as well as its delivery to customers in America. That Noriega was directly involved in the shipments of cocaine to the United States was central to the indictment.

For Bilonick, the slide into drug trafficking was a matter of greed. Bilonick said he was aware that smugglers operated almost freely in Panama. But the idea repulsed him. He said he remembered speaking to Noriega shortly after César Rodríguez had crashed in El Salvador.

"Why do you keep these people around?" he asked Noriega, who responded that "he needed some people to do the dirty work."

Bilonick came to understand the lure of smuggling in 1981 while on a business trip to Colombia. There, he said, a fellow diplomat introduced him to the Ochoa family.

On a visit to the Ochoas' ranch, Bilonick said, Jorge Ochoa made him a proposition he could not refuse: Ochoa would pay Bilonick 7 percent of every dollar he could smuggle out of the United States to Colombia. With a diplomatic passport and frequent trips between the United States and Panama, it would be an almost effortless way to make money. Ochoa was talking about smuggling as much as $60 million out of the United States each week. Bilonick agreed.

Bilonick said he introduced Noriega to the cartel in December 1981, shortly after the M-19 guerrillas kidnapped Marta Ochoa. Bilonick said he flew to Medellín and offered his services.

As a representative of the Ochoa family, Bilonick first went to the ex-president of Venezuela, Carlos Andrés Pérez, who said he understood the M-19 on a philosophical level, but if the goal was to negotiate Marta's release, practically speaking no one could be better suited than Noriega, who, after all, had everyday experience dealing with and meeting the needs of guerrilla groups.

Bilonick went to Noriega. "I explained to him what the situation was, that I was working with brothers, that the brothers were bringing a lot of money into Panama that was very beneficial to me. . . . I also told him that it was so important to him that I would offer to pay him some money if he would do something for me because it was helping me, actually, as well as the girl."

Noriega arranged a meeting. Bilonick paid him $125,000. On February 16, 1983, Bilonick said, he finally went to a park in a provincial capital of Colombia where Marta Ochoa was released by her captors.

Bilonick said that when he arrived back in Medellín with Marta, her father kneeled down in a puddle of water and embraced his knees. From then, Bilonick said, his relationship with Jorge Ochoa and his brothers changed from one of business to one of "brotherhood."

Noriega, Bilonick said, had only arranged the negotiations between the Ochoas and the M-19. He never attended. But later, Bilonick said, he was directed to deliver $1,256,000 to Noriega. The Ochoas and Noriega had agreed secretly that Noriega should be more fully rewarded for Marta's release, Bilonick said.

After Marta's release, Bilonick and Jorge Ochoa jointly purchased Inair airlines. Shortly after, Ochoa transferred his part-ownership to Pablo Escobar. On February 28, 1982, Escobar met with Bilonick and said the airline was sure to be profitable. "I want to work the airline because we have an agreement to work with Panama and to work with Noriega," Bilonick said Escobar told him. Inair would be used to transport cash and cocaine, Escobar told Bilonick. Ochoa and Escobar told Bilonick the deal had been cut with Noriega himself. "If you don't want to use the airline for that, I will do it without you," Bilonick remembered Escobar saying.

Others had testified that Noriega had approved and had been paid for the protection of precursor chemical shipments and the transport of drug proceeds. Now Bilonick was saying that Noriega was also paid to protect cocaine shipments.

Between December 1982 and June 1984, Bilonick said, nineteen DC-8 Inair flights hauled fifteen tons of cocaine to Miami. Most of the loads were stashed in shipments of domestic appliances. For each load, Bilonick told the Miami jury, Noriega was paid $500,000. In a year and a half Noriega earned almost $10 million.

"Now, what was the $500,000 for? What type of protection? What would it buy?" Malman asked.

"It would imply a secure landing strip, secure transit through the streets and roads and highways of Panama, and secure entry into the airport," Bilonick said. After a pause he added, "And silence."

Bilonick said Inair's success bred boldness on the part of the cartel. In late May 1984, shortly after the May 21 raid on the Darien lab, Bilonick told Escobar that he was against further loads going to Miami on Inair. But Escobar insisted that the PDF was not growing more vigilant. "Get it ready. Get it ready and we will ship it," Escobar told Bilonick. Escobar said he had Noriega's assurance of protection, and changed the subject. Could Inair fly cocaine to Nicaragua? That would mean a new transshipment route. Escobar told Bilonick that arrangements had already been made with Daniel Ortega, the leader of Nicaragua's Sandinista government. Escobar was introduced to Ortega by Noriega, Escobar told Bilonick.

Bilonick's testimony was not a surprise. Floyd Carlton had testified earlier that he once flew to Nicaragua with Escobar and several million dollars in cash.

But the Nicaraguan connection never materialized. Two weeks later, on June 15, Inair's cargo and jet were seized in Miami, and the Panamanian government permanently closed Inair. Malman was pleased with the direct examination. Bilonick had put together Inair and the birth of the cartel. Bilonick knew Noriega; he was a lawyer and smart. That had to impress the jury, Malman thought.

"Now, your job, I think you told us, was to export the cocaine from the country of Panama to the country of the United States, correct?" Frank Rubino asked on cross-examination.

"Yes, sir," answered Bilonick.

"Now, you tell us that Ochoa had to bribe Noriega to get the cocaine into Panama, correct?"

"Yes, sir."

"Who did you have to bribe to get the cocaine into the United States?" Rubino asked. If the prosecution's theory was to be believed—that Noriega had been bribed to let the cocaine out of Panama—then surely someone in the United States must have been bribed as well to let it in. After all, Customs in almost every country checks incoming flights, not outgoing.

"If I could have found one man that controlled the United States, I probably would have bribed him," said Bilonick.

Rubino stepped toward Bilonick. "How about the president of the United States? Doesn't he control the United States?" Rubino asked.

"He does not control the United States," Bilonick said. Rubino's logic, however, was not lost on Bilonick.

"Don't tell him that," Rubino said.

Rubino's impertinence made Malman bristle, and he objected.

"I am sorry," Rubino said. He turned back to Bilonick: "So is it your testimony that you did not have to bribe anyone to bring drugs into the country of the United States?"

"It's the testimony and a fact," said Bilonick. Preposterous, thought Rubino. Noriega was the leader of the country, not a customs agent or street drug enforcement agent. The general was being blamed for nineteen loads of cocaine that came to the United States, but eighteen of the nineteen loads had gotten past U.S. officials. Noriega had a whole government to worry about—labor, agriculture, health care—not just drug enforcement.

Bilonick said that in his business with the cartel he earned $47 million. But he never once paid Noriega a bribe.

"Are you telling the jury you weren't giving General Noriega one single dime?" asked Rubino.

"Yes, sir," responded Bilonick.

"And I think you told us that General Noriega said in your presence that 'whatever Bilonick wants, he should have'?"

"Basically."

"This is the same man who shuts down your airlines, right?" Rubino asked.

"After a major drug seizure, of course," Bilonick answered.

"So you didn't quite get from him what the general promised you, did you?" Rubino said.

"That could be a fair statement," Bilonick said.

"And at no time whatsoever have you ever given, personally given, General Noriega one penny for his aid to facilitate any of your drug operations, correct?"

"I have always stated that I never gave him the money personally."

Well, if the cartel was paying off Noriega, Rubino went on, then "when General Noriega shut down Inair airlines, if he were receiving $500,000 per load, he effectively closed himself out of that money, did he not?"

Again, Malman objected to Rubino's impertinent tone.

"Sustained," Judge Hoeveler said.

CHAPTER 28

★★★★★★★

The Cartel Connection

Carlos Lehder was locked in a seven-by-eight-foot cell at the Marion, Illinois, Federal Penitentiary, the most secure federal prison in the United States. Lehder's entire cell block included just eleven other prisoners, each in solitary confinement.

Since arriving at Marion, Lehder had not once spoken to another prisoner. He tried to smuggle a note to an inmate housed on the tier above him. The note, which was intercepted, simply offered his weekly allotment of commissary cigarettes.

When Lehder went for exercise—a total of five hours each week—he was accompanied by three guards. He exercised in a cage alone. He learned how to paint, but he did so by correspondence. Every night Lehder prayed that he would not spend the rest of his life in Marion.

After a seven-and-a-half-month trial in a Jacksonville federal court in 1988, Lehder was convicted of conspiracy to import three tons of cocaine into the United States and sentenced to life plus 135 years in prison. Lehder had been arrested following a gun battle between his bodyguards and Colombian police. Soon after, when a crack opened in the on-again, off-again narcotics extradition treaty between the United States and Colombia, Lehder was the first to go. He came to the United States locked in the pitch-black toilet of a DEA plane, on his knees, his arms handcuffed around the stool. He had promised to kill a federal judge for every week he spent in jail. Still, Lehder ended up in Marion.

In Jacksonville the government had worked overtime to convict Lehder. Tampa U.S. Attorney Robert Merkle, who signed the 1988 Tampa indictment of Noriega, tried Lehder personally. He called 115 witnesses to put Lehder away.

The prosecution's decision to call Lehder as a witness against Noriega on Tuesday, November 17, had been difficult. Lehder's journey to the witness stand had begun shortly after Noriega's arrest. As witnesses were gathered, many began saying that Lehder knew about Noriega. Go see Lehder, the doppers kept telling DEA supervisor Tom Raffanello's agents. Sitting in Marion, it wasn't long before Lehder himself also said he might, for the right deal, have something to say about Noriega's relationship to the cartel.

322

But before Lehder made his offer to Noriega's prosecutors, he had some advice for the general. "Give it up," Lehder told Noriega in a letter. Lehder said he had spent $7 million on his defense in Jacksonville and had only the rest of his life in prison to show for it. Plead, don't fight, Lehder told Noriega.

From the first, Pat Sullivan knew that the one thing that the prosecution lacked was someone who could say Noriega personally had been in contact with the cartel. Looking at the prosecution's case was like looking at a house without a foundation, Sullivan thought. Lehder could provide the foundation. He could say that the cartel had made arrangements with Noriega to bring ether and acetone through Panama. He could say Noriega sold cocaine seized from the cartel back to the cartel. Lehder could even put a dollar figure on Noriega's dealings. He could put the cartel's dollars in Noriega's hands.

Just after the completion of the Saldarriaga and Davidow trial in May, Sullivan put out feelers to see what it would take to get Lehder on the witness stand for the prosecution. But the first hurdle was not Lehder. It was getting the U.S. government on board, lining up support within Justice and the DEA. Sullivan leveled with Malman and Lewis. "We need this guy," he said. The three talked with DEA supervisor Raffanello, and agents Steve Grilli and Lenny Athas. They agreed. Raffanello quietly sent Colombian-born DEA agent Henry Cuervo to Marion to see Lehder, at the same time Raffanello, the agents, and Sullivan talked to Tom Cash, the DEA special agent in charge in Miami.

Cash had been around a long time. He had been the deputy assistant administrator for enforcement at Main DEA in Washington when the Noriega indictment had been handed down. He shook his head as he listened, but he promised to take the idea to Judge Robert Bonner, the DEA administrator.

"What carried the day for both me and Judge Bonner was that this was a criticial part of the indictment," Cash said later. "We looked at the witness list we had and then we asked ourselves, 'Do we want to give Rubino the opportunity to say not one member of the cartel testified?' In a perfect world we would have wanted a different indictment, one without the cartel aspects. In the end, we agreed with Sullivan. We chose Carlos."

At Main Justice there was also hesitation. After all, Lehder had been the most significant drug conviction in U.S. history. Now, the idea was to enlist him as a witness. Understandably, a significant amount of opposition was coming from Tampa and the prosecutors who had put Lehder in prison. Ernst Mueller, one of the lead prosecutors against Lehder, prosecutor Doug Kehoe, and Robert Ginzman, the U.S. attorney for Florida's Middle District, were not keen about giving Lehder up. But Mueller, in a memorandum to Ginzman, advised caution in opposing the idea. If the Noriega case is lost, he warned, we don't want to be sucked into the blame.

The final decision was the attorney general's. Bob Mueller at Main Justice, the AG's top assistant, finally passed the go ahead down to Sullivan. Whatever it took, Sullivan was told, convict Noriega.

Sullivan sent Henry Cuervo along with Guy Lewis back to Marion to see Lehder. Lewis recollected the first time he saw Lehder in person. Lehder had gotten off a prison elevator with three guards. There, in America's most secure prison, Lehder was shackled at the ankles, waist, wrists, and around the neck. It was a picture out of a B gangster movie.

Lehder spoke perfect English. He was hip and intelligent. Cuervo and he had come from the same part of Colombia. All three were young. There was a near instant rapport. Most important, Lehder had a story to tell and it was credible. "Officer Noriega was just another crooked cop," he told Lewis and Cuervo. But Lehder insisted he wouldn't testify for free. He wanted time off and out of Marion. Maybe out of Marion, Lewis said shaking his head, but no time off.

Three months later, on August 24, after several visits and with only two weeks to trial, Lewis and Cuervo came back to Marion with Sullivan. The prosecution could get Lehder out of Marion, into a cell that wasn't buried underground, Sullivan said. That was the deal. Reluctantly, Lehder agreed.

Days later, Sullivan echoed Lehder in his opening statement to the jury. Noriega was just another "crooked cop," he said.

Lehder, forty-two, wore a gray suit, white shirt, and red paisley tie. His wavy black hair was stylishly cut, but his tan had long faded to a prison pasty white.

Following Lewis's questioning, Lehder said he began his life of crime by selling stolen cars. In the early 1970s he set up a Medellín car dealership and soon met Jorge Ochoa and Pablo Escobar. The two introduced Lehder to drug smuggling. Business was so good that by 1978, Lehder bought his own Caribbean island. From the island he ran one of the cartel's most profitable cocaine routes into the United States.

"I was a smuggler, I was a criminal, and I was a rascal," Lehder told the jury. He added, "It is my intention to cooperate with the United States government and rehabilitate myself."

Lewis directed Lehder to the cartel's relationship with Noriega.

The Medellín cocaine "mafia," Lehder said, first became aware of Noriega in the late 1970s when one of the city's older and respected traffickers was arrested in Panama, tortured, and fined. Noriega was the officer in charge. "This particular incident was so close to us that it filled up the cup," said Lehder, testifying in English. "I mean, we had to do something about it."

The Medellín traffickers discussed their choices, said Lehder. They could either bribe Noriega or fight him. They decided to bribe him. "We knew he was in control of the G-2 and narcotic police. My knowledge was that he was just another criminally corrupt police official in Panama." The traffickers' relationship with Noriega changed after the kidnapping of Marta Ochoa and Noriega's helping to negotiate her release, Lehder said. The cartel's representatives at the negotiations returned to Medellín with greetings from Noriega and "the offer that if any desire to conduct any affairs in Panama was wished, he was willing to listen."

In March 1982, a month after Marta's release, the cartel, which had taken form in reaction to the kidnapping, met and plotted its course. Among the issues debated at the cartel "round table," Lehder said, was "the fact that Officer Noriega did have, as a matter of fact, control over law enforcement in Panama," and that could be helpful for the cartel. In short order the cartel met with Julian Melo of the Panamanian Defense Forces and began to deal with Noriega, Lehder said.

Because Lehder's cocaine route to the United States through the Bahamas had recently been closed down by the DEA, the cartel looked to Panama. Ochoa and Escobar soon purchased Inair airlines. "The main thing was that the cartel had access to an airline that it had purchased and wanted to use that airline, called Inair, as a pipeline to the United States for our cocaine." For $1,000 per kilo, Noriega guaranteed protection. "We were given access to special members of the tower, a special radio frequency, which we could call before we approached the territory. Our airplanes were to park at the government facility, which is a police military facility, in hangars, and that's where the cocaine was unloaded." The operation, Lehder said, would be protected by the G-2.

"There were several meetings, specifically with Officer Melo arranging for our bankers and accountants to meet Mr. Noriega's accountants and bankers, in order to arrange for these loads of money to come into Panama from the United States. The agreement was that Officer Noriega would receive a percentage, about 5 percent, on every dollar that we flew in from the United States into Panama."

By 1983, 60 percent of the cartel's cocaine was flowing through Panama to the United States, said Lehder. Soon Noriega sent his "intimates" around to get a cut of the pie. That's how César Rodríguez and Floyd Carlton went to work for the cartel, said Lehder, who further explained why the testimony of many of the government's witnesses had not perfectly fit: None knew the full story of the cartel and its work. Pilots and operatives knew only what they needed to know.

"In an organization like the cartel, one has to compartmentalize information for different reasons. One, if the person happens to be a thief and likes to steal the cocaine or the money, well, he can do so much damage because he just got limited information. Also, if this person happens to be arrested and decides to spill the beans, as we say, he can just spill the beans in certain aspects of the operation and just certain people. And, third, and no less important, if this person happens to be kidnapped for ransom, and tortured or threatened with death if he doesn't give up where the cocaine is or where the monies are, he has—although he might want to tell—he has very limited information about the entire operation."

The cartel's protection money was not wasted, Lehder said. Noriega's agents provided the cartel with pictures of U.S. DEA agents assigned to Panama and warned the cartel to use bigger planes when the number of small aircraft from Colombia landing in Panama City grew large enough to arouse suspicion at American military bases in the Canal Zone.

Noriega sold confiscated cocaine back to the cartel, and after one load had been confiscated by PDF forces, Lehder said, Noriega ordered it stolen back for the cartel by the G-2.

The 1984 raid on the Tranquilandia resulted in a crisis for the cartel leadership, Lehder said. There was an immediate need to establish a new lab to ensure the continued flow of finished product.

"It was decided that we should try to persuade Officer Noriega to allow us to build a laboratory in the jungles of Panama. We decided to send our team of envoys, our ambassadors, over there to talk, negotiate, and persuade Officer Noriega to allow us to build a cocaine industrial complex in the jungles of Panama." Lehder said the cartel paid Noriega $5 million to allow the Darien lab to be built and an extra $1 million to ensure a sanctuary for the cartel leadership in Panama.

Traffickers Gustavo Gaviria, Alonso Cardenas, and Pablo Correa negotiated the deal. Just ten days after the destruction of the Tranquilandia lab, the cartel had the "green light" to begin construction in the Darien jungle, Lehder said. The assassination of Bonilla, the relocation of the cartel to Panama, and the establishment of the Darien lab seemed to give Noriega a heightened sense of self-importance, said Lehder. "Now that the cartel was based in Panama, he wanted to invest in the cartel," Lehder said. "He wanted a bigger piece of the pie." But that soon changed after the Darien raid. The cartel quickly moved to establish new transshipment routes through Nicaragua. That was done with the help of the Cuban government, said Lehder. "The Cubans were in charge of that cocaine conspiracy in Nicaragua, sir. It was not the Sandinista government, but it was the Cuban government."

Lehder said the settlement of the dispute between the cartel and Noriega over the Darien lab was negotiated by Fidel Castro and former Colombian president Alonso López. The cartel got $2 million of its $5 million back. Even so, after the raid and then the Inair seizure in Miami, the Panama connection was never the same for the cartel.

Lehder's direct examination spilled into Wednesday, November 20. When Guy Lewis said he had no further questions, Frank Rubino asked for a sidebar.

For two and a half months Rubino himself had cross-examined each witness. The prosecution had gone forward as a tag team, dividing up the witnesses. Sullivan, Malman, and Lewis often had two days off between their respective witnesses. Not so for Rubino; Jon May was sequestered preparing the defense case.

Rubino told Judge Hoeveler that he was not ready to question Lehder. The defense's material on Lehder was four inches thick, but Rubino said he simply had not had time to prepare. "I cannot render effective assistance of counsel if I have to cross-examine this witness today," Rubino told the judge.

Hoeveler was not happy. It was barely past the noon hour. "I'm not going to lose a day in this case," the judge said.

Rubino said the government had not given him notice that Lehder would appear. "I spent this weekend preparing other witnesses, honestly," said Rubino. "He was not on my list of the next five people. I have plenty of material, and I need to read the material."

Sullivan was less than sympathetic. Lehder's appearance had been no secret. It was only a matter of when. "I recognize the difficulty Mr. Rubino has with preparing for every witness, but since we've been in trial for three months, he knew, by process of elimination, Lehder had to come soon, and that's where we are," Sullivan said.

"I knew Lehder was coming," Rubino responded. "That's not in dispute. But the court has to take notice that I'm trying this case essentially single-handed. I don't take turns doing cross-examinations. I don't have other lawyers helping me. I spend from nine-thirty to five in this courtroom every day, and I try to prepare every night and weekends."

In three months, Rubino said, he had taken just three days off. "The court is aware that testimony-wise, this is probably the single most important witness that my client faced yet in this trial. I'm asking for one afternoon. So instead of five months and three days, it will take five months and three and a half days, but my client will have a fair trial."

Hoeveler half-smiled. "You're just tearing me up," the judge said. "You be ready tomorrow morning. Ready or not, we go tomorrow."

"I promise I'll be ready," said Rubino.

Rubino prepared. Lehder was a model of decorum, but every action he had ever taken as a member of the cartel had been marked by extremes. While Jorge Ochoa had shunned public attention, Lehder had sought public interviews. He had fashioned his own paramilitary group and had tried to start his own political party. His flamboyance and volatile temper were legendary in Colombia. The jury had seen none of the real Carlos Lehder.

The next morning Rubino wasted little time pressing Lehder:

"Good morning, Mr. Lehder. Sir, yesterday toward the very end of your examination, Mr. Lewis asked you how was it that you got to the United States. And your answer was, 'I was extradited under the rules of an extradition treaty between the United States and Colombia.' Do you remember that question and answer?"

"I do," said Lehder.

Rubino's tone became less conciliatory. "Have you not publicly stated that you were kidnapped to the United States?"

"There [are] different opinions regarding that, sir," said Lehder.

"Have you publicly stated, 'I was kidnapped when there was no treaty'?"

"I think that's a legal issue which is [in] the appeals court, sir."

"Sir, my question is, did you say it or didn't you say it? That's all."

"Do you have a transcript regarding that, sir?" Lehder asked.

"Sir, let me explain to you how this court works, in all due respect," said Rubino in irritation. "I ask the questions, and you give the answers. Okay?"

Lehder was flushed. "Yes."

"My question very simply stated is, have you said that you were kidnapped?"

"Yes, sir. I did," said Lehder.

Rubino pushed on. Lehder confirmed that he had claimed he'd been kidnapped from Colombia by U.S. Attorney General Edwin Meese. The United States had brought him to trial not because he was a drug dealer but because his views were in political opposition to the U.S. government's, Lehder had said. In January 1989, Lehder conceded, he sued the United States for $92 million, claiming he'd been illegally extradited.

Now he tried to explain: "Mr. Rubino, for many years I was on a political, judicial, ethical, and philosophical confrontation with the United States government. For many years that happened." He added, "And I am glad it is over."

But wasn't it true, Rubino asked Lehder, that he dropped the suit after he reached his cooperation agreement with the United States, the agreement that now had freed him from Marion? "Wasn't its purpose to blackmail the United States to come to some type of an agreement with you?" Rubino asked.

"That [would] be a very unfair statement, sir," said Lehder.

"In fact, you did come to some type of an agreement with the United States government, did you not?"

"Yes, sir."

"That agreement is why you are here today, correct?"

"Yes, sir."

"And you dropped the lawsuit?"

"I did, sir."

"It worked, didn't it?" pressed Rubino.

"I object to the question, Judge," said Guy Lewis. Here was a U.S. prosecutor in the uncomfortable position of coming to Lehder's defense.

The judge sustained the objection. After all, Hoeveler explained, Rubino was asking the witness to explain the government's mind.

But before Lehder could relax, Rubino reworded the question and attacked again.

"You have now made an agreement with the United States government, have you not?" he asked.

"Yes, sir," Lehder answered.

"And now that you are cooperating with them, you have dismissed this lawsuit, correct?"

"Yes, sir."

Rubino pressed the parallel. Of the government's 115 witnesses called to testify against Lehder at trial, 22 were fellow drug smugglers. Hadn't each traded his testimony for reduced jail time or better prison conditions? Rubino asked.

"I believe that's accurate, sir," Lehder answered.

"And they were all pardoned for every sin they ever committed, correct?" Rubino pushed.

The refrain could have been, "Just like yourself," but again Lewis forestalled it.

"Judge, I object to that question," said Lewis, his arms outstretched.

Hoeveler half-smiled. "Sustained as to the form of the question," he said, looking at Rubino.

Rubino was ready to turn to Lehder's long history of making wild accusations and not telling the truth. Through a litany of questions the jury would see that Lehder had a habit of making inconsistent statements. Why wouldn't his testimony against Noriega be more of the same, an attempt to please the government to receive better prison conditions?

Rubino came to sidebar and explained where his questioning was going.

"He has said false evidence was used against him to convict him illegally. He was not guilty. Paid witnesses were used. He went through this whole big thing about he's not guilty. Now, today, he says he's guilty. If this isn't a prior inconsistent statement—"

"It is," agreed Judge Hoeveler. "What you are doing is trying to get at subterranean purposes here. You want him in effect to lay the groundwork for your arguing that all of these witnesses were apparently in this case lying."

Hoeveler invited Rubino to proceed.

But Rubino's next question took the prosecution by surprise.

"Sir, did you not make the statement that the federal prosecutor in your case concealed evidence?" he asked.

"I don't particularly recall that statement, sir," said Lehder.

Pat Sullivan did not wait for Lewis to object. "Your Honor, may we go sidebar on this?" Sullivan asked.

This was not the impeachment of a statement Lehder had made on direct examination, Sullivan protested.

"It is for impeachment of us," Myles Malman said.

"It is obviously for impeachment of prosecutors in their honesty," Sullivan said.

"What about that?" asked Hoeveler, turning to Rubino.

"Your Honor," Rubino said, "absolutely not."

"That goes to his credibility if he's making false statements against people," Jon May said, who had come to court for the cross-examination. "Your Honor, if this man has made false accusations against people, that goes to his credibility. Mr. Lehder has claimed that the Central Intelligence Agency was delivering letters to him in the jungle from the vice president's office. He has claimed that Edwin Meese was going to or had agreed to drop the charges against him if he would make his islands available to the United States government for their efforts against the Contras so that the United States government could import cocaine into the United States."

"Here we go," said Malman.

But May pressed on: "These are not positions that we believe are true. These are positions which are manifestly false. These are false statements, false accusations that this man has made. We are not introducing those to prove that the vice president was sending this man letters. We are doing it to prove just the opposite, that this man has made up statements about all sorts of people, not just our client, and that definitely goes to his character for truthfulness."

Hoeveler overruled the objection and allowed Rubino to go forward.

Lehder confirmed that he had told a reporter that U.S. authorities in 1982 offered to give him the "green light" to smuggle cocaine into the United States in return for using his Caribbean island to ship guns to the Contras via Costa Rica and Honduras. The U.S. vice consul in Cali, Colombia, himself had offered the deal in 1982, Lehder said. Lehder had made the comment in an unpublished *Playboy* magazine interview. Lewis and Sullivan looked at each other. This was the first they had heard of the interview.

Lewis objected. The questioning was far afield, he protested. Again the attorneys came to sidebar. Turning away from the jury and the witness, the judge could barely contain a chuckle.

"I appreciate the court is laughing," said Rubino.

May took up the defense position again: "If he makes the allegations that the attorney general is going to drop charges against him and allow him to import cocaine if he agrees to let his island be used by the United States government, that goes directly to this man's credibility, his ability to tell the truth."

Hoeveler was still smiling. "That is not what you are trying to prove here," the judge said. "What you are trying to prove here is (a) he's a liar, (b) if he isn't, the government is, has been. We are getting into your pipeline theory."

"Yesterday and the day before, this man looked very reasonable," May said, "very clean-cut. He is saying things about General Noriega that a lot of these people are prepared to believe because it is General Noriega. They have to understand that he's making the same kind of allegations against Ed Meese that he's making against General Noriega. You have to understand the context." Rubino privately called Lehder the Charles Manson of the dope world. He was crazy and dangerous. He could not believe the government was dealing with him.

Hoeveler allowed Rubino to press his cross-examination.

Lehder said he became suspicious of the U.S. government's offer since he was already under indictment for using his island to smuggle drugs. "I came to the conclusion that this was a U.S. government sting to have me arrested, so I cut all relationships with them," he said.

By late in the afternoon Rubino shifted the questioning to the cartel payoffs to Noriega, which Lehder had spoken of on direct examination. "You have never paid any money, to use your words, directly to my client, General Noriega, either, have you?" Rubino asked.

"The cartel did, sir," responded Lehder.

"That wasn't my question," Rubino said. "Would you please answer my question."

"Yes, sir."

"My question very simply stated was, you have never paid any money directly to my client, General Noriega?"

"Not directly, sir."

"Tell this jury what you, with your own two eyes, have actually seen General Noriega do."

"Sir, your multimillionaire police officer client was a high police official. He wasn't a gangster in Medellín, running around," Lehder shot back, frustrated. "So we're talking about two different countries, sir. I didn't live in Panama, and he didn't live in Medellín. I never met your client, sir."

Rubino pressed again: "Is it a fair statement, sir, to say that since you have never met General Noriega and never talked with him, that all of your testimony is based on hearsay, innuendo, and secondhand speculation?"

Once again Lehder grew flush. "That would be very inaccurate and unfair to say. Everything I have said here is the truth and nothing but the truth, sir."

Before Lehder could be called back to the witness stand on Monday morning, November 25, Judge Hoeveler pulled the attorneys into his chambers.

"I looked in the paper this morning, and, frankly, I really don't read a whole lot about this case in the newspaper, nor do I watch it on television because I am generally home too late to watch the local news, but I noted in the paper this morning that Mr. Rubino, for the first time since the case started, violated the standing rule against talking with the press and stated publicly that he thought Mr. Lehder was a liar," the judge said. He turned to Rubino. "Did you do that?"

Rubino moved to the edge of his chair. "I will tell you what happened, Your Honor. I did not give any kind of interview or press conference in any way, shape, or form." Rubino explained that as he was leaving the courthouse he was dogged by a reporter. He never stopped. He kept walking. The reporter kept asking questions. "I did say, 'I don't believe him,' or something to that effect, yes, and then I kept walking, and that was the entire extent of it."

"Right," said Hoeveler.

"But I just want you to know it was not an interview. It wasn't like I stopped and had a conversation. I was just on my way walking. You know how they yell at you, and I did reply back. I am not going to tell the court I didn't reply. I did, and I guess I should not have."

"Well, it is not a question of guessing," Hoeveler scolded. "You shouldn't have. It is a clear violation of the rule." He turned to Sullivan. "Does the government have any comment?"

Sullivan was sympathetic to Rubino. For nearly two years no attorney in the case could walk in or out of the courthouse without being followed and questioned by reporters. A reporter had once followed Sullivan on his four-block walk from the U.S. attorney's office to the courthouse. At recesses, reporters leaned over the rail and asked questions. Every evening when he returned to his office after a day in court, Sullivan had a stack of pink message slips seeking comment. So did every other attorney in the case.

"These things kind of roll off our back, but if we could, we would prefer naturally that the rules of court be followed," Sullivan said. He remembered that during the codefendants' trial a reporter had asked him about the untimely death of prosecution witness Ramón Navarro.

"What are you going to do now?" someone asked. "Just try the case," Sullivan responded. The next day the comment was in the *New York Times*.

"We would prefer to see it not happen," Sullivan told the judge.

Hoeveler turned back to Rubino. It was three days before Thanksgiving. "In the spirit of the season, I am going to forgive you," he said. But he added that if it happened again, he would fine the offending attorney.

"I am sorry," Rubino said again. "It was kind of one thing that slips out of your mouth as you are walking to your car."

"I want this case to finish," the judge said sternly. "I don't want to have to try it again. Okay. Let's go to work."

With the jury again seated, Hoeveler greeted them and, as he had each morning, asked whether they had seen any media coverage. "There has been some media publicity about the case over the weekend," the judge said. "I trust none of you have seen it or heard it. If you have, please tell me. I assume no one has talked to you or that you have not discussed the case with anybody, unless you tell me differently." The jurors shook their heads no.

"No answers. That means you haven't," the judge said. "Thank you."

Rubino turned to Lehder's claim—in a March 1990 prison interview—that the cartel gave the U.S.-backed Contras $10 million in the early 1980s.

"To the best of my knowledge, there was some contribution to the Contra anticommunist movement," Lehder told Rubino. "It could be around $10 million."

Since the prosecution's objections to Rubino's cross-examination the week before had worked to support Lehder's credibility, Rubino was more than happy to turn that seeming support back on the government. If the cartel paid money to the Contras, perhaps the Contras allowed drugs to be shipped to the United States on planes that had first brought guns to the anticommunists. It was the pipeline theory that the traffickers and Contras worked together. Rubino did not intend to let the government have it both ways. Either Lehder was a liar or he wasn't.

"Did the cartel receive any guarantees from leaders or commanders of the Contra forces that they could protect cartel drug shipments through Costa Rica?" Rubino asked.

"I don't recall that, sir."

"Was the cartel shipping drugs through Costa Rica to the United States in exchange for shipping weapons from the United States to the Contras?" asked Rubino.

"Not to my recollection, sir." But, Lehder added, "I do recall that there were shipments going through Costa Rica."

The questioning drew repeated objections from Guy Lewis. The subject was irrelevant, he protested.

At sidebar, Jon May made the defense's point: "The relevance is that the cartel, being capitalists, aren't going to pay somebody if it is not necessary. Panama is next door to Costa Rica. If they had a secure route to go to Costa Rica, they would not have gratuitously paid General Noriega the millions they say they would have paid him. We are saying there was no need to pay Noriega because they had another pipeline through Costa Rica right next door."

May explained where the defense was going: "The government has repeatedly said to the court—and what they have tried to convince the court of—is that it is our theory that the CIA was involved or that the United States government was involved in cocaine shipments to the United States. That's not our theory. Our theory is very simply a piggyback theory, that certain Contra individuals, certain drug pilots, took advantage of an arms pipeline, not with the sanction of the United States." May's comment was a preview of things to come.

Rubino had one final area of questioning.

Was it true, Rubino asked Lehder, that he had congratulated Pablo Escobar following the assassination of Rodrigo Lara Bonilla?

"Yes, sir," answered Lehder.

"Did you— Were you telling this jury that you actually congratulated Pablo Escobar for murdering somebody? Is that what you are saying?"

"Sir, I congratulated Escobar because I was a member of the cartel, sir," Lehder answered. "I congratulated him for what he had done, sir."

"Which was killing a human being, correct?"

"Which was, unfortunately, executing one of his enemies, sir."

"And you were so pleased about this—" Rubino began.

Guy Lewis again stood. "Judge, I am going to object to any[thing] further. He's made his point with the jury."

Rubino asked why the cartel had Bonilla assassinated.

"Sir, those are kind of internal matters and political matters that might be hard to explain here to an American jury, but Colombia was engaged in a tremendous civil war. And an abnormal amount of people was being killed, but some of his agents were killing a lot of people. And there was, in the revolutionary and political context, it was justified, sir. That's all I can tell you."

Rubino looked flabbergasted. "Just snuffing him out like stepping on a cockroach, correct?" he asked.

"Now Mr. Rubino," said Hoeveler, interrupting. "I've sustained objections to the inflammatory matters. Do I have to say another one?"

At sidebar Rubino explained himself: "I think this jury should know that he is a political anarchist. He says . . . in certain areas that he is waging war against the United States and he [will] flood the United States with cocaine in order to achieve this war of his. He makes other statements that the end justifies the means." Lehder had maneuvered himself into testifying and had used the prosecution, Rubino said. In Colombia, Lehder had called cocaine and marijuana a "revolutionary weapon in the struggle against North American imperialism," Rubino said. "I think the man is suffering from delusions of grandeur, and I think I have the right to show—if this man fabricates stories about the Russian embassy, the vice president, and the CIA—I have a right to show that he's not as stable as he says he is."

Judge Hoeveler looked first at Lewis and then at Sullivan. "I may, at some point, order this gentleman examined before we get into this sort of thing." Then Hoeveler added, "I'll tell you frankly, from my watching him, it would appear—and I'm quite willing to say this on the record—that the man is far from demented. As a matter of fact, he is, I would say, quite alert."

Rubino smiled. "Then maybe the vice president's press secretary did send him a letter . . ."

Hoeveler grinned. "That doesn't mean he's not off the wall."

There were others who agreed. "The inexplicable aspect of all this is how U.S. justice solicits this type of statement, offering reductions of sentences to people who break all records in slandering people, people . . . who have made deals to save their scalps," observed Alfonso López Michelsen, the former Colombian president whom Lehder described as a friend of the cartel's.

In Miami, former Contra leader Adolfo Calero also denounced Lehder: "It's absurd to pay attention to what a convict says. It's a lie, an absolute lie that the resistance has accepted money. That amount of money is impossible to hide."

Even Robert Merkle, who had put Lehder in prison, was amazed by Lehder's appearance on the witness stand. "He started the cartel, for crying out loud," said Merkle. "He was the guy who really triggered the American appetite for cocaine."

But Lehder's testimony was not alone before the jury. Like the witnesses who had come before, Lehder claimed the cartel paid $5 million to permit the construction of the Darien lab; also like others, he could trace the money only as far as Julian Melo. He also corroborated Ricardo Bilonick's testimony that the cartel "bought" Noriega, even though he acknowledged that he had never met Noriega.

Still, the parade of witnesses offering dates and places, detailing payoffs, and discussing the mechanics of cocaine trafficking was making it difficult for the defense to argue that the events in the indictment had never taken place.

CHAPTER 29
★★★★★★★

Guns for Drugs

With the testimony of Carlos Lehder complete, the government was ready to turn to the *Krill*'s guns-for-drugs voyage from Panama to Colombia in March 1986. Like the now-convicted Brian Davidow and William Saldarriaga, Noriega was charged with trying to use the *Krill* to import cocaine into the United States. Additionally, though, Noriega was alleged to have protected the *Krill*'s voyage and to have helped set up the *Krill* smuggling conspiracy.

There were witnesses who connected Saldarriaga and Davidow to the *Krill*, but there were no witnesses that put Noriega on or near it. The case for Noriega's protection of the *Krill* was based almost wholly on the testimony of Davidow and Amet Paredes, the son of the former Panamanian military leader, Rubén Dario Paredes, whom Noriega shunted aside in 1983.

The voyage of the *Krill* was the last illegal act alleged in the Miami indictment. The obvious question seemed to be: Why would Noriega—who others testified received millions of dollars from the cartel—protect the *Krill* for just a few hundred thousand?

Davidow, who wanted to lessen the possible fifty-five-year sentence Judge Hoeveler could give him at his sentencing following the Noriega trial, testified on Monday, December 2, that he went to the Panama City office of César Rodríguez in March 1986, where Rodríguez told Noriega, "My general, the yacht is ready." Davidow heard the conversation via speakerphone.

"You're responsible for my share," Davidow said he heard Noriega reply. "Don't screw up this time."

Noriega would be paid to protect the *Krill* as it sailed from Panama to Colombia. The *Krill* would sail to Colombia with a load of M-16 rifles. There the rifles would be exchanged for cocaine, which would then be taken to Miami. Drugs were never mentioned during the conversation in Rodríguez's office, Davidow said. But the conspirators, including Noriega, each would receive $300,000 to $400,000 for their part in the venture.

On cross-examination Frank Rubino asked if, other than the alleged March meeting, Davidow had ever heard Noriega's voice.

"No," said Davidow, adding, "I never spoke to him."

On redirect, Malman asked Davidow why he decided to testify against Noriega. Was it just in the hope of receiving lesser jail time? Malman asked.

It wasn't, Davidow said. "It can be hard to sleep with yourself sometimes, knowing you have been involved with these things in the past. It's a very nice thing to say them out openly and be able to be absolved in a way, as long as you tell the truth, and to state all the previous items you've done in the past."

"All this drug dealing you did, how old were you when you started?" asked Malman.

"I was twenty-two when I started," Davidow answered. Now he was thirty.

Amet Paredes had been the prosecution's star witness against Davidow. He followed Davidow to the witness stand.

The speakerphone conversation with Noriega had taken place not in Rodríguez's office, said Paredes, but in the corner of a nightclub owned by Rodríguez.

As he had done during the codefendants' trial, Paredes told of how he and his brother, Rubén Paredes, Jr., hoped to sell the *Krill*. The sale became complicated, however, and Paredes said he soon learned the boat was tied to a drug transaction. "They were going to use the *Krill* for another business, the cocaine business," Paredes said under questioning by Pat Sullivan. "I asked them, 'How are we going to do this?' They say, 'Well, we have protection from Mr. Noriega to do that.'"

At a follow-up meeting, Paredes continued, Rodríguez said, "We are going to have a meeting here and call *El Man* to let him know that everything is under control."

"General, everything is ready in Colombia," Rodríguez told Noriega. "We have the cocaine waiting, and we just need to hurry."

To that, Paredes said, Noriega replied, "Just keep doing the things, and if you have any problem, call me back."

Later, Paredes continued, there were problems. First, the *Krill* could not sail without a certificate verifying that its unpaid taxes had been satisfied. Noriega cleared the paperwork. Then when the guns that were to be traded for cocaine did not arrive, Noriega arranged for the delivery, Paredes said. All of the arrangements for Noriega's assistance were made on the speakerphone, said Paredes.

Anticipating that Rubino would find Noriega's speakerphone conversations not prudent and unbelievable, Sullivan asked Paredes to explain.

"Does General Noriega know that he's on a speakerphone and—what is there?—six or eight people sitting around, hushed up, listening to his words? Does he know this?" asked Sullivan.

"I don't know that," said Paredes.

"Was more than one person talking at once on your end of the conversation, your side of it, if you know what I mean by that?"

"Yes, sir."

"Was there more than one person speaking at once?"

"Yes, sir."

"So, based on that, it would be pretty obvious to General Noriega, if he was ever there on the phone, that he was on a speakerphone?"

"I think so."

"Didn't he ask who was on the other end since he knew it was a speakerphone?"

"No, because César told him, 'We're here, we're all here.'"

Paredes's account was ridiculous, Rubino thought. If Paredes was to be believed, then everywhere Noriega went there was a speakerphone. Paredes would lie when the truth would serve him better, Rubino thought.

Rubino left aside the unbelievable contention that Noriega would discuss drug trafficking with people he could not identify. On cross, Rubino made another point.

"In any way, shape, or form, did General Noriega help you bring any of that cocaine to the United States?"

"No, sir," Paredes answered.

"Did you believe that General Noriega had the ability to protect the vessel Krill when it was in the territorial waters of the country of Colombia?" Rubino asked.

"Yes, sir," said Paredes.

"You believed that he had that ability?"

"Yes, sir, because the boat had to go through the canal."

"Would you explain to the ladies and gentlemen of the jury how you believe General Noriega was going to protect that vessel as it went on its passage to the United States."

"I don't know that, sir."

Rubino next guided Paredes through his decision to cooperate with the government. For three years after the delivery of the indictment, Paredes refused to cooperate, even declined an agreement that would have given him immunity from prosecution. In six different statements Paredes denied knowing of Noriega's involvement in the Krill venture. He denied that Noriega was present in person or on the speakerphone at the planning meetings. But then he changed his mind.

"Now, after you told the prosecutors and the DEA agent that General Noriega was not involved, they didn't want to use you as a witness, did they?" Rubino asked.

"I don't know that," replied Paredes.

"Well, they didn't make a deal with you at that time, did they?"

"No, sir."

"But eventually you changed your testimony. You changed your statement, and you said General Noriega was involved, correct?"

"Correct."

"And you said you overheard General Noriega on a speakerphone?"

"Correct."

"And after you changed your testimony, you got a plea agreement, did you not?"

"Yes, sir."

"Reducing you from what? Ninety-five years to twenty with a cap of ten, correct?" Rubino asked. The government had agreed to drop four of the five counts against Paredes.

That was correct, said Paredes.

Rubino referred back to the meetings in Rodríguez's office, meetings where all of those who had been present except for Paredes, Davidow, and Saldarriaga were now dead.

"Today in court you maintain that you—in the presence of a group of people who are now dead—overheard General Noriega on a speakerphone?"

"Today is the truth, Mr. Rubino," said Paredes, growing angry. "It is over. There is no more lies here. This is the truth."

Rubino pressed on. "So your testimony here today is that when you met with the prosecutors and the agents, you were lying then?"

Sullivan stood. "I object. Repetitive and argumentative," he protested.

"Sustained," the judge ruled.

Rubino had one further area of questioning. In 1988, Paredes had been detained in Panama for his involvement in a separate cocaine-dealing incident. He was taken to jail and there called his father. Paredes did not know that his call was monitored.

"Do you remember, in essence, having a conversation with your father on the eighth of March where your father said to you, in so many words, that you were going to 'send Noriega to hell' and you agreed with that?" asked Rubino.

"I don't remember that," answered Paredes.

"General Noriega is the same man that destroyed your father politically and destroyed your family economically, correct?" Rubino pushed.

Again, Sullivan objected. "Repetitive. Argumentative."

"Sustained," said the judge.

Following Paredes to the stand was Manuel Sánchez, a San Blas Indian who was the captain of the *Krill*. Sánchez testified that he worked for the Paredes family and was asked to captain the *Krill* to Colombia in March 1986.

Sánchez had testified at Davidow and Saldarriaga's trial and was instrumental in placing the two at key points in the *Krill*'s voyage. But when it came to Noriega's involvement, Sánchez could only say that he was told Noriega protected the voyage. Sánchez said he did not know for certain that was true.

Noriega's direct link to the *Krill*, according to the prosecution, was an autographed picture of Noriega that hung in the boat's cabin. Myles Malman asked Sánchez about the photograph.

"Now, when you first began to work on the *Krill* in '85, was that photograph on the *Krill*?" Malman asked.

"No, sir," Sánchez replied.

"When you prepared to leave on your voyage to Cartagena, Colombia, was the photograph on the *Krill* then?"

"Yes," Sánchez said.

One of the coconspirators, Ramón Navarro, had brought the photograph to the *Krill*. Navarro had gotten it from César Rodríguez.

Malman also asked Sánchez about the load of rifles the *Krill* carried to Colombia. Sánchez said that two boxes were brought from Orlando Villarreal's warehouse and placed on the *Krill*. Sánchez said they were heavy and had to be handled by three men, but he never looked inside.

The government alleged that the two boxes contained one thousand M-16s.

On cross-examination, Rubino asked Sánchez about the photograph of Noriega: "Isn't it true that that photograph had been hanging in César Rodríguez's office for two years before the *Krill* incident?" he asked.

"I don't know," said Sánchez.

Rubino asked about Sánchez's arrest in Colombia and the seizure of the *Krill* by Colombian police when the cocaine was discovered on board. When the Colombian police saw the picture of Noriega, had that stopped them from performing their duties? Rubino asked.

"No, sir," replied Sánchez, who ended up spending a year in a Colombian jail.

Colombian police Capt. Carlos Malaver followed Sánchez to the witness stand. Malaver said a wiretap revealed that two Colombian traffickers awaiting the arrival of the *Krill* in Cartagena spoke about the "security" they had arranged for the voyage. But neither ever mentioned Noriega.

The final *Krill* witness was a Cuban-American drug trafficker named Héctor López who said he had worked with Saldarriaga receiving cartel cocaine in Miami. They sent the proceeds to Panama.

López said that when smuggling cocaine through the Bahamas became too expensive, he relocated to Panama. There, he said, he paid money to Pascual González, the head of civil aeronautics in the PDF, to guarantee the safety of his drug shipments. Even so, said López, one of his planes was confiscated. López said González urged him to buy further protection by paying Noriega $100,000. López said he sent the money to Noriega but never met him.

On cross-examination, López conceded to Rubino that his testimony against Noriega would be counted as a "credit" against an eight-year drug-trafficking sentence. After testifying in six other trials and providing information in twelve other cases, López had reduced his jail time to just three years, he said. But waiting to testify against Noriega, López complained, had actually lengthened his sentence. If he had been called early in the trial, he would already be free.

CHAPTER 30

★★★★★★★

Pieces of the Puzzle

The final phase of the government's case began on Thursday, December 5.

Amjad Awan was Noriega's personal banker and had accepted millions of dollars in deposits from him, beginning in January 1982, in the Bank of Credit and Commerce International, commonly called BCCI.

BCCI was founded in 1972 by a Pakistani banker with just $10 million and a loan from the Bank of America. A privately held bank, BCCI grew to have assets of $20 billion by the 1980s—a modest size by international banking standards. Headquartered in London and the Persian Gulf emirate of Abu Dhabi, BCCI's principal operations were in Luxembourg and the Cayman Islands, both countries with light banking regulations. By the mid-1980s the bank had established branches in sixty-nine countries with 1 million depositors and had built a reputation as a lender in the Third World, particularly to small businesses in Africa and Latin America. In large part, BCCI's growth was attributable to the aggressiveness of its executives, executives such as Awan who sought out businessmen and leaders of small countries—such as Noriega—with large amounts of money to deposit.

By July 1991, three months before Noriega's trial began, the full nature of BCCI's business had become clear. On July 5, the Bank of England and other international banking authorities moved to curtail BCCI's operations, acting on evidence that as much as $15 billion had fraudulently vanished from the bank.

In the United States, investigators in New York, Miami, Tampa, and Washington began trying to determine to what extent BCCI had become a tool for money launderers and international drugs and arms dealers, and to what extent BCCI concealed its assets, the identities of its loan recipients, and interest in other financial institutions.

BCCI—because it was privately held and operated chiefly in countries where banking regulations limited public disclosure of its business—had never been allowed to accept deposits in the United States. By the middle of 1991, investigators suspected that the bank had circumvented U.S. banking rules by secretly acquiring at least a quarter interest in the parent company of First American Bankshares, Inc., the largest banking company in Washington, D.C.

By the start of the Noriega trial, BCCI's notoriety was well established. Iran-Contra investigators suspected the bank had assisted former National Security Adviser Oliver North in financing arms deals with Iran. Others linked BCCI to a multi-million-dollar CIA fund to finance anticommunist rebels fighting in Afghanistan. And still others pointed to evidence that the renegade Palestinian guerrilla and terrorist Abu Nidal purchased arms through BCCI accounts.

In the United States the bank had first come under suspicion in 1986 when a U.S. Customs Service agent posing as a money launderer was told by a Colombian drug trafficker that he could launder more money if he opened an account in an international bank with a branch in Panama. The agent selected BCCI at random. That investigation led to an indictment of BCCI and five of its employees, including Awan. The indictment alleged a scheme to launder $32 million in cocaine profits.

In January 1990 two divisions of the bank pleaded guilty in federal court in Tampa to laundering $14 million in drug money from the Medellín and Cali cartels. The bank admitted it had used international loans and withdrawals and wire transfers to hide the trail of drug money. Seven months later, Awan and his colleagues were convicted of the laundering conspiracy.

When Awan walked into court on December 5, the forty-four-year-old bespectacled and bearded Pakistani-born banker was serving a twelve-year sentence for his role in the scheme. Dressed in a gray prison outfit, Awan, like many of the witnesses before him, hoped to trade his testimony for reduced jail time.

Soft-spoken and with a British accent, Awan said that he became the head of the Panama branch of BCCI in 1981. He pursued Noriega, who then headed Panama's G-2 military intelligence unit, and opened Noriega's first account with the bank in January 1982. The account was a numbered or "manager's ledger" account, Awan said. It was opened with the proviso that it would be maintained in "strict secrecy and confidentiality at all times." The first deposit, he said, was $42,000 in cash, bundles of $100 bills.

In the next year or two, Noriega made additional cash deposits, as much as $2 million but rarely less than $100,000, Awan said. The deposits came every two or three months and usually were brought to Awan's private office in suitcases or briefcases by a member of Noriega's staff.

In December 1983, Noriega requested that his accounts—which then totalled $5.4 million—be transferred to London where there was "better confidentiality." There, Panamanian bank employees would not become suspicious of the accounts, Awan said.

The accounts were opened for G-2 in Noriega's name. Even so, said Awan, in July 1984, Noriega instructed Awan to transfer more than $308,000 out of one of the G-2 accounts and into another belonging to Noriega's daughter, Thays. A few months later, in September 1984, Awan said, Noriega requested a $400,000 loan to buy a Paris apartment. In his loan request Noriega identified the BCCI accounts as his own. Awan said Noriega had also guaranteed a $2 million loan to César Rodríguez using the BCCI accounts and the Noriega family paid its monthly VISA bill through the accounts. Those bills sometimes ran to more than $25,000 a month, Awan said. By 1988, when Noriega was indicted, the accounts had grown to $19.3 million. Three days after the U.S. indictment, Noriega requested the accounts be moved from London to Luxembourg to take further advantage of bank secrecy laws, Awan said.

Through two days of direct examination in which he entered thousands of bank records into evidence, Pat Sullivan never asked Awan to explain where Noriega's money might have come from. To this Frank Rubino lodged a standing objection, arguing that the banker's testimony was irrelevant. The prosecution simply had not shown ties between Noriega's accounts and the drug trade.

"I don't think just because a world leader has a fortune, ergo [that] makes him a drug dealer," Rubino told the judge at sidebar. "There are other opportunities. There are other ways to make money." The implication—that Noriega could have accumulated millions through misappropriation—was one Rubino was willing to concede and even propose on cross-examination. And, Rubino suggested, Noriega might also have spent that misappropriated money on himself and his family.

"There are personal expenses run up by the general's daughters, correct? And probably his wife? And maybe some himself, correct?" Rubino asked Awan.

"Possibly, yes," replied Awan.

"And that was not the intention for which this account was opened when it was opened, was it?"

To that Sullivan objected.

Much of the BCCI-deposited money was spent legitimately, Rubino suggested. Many of the records showed embassy expenses, and one BCCI account payout was to the Boeing airplane company for $900,000.

As for the series of account switches following Noriega's 1988 indictment, there was a purpose, Rubino suggested.

"Prior to that, the United States had been putting great economic pressure and sanctions upon the government of the country of Panama, had they not?" Rubino asked.

"Yes, sir."

"Some of the things the government of the United States had done to bring down the government of Panama was impose sanctions upon not paying taxes, correct?"

"I object," Sullivan said.

"Did he tell you why he wanted it moved?" Rubino asked, taking a different tack.

"Yes, sir, he did."

"What did he tell you?"

"In brief, he wanted it to be in a safe place."

"He didn't want the government of the United States to seize it, did he?"

"Correct," Awan answered.

Drug Enforcement Administration financial analyst Lenore Sowers followed Awan to the witness stand. Using BCCI records and Awan's testimony, Sowers traced $23 million that had flowed though Noriega's secret accounts. Sowers said that $7.1 million of Noriega's BCCI deposits were in cash, and another $7.5 million went through BCCI's Panama branch. It was unclear where another $4.5 million had come from. As Sowers stood at a flowchart and testified, Rubino stood and objected.

"Unless this particular chart, somewhere on it, can show it's drug income, it just becomes totally irrelevant," Rubino said.

Judge Hoeveler stopped Rubino. "Now, I think you're arguing your case." The judge called the attorneys to sidebar.

"We're playing with smoke and mirrors and dazzling the jury with the pretty charts," Rubino continued. "Contrary to what the DEA believes, people make legitimate income. The DEA is so paranoid that their opinion is if you make more than they do, you're dealing in drugs."

"I know he had a legitimate job as general, but there are no known sources that can possibly justify the accumulation of this wealth," Sullivan responded.

Hoeveler suggested that Rubino develop the thrust of his objection on cross-examination.

Rubino turned first to a heading on Sower's chart labeled: "Sources of funds that are not indicated on the various types of documents."

"Would drug money be up here? If Floyd Carlton paid the General money, would it go up here in this 'other source'?" Rubino asked.

"I don't know," responded Sowers. "Unless they had Floyd Carlton's name on the document, I could not indicate."

Rubino pointed to another entry on the chart. "Now, if General Noriega received $5 million from the Medellín cartel to protect the lab in April of 1984, it couldn't be part of these two, $3 and $2 million, deposits received in '83, could it?" he asked.

Sowers began, "Not if he received—"

"Judge, I object," Sullivan said. "It calls for speculation on what it could or could not have been."

Hoeveler agreed. "You are into argument again, Counsel," he told Rubino.

"From April of '84 right up to and including today, is there any $4 or $5 million cash deposit?" he asked.

"The highest one is $1.1 million," said Sowers.

"Is there any check in from the Medellín cartel here for $4 or $5 million bribing General Noriega to protect the laboratory?"

"Not that I have knowledge of."

"Is there any check in here around any time after April of '84 for $4 or $5 million?" Rubino asked.

"There is not," Sowers answered.

"Talking about sources, were you able to determine if any money was received into any account that was a payment by a foreign government to General Noriega individually or in his role as head of G-2 or in his role as leader of the country of Panama?"

"There is not any documentation that states it is from a foreign government."

"Any indication of payments from the United States Central Intelligence Agency?" Rubino pressed.

"Not that I know of."

"Any indication of payments from the United States military intelligence?"

"I object," Sullivan said. "He could go several days making up things that he'd like to suggest."

Hoeveler called the attorneys to sidebar. "Why don't you simply, if you are in good faith, ask, 'Do you know the source of these monies?'" the judge suggested.

"Simply throwing out all this money and [not having] the faintest idea where it came from, she cannot prove this is drug money," Rubino responded.

"You are trying to argue your case to the jury through a witness who only knows the numbers she has looked at," Hoeveler said sternly. "I don't want you to do it anymore."

Rubino resumed his examination.

"Have you ever reviewed accounts of agencies of foreign governments?"

"No, sir."

Of the unaccounted funds that had been added to the accounts, Rubino asked, could some have been interest on the millions deposited?

"One of the purposes, I am sure, is to generate interest," Sowers answered. "Approximately $4 to $6 million, I think, would be a fair assessment."

"So then the $23 million is really $19 million plus $4 million interest or $17 million plus $6 million interest. It is around that range?" Rubino asked.

Sowers agreed.

Pointing to further entries, Rubino asked about $2 million that had been transferred into the accounts from Mrs. Noriega's accounts at Citibank in New York and the Korea Exchange Bank in Seoul. Other entries from Mrs. Noriega included a steady income of $35,000 a month with some payments of up to $135,000 in a month's time. Sowers agreed she knew nothing of Mrs. Noriega's family wealth, trust funds, or business annuities.

"Now, part of your job in going through records for the Drug Enforcement Administration, I think you have told us, is to look for 'unexplained wealth.' Is that true?" Rubino asked.

"Correct."

"Now, in order to do this, you have to look, don't you, at a person's income and a person's expenditures?"

"Correct."

"And, further, after you do this, don't you have to rule out all legitimate sources of income to see if you have some unexplained income?"

"That is correct."

"Now, in order to do that, don't you have to have . . . some knowledge about the person whose records you are analyzing?"

"Correct," Sowers answered.

"Can you say any of this is drug money?" asked Rubino.

"No," Sowers said.

After three months of trial, the evidence against Noriega amounted to the recollections of nearly sixty witnesses, all of which was testimonial evidence at best. Apart from Steven Kalish's letter to Noriega, which was discovered in Felicidad Noriega's Paris safe-deposit box, tangible evidence directly linking Noriega was lacking, except for some generic photographs of cartel cocaine packages. The prosecution had held it back until the end.

On the witness stand was Fernando Dilacova, a special agent in charge of the Drug Enforcement Administration in Panama at the time of the invasion. On December 22, 1989, as the invasion fighting still raged, Dilacova with military personnel went to Noriega's Panama City home.

In Noriega's home office, in a file cabinet behind a desk, there was $5,822,619 in cash in $100, $50, $20, and $10 bills, Dilacova testified. The cash was used, and some of it was found in a brown envelope inscribed, "To my General. Personal and Confidential."

When Guy Lewis completed his brief direct examination of Dilacova, Rubino asked why the money had been seized. Was there proof it was the proceeds of drug trafficking?

"No," Dilacova responded.

In fact, the money was returned to the government of Panama, Rubino pursued.

"Yes," the agent responded.

Rubino asked about the DEA's search of Noriega's residence and the presence of the military.

"Now, does the DEA normally function in time of war?" Rubino said.

Lewis objected, and Rubino asked to speak to the judge at sidebar.

"Under what right or authority— I think the jury has a right to know how this man can walk into my client's house and seize things from him—when he's an American agent in a foreign country—other than by an act of war. I think I have a right to develop that and let the jury think about it and mull that over. What are we doing there, searching people's houses in a foreign country?"

The question was not one for the jury, Judge Hoeveler told Rubino. The law was clear; the Supreme Court had only recently ruled that warrantless searches by U.S. agents working in foreign countries was not a violation of the Fourth Amendment prohibition against illegal searches and seizures.

There was no evidence, Rubino said, that the money was drug proceeds. With U.S. economic sanctions taking a toll in Panama prior to the invasion, Noriega had stashed the money to pay his soldiers. "There are many reasons why a de facto leader would have that amount of money on hand," Rubino told the judge.

"I didn't mean for the jury to decide whether the search was legal or illegal," Rubino told the judge.

Hoeveler studied Rubino a moment. "You kind of want to upset them," the judge observed.

"Oh, yes. I'm not going to tell you differently. I do," Rubino said.

It was not a matter for the jury, the judge said, ending the sidebar.

On the morning of December 21, 1989, the day before Dilacova searched Noriega's home, U.S. Army Intelligence Officer Kenneth Webb had led six soldiers on a search of Noriega's offices at the PDF *comandancia*. Webb's unit had followed Army Rangers into the command center in the midst of a firefight surrounding the headquarters. On the second floor, Webb's unit proceeded with chemical lights down a long hallway. Two men checked for booby-traps as the unit proceeded. On one side of the hallway was a large reception hall with draperies and a wooden floor, an officers' dining room, and a covey of small offices and secretarial stations. The last office on the left was Noriega's, and it had a small den leading to a bedroom. There, next to a closet filled with Noriega's dress uniforms, Webb found a small yellow piece of paper, a handwritten note.

"There were monetary figures noted on the document and some large figures," Webb said. "That's what caught my eye."

Before Webb could continue, Rubino stood. "Your Honor, so that there is no confusion for the jury, we are prepared to stipulate that the area that the officer has testified about is, in fact, General Noriega's personal office/apartment, if you will, contained in the *comandancia*. We are further prepared to stipulate that the document that the gentleman found, the officer found, on top of the dresser is, in fact, the document written by General Noriega in his own hand."

It was a preemptive strike. Rubino had already seen a photocopy of the document.

Myles Malman had no further questions. A government handwriting expert would be called to interpret the document.

Rubino again moved preemptively: "This piece of paper that's in evidence was not found hidden in the safe, was it?" he asked.

"No, sir," Webb answered.

"The paper was right on top of General Noriega's own dresser, correct?"

"That's correct, sir."

"Well, since the letter is in evidence, let's take a look at the first line of the letter."

"In English, does it say, 'Carry politics to a strong force?' Is that the translation of what it says?"

Webb said he could read Spanish, but he was not sure of the translation.

Rubino pressed on: "And below that it says, 'Fifty thousand dollars a kg, a kilogram.' Does it not?"

Webb looked at the exhibit. "It says $50,000 kg. Yes, sir."

And it also said "$30,000/$35,000 kg" and "17,000 55 GLS," which could stand for fifty-five-gallon drums, Webb and Rubino agreed.

"Below that, does it not say, 'Eighty-four thousand kilograms de cocaine'?" Rubino asked.

"It says eighty-four thousand kg de— It looks like cocaine, yes, sir," Webb said.

Malman stood and objected. Rubino was trying to adopt the witness as his own, Malman protested. The cross-examination had moved beyond the scope of the direct examination.

Rubino smiled. He had no further questions.

The prosecution's case was now complete.

On Friday, December 6, Frank Rubino and Jon May went to Judge Hoeveler and argued that they would not be prepared to go forward with Noriega's defense before January 13. The judge had asked Rubino and May to go forward immediately after the conclusion of the government's case, probably in the week or two before Christmas.

But May said the defense planned to call as many as a dozen DEA agents and administrators to testify, few of whom had consented to pre-appearance interviews. "Most important, the defense has been hampered by the fact that most of our witnesses have refused to be interviewed," May told the judge. "We [do] not have to tell this court that these particular witnesses are exceedingly hostile to the defense." There were also witnesses in Panama who were afraid to travel to the United States for fear they might be jailed, May said. The defense believed it would have to travel to Panama to take depositions from Panamanian witnesses.

Pat Sullivan said the prosecution opposed a delay. "It's taken the government three months to put on its case, and we're into our fourth month, and that should have provided defense counsel with sufficient time, with their numerous investigations, to develop the testimony and evidence they think would benefit their case. We heard that Mr. Rubino started the defense of this case in 1988, when he had the whole PDF to draw upon. Maybe part of the problem is that—the way I detect it—they have gone through a number of potential defenses . . . disregarding them, deciding they really weren't too viable, and now, we're down to something that may be viable, but they wasted their time on a bunch of other things—proving the history of World War II and Burma and Thailand."

Rubino said there was another reason to delay the defense: It would be unfair to give an opening statement, examine one witness, and then take a break.

"To come back two weeks later and say to that witness, 'Sir, do you remember the last question that I asked you when we broke two weeks ago?' You almost have to start all over again," Rubino said.

"The General sat in jail for a year and a half, two years before the trial ever came. He doesn't mind sitting in jail another two weeks so I can do a good job," Rubino said. "He's not going to come back later and say, 'My trial was dragged out longer than it should.'"

Hoeveler was not greatly sympathetic. "We have been at this for two years now," he said. "We're running out of time. Let's talk about the jury. These people have a right to live their lives. I never heard of a case where the defense asked for a month to start their case."

Hoeveler asked May and Rubino to be ready to begin during the week before Christmas. The holiday break would give them ten days for additional preparation. The trial, Hoeveler hoped, would finish by the end of January.

But on Monday, December 16, two days before the defense was to begin its presentation, Rubino and May returned to Hoeveler.

On Saturday morning, December 14, just four days before the judge had asked Rubino and May to make their opening statement and begin the defense, Sullivan and Guy Lewis sat down with James Bramble, a DEA agent who headed the agency's in-country Panama operation during part of the early 1980s. Bramble was scheduled to be called by the defense as one of its first witnesses. He had refused to be interviewed by Rubino and May, but was telling the prosecutors what he knew about Noriega's work with the DEA.

Sullivan and Lewis had copies of the DEA 6's—incident reports—spread before them. Bramble was explaining what the reports meant. "This was all done consistent with Operation Negocios," Bramble said.

Sullivan and Lewis looked at one another. "Operation Negocios? What's Operation Negocios?" Sullivan asked.

Negocios is the Spanish word for business, and Operation Negocios was a cooperative effort between Noriega's drug enforcement units and the DEA conducted between 1983 and 1987. Noriega's agents monitored flights carrying drug money to Panama. The G-2 and DENI provided the DEA with extensive information on cartel money couriers entering Panama through the airports.

Sullivan was dumbfounded. This was the first he had heard of Operation Negocios. Bramble had briefly outlined what seemed to be a close cooperative effort between Noriega and the DEA to stymie the cartel's work in Panama. That cooperation ran counter to almost everything the prosecution had just spent more than three months telling the jury. Sullivan called Steve Grilli. "Tell me about Operation Negocios!" he yelled into the phone. Guy Lewis had never seen Sullivan more upset. Grilli said he had never heard of the Negocios effort. "Well, find out!" Sullivan yelled.

Sullivan had spent almost two years pleading with the DEA and its investigators to disclose every facet of Panamanian cooperation in the drug war. Now on the eve of the defense case, it looked as though new evidence—that neither the prosecution nor the defense had known about—would be brought to the jury. The revelation could go beyond embarrassment; it could border on obstruction if agents had witheld information. Within minutes of the end of the hearing, Sullivan ordered an extensive search of DEA files regarding Negocios.

Sullivan phoned Rubino and May that evening and disclosed what he had learned. He said he had ordered an immediate and thorough investigation into the details of Negocios.

(Immediately after Christmas, Sullivan, Lewis, and DEA agents Tom Raffanello and Lenny Athas went to Washington to DEA headquarters. A special room was segregated for agency files pertaining to Panama. The room was stacked to the ceiling with boxes. Sullivan personally led the search. Every relevant bit of information was to be turned over to the defense as required by the rules of procedure.)

"I am expecting the worst," Sullivan told Lewis and the agents.

Before the judge on Monday, May called Operation Negocios "one of the most significant operations run out of Panama in cooperation with the Panamanian Defense Forces, an operation which tracked the movement of millions of dollars of cartel money from Colombia to Panama." Not only must the defense be given time to examine the documents and interview the DEA agents involved, he said, but the question of sanctions against the government and even a mistrial might be considered. "We were about to embark upon the examination of these DEA agents without having the most critical information needed for our examination. This is beyond question the most significant discovery given to us in the course of this case."

The only way to guarantee a fair trial, May continued, was to allow a full examination of the newly discovered material. "This trial has gone on three and a half months," May said. "It is going to go on at least through January. There should be no rush to judgment here."

Though clearly embarrassed by the revelation of the material, Sullivan argued a delay was not warranted. Noriega had had three years since his indictment to prepare his defense. If the PDF had been cooperating with the DEA, then Noriega's own agents should have known about Operation Negocios. It should not be a surprise now. Even as the trial progressed, Sullivan continued, the defense had insisted its investigators were working in Panama. One investigator was Luis Quiel, a PDF inspector who had worked narcotics enforcement for the PDF for years. Why hadn't either Quiel or Noriega himself told Rubino and May about Operation Negocios? Sullivan asked. "This does not take the defense by surprise," Sullivan told the judge. "I don't believe it does."

"Are these Quiel's documents?" Hoeveler asked May.

"No. These are not Quiel's documents," May responded. "There was an invasion. All of General Noriega's records were seized by the United States government. They have not been able to locate Quiel's records." Exculpatory records were all in the possession of the invader, the United States government, May said.

"I don't want you to suffer any prejudice, nor will I permit you to suffer any prejudice," Hoeveler said. "I am just trying to keep the matter going."

"We want to get our case on," May said. "We want to do it effectively."

On Tuesday, December 17, Hoeveler waited for the jury to be seated. Out of consideration for the defense and out of consideration for the jurors who had spent three months in court, the judge announced that the case would be in recess until January 6.

"You are to decide the case on the evidence that comes from the witness stand and the exhibits," Hoeveler told the jurors. "So it is vital that you not discuss this case with anyone or let anyone discuss it with you or read anything in the newspapers or listen or see television. Be very careful about that. On behalf of the parties, we all wish you a very merry Christmas."

Rule 29 of the Federal Rules of Criminal Procedure allows a court to enter a judgment of acquittal on some or all of the offenses charged in an indictment after the close of the prosecution's case, provided the evidence presented has been insufficient to reach a conviction.

Defense attorneys routinely make Rule 29 motions, and on December 17, Frank Rubino made his.

The next day, after the jury was dismissed, Judge Hoeveler ruled on the motion.

Rubino argued that the government had failed to clarify a central aspect of the indictment—the alleged payment of $5 million by the cartel for protection and the right to build the Darien lab. The government's witnesses had offered differing accounts of the surrounding events. Some said the money was paid to Noriega. Others said it was paid to Julian Melo. Some said Noriega agreed to return part of the money to the Colombians after Fidel Castro settled the matter. Others said there was an agreement to make Melo the scapegoat. The government had never made clear who ordered the raid or why. "General Noriega is the leader of the PDF, but that does not make him responsible for every single act of every single member of the PDF," Rubino told Hoeveler.

Just as unconvincingly, Rubino argued, the prosecution had failed to trace the cartel's cocaine to the United States. Even in a light most favorable to the government, Rubino said, Noriega was never told where the cocaine he was to protect was going—not to Panama, not to Europe, not to the United States.

In response, Pat Sullivan argued the evidence taken "as a whole" pointed to Noriega's involvement in a broad smuggling conspiracy.

"The government has attempted to prove, for the RICO counts especially, an overall conspiratorial agreement between General Noriega and the Medellín cartel," Sullivan said. "It has separate parts. Some of it relates to protection of ether shipments going to labs. The major part, of course, had to do with protection or at least permission for cocaine flights to enter Panama to be sent on to the United States. Those are all part and parcel of the overall agreement, and proving one part of that agreement, I suggest, Your Honor, tends to prove the other parts as well."

For Hoeveler, there was sufficient evidence that the defense motion for acquittal should be denied. Some of the counts were weak and some of the evidence—particularly in the instance of the Darien lab—"goes in all different directions," Hoeveler noted. "But, giving the government the benefit of the doubt, there is sufficient evidence to go before a jury," he concluded.

During the next three weeks, Hoeveler told both sides, he expected the case to move forward. Rubino and Sullivan agreed that both sides would travel to Panama to take the depositions of defense witnesses sitting in prison. In January, the judge said, the defense would open. "In the meantime," Hoeveler ended, "I am going to be here. If you need to see me, I will be glad to see you."

Bill Hoeveler had been at this case full-bore for two years. It had been a constant wrestling match, keeping it all on line for trial—and once trial began, keeping it all on track. The judge was sixty-nine years old. He hadn't cut back a bit, still carried a full load, in the neighborhood of four hundred cases, and a lot of those were criminal cases, the most stressful of all.

As the Noriega trial date had approached the previous summer, Hoeveler raced to close out his trial calendar. The Speedy Trial Act said a defendant had a right to go to trial in a reasonable amount of time. That meant there were cases that had to be finished before the Big One took off, cases that under the law had to be tried.

But the Noriega case was a four-hundred-pound gorilla. It did what it wanted to do. It had a way of running over everything else. Still, Hoeveler was adamant about finishing out as much of his trial calendar as he could before he was forced by the constraint of time to send cases off to other judges. On the Saturday before the Noriega jury selection got under way in September, Hoeveler finished one trial. The next Tuesday, the prospective Noriega jurors were in court.

This schedule meant there wasn't time for tennis anymore. The Saturday afternoon sets had been a staple for years. Now there was barely time for walking Nisei, the Hoevelers' one-hundred-pound Akita. There were some obligations Hoeveler could not ignore. Saturday morning was still reserved for reading law books onto tape for blind and visually impaired law students. Sunday was church. The judge was a chalice bearer and served on the parish vestry at Saint Stephen's Episcopal Church in Coconut Grove, just a few minutes' drive from home.

September and October had not been bad. For the first two months of the prosecution's case, things had actually gone well. The case was on a four-day-a-week courtroom schedule. That left Fridays for sentencings and hearings in other cases, for motion work, opinion writing, and management of the office. Janice Tinsman, the judge's secretary, and Maria Conboy, his courtroom deputy (Hoeveler liked to call them "the girls" because they could have been his daughters) kept things running smoothly and generally made life pleasant. And Sandra Cavazos, the law clerk whom Professor Arthur Miller at Harvard Law School had recommended to help handle the Noriega case, was great. At the start there had still been time for games of Pig, a Nerf basketball game that had been played in chambers between the judge and all comers for years.

But by November it seemed as though the Noriega case was turning into more and more of a Sisyphean labor. At night, about seven or seven-thirty, after he arrived home from work, Hoeveler would take Nisei out for a walk, and frequently he would complain about the tightness in his chest. "I don't think I'm getting enough exercise," he would tell Griff, his wife.

With the Rule 29 out of the way and the trial in recess for two weeks, Hoeveler decided to give Franz Stewart a call. Stewart was a cardiologist and a friend. "I want you to get in here for a stress test," Stewart told Hoeveler. "Come in Monday."

On Monday, December 23, Stewart looked over the results of the stress test. Not good. He sent Hoeveler around for a catheter procedure. The technicians injected dye into his arteries to check for blockage. They sent a little camera in for a look. The results were dire. One of the major vessels to the heart was 99 percent blocked. How could this be? Hoeveler wondered. I don't smoke; I don't drink; I'm an avid tennis player.

This was serious business. Immediate surgery was truly the only solution, the only way to go on living. Stewart took Griff aside. "He runs more of a risk by going home, by walking out of here, than he does from an operation," he told her.

On Christmas Eve morning, in a two-and-a-half-hour operation, the surgeon removed an artery from Hoeveler's leg and used it to replace the damaged artery connected to his heart. By the time it was over, the operation had turned into a triple bypass.

Hoeveler awoke on Christmas morning. Griff was there. She was a beautiful sight. It was a great Christmas.

The room soon filled with cards and bouquets and fruit baskets from wellwishers. As the news spread, the gifts piled up. Hospital security stood watch in the hallway.

By the day after Christmas, word of the surgery had reached the press. How serious was it? What about the trial? Stewart had already told Hoeveler there was no going back to work on January 6, as the judge had planned. At least four weeks were needed for recovery. The soonest he could get back on the bench would be the end of January, Stewart said, and even then, only half days for a while.

"I'm determined to finish it," Hoeveler told reporters who squeezed into his hospital room. But one had to follow the doctor's orders. At the judge's bedside was the devotional *The Imitation of Christ* and his well-worn Bible.

By the middle of January it was clear that Hoeveler would not be back on the bench as soon as he hoped. Dr. Stewart ordered the date of the trial's resumption to slip from January 27 to February 3. That was a solid six weeks of recovery.

As it turned out, the delay was not wasted on Frank Rubino and Jon May. Rubino was exhausted from going head to head with the three prosecutors for nearly four months. The defense had planned to use the two-week break to regroup. Now Rubino and May went into high gear.

With Hoeveler's consent, they arranged to travel to Panama to take the testimony of three imprisoned aides to Noriega. They hoped the three— Nivaldo Madrinan, the former head of DENI, Panama's equivalent of the FBI; Lucinio Miranda, the former head of narcotics investigations for the Panamanian military; and Cleto Hernández, once an officer in G-2, military intelligence—would discredit the government's testimony regarding the alleged $10 million payoff. All three would know in detail the workings of the just-revealed Operation Negocios. The judge agreed that videotaped testimony of the three prisoners could be used in court as long as the prosecution was allowed to travel to Panama to conduct cross-examination.

On Thursday, January 30, Sullivan, Malman, Lewis, Rubino, and May returned from Panama. In three days they had taken nearly twenty hours of videotaped testimony. The following day the group went to the judge's chambers. It was the judge's first visit back to the courthouse. He looked a bit drawn, a bit pale, but not incredibly worse for the wear. All five attorneys were happy to see him. Not one wished the judge off the case. The trial would commence the following Monday on a half-day schedule for two weeks, Hoeveler told the group.

"You're probably more ready than I am, but we're going to take a shot at it," he said.

"We want to recall all of our previous witnesses," Pat Sullivan joked.

Hoeveler smiled. "I had a feeling that you would have a rebuttal case, especially in view of the delay. We'll see if we can get to the jury sometime in early March."

CHAPTER 31
★★★★★★★

In Defense of Noriega

The prosecution had failed to make a direct link between Noriega and drugs and drug money. But the defense's case was not perfect either. Jon May and Frank Rubino had failed to find a solid link that said the American government allowed drugs to travel uninhibited into the United States as payment for the delivery of guns and other assistance to the Nicaraguan Contras or other U.S.-backed groups in Central America.

Late in the fall of 1991, Rubino and May had threatened to subpoena the Joint Chiefs of Staff, military intelligence officials, and most of the president's National Security Council. A subpoena had gone out to former NSC senior staff member and Iran-Contra planner Oliver North, but by the middle of January 1992, thoughts of an Iran-Contra defense were dead.

The judge had stymied each of Rubino's attempts to broaden the case into the realm of politics on cross-examination. Rubino had tried to use innuendo as a lever to open the range of inquiry, but the judge had turned the effort back. While the prosecution made its case, May had spent most of his time locked in the courthouse basement with secret government documents. But there was no smoking gun.

The defense's Classified Information request had spoken of CIA-backed international gunrunning as part of the fight against communism, but May had found nothing to substantiate the charge. The search had been reminiscent of prosecutor Richard Gregorie's first visit to the CIA in 1987. Whatever CIA or NSC trail there was had not been neatly archived.

Even with the extra six weeks to search, while Judge Hoeveler recovered, the Operation Negocios lead had not panned out for the defense, either. Negocios had proven beyond a doubt what many had suspected for years: that the DEA's in-country agents and domestic agents rarely shared information. Turf wars and distrust within the agency were magnified by the Noriega investigation where so many careers and reputations seemed at stake.

But the Negocios files—in the end four volumes of about two inches thickness each—turned out to be a compilation of bits and pieces of information that, in fact, the defense had gotten from the prosecution before and during trial. As a whole, the Negocios file was only barely more impressive than its parts.

Negocios had served to solidify Rubino and May's resolve to present a cooperation defense. But the cooperation, in the end, did not look to Sullivan as though it would contradict the whole of the government's case. On cross-examination, the prosecution could easily argue that Noriega's Negocios cooperation was just another part of his double dealing. That's how Sullivan intended to counter the defense. That, however, would not keep Rubino and May from playing up the operation's late discovery. Rubino and May were resigned that the defense would have to take a more predictable turn.

"If he didn't let us do it in the front during the government's case, do you think he'll let us do it in the back?" Rubino told reporters who asked about a defense development of the Iran-Contra connection. It was a rhetorical question. The answer was, of course, no. The cooperation defense had become the key. It was not strong, but with Negocios it was at least not puny.

Rubino had already done what he could to attack the credibility of the government's witnesses. They were, for the most part, drug traffickers and convicted money launders, and on cross-examination he had not let them off scot-free. Without the smoking gun connection—the U.S. government's knowing involvement and support of criminal activities in aid of a Central American freedom fight—the challenge now was to build on Rubino's cross-examinations of the witnesses to demonstrate Noriega's full cooperation with the U.S. antidrug effort.

To counter the prosecution's inmate witness list, what better defense than to call the jailers? By Monday morning, February 3, May and Rubino had lined up sixteen past and present U.S. government officials to take the witness stand for the defense. It was a dangerous course for a defense to call government agents. But it was the only course because the defense *was* government agents, Rubino would say. The subpoena list included three former chiefs of the DEA, nine DEA agents who served in Panama, a former U.S. ambassador to Panama, a retired Army general, a retired Navy admiral, and two CIA agents. And as if to underscore just how different the defense would be from the prosecution, Rubino and May settled on a slight twist. May would deliver the opening statement.

After three months, Rubino's role as a street-smart and sometimes wise-cracking foil to the studious and ultra-serious prosecution team had no doubt left its mark on the jury. May would lend an earnest, scholarly imprimatur to the defense. The message would be that the defense was able to do its homework. The tack would also introduce May to the jury and allow him later to examine witnesses, which his long preparation had made inevitable. The downside was that in sixteen years of practice as an appellate court specialist, May had not once delivered an opening statement, even though he was an expert in the complex questions of legal appeals. "If I have a tendency to get tongue-tied or to lose my place or stare off," May told the jury, "I hope you will be understanding."

What the jury was about to hear would not fit together neatly like the plot in a movie or television drama, May outlined. Rather, it would be bits and pieces that would in the end fit together. To start, May said, the defense would call former top administrators of the Drug Enforcement Administration.

"What these three men will tell you, ladies and gentlemen, is that the level and quality of the cooperation given by General Noriega to the United States in its investigation of narcotics and money–laundering offenses was unprecedented among the leaders of Central and South American nations."

After six weeks away from the case, the jury seemed especially alert. They followed May closely.

Next, May said, would follow the DEA agents who had fought the drug traffickers on the ground and in person in Panama and in Central and South America. "These men will tell you that they placed their lives in the hands of General Noriega."

U.S. agents working overseas during the 1970s and 1980s were injured and killed doing their jobs. But in Panama, the DEA "could operate knowing that they were safe from harassment, from intimidation," May said. "The evidence will show that General Noriega over and over again provided these agents with the assistance and the support and protection that they needed."

The former U.S. ambassador to Panama and the former head of the vice president's Task Force in south Florida would testify. "They will tell you that over and over, the United States came to General Noriega for assistance. They will tell you that General Noriega was our ally in the war against the drug traffickers." That assistance came in the interdiction of drugs arriving on freighters, in the locating and destroying of precursor chemicals, in the elimi-nation of marijuana production, in the identification of cartel money couri-ers, and in the apprehension and expulsion of criminals wanted in the United States. Between 1977 and 1988, May said, Noriega had permitted the United States Coast Guard to board two hundred vessels of Panamanian registry. Over 2 million pounds of marijuana was seized and destroyed as a result. One million gallons of chemicals used to produce cocaine had also been seized and destroyed in Panama during the same period, May said. The amount of chemicals seized was so vast that Panama was forced to ask the United States for expert advice on how to destroy large quantities of ether and acetone without causing an ecological disaster, May said.

"The quantity of ether and acetone destroyed was a significant blow to the operations of the Medellín cartel," May continued. "These agents will also tell you that another way of getting to the drug traffickers, another way of stopping this business, is to identify and seize the money that is used to finance both the production of the cocaine as well as to finance the efforts of distributing the cocaine. You will hear a great deal of testimony about an operation called Negocios, an operation which began in 1983 and continued through 1987, an operation which targeted individuals who were coming into the airports in Panama sometimes carrying millions of dollars of narcotics proceeds." The couriers were stopped and identified, and "this intelligence information resulted in the discovery of some of the most significant cartel operations in the United States."

Operation Negocios was so secret, May said, that even top DEA administrators did not know about it. The reason the operation was so secret was that General Noriega and the Panamanian Defense Forces were providing to the DEA information "which they were prohibited from providing under the bank secrecy laws of Panama. In assisting the United States, General Noriega and the Panamanian Defense Forces went beyond the expectations of any of these agents and also beyond what they were permitted to do under the laws of Panama," May said.

At the very time that General Noriega is alleged to have been in bed with the Medellín cartel, the evidence would show that the PDF raided and destroyed the Darien lab, identified through Operation Negocios the very money couriers who were alleged to have delivered money to Noriega, and seized vast amounts of precursor chemicals. "Six weeks after the raid at Darien, General Noriega, through his antinarcotics unit, was providing the Drug Enforcement Administration information pertaining to an offer by the Medellín cartel to pay the Panamanian Defense Forces $5 million if they would stop the seizures of cocaine," May said. The DEA learned about the cartel bribe not from the prosecution's witnesses but from the PDF.

Eight weeks after the raid at Darien, May continued, Jorge Ochoa's chief lieutenant in Panama was under arrest, and soon after, the cartel's main bank in Panama was closed. The lab workers arrested in Darien were made available to the DEA for interviews and interrogation, May said. They were returned to Colombia in handcuffs and under armed guard. May paused for a moment and looked up from his notes. His presentation was direct. The message was simple: Noriega had cooperated. "The evidence will show that some of the most significant operations against the Medellín cartel, operations conducted by the Drug Enforcement Administration, occurred, were made possible, as a result of assistance that General Noriega and his antinarcotics unit provided to the DEA."

Because of information provided by Noriega, May told the jury, the cartel's most important money launderer had been arrested in May 1983. Ramón Milian Rodríguez had laundered more than $200 million of cartel money before his arrest.

May shifted directions. "You have heard that General Noriega made a trip to Havana. That is true. General Noriega did go to Cuba in July 1984," May said. "The evidence will show that Castro invited General Noriega to Cuba. The evidence will show that this invitation was extended before General Noriega left on his trip to France and Israel. The evidence will show that Castro invited General Noriega to Cuba, not to talk about the Darien lab, not to talk about assassins, but to discuss the dangerous and explosive situation in Central America. You will recall there were wars going on in Nicaragua and El Salvador at the time. You will hear that Castro's invitation to General

Noriega was communicated to the Central Intelligence Agency. He received a briefing from the Central Intelligence Agency on what they wanted communicated to Castro. Ladies and gentlemen, when General Noriega returned from the trip to Cuba, he met with the Central Intelligence Agency. He told them in detail of his conversations. You will hear from the Central Intelligence Agency. This was not an isolated event. General Noriega over the course of twenty years had numerous contacts with Fidel Castro, many trips to Cuba. These contacts, these trips, were known by the United States and on occasion encouraged by the United States."

When Marxist revolutionaries took control of the island of Grenada in October 1983 and threatened the lives of American students there, the United States asked Noriega to contact Castro and urge him to order the surrender of Cuban troops stationed on Grenada. "During the course of this trial you will hear of other incidents where General Noriega was relied upon by the United States." May paused and slowly looked from one end of the jury box to the other.

"Ladies and gentlemen, none of the witnesses we present has received immunity for his testimony. None of the witnesses we present was allowed to plead to a reduced charge. None of the witnesses we will present received a reduced sentence for his cooperation or was allowed to keep his drug profits in exchange for his assistance. None of the witnesses we will present is being moved to the prison of his choice or let out of prison on a reduced bond or placed in the Witness Protection Program. Ladies and gentlemen, the evidence will show that General Noriega was a friend of the United States, but he was also the leader of a sovereign and independent state. The evidence will show that he fought the drug traffickers, not as a favor to the United States but because the traffic in marijuana and cocaine was and is as much a threat to his nation as it is to ours. At the end of this case you may wonder why General Noriega was indicted."

Again May paused for a moment. "But that is not an issue for you to determine. The sole issue for you to determine, for you to decide, is whether or not the government has proved its case beyond a reasonable doubt." Again May paused. "After considering all the testimony to be presented, we believe that you will find General Noriega is not guilty." May adjusted his glasses, folded his notes, and then turned and walked back to the defense table.

The statement had taken slightly less than twenty-five minutes, a fraction of the time Pat Sullivan had taken to deliver the government's opening statement five months before.

At the defense table, Noriega smiled slightly as May returned. Noriega, who every day had come to trial in his dress general's uniform, now had added a pair of dark reading glasses. Before him was a small stack of yellow legal pads. By Noriega's side, Rubino also half-smiled with satisfaction at May's opening, reading glasses, too, perched halfway down his nose. It looked as though the defense was rolling up its intellectual shirt-sleeves to get on with the fight.

The moment, however, was short.

"All right," said the judge without hesitation. "Gentlemen, are you ready to proceed with your first witness?"

"Yes, sir," Rubino said, standing.

And then Jon May stood again. For now, he would take on the defense's direct examinations as well. He called former DEA Administrator Peter Bensinger.

There is an adage among lawyers that there are no substantive gains to be made on cross-examination. Even when a witness is turned around on cross, the most that a jury sees is that the gains that were made on direct are nullified. That meant that as May walked back to the lectern to begin the defense's direct examinations, the best he and Rubino could hope for was that, so far, the case was a draw.

Even though a defendant comes to trial under presumption of innocence, the weight of government officialdom almost always takes an immediate toll. In Noriega's case, the president had launched an invasion to bring him to trial. Certainly, it could have been in the back of any juror's mind that the president would not take such an action were not Noriega guilty of something. And there had been the length of the government's case. That, too, would make an impression, whether or not the government had actually won its points.

Many defenses might decline to call witnesses at all and simply let the jury grapple with its reasonable doubts. But there was no question that after nearly fifty witnesses and three months, the defense had to counter—and do it dramatically.

Using witnesses gathered from the government to help build up its case on direct examination and pitting the government's prosecutors against other government law enforcement agents on cross was part of Rubino and May's strategy.

Calling the government's own agents to offer testimony on behalf of the defendant all but guaranteed the defense's witnesses would be hostile. Peter Bensinger, the former DEA chief, had declined to be interviewed by May and Rubino prior to taking the witness stand. While witness interviews afford attorneys an opportunity to measure a witness's effectiveness and recall, they cannot be required. Once on the witness stand, Bensinger took the earliest opportunity to make his position clear.

"I have been subpoenaed as a witness to this case, in the sense as a hostile witness," he told May, who had asked if the government had interviewed him beforehand. "I want to provide whatever information is required during this trial, factually and honestly. It is not my obligation to provide an interview with you."

Since Bensinger, of his own description, was hostile, court rules allowed May on direct examination to ask otherwise unacceptably leading questions. He quickly guided Bensinger to three letters that he had written during his tenure as DEA chief from 1976 to 1981. The letters were either to or about Noriega and his narcotics enforcement troops.

The first, addressed to Senator Robert Dole of Kansas, was sent in the late 1970s. May asked Bensinger to describe its contents. "The letter indicates good cooperation does exist between the DEA and the Panamanian National Guard," Bensinger said, paraphrasing his letter. "The letter goes on to say that there have been bilateral enforcement efforts interdicting drug shipments and individuals have been arrested as a result of those efforts. Expelled from Panama to the United States." Bensinger added, "My view was, 'Let's get whatever we can get in the way of cooperation and information and seizure.'" Bensinger said of Noriega's G-2: "But I was not under the impression that this was an agency, an organization, that was without the suspicion of corruption or looking the other way."

Bensinger had also sent a Christmas greeting to Noriega in 1986. "The professionalism of your agency is well respected by us as well as your leadership," the letter said.

"At this period of time, when you wrote this letter, did you regard General Noriega as a professional involved in the same sorts of activities that you yourself were involved in with your agency? Is that not true?" May asked.

It was a softball question for Bensinger. He took the opportunity.

"I always regarded Colonel Noriega with suspicion since taking office as the administrator," he replied. "I base that on the files I had seen, anecdotal information, even the size of his house."

Bensinger added that during 1977 and 1978, while the Panama Canal Treaty negotiations were in progress, the Panamanian government. including Noriega, had worked hard to be cooperative. But there were ulterior motives, Bensinger suggested. "I would not characterize Colonel Noriega during that period as a true, outstanding, professional law enforcement officer," Bensinger said. "I looked upon the cooperation that we got as gravy."

On cross-examination, Bensinger told Myles Malman that his letters to Noriega had not been more than "goodwill salutations." They were letters that went to other law enforcement and world leaders as well, he said. "Those words that appear in that letter are not unique for Colonel Noriega, were not unique for Panama."

May came back on redirect. "Was it your practice to allow letters to go out under your signature which were not true?" he asked.

"That would not have been my practice," Bensinger replied.

The defense's second witness, Jack Lawn, had headed the DEA from 1985 to 1990. He was no easier to get along with.

After Lawn left government service, he became operations manager for the New York Yankees. Now, early February, was the start of his busiest part of the year. He was none too thrilled about going to Miami to appear on behalf of Noriega.

Jon May had been in New York in late January and had contacted Lawn by telephone. Lawn said he would not be adverse to meeting in preparation for his testimony, but his schedule right then would not allow it. He agreed to meet May the Sunday before he would be called. May offered to meet Lawn at the airport, but Lawn declined and suggested they meet at his hotel. When May arrived at the Miami Sheraton, Lawn begged off, saying he was tired. He offered to talk at another time. Three unanswered phone calls later, May gave up. In the meantime, Lawn sat down with Myles Malman and reviewed his recollections.

On direct examination, May once again presented his witness with a collection of official letters. The first, written in July 1985, wished Noriega continued success in his fight against the drug menace.

"I would have to say that the letter was written while I was wearing my diplomatic hat and that I was writing a letter hoping that we would continue in a working relationship with the government of Panama," Lawn explained after reviewing the letter.

Lawn was asked about the DEA and PDF's joint venture, Operation Chemcom, which had seized and destroyed millions of gallons of precursor chemicals used in the manufacture of cocaine. The operation was successful but not overwhelmingly so, Lawn said. "I am aware that the chemicals were seized by the Panamanian Defense Forces. And, as I say, sometimes very successfully." But, he added, "sometimes not so successfully in that the chemicals were later released."

There was another letter written in 1986 that said: "I would like to take this opportunity to reiterate my deep personal appreciation for your vigorous anti-drug-trafficking policy that you have adopted, which is reflected in the numerous expulsions from Panama of accused traffickers, the large seizures of cocaine and precursor chemicals that have occurred in Panama, and the eradication of major cultivation in Panama territory."

And another thanked Noriega for expelling Jack Carlton Reed from Panama. Reed had been Carlos Lehder's partner in trafficking. The expulsion sent Reed to the United States to stand trial.

Another letter thanked Noriega for his cooperation in the DEA's Operation Pisces, a money-laundering sting that resulted in the roundup of 115 drug traffickers and the seizure of ten thousand pounds of cocaine. "Drug traffickers around the world are now on notice that the proceeds and profits of their illegal ventures are not welcome in Panama," Lawn told Noriega in his letter. There were a half-dozen letters of praise.

"The DEA has had a long and successful relationship with the government of Panama, has it not?" May asked.

"Yes, sir. I have so testified many times," Lawn responded. But still, Lawn insisted, Noriega had to be coaxed to cooperate. Thousands of similar letters were sent to foreign officials every year, Lawn told May. "I certainly wouldn't characterize General Noriega's cooperation as unprecedented in a positive way."

On cross-examination, Myles Malman asked Lawn about the timing of the letters. Two, Lawn told the jury, were written at the very time Noriega was under investigation by prosecutors in Miami and Tampa. Lawn said he was fully aware of the investigations but sent the routine letters anyway. Noriega's antidrug efforts often seemed ceremonial, Lawn said. At a regional drug enforcement conference in Brazil in 1987, Noriega insisted he would attend the conference banquet only if he could be seated at the head table next to Lawn. "The general arrived at the banquet and was followed by a number of television cameras and photographers," Lawn said. "It was a first-rate photo opportunity."

When the establishment of a regional drug-fighting intelligence center was proposed by a Colombian police official in 1987, Noriega stepped forward to suggest the center be built in Panama, Lawn said. But the idea got nowhere because "through the years there were many allegations made about certain corruption in Panama." Lawn said he insisted the intelligence center be built where it would be secure. Panama was not that place, he said.

On the defense's second day, May called his third witness. Arthur Sedillo had been the DEA's in-country attaché for Panama from 1977 to 1979. His job had been to advise the U.S. ambassador on narcotics matters and to coordinate enforcement efforts with Noriega's G-2. This time May introduced more than a dozen DEA letters and documents into evidence. All, again, showed Noriega's cooperation. One telex from Bensinger to Noriega offered personal congratulations for the PDF's seizure of two hundred pounds of cocaine. May asked Sedillo his opinion of the telex.

"This incident was not simply gravy or for show, is that correct?" May asked.

"That's correct," Sedillo responded.

Sedillo himself had written many letters requesting Noriega's assistance in drug enforcement. They included requests for the expulsion of traffickers and requests for information on traffickers' deposits in Panamanian bank accounts. Sedillo confirmed that one intelligence tip from Noriega's officers resulted in the indictment of traffickers in Minneapolis and New York. "Permit me at this opportunity to thank you for the assistance rendered in this matter," Sedillo wrote, thanking Noriega for his assistance. "The action taken by your people again has proven their professionalism and dedication to this world drug-trafficking and abuse problem. By your efforts these traffickers, who have made millions of dollars at the cost of the misery and death of our youth in the United States, will finally be brought to justice."

Pat Sullivan was direct and short on cross-examination. "Was there a problem in Panama when you were conducting investigations about leaks occurring and compromising the investigations?" he asked Sedillo.

"I suspect that, but I never had anything to confirm my allegations," Sedillo said.

On the third day of the defense case, Wednesday, February 5, Frank Rubino took May's place as the defense's direct examiner.

"Good morning," Rubino began, stepping before the jury. "I hope you haven't forgotten me over the last seven weeks."

The jurors smiled, and the judge interjected, "I think the government hopes they have."

Rubino grinned and shrugged his shoulders.

"Now let's proceed." Judge Hoeveler motioned to Rubino.

The defense called DEA agent James Bramble to the witness stand. Bramble headed the agency's Panama office from 1982 to 1984. He now was chairman of the agency's professional conduct board.

If Jon May's quiet, unassuming manner had lulled the jurors, Rubino wasted little time reclaiming the edge that had marked most of the defense's cross-examinations.

"You have been subpoenaed here by me as a defense witness, that is, to testify for the defense, right?" Rubino began.

"Yes, sir," Bramble answered.

"It is kind of like your most dreaded nightmare, right?" Rubino asked.

Guy Lewis objected. The courtroom broke into laughter.

Hoeveler laughed along. "I can see you are back," he said. "With a vengeance," Rubino said with a smile.

Bramble, like the DEA witnesses, also had refused to be interviewed in advance of his testimony. Rubino, using DEA documents, guided him through his two years in Panama. Reviewing a series of his agency's reports, Bramble conceded that Noriega had assisted in the capture of Ramón Milian Rodríguez, a cartel money launderer. Information provided by the PDF led to Rodríguez's arrest in Fort Lauderdale and the seizure of $5.5 million in cash and sixty-one pounds of cocaine. Noriega could make investigations and produce results, Bramble said. Whether it was confiscating legal shipments of ether or circumventing banking laws to help catch a money launderer, Noriega could deliver, he testified. "We had a saying, 'There was the law, and there was the general,'" Bramble said. "When he made a decision, it didn't make any difference what the law said, we went with his decision."

As Rubino questioned Bramble, he asked the agent to note the reports' dates. Rodríguez's May 1983 arrest, for instance, came at the same time that Noriega, according to the government's indictment, was accepting payoffs to protect the cartel and its operatives. "'As you are aware, the information that has been provided by Inspector Quiel's office has contributed greatly in the U.S. government investigation of Ramón Milian Rodríguez and his money-laundering operation,'" Bramble said, reading to the jury from a letter he had written to Noriega in July 1983. "'This has been a very significant investigation and would not have occurred without the input from Panamanian authorities.'"

And during the same period, Noriega's troops increased drug surveillance at the Panamanian port of Colón, assisted in the inspection of Panamanian flagged vessels suspected of drug running, eradicated marijuana crops in

Panama, and expelled fugitives to the United States. Yes, Bramble said, referring to his own reports, that was all true. In one memorandum written to U.S. Ambassador to Panama Everett Briggs, Bramble complained that a cartel trafficker and fugitive had been released by the PDF only minutes before he was to be put aboard a flight for the United States and expelled. But the fugitive's release, Bramble noted, was at the direction of PDF Col. Roberto Díaz Herrera, not Noriega. That was the same person who had first accused Noriega of drug involvement and who was ousted by Noriega as a candidate for leadership of the PDF.

Bramble said that he had never feared putting a fellow agent under cover in Panama and informing the PDF. PDF Inspector Luis Quiel was the first to call him about the Darien raid, and he invited Bramble to visit the lab site shortly afterward. The DEA was allowed to interview the twenty-three Colombians who had been captured and arrested near the lab, Bramble confirmed.

Bramble's testimony on direct examination took most of two days. Lewis had repeatedly objected to the letters and reports offered into evidence. The confidential DEA reports, which spoke highly of Noriega's cooperation, were hearsay and inadmissible, Lewis complained frequently.

By Monday, February 10, Rubino was close to completing his questioning. Bramble confirmed that he had initiated Operation Negocios. One related document showed that Medellín cartel money launderer Eric Guerra, who had testified during the prosecution case, was among those identified during the Negocios surveillance.

Finally, Rubino asked about Noriega's efforts to control money laundering even though Panama had tough bank secrecy laws. Rubino asked about Noriega's closing of Panama City's First Inter-Americas Bank. "That particular bank was alleged to be owned by the Medellín cartel, was it not?" Rubino asked.

"No. I think it was associated with the Cali cartel," Bramble responded.

"Still drug dealers?" Rubino rejoined.

"That's what I believe," Bramble agreed.

"Eventually that bank was shut down by the Panamanian Defense Forces, was it not?"

"That's correct," Bramble said.

Bramble had not cooperated with the defense, but his testimony clearly hurt the prosecution. Bramble had not fenced with Rubino as Bensinger and Lawn had. His straightforward answers left the impression that he did not disagree with the defense's points.

Guy Lewis knew he could afford to lose little time or ground on cross-examination. He immediately stepped to the lectern.

"Certainly, shutting down a Cali cartel bank wouldn't have hurt the Medellín cartel, would it?" he asked, trying to shift the focus to Noriega's cooperation with the Medellín traffickers.

"Not to the best of my knowledge. No, sir," Bramble replied.

"To your knowledge, did the PDF ever shut down a Medellín cartel bank?"

"No, sir."

Lewis seemed to take inspiration from Rubino's no-holds-barred aggressiveness. He tried to turn it back on the defense. "It is not unusual that a crooked cop continues to make arrests, is it?" Lewis continued after asking Bramble about work for the DEA.

"No, sir," Bramble replied.

"It is not unusual that a crooked cop continues to seize drugs, is it?"

"No, sir. It is not."

"And that crooked cop continues to gather financial information?"

"That wouldn't be unusual."

"And in fact, Agent Bramble, what better way to disguise your activity, your crooked activity, than to continue this law enforcement activity?"

"That's certainly a cover, sir. Yes, sir."

Lewis paused only for a moment.

"Now in Panama, was there anybody that was a higher law enforcement official than General Noriega when you were there?"

"He was in charge of the police function. Yes, sir," Bramble replied. All of the DEA's work in Panama had to be conducted through the PDF. The agency could not proceed independently. That meant, Bramble said, that one of his biggest jobs was to be diplomatic, to seek Noriega's support and not upset him. Noriega had become angry in the past when the DEA sent agents to Panama who conducted unapproved unilateral investigations, Bramble said.

Lewis asked about the letters of praise that Bramble had written to Noriega.

"The letters themselves, do they have a name among the law enforcement community?" Lewis asked.

"Well, they are normally referred to as 'atta-boy letters,'" Bramble replied. "You pat somebody on the back for doing a job that you've asked them to do."

"In fact, one of your jobs down in Panama certainly was to continue to encourage, to get as much as you could out of the PDF, correct?" Lewis asked.

"That's correct," Bramble answered.

"And if you thought that the letter could help you tomorrow, certainly it is worth telling them thank you for responding to your request today, correct?"

"That's correct, sir."

In fact, Bramble continued, sometimes Quiel and even Noriega would specially request that an "atta-boy letter" be written on their behalf. One time, Bramble recollected, Noriega requested a letter when the political opposition was questioning his drug enforcement resolve. Bramble said his letters sometimes appeared in government-backed newspapers within twenty-four hours of being delivered to Noriega. That, Bramble said, was "quite embarrassing."

It was difficult to know whom to trust in Panama, Bramble continued.

The head of Panama's equivalent of the FBI, Nivaldo Madrinan, was not trustworthy, Bramble said, and neither was Lucinio Miranda, the chief of Noriega's narcotics squad. Bramble said he never shared confidential intelligence information with the PDF.

Even though PDF information led to the arrest of money launderer Ramón Milian Rodríguez, reports also showed, Bramble said, that Rodríguez made dozens of trips to Panama and that Noriega's G-2 not only "sanitized" its money-laundering reports but sometimes helped Rodríguez unload his currency cargo.

Lewis asked about the release of trafficker Rómulo Betancourt by Col. Robert Díaz Herrera.

"To your knowledge was Colonel Díaz Herrera ever court-martialed?" Lewis asked.

"No, sir."

"Was he ever prosecuted?"

"No, sir."

"To your knowledge did anything happen to him?"

"To my knowledge, no, sir."

Lewis seemed to mimic Rubino's wisecracking when he said: "Kind of like what happened to Melo, isn't it?"

Lewis pressed Bramble: "Now, to your knowledge, was one fugitive in your entire time in Panama, one fugitive that you associated with the Medellín cartel, was he shipped to the United States for prosecution that you know of?"

"Not to my knowledge, no, sir," Bramble responded.

Lewis asked about a DEA request to wiretap the phone of Inair owner Ricardo Bilonick. Noriega's aide, Luis Quiel, turned down the request, Bramble said.

Lewis asked about Operation Negocios. Bramble responded that Negocios did have successes, but the DEA eventually went out on its own and hired an undercover agent working at a Panama City airport to get the names of money couriers whom the PDF failed to identify. Bramble said that while the PDF worked the Tocumen airport, they left the Paitilla airport, the country's second largest, unchecked.

Among those the DEA's undercover source identified were César Rodríguez and Steven Kalish, Bramble said. The source told Bramble that Kalish and Rodríguez were protected by Noriega. Bramble tried to find out why. "I asked Luis Quiel if César Rodríguez was working for General Noriega, and he answered in the affirmative, said he had some sort of contract to supply parts for the aircraft in the country or something, but he was officially connected to the PDF," Bramble remembered.

"You couldn't touch him, is that correct?" Lewis asked.

"Absolutely not."

Lewis showed Bramble additional DEA reports. Nowhere had the PDF reported that Jorge or Fabio Ochoa ever entered Panama.

★   ★   ★

Rubino had all but gloated over his success with Bramble on direct examination. He and May rejoiced privately that they had managed to get out through a DEA agent that Noriega had cooperated with U.S. drug enforcement efforts. But Lewis's cross-examination had inflicted damage. During one break in Lewis's cross, with the jury out of the courtroom, Rubino pulled Lewis aside. "You're killing us," he said. When Lewis finished, both Sullivan and Malman flashed him the thumbs up.

Rubino renewed his self-described "vengeance" on redirect, turning first to the "atta-boy letters."

"Is there anything in the letters that is untruthful, that is a dirty, filthy lie?" Rubino asked.

"No, sir," Bramble answered. One could call them diplomatic, but they were also true, Bramble said.

It was true that the cartel leadership had not been arrested in Panama, but wasn't it also true they hadn't been arrested in the United States? Rubino asked. He listed the Medellín bosses: Jorge Ochoa, Fabio Ochoa, José Gonzalo Rodríguez Gacha, Carlos Lehder.

"No, sir," Bramble replied to each name. The DEA had not made the arrests either.

Rubino was angry. "They just couldn't devote their life to your whim and wish and give you everything you wanted, could they?" Rubino pressed Bramble.

Lewis objected. "Judge, I ask for an instruction of Mr. Rubino to quit asking these questions. He is going to get a chance to argue his case at the end, just like we will," Lewis protested. The judge sustained the objection.

"How many times did you go to that man sitting there," Rubino said, turning and pointing to Noriega, "and say, 'I want to interview any one of these people on this list,' and he said you cannot do it?" Rubino asked.

Bramble sat a little taller in his chair. He hesitated and looked at the prosecution table. "Most of the people on the list I didn't even know existed, sir, and I didn't go to him at all," he answered.

CHAPTER 32

★★★★★★★

DEA Agents and Cooperation

Thomas Telles followed James Bramble to Panama as the DEA's in-country attaché, serving from 1984 to 1986. He now followed Bramble to the witness stand. He would be no more conciliatory to Frank Rubino than his colleagues had been.

"Sir, let me ask why you would discuss these matters with the prosecutors but refuse to discuss them with me since I have, in fact, subpoenaed you?" Rubino asked after Telles took his place on the witness stand.

"It was a decision I made, and I chose not to speak with you and speak with the prosecutors, sir," Telles answered matter-of-factly.

"I appreciate that," Rubino responded. "But would you tell me why you chose that?"

"I understand it was my privilege and my right, and I chose that right."

Rubino was determined to discover the source of the agent's recalcitrance. "Can you tell me why you chose that right?" he pursued.

"I feel comfortable speaking with the prosecutor," said Telles.

"In some way have I made you uncomfortable in the past, since we've never met?" Rubino asked.

"You don't make me uncomfortable. No, sir."

"Okay. Well, let's see," Rubino said. "I am going to now go through an examination with you as best I can."

Rubino's first objective was to cast further doubt on the prosecution's assertion that Noriega had protected the cartel's operations.

Looking at a string of DEA reports, many of which he had authored, Telles agreed that Noriega's assistance was essential in the seizure of $5.8 million from a Texas company that the PDF had identified as laundering $2 million each month in Panama. Telles also agreed that the closing of the Cali cartel–run First Inter-Americas Bank came after DEA agents, with the assistance of the PDF, watched José Rodriguez Gonzalo Gacha, the Medellín cartel leader, launder $10 million a month there.

If, through Bramble's just-completed testimony, the prosecution meant to imply that somehow the Medellín cartel was spared or even helped with the closing of Inter-Americas, Telles's testimony on the point aimed to reject the notion. With the closing of Inter-Americas, the Medellín bosses lost an important laundering center as well. Still, Telles insisted he'd never heard of the Medellín boss Gacha. "I wasn't working in Colombia," the veteran agent testified.

But Telles agreed, after poring through stacks of DEA reports at Rubino's prompting, that the PDF provided intelligence on small planes going into Paitilla airport and helped track cartel smuggler Steven Kalish. Document by document, Rubino's questioning was designed to prove Noriega's assistance to the U.S. agents. Four hours after he had begun, Rubino was up to document number 62.

The questions followed a pattern: "Did you ever request the PDF to do surveillance for you to see not only after the money arrived at the airport but where it was going and things like that?"

"Yes, sir," Telles answered.

"And it was important to you to know which particular bank this money was being deposited in, was it not?"

"Yes, especially."

"And reports like this, furnished to you by the PDF, fulfilled your need to know this information?"

"It helped. Yes, sir."

"And this information was furnished to you by the Panamanian Defense Forces during the period of time when General Noriega was, in fact, its leader, correct?"

"Yes."

When Telles returned to the witness stand the next day, Wednesday, February 12, and again the day after that, Rubino continued to confront him with documents. It was as though Rubino intended literally to match with DEA reports and documents the full weight of all the government's witnesses.

Telles conceded that he often turned to the PDF for help. He even trusted the PDF to provide his own security when he went undercover to arrange a sting on Bolivian traffickers in April 1985. Telles said that Noriega helped target the top leaders of the Medellín cartel, including Pablo Escobar and Carlos Lehder, in a 1985 money-laundering probe called Operation Plata—Spanish for silver or money. Even though Noriega and the attorney general of Panama approved the plan and made the unusual concession of allowing phony shell corporations to be established to further the sting, Telles said the operation never happened. But it wasn't the PDF that backed out. "My headquarters decided not to do it," Telles said.

Rubino asked the agent about a letter he had written to Luis Quiel, Noriega's narcotics chief. The 1985 letter thanked the PDF for arresting a fugitive and sending him to Miami to stand trial.

"Is this just an atta-boy letter?" Rubino asked.

It wasn't, Telles said.

"These letters are fair representations of your requests to them?" Rubino hammered.

"Yes, sir," the agent conceded.

Rubino's parade of documents continued unabated for nearly two full days. Finally, the judge called the attorneys to sidebar. "I really want to finish this case by April," he said. "If we go into every one of these events as though we were trying the case again, we are never going to finish."

By this time Rubino was covering the Miami seizure of the Inair cocaine load. As with each document before, Rubino asked Telles to read it over and then followed with questions on almost each paragraph.

"You do appreciate the Inair as being part of the indictment," Rubino said, responding to the judge's prodding. "It is not just any old arrest."

Hoeveler tried to be stern. "What I am suggesting to you is that if we take this much time on many of these things, we are going to be here for a long, long time," he told Rubino.

Perhaps the reams of DEA paperwork could be condensed before the witness looked at it and Rubino offered them into evidence, the judge suggested. "They are not going to read all of these documents," the judge said.

"I hope they will," Rubino countered.

Hoeveler offered more advice. "You want it to be punchy from your standpoint. The fewer the documents that make your point, the better, I would think."

Rubino explained that he was only looking ahead to closing arguments. Wouldn't it be to his advantage to stand up on closing and say he had two hundred documents to support his case and the government had only six to support its own? There was no point arguing, Hoeveler decided. "We do need to keep the case moving," he ended.

The next morning Rubino attempted to heed the judge's suggestion. He offered only a handful of documents. One showed that Telles attended a 1985 meeting with Noriega and a leader of the Colombian police that resulted in increased patrols of the San Andrés and Rosario islands. It was near San Andrés Island that the *Krill* was seized in 1986, Telles conceded at Rubino's prompting.

Telles also confirmed that the PDF went to the DEA and reported that a Colombian had offered a $5 million bribe to PDF officers if they would protect the transport of chemicals and cocaine through Panama. The payoff was offered as Noriega's police seized hundreds of thousands of gallons of ether and acetone destined for Colombia in 1984.

"The seizures continued after this date, this report, did they not?" Rubino asked.

"Yes," Telles answered.

Telles had not been a willing witness, but Rubino felt confident that the jury was getting his point. Perhaps the $5 million bribe was one Col. Julian Melo accepted and kept.

On cross-examination, Pat Sullivan took his openings where he could find them, and on cross that meant going to the documents Rubino had offered on direct.

Telles said that while watching television in 1984 he was surprised to learn that the PDF had expelled the twenty-three Colombians captured near the Darien lab. Telles said he had hoped to get a prosecutor in the United States to file conspiracy charges against the lab workers, but suddenly, five days after their capture, they were sent home.

Telles said he called Luis Quiel and asked for an explanation.

"The boss," Quiel explained, had ordered the Colombians expelled.

"And who did you understand the boss to be?" Sullivan asked Telles.

"General Noriega," the agent replied.

Gone with the workers was also the lab's chief, Otalvaro Cabrera-Medina. Cabrera had confessed that he not only ran the Darien operation but was responsible for supplying chemicals to the just-raided Tranquilandia lab as well.

Almost immediately after the lab workers' expulsion, another cartel operative, a Colombian named Eduardo Zambrano, who, Telles said, was believed to have supervised the cartel's chemical and bank operations in Panama, was also expelled by Panama.

"At that point I don't think there was any further assistance given to us," Telles said of the PDF. "I was very disappointed."

The PDF operated on Noriega's whim, Telles told Sullivan. PDF cooperation with the DEA depended on the boss's attitude. When the DEA requested a wiretap on a member of the Cali cartel, Quiel at first agreed. After checking with Noriega, though, Quiel returned and reported wiretaps were illegal in Panama.

And as for the closing of the Inter-Americas Bank, Telles said, that was as much a result of the media's coverage of the November 1984 arrest in Spain of Cali cartel leader Gilberto José Rodriguez Orejuela as it was the work of the PDF. Public outrage in Panama over the revelation that a cartel boss owned a bank all but forced the PDF to order the closing, Telles said.

On Monday, February 18, Jon May took up the redirect for the defense. He asked about the expulsion of the twenty-three Darien lab workers to Colombia. The government of Colombia had requested their expulsion.

"Are you aware that in addition to honoring requests by the United States government to expel fugitives that Panama honored requests by other nations to expel fugitives to other nations?" May asked. The world did not revolve around the United States.

"Yes," Telles answered.

Daniel Murphy read every intelligence report and briefing paper that came to Vice President George Bush between 1981 and 1985. "I saw no intelligence on transshipment of drugs through Panama. Leave out money laundering for the moment," he had said on July 14, 1988, when he testified before Senator John Kerry's Subcommittee on Terrorism, Narcotics, and International Operations. "Panama had a very high reputation in the fight against drugs because of their great cooperation in letting us go aboard ships with their flag. My whole impression of Panama throughout this whole period, right until April 1985, was that Panama was a fine example of a cooperating sovereign country in the United States' effort to fight drugs. Now, I would not have that impression if I had been reading intelligence that said that this bum Noriega was pushing drugs or that he was transshipping it through or that we had hard evidence that they were doing this much money laundering."

Murphy was Vice President George Bush's chief of staff and before that his second in command at the CIA. What he seemed to be saying was that Bush at least knew about Noriega-sanctioned money laundering in Panama. This contradicted Bush's 1988 election campaign claim that he was not aware of any wrongdoing on Noriega's part prior to the delivery of the indictment in 1988.

Murphy had said it didn't make sense that Panama would be a cocaine shipping center. Why would the Colombians fly their cocaine only a few miles north, unload it, reload it, and then send it the rest of the way to the United States?

In 1981 the vice president named Murphy the operational chief of the South Florida Task Force, the Reagan administration's front-line defense against cartel trafficking. The task force operated, in part, with intelligence gathered by the DEA and the CIA. If the CIA knew that Noriega was involved with drug traffickers, the vice president was never told, Murphy said.

The Kerry committee also wanted to know about two visits Murphy made to Panama in the second half of 1987, visits that happened to coincide with the Miami grand jury's work on the Noriega indictment. Murphy had been out of government service for nearly two years, and he went to Panama, he said, as a business consultant. But in his meetings with Noriega in August 1987 he talked about more than business. "They were closing in on him. I told him why the United States had such a low opinion of him. I said, 'You're a drug guy, you're a murderer, you are considered to be a rapist, you are importing aliens into the United States, you're playing footsie with Castro and possibly Ortega, and you're selling arms to the M-19.' I said, 'You know, that's the kind of reputation you have in the United States.'"

Murphy said he told Noriega to get the military out of politics in Panama. Turn the government over to civilians. Provide for fair elections. But Noriega could offer only excuses, Murphy said. Nothing changed. Still, Noriega asked Murphy to return in November 1987. "I told him of U.S. attitudes at that time, that it was a solid position of still wanting him out, that that hadn't changed," Murphy said of the November meeting. Noriega replied, "I am not inflexible."

Murphy said that before and after both visits he met with Richard Armitage, the Pentagon's assistant secretary for international security affairs; Elliott Abrams, the undersecretary of state; Donald Gregg from the vice president's office; National Security Adviser Frank Carlucci; and Richard Kerr, the deputy director of intelligence at the CIA.

After Murphy's November meeting, Noriega fired his New York ambassador, José Blandon, and dumped Blandon's plan for a transition to a civilian government. Some said Murphy's visit gave Noriega the impression that there was still room for negotiation.

"But I no sooner got home," Murphy told the senators, "like now we're talking about December, January—it became apparent that the United States was working much more closely with the opposition than I understood. I had never been briefed on any of the ongoing relationships. And then, of course, came the sanctions and then came the indictment, and it became quite evident to me that this was an area that I didn't want to be operating in."

Jon May said ahead of time that most of the defense's questions for Murphy would have to do with his task force duties. The judge had pretty much precluded any great exegesis on Noriega's cooperation or what the president knew and when he knew it. Still, Murphy was the highest-ranking former U.S. government official to appear at the trial. He was called to the stand on Wednesday, February 19.

"We publicized the hell out of it, and almost overnight the murders stopped in Miami," Murphy said of the South Florida Task Force. Additional federal agents and prosecutors were hired in Miami in 1982; Coast Guard patrols were supplemented with military units. "It was quite evident that what we call the bad guys backed off, given this force that they were facing," Murphy told May on direct examination. The vice president was the only one to have an "action plan," Murphy said.

"To the best of my knowledge, the Panamanian government cooperated in all our requests to board Panamanian vessels on the high seas that were suspected of carrying drugs," Murphy said.

Murphy looked at a chart which showed that between 1981 and 1986, 1.9 million pounds of marijuana had been seized on the high seas with Noriega's help.

"In the years 1982, 1983, and 1984, was Panama a major transshipment point for narcotics?" May asked. The question had come almost word for word from the 1988 Senate hearing transcript. Murphy's answer would have to be "Not to my knowledge."

But Myles Malman immediately objected. Murphy had been the Reagan administration's point man in the drug war during those years. Yet in 1982, 1983, and 1984, he had had no idea that Panama was the cartel's cocaine shipping center as the prosecution was now claiming. Malman knew that and was trying to keep Murphy out of trouble.

"I don't want to get into any of this because it is beyond the scope," Malman told the judge at sidebar. "This witness does not have a sufficient basis of knowledge." Malman argued that the task force's mission was interdiction, not intelligence.

Pat Sullivan joined the sidebar. "It is obvious that what he thought in 1984 does not have a whole lot of probative value to what the DEA discovered when they conducted an investigation in 1987 and 1988," he added.

May could see a downside to letting Murphy go forward. The question could open the field to cross-examination on Murphy's 1987 visits to Panama. It could lead to Murphy's revelation that he then had some worries about Noriega's reputation. But May wanted to portray Noriega as a drug fighter. Any exploration of a subtext to the 1987 meetings between Murphy and Noriega, any insinuation that Noriega believed he was cooperating or acting on behalf of the U.S. government, could not come in; the judge had made that clear. Better to leave this question in the jury's mind: How could Noriega have offered significant assistance to the South Florida Task Force and the DEA while also working to protect the cartel?

"On the basis that the court might well permit the government to get into the 1987 meeting, I will withdraw the question," May told Hoeveler. "It was a very controversial trip described by various people for different reasons. To get into that particular meeting opens a big can of worms. There is a basis to believe that Admiral Murphy's trip to Panama was really a quasi-official trip."

May ended with another atta-boy letter from Murphy to Panama's ambassador to the United Nations, Aquilino Boyd: "Panama's willingness to respond to the request of U.S. agencies and to cooperate in controlling the trade of illicit narcotics is greatly appreciated. I'm well aware of the particularly good working relationship between the Panama Defense Forces and the United States Coast Guard."

There was little room for Malman on cross-examination. Again, the prosecution fell into the position of having to downplay the competence of its own agents. The U.S. government's top drug fighter during the years in question could not have known what the prosecution said should have been obvious to law enforcement in Panama, that Noriega authorized major drug flights to the United States.

"You had no formal training, nor do you today, in actual law enforcement, is that correct?" Malman quizzed Murphy.

"None at all.

"And the job of investigating criminals or persons suspected of criminal activity, gathering evidence, collecting evidence, analyzing investigations, is something that you, in your role, left to others, is that correct?"

"That's correct," Murphy responded.

Three men who had not left criminal investigations to others were locked in Panama's Modelo prison. Nivaldo Madrinan directed Panama's equivalent of the FBI, called DENI, during Noriega's rule. Lucinio Miranda was the chief of DENI's narcotics investigation unit. And Cleto Hernández headed the counter-intelligence unit of the Defense Forces' G-2. The three were imprisoned following the American invasion on charges ranging from civil and human rights violations to torture and murder. Now, two years later, they still awaited trial.

Their involvement in Panama's drug enforcement effort made them the Panamanian counterparts to the DEA agents and administrators whom Frank

Rubino and Jon May had already called. Their impressions of Panama's drug enforcement cooperation with the United States were bound to be more rosy and would dovetail nicely with Murphy's generally positive testimony. The defense lawyers were confident. In late January, with Judge Hoeveler's permission and while the judge was still recuperating, Frank Rubino, Pat Sullivan, Myles Malman, and Guy Lewis flew to Panama City to take the depositions of the three former PDF officers. The three prosecutors were equally worried about confronting Noriega's close cronies. If they came across as credible, "They could put a real hurtin' on us," as Malman put it.

The Panamanian government agreed to make each of the prisoners available for one day. A Panamanian magistrate would preside over the sessions, with the defense conducting its direct examination for three hours and the prosecution getting an equal period for cross-examination. There would be no redirect or recross-examinations, the Panamanians said. The testimony would be videotaped for the Miami jury.

To one extent or another, the three officers' names had already surfaced in the course of the trial. Inair boss Ricardo Bilonick accused Madrinan of coordinating a $500,000 cartel payoff to Noriega. Miranda and Hernández, witnesses testified, assisted in the investigation of Julian Melo and the cartel operatives who had allegedly plotted Noriega's assassination following the Darien raid in 1984. Hernández was linked to the Krill as Noriega's errand boy. During its case, the government implied that all three were essentially unindicted coconspirators, that they had acted to further Noriega's demand and receipt of cartel protection money.

A seven-by-eight-foot screen was set up in the Central Courtroom, and Hernández's taped testimony was played for the jury on Wednesday, February 19, directly following Murphy's ninety minutes on the witness stand.

Hernández had risen to the rank of major in the PDF. As part of G-2, he had regularly collected intelligence from countries throughout Central America and, in turn, passed that information on to American military intelligence officers assigned to the United States Embassy in Panama and also to the CIA. For his own government he monitored labor and student movements but would also track anti-American demonstrations for the CIA.

Hernández said it wasn't true that he had provided protection to cocaine traffickers on Noriega's orders. Rather, he said, from 1972 until the late 1980s he and Noriega had regular "contact with the CIA directly" about traffickers operating in Panama and throughout Central America. The former PDF officer rebutted prosecution witnesses who alleged he had helped the voyage of the Krill by delivering special papers to César Rodríguez that permitted the Krill to leave Panama. He said his only contact with Rodríguez had been to pick up rental cars from Rodríguez's auto dealership. Hernández insisted that three years before the Krill voyage, Noriega curtailed his relationship with Rodríguez.

"It was a friendly relationship up until after he was made a general,"

Hernández said of Noriega and Rodríguez. "After he took over in 1983, he said he had to change his life-style." Then Noriega all but ignored Rodríguez and others he had associated with before.

"In 1985 the general told me to tell all his friends who were using his name to cease using his name."

Hernández confirmed that on Noriega's 1984 trip to France and Israel, following the news that Julian Melo had plotted with the cartel to assassinate Noriega, Melo was detained and sent separately back to Panama. When Noriega's entourage followed, Hernández said he was surprised to learn that an unscheduled stop in Cuba had been added to the trip. The testimony was a surprise for Rubino as well. It went counter to the defense's contention that the stop had been planned.

On cross-examination, Guy Lewis set out to undercut the career officer's impartiality by showing his continuing allegiance to Noriega. The insinuation that he was somehow protecting Noriega irritated Hernández. "Are you still holding any loyalty to General Noriega?" Lewis asked Hernández.

"May I ask you, do the Defense Forces exist?" Hernández replied curtly.

"Do you still hold any loyalty to Mr. Noriega?" Lewis pressed.

"He's no longer the general. There is no army. There is no institution. I used to belong to an institution," Hernández answered shortly. He added, "I believe in Panamanian justice, and I am proving my innocence with whatever little justice there is."

Lewis moved on to questions about César Rodríguez and Floyd Carlton. He first asked what association Hernández had had with Carlton.

"I never met him," Hernández replied, "nor do I know what he looks like, whether he's white or black, tall or short, thin or fat."

"How long were you in G-2 Intelligence?" Lewis continued.

"For approximately ten years, and I don't have to know everyone in Panama. There are two million of us," Hernández responded.

Hernández turned to the Panamanian magistrate who was overseeing the depositions and complained that the prosecutor's questions were impertinent and implied that he was stupid. The magistrate motioned Hernández off.

Lewis picked up the pursuit, asking if Hernández had been aware that millions of dollars were being flown into Panama each day. Wasn't the G-2 supposed to know about such flights?

"That's what I read in the newspapers, but I ask myself, how come all that money was coming in, and there is poverty here?" Hernández said.

Throughout his testimony Hernández would stand and then sit. A wound inflicted in the course of the invasion still continued to bother him, and he was unable to sit for more than an hour without pain.

The following day came the testimony of Nivaldo Madrinan, the former head of DENI. Madrinan had risen in the PDF to the rank of lieutenant colonel.

"He gave his unrestricted and unswerving support," Madrinan said of Noriega and his participation in the drug fight.

Madrinan claimed that the PDF's efforts were important to the DEA. He said his men helped U.S. agents track money couriers and drug traffickers, and also discovered the Darien lab. Madrinan said he personally told DEA agent Tom Telles about Panamanian investigations of Carlton and Rodríguez. Once Carlton was jailed, Noriega refused to set him free, Madrinan said. Madrinan called the Melo case "a blot upon the institution of the Defense Forces." Of Melo, Madrinan said, "He was a member of the general staff, and he found himself involved in shady activities."

Madrinan said he personally interrogated cartel operative Ricardo Tribaldos about the $5 million cartel bribe. He said the investigators assumed that Melo had agreed to pass a portion of the bribe to Noriega, but during the investigation, Madrinan said, Tribaldos complained that the protection the bribe was supposed to buy never came. That Melo acted alone, Madrinan said, was proved when PDF investigators were dispatched to the home of Melo's mother, and there they recovered two suitcases full of money. The investigation was no secret, Madrinan testified. "All drug-related investigations, and this one in particular, were reported to the DEA," he said. Madrinan also asserted that small Colombian planes were not ignored by PDF security agents. Rather, they were searched for fear they might be transporting weapons. The vigilance of the PDF was much greater than the prosecution had portrayed, Madrinan insisted.

Rubino asked if Madrinan had ever been convicted of a felony.

"No sir, and I am glad that you should ask that question," Madrinan said, his voice rising, "because I have been held for two years. In this case, and exposing myself to any repercussions, anything that may increase the vindictiveness with which we have been judicially treated in this country, I have dared give this testimony."

Rubino and the prosecutors agreed in Panama that objections raised during the course of the depositions would be taken up later before Judge Hoeveler. If the judge sustained an objection, the testimony would not be given to the jury.

On cross-examination, Myles Malman asked Madrinan about the difference between the way Melo had been dealt with for plotting Noriega's assassination and the way another officer, Moises Giroldi, had been treated for leading a coup attempt against Noriega in October 1989. Melo had been confined to quarters and then discharged from the PDF. Giroldi, who had tried to retire Noriega without firing a shot, was executed.

While the questioning had gone forward in Panama, Rubino had objected. Now he asked for a sidebar.

"There is absolutely no reason, at this point in the case, to get into testimony like this," Jon May told Hoeveler. "It's not relevant to anything in this indictment, and extraordinarily prejudicial. If we start getting into questions having to do with the coup attempts, we get into the various kinds of political issues that the court has certainly precluded us from getting into."

Politics was not the issue, Malman responded. Rather, the question was the seriousness with which the PDF treated a major drug investigation. If the Melo affair was, as Madrinan claimed, the most important criminal investigation he had ever undertaken, why was Melo simply detained and then discharged from the PDF? The case involved not only a $5 million bribe but an assassination plot as well. On the other hand, in 1989, Giroldi had plotted a bloodless coup and was executed. Melo had gotten off so lightly, Malman argued, because of Noriega's link to the cartel.

More than anything else, what the Giroldi episode demonstrated was Noriega's deep concern, a fear, over a U.S.-backed coup, May said. What this all showed was that Noriega took the United States far more seriously than a plot cooked up by the Medellín cartel. "It does put us in a position of having to introduce evidence surrounding the circumstances of that coup and the politics going on in 1988, '89," May told the judge.

The argument struck a chord with Hoeveler. "I don't want to get into the pressures being put on Panama in 1989 and the 1980s," the judge said. But while politics had been irrelevant so far, Hoeveler said, there could be a case for discussing the coups if they reflected on the PDF's dealings with drug dealers. "They say the relevance of this has been created by Mr. Rubino in developing what he did about Melo. It's a troubling point because I really don't want to get into it, but I'm not sure that I can deny them the right to let it in."

"If we go into the politics of the events, we'll get into such things as the election of 1989," May countered. "We also have the invasion."

"I don't want to get into that, either," Hoeveler said.

Rubino decided to up the ante. "It appears to me," he said, "that if this comes in, it will open doors, that we will have to show the United States' involvement in this, which was the United States sent helicopters to aid and assist this coup." Rubino's reference was to the U.S. Southern Command's blocking of bridges and roads to aid and assist in the October 1989 coup attempt. The United States had barely sat on the sidelines, Rubino said. "It was an actual attempt to overthrow a seated government," he said.

Hoeveler thought for a moment. Both sides had made their points.

"If I let this in," Hoeveler said, looking at Malman, "I do not see how I can foreclose the defense presenting as much detail about that event as possible, including possibly the involvement of another government in it."

Rubino shook his head. "We will have to go through this whole thing to justify a death penalty," he said. "Probably bring in photographs which we have available of the coup: the people in the streets, the machine guns, the whole thing."

Videotape of U.S. helicopters hovering over Panama City in support of the overthrow of the Panamanian government was more than Malman or Sullivan wanted. After a short recess, Malman withdrew his request to show Madrinan's testimony about Giroldi's execution. But he asked the judge to reserve the right for further inquiry should Noriega later take the stand.

Rubino and May counted the ruling a blessing. Madrinan had even less appeal on video than he did in person.

The video continued. Malman asked Madrinan why DENI had not informed the DEA about the convergence of the cartel leadership in Panama following the 1984 assassination of Rodrigo Lara Bonilla. Madrinan said his department was not aware that the Colombians were wanted. Madrinan explained that a separate $4 million seized from traffickers in 1984 was used in part to help fund his department. It was not a payoff that he had split with Noriega, as the prosecution asserted. Madrinan also complained that his arrest and imprisonment were largely political.

"Are you a political prisoner now?" Malman asked Madrinan.

"I believe I am," Madrinan replied. "We all believe we are. We are being held in a prison as a result of a United States invasion. "We were imprisoned in American jails, where we were not allowed the right to a defense, where it was only after a month that our families found out that we were being held. And we continued to be held without having been brought to trial." Even now, giving testimony was a danger, Madrinan said. "We are exposing ourselves to political and judicial retaliation as well as other calamities that have befallen us in the force of these two years of illegal detention."

The taped deposition of the defense's final Panamanian witness, Lucinio Miranda, was shown to the jury on Thursday, February 27.

Miranda said that there was a "constant exchange" of information between the PDF and the DEA. He said the DENI narcotics team that he headed kept track of not only small plane traffic from Colombia and the south but also plane traffic from the north. But it was not a crime in Panama to fly cash into the country from the United States, Miranda testified.

Cartel money launderer Eric Guerra was almost constantly under surveillance, Miranda said. Whatever the PDF knew about Guerra it told the DEA, he said. Noriega was fully informed about suspected money launderers, Miranda testified.

"At any time did General Noriega ever interfere with these investigations?" Rubino asked.

"No, never," replied Miranda. "Quite to the contrary. He was always concerned that information be supplied to the DEA."

The same was true for the Inair investigation. Noriega had not stood in the way. "Quite the contrary," Miranda said. "He authorized it, and he was very keen on the case being developed together with the DEA."

As for the Melo case, Miranda said, he was present when the cartel's operatives were questioned about the assassination plot. Noriega's only instruction to the investigators was that the investigation proceed to its "ultimate consequences."

On cross-examination, Sullivan questioned Miranda about the success of his narcotics investigations. It was true, Miranda conceded, that the DENI efforts to prosecute Floyd Carlton and Ricardo Bilonick had failed.

"Mr. Miranda, is it your hope that General Noriega is acquitted at his trial in Miami?" Sullivan asked.

"Well," Miranda answered, "to hope for something is like when you are waiting for something to happen, but to tell you—how can I put this to you?—I really have no expectations in connection with that."

At sidebar, Rubino complained to the judge that the defense's efforts were being continually hindered. The night before the first of the three Panamanian witnesses gave his deposition, all three were visited by Panamanian justice officials and threatened with additional human rights charges if they testified. The threat had been carried out, Rubino said.

Now, Rubino continued, Luis Quiel, who had been Noriega's liaison to the DEA, had gone into hiding in Panama. He, too, had been charged and threatened with arrest after the Panamanian government learned he had sought permission to travel to Miami to testify for the defense. Any hope the defense might have had of calling Quiel was now gone.

It was March 2, and six full months had now elapsed since the trial began. Juror Waymon Jackson's eighty-three-year-old father-in-law had just died. It was Monday; the funeral was set for Thursday.

There were only three alternate jurors left. If Jackson was dismissed from the jury, there would be only two alternates left. Anything could happen before the end of the trial. In no time, there could be no alternates and fewer than twelve jurors. The week before, Mirtha Alberto, a twenty-four-year-old Hispanic woman who sat in the second row of the jury box, had been excused. On Thursday, as Alberto left court, she stumbled down a flight of stairs. A few minutes later a television reporter found her disoriented and wandering on Miami Avenue. She had almost been hit by a car. "I haven't slept in forty-eight hours," Alberto kept repeating after court security officers brought her back to the judge's office. Her words were slurred. Janice Tinsman, the judge's secretary, called paramedics. Alberto should go to the hospital, they said. Alberto refused. The next morning the young woman called in sick again.

Hoeveler was concerned. There were other jurors and alternates to worry about. There were witnesses scheduled. The judge called the attorneys into his chambers. How much more delay are we willing to put up with? Alberto was still refusing to see a doctor, the judge told them. She also wasn't saying when she would be back. Rubino, May, Sullivan, Malman, and Lewis all agreed the trial must proceed. Alberto was dismissed.

But Jackson was healthy. The judge again asked the attorneys what should be done. If testimony was suspended while Jackson traveled to his father-in-law's funeral, another week would slip by.

"We would just as soon keep as many jurors as we can," Sullivan told Hoeveler.

The defense's witnesses could be shuffled, Rubino offered. Three "live" witnesses from Panama had been delayed in getting permission to travel to Miami. They might not be available in the next two or three days anyway. The defense could wait for Jackson, Rubino told the judge.

But five or even four days off could bring more problems, Hoeveler said. Some of the jurors were elderly. One, Thelma Sturdivant, had been on crutches for the past two weeks. Every week it seemed an hour was taken from the schedule for one juror's or another's doctor's appointment.

"If tragedy struck somehow and we lost three people, would you be willing to go with eleven?" Hoeveler asked, looking first to Rubino and then to Sullivan. Federal juries were usually made up of twelve jurors, but with the attorneys' agreement and Noriega's, deliberations could go forward with less than a full jury box.

Rubino was hesitant. He didn't like the idea. "I might go with eight, if I can get the right eight," he said and smiled. Sullivan and Malman smiled. They would take the right eight, too.

"I hate to lose a week," the judge said again. "Every time we enlarge this— of course, it has been largely my fault, but every time we enlarge this, we run the risk of losing someone else."

Malman leaned forward in his chair. "The deliberations could be very long," he said. "Some of the deliberations could be very trying and exacting on some of them, and I just have a lingering, nagging concern that we could go through three and then—"

"Do you mean during the deliberations?" the judge interrupted.

"Or around the final phase it could potentially be a lot of pressure and stress," Malman said. "We already had one juror, an alternate juror, that had a heart attack."

Jon May was leaning back in the judge's sofa. "Your Honor, everything unimaginable has seemed to have happened in this case. While it may be almost unimaginable, we could go through that many jurors. It would only be the latest in a series of unexpected, crazy things to happen in this case."

Hoeveler nodded in agreement. He considered a moment. "Well, I don't want to lose a week, is the long and the short of it. We've got to finish this case. We are just extending the risk by extending the time," he said, reaffirming his own position.

If Jackson could return by Friday, Rubino said, the defense would be willing to work on Saturday. Sullivan agreed. The judge sent a court officer to ask whether Jackson could return directly after the funeral and be back in court by Saturday.

It was a fourteen-hour drive, Jackson replied, and with the grandchildren in the car, it would be difficult to be back on Saturday. The reply sealed the decision. Hoeveler called the balance of the jury into the courtroom.

"We would very much like to keep Mr. Jackson, but we just simply cannot afford to lose a week," he told the jurors. "So we offer you our condolences, Mr. Jackson, and we are going to excuse you from the jury."

Jackson stood, shook a couple of hands, and followed the security officer out of the courtroom. It was a long way to come to turn and go home. Now, there were two alternates left.

"I would like to say this, folks," Hoeveler said to the jury, "and I say it, of course, with a certain amount of humor, but I am going to order that none of you get sick." The remaining jurors smiled.

"We are looking now at the end of the road fairly soon," the judge added.

CHAPTER 33

★★★★★★★

Working for the CIA

On Friday, February 28, Jon May handed Pat Sullivan a handwritten list. The defense case would last another week, perhaps a few days more. There were either nine or ten more witnesses. Sullivan scanned the list. At the bottom was Noriega's name. After it was a question mark.

If Noriega took the stand, there would be little Rubino could do to control the cross-examination. Sullivan had been preparing to cross-examine Noriega for months. Noriega would be attacked not just on the evidence but also on his character and credibility. Rubino knew there was no telling what would come in.

Still, Noriega was no stranger to public speaking, and he did have stories to tell. His own story was likely to be his most compelling. If Noriega took the stand, the jury would see that the defendant was not afraid to make his own defense.

But first, the defense would offer a rebuttal to prosecution allegations that were hanging. Rubino planned a rapid-fire, staccato near-summation emphasizing Noriega's dedication to drug enforcement efforts.

First up was DEA agent Alfredo Duncan, who had headed the U.S. agency's Panama office from July 1986 to December 1988.

Duncan confirmed that Noriega and Luis Quiel worked closely with the DEA. The efforts of the Panamanians were essential to the drug war in Central America, Duncan said.

"How many operations were conducted during the period of time when you were the country attaché?" Rubino asked.

"I could not begin to give you a number," Duncan answered.

"When you did these undercover operations, when your office conducted them, it required the assistance of the Panamanian Defense Forces?" Rubino asked.

"That is correct," Duncan replied.

"Did they actually go out there and protect you or your agents?"

"Yes, sir."

"Did they go with you and aid you, assist you, in the seizing of drugs during these undercover operations?"

"Yes."

"This required a certain amount of faith, trust, and confidence in the PDF, did it not?"

"Yes."

Rubino loved it. There was nothing that could take away from so many "yes" answers. It spelled cooperation, clear and simple.

Duncan said that it was Noriega who deported cocaine trafficker Jack Carlton Reed to the United States for trial in 1987. Reed had been Carlos Lehder's codefendant at the Jacksonville trial. Lehder himself had gone to prison through the efforts of the DEA, but there was no taking away from the fact that Reed stood trial and had gone to prison almost wholly because of Noriega and the PDF.

Next up was DEA agent Douglas Driver, whose tenure in Panama partially overlapped Duncan's and had lasted from 1985 to 1987.

Rubino guided Driver through a sheaf of agency reports that cataloged PDF support for the DEA. One 1986 cable from the commandant of the U.S. Coast Guard called Panama's assistance in stopping drug ships "a milestone in high seas law enforcement."

Rubino next asked Driver to read from a 1986 letter in which he praised the PDF for its assistance in the arrest of Bolivian trafficker Roberto Suárez. "DEA considers this to be one of the most successful cases done anywhere in the world in recent years and looks forward to continued cooperation with your office," Driver read aloud. The effort, which resulted in Suárez's conviction in a Virginia federal court, was "one of the finest examples of international cooperation that can be found anywhere," Driver had written. Driver testified that he, too, like Duncan, trusted the PDF to provide security when he had gone undercover in Panama.

But on cross-examination, the two agents' begrudging praise on direct was tempered. Duncan, following Guy Lewis's cross-examination, said that Operation Negocios was in time phased out. That effort, Duncan said, ended with no Panamanians or Americans ever being prosecuted. Lewis took Duncan across that ground twice. No Panamanians or Americans had ever been prosecuted.

Driver, who was cross-examined by Pat Sullivan, said his letter regarding the Suárez case had been solicited by Luis Quiel. The letter was accurate, Driver said, but Quiel "told me pretty much what he wanted me to put in it, and I did."

The PDF's assistance was not always forthcoming, Driver told Sullivan. In one effort to crack a money-laundering ring fronted by a Panama City jewelry store, Driver said he was frustrated by the PDF's lack of action. "I went to the Panamanians, literally, dozens of times," Driver testified. "They just would not respond. It was like talking to a cow; they just looked right through me. They wouldn't tell me 'No.' They didn't like to tell me 'No.' They just looked at me with a blank look and did nothing."

Driver said he went to Quiel in frustration and asked for assistance in getting a wiretap to help break the case. "He told me that the PDF could only conduct wiretaps in matters of national security. So we had a discussion about exactly what involves national security for a country like Panama," Driver said.

"Does narco-terrorism, does drug traffickers and drug dollars, and that type of activity, constitute national security in the minds of Panamanians?" Sullivan asked.

"It appeared that at times it did and at times it didn't," Driver said.

Francis Mullen was the DEA's top administrator from 1981 to 1985. In response to Rubino's questioning, Mullen said that during his time at the DEA, Noriega assisted U.S. drug agents every time they asked for help.

Rubino asked Mullen to read from a March 1984 letter he had written to Noriega. Mullen read that one of his agents "has advised me of no small number of instances in which you have lent your personal support. It is very meaningful to us."

"In the time you were the head of the agency, did you ever receive any credible information that General Noriega was involved in drug trafficking?" Rubino asked.

"No," he said.

"Whenever you asked General Noriega for help, would he always give it to you?"

"Yes," Mullen said.

Rubino loved that answer. There was no getting around the fact that the United States' top drug fighters had gotten along just fine with Noriega at the very time the government now alleged he was cooperating with the world's most notorious drug traffickers. Rubino was confident the jury was asking itself, How come the DEA didn't know about Noriega? Why was the same government that had praised his cooperation now accusing him of trafficking?

Guy Lewis picked up the cross-examination, trying to counter Mullen's testimony.

Referring to the investigation that had led to Noriega's indictment, Lewis asked, "Did you participate in the investigation that led to this indictment?"

"No," Mullen answered.

"This case was made after you left the administration?"

"Yes," Mullen answered.

Interspersed with the three DEA agents were five Panamanians, each of whom Rubino hoped would counter one or more of the prosecution's earlier witnesses.

Luis Ellis had directed a small Panamanian port in 1984. Cartel businessmen allegedly had gone to him and used Noriega's name to help open the port for ether shipments to Colombia. But Ellis said the prosecution's witness who had alleged his help, Jaime Castillo, never approached him. He said Noriega hadn't, either. "General Noriega never called me or talked to me about any of this," Ellis testified. "In fact, he never talked to me about any other matter."

On cross-examination, Ellis conceded that his wife once worked as Noriega's secretary. But he also insisted "My purpose in coming here has been to tell the truth."

Next came Ricardo Bermudez, the former director of Panama's civil aviation department. Bermudez had supervised air traffic controller and prosecution witness Anel Pérez, who had testified about the PDF's loading and unloading of cartel planes and the arrival of cartel leaders at Panama's two largest airports. Bermudez said it would not have been unusual for PDF officers to meet Colombian and other planes at Paitilla or Tocumen airport. The PDF, by regulation, was required to meet all incoming flights as a matter of general security, he said.

"In your experience did G-2 only meet selected Colombian aircraft?" Rubino asked.

"No, sir."

"What aircraft did they meet?"

"They met all general small aircraft," Bermudez replied.

Bermudez said it would have been possible to see planes loaded and unloaded from the control tower, as Pérez had testified, but it would have been very difficult even with binoculars to know what the cargoes were or to specifically identify individuals.

"Is it your testimony that Floyd Carlton and César Rodríguez did not receive special privileges at the airports?" Guy Lewis asked on cross-examination.

"It is my testimony, sir," Bermudez replied. "Nobody could."

At sidebar, Rubino told the judge, "It is my position that Anel Pérez is a disgruntled person, a busybody who could hardly wait to get up here and testify against the general."

Rubino next called Balbina Herrera, the woman whom Max Mermelstein had identified six months before as a Noriega crony who allowed cartel traffickers and money launderers free access to Panama's airports. Mermelstein had pointed her out in a videotape in which Herrera stood next to Noriega, the two waving to a cheering crowd. Herrera, Mermelstein testified, was a corrupt customs official who had been bought off by Pablo Escobar and Jorge Ochoa.

From the moment Herrera took the witness stand she seemed consumed with anger. She told Rubino she had been trained in agricultural science and then to be a high school teacher. After college she had become the administrator of a student aid program.

"What if anything did your job have to do with airports in Panama?" Rubino asked.

"Nothing whatsoever," Herrera answered.

She said she was now a member of Panama's legislature. She had never met Pablo Escobar or Jorge Ochoa or ever heard of Max Mermelstein until the start of Noriega's trial.

Herrera was not apologetic when Pat Sullivan questioned her on cross-examination. She called the trial a political prosecution.

"You've been a long-time supporter of General Noriega, have you not?" Sullivan asked Herrera. Sullivan privately conceded that the prosecution had misidentified Herrera. She had not been a customs official. "We were caught with our pants down," he said. Nonetheless, he did not intend to give ground in front of the jury.

"I have supported my country, Panama," the legislator replied sternly.

"And you fully supported him while he was leader of your country, didn't you?" Sullivan asked.

Herrera became insulted by Sullivan's patronizing tone.

"I understand that there was a political confrontation between your government, the one that you are representing here today, and my government; and that war dating back to 1987 through 1990, when you invaded Panama," she replied, refusing to back down. She paused a moment. "Obviously I am on the side of my country." She was almost yelling at Sullivan.

"Were you on his side when General Noriega was indicted for drug trafficking?" Sullivan asked, uncharacteristically raising his voice to counter Herrera's confrontational tone.

"General Noriega was not indicted for drug trafficking," Herrera shot back. "The United States was going to strangle my country. And I as a Panamanian, I took the side of my country. I as a legislator took the side of my country, and I would have supported my country whomever. I would have been on the side of my country."

"Isn't it true, ma'am," Sullivan asked, almost yelling as well, "the reason you are here is to support your general, as you have all your adult life?"

"I am here today because one of your witnesses said that I was their contact in 1983 and that I was there as a representative of General Noriega. I do not know the people who gave testimony here, and if that is helpful to General Noriega, that's not my problem, but I am telling the truth."

The exchange continued. Malman and Lewis looked at each other. To make Pat Sullivan visibly mad was no small task. Sullivan later quipped that crossing Herrera was akin to getting into a barroom brawl.

Rough questioning on cross-examination also followed for Rodolfo Castrellon, a former Panamanian air force officer who was called by Rubino to rebut the charge that the twenty-three lab workers arrested near the raided Darien lab had been returned to Colombia aboard Noriega's personal jet.

Castrellon testified that he had assigned the crew and selected the plane aboard which the arrested workers would be flown. The aircraft was a cargo prop-engined plane with no seats, not a luxury jet. Noriega did not give the workers a free pass. They boarded manacled and under guard, Castrellon testified.

Myles Malman's cross-examination directly attacked Castrellon's credibility. Rubino had put Castrellon on to testify about the plane. But the prosecution's investigation had turned up holes in Castrellon's credibility. Malman wanted nothing less than to shred Castrellon. The witness was a close friend of the Noriega family and had chauffeured Mrs. Noriega around Miami during the trial, Malman pointed out. Castrellon had sought political asylum in the United States. "What you really fear is prosecution for crimes you committed," Malman suggested.

That was not true, Castrellon said.

Malman asked Castrellon about a 1983 scheme to sell arms to Colombian guerrillas. A Panamanian investigation said Castrellon and César Rodríguez were partners, and Castrellon had been castigated by Noriega for entering the scheme. Rubino was shocked by the question. He had never heard anything about this.

Castrellon first unconvincingly denied his participation and then reluctantly agreed. Something had gone wrong with the background investigation of Castrellon prior to putting him on the stand, Rubino kept thinking. Castrellon was a sitting duck, and Malman was taking full advantage of his chance to explore his inadequacies.

Rubino watched his witness being torn apart. Finally, he objected. Malman's questions were wide of the direct examination. "I don't see how this goes to whether that's the airplane that flew the people back or not," Rubino said, standing at the defense table. Not only had Rubino broken Malman's flow, but he had gone beyond objecting to speechmaking.

Hoeveler called the attorneys to sidebar. The manner of the objection was out of line, Hoeveler told Rubino angrily. "I don't want to chastise you publicly, but those objections of yours, stating what you conceive to be the issue, are argumentative objections."

Rubino resisted the rebuke. "This witness testified about actually one simple issue," he told Hoeveler, trying to regain the high ground. "It was not a 727. If the government is not disputing that issue and this is just witness bashing, then I think it is wrong."

Malman, Sullivan, and Lewis were all smarting from Rubino's final string of witnesses. Rubino had been scoring points. He was moving the witnesses on and off the stand and keeping their testimony short. It was a new tactic, given Rubino's drawn-out cross-examinations.

"Cross-examination," Malman said, "is designed to press, probe, and pry the witness's bias, motive, and interest to tell the truth. He actually has offered no real testimony other than the fact, 'I picked the airplane.'"

Weak, Rubino thought, very weak. The prosecution's questions were pure and simple harassment. "The government has to have a good faith basis to believe this man was lying," he stated. "If they won't say he's lying and that wasn't the plane, then they don't have the right to do this."

Hoeveler split the baby, overruling the objection but warning Malman to get to the point.

Wasn't it true that he had sought political asylum in the United States because he was a friend of Noriega's, Malman asked Castrellon.

"I am a friend of General Noriega. I do not deny it," Castrellon responded.

Rubino used his redirect to take Malman's cross-examination to task.

"The government asked you questions about whether you knew General Noriega's wife, whether you drove her around on various errands and things of that nature. Do you remember that line of questioning?" Malman asked.

"Correct."

"When you chose which aircraft you intended to send back the prisoners to Colombia in, was that decision based upon the fact you knew General Noriega's wife?" Rubino continued.

"No," Castrellon replied.

"Was that decision based upon the fact of whether or not César Rodríguez had a Porsche?"

"No, sir."

"You were asked questions by Mr. Malman about international arms dealing. Do you remember those questions?" Rubino continued.

"Correct."

"And you were more specifically asked questions such as whether you needed General Noriega's permission to sell arms. Is that right?"

"Correct."

"Do you know if, when Oliver North sold arms to Iran, he had President Bush's permission?"

A frown immediately spread across Hoeveler's face. He called the attorneys to sidebar. Rubino was on a desperate roll, and now was the time to put a stop to it. "You must have had something for lunch that affected your thinking," the judge said, wagging his index finger at Rubino.

"That cross had no bearing on what airplane was used," Rubino replied curtly.

"That question was so obviously improper that I couldn't believe it," the judge said. No more, Hoeveler told Rubino.

Rubino walked back to the lectern. "Sir, are you absolutely positive that the twenty-three prisoners from the Darien lab were not shipped back to Colombia in a luxury executive jet?"

"I am positive," Castrellon answered. "Those two planes are not similar to each other in any way." Rubino had hardly reclaimed his witness. As he sat down, Malman looked away from the jury with a grin of victory on his face.

Panamanian legislator Jerry Wilson followed Castrellon to the stand. Wilson had helped draft a tough drug law in Panama in 1986. The measure was the first to outlaw money laundering in the country, Wilson testified.

Noriega lobbied for passage of the measure, Wilson said. Panama's current foreign minister, who had come to power following the 1989 invasion, opposed the law.

★   ★   ★

Donald Winters was the CIA's senior officer in Panama from 1984 to 1986.
During the classified information hearings the previous summer, Jon May
had agreed that the defense would go no further than to question the intelligence agency's officers about specific and relevant meetings that they had
had with Noriega. But a defense that would explore the general tenor of relations between Noriega and the CIA had been abandoned. Hoeveler made it
clear he intended to keep the defense focused on events related directly to
the indictment. Winters had met with Noriega once every ten days or so, but
only three of their meetings would be discussed in the direct examination,
Rubino and May agreed at the hearings.

Before Rubino began his direct examination of Winters, he read to the
jury an agreement reached by the defense and the government stating that
between 1971 and 1986, CIA officials made contact with Omar Torrijos and
Noriega relating to Castro and communist Cuba. Noriega became the intelligence liaison between the agency and Panama. Noriega frequently met with
Castro in the course of his government's business. Related to those contacts,
Noriega would then brief the CIA. One meeting between Castro and Noriega
in July 1984, the stipulation continued, became an overt act named in the
indictment.

"On some occasions Noriega would contact the United States government
representative, either directly or though an intermediary, with information
about a particular meeting or contact he had with Castro," Rubino read
aloud.

"He did that following his July 1984 meeting with Castro. United States
intelligence agencies encouraged and appreciated this assistance from
Noriega in matters relating to Fidel Castro."

Winters wore a gray suit and red tie. He was gray-haired. Shortly before
Noriega's visit to Havana in July 1984, Winters met with Noriega at the general's home. Noriega told him that Castro had requested a meeting in two
weeks' time.

"The rationale that was expressed by General Noriega," Winters said, "was
that Fidel Castro was eager to discuss with General Noriega the situation that
existed at that time in Central America, particularly in Nicaragua and El
Salvador."

Winters's testimony was calm and measured. Unlike almost all of the
other agents who had preceded him, he had agreed to discuss his testimony
with the defense before taking the stand. Rubino liked Winters. To begin
with he was not a cop. CIA agents took the big picture view. They were
worldly. DEA agents saw crime under every rock, to the point of paranoia,
Rubino thought. Winters and the CIA could appreciate what Noriega had
done. But Rubino soon found that what Winters said in private was no more
revealing than what he was saying now. Still, if Noriega had told the CIA
about his meeting with Castro two weeks before it occurred, it could hardly

have been the spur-of-the-moment visit the prosecution claimed. And it meant Noriega had had nothing to hide. That point would not be lost on the jury, Rubino was confident. The testimony tore right at the heart of the government's case, Rubino and May agreed.

Winters said Noriega requested briefing points to take to Cuba, topics of discussion the U.S. government wanted brought to Castro's attention. Winters described his contact with Noriega in the third person, reading from his own report to his superiors at the CIA, and then said he forwarded Noriega's request for a briefing paper to the CIA's headquarters in Langley, Virginia. Forty-eight hours later, Winters said, he delivered the briefing points in a sealed envelope to Noriega at home. When Noriega returned from Havana, he reported back to Winters. Again Winters filed a report on his discussion with Noriega. There was no discussion with Castro regarding the drug cartels, according to Noriega, Winters said.

About three weeks after Noriega returned from Cuba, Winters met with Noriega again. The meeting was held on August 1, 1984, in a private room at a U.S. military base in the Canal Zone.

"Was anyone else from the Central Intelligence Agency besides yourself present for this meeting?" Rubino asked Winters.

"Yes, sir," Winters replied.

"Who was the highest-ranking officer there at this meeting?" Rubino asked.

"The director of Central Intelligence, Mr. William Casey," Winters said. The meeting lasted an hour and a half. Winters said Noriega did not report any discussion with Castro regarding the Colombian drug cartels.

Rubino offered the jury another stipulation: that from 1981 to 1986, Noriega was aware of extensive U.S. eavesdropping operations conducted in Panama. "General Noriega permitted these operations and actively participated in them. In 1979 he encouraged the United States to use this capability in the investigation of drug trafficking," the stipulation said.

Myles Malman rose, buttoned his suit coat, and walked to the lectern to take up the cross-examination.

"Were you told by General Noriega that he discussed [with Castro], amongst other topics like El Salvador and arms in Central America, and Honduras—were you told that what was also discussed was a dispute between the Medellín cartel and then-General Noriega?" he asked.

"No, there was nothing of that nature mentioned," Winters answered.

"Are you familiar with something called a cover story or the term 'cover' in the intelligence business?" Malman asked next.

"Very much so," Winters replied. "If you go to see your mistress, you usually have a cover."

On redirect, Rubino followed Malman's inference regarding Noriega's visit to Havana.

"During the period of time you dealt with General Noriega, did you ever

know him to possess a crystal ball?" Rubino asked. The question was designed
to get under Malman's skin.

"No."

"Now the invitation that he told you about, he received an invitation on
June 11. Am I correct?" Rubino followed.

"That's correct," Winters replied.

"Did he tell you that the people from the Darien lab made the complaint
on June 24, some thirteen days after he told you about the invitation?"

"No," the CIA officer answered.

Four cables to CIA headquarters from agency officers in Panama were turned
over to the defense by the government. Sections of the cables were heavily
blacked out by agency censors. The cables were consolidated with an agreement of the prosecution and the defense, and they were offered as substitutions in lieu of live CIA witnesses. Hoeveler explained how the substitutions
worked: "This information was put in reports which have been produced for
the defense by the government, and rather than put in all of those documents, what is called a substitution, a consolidation of those reports, has
been made." The substitution was a narrative of four paragraphs.

As Rubino read it into the record, it became obvious the defense had
adopted its contents as gospel. It said that Noriega received no part of the
cartel's $4 million bribe, that the bribe was paid to protect the Darien lab,
and that another $2 million payment was made to protect the shipment of
six thousand barrels of ether passing through Panama in 1984. "The
Colombians gave Melo the $4 million and assumed that he would arrange for
the necessary cooperation from the PDF," the narrative said. The CIA reports
said Melo never passed any of the bribe money to Noriega.

Though the narrative did not identify the CIA's sources, both the defense
and the prosecution knew from the original cables that one source was
Noriega himself. The narrative was based, in part, on the defendant's own
account.

When Rubino had finished reading the substitution, Sullivan rose and
asked Hoeveler for an instruction to the jury. The prosecution agreed only
that the CIA had received the information offered, he said. He asked the
judge to tell the jury that the veracity of the CIA's information could not be
determined.

Still, if the cables were taken at face value, they contradicted the core of
the indictment's racketeering charge—that Noriega had taken money to protect the cartel.

Noriega was anxious to testify and sometimes even adamant that Rubino
should put him on the witness stand. His speech to the court following the
prison tape debacle—the "level playing field" speech—had been well received
in court and in the press. Noriega had shown that he was not the raving mad-
man the Bush administration made him out to be. "A most interesting per-

formance," Judge Hoeveler said after listening to Noriega. "He's a small man. When he spoke, you could see he had the commanding presence that probably got him where he got to." But Noriega spoke with notes then, and his words were as much Rubino and May's as they were his own. On the witness stand there would be no notes. It would be Noriega and Sullivan, and Sullivan, well versed in the art of cross-examination, would have the advantage. The assumption among the prosecutors was that Noriega would testify. Preparation for a Noriega cross-examination had been going on for months. Tom Raffanello had agents in the field conducting interviews on Noriega until a week before the government guessed Noriega would be called. Sullivan's chief objective in crossing Noriega would be to confront him with his unexplained wealth. Where had those millions of dollars that flowed through BCCI come from? If the money belonged to Panama, why had Noriega treated it as his own? The betting was that Noriega would grow flustered under Sullivan's questioning and in the end self-destruct.

Rubino and May had vacillated about letting Noriega take the stand. Three months before the start of trial, Rubino thought Noriega would probably testify. ("He made a dramatic statement, and he told the truth," Rubino said of Noriega's pretrial speech.)

The lawyers had carefully shielded Noriega from probing public scrutiny. Every day since his capture Noriega had received one or two requests for an interview. Every day. There was no point in talking to the press. If the time came for Noriega to talk, it would be at the trial.

Letting Noriega tell his own story could be quite effective, and Noriega wanted to. Rubino always believed a defendant should testify on his own behalf. "A jury wants to hear and see the defendant." he said. It was a way to humanize the case. But the problem, both Rubino and May could see, was that Noriega on the witness stand would be clearly out of his league. He had almost no understanding of how the American justice system worked; it was not like being a dictator. And testifying would not be speechmaking. Force of personality would have some effect but not that much. Answering questions really meant taking some direction. Noriega was versed in giving directions but not taking them. Even during trial preparation, the problem was evident. If you asked him what day it was, Noriega could not be counted on to answer correctly. He might say "green" as readily as "Monday." That was a dictator's way, Rubino and May agreed. Weeks of practice questioning in which May and Rubino took turns grilling Noriega just as Sullivan would on cross-examination had not paid off. Noriega simply could not learn how to be a good witness. The two attorneys finally agreed that putting Noriega on the stand was not worth the risk. It was now obvious that Noriega would not have the opportunity to make good on his threat: "I realize that this case has implications to the highest level of the United States government, including the White House," he had once boasted.

Rubino knew that Sullivan on cross would try to seek answers to the murder of Hugo Spadafora, the Panamanian dissident, and the execution of Maj.

Moises Giroldi, the leader of the October 1989 coup. Sullivan would want to know all about Julian Melo and the $5 million bribe. There might be no end to the downside.

What Noriega most wanted to talk about—his friendship with Bill Casey, his face-to-face meetings with Oliver North and John Poindexter—would not be on the agenda. That universe of Noriega's possible testimony had been rejected by the judge. There would be no opportunity to talk about his prisoner-of-war status. There would be no discussion of the invasion or the U.S.-imposed economic sanctions against Panama.

By Monday morning, March 9, the defense had just two witnesses left. If Noriega was going to take the stand, it would be either that afternoon or the first thing Tuesday morning. Speculation was running high. The ranks of the press had thinned over the past few months, but now the gallery was full again. Rubino and May were not afraid to tease the media, keeping the prosecution off guard.There would be an announcement on Monday, May had promised the Friday before. Most reporters thought that Noriega would go on. Who better to tell the story of cooperation than the man who had cooperated?

But on Monday, in chambers, shortly after 9 A.M., Rubino told Hoeveler and Sullivan that Noriega would not testify. The defense would call its two additional witnesses and then rest.

Sullivan and Malman looked at each other. Could they trust a defense lawyer? Rubino had changed his mind more than once. Sullivan asked Hoeveler for a Teague inquiry. (*Teague* was an Eleventh Circuit Court of Appeals case that addressed a defendant's right to take the stand in his own defense. The appeals court said a defendant should be instructed by the court about his right to testify, not just by his attorney.) "A defendant has an absolute right to take the stand if he is compelled not to by his attorney," Sullivan recited from the case. It is automatically ineffective assistance of counsel and a denial of the Sixth Amendment right if a defendant wants to testify but is not allowed to, Sullivan continued. A Teague inquiry would ensure that Noriega was making a voluntary and intelligent waiver of his right. This way there would be one less appeal issue.

But Rubino's mind was made up. After five weeks and eighteen witnesses, the defense was done. The burden of proof rested with the prosecution, not the defense. Rubino was certain his evidence showed that Noriega had not turned Panama into a racketeering enterprise, as the government had charged. Though Rubino was convinced the government still had not come clean with all the documents it could have turned over on discovery, the defense had little more to gain. The standard instruction to the jury would be that Noriega had no legal obligation to testify. "The desire to testify is different from the necessity" was Rubino's philosophy. The decision was a lock, Rubino assured Sullivan. The defense would finish its case this afternoon. The judge could then quiz Noriega, and the defense would rest.

Hoeveler agreed a Teague hearing was in order. The next morning, March

10, Hoeveler called the attorneys and Noriega to his chambers. Noriega was given a chair directly across the desk from the judge. The prosecutors and the defense team sat to the side.

"Good morning, sir," the judge said.

Noriega smiled at the judge and took his chair. He genuinely liked Hoeveler. "Good morning, Your Honor," he replied.

Hoeveler leaned slightly forward and folded his hands before him. "I want to go over a matter with you that I think you have already discussed with your attorney."

Noriega nodded. "Yes."

"Do you understand, sir, that under the Constitution of this country you have an absolute right to testify if you wish to?" Hoeveler asked.

"Yes, sir."

"You also have an absolute right not to testify if you do not wish to," the judge continued.

"Yes, sir."

"Have you discussed this with Mr. Rubino?"

"I have been advised by my attorney," Noriega replied.

"Now, I am not going to ask you what advice he has given you or what your discussions were, but I want you to understand that the final decision as to whether or not you are going to testify is, under our law, entirely up to you. Do you understand that?"

"Yes, sir," Noriega replied. His hands gripped the arms of the chair. He had assured Rubino and May that he was satisfied that they were recommending the right course.

"All right. Now, what is your wish? Do you wish to testify or do you not wish to testify?" Hoeveler asked.

Noriega paused a moment, considering not his decision but rather how to tell the judge what he felt. "If you would also allow me to," Noriega began, "I am prepared to testify mentally and spiritually. I am fully composed to testify, but based on the laws of the country of the United States, based also on the Geneva Treaty of the treatment allotted to prisoners of war, and also in my condition as a prisoner of war, I would take my right not to testify."

Noriega stopped again, and the judge leaned further forward. "Is this a decision that you have made freely and voluntarily?" Hoeveler asked.

"It is a decision that I am expressing to Your Honor," Noriega answered.

Hoeveler was impressed by the plight of the man sitting before him. Being a judge was as full a measure of the human experience as Hoeveler had ever known; it was something one could never take too seriously. It was at moments like this that he felt genuine empathy for the people before him.

"I recognize the fact that you have been brought to the United States against your will," Hoeveler said, "and that you are in custody against your will, but beyond those points, has anyone coerced you or intimidated you or forced you in any way to make the decision you are making?"

"No one would be able to do that," Noriega answered adamantly.

"All right," Hoeveler said, "and have you had sufficient opportunity to discuss this matter with your attorney, Mr. Rubino, and your attorney, Mr. May?"

"I have discussed the subject with them," Noriega said. "I have also been explained as to the limitations within which I would be able to express my points of view, which are the laws to which this case is subject to; and my presentation would have to be limited not to include political matters, matters that have to do with the invasion, matters that have to do with war, and that's within the rules of this trial over which you have presided in such a dignified manner."

It was close to speechmaking, Hoeveler thought, but the general was correct. The limits of the case were in place.

"I wouldn't presume to explain to you the limitations of any examination and cross-examination that you might face," Hoeveler said. "For that advice you will have to rely on your lawyers. I simply want to make sure that you have had sufficient opportunity to discuss this with your lawyers."

"Yes, sir," Noriega answered and nodded.

Hoeveler turned to Rubino and asked if he, too, was convinced that Noriega was making a willing and voluntary relinquishment of his right to testify.

"Yes, sir," Rubino told the judge. "This is not a decision that was made overnight. This is something that has been discussed with the general as the case has progressed. The decision was ultimately and independently made by the general, but I must say to the court, it was made after much discussion with Mr. May and myself. I think that's something—that any client looks upon his lawyer for advice. I did advise the general of my belief of certain limitations of testimony, as to what I would call the law of the case, as it has developed through this case, and I have advised him of particular areas that I felt the court would accept as relevant areas and certain areas that the court, in my concerted belief, would find to be irrelevant areas, based upon certain decisions previously made. So I have tried to give him a total view," Rubino said.

Hoeveler turned again to Noriega. There was a matter of setting the record. "There [is] one other thing," the judge continued. "Do you feel well today?"

"Thank God, fine," Noriega replied.

"Have you had any medication of any type this morning?"

"No. Not ever."

"Have you been under the care of a psychiatrist or psychologist within the two years you have been here?"

"No," the general replied. "Last year at the date of the anniversary of the invasion, the director's office of the MCC sent a psychologist to me to see how I was reacting. However, I told him that it was not necessary."

Hoeveler again turned to Rubino. "Mr. Rubino, in your opinion, is your client fully competent to make the decision that he has made?"

"I have no question that he's making a knowing and intelligent waiver of his right, after discussing it with both his counsel and receiving advice," Rubino answered.

The judge turned to Noriega and smiled. "I ask that question, not because I think you have any problems, but only as a matter of putting it on the record that there is no question about your competency or willingness to do what you have done," he said.

Noriega nodded. "I understand that, Your Honor."

There was a momentary pause, and then Noriega asked if he might make a further comment.

"Go ahead," Hoeveler said.

Noriega sat up in his chair and looked at Sullivan and then Malman. "Please excuse my ignorance as to these legal matters," he began. "I would not want the prosecutors or the lawyers present here to interpret that my waiver to the right to testify is in any way a way of not answering questions because I had and I have sufficient documents and sufficient mental recollection to answer any question to any of the questions that I have seen that have been formulated during the months that I have been sitting over there."

Sullivan remained expressionless. Malman and Guy Lewis looked at each other.

"That's all I had to say, Your Honor," Noriega finished.

"All right," Hoeveler said, leaning back in his chair. "Thank you."

Sitting in the back of the room were three pool representatives of the media, a CNN reporter, a reporter from United Press International, and an international reporter from South America. The three stood and left Hoeveler's chambers. Within minutes Noriega's decision was news around the world.

Walking out of the judge's chambers a few minutes later, Rubino was surrounded by reporters. "Certain restrictions have been placed on certain areas of inquiry," he explained. Those restrictions would have limited Noriega's testimony. The restrictions were born of "certain secret decisions I cannot discuss with you," he said. A few minutes later, back in open court, with the jury again present, Rubino announced that the defense would rest.

CHAPTER 34
★★★★★★★

Drawing Conclusions

There hadn't been many surprises for the prosecution during the defense's case. Pat Sullivan felt the cross-examinations had gone well, and for the most part the "cooperation" testimony of the DEA agents seemed to have been effectively countered. Now, after six months of trial and three months since the prosecution rested, Sullivan was anxious to take advantage of the prosecution's rebuttal time. Rebuttal meant just that: There wasn't to be any introduction of new issues. The effort was to be a response to the defense's witnesses. Sullivan estimated his witnesses would take a week. One always had to be concerned about a jury's interest flagging, but this group seemed to be paying attention. There was a stony concentration in the jury box, but it had not turned to a glaze. They were still listening.

Frank Rubino, of course, expected the worst. If it were his rebuttal, he'd put in whatever he could, including new issues. After all, this was battle. Why would Sullivan and Malman be any different?

The defense rested before lunch. At 1:30, Myles Malman called the government's first rebuttal witness, DEA analyst Carol Cooper. Cooper had worked Operation Chemcom, which tracked precursor chemicals from Chicago to New Orleans to Tranquilandia in 1984. Defense witness Nivaldo Madrinan, the DENI chief, claimed the PDF had helped track the ether to Tranquilandia. That, in turn, had led to the Tranquilandia raid that netted ten tons of cocaine. Cooper said the ether never went through Panama. DEA satellite-activated beepers showed it was in the Colombian jungle forty-eight hours after it left New Orleans.

Noriega, Madrinan, Luis Quiel, and the PDF couldn't have helped track the ether if it never landed in Panama, Cooper testified.

Rubino's cross-examination was simple.

If the ether never landed in Panama on its way to Colombia, then Noriega could not have given it safe passage, either, could he?

"No, sir," Cooper answered.

A U.S. Customs' agent and a Customs' analyst followed Cooper to the stand. Both claimed that the Customs Service, not Noriega's police, had initiated the investigation of cartel money launderer Ramón Milian Rodríguez.

But on cross Rubino countered by asking them to read aloud Panamanian customs reports sent by the PDF to James Bramble of the DEA that said Rodríguez was shipping cash.

Group 9 DEA agent Henry Cuervo, who had been on the ground in Panama during the invasion, came to the witness stand at the end of the first day of rebuttal. Cuervo had testified earlier during the government's case. Now he returned with flight records captured in the invasion. The records showed that U.S. marijuana smuggler Steven Kalish visited Panama in 1983. But the records failed to show that Kalish was under investigation by the PDF for trafficking. That, of course, ran counter to defense testimony, which suggested the PDF was tracking Kalish, who was bringing millions of dollars in drug proceeds into Panama for laundering.

On cross-examination Rubino asked Cuervo to look at the reports a second time. The files, which the government was now entering into evidence, were incomplete. The prosecutors had removed PDF Narcotics Division reports from the files. When those reports, which Rubino had introduced during the defense case, were meshed with the flight records, they showed that Kalish, in fact, had been tracked by the PDF.

"The ones the government put in do not show anybody bringing money through the airport; the ones the defense brought in do show someone bringing in money, is that right?" Rubino asked.

"I believe so, yes," Cuervo said.

"So, essentially, if we put the two together, you get the whole picture, don't you?" Rubino observed.

On the second day of rebuttal, Wednesday, March 21, Eduardo Martínez, the Medellín cartel's top money man, took the stand. Martínez had been rounded up with 127 other cartel operatives in 1989. His arrest and conviction was one of the fruits of the massive money-laundering sting known as Operation Polar Cap. Atlanta federal prosecutors showed that Martínez had laundered between $200 million and $300 million for the cartel between 1985 and 1989. Martínez was now trading his testimony for a reduction in a possible thirty-year jail sentence.

On the stand, Martínez challenged the credibility of Nivaldo Madrinan. Martínez said he had paid $200,000 through intermediaries to Madrinan in March 1989. The payoff was made for assistance in eluding the DEA in Panama. The bribe had gone through Madrinan's cousin, Pedro Madrinan, Martínez testified.

Rubino objected. The events the Colombian was testifying to fell three years beyond the period of the indictment and should not be admissible, Rubino argued.

Hoeveler considered a moment. The testimony helped show how Madrinan had operated his narcotics squad, the judge said. That could lend perspective to his credibility. The objection was overruled.

On cross-examination Martínez conceded to Rubino that once he had bribed his way out of Panama, he never went back. He knew, he said, that he might not be so lucky with the PDF the second time.

Madrinan's cousin Pedro followed Martínez to the witness stand the next day. He said he had passed $100,000 of the $200,000 bribe to Nivaldo. The police chief then freed Martínez and two others, he claimed.

Wasn't it curious, Rubino asked Pedro on cross-examination, that he had conveniently recorded the bribe in his daily diary among common chores like getting the oil in his car changed?

"Did you write down other criminal activity in there?" Rubino asked.

"No," the witness answered.

On Monday, March 16, the third day of government rebuttal, Guy Lewis called Panamanian Felipe Pena to the stand. Pena had worked in Madrinan's antinarcotics unit during the early 1980s. He said that in May 1984 he drove Medellín cartel leader Julio César Correra, who was then visiting Panama, to see Noriega. Also at the meeting, Pena said, was Julian Melo. The upshot of Pena's testimony was that Melo had not acted alone. It was another face-to-face meeting between the cartel and Noriega. In addition, Pena said that on April 30, 1984, he picked cartel leader Pablo Escobar up at a Panama City hotel and drove him to a meeting with an aide to Noriega. That was the same day Colombian Justice Minister Rodrigo Lara Bonilla was assassinated, Pena remembered. Pena's testimony was curious because the prosecution's previous witnesses claimed Escobar had not arrived in Panama until a few days after the assassination, fleeing Colombia with the rest of the cartel.

Rubino scoffed at Pena's testimony. Wasn't it true, Rubino asked, that Pena contacted the prosecutors when he read about Noriega's trial in the newspapers? Wasn't it true that he had everything to gain by testifying against Noriega? In Panama, Rubino noted, Pena had been linked to the planting of a kilogram of cocaine in the car of an Ecuadoran presidential candidate then visiting Panama. Wasn't it true, Rubino asked, that he was trading his testimony against Noriega for a deal with Panamanian prosecutors?

"That's not true," Pena protested. "I don't have any pending case." But Pena conceded that his seemingly certain and recent identification of Correra came even though the man he claimed was Correra had sat in the back of his car for only about an hour seven years before.

Pena's testimony upset Jon May. It was a wholly new meeting, a meeting the defense had not heard of before. At sidebar he complained that the government was breaking its word and introducing new evidence. "It is very much in the nature of the government reopening its case to present new evidence." Putting Noriega at another meeting with a cartel boss expanded the case, he told the judge. "We are severely prejudiced." There was no way to defend against Pena's testimony on cross-examination without investigating the allegation. The new evidence would effectively deprive Noriega of his Sixth Amendment right to effective assistance of counsel, May complained.

The point was fair, Hoeveler said. The judge ordered Pena to remain in Miami for a few additional days. The defense could reopen its cross-examination if necessary. But Hoeveler warned that the government's rebuttal was drawing to a close and time was running out.

To rebut the testimony of Noriega aide Cleto Hernández, the prosecution next called the former Panamanian roommate of Colombian drug trafficker Nubia Pina. Pina had been a partner of César Rodríguez in the *Krill* smuggling voyage. The roommate, Doris Fernández, testified that she was certain Hernández knew about the *Krill* and its intended voyage ahead of time. Hernández often visited Pina, she said. Fernández also said she had heard that César Rodríguez was involved in sending cocaine-refining chemicals to the Colombian traffickers. Noriega, she said she was told by Pina, was also involved. On cross-examination Fernández conceded that all she knew she had learned second- or third-hand.

DEA agent and analyst Charles Vopat next testified that Noriega's antidrug efforts—the ones headed by Madrinan and Miranda—were not what they appeared to be. He said he had put an end to Operation Negocios in 1986 because Panamanian officials quit cooperating. Despite repeated requests, Vopat said, the information the DEA really needed was never forthcoming. He said he got more information out of the DEA's own paid informants than he did out of Noriega's G-2. The PDF's cooperation was not all that the defense made it seem, Vopat said.

With his testimony, Vopat offered scores of reports that he asserted clearly showed the PDF had provided only about one-third of the information received by the DEA in the course of Operation Negocios and other money-laundering probes. Most of the intelligence, Vopat claimed, was generated by the DEA itself.

On cross-examination Rubino asked Vopat to look more carefully at the agency's reports and his own analyses. Many that Vopat had attributed to secret DEA sources had little if anything to do with money laundering. To say that the PDF offered little assistance meant nothing when the reports showed the subjects reported on didn't even concern Panama.

Rubino held out a stack of the reports. Referring to one that described orange-and-white automobiles in Miami, Rubino pushed Vopat. "The bottom line is, it doesn't say a word about bringing money into Panama through Tocumen or Paitilla airport. It talks about people driving around in Miami." His point was made.

By Thursday, March 19, the prosecution was all but finished with rebuttal.

Guy Lewis called Evaristo Gómez to the witness stand. Gómez had been a PDF officer working as a liaison between the PDF's narcotics unit and the DEA from 1981 to 1989. He had been developed as a witness before the start of the trial, but Sullivan had insisted he be kept in reserve for just the right moment. Now was the time. His testimony, Sullivan was certain, would be as strong as any the government had put on in the course of the trial.

Gómez testified that he had been ordered to provide the DEA with "sanitized" intelligence reports on drug couriers and fugitives. Contrary to what his bosses in DENI claimed, Gómez said, the cooperation of the Panamanian police was a sham. No information that had not been reviewed first by Luis Quiel and Noriega was to be handed over to the Americans, Gómez said of his orders. The information was screened, collected into what the PDF hoped would be impressive batches, and then passed to the DEA, he said.

"The captain would always tell me that we needed to keep the people from the DEA happy because they used to demand a lot," Gómez said on direct examination. No files concerning Floyd Carlton, César Rodríguez, or Steven Kalish were turned over to the DEA, Gómez said.

And in the year following Noriega's 1988 indictment, Gómez continued, PDF narcotics police rounded up drug documents that might incriminate Noriega. The documents were routed into Gómez's office, and some were copied and sent to Noreiga's attorneys in the United States, he said. But then one day the papers disappeared. Gómez said he never saw them again.

At sidebar, Rubino confirmed that many of the files that Quiel had collected following the indictment were turned over to him. They were attorney-client work product. Rubino said he resented the insinuation that somehow he was involved in a so-called cover-up.

Lewis enjoyed watching Rubino squirm. No offense intended, he told Rubino. Gómez's testimony was electric. The files that made up Negocios had been doctored, if what Gómez said was true. He belied the defense contention that Noriega had cooperated with the Americans. The cooperation was replete with treachery and betrayal. The Panamanian leader had shorted the DEA.

Rubino considered Gómez's testimony devastating. He had made a sham out of the Negocios-cooperation defense. Gómez had no axe to grind with Noriega. His testimony was totally believable. Rubino had nothing to counter Gómez with.

The former Panamanian attorney general Rafael Rodríguez next testified that he was forced to resign at gunpoint in July 1983 as he investigated corruption in his country's military. Noriega, Rodríguez testified, told him his investigation was hurting Panama. Resign or "become a friend of the defense forces and cover up everything that smelled," Noriega told him.

"Colonel Noriega expressed to me that the prosecutor had to be a friend of the Defense Forces," Rodríguez said. "Not even a mosquito could get into Panama if Noriega didn't allow it," he added.

Rodríguez said he resisted resigning as long as he could and then finally fled to the United States.

Who was the commander in chief and the leader of Panama when he had been forced to flee? Rubino asked Rodríguez on cross-examination.

Gen. Rubén Dario Paredes, Rodríguez replied.

★   ★   ★

In total, fourteen rebuttal witnesses testified for the government in its week-long rebuttal case.

The prosecution, Sullivan told Hoeveler, was again finished.

But the defense wasn't.

Rubino and May were still upset about the testimony of Felipe Pena, and his allegation of a newly discovered meeting between Noriega and the cartel.

"We sincerely believe these do not rebut anything but are brand-new charges," Rubino told Hoeveler.

May said: "Now the government has suggested that this is proper rebuttal testimony. They have argued that this was rebuttal to our allegations that Julian Melo traded on General Noreiga's name as well as the issue of whether General Noriega fully cooperated with the Drug Enforcement Administration." Then why had the government waited until its rebuttal case to offer a new meeting? May asked.

"I think that the question here is a question of fairness. Shouldn't the defense be entitled to show that at the time when Pena says Correra and General Noriega met, General Noriega was elsewhere?" In fact, May continued, of all the weekends that Pena could have picked to claim Noriega was meeting with the cartel, the first weekend in May 1984 was the one that the defense could most convincingly show Noriega had *not* met with Correra. That weekend had come just days before Panama's first free election in sixteen years. Noriega had spent that weekend campaigning for his hand-picked candidate Nicolas Barletta. New defense witnesses, May told Hoeveler, could account for Noriega's every move. Pena, he said, was lying. The defense was taking the unusual step of requesting a surrebuttal, May said. It wanted to reopen its case to call additional witnesses.

Hoeveler was not happy. This case might never end. Surrebuttal was almost unheard of. Exasperation crept across the judge's face. "You know, every witness the government puts on, if there is evidence to counter it, we could just keep the trial going," he told May. "There has to come a time when the testimony stops and the jury decides the facts. I have been on the bench almost fifteen years. In that time I think I have granted surrebuttal maybe one time, and that, obviously, was in a case of considerable need and good cause."

May conceded that the challenge was on a very narrow point. However, he continued, "it will not significantly delay this trial. It is in the interest of justice."

This was nonsense, Sullivan said. Pena's testimony, like others, was offered to rebut the testimony of Miranda and Madrinan that they had never seen or known of the presence of the cartel in Panama. Pena also testified that Correra had met with Madrinan. Both Panamanian police officials knew of Escobar's presence in Panama, Pena testified. It was clearly rebuttal, Sullivan argued. And, Sullivan said, Pena was developed as a witness in January, just three months before. There was no way he could have been called to testify during the prosecution case. The prosecutors hadn't known about Pena then.

May and Rubino knew they had a good shot at reopening their case.

Hoeveler's tenure on the bench had been notable for the fact that he would go the extra mile for a defense. That was one reason verdicts in his court were so seldom overturned on appeal. Everyone, especially criminal defendants, received the benefit of the doubt; there were few points on which to appeal.

When May finished his argument, Hoeveler considered only a moment or two. "At this point I am resigned to the fact that we will finish when we finish," he said. The words came in a measure and cadence that Rubino and May could easily mark as their very last chance. "If it isn't this week," Hoeveler continued, "it will be next week."

Hoeveler looked at the two defense lawyers. "We've done some most infrequent things in this case before, to assure your client a complete defense, such as taking depositions during the course of the trial, for example, and giving you time to prepare for witnesses presented by the government. But I do want to make sure that you have an opportunity to present all that you wish to present." For the record, Hoeveler now offered his justification. "Your client did not take the stand, yet the point that you wish to rebut in surrebuttal was really testimony about him, which could, I suppose, essentially be considered evidence that should not have come in on rebuttal. . . . I think that surrebuttal is properly appropriate under those circumstances." The judge paused. "So do what you have to do," Hoeveler told Rubino. "Go ahead." But the limit was two additional witnesses. That was all.

Ignacio Occhi, a Spanish magazine distributor living in Panama, had escorted a group of Spanish journalists to interview Noriega the weekend before the May 1984 election. Fernando Jaen, a civilian aide to Noriega, had also been with Noriega that weekend. The two could say it would have been impossible for Noriega to have met with the cartel when Pena claimed. Noriega had been giving interviews to journalists almost the whole weekend. They would be very effective. Their testimony was set for Monday, March 30.

But the day before, as Occhi and Jaen prepared to board a plane for Miami on their way to testify, they were detained by Panamanian officials. In the end, Occhi was permitted to leave, but Jaen was thrown in jail.

"I must say to this court that we find the circumstances and the timing of these events to be more than coincidental," Rubino protested to Hoeveler on Monday. The arrest of Jaen gave Noriega only a partial alibi for the time period Pena had testified to, Rubino explained.

Myles Malman stepped forward for the prosecution. Rubino was wrong, he said. The government had made a Herculean effort to assist the defense in bringing witnesses from Panama, he told Hoeveler. Defense had waited until the last moment to bring its witnesses forward and time had run out, Malman said with a profound lack of sympathy.

It was obvious, there was nothing to be done.

Rubino called Occhi to the stand.

Occhi said Noriega definitely had participated in the press interviews that weekend. For at least half of the weekend, he said, Noriega had rarely been out of his sight for more than a few minutes.

Malman's cross concentrated on Occhi's friendship with Noriega's family, a friendship he had struck up as a result of Noriega's daughters' interest in Spanish magazines. But Occhi insisted his friendship with the Noriegas was hardly a reason to come to Miami to lie on the witness stand.

Before Occhi stepped down, Rubino came back on redirect. He directed Occhi to the previous day when Jaen had been arrested in Panama. This smelled of obstruction, Rubino suggested.

Malman objected, and the objection was sustained.

To no end, Rubino protested anew at sidebar: "Short of another invasion to snatch him and bring him here," Rubino complained in frustration, "there isn't very much we can do about it."

In the final two weeks of the trial, things got messy. First, the press: Richard Cole, the Associated Press correspondent, had been sitting in the first row of the gallery for six months. Cole had been on top of the case for two years. Even other reporters would go to him for help on trial stories. He'd broken his share of stories, putting the *Miami Herald,* the *New York Times,* and the *Washington Post* in their places. But on March 15 another reporter passed a note to the judge claiming that Cole was feeding information to the defense. The judge was angry. He liked Cole, but he didn't much care for the ethics of a reporter who would take sides, and he particularly didn't care that the defense—which was getting a government stipend to cover its costs, including investigators—was taking handouts from what was supposed to be an unbiased media.

Hoeveler invited Rubino and the prosecutors into chambers.

"You were unaware of the background of one of the Colombian witnesses, and Cole did a background check and supplied you with information—'you' being Frank Rubino," Hoeveler accused Rubino. While Cole was doing the background check for the defense, Rubino had stalled a cross-examination waiting for the information, the judge charged. "Now, what about that?" Hoeveler demanded in a louder voice.

Rubino couldn't lie to the judge. The fact was that both he and May had cultivated the press from the beginning. Reporters wanted a story to report. The defense had a story. The object was to get Noriega's side out. Rubino knew he would be picking a jury; potential jurors read newspapers and watched television news. Helping reporters see that Panama and Noriega had not always existed at the pleasure of the U.S. government could help potential jurors appreciate Noriega's position.

But just as important, both Rubino and May appreciated, some reporters knew as much or more about Noriega, Panama, and the United States' history of involvement in Panama than any of the attorneys or investigators working the case.

"Your Honor, I have gathered information from numerous reporters," Rubino told Hoeveler. "I found newspaper reports, TV reports, and videotape to be very helpful in the preparation of not only this case but numerous cases."

It was true, Rubino said, that he had asked Cole to do a computer check on one of the government's rebuttal witnesses, but what difference did it make? He could go to the Associated Press or to any other news operation, stand in line, and get the same information. All he was guilty of was using a shortcut.

"I didn't know reporters were a taboo source of public records," Rubino told the judge.

"I just don't think that it's professional for a reporter to be acting as investigator to either side," Hoeveler responded sternly. "In my mind, it's highly unprofessional. If you were stalling, waiting for information, it's unprofessional, and if I was convinced of it, I would fine you."

"I don't see what's wrong with me checking public sources to get information," Rubino reiterated.

"You're missing the point," Hoeveler shot back. "There is nothing wrong at all with you checking sources, but when you start getting a reporter to do investigations for you, he's going well beyond that which he's employed to do."

Hoeveler knew there was little he could do. It was an ethical, not legal, issue.

"If I thought he was acting as an investigator for you, I'd bar him from the trial, if I could. I just don't think I can. Apparently it bothers the other reporters. Apparently the press pool is upset by what you and he are doing. I suggest that you be a bit more discreet about your dealings with the press."

Rubino's attitude irritated Hoeveler. It was clear Rubino was resisting his deeper meaning. "That's really all I have to say," said Hoeveler.

Three days later, Hoeveler again called the attorneys into chambers. He had received a call from *Washington Post* reporter Michael Isikoff. "The information they have is that I was picked up by a limousine sometime last week when President Bush was in town; that I was taken to meet the president, at which point the president impressed upon me the importance of the government winning this case."

Rubino was the first to respond. "Are you serious?" he asked.

"That's unbelievable," Myles Malman said.

"Are you serious?" Rubino repeated.

Hoeveler said he would be returning the reporter's phone call. "I want to assure you that I have never met President Bush at any time or under any circumstances."

"We've seen him in a photograph in this case," Sullivan added, referring to the photograph of Bush and Noriega taken in Panama in 1982 that Rubino had been desperately and fruitlessly trying to admit into evidence since the start of the trial.

But it was also more than the press. There was the curious story of F. Lee Bailey, Jr., the noted Palm Beach criminal defense lawyer.

One morning during the previous October, Bailey was reading a newspaper account of Noriega's trial and recognized the name of a former client, Gabriel Taboada. The convicted Colombian cocaine trafficker had testified for the prosecution that he had been in Medellín when Fabio Ochoa and Gustavo Gaviria presented Noriega with $500,000 stuffed in a suitcase.

That couldn't be right, Bailey thought to himself. Taboada had been his client for a short time in 1988. Before agreeing to represent Taboada, Bailey queried the Colombian about dealings with Noriega. Because Noriega had hired Bailey in early 1988 to deliver documents to the U.S. State Department in an effort to negotiate a dismissal of his indictment, Bailey was careful to avoid a conflict of interest with someone like Taboada. If Taboada had had any dealings with Noriega, Bailey remembered telling Taboada, he would be precluded from representing him. There were no conflicts, Bailey remembered Taboada saying.

But, in October 1991, Taboada was testifying that he had been with Noriega in Medellín.

On February 3, 1992, Bailey wrote to Pat Sullivan. "Because he claimed to know other Colombians well up on the drug totem pole, I queried him carefully in order to avoid an ethical conflict on my part," Bailey wrote. If Taboada had told Bailey the truth, that he had not dealt with Noriega, then he had perjured himself on the witness stand, Bailey suggested. It was a serious development because Taboada was the only witness who said he had actually watched Noriega receive a bribe from the cartel. From Palm Beach, Bailey waited for something to happen. It didn't. On Friday, March 13, Rubino received a call from Bailey, who suggested that Rubino ask Sullivan about Taboada's testimony.

On Tuesday, March 24, Hoeveler took up a motion filed for the defense by Jon May. The defense requested that Hoeveler determine if the government had been aware of a possible inconsistent statement by one of its witnesses. The hearing must go forward out of deference to Noriega's right to a fair trial, May argued.

Hoeveler was skeptical. "I have got to say to you, Mr. May, that I have a certain reluctance to get into the testimony of a lawyer who has represented both the defendant and the witness, whom he is apparently about ready to testify against," Hoeveler said. Bailey was saying that he had been aware of Taboada's testimony for months and only now informed the defense. "I have to tell you that the posture in which this comes before the court is a very strange and interesting posture," he told May.

Sullivan spoke for the government. He said he had spoken to Bailey the previous February and had followed up on the lawyer's allegation. But the FBI agents and the U.S. attorney in South Carolina where Taboada was held in 1988 said they had debriefed Taboada then and that he had never been questioned about Noriega. "The bottom line is, we determined that there are no evidences or possibilities that Mr. Taboada made prior inconsistent statements to the effect that he knew nothing about Noriega," Sullivan told the judge. The government remained satisfied with Taboada's testimony.

Hoeveler called for a hearing on the matter the next day. At noon, during the jury's lunch recess, the judge called the attorneys into court. The only way to determine if Taboada had perjured himself was to hear from both the client and his lawyer. For Bailey to testify about exactly what Taboada had told him, Taboada would first have to waive attorney-client privilege, Hoeveler said. In effect, Taboada would have to allow his lawyer to testify that he was a liar.

Taboada was brought to court. "It appears your former lawyer may testify to things that contradict what you said in this courtroom. Are you willing to give up your rights and let Mr. Bailey testify?" the judge asked him.

"No objections," Taboada answered through an interpreter. Hoeveler looked puzzled. Waiving the attorney-client privilege could be injurious to you, he told Taboada.

The Colombian did not respond. He looked quizzical.

"I don't feel he is aware of the consequences of his decision," Hoeveler said.

Hoeveler asked Taboada's new attorney, John Mattes, to take Taboada aside and make sure he understood what was going on. After Mattes spoke to Taboada, Hoeveler took up the questioning again. Taboada reasserted that he had told the FBI in May 1990 of the meeting in Medellín and of Noriega's presence. But now, he said, he wanted his conversations with Bailey kept private. He did not wish to waive privilege. And he was not lying, he insisted. He would allow Hoeveler to question Bailey in private, but Bailey's answers must be "kept private between Mr. Bailey and the judge, forever," he insisted.

Hoeveler looked at Rubino and May and then at Sullivan. As usual in this case, they were in uncharted waters. "I think he is declining to waive privilege," Hoeveler observed. Mattes agreed that that was what he believed was Taboada's wish.

That left little recourse in determining for the official record whether Taboada had offered perjured testimony. The hearing was essentially a lost cause for the defense. Hoeveler turned to Rubino and May for suggestions.

The defense would accept the judge's determination, but they preferred that Hoeveler go forward with the questioning of Taboada and Bailey in private. A half hour later, Taboada and Bailey left Hoeveler's chambers. Hoeveler called in the defense attorneys and prosecutors.

"I'm not sure how to handle it, but I think it's a tempest in a teapot," the judge said. "The impression I get is that it's a matter of miscommunication rather than one person lying to another person."

Taboada, the judge said, had agreed to a polygraph test. He insisted he had never misled his former lawyer and that he had told the truth in court.

When Taboada and Bailey had first met in 1988, the two spoke in English, the judge related. The fact was that Taboada was more comfortable speaking Spanish. The two probably had not understood each other, the judge suggested. "He did make it clear at the end he does not want Bailey to talk about anything they talked about privately," Hoeveler told the attorneys.

There was no waiver of confidentiality or privilege, Hoeveler said. Taboada never mentioned Noriega to Bailey in 1988. It wasn't clear whether Noriega's name had ever come up between the two, the judge suggested. In short, the whole issue was odd. And it was now closed.

The Look Shop on the lower level of Burdine's department store at the sprawling Dadeland Mall was a ten-minute drive from where Ramón Navarro had crashed and died; it was around the corner from where William Saldarriaga had been arrested on a traffic violation in October 1989; and it was fifteen minutes north of the Metropolitan Correctional Center where Noriega was in his cell.

On Friday, March 20, at a few minutes past 8 P.M., Felicidad Noriega, the general's wife, and Rosa Busto, a friend, were snipping buttons off designer jackets. The buttons didn't even match. They were different shapes and sizes, twenty-seven in total, cut from ten different jackets. When Noriega and Busto walked out of the shop and then out of the store, store detectives called Metro-Dade police. The buttons were valued at $305, and the ruined jackets, $1,242. The charge was third-degree grand theft. On Monday the defense would begin its surrebuttal. The next day, Tuesday, the incident was all over the television news.

Wednesday, a weary Frank Rubino asked Hoeveler to poll the jury. Rubino wanted to know if the jurors could still decide the case without prejudice. Polling the jury could take two hours, Pat Sullivan complained.

"So what if it takes two hours?" Rubino snapped. "He is on trial for one hundred and forty years. A fair trial cannot be measured in terms of a clock."

When the jury took its place in court, Hoeveler turned to them. "Now, I want to ask you if you have seen, read, heard, viewed any matters concerning a member of the defendant's family?" he asked. Almost every hand went up. Rubino shook his head.

"Obviously, it has no relation to this case, but nonetheless I do want to discuss with you briefly that particular item," the judge said. Each juror would be called aside individually.

Jean Hallisey, the juror sitting in the number one chair, was called up first. What did you hear? the judge asked.

"I walked in the house last evening, and my husband said, 'Did you hear about Mrs. Noriega?' And I said, 'No.'"

"Do you have any opinion about that that would relate to the case?" Hoeveler asked.

"Not really, because I know, being a woman myself, I thought, well, maybe she just had some buttons missing on her clothing," Hallisey said. "I mean, it seemed like it was a little bit blown out of proportion for me. They are two different people."

"I hated to hear that about anybody," Bernadine Cooper, the juror sitting in the number four chair, told Hoeveler.

Other jurors had heard bits and pieces of the story on television. Some had heard on the train riding to the courthouse. Only two hadn't heard. None said it would affect their judgment.

After all the jurors had been questioned, Hoeveler was satisfied. So, too, was Frank Rubino.

"As you all pointed out to me, this has absolutely nothing to do with this case or the issues in this case," Hoeveler said when he called all of the jurors back together. "I want to make sure that it will have absolutely nothing to do with your decision on the issues in this case."

CHAPTER 35
★★★★★★★

Closing Arguments

The trial was now going into its seventh month. It had been fifteen weeks since the prosecution rested. On Tuesday, March 31, the Central Courtroom was packed.

Felicidad Noriega had paid a fine, and her lawyer was settling the buttons theft charge. As they had for almost every day of the trial, her daughters, Thays and Sandra, sat at her side, directly behind their father, who was now leaning back against the defense table awaiting the judge.

Winston Spadafora, the brother of murdered Panamanian dissident Hugo Spadafora, had flown in from Panama and sat two rows over. "I hope he rots in his jail cell," Spadafora said, looking toward Noriega. Danny Moritz had flown in from the DEA field office in Detroit. He shook Steve Grilli's hand and sat in the first row in the middle, next to DEA SAC Tom Cash and agents Tom Raffanello and Ken Kennedy. The parents of two U.S. soldiers killed during the 1989 invasion sat behind them in the gallery.

The press of the world occupied twelve full rows. Print reporters and broadcast journalists filled in the seats behind the dozen reporters who had been in court each day since the beginning.

At the prosecution table, Myles Malman leaned back in his chair; he stroked his mustache and looked through his notes. He had been preparing this closing statement since October 1989. That was the way Malman worked. He always began thinking about the closing argument when he took on a case. His notebooks were jammed with references to the witnesses. His office was piled with marked trial transcripts. Now it would all come together.

Pat Sullivan and Guy Lewis sat at either end of the prosecution table, flanking Malman. Lewis looked over his shoulder. Other assistants from the U.S. attorney's office were filling in the open seats along the side of the gallery.

Next to Noriega at the defense table, Jon May sat in Frank Rubino's chair. Rubino still had not come up from the defense's office in the courthouse basement. He had only just begun to shape his closing. He had been working almost every day for seven months.

Malman would deliver the government's closing argument. Rubino would

411

follow with the defense's closing. Sullivan would speak last, giving the government's rebuttal.

In the jury room, the jurors took their usual places around the long conference table. Christopher Johnson, an alternate, had been dismissed two weeks before because of a foot infection. There were twelve jurors and only one alternate now; five jurors and alternates had been lost along the way. But there was relief in the air, with only a few more days for closings and deliberations. It was almost over.

In chambers, Bill Hoeveler put on his black robe. Sandra Cavazos, his law clerk, stood off to the side. She had clerked the case for two years. She smiled as Hoeveler finished buttoning his robe.

"This is it," Hoeveler said. It was as though the burden was already beginning to lift. Hoeveler and Cavazos walked into court.

"All rise," the deputy marshal called.

When the judge had taken his seat, he called for the jury.

First, there were a few evidentiary matters to be put into the record. Sullivan and Rubino ran through their lists. By a little after 11 A.M. they had finished. Hoeveler turned toward the jury. "Ladies and gentlemen, that completes the evidentiary phase of this case." He looked to the defense table and then to the prosecution.

"All right, Mr. Malman," the judge said, inviting Malman to come forward.

Malman stood and buttoned his suit coat. Guy Lewis leaned back in his chair to make sure Malman wasn't wearing the argyle socks he favored with those $1,200 suits. Lewis hated those socks.

Steve Grilli sat at the end of the prosecution table. He looked over his shoulder at Ken Kennedy. Malman's persnickety ways had grated on Grilli for two years. But Grilli knew there was no better choice than Malman for the closing. Malman loved detail; he knew the law; the closing was in good hands.

Malman walked to the lectern and set down his notes.

"Ladies and gentlemen of the jury," he began, "Manuel Antonio Noriega was a man of great, great power. He had the ear of Cuban premiers and Colombian ex-presidents. He used his power to deceive the DEA on a daily basis with sanitized and controlled information. While he used his power to trick and fool the DEA, the CIA, and the gringos with phony cooperation, he sold his uniform, his army, and his protection to a murderous international criminal gang known as the cocaine cartel of Medellín, Colombia. For millions and millions of dollars in cash, they bought that man, that man and his uniform, to do their corrupt and dirty bidding.

"He was the classic military dictator, but as the evidence unfolded before you over these past months, it proved Manuel Antonio Noreiga was nothing more than the corrupt, crooked, and rotten cop—Officer Noriega, as Carlos Lehder called him. Nothing more. Nothing less."

Malman spoke softly and evenly, hardly looking at his notes. He stood to the side of the lectern where the jurors could take his full measure.

"After all the showboating and the smart remarks and the double-talk and the flash and the glitter is over, ladies and gentlemen, the trial is one thing and one thing only: a search for the truth. I will attempt to the best of my ability to present arguments to you, arguments that flow from the evidence, from the sixty-one witnesses called by the United States and the nineteen called by the defendant and the thousands and thousands of pages of evidence.

"The issue in this case is one and one alone, and that is, that Manuel Antonio Noriega, using his position and his role as the general of the Panama Defense Forces and the general of the G-2 intelligence of Panama, took part in this conspiracy, and a criminal enterprise. The issue is not whether or not Manuel Antonio Noriega could play the good cop when he wanted, to the extent he wanted, in his own backyard and on his own terms. That's not an issue, and we'll discuss that later on. The issue is not whether or not some of the amounts of cocaine charged are different [from] those in the indictment. The actual amount of cocaine is not an issue in the case. What is an issue is that it was cocaine and it was sent here," Malman said emphatically.

There was no issue of jurisdiction, Malman told the jurors. The judge had decided that. That was not their concern. The issue was not politics. Politics, the judge had also ruled, played no part in this case, Malman said. "The issue at hand," he said, looking at the first row of the jury box, was simple: "Did Manuel Antonio Noreiga commit these crimes?" Malman paused a moment again.

"You're probably saying, 'Well, we're about to begin our deliberations, how do we go about doing this task?'" His voice became reassuring. "Well, jurors have been reaching verdicts in American courtrooms for two hundred years. The most important tool that you need to decide this case—it's something that each and every one of you has brought to us in this courtroom—that's your God-given common sense, reason, intelligence, judgment. When it comes to those facts, when it comes to deciding who is telling the truth, when it comes to deciding what's what and what happened and searching for the truth—common sense. There's no substitute for it."

When they looked at the evidence, Malman told the jurors, they should first look to the witnesses' credibility. Not every witness's testimony had to mesh with another's. Not every witness had to come to trial clean. Plea agreements were an unfortunate tool of law enforcement. "You take a small fish, put him on the hook to catch the big fish. These plea agreements, these cooperation agreements are not done in some back alley behind some closed doors. They are done in courts, open courts. If you have a robbery in the church on Sunday, the witnesses are going to be churchgoers and preachers," he said. "You have a crime committed in the inner sanctums of the Medellín cartel, who are the witnesses going to be? The pilots. The distributors. The bankers. The cartel leaders. You should not be shocked to see the coconspirators of Mr. Noriega come in and testify. You should not be shocked to see a leader of the Medellín cartel, Carlos Lehder, come in here and testify. We make no apologies for this," Malman said. "Plea bargaining is lawful and proper and a traditional law enforcement technique. You go up the ladder to get the top men. Yes, these people are criminals," he said, but "these are people . . . not some form of subhuman life."

Credibility was nearly guaranteed, Malman suggested. Bargained witnesses have to tell the truth, he said. Once they are on the witness stand, they are marked by the cartel. They have nowhere to turn. They give up their past lives. They face maximum jail sentences. Cooperation and telling the truth are their only chances to turn their lives around.

There were inconsistencies in the witnesses' testimony, Malman conceded. "It's a reality of life in a case like this with eighty witnesses that there are going to be inconsistencies. Inconsistencies in a criminal trial are badges of the truth." But the evidence added up, Malman told the jurors. Piece by piece, it added up.

"How did he get $23 million in secret bank accounts in Europe?" Malman asked. There was no clear answer, but all of the facts added together said Noriega broke the law.

And why were Noriega and Panama essential to the cartel? Malman asked. How did Noriega make himself important to the cartel? The answer was obvious: The cartel could not do business in a country unless it had protection, Malman asserted. "He may chitchat with the CIA now and then to keep them happy and to kind of juggle all the balls. One minute he's embracing Castro. The next minute he is embracing Reagan, and the cartel. He always kept those cartel fellows on their toes. He would sometimes seize a little money. They would have to pay to get it back. He'd take their plane. They would have to pay to get it back. That is the way that Noriega controlled Panama," Malman said.

Noriega was the right man in the right place, he continued. The Medellín cartel was born as a result of the Marta Ochoa kidnapping. Noriega was the man who assisted the traffickers in negotiating her release.

"So the cartel is born, and from the Marta Ochoa kidnapping, so is the agreement with Manuel Antonio Noriega. The agreement which was loose before is now tight and the cocaine pipelines are established, and Noriega provides protection to the cartel."

DEA agent Lenny Athas placed large multicolored charts on the courtroom easel near Malman. They outlined the government's case and its witnesses. Name by name, Malman pointed down the chart. He reviewed each one and the importance to Noriega's trafficking conspiracy.

Floyd Carlton was the "bus driver." He flew the cocaine. Malman read from Carlton's testimony: "Nobody inspected our airplanes. Nobody did anything to us," Carlton had testified.

G-2 security guard Rodolfo Carcamo and Air Force Col. Lorenzo Purcell had backed up Carlton's testimony. Both said Carlton and his partner, César Rodríguez, were "friends with the general." They enjoyed unhindered access to the airports.

Remember, Malman said to the jury, Ricardo Bilonick questioned Noriega about surrounding himself with people like Carlton and Rodríguez. Bilonick recalled Noriega replying that he "needed some people to do the dirty work." Remember that Carlton kept Noriega's home phone number handy and that Noriega encouraged Carlton to charge more for his drug flights.

And Malman asked the jurors to recall the time cartel pilot Roberto Striedinger landed at Pablo Escobar's Medellín ranch. "*El Tigre* is here, Noriega is here," ranch workers rushed to tell him.

Noriega's long-trusted military aide, Luis del Cid, testified that he had delivered part of Carlton's drug payoffs to Noriega, Malman reminded the jurors. He read from del Cid's testimony: "I knew it was drug money. Floyd was a dope dealer. Noriega sent me to get the money." Remember, Malman said, that del Cid had obeyed his general in just the way he snapped to attention in the courtroom that day.

The Paitilla airport and Inair pipelines were established, and nothing came through Panama's airports without Noriega's knowing, Malman reminded the jurors. David Rodrigo Ortiz had testified to flying two trips with Carlton. Noriega's security protected the airports. "One could feel the presence of those people there," Ortiz had said.

Noriega's people "were always in control of everything at the airport," flight controller Anel Pérez had testified. Cartel money launderer Eric Guerra had said he could pick up the cartel's money with "all the freedom. . . . They even gave me protection at times."

"Now, I don't know if you remember" or "I know this happened a long time ago, and you may not all recall it," Malman would say as he wound his way through the testimony of each witness. He had searched out each of the witnesses' most damning words, and he read through pages of direct quotations from the witnesses' testimony. The closing pressed through the morning and into the late afternoon.

After each break, the jury seemed ready for more, and Malman seemed reinvigorated.

He turned directly to Noriega's relationship with the cartel: "One of the most startling pieces of evidence in this trial—Manuel Antonio Noriega goes to Medellín to rub shoulders with the cartel leadership," he reminded the jury. Remember, he said, Noriega's joking with Fabio Ochoa and Gustavo Gaviria over the importation of a red Ferrari. And at the end of Noriega's visit, there was $500,000 in a briefcase. Later, Malman recollected, Carlos Lehder testified that Noriega was paid $500,000 for the return of cocaine to the cartel, cocaine that had been confiscated from other traffickers. "Here's the five hundred, Manuel," Gaviria told Noriega. "He doesn't say, 'Here's the five hundred for cocaine.' He doesn't say that because that's not the way these conspiracies work," Malman told the jury. "They don't write it down."

And remember, Malman said, "the defendant need not ever have stepped one foot inside the United States. If his crimes, the many crimes that he committed that he's charged with here, affected the United States, affected this district," then that was enough to convict.

Did any one witness know all that happened? Malman asked. Could one witness alone link Noriega to the conspiracy? No, Malman said. "Compartmentalization. The cartel practiced it. Noriega practiced it. Del Cid told you Noriega invented it. The right hand didn't know what the left hand was doing. That way, if you are ever accused, you remove yourself. If some of your people get burned or caught, then it doesn't reverberate all the way back." Malman had not even unbuttoned his suit coat throughout his argument.

Remember, Malman said, Jorge Ochoa had a phony Panamanian passport. Steven Kalish had a Panamanian diplomatic passport. That helped 1984 become a very busy year in Panama, he said. "The cartel and American dope dealers are running around Panama with phony passports provided by Noreiga. Ether is flowing to Tranquilandia. The Tranquilandia raid led to the assassination of Bonilla. What do these people do? They flee. Where do they go? Panama.

"The ether and the lab and the presence of the cartel and the murder of Lara Bonilla are all interconnected," Malman said. "The cartel decides it has a problem. It wants to move out of Colombia. There is no question that the cartel would never ever, ever, especially after Tranquilandia, have constructed a lab in Panama without protection.

"And there is no question that they would have gone to the very top, and that's why Julian Melo was in Cali. The Ochoas said, 'We will pay, but we have to make sure that Noriega is in on this because with our experience in Panama, if Noriega is not in the play, it is a no-go.'" Melo was Noriega's point of contact with the cartel, Malman reminded the jurors. Melo had gone to school and then served as a Panamanian military attaché in Colombia. So the bribe was paid. "Things progressed. The money was split up, and we come, of course, to the great question that must have been going through everyone's mind: If Noriega got a few million dollars, then why was the lab raided? It is a good question," Malman said, pausing. "That's why sometimes this case is a little tricky." He paused again. "You have to think back in time to find out why the Darien lab was raided."

The key, said Malman, was in the testimony of PDF Col. Rogelio Alba. Alba and his troops were stationed in the dense Darien jungle. He had 130 men to patrol twenty-one thousand square kilometers. Alba had no scout planes and no radios. His men were stationed at "this little sleepy outpost in the south on the Colombian border. Nothing ever happened there. A perfect place for a lab." Only because a fishing boat had reported unusual activity near the coast had Alba sent an eleven-man patrol into the Darien, and only because the patrol became lost was a search mounted. A search plane was the first to discover the lab. Why was there an overreaction to the discovery of the lab? Was it because it was thought to be a guerrilla camp? Or because members of Noriega's staff knew exactly what had been found?

Whatever the answer, a member of the top Panamanian command was sent to lead the raid. And when it was discovered to be a cocaine lab and the lab workers were arrested, none were ever prosecuted in Panama. "No prosecution in Panama for building the cocaine lab. No prosecution in Panama for illicit or illegal association," Malman told the jury. "The Colombians are furious. They have paid for that protection. What is going on here? Well, we submit, and the evidence shows to the exclusion of any reasonable doubt, that the lab raid was an accident." Malman read Alba's words: "The laboratory was discovered accidentally." And others agreed. Ricardo Tribaldos said Julian Melo told him the raid was a "mistake." Carlos Lehder testified, "The lab got destroyed, I understand by mistake."

Malman said the lab raid caused a chain reaction. Ether started piling up in Panama's ports. Noriega's reaction was to seize the ether. Almost at the same time, Noriega began demanding higher fees for each kilo of cocaine he allowed to be smuggled through Panama. What happened next? Malman asked. The cartel got mad, and Noriega agreed to send his representatives to meet with the cartel's representatives in Havana. But when Noriega learned that Julian Melo had plotted with the cartel to assassinate him, he decided to go to Cuba himself. That is where Melo was made the scapegoat for Noriega's wrongdoings, Malman said.

"In this case the defense put forward basically two defenses," Malman went on. "One that the government witnesses, because they made deals, were all lying. Secondly, that because Manuel Antonio Noriega was a great cooperator, that therefore, he didn't do these crimes.

"The cooperation defense was proven to be exactly what it was—a fraud and a sham," Malman said. "Just what Noriega wanted it to be—a cover for his criminal activities."

Noriega was a master at covering his tracks, he told the jurors. First, he said he was sending envoys to Cuba to deal with politics, then he went himself. "The same cover and deception and deceit that was put forward in this cooperation—give the DEA just enough to keep them happy, just enough. There was cooperation, therefore Manuel Antonio Noriega is not guilty," Malman scoffed. "That defense has nothing to do with the crime charged, ladies and gentlemen. We never have to prove motive in a case—the reason why somebody does something. We just have to prove intent, that there was willful desire to accomplish the criminal objective. Why did Manuel Antonio Noriega do this? The answer is rooted and founded in common sense—money, pure and simple greed—nothing more, nothing less."

Malman paused a moment and then began again: "It's kind of interesting that of all the banks in Panama, Noriega goes to the most infamous bank known for money laundering, the BCCI, the Bank of Crooks and Criminals. You must look at the whole picture," he said, "and that is that Mr. Noreiga was sharing in drug money by protecting cocaine shipments through Panama and members of the Medellín drug cartel themselves." Malman put his hands on the lectern and looked across the jurors' faces.

"It is over, ladies and gentlemen, because now is the time that Manuel Antonio Noriega must be held accountable, because it is over. The deception is over. The plotting is over. The manipulation is over. The cover stories are over. It's all over." He paused and then rested his hands at his sides. He let his final comment sink in. He looked at the jurors' faces, then turned and walked back to the prosecution table.

Malman's nearly four hours of closing had gone on through the afternoon and spilled into Wednesday morning. Noriega had sat expressionless the entire time. Hardly moved. Sometimes he rested his chin in his hand. Jon May, at Noriega's side, and later Rubino scratched notes on long yellow pads as Malman spoke. Not once had the defense risen in objection.

When Malman finished at mid-morning on Wednesday, April 1, Hoeveler recessed the jury for fifteen minutes and called the attorneys to sidebar.

"You did a good job," the judge said to Malman. He turned then to Rubino. "I am sure Mr. Rubino is going to do a good job, too," he said.

"I am going to try," Rubino said. He hoped the judge's comment was not intended to be patronizing.

"Now, the other comment I want to make is a friendly observation," Hoeveler continued, still looking at Rubino. "I've gotten to know you over the months. I know there are times when you get excited and flamboyant, and that's not by way of criticism. It would be nice if there were no objections during [your closing]." Hoeveler paused a moment. "So I am going to ask you to do basically what Myles did, and that was stay within the record."

Rubino only half-smiled. There was no doubt he was sorely tempted to work out the deep anger he still felt over the invasion and the treatment his client had been afforded by American politicians. It was all politics, Rubino thought; even the judge must think that in his heart.

Rubino didn't want Hoeveler and especially the prosecutors to get the impression he was about to roll over. "We advised the government in advance, unless they did something that we considered just to be absolutely outrageous, we were not going to object," Rubino responded, heading for the high ground. "We felt we gave them some liberal interpretations, but in an argument they are allowed to state what their opinion is." The government might consider doing the same for him during his closing, Rubino would have liked to add but didn't. Rubino told Hoeveler his closing would take the final two hours of the day and would probably stretch through much of the next day.

Hoeveler called the jury back into the still-packed courtroom. Noriega sat attentively at the defense table. Hoeveler invited Rubino to begin.

Rubino was dapper, as usual, his hair combed back along the sides and wearing a dark suit, white shirt, and a modest tie chosen by his wife, Anne. He held a black pen in his left hand.

"Almost the first words out of Mr. Malman's mouth in his argument to you were 'General Antonio Noriega was a classic military dictator.'" Rubino paused to let his first words soak in. Then he said, his voice raised and filled with righteous indignation, "Is that a crime in the United States, we ask? Is that what this indictment is all about? Is that why we are having this trial?" Rubino paused again, letting his argument establish a rhythm. "If not, why did he say that? Was it a slip of the tongue? Why didn't he call him a drug trafficker?"

Rubino turned and picked up a copy of the indictment from the defense table. He held it over his head and then waved it. "This indictment stinks. It stinks like a dead fish. It smells from here to Washington. The government's theory is that if you throw enough mud against the wall, maybe some of it will stick. They told you in their opening statement that they would put the pieces of a puzzle together and you would see the picture. What they have done, actually, is taken two or three puzzles, mixed all the pieces up, and said to you, 'Figure it out. See if you can make a picture out of it.' Well, it is not a game show here, it is a trial, and the general's future is at stake.

"They have given you numerous versions of events. If you don't like this version, let me give you another one, they say. The standard to use to judge the evidence is one of reasonable doubt. Two words you won't hear a whole lot about from the government. What is reasonable doubt? It is a real doubt. Not an imaginary doubt. Not some crazy idea. It is something you can honestly assign to reason. The burden is on the government to prove its case beyond a reasonable doubt. In this case they have failed to do that. Proof beyond a reasonable doubt is proof so convincing that you would be willing to rely upon it and act upon it without hesitation in the most important of your personal affairs. The government's proof has not arisen to that level. It has missed the mark by a mile.

"The government pursued the very informants in this case with a vengeance. They followed them. They stalked them. They cursed them. They hated them. And ultimately they caught them. On the day they agreed to testify for the government, suddenly those hated and hunted criminals were transformed into paragons of virtue. The liars became truth tellers. The drug traffickers became drug fighters. The accused became the accusers." Rubino put his hand on the lectern and stood off to its side. He placed an enlargement of a portion of the jury instructions on an easel. The jury instruction was a warning, he said, pointing to its words. The testimony of paid informers and witnesses with plea agreements should be considered with caution.

"Mr. Malman, in his argument, told you that these people aren't subhuman life." Rubino again paused for effect. "They sure are," he said, his voice filling again with indignation. "They are the scum of the earth." Take Max Mermelstein, Rubino suggested. Mermelstein stalked one man who was later murdered and was present when another was murdered and even helped dispose of the body. His jail time after making an agreement with the government: two years and twenty-one days.

"We've got poverty in this country, we've got people on food stamps. We have homeless people, and we've got Max Mermelstien getting $670,000. If that doesn't disgust you, nothing will," Rubino said. "The gem of them all," he continued, "[is] Carlos Lehder. You know, when they brought Carlos Lehder in here, the only way they could have outdone that was to bring in Charlie Manson. The maximum sentence he could possibly receive in

Jacksonville was life plus one hundred and thirty-five years. The judge in Jacksonville realized just what Carlos Lehder was, and he realized the seriousness of his offenses. He sentenced him to life in prison plus one hundred and thirty-five years." Floyd Carlton, Luis del Cid, David Ortiz, Brian Davidow, all cut deals with the government.

Rubino looked at the jurors, pleading. "You know, some fifty years ago my parents came to this country, and at that time coming to the United States and becoming a citizen required you to be of good moral character. Now, you've just got to be a major Colombian drug dealer."

And there were others who had testified, who with their testimony planned to cut deals with the government, Rubino said. "You know, I was going to make a chart of who didn't get a deal, but it would have been about the size of a postage stamp." Rubino set aside his chart of witnesses and walked back to the podium.

"It seems to be the government's theory of the case that drugs couldn't move through and the cartel couldn't function and nothing could happen in Panama without General Noriega's protection. But according to the testimony we've heard in this case, drugs flowed through Costa Rica, Nicaragua, the Bahamas, Bolivia, Colombia, and the United States. Why only in Panama would you have to have the leader's permission?" Rubino asked. There was no explanation, he suggested, just as there was no explanation for many of the government's theories.

Floyd Carlton insisted that he paid Noriega. Paid him for what? Rubino asked. He read from Carlton's testimony: "'You never told General Noriega when you were coming with the airplane full of what you believed would be dope?'

"'No, sir.'

"'And, in fact, to the best of your knowledge, he didn't have the faintest idea you were coming?'

"'Indeed.'"

Rubino looked up. Carlton had insisted he paid Noriega $100,000 to do that, he said. "Does that make sense?" Rubino asked. "It just doesn't make sense." And Carlton, who insisted he was a friend of Noriega's, claimed his payoffs included the right to land at clandestine airstrips in the jungle, while others had testified that Noriega allowed unknown Colombians to land at Panama City airports and receive special G-2 protection as well. "Doesn't make sense, does it?" Rubino said, looking at the jury. "This doesn't make sense. Trials have to make sense. People don't do things without a reason."

Gabriel Taboada told of Fabio Ochoa wanting a red Ferrari. "The five members, the heads of the Medellín cartel, all came together to discuss getting this kid a Ferrari?" Rubino asked sarcastically. "Does that make sense to you? And then General Noriega comes in to make this Ferrari meeting even more important." The government's only proof of the alleged meeting was a picture of a red Ferrari. It made no sense, said Rubino.

"The Darien lab—the government propounded two separate and distinct theories. There is the Alba mistake theory, and there is the Carlos Lehder retaliation theory. Alba: It was just a mistake, and they stumbled on it. Carlos Lehder is the opposite. Carlos said the general now wanted to be part of the cartel. He wanted a piece of the action, and they wouldn't let him, so he raided the lab to retaliate against the cartel. Which is it? This isn't a menu at a Chinese restaurant where you can pick one from column A and one from column B. Which is it, or is it the truth?"

If Noriega was protecting the Darien lab, there would have been Panamanian troops close by. There was nothing. "Is this how General Noriega would protect this lab?" he asked.

And what about Noriega's visit to Cuba? By the time of Noriega's visit on July 5, 1984, the Colombian prisoners had already been sent home. Melo had been detained and court-martialed. The general staff had returned the money to the cartel. "What did he need Castro's help for?" Rubino asked. "All of the problems occurred before he went to Cuba.

"No one has ever denied Melo took a bribe, but no one has ever told you that Melo did anything more than line his pockets with money," said Rubino, raising his arms and his voice together. "Has one person taken that witness stand right here and said to you Colonel Melo gave General Noriega the money? It is a leap of faith. There is a missing link."

Malman had been measured in his delivery. Rubino loaded his sentences with sarcasm, drawing out the words—"leeeeap of faith"—theatrically. And Rubino was constantly in motion. He walked to the jury box and then back to the lectern. He stood next to the witness stand and then walked across the courtroom to the defense table. But he always kept his eyes on the jury.

There were other pieces of the government's case that didn't fit, Rubino said, other pieces that didn't make sense. "Mr. Winters, the CIA representative who testified here, told you that General Noriega met with Bill Casey, the director of the CIA. That's how important an asset to America General Noriega was—that he met face-to-face with Bill Casey." Rubino's voice was again rising in indignation.

Sullivan jumped from his chair. "I object and move to strike the last comment," he protested, cutting Rubino off. Winters, said Sullivan, never testified that Noriega was an asset.

The objection was sustained, Hoeveler said.

Rubino shrugged his shoulders and smirked, turning back to the jury. "You decide, then, why General Noriega met with the director of the Central Intelligence Agency." The government's case was built on shallow hearsay, Rubino said. Ricardo Bilonick came to court and said, "'Pablo and Jorge' told him." Rubino smiled and pointed at Noriega. "Isn't there anybody who's going to say, 'I dealt with him, with this man sitting here?' Why is everybody telling us, 'He told me that he said'? Is that proof so clear and convincing?"

The proof of the *Krill*, Rubino said, was an example of how weak the government's case truly was. "General Noriega knows that the United States is conducting eavesdropping operations in Panama, and he speaks on the tele-phone and talks about cocaine?" Rubino let out a mock laugh. "No. He's not a stupid man." He raised his arms in suggestion. "Reasonable doubt," he said.

The DEA agents came to court and complained about Noriega's assis-tance. "They were darn lucky to have an office there, they were darn lucky to get all the information they did, and now they kick the gift horse in the mouth. Corrupt cops do not arrest the person whom they committed crime with. Think about that," Rubino said, walking toward the jury. "The Inair incident they sent up to the United States to stand trial. General Noriega made it easy for Panamanian-registered vessels to be boarded and searched by the Coast Guard. Reasonable doubt," said Rubino.

Through the afternoon of Wednesday, April 1, and through the morning of the next day, Rubino wound his way through the testimony and issues of the trial. Witness after witness, point after point of the government's case, none of it made sense, he complained. It made no sense because that was not the way it happened, he said. Only when Noriega's usefulness to the U.S. gov-ernment waned did he suddenly become a liability rather than an asset. "Francis Mullen, the head of the Drug Enforcement Administration at the time, said to you, 'No,' he was not aware of any credible evidence that General Noriega was involved in drug trafficking."

Rubino circled back to his opening comments. It is not a crime against the United States for Panama to have been a military dictatorship, he said. "Why does the government want to show you, beyond and to the exclusion of any reasonable doubt, that Panama was a military dictatorship controlled by General Noriega? It's not one of the counts in this indictment. It's not a vio-lation of United States law. Are we here because General Noriega is a drug trafficker, or are we here because he was a military dictator?

"They haven't proved this," Rubino said, holding up the indictment. "But they have proved beyond and to the exclusion of every reasonable doubt that General Noriega, this man here"—Rubino walked quickly to Noriega's side and put his hand on Noriega's shoulder, telling him to stand up—"this man was a military dictator." Rubino paused.

As Noriega stood, Rubino wrapped his arm around Noriega's shoulder. Noriega's faced reddened slightly, and then he began to weep. It was the first emotion he had shown in public since his arrest. Rubino comforted him. "Are you going to find him guilty of being a military dictator, or are you going to find him guilty of that indictment? Go through that indictment and come back and find him not guilty of each and every one of these ten counts."

Rubino took his arm from Noriega's shoulder. Behind Noriega, his two daughters were also weeping. Noriega wiped his eyes and sat down. Rubino walked back to the lectern and slowly looked across at the jury. "Thank you," he said and turned to the judge. "I have nothing further."

Rubino's closing had taken six hours.

★   ★   ★

The next morning, Friday, April 3, Hoeveler invited Sullivan to deliver the government's rebuttal. Where Malman laid out the trial in a narrative account, Sullivan now took on Rubino's argument point by point.

Sullivan's rebuttal was like his opening statement—workmanlike, no flash.

This case, he began, "has nothing to do with politics. It has everything to with Manuel Noriega's ability to facilitate drug trafficking through Panama on behalf of the Medellín cartel. He controlled everything in that country, from the airports to the seaport in Colón. He controlled the attorney general's office. He overthrew the president. He could make anyone do his will in Panama. Isn't that a commodity worth buying for the chieftains of the cartel? All they did in all their business was buy crooked cops."

The point was not that Noriega was a dictator, said Sullivan, but what he "was capable of doing in Panama. Of the prosecution's sixty-one witnesses, he said, eleven testified about first-hand contacts with Noriega and $24 million in alleged bribes. The others offered circumstantial but not direct evidence of the meetings and payments.

Floyd Carlton paid for an insurance policy, said Sullivan. If he got into trouble, he would be covered. The release of the Darien twenty-three in four or five days was also an insurance policy at work, he said. The lab raid was a mistake, but the policy kicked in. "Why would the cartel believe that Julian Melo would protect the lab? Why would the cartel believe that Julian Melo would deliver the bribe money to Noriega? The cartel is not made up of stupid people," Sullivan said. "They are ruthless businessmen. The cartel trusted Julian Melo because he had been an envoy to them from Noriega since 1982."

Why would the cartel trust Noriega to accept the money? The same reason it trusted Melo to offer the bribe, said Sullivan. "The cartel had a long and happy relationship with Manuel Antonio Noriega." And that was the bottom line. Sullivan touched on each of Rubino's arguments and included a statement about each of the defense's witnesses. His response took slightly more than three hours.

Melo met the cartel on Noriega's behalf. Melo worked with Noriega and was secretary of the general staff. The cartel "had a long and pleasurable history with Julian Melo doing the bidding of the general staff as the envoy of the cartel."

Looking first at the jury and then toward Noriega, Sullivan said, "Whatever happens, the defendant has had due process. That's all anyone can ask."

CHAPTER 36

★★★★★★★

The Jury's Work

When Sullivan completed the government's rebuttal, court recessed for fifteen minutes. At 3:30, Judge Hoeveler moved from the bench to a table set before the jury. He would now charge the jury and then dismiss it to deliberate.

"Mention has been made during the trial as to the manner in which the defendant was brought here," Hoeveler told the jurors. "That is not an issue in this case and is not for you to consider." The court had ruled on the issue of jurisdiction. "And I say respectfully, ladies and gentleman, you are not allowed to second-guess. The fact that the defendant is a Panamanian and not a United States citizen" is irrelevant, he continued. "I have decided that issue, and I have concluded that this court does have jurisdiction to hear this case. While you can consider the defendant's status as the leader of his country, insofar as that status may affect some of the factual issues in the case, the defendant's leadership role in no way affects the jurisdiction of this court to try the case. Moreover, politics and policies should play no part in your deliberations.

"The defendant is never under any burden to prove anything," the judge told the jurors. "The burden of proof is upon the government at all times in making your determination. The defendant is not on trial for any act or conduct or offense which has not been alleged in the indictment."

Hoeveler coursed his way through the ten-count indictment, reviewing the charges and outlining the law that the jurors were to follow. The charge took nearly two hours. At times Hoeveler read from his notes and from the instructions that would be sent to the jury room with the jurors, and at other times he spoke without notes; his instructions to scores of other juries were exactly the same. He explained the verdict form and how there would be a space for each count of the indictment, a space to check "guilty" or "not guilty."

To reach a guilty verdict on the most serious of the charges, count one and count two, the RICO counts, which alleged a racketeering conspiracy and racketeering, Hoeveler told the jurors that they would have to find that Noriega and at least one other person had in some way come to a mutual understanding to try to accomplish an unlawful plan. Further, Hoeveler said, to reach a guilty verdict under RICO they would have to find that the conspirators committed at least two of the eleven specific "predicate acts" or

424

offenses alleged in the indictment. "Like every element of the offenses I am describing, you must find these facts beyond a reasonable doubt," the judge said. He added, "You must be unanimous" in finding "the offenses the defendant committed." It was not acceptable, he told them, for part of the jury to find Noriega guilty of two or more of the alleged offenses. To bring a guilty verdict the jurors must be unanimous on specific counts.

The jurors paid close attention to Hoeveler's words. Still on crutches from a hip operation, Thelma Sturdivant watched the judge closely. But Hoeveler had had triple bypass surgery. "If he can go through with this, so can I," she had told other jurors.

Count three, count seven, and count eight charged Noriega with conspiracy to distribute and import cocaine to the United States. These were not racketeering conspiracies under the RICO law, Hoeveler explained, but crimes nonetheless. The judge noted that count four, count five, and count nine also charged Noriega and others with distribution and aiding and abetting the distribution of cocaine. "The conspiracy counts have to do with the alleged agreement to get together to do criminal acts," the judge said. The other counts are called "substantive counts." Substantive meant that the alleged conspiracy acts were alleged to actually have been committed.

Count seven alleged that Noriega and others had helped manufacture cocaine in Colombia with the intent to distribute it in the United States, and count ten charged that Noriega and others were involved in flying drug proceeds from Florida to Panama. For all of the counts, Hoeveler explained, the government need not have established with certainty the exact dates of the alleged offenses but that, beyond a reasonable doubt, they had occurred.

Intent and motive should not be confused, the judge told the jurors. Motive is what prompts a person to act or fail to act. Intent refers to the state of mind with which an act is committed. In this case, Hoeveler said, the government was not required to prove motive, only intent beyond a reasonable doubt. Hoeveler looked up from the instruction booklet.

"Folks, a separate crime is charged in each count of the indictment, and each charge and the evidence pertaining to it should be considered separately. The fact that you may find the defendant guilty or not guilty as to any one of the offenses charged should not control your verdict as to any other offense charged. I caution you that you are here to determine the guilt or innocence of the accused from the evidence in this case."

At 5:15, a late afternoon for the jury, Hoeveler was reaching the end of his charge. He spoke solemnly. "I am the only one who wears black robes in this case, but I want to assure you that you are judges in this case, just as much as I am, in every sense of the word. Indeed, your responsibility is greater than mine. You will decide the case, and I simply assist you in arriving at that end." Tomorrow their work would begin, Hoeveler said. Now they should relax and get a good night's rest.

Three weeks before, the jurors had agreed to be sequestered during their deliberations. They had arrived at the courthouse this morning with their suitcases packed. They would now be together until they reached a decision, spending their nights under the watchful eyes of the U.S. Marshals Service at the Everglades Hotel, four blocks from the courthouse. Each morning they would be brought to the courthouse to deliberate, and each evening until they reached their verdict they would return to the hotel. Tomorrow morning, Saturday, April 4, they could begin their deliberations in earnest; the judge suggested that they not work on Sundays.

"I will leave you with one last thought," he said. "The word 'verdict' is a derivative of the Latin. It means to speak the truth. Let your verdict speak the truth."

Preparation of the jury instructions had been a collaborative effort. For three weeks Jon May, for the defense, and Guy Lewis and Michael Olmsted, for the government, hammered out the exact wording of the instructions under the direction of the judge. Much of what Hoeveler read to the jury during his charge had been agreed upon by both sides.

The defense agreed to the renumbering of the charges in the indictment. There was no sense including for the jury the original count eight, which charged only Ricardo Bilonick and Gustavo Gaviria, not Noriega, with cocaine importation; and the original count twelve, a Travel Act violation involving a flight by Tony Azpruia. The government had dropped count twelve before the start of trial when it decided Azpruia, who had testified before the grand jury, was not telling the truth. What Hoeveler did not tell the jury on Friday afternoon as he delivered the charge was that a squabble had erupted between the government and the defense over the ordering of the indictment.

When May and Rubino read through the newly organized indictment on Thursday afternoon, they found that more than renumbering had occurred. Lewis and Olmsted had trimmed and reshaped it.

Gone from the list of overt acts committed "in furtherance of the conspiracy" were the allegations of grand jury witness Boris Olarte, who had testified that he personally delivered $4 million to Noriega. Gone also were Olarte's allegations that he discussed the purchase of cocaine-processing chemicals with Noriega.

Richard Gregorie had used Olarte extensively to help build the indictment in 1987 and 1988, but when Sullivan, Malman, and Lewis interviewed Olarte, they came away convinced he was a liar. The connections to Noriega weren't there. Olarte had not been called to the witness stand, and the government had not presented his allegations to the jury. But dropping the charge now seemed to strengthen the government's case; it was a loose end the jurors would not get to consider.

Rubino and May felt that every time they turned around, the government was trying to pull something. Both thought immediately of the freezing of Noriega's bank accounts, which had stymied the defense for months, the taping and release of Noriega's prison telephone conversations, as well the interception of the defense subpoenas by the State Department.

Now, at the last minute, without saying a word, the government was trying to make itself look good by sending the jury only those portions of the indictment for which the prosecution had presented proof. It was true that the government was conceding it could not prove the offenses it had trimmed, but by presenting only the counts it wanted, it was suggesting the case was more solid than it was.

After the jury was charged, May and Rubino took their complaint to Hoeveler. They were convinced the jury should have to decide for itself why the indictment didn't match the evidence. They were convinced an ensuing discussion among the jurors would underscore the holes and gaps the prosecution had failed to fill.

"I just saw the redacted indictment for the first time," May told the judge. The government had essentially rewritten the indictment to fit the prosecution's proof. May called the removal of the Olarte allegation "unprincipled."

"How dare you?" Rubino demanded.

Sullivan charged, in turn, that the defense hoped to "mislead the jury" to consider allegations the government had not proved.

But Rubino said that the government filed the indictment and brought its case. Now it should live with its own indictment.

Sullivan turned to Hoeveler. "Judge, if we have fifty overt acts charged in an indictment and we really don't want to go with fifty, we only want to go with twenty and therefore forget about the other thirty—there wasn't proof of them, we don't want them—how does that possibly prejudice the defendant?"

Rubino said, "Your Honor, the indictment is not just a charging instrument. It is the document that we had to defend against. If you are going to let them take stuff out and let them rewrite the whole thing so it perfectly fits their proof, you should rewrite the whole indictment so it is perfect."

"Then it will really serve their purpose," May added. "If we get some kind of benefit from the jurors saying, 'Well, they never presented evidence of this happening in this way,' well, Your Honor, that's only fair," May argued. He asked Hoeveler if he would hear from Noriega on the issue. Hoeveler agreed.

Noriega rose from his chair. As usual, he wore his freshly pressed uniform.

"These were the same charges that in 1989, as the end result, brought fire, blood, and tears between two countries," Noriega told the judge. "These were the same charges that forced the papal nuncio to bring me out and hand me over to the U.S. government. I continue up to this moment waiting to see the evidence of these charges, as I continue to wait for the evidence of other charges." Noriega reflected a moment. His voice was soft but still assertive. "All the indictment or nothing," he said.

Hoeveler thought a moment and then said plainly, "We cannot make a silk purse out of a sow's ear." The original indictment, less the two counts dropped before trial, would be sent to the jury, he said, just as the defense requested. But the instruction that the "government is under no obligation to prove every item in the indictment, and you are to consider only the evidence in relation to the charges about which the government has offered evidence" would also be submitted. It was a bit of "baby splitting," Hoeveler said, but it was time for the jury to do its work.

There hadn't been much chatting in the marshal's van during the three-minute ride to the courthouse from the Everglades Hotel that morning. Sleep on Friday night had been restless. The Everglades wasn't the fanciest hotel in downtown Miami, and there was a lot on everyone's mind. The deputy marshals were monitoring the telephones, limiting conversations. There were holes in the newspaper where stories on the Noriega trial story had been. Curfew was 11 P.M.

Jury Room 405 was off the back hall of the Central Courtroom. Actually there were two rooms. One room was filled with the exhibits: the charts, photographs, and boxes of documents, more than seven hundred pieces of evidence, that had been admitted in the course of the trial. The other room had a long oval table, twelve chairs, and a chalkboard.

The first thing to do, the judge had suggested, was to elect a foreman. The jurors folded small squares of paper with their choices. It wasn't unanimous but close. Lester Spenser had sat in the middle of the second row of the jury box. He was juror number eleven. Spenser, a black man of medium height and a thin athletic build, was thirty-nine. He had worked seventeen years as a senior field rater for an insurance company. He was gregarious and good-tempered. Voting took only a few minutes. Spenser would be the foreman.

Then the jurors waited for the indictment. The judge had promised it by 10:30, but it still hadn't been delivered. Spenser paged through the nearly fifty-page instruction booklet, which was virtually cross-referenced to be read with the indictment. There was no point in starting without the indictment. At 10:50 the judge called the jurors into court, where each received a copy of the indictment. "I think you are all set now to deliberate," Hoeveler said. "You have the verdict form. With that I ask you again to retire and deliberate."

There was only one way to begin something like this, they all agreed: prayer, guidance, silence. Two minutes of silence to get in touch with what lay ahead.

Bernadine Cooper bowed her head. So did Thelma Sturdivant. So did almost all of them. Every eye was closed for two minutes. "I asked the Lord to guide me to the right decision," Elena Harden said later. "I didn't want to go on my own and make a mistake."

When Lester Spenser looked up, he adjusted his glasses and glanced around the table. He began reading the instructions. It took nearly two hours. Reading the indictment aloud took another hour.

Saturday afternoon the discussion around the table was free-ranging. Almost everyone had something to say about one or the other of the ten counts. This was the first time they had the chance to talk as a group about the case.

They had all heard the same witnesses, the same evidence, but even now, this early, it was clear there were major differences of opinion. They went around the table again, one count at a time, evaluating what made sense and what didn't.

Count one, the RICO conspiracy, was difficult. That count would fall in place if the others did. The next most difficult were counts six and seven, the Tranquilandia and Darien counts.

Tranquilandia was in the south of Colombia. It was hard, given the testimony, to trace the cocaine that was manufactured there. One couldn't say for certain that the drug had reached the United States; it was also a stretch to connect the ether and acetone in Panama to cocaine in the United States. There wasn't a direct link. The Darien count was just as tough. The prosecutors said the complex was built after the payment of a bribe, but the dozen witnesses who testified about the scheme contradicted one another.

Rubino had charged that the Darien lab was the result of Julian Melo's "trading on General Noriega's name" without permission, and CIA cables supported Rubino. But the government said the CIA cables were the product of a misinformation effort by Noriega's intelligence apparatus. Nowhere in the testimony did the money directly change hands.

The *Krill*, the boat counts, eight and nine, on the other hand, were easy. Where was the proof Noriega was involved? There wasn't any. It didn't even seem close. There hadn't been two witnesses who agreed with each other when it came to the *Krill*.

Each of the jurors seemed absorbed by the discussions—everyone, that is, except Bernadine Cooper, a sixty-four-year-old black housewife. She was one of only a few jurors who had served on a jury before. Ironically, she had sat on a murder case in which Frank Rubino had been the defense lawyer. Each of the jurors spoke about the indictment, but Cooper passed every time. Many leafed through their stenographer's notebooks, matching their notes to the points under discussion. Several had filled more than a half-dozen pads in the course of the trial. Cooper, however, had only one notebook. "I don't take any notes; I have it all here," she said once and then twice, tapping the side of her head. And then she pointed up. "Up there, He's going to make the decision for me," she said.

This worried Spenser. Jean Hallisey, a transplanted New Englander who had sat in the first seat of the jury box, didn't care for Cooper's comment. Hallisey considered Noriega "a greedy, uneducated, grab-all-I-can person" with a big ego. She'd stared across the courtroom at him with disdain throughout the trial. The way Hallisey saw it, Noriega had this emotionless "nobody can touch me, nobody can get to me" look about him. Now Cooper was leaving her decision to God. But, Hallisey thought, someone right *here* is going to have to make a decision. At 2:45, Hoeveler tapped on the door and poked his head in. He said he was going home for the balance of the afternoon. He reminded the jurors that when they were not in the jury room, they were not to discuss the case in any way. It was important, the judge said, to rest the next day, Sunday. Go to church or visit with family, but get your minds off the case, he told them. The marshals would make the necessary arrangements.

On Monday morning there were no disagreements on counts eight and nine, the *Krill* conspiracy charge and the related cocaine distribution charge. At mid-morning the jurors folded their ballots and passed them to Spenser. The vote was unanimous, 12-0, not guilty on both counts.

The *Krill* and Noriega: It hadn't happened. If it had, it sure wasn't in the testimony. Depending on the witness, Noriega had participated in the *Krill* planning meetings by phone, speakerphone, or in person. The indictment said in person. The witnesses weren't sure.

The remaining eight counts were going to be much more difficult.

Spenser called for a ballot. The count was surprising. There wasn't much disagreement. Spenser announced the results: 11 to 1, guilty on every one of the other eight counts. It wasn't even noon yet, and this was only the second day of deliberations. As long and as complicated as the case had been, maybe reaching a verdict would not be too hard. Spenser picked up the jury instructions and began reading again, starting again with count one. Then the discussions began again.

It was soon clear that Cooper was the lone juror not in agreement with the others. The sticking point was right at the top with counts one and two. "I didn't see any money pass," Cooper said when her turn came. "I didn't see any drugs pass."

Rosebud Scott, a fifty-year-old elementary school teacher who from the start had wished she was back with her first grade class instead of sitting through the trial, turned to Cooper and tried to explain. To understand how the money had passed it would take putting the testimony of two or three witnesses together, she told Cooper. There were the witnesses in Medellín, the PDF officers, Noriega's friends. Each contributed to the story. "Do you see how these witnesses come together?" Scott asked. Nova Rodríguez, a thirty-four-year-old Filipina American postal worker, and Hallisey added to Scott's explanation, but Cooper could only repeat, "I didn't see any money pass."

Other jurors joined in: It wasn't any one witness or any one piece of evidence, it was all of it put together, fifty witnesses saying something was going on. But Cooper had a way of turning away when the others talked, as if she wasn't listening.

Lester Spenser read through the instructions for counts one and two again. That afternoon they agreed to take another straw ballot. Maybe Cooper had seen the light. The ballots now came back 10 to 2.

Jim Hogan, a thirty-year-old power plant firefighter, was wavering. Perhaps Cooper was right. Hogan hadn't seen any money change hands, either. "I have some questions," Hogan said. "A lot of people are dead—a lot of the people that are supposed to know about all this. What happened to Julian Melo, and what happened to Inspector Quiel? There are some unanswered questions here." Hogan's point was well taken. Melo and Quiel had not been heard from. Melo had been interviewed by both the prosecutors and defense as a potential witness. Neither side believed he was reliable. Quiel had disappeared during the invasion and had remained in hiding.

Jean Hallisey shook her head. This was crazy. The jury was moving backward. No one wanted to believe the worst, but there were just too many witnesses and the evidence added up.

Leslie Allen rested his head against his hand. Allen, juror number seven, second from the right in the front row of the jury box, was a sixty-four-year-old retired construction worker. It all seemed perfectly clear to him. All you had to do was look at the overall picture. There were witnesses from Panama and Colombia who hadn't agreed perfectly, but they were close.

Hogan went to the blackboard at the end of the room and picked up the chalk. He started drawing squares. One box was the cartel, the other was Noriega. How did one make the link? How did the money change hands? "I just don't know how I can put it together," Hogan said. "There is a missing link somewhere."

Late Monday afternoon Spenser sent a note to the judge: "Judge Hoeveler, please provide transcripts of the following: (a) Floyd Carlton, (b) Amet Paredes, (c) Amjad Awan, (d) Ricardo Bilonick, (e) Roberto Steiner, (f) Eduardo Pardo, (g) Gabriel Taboada, (h) Enrique Pereira, and (i) Enrique Pretelt." Hogan wanted to look more carefully at the testimony. Steiner (Roberto Striedinger) and Taboada had been in Medellín when the $500,000 was allegedly passed to Noriega. Carlton and Bilonick said there had been bribes. Pereira said he had delivered cash to Noriega. Hogan wanted to convince himself that this all fit.

On Tuesday morning, Hoeveler called the attorneys together in his chambers. He told them about the note. All agreed the transcripts of both the direct and cross-examinations should go to the jury. Privately, Sullivan, Malman, and Lewis agreed that the request for prosecution witnesses' testimony was probably a good sign. It meant the jury had paid attention. What they wanted was key to the overall conspiracy.

Rubino and May knew that second-guessing these things was like trying to read tea leaves, but they agreed there was little need to worry about the jury's request. The jurors were stuck on some part of the government's case, and that couldn't be bad for the defense.

Hogan spent much of Tuesday morning again standing at the chalkboard, drawing the same diagrams, trying to make the testimony fit. Down the table, Bernadine Cooper was sticking by her analysis of the events. "I didn't see any money pass. I didn't see any drugs pass," she kept repeating. The jury instructions insisted on unanimity. But there was also supposed to be give-and-take, the judge had told them. Cooper was hardly participating. "The law is very harsh," Cooper said. "I can't accept how harsh it is. This man is not a U.S. citizen. I just can't understand how this U.S. law can be so harsh on the man."

Ten people were in agreement and were ready to go home. The other two were spoiling the proceedings. Hogan kept trying to make the boxes meet. "We have to be sure," he said.

Hallisey and Rodríguez couldn't take it anymore. "Sit down," they snapped at Hogan. "Sit down."

Ethel Johnson and Evelyn Reid had sat in the front row of the jury box with Cooper. Johnson, a forty-six-year-old black woman, was adamantly opposed to drugs—it was a "strong moral belief." Reid, also black, a fifty-one-year-old nurse at the Veteran's Administration Hospital, had sat next to Cooper throughout the trial. It was the whole picture, Reid tried to explain to her; not the specifics but the whole that fit together for a conviction. But Cooper insisted that Noriega was not guilty.

Hogan wasn't sure. He thought Noriega was guilty, then not guilty, then guilty. After lunch, at 1 P.M., Spenser sent another note to the judge: "Judge Hoeveler, please confirm the following statement and question: (a)Twelve jurors must agree on each count listed within this indictment in order to return a verdict of guilty; (b) What other options do we have of returning a verdict of not guilty on any or all counts if we cannot arrive at a unanimous verdict?"

For the prosecution team, the note was disheartening. When the requests for the transcripts came out, it appeared as though the jury was on track. The order of the transcripts indicated the jury was being methodical, going through the indictment point by point. But now, only four hours later, it looked as if there was a stall.

Pat Sullivan suspected a problem with either count six, the Darien lab charge, or count seven, the Tranquilandia charge, or both. The fact of the matter was, there had not been a shred of direct evidence on either count. There had been enough evidence for Hoeveler to let the two counts pass on the Rule 29 motion, but Sullivan thought in the jury's place that he might not convict on those counts.

For Rubino and May the note sounded like good news. A deadlocked jury wasn't a win, but it was close. If the government had to try the case again or retry specific counts, it would never do as good a job the second time around. The case would never be as strong. Witnesses disappear and forget. Another important point: The defense would know the prosecution's best evidence and would be prepared. A stall on the two RICO counts would be great, Rubino and May agreed.

Hoeveler looked over the jury's note. He asked for the attorneys' observations. All agreed that unanimity was required on each of the individual charges. The jury should know, they said, that the alternative to a unanimous verdict of guilty or not guilty was simply "can't reach a verdict." The jury could convict Noriega on specific counts, find him innocent on others, and not be unanimous on still others. "But after only three days, I would not encourage [the idea] that they can come back a hung jury," Rubino said. Sullivan agreed.

Hoeveler brought the jury into court at 2:20. "There are ten counts in the indictment," he said. "Each of those counts is a separate case, just as if we had taken ten different cases. We could have tried them separately, but in the interest of time and expense, we tried them all together. But each count presents a separate case, and you may do with each count what you think is proper. You do not have to find the defendant guilty or not guilty in connection with all of them in order to return a verdict. Your verdicts can be mixed or all the same. You must agree unanimously on any verdict whether it is a not guilty verdict or whether it is a guilty verdict. You must agree unanimously on any verdict you return on any count. Now, while I am reluctant to say this, I will, in the interest of telling you the complete picture: If you cannot agree on any particular count, you cannot agree on it. We would declare a mistrial as to that particular count. The matter is in your hands," Hoeveler said, "and whatever your findings are, we must accept." Hoeveler asked if he had made himself clear.

"Somewhat," Lester Spenser replied. "After we deliberate for a while, we are debating and debating. If we can still not necessarily reach a unanimous decision on a particular count or case as is indicated, do we send out and say we cannot reach a decision?" The jurors all stared at the judge.

"We've been at this six months," Hoeveler said, almost lecturing the jury. "If, as to any count, you feel you cannot reach a decision, then send me a note and tell me that, and I will take the matter up with you further." Hoeveler sent the jury back to the jury room at 2:30.

By five in the afternoon, little had changed. Jim Hogan had decided the big picture was probably the right way to go. The connections weren't going to be perfect, but the big picture, the big puzzle, made sense. But Bernadine Cooper still was not budging.

On Wednesday morning, April 8, before the van left for the courthouse, Nova Rodríguez told the deputy marshal she did not want her room made up that morning. Her bags were packed and sat on the bed. No maid service, she said; she was going home that night.

Less than an hour after the jury went to the courthouse, before their morning break, Elena Harden took one of the deputy marshals aside. She said she wanted to speak to the judge. Two of the jurors were bickering, Harden complained; "something that bothers her conscience," the deputy told Hoeveler, relaying the message.

Inside the jury room, Cooper was now saying she had made up her mind before the deliberations started. She was not changing her mind, she insisted.

"If we can show you how he was involved," Harden asked Cooper, "will you reconsider?"

"No, no, no. You can say all you want. I have made up my mind," Cooper said.

Spenser suggested they go around the table again and have each juror explain his or her position. Again Cooper declined. "No, no, no," she insisted.

Jean Hallisey had had enough. The government had buried Noriega in evidence, and Cooper was dug in. At ten minutes to eleven she told Spenser that it was time to get the judge involved. It was a deadlock, and everyone was waiting on Cooper. Two counts were decided, and the other eight were deadlocked. "You have to see the judge or I am going to walk out of here right now, and I don't care if they arrest me," Hallisey told Spenser, who handed her a pencil and paper. "Go ahead," he told her.

Hallisey wrote the note: "We have a serious problem. Apparently there is a juror who has testified two days ago that their mind was made up before we reached this room. We are deadlocked. We feel that we are wasting time in fairness to everyone." Hallisey decided to soften her irritation. "Everyone in this room is honest, bright, and reasonable. What should we do? It is affecting all of us because of the seriousness of this case."

When Hoeveler read the note, he cringed. He often said his worst fear in any case was a hung jury. In this case a hung jury would be a nightmare. If there was anything that could be done to avoid a mistrial, then it had to be done. The leatherneck in Hoeveler came out. If this jury thought it was going home, it had another think coming. Hoeveler had presided over the 1979 Miami Longshoremen's trial. That trial had lasted seven months, as long as Noriega's, and the jury was out six weeks before it reached a verdict. And in that case the government's evidence was even stronger. No, Hoeveler thought, these jurors were not going home. Not yet.

Hoeveler called the attorneys in, and at 10:25 the jury was brought back to court. He read the note aloud and then looked up at the jurors. It was lecture time.

"Now, in arriving at a verdict, each of you must make up your own mind, after consideration of all of the evidence as it is recalled by you. That consideration should include the opinions of your fellow jurors, as well as your own. In this court, in order to render a verdict in any case, and in any count in the case, all of the jurors must concur. That means that each and every one of you must agree, must concur in the verdicts you return in this case." Hoeveler paused.

Lester Spenser used the moment to speak up: "We have read that over and over and over and over again." The frustration in his voice was deep.

"Now, I have read it to you once more," Hoeveler responded sternly. The scolding was not for Spenser but for the entire jury. There was more than a tinge of anger in the judge's voice.

An "Allen charge" was an instruction advising jurors to listen to one another with a disposition to be convinced. It was a direct instruction that reminded jurors of the "time, effort, money, and emotional strain" of a case. It said failure to reach a verdict would mean leaving the case open to be tried again. Some judges called it the dynamite charge, the shotgun instruction, or the third-degree instruction.

This wasn't an Allen charge. Hoeveler wasn't giving the twelve the third degree, but he was getting close. The judge called this his modified Allen: "This, ladies and gentlemen, is serious business. We have been here for over six months. You should carefully consider the view of each other. That's the purpose of deliberations. Please look at this case reasonably. Talk about it, discuss it." Then he turned up the heat. "Let me assure you, you are not going home today. If you think I am going to give up easily, you are wrong. Now, I am saying this to you: I don't want anyone on this jury, after having carefully considered the opinions of each other, to recede from an opinion that you honestly feel should be the case. I would not want you to do that. Neither do I want you to say, 'I've reached a conclusion. I am not going to think about what the rest of you think.' You should not do that."

Spenser raised his hand. "That has happened," he said.

"Well, I am hoping that that juror will reconsider and follow my instructions," Hoeveler responded. After all, he continued, the jury had requested thousands of pages of testimony, and the evidence was all in the jury room. "I want you to think about that testimony," Hoeveler said, "and all of the other testimony in this case and every exhibit that's been submitted to you."

"We will try again," Spenser told the judge.

After the jurors had filed out of the courtroom and were secured again in the jury room, Hoeveler ran his hand through his hair. He looked at the attorneys still seated before him. "It is a pity if one juror blows this case," he said. All nodded in agreement.

After court had recessed at 10:35, the judge went back to his chambers. Outside in the long, narrow corridor he could hear the reporters who had gathered. He opened the door and stepped out. "For those of you who have faith in the Almighty," he said, "I hope you'll solicit a speedy end to the trial. The worst thing that can happen is a hung jury. I cannot conceive that will happen."

Almost any story would have suited the reporters: conviction, no conviction, hung jury. Without daily courtroom stories to file, the press had already busied itself with estimating just how bad a hung jury would be. The cost in emotional energy was evident on Hoeveler's face. The fun part was putting a monetary figure on the proceedings. In terms of cash, and discounting the cost of the 1989 invasion, some reporters had pegged the prosecution costs at $3 million to $4 million. The cost of the defense was probably about half that. The cost of informants' fees and Witness Protection Program payouts would probably reach $1.5 million, some reporters figured. A hung jury would mean starting all over again. Figure another $8 million. At least the government wouldn't have to pay for another invasion, some reporters joked.

No one on the government side wanted to think about a loss. A loss would be devastating. Tom Cash, the special agent in charge of the DEA's Miami field office, said the impact of a loss on the DEA would be a disaster. Almost the whole of federal law enforcement had divorced itself from the Noriega case. The burden rested on the DEA alone. Cash said privately that a loss at trial could mean the end of the DEA. It would make a joke of the drug war. Pat Sullivan and Myles Malman knew a loss would be a burden for the rest of their careers. Of course, a victory would be a different thing. Victories had a way of rolling uphill. Credit for a victory would be embraced at the top, but a loss would rest squarely on the trial team: They weren't smart enough or hadn't worked hard enough; Main Justice should have jumped into the case from the get-go. Even Leon Kellner, the Miami U.S. attorney who with Richard Gregorie had filed the indictment, was sweating this one, and he had been in private practice in Washington, D.C., for the last two years. As the days went by and there was still no word of a victory, Kellner sat in his office just a few blocks from the White House thinking about the White House press release that would come with a loss. The release, Kellner imagined, would say, "This was all Leon Kellner's fault."

Late Wednesday afternoon in the jury room, Hoeveler's stern words were having their effect. When the judge had said no one was going home today, there was nervous laughter in the jury box. There was serious decision-making to be done. There had to be some give-and-take. Spenser picked up the instructions and read them aloud again. Then he read the indictment. Again the discussion proceeded around the table.

"I could understand that a lot of the witnesses were just trying to save their necks," Thelma Sturdivant said, "but when you have so many of them, coming from different places, and they repeat over and over the same story, there is something to think about. Besides, there were witnesses that testified and corroborated their testimonies who had no plea bargain."

Consider the witnesses, Sturdivant said. Luis del Cid "was a plain person. He was a serviceman. He followed orders. He wasn't trying to say things different [from] the way they were." Sturdivant looked at Cooper. "I believed what he told," she said. "There was money. It was in a box or a bag, and he passed it on."

Carlos Lehder was another, Sturdivant said. "I felt impressed by his testimony. He was just a cruel man who did not care about anybody, not even about himself. But usually those are the ones who tell the hardest truth. He said a lot of things. He must have been there."

Nova Rodríguez's turn came. She talked about Roberto Striedinger, the cartel pilot, and Gabriel Taboada, the car dealer. They had been in Medellín and had seen the suitcase filled with $500,000. Noriega had walked into the room and joked with the Ochoas. Then Carlos Lehder testified that Noriega was paid $500,000 for the return of confiscated cocaine.

"Do you see how the suitcase with the $500,000 fits in with Carlos Lehder?" Rodríguez asked. "That was three different people, but they all knew about the money and it went to General Noriega. Do you see how one's testimony supports another's testimony?"

Cooper looked up. "Well, what about the people who are dead?" she asked, perhaps thinking about César Rodríguez.

"We have to go by what the living are saying," one juror said.

Cooper couldn't see who was talking, but she looked down the table.

No one wanted the man to be guilty. No one wanted to point a finger. But that was the life he chose. "If you chose that way, you have to live with the consequences," Rodríguez said.

The judge's talk had already made Hogan solid for conviction. He was done drawing squares on the chalkboard. "It wasn't one person. It was like a big puzzle," he said.

That evening, on the ride back to the hotel, everyone was a lot calmer. Cooper had not come around, but they would try again tomorrow. After dinner, Ethel Johnson and Jean Hallisey sat with Bernadine Cooper. "Maybe the Lord will direct us. Maybe we should pray," they said. They prayed for guidance. Later, Hallisey spoke to Cooper alone. "The whole world is waiting for this verdict," Hallisey told Cooper. "President Bush is waiting for this verdict." Cooper pursed her lips and walked back to her room.

On Tuesday morning, April 9, Spenser read the instructions aloud again. He began with count one and then went to count two. His voice was growing hoarse. Discussion started around the room again. When Cooper's turn came, she lifted her head. "I can see now what it is all about," she said.

The jurors all turned toward her. "He's a bad man who deserves to go to prison," Cooper said.

A smile came to Spenser's face.

It was almost as if they couldn't take the vote fast enough. Still, they took each count one at a time.

Count one: the racketeering conspiracy that said Noriega and others helped the cartel set up its manufacturing, distribution, and money-laundering operations in Panama. The count that said Noriega protected cocaine shipments from Panama to the United States; sold ether and acetone that had been seized in Panama; hid the cartel leaders after the assassination of Rodrigo Lara Bonilla in 1984; took a $4 million bribe to allow the establishment of the Darien lab; protected money-laundering flights from south Florida to Panama; and supported the cartel's effort to import cocaine into the United States. The vote: 12-0. The maximum sentence: twenty years. The verdict: guilty.

Count two: the "substantive" or actual racketeering charge which said that between October 1981 and March 1986, Noriega engaged in the illegal activities planned by the conspirators listed in count one. The vote: 12-0. The maximum sentence: twenty years. The verdict: guilty.

Count three: the conspiracy with members of the cartel to import cocaine into the United States between October 1981 and January 1984. The maximum sentence: fifteen years. The verdict: guilty.

Count four: the distribution of four hundred kilograms of cocaine flown by Floyd Carlton from Colombia to Panama in May 1983. The maximum sentence: fifteen years. The verdict: guilty.

Count five: the distribution of another four hundred kilograms of cocaine flown by Carlton from Colombia to Panama in January 1984. The maximum sentence: fifteen years. The verdict: guilty.

Count six: helping Pablo Escobar, Jorge Ochoa, and others obtain chemicals to manufacture cocaine at Tranquilandia, the giant cocaine lab in southern Colombia, between September 1983 and March 1984. The maximum sentence: fifteen years. The verdict: guilty.

Count seven: conspiracy to manufacture cocaine at the Darien Province lab in southern Panama and to distribute and ship the cocaine to Florida using Ricardo Bilonick's Inair cargo airline during May 1984. The maximum sentence: fifteen years. The verdict: guilty.

On count eight and count nine, the *Krill* conspiracy and distribution counts, the verdict was already in: not guilty. For each charge Noriega had faced a twenty-year maximum sentence.

Count ten: causing travel in furtherance of the conspiracy; the flight of two drug pilots carrying $800,000 in drug proceeds from Fort Lauderdale to Panama. The maximum: five years. The verdict: guilty.

It was slightly before 2 P.M. on Thursday when Spenser announced that verdicts had been reached. He immediately went to the door and informed the deputy marshal standing in the hall. Spenser handed the note to the deputy marshal: "We have reached our verdict."

Just after 2 P.M., two deputy marshals arrived at Hoeveler's chambers on the ninth floor of the new courtroom tower. Courtroom deputy Maria Conboy took a note into court where the judge was now in the middle of a sentencing hearing. Hoeveler opened the note. "Hallelujah," he said under his breath. "Hallelujah."

Conboy called the attorneys. Court would reconvene in half an hour.

Pat Sullivan was sitting in his office four blocks away when the news came.

"Yes!" Sullivan said aloud. "It's a conviction." Sullivan was convinced the jury could not have hung; a hung jury would have struggled longer. There were convictions, Sullivan was sure, probably on half of the counts. Sullivan, Myles Malman, Guy Lewis, and James McAdams gathered and with an entourage of a dozen lawyers and secretaries from the U.S. attorney's office began the walk to the courthouse. Half a block from the courthouse they were engulfed by dozens of reporters.

Frank Rubino and Jon May had just returned from lunch when the news came. Both were nervous during the ten-minute drive to the courthouse from Rubino's Coconut Grove office. Rubino said he was sure the jury had hung on counts one and two, and probably on the Tranquilandia and Darien counts as well. The evidence was just not there. He was sure he had gotten through to at least two of the jurors. They had to hang. Maybe it was even an acquittal.

"Let's go," Hoeveler said at 2:20 when he had stepped down from the bench and walked back into his chambers in the tower. Sandra Cavazos, his law clerk, took a place at Hoeveler's side. They had been together on this case for two years. The whole office staff and two deputy marshals followed them down to the first floor, across the courtyard to the old building, and into the judge's second chambers off the Central Courtroom.

Sandra, Thays, and Lorena Noriega sat in the front row of the gallery, flanking their mother.

By the time Rubino and May arrived, Sullivan, Malman, Lewis, and the rest of the prosecution team were already in court. Noriega had been escorted up from "the submarine." He was now in the holding room off the courtroom. He was somber and nervous when Rubino and May walked in.

The first two rows of the center section of the gallery were filled with network television sketch artists. Many of the same visitors who had come for closing arguments were back in court. There were dozens of reporters. By 2:25 there were no seats left in the court.

Hoeveler took the bench and called for order. The room grew silent. Conboy handed the judge the jury's penciled verdict form. Hoeveler opened it.

Eight guiltys, two not guiltys, no undecideds. Hoeveler was surprised. Eight counts guilty. It was clear, Hoeveler thought to himself, that the jury had paid close attention. The *Krill* counts were obviously weak. But Hoeveler would not have guessed guilty on the Darien and Tranquilandia counts. The jury system was solid, Hoeveler believed. It had worked again.

When the verdict on count one was read aloud, Jon May sensed the emotion shooting through Noriega, who was sitting next to him. It was like receiving the news that someone very close had died. They both felt it at the same instant. Noriega straightened and sat bolt upright in his chair, taut with nerves.

Rubino heard the first guilty and then the others. This was wrong, he thought. Wrong, wrong. Felicidad Noriega's hands were clasped in her lap. Her face grew expressionless. Sandra and Thays began to weep and then to sob. In the jury box, the twelve jurors stared straight ahead, somber.

When the last verdict was read at a few minutes before 3 P.M., Hoeveler paused. "Thank you," he said to the jurors. He excused them for the last time. Each rose and walked quietly and quickly from the court.

When they were gone, Hoeveler turned to Noriega. The general was stunned. "General Noriega, the jury has found you guilty as to count one, and it is the judgment of this court that you are guilty as to count one. The jury has found you guilty as to count two, and it is the judgment of this court that you are guilty as to count two." He proceeded through the remaining eight counts.

Noriega remained at attention in his chair. Rubino leaned over and put his arm around Noriega's shoulder. Eleven hours after the jury had said it was deadlocked, after thirty-five hours of deliberation over four and a half days, the trial was over. Hoeveler announced that the sentencing would come on July 10, three months from now.

The deputy marshals led Noriega to a small sitting room off the courtroom. Before he turned to his family, Noriega shook hands with Rubino and May. He had nothing to say. Alone with his wife and three daughters, he cried, a gut-wrenching cry of emotion, deep and long.

On the thirteenth floor of the Everglades Hotel, most of the jurors were packing their bags. The live television news bulletins had already begun. When room service arrived with sandwiches, Thelma Sturdivant was praying.

On the elevator ride up, reporters had crushed Jim Hogan and Lester Spenser against the back of the car. The jurors had agreed not to comment, but it was clear the press would not leave them alone. "Give us a few minutes, and we'll come down and talk," Spenser and Hogan promised.

"As you know, it's been a long trial," Spenser said later. Hogan added, "This decision was difficult, and it was a decision that was heavily debated back and forth. The verdict speaks for itself. We examined all the evidence, and we are all looking forward to returning to our normal lives."

On the front steps of the courthouse, Acting U.S. Attorney James McAdams (Dexter Lehtinen had left office four months before) crumbled his notes for a concession speech, the one that said the prosecution had done the best job it could and would try the case again.

McAdams told reporters that after sentencing, Noriega would be taken to Tampa to stand trial on the marijuana-smuggling and money-laundering charges of the 1988 indictment. He promised that the United States would work with foreign governments to retrieve the millions of dollars Noriega had stashed away in European bank accounts.

Pat Sullivan stepped forward next, flanked by Malman and Lewis. Sullivan allowed himself a grin before he began. "It was worth it all," he said. "We are surprised at the enormity of the victory. We knew we had some counts weaker than others. We had some doubts."

Reporters asked about the manner in which the government had won, the use of dozens of convicted felons. "You can't convict without those people at the bottom agreeing to testify against those people they worked for," Sullivan said. "There was no plea bargain in the case that provided that anyone would go free. In virtually every case tried in federal district court in which we try to convict a kingpin, we invariably have to use the soldiers and the underlings in order to convict the higher-level defendants. You don't get to the top without starting at the bottom."

At the headquarters of the Drug Enforcement Administration in Washington, Judge Robert Bonner, head of the agency, said, "Manuel Noriega's past has finally caught up with him. His day of reckoning has arrived. He must now pay the price for colluding with the Colombian drug lords."

At Main Justice, Attorney General William Barr stepped into the briefing room. "This is an important message to the drug lords. There are no safe havens; their wealth and their firepower cannot protect them forever. As came out clearly in court, this was a case of a corrupt cop. The full extent of his corruption or his involvement in drug trafficking was not evident to the United States at the time there was cooperation."

At a White House picture-taking session, President Bush paused for a moment and told reporters, "He was accorded a free and fair trial, and he was found guilty. I hope it sends a lesson to drug lords here and around the world that they'll pay a price if they continue to poison the lives of our kids in this country or anywhere else. Now that he has been convicted, I think its proper to say that justice has been served."

Frank Rubino was angry when he and Jon May walked out the front door of the courthouse an hour after the verdicts were read. First, he praised the jury for being "fair" and "honest." Then his voice filled with a mixture of deep personal hurt and indignation. "This, in our opinion, is the modern-day version of the Crusades. The United States will now trample across the entire world, imposing its will upon so-called independent, sovereign nations. Unless leaders of foreign governments are willing to kneel once a day and face Washington and give grace to George Bush, they, too, may be in the same posture as General Noriega." Rubino looked around at the press that he had so effectively managed for two years. This seemed like his last hurrah.

"A new page has been written in American history," Rubino charged. "The U.S. government, in its role as world policeman, saw fit to invade a country and seize its leader. The jury has condoned that action and sent a message to the rest of the world's leaders that you, too, may soon be in our courthouse. This was not a drug case. This was a political case. It always was, it always will be. We only wish we had been allowed to present the evidence to address this case."

Tom Cash, the agent in charge of the DEA's Miami office, shook agent Danny Moritz's hand after the verdict was read. It had been almost seven years since Moritz had first gone undercover to track Noriega and the cartel.

Cash gripped Moritz's hand. "Well," he said, "the good guys won and the bad guys lost."

CHAPTER 37

The Summer of the Year 2016

Three months later, at Noriega's sentencing on Friday, July 10, 1992, Frank Rubino's ire had not abated.

"Your Honor, before the court today is General Manuel Antonio Noriega, the ex-leader of the Republic of Panama, once a sovereign nation, a nation obviously not militarily as strong as the United States, the mightiest war machine the world has ever known, but still an independent republic of the world. This man was once our friend, once our confidant, once our political ally. All this has changed. Do we want to know the truth? I think not, at least not today.

"For reasons that were not allowed to be brought out in this courtroom, General Noreiga was threatened by the United States. Eventually the threats were made true, and he was indicted in the United States district court. Was this a real indictment or a coercive means to accomplish a political goal? Years ago when our government wished to discredit someone, they called him a communist. Today they call him a drug trafficker. For reasons never articulated in this courtroom, the government of the United States set out to discredit General Noriega and destroy the sovereign nation of Panama."

Rubino stood at the lectern. His voice was forceful and angry. Noriega, sitting behind Rubino at the defense table, next to May, was wearing his dress khaki uniform, as usual.

Rubino knew this was his last chance.

"Panama posed no threat to the security of America," he said. "We condemned the Panamanian government and its politics because this was a political prosecution. All the while the world's most heinous drug traffickers were running wild in Colombia. They could grow, manufacture, process, package, and transport drugs in Colombia with impunity. If we really wanted to stop drug trafficking, we should ask ourselves: Did we invade the wrong country? But Colombia doesn't have the canal. In the words of President Reagan, and I quote, referring to the Panama Canal: 'We built it, we paid for it, and it's ours.'"

Rubino turned and motioned toward Noriega.

"Before the court today is a man who has never committed a crime on the soil of the United States. If the court wishes to impose an excessive sentence, it really doesn't matter. If you give him thirty years, forty, fifty, sixty, seventy, who cares? He'll die in prison anyway." The only just sentence was time served, Rubino told the judge, time served and the return of Noriega to Panama. "Send him to Panama to be judged by Panamanians," Rubino said. "Let's stop insulting Panama. Let's stop treating Panama as a colony. Send General Noriega back to Panama. If he committed crimes in Panama, he should pay for them there."

Before Rubino began, Jon May had argued to Hoeveler that Noriega should not be sentenced to a federal penitentiary but instead should be turned over to the Department of Defense and interned in a special prisoner-of-war camp. The Geneva Convention outlined the treatment of prisoners of war, May told Hoeveler. International law "explicitly prohibited" sending Noriega to a penitentiary, he said.

May and Rubino hoped more than anything to keep Noriega out of the federal prison at Marion, Illinois, the maximum-security prison where Carlos Lehder had been jailed. Prisoners there existed in solitary confinement, some in cells underground. Prisoners at Marion received only one hour of exercise each day and lived the rest of the time in eight-by-seven-foot cells.

May believed that if Noriega had to be locked up, he would be better off at a military stockade like the one at Leavenworth, Kansas. As a prisoner of war among military men, May hoped, Noriega's high rank would afford him a modicum of respect.

Hoeveler himself thought that Noriega was indeed a prisoner of war. The Bush administration and the Justice Department had conceded as much during the litigation over jurisdiction in the spring of 1990. But the judge knew that what he thought might have only a partial bearing upon where Noriega was imprisoned, if he was. Prison assignments were ultimately made by the Federal Bureau of Prisons. Hoeveler could only make a recommendation.

Pat Sullivan followed Rubino to the lectern. Rubino had requested that Noriega be allowed to address the court on his own behalf before the sentence was imposed. Hoeveler thought it fair that Noriega get almost the last word. The judge invited Sullivan to comment on behalf of the government.

The prosecutor, as usual, was direct and plainspoken: "The general and Mr. Rubino just don't get it," Sullivan began. He rested his hands on the edge of the lectern and leaned forward as if he were giving the government's case a final push. "This was never a political trial. He was tried under the rules that every defendant who appears in this courthouse is tried."

Sullivan motioned toward Rubino. "He could have put on any evidence to convince the jury that the general didn't do what he was charged with doing. The general could have taken the stand in an attempt to convince the jury that he didn't do what all the witnesses said he did." Sullivan paused. "The evidence had nothing to do with politics, had nothing to do with the Panama Canal. Nothing ever occurred in a political context that had anything whatsoever to do with the general reaching an agreement with the Medellín cartel to transship cocaine through Panama to the United States, and that makes it not a Panamanian problem but a problem for the United States, the Southern District of Florida, to deal with. I ask the court to sentence the general to a maximum term of imprisonment on every count to run consecutively for a term of a hundred and twenty years."

Noriega sat motionless, his face blank, as Sullivan walked back to his seat. A hundred and twenty years. He had not flinched; Rubino and May had already warned him to expect the worst. Sullivan was only doing his duty as a prosecutor. Noriega understood the concept of duty.

Hoeveler turned to Noriega. "General," the judge said, inviting Noriega to address the court.

Noriega stood and turned sideways, toward his wife and three daughters in the first row of the gallery. He blew a kiss to them. He had been preparing his comments for weeks. His speech to the court was typed in large print, in Spanish, and ran just slightly longer than forty-one pages. With the interpreter interrupting to deliver the translation, Noriega's comments would run about an hour.

Rubino and May had coached Noriega. The speech was well written, to the point, and certainly would not detrimentally affect the judge's sentence.

But when Noriega took his place, standing at attention before the judge, he looked away from his text.

"I would like to deviate slightly from the context of my original speech," he began in a firm voice. "We are now addressing history. You are a man of history," Noriega told Hoeveler. "Dr. Sullivan is also a part of history. I would like to correct Dr. Sullivan. The government imposed in Panama by way of an invasion which caused the destruction of the Panamanian Army by the United States." Noriega paused as the translator followed his words. The comment had not been a complete sentence.

"How can it thus degrade a general of an army that has been destroyed? That is going against reality. And it also is a lack of respect to Your Honor and the truth of the matter." The general was not following his notes. At the defense table Rubino and May grew uncomfortable.

Noriega continued: "When can he say that the present military forces, or as he said, how is it that a military council or even a court-martial was given to Mr. Melo? Do you recall that, Your Honor? How could they have formed a military council if there are no more military men there after the invasion? It ended after the invasion."

Rubino and May knew that what they were hearing was not a failure of the translation. This was Noriega's way. They had seen it over and over again in their preparation of the case. Noriega lacked the sophistication to speak extemporaneously. He was an egotistical man, and proud. He was not a highly educated man. He was a soldier. He was a military man who for decades had given orders, not taken them. He was a man who had failed to understand how he could best help himself. For two years he had been in custody, and during the months of negotiations that had preceded the delivery of the 1988 indictment and later during the invasion, he had failed to understand how he could best help himself. Putting Noriega on the witness stand would have been a disaster, Rubino and May knew. There would have been no predicting what he might have said. Noriega's mind was flooded with tangential concerns. He could not be controlled. That's what was happening now.

More than two hours later, Sullivan, in a few short sentences of rebuttal, would call Noriega's speech a "farce" and a "diatribe," saying that "due to his overweening pride and arrogance, he merely vented his spleen with petty fulminations. He didn't deal with the evidence in the trial. He didn't deal with anything but with figments of his imagination."

"So please," Noriega continued, "let's not lack respect and treat ourselves with respect here. I would like to invoke upon God, on his straight and narrow path, and the two Bibles which you have, Your Honor, which you follow, one Bible being that of human rights and righteousness, and your Christian Bible."

In his often rambling statement, Noriega mixed quotations from figures as diverse as Socrates, the Chinese philosopher Lao-tzu, the biblical prophet Jeremiah, and the wife of presidential candidate Bill Clinton. He claimed that the Reagan administration had plotted the airplane explosion that killed his predecessor, Omar Torrijos, in 1981. He spoke of National Security Adviser John Poindexter and the Reagan administration's efforts to overthrow Nicaragua's Sandinista government. He spoke of an American plot to murder the deposed Shah of Iran in Panama in order to help free American hostages in Iran during the closing days of the Carter administration.

His message was that he would not admit guilt and would not grovel in front of the United States. "My indictment was orchestrated by those who fear me, men who sought to discredit me through accusations or kill me by means of an invasion. Since they were unable to kill me previously—not with the commando group that was trained in the Caribbean, not with two military coup attempts, not with the invasion when fifteen thousand American soldiers were looking for me dead or alive—since they were unable to kill me yesterday, they bring me here today so that you can do them the favor of killing me alive. For thousands of years powerful nations have caused these types of activities to initiate wars or to persecute leaders that are considered as obstacles in their objectives. I forgot that, and I fell into the trap of the United States' harassment in my own country. Panama was not invaded because its canal was threatened. Panama was not invaded because the lives of American citizens were in danger. Panama was invaded because I was an obstacle and damaged the historical souvenirs of your President George Bush, who preferred me dead! Panama has its own history. It was portrayed here as though I had just created an army for the first time. Panama is not a colony of the United States. It never was nor will it ever be. The jury could not truly understand that Panama had its own laws, its own way of life, its own culture, its own customs, its own history, and its own political and economic interests.

Panama enters with a sphere of interest to the United States because of its geographic location as being the shortest route for going between the Atlantic and the Pacific. The 1903 treaty was imposed and never signed by any Panamanian. The Reagan-Bush administration confused my friendship and my professional coordination with them as being submissive, dependent, and subservient. We had worked together on many different levels for the benefit of both nations, but when they wanted to go against the interests of my country, I did not accept. Yes, Your Honor, there is a strong political odor that can be felt in the development of this case. The Chinese Wall of the government, the national security hearings, the conferences and permanent consultations with Washington are 'political overtones' before, during, and after. I am now in the belly of the Leviathan. What justification can this country have in causing the death of more than three thousand people in order to capture only one man? When during the history of civilized nations of America has a country been invaded with the result being a destruction in order to overthrow and arrest a foreign leader who is fulfilling his mandate? What justification can this administration give its citizens for an expenditure of more than $250 million to carry out an arrest? How can you explain that among the two hundred and fifty thousand photographs captured during the invasion there exists not a single one of me with the heads of the Medellín cartel in the supposed meetings that have been spoken of so much in this chamber?

"Nevertheless, there remain photographs in the files in intelligence that were never brought here, such as this photograph." Noriega held a photo taken of himself and George Bush in Panama in 1983. "This photograph has an explanation, Your Honor. What is President Bush doing in this photograph with General Manuel Antonio Noriega? Noriega was not someone strange. He was not a criminal when they went to visit him. The millionaire propaganda machinery that was used against me by the Reagan-Bush administration for almost four years did not allow any of the citizens of this country to escape its claws. There could not have been an impartial jury who did not have any preconceived notions about this trial.

"Of the mysterious trip to Cuba, it was not permitted to say that this included a request for a visit by a high emissary of the Reagan-Bush administration and that after my visit he went to Cuba to open a channel of conversation. But it is not convenient to the administration that this be known because the Cubans in exile would criticize it. And here it was not permitted to say the name of this high official sent by Reagan and Bush and received by Castro after my intervention.

"The visits to Medellín, had they been true, the intelligence service of Colombia would have had details or would have had confirmation of them.

"Did you know, Your Honor, that from the beginning of May 1988 until October of 1989 these two administrations were prepared to agree to the cancellation of all the criminal charges against me in exchange for my handing the country over to them so they could impose their government, courts, and administrator on the Panama Canal?

"If the people had known this proposal . . . they would have felt the nausea, the repugnance that I lived [through] at that moment. I do not lament the consequences. If this is the price that I am paying in exchange for my loyalty to the country that saw me born, that price is very, very low.

"The question is: Why weren't the real drug traffickers offered this? The answer is simple: Besides being criminal, they weren't Panamanians and couldn't offer anything of interest in exchange. They couldn't offer territory for military bases, nor could they offer the canal beyond the year 2000.

"That is the reason they wanted me dead; that, in the middle of the twentieth century, one stop from the third millennium, the president of the most powerful nation in the world, his chest swelled up, put a price on my head of $1 million.

"Being the policeman of the world is a highly expensive proposition. How many internal problems of this country has it cost—the homeless, the unemployed, families that have no homes in Los Angeles, in New York, those people with AIDS in Miami? All of this could have been solved. This administration was indifferent toward crime, corruption, and violence on its own streets.

"For my part, I accuse George Herbert Walker Bush of exercising his power and authority to influence and subvert the American judicial system in order to convict me.

"I accuse George Herbert Walker Bush of genocide for having ordered the massive bombardment of the civilian population of Panama and causing the deaths of more than five thousand people.

"I also accuse George Herbert Walker Bush of making the Panamanian people poor through lies of economic assistance, which they very well know will never be fulfilled.

"I accuse George Herbert Walker Bush of planning the destruction of Panama's sovereignty and the destruction of the Defense Forces of Panama in order to retain those military bases after the year 2000 and in order not to have to return the Panama Canal to its true owners, the people of Panama.

"Of this and more, he is guilty, and today I denounce him before the United States people and the world. I would have preferred to take that seat there during the trial so that we may have heard more. Nevertheless, I give my thanks to God for having chosen me from among so many Panamanians to find myself here undergoing this very difficult analysis. I praise God for all of these circumstances, knowing that He is the only director of the circumstances. I praise the Lord for having been my pastor and for having maintained me alive during the invasion of Panama.

"I confess to you and the world that I am at peace with myself."

When Noriega sat down, the hearing had been going on for more than four hours. Judge Hoeveler looked tired. He had thought hard about Noriega and the sentence he was about to impose. He had prayed about his decision for days. He had sat in the back pew of Saint Stephen's Episcopal Church, rested his head in his hands, and prayed for compassion and wisdom. Now he had to do what he must.

"If some of the things happened that General Noriega says happened," Hoeveler began, looking out over the courtroom, "that burden is on someone else. The beauty of this system is that a case that comes into court is and should be uninfluenced by anything except the charges that are made and the defenses that are presented. The politics of this case were not a part of the case, should not have been a part of the case, and I think everybody did all they could to keep them from being a part of this case, and as I say, what happened outside the four corners of this case and this courtroom is somebody else's burden, not mine.

"But now I'm called upon to make a decision on sentencing, and again, I must look not to what the general mentioned but to what happened in this courtroom. The real reason why we're here today is because a jury of twelve men and women decided that the government had proved beyond a reasonable doubt that the charges were indeed proved." Hoeveler paused. "With that conclusion, I will ask the general to please rise."

Noriega, with Rubino and May on either side of him, stood.

"As to count one of the indictment, the defendant will be committed to the custody of the attorney general of the United States for the confinement of a period of twenty years," the judge began. Concurrent to the sentence of twenty years on count one, Noriega would serve twenty years for count two. For each of the following five counts of cocaine distribution and manufacturing, Noriega would serve fifteen years concurrently but consecutively to the twenty years for the first counts. And for the one travel count related to the flight of drug profits to Panama, the judge sentenced Noriega to serve five years consecutive to the sentences imposed in counts one, two, three, and seven.

The sentence was forty years in prison and, in addition, three years of special probation upon release and a fine of $100.

Certainly there were issues of appeal:
  *The legality of the U.S. invasion and the death and destruction wrought in Panama
  *The United States' right to seize a fugitive in a foreign country in violation of an extradition treaty
  *The jurisdiction of the court to try a foreign head of state
  *The interception of Noriega's telephone calls from prison and whether the attorney-client privilege was violated; the interception of the defense team's witness list before trial
  *The government's introduction of evidence that might be considered irrelevant or inflammatory, such as testimony about the six French dancing girls who were given to Noriega as a gift

Jon May would carefully pick from the choice of appeal issues. A winning appeal was almost always founded on a single issue. A shotgun appeal would be unlikely to persuade the Eleventh U.S. Circuit Court of Appeals or, following that, the U.S. Supreme Court.

But May was certain that someday the Supreme Court would take up Noriega's case.

On the day of his sentencing, Noriega was fifty-six years old. At the earliest, he would be eligible for parole after ten years. He had already served two years. He would likely seek release in January 2000.

But because of the nature of the crimes, his notoriety, and a concern that he might return to Panama and seek out his former supporters, it is more likely that he will serve two-thirds of the sentence, a total of 26+ years.

Noriega would never be tried on the Tampa marijuana-smuggling charges. On Friday, March 23, 1993, a federal judge, upon the motion of prosecutors, dismissed the 1988 Tampa indictment.

"The government's interest has been vindicated and the cost of a second trial would not be warranted," said Tampa U.S. attorney Robert Genzman.

Manuel Antonio Noriega, assuming he lives and is not tried and convicted on the charges awaiting him in Panama, will be free at the age of eighty in the summer of the year 2016.

ACKNOWLEDGMENTS

This book is based on more than 30,000 pages of official records, including court pleadings, trial transcripts, Executive Branch documents, and congressional testimony. It also is based on my own observation and scores of hours of personal interviews with persons directly involved.

Because almost all of those who helped make the telling of this story possible are identified within the text, it would be redundant to name them here. I thank them for their long patience and cooperation. I note that some of the sources who provided information for this book requested anonymity or asked that the information they provided not be directly attributed to them. None of the dialogue or description has been invented. My rule was to check quotations and descriptions with the source or with direct witnesses.

I acknowledge the reporting of dozens of journalists who were involved in covering this case and the events leading up to and surrounding the trial. Their hard work added background and detail to mine. Among them were reporters for the Associated Press, *The Miami Herald*, the *Fort Lauderdale Sun Sentinel*, the *Miami Review*, *The New York Times*, *The Washington Post*, the *Los Angeles Times*, and *The Miami News*. I acknowledge particularly the reporting of Milt Sosin, Warren Richey, David Lyons, Richard Cole, John Dinges, and Frederick Kempe.

I wish to thank certain persons whose contributions to my work were very specific: Denise Sanders and Linda Datko at the federal court library in Miami; Paul Gamble for technical assistance in San Francisco; in New York, my agent, Jane Dystel, and at Charles Scribner's Sons, Bill Goldstein, Hamilton Cain, and Brian Desmond. I am particularly grateful to my reporter colleagues in Miami, Susan Postlewaite and Keith Donner.

Of course, there are many others whose assistance, hospitality, friendship, and advice were essential and for which I am grateful; but foremost is Bruce Albert for his encouragement through the long middle course of my work, and Deanna Wilson, who encouraged me to undertake this project and whose example stood me in good stead at the first and last.

INDEX